An Invitation to Political Thought

AN INVITATION TO POLITICAL THOUGHT

Kenneth L. Deutsch
State University of New York at Geneseo

Joseph R. Fornieri
Rochester Institute of Technology

THOMSON
WADSWORTH
Australia • Brazil • Canada • Mexico • Singapore • Spain
United Kingdom • United States

An Invitation to Political Thought
Kenneth L. Deutsch, Joseph R. Fornieri

Publisher: Michael Rosenberg
Managing Development Editor: Karen Judd
Senior Editorial Assistant: Megan Garvey
Marketing Manager: Trent Whatcott
Marketing Communications Manager: Heather Baxley
Senior Content Project Manager: Josh Allen
Art Director: Linda Helcher
Print Buyer: Linda Hsu
Permissions Editor: Tim Sisler
Production Service: International Typesetting and Composition
Cover Designer: Jen 2 Design
Cover Image: Elizabeth Michaud
Compositor: International Typesetting and Composition
Printer: West Group

Printed in the United States of America
1 2 3 4 5 6 7 11 10 09 08 07

Library of Congress Control Number: 2007931741

Student Edition:
ISBN-13: 978-0-534-54563-5
ISBN-10: 0-534-54563-7

Thomson Higher Education
10 Davis Drive
Belmont, CA 94002-3098
USA

For more information about our products, contact us at:
Thomson Learning Academic Resource Center
1-800-423-0563
For permission to use material from this text or product, submit a request online at
http://www.thomsonrights.com.
Any additional questions about permissions can be submitted by e-mail to
thomsonrights@thomson.com.

This book is dedicated to our teachers
who instilled in us a love of political philosophy.
Joe Fornieri would like to make a personal dedication to
two of his teachers who appear in this volume:
Kenneth L. Deutsch and David Walsh

CONTENTS

Preface

This text reader has been developed to draw students into the fascinating world of political philosophy with its critical reflections on state power, freedom, equality, and justice. We are convinced that the best way to guide people in their study of this field is to examine the diversity of great political thinkers over the past 2,500 years of Western intellectual history.

This volume is unique in combining key texts from the great thinkers with expert commentary on these texts from distinguished teachers in the field of political philosophy. In addition to key primary sources and commentary, each chapter is organized thematically around the core teachings of the political thinker. Other helpful pedagogical features include highlighted key terms, case studies that apply the thinker's ideas to current events, questions for reflection, Web sites, and suggestions for further reading.

Based on our combined teaching experience of forty years, we are further convinced that the best way to provide a guide to these thinkers is to choose someone who has mastered the texts of each thinker, who has a great passion for the issues raised in those texts, and who has a great commitment to communicating those thoughts to others. Notwithstanding the editors' own contributions, we have selected guides who we are convinced meet our expectations.

We very much hope that this book has the quality of an invitation. We especially hope that our readers enjoy the intellectual journey.

We wish to thank Michael Rosenberg, Megan Garvey, and Karen Judd at Cengage Learning; Deepti Narwat and Meg McDonald for their excellent copy-editing work; Adam Botzenhart for his outstanding and diligent services as a student research assistant; Liz "the artist" Michaud for her gifted illustrations; Angelo Valente for his assistance; the Earhart Foundation for its generous support; and Pam Fornieri for her love and support throughout the years.

We would also like to thank Douglas C. Nord, Wright State University; Bruce Frohnen, Ave Maria Law; and Walter J. Nicgorski, Notre Dame for their critique and guidance to us in the review process.

About the Authors and Contributors

Kenneth L. Deutsch is Professor of Political Science at SUNY Geneseo. He has taught at Geneseo for 35 years. He has published numerous books about issues including political obedience and resistance to the state, Indian and American political thought, and constitutional rights and liberties, as well as three books assessing the political teachings and intellectual influence of Leo Strauss, one of the 20th century's great political philosophers. He is an avid opera fan and collector. Over the past 40 years he has collected thousands of records and CDs of live opera performances and recorded vocal concerts. He reads books about religion and philosophy for fun.

Joseph R. Fornieri is Associate Professor of Political Science at the Rochester Institute of Technology. He is the author of several books about Abraham Lincoln, including *Abraham Lincoln's Political Faith,* a work that explores the 16th president's religion and politics. He received the Eisenhart Outstanding Teacher Award in 2002. He sings, plays harmonica and guitar with his brother Peter in *The Dynamics,* a local blues band in the Rochester area. He lives in Fairport, New York, with his wife Pam and their two daughters, Isabella and Natalie.

Ralph C. Hancock is Professor of Political Science at Brigham Young University. He is the author of *Calvin and the Foundation of Modern Politics* and of various studies of Tocqueville and other thinkers, concerning the relationship between philosophy and the moral–political–religious realm. He enjoys playing basketball and tennis, as well as translating works from French. He and his wife Julie have five children and four grandchildren.

Andrea Ciliotta-Rubery is Associate Professor of Political Science at SUNY Brockport. She earned a doctorate in political theory at Georgetown University, Washington, D.C., and is the author of several articles addressing Machiavelli's piety and 16th-century politics and literature. An avid cook and antique collector, she lives with her husband and four children in Rochester, New York.

Ethan Fishman is Professor of Political Science at the University of South Alabama. He is the author of numerous books and articles, including *The Prudential Presidency and Likely Stories,* that examine the relationship between classical Western ideals and contemporary American politics. He was recognized as an outstanding teacher by the student honor society Mortar Board. Among the groups to which he belongs is the Old Farts Athletic Club.

Gary D. Glenn is Distinguished Teaching Professor Emeritus of Political Science at Northern Illinois University, where he has taught since 1966. As a teacher of the history of political philosophy, he has continually created new courses while trying to make the subject's books accessible to each generation of students. As a scholar of that tradition, he has written about the ideas of inalienable rights and limited government; the thoughts of Xenophon, Hobbes, Locke, Burke, Bellarmine, Leo Strauss, and Walter Berns; aspects of the American regime; religion in political campaigns; aspects of Catholic political philosophy and social thought; and the teaching of political science. He and his wife Ann have enjoyed, in their 44 years of marriage, raising their four children and welcoming into the family their spouses and seven grandchildren.

Samuel Gregg is Director of Research at the Acton Institute. He is the author of many articles as well as six books, including *Morality, Law, and Public Policy; On Ordered Liberty; Banking, Justice, and the Common Good*; *A Theory of Corruption;* and *The Commercial Society*. He is an editorial consultant for the Italian journal *La Societá,* as well as American correspondent for the German newspaper *Die Tagespost*. He writes extensively about matters of ethics in law, finance, and medicine. In his spare time he writes and lectures about the life and thought of Sir Thomas More.

Carson L. Holloway is Assistant Professor of Political Science at the University of Nebraska at Omaha. In 2005–2006 he was the William E. Simon Visiting Fellow in Religion and Public Life in Princeton University's James Madison Program in American Ideals and Institutions. His books include *All Shook Up: Music, Passion, and Politics* and *The Right Darwin? Evolution, Religion, and the Future of Democracy*. He is currently at work on a book about the thoughts of John Paul II and modern political philosophy, which will be published by Baylor University Press. He lives in Omaha with his wife Shari and daughters Maria, Anna, Elizabeth, Catherine, and Jane.

Peter Augustine Lawler is Dana Professor of Government at Berry College. He is author or editor of 12 books and 200 articles and chapters. His *Homeless and at Home in America* just appeared in print. He is executive editor of *Perspectives on Political Science* and a member of the President's Council on Bioethics. His favorite TV show is HBO's *Big Love* and he loves basketball.

James V. Schall, S.J., is a Professor in the Department of Government at Georgetown University. His books include *Reason, Revelation, and the Foundations of Political Philosophy; At the Limits of Political Philosophy; On the Unseriousness of Human Affairs; Roman Catholic Political Philosophy; The Life of the Mind;* and *The Regensburg Lecture.*

Sean D. Sutton is Assistant Professor in the Department of Political Science at the Rochester Institute of Technology. He earned his Ph.D. from the University of Dallas. He is currently working on a book exploring the enlightenment foundations of rational choice theory. He enjoys practicing martial arts and is an accomplished chess player.

David Walsh is Professor of Politics at The Catholic University of America, Washington, D.C. He is the author of a three-volume study of modernity addressing the totalitarian crisis, the resurgence of liberal democracy, and the philosophical revolution of the modern world. The first two volumes were published as *After Ideology: Recovering the Spiritual Foundations of Freedom* (1990) and *The Growth of the Liberal Soul* (1997); the third volume, *The Luminosity of Existence: An Outline of the Modern Philosophic Revolution* is forthcoming. A native of Ireland, Walsh returns frequently to the Emerald Isle, where he takes pride in being mistaken for an American.

Introduction to *An Invitation to Political Thought*

By Kenneth L. Deutsch

WHAT IS POLITICAL PHILOSOPHY?

Ambrose Bierce in his humorous Devil's Dictionary writes that politics is "a strife of interest masquerading as a contest of principles." Bierce certainly speaks for the cynics of every generation. However, the phenomenon of politics is not exhausted by the cynical point of view. When we talk about politics, we cannot avoid questions of truth or falsity, good or bad, better or worse. If the cynics are correct, then Al Qaeda—the Islamist terrorist group—cannot be condemned for its hijacking of American jets and using them to destroy the World Trade Center, killing thousands of innocent people. Talk concerning the legitimacy of terrorism, affirmative action, abortion, outrage against political and financial corruption, and many other issues cannot be stripped of all moral reference; we cannot really believe that politics has nothing to do with morality or moral standards. Ambrose Bierce was at least partly wrong: Politics is also the contest of moral principles!

The enterprise of *political philosophy* is the serious search for comprehensive knowledge or wisdom about political things. We seek knowledge concerning the following problems:

1. Human conflict—the nature and causes thereof.
2. The pursuit of power—the capacity to make others do our bidding.
3. The best or best possible cooperative social arrangements, capable of resolving or diminishing society's common problems.
4. The moral foundations of political legitimacy, liberty, equality, justice, and human rights.

5. Who should govern—one, few, or many.
6. The state and its nature, proper purpose, and limits.

These six issues, among others, require comprehensive knowledge of the facts about human nature and human social relationships. These facts constitute the *descriptive dimension of political philosophy*—the aspect of political philosophy that describes how things are. We also need knowledge concerning the principles of evaluation that enable us to construct and apply a standard to judge politics. The principles of evaluation and the standards offered to judge politics are known as the *prescriptive or normative dimension of political philosophy*—the aspect of political philosophy that prescribes how things ought to be. These two dimensions are related: The facts that we identify as worth describing in the human condition profoundly affect our evaluations and prescriptions. At the same time, what we establish as a sound basis for prescription leads us to focus on certain facts concerning the human condition.

The six issues and questions just listed are neither understood nor answered spontaneously if we simply gather social science data. Though these data are often relevant, we need to know whether the facts of economic, social, religious, or political practices support or refute our standards about human flourishing or welfare, human dignity or fair treatment. Political philosophy is, then, fundamentally evaluative. We need to know which standard we should affirm in evaluating the facts—and which facts contribute to the construction of our standards. Facts and evaluations are thus closely related.

The political philosophers we explore in this book claim to have good reasons for the facts they consider significant and the moral standards they apply to evaluate these six great political issues and questions. Some political philosophers offer good reasons or arguments based primarily on extensive empirical social science evidence or historical case studies; others base their arguments on a certain logic or pattern of ideas; and still others emphasize the existence of moral claims based on either unaided human reason or divine revelation, both of which offer humanity blueprints for the good life.

Political philosophy begins with the assumption that such public questions as obedience to the law, the best possible government, or the justice of public policies are in need of justification. We cannot imagine a human world without conflict over these questions. As Sir Isaiah Berlin put it, political philosophy is possible "only in a world where ends collide."[i] This is a world in which there is never-ending conflict over public goals and power. Given such conflict, we need wisdom about political matters that might enable us to persuade others whether particular political institutions or policies are better or worse for society. Harvey Mansfield argues that politics and political philosophy have one thing in common, and that is argument.[ii] Political philosophers seek to judge partisans engaged in political debate, to make their claims serve the public good, and to provide norms to evaluate the significance of facts that political scientists submit to society.

---

[i]Sir Isaiah Berlin, "Does Political Theory Still Exist?" in *Philosophy, Politics and Society*, Second Series, (eds.) Peter Lastett and W. G. Runciman (Oxford: Basil Blackwell, 1962).

[ii]Harvey Mansfield, *A Student's Guide to Political Philosophy* (Wilmington, Delaware: ISI Books, 2001), 1–8.

Political philosophers pursue their questions about political matters in response to the specific problems of disorder and crisis found in society. They seek to present us with a comprehensive vision of an ordered whole—a vision of a society that can be better ordered or better governed. This comprehensive vision encompasses an attempt to understand the human necessities, passions, and ambitions that propel us to exercise political power, construct political institutions or constitutions, and pursue justice or fairness in human relations. Leo Strauss, one of the most important 20th-century political philosophers, puts it well when he states that political philosophy is "an attempt to truly know both the nature of political things and the right to the good, political order."[iii] To be sure, the nature of political things and the good political order are highly contested by both political philosophers and political partisans.[iv]

POLITICAL PHILOSOPHY: CONFLICT, DIAGNOSIS, ORDER

Political Philosophy and Conflict

Situations of political conflict arise over differences in religion, gender, class, economic interests, race, social status, and so forth. More specifically, political conflict may occur over affirmative action, taxation, regulation of business, government aid to parochial schools, Social Security, health care, terrorism, multiculturalism, and many other subjects. Such conflicts can produce urgent social problems and disorder. Edmund Burke argues that the pursuit of political philosophy takes place in a condition of political disorder or decay, and that "the bulk of mankind are not excessively curious concerning any theories whilst they are really happy; and one symptom of an ill-conducted state is the propensity of the people to resort to them."[v]

Indeed, many of the great or epic political philosophers have pursued their inquiries as a result of profound social conflict and decay in which, according to Thomas Spragens, their respective political philosophies and comprehensive visions "are like pearls: they are not produced without an irritant."[vi] We will be examining Plato's political philosophy, which resulted from the death of Socrates; St. Augustine's political philosophy, which emerged as a result of the fall of Rome; Machiavelli's political philosophy, which sprang from Italy's disunity; and Hobbes's political philosophy, which came from the English Civil War. Contemporary political philosophies have resulted from the Nazi Holocaust, the crisis of liberal democracy, the emergence of the bureaucratic state, globalization, gender inequality, political correctness, nuclear proliferation, terrorism, and various threats to individual liberty. Political philosophy is not the study of great texts simply for antiquarian interest, as if they were simply museum pieces. The great books of a Plato or a Machiavelli might

---

[iii]Leo Strauss, *What is Political Philosophy? and other Studies* (Chicago: University of Chicago Press, 1988), p. 40, 172.

[iv]Harvey Mansfield, *A Student's Guide to Political Philosophy* (Wilmington, Delaware: ISI Books, 2001), pp. 1–8.

[v]Quoted by Daniel Boarstin, *The Genius of American Politics* (Chicago: University of Chicago Press, 1953), p. 1.

[vi]Thomas Spragens, Jr., *Understanding Political Theory* (New York: St. Martin's Press, 1976), p. 20.

have emerged as a result of a particular historical irritant; yet their texts also transcend their own times and continue to challenge contemporary political thinkers and partisans to consider the richness of their alternative teachings as part of our contemporary dialogues about our own political problems.

The comprehensive visions of these "epic"[vii] political philosophers challenge us to encompass the complexity of human nature, the social good, and politics by being open to their profoundly diverse questions and diverse prescriptions for a truly decent political order. To seek knowledge of the real complexity of human needs, aspirations, and relationships is to pursue the *philosophical approach to politics* that seeks wisdom. The *historical approach to politics* is most useful in helping us understand the "irritants" that contributed to political philosophers' desires to write texts with comprehensive visions. The historical approach also lets us see the extent to which there has been a dialogue in Western history over the past 2,500 years about certain perennial issues of liberty, justice, gender, equality, the state, and so on. Finally, the historical approach enables us to form our own dialogues about certain issues found in Plato's and Rousseau's texts concerning equality, democracy, education, and the common good. Reading their texts comparatively is an excellent way to begin the pursuit of knowledge and wisdom about politics. The approach to these epic political thinkers and their great teachings is primarily philosophical in that it assumes that our democracy is enhanced by many citizens being intellectually capable of challenging both the ignorant and the powerful.

Political Philosophy and Diagnosis

Political philosophers provide a comprehensive vision of the political when they raise questions and provide some (often tentative) answers about the most important factors that cause conflict, disorder, corruption, violence, terrorism, exploitation, or revolution. By so doing, they lead us to focus on the particular factors that cause political disorder or order. For example, Hobbes examines human passions; Plato discusses differences as the basis for justice; Machiavelli focuses on human deception and its relevance to successful political leadership; and Marx addresses the role that economic inequality and class conflict play in forming a political system. The epic political philosophers are not satisfied in simply describing public disorder or discontent: They seek to diagnose the causes of human conflict. For example, Marx is not satisfied simply to describe economic class conflict in society; he shows that the unequal material distribution of resources causes that conflict. Such descriptions of human conflicts and disorder are united with the political philosopher's diagnosis of the disorder's causes and then related to his or her prescription for a political therapy that will make public life better. Indeed, as Thomas Spragens puts it, "the causal analysis which a political theorist provides in his examination of the sources of political disorder decisively shapes his prescriptive conclusions. Sound diagnoses must precede beneficial therapy."[viii]

[vii]Sheldon Wolin, *Politics and Vision* (U.S.A.: University Presses of California, Columbia, Princeton, 2006).

[viii]Spragens, p. 75.

Political Philosophy as Prescription or Political Therapy

The political philosopher offers his or her prescription or therapy by identifying appropriate norms or standards, which help to resolve or diminish human social conflicts, thereby creating a better political order. Which is the best form of government? Are there proper limits to freedom? What type of equality should be the basis of public policies—equal rights, equal opportunities, equal results? What should be the basis for just treatment of individuals or groups? In addition to establishing a norm or standard for the best form of government, many political philosophers discuss the conditions under which the best is achievable and workable. If the best form is not achievable, what is the most workable or best possible form under particular conditions?

Among the political philosophers, various conflicting norms are claimed—such as Plato's "justice," which is the harmony of individuals in society in which all pursue the tasks they are most capable of performing—("minding one's own business"); or Marx's social "justice," which occurs when each person gives freely of his or her different talents for the public good and everyone's basic needs are equally provided for; or finally Hobbes's "justice," which is the social situation in which the state's sovereign is obeyed absolutely. Which of these conflicting norms concerning justice is true or workable in terms of human needs, talents, and resources? Leo Strauss is convinced that human beings will never create a society free of contradictions—perhaps even including contradictory norms. When we read political philosophers and their different and conflicting norms, we are invited to reflect upon the norms we hold, or to discuss with others whether we should accommodate, tolerate, integrate, or reject these norms in our own imperfect public life.

In summary, we can say that a political philosophy has factual (descriptive), diagnostic (causal), and evaluative (prescriptive) dimensions to its comprehensive vision of politics as conflict over power and modes of social cooperation. Although we can and should separately analyze these three dimensions in each political philosopher's teachings, we would be missing a great deal if we did not also examine the comprehensive vision of an ordered whole that each political philosopher seeks to convey. To see this comprehensive vision, we must notice to what extent a political philosopher identifies facts about human conflict that he or she regards as significant; conditions that cause conflict; and norms that will provide therapy in evaluating, resolving, or diminishing that conflict. The norms help us identify which facts of human life are truly salient in understanding both human conflict and cooperation. Understanding certain facts of human life helps us justify the validity of norms as we evaluate the six major political issues discussed earlier. For example, to St. Augustine a crucial fact of human life is the original sin of Adam and Eve and our inheritance of that sin of human rebelliousness against God. That fact is directly related to his view that a valid norm of the state and its power must be to serve as a divine remedy for human sinfulness. To be sure, there is much more to St. Augustine's view of the state than this simple statement. Yet we can read St. Augustine's text to see how his facts, diagnosis, and norms create a comprehensive vision of an ordered whole.

EXPLORING THE WORLDVIEW OF A POLITICAL PHILOSOPHY: THE MAJOR QUESTIONS

The great books of the political philosophers come to us from the problems and crises of their times. And they emerge from the sense of wonder of the political thinker who is open to the possibility of truth regarding (1) wisdom about the nature of the cosmos; (2) human nature and its relation to the cosmos; (3) the good society; and (4) the role of politics in human life (the philosophical approach). These four dimensions comprise the *worldview* of the political philosopher. This four-part structure of the worldview helps us unpack the comprehensive vision of each political philosopher to compare them historically—from Plato to Mill to Nietzsche. Studying political philosophy, according to Leo Strauss, "consists . . . in listening to conversations between the great philosophers . . . the greatest minds, and therefore in studying the great books."[ix]

For thousands of years human beings have asked questions about themselves, their role in the universe, and the purpose of their existence. Aristotle called this our sense of wonder—an innate and impelling necessity to seek the answers to these fundamental questions. Questions about the cosmos include the following: What is ultimate reality? Is it spirit or matter? Is the universe ordered or chaotic? Does a God or gods exist? Is life random or providentially guided? Is the universe inclined toward the good and the just, as St. Thomas Aquinas claims, or is it devoid of objective moral purpose, as Nietzsche claims? Can we know the answers or tentative answers to these questions? If so, how? By empirical evidence? By reason? By faith and divine revelation? G.K. Chesterton explains the practical relevance of our wider view of the universe:

> There are some people—and I am one of them—who think that the most practical and important thing about a man is still his view of the universe. We think that for a landlady considering a lodger it is important to know his income, but still more important to know his philosophy. We think that for a general about to fight an enemy it is important to know the enemy's numbers, but still more important to know the enemy's philosophy. We think the question is not whether the theory of the cosmos affects matters, but whether in the long run anything else affects them.

HUMAN NATURE

Only by focusing on political philosophers' teaching about human nature can we explore their response to the six fundamental questions of politics discussed previously. Human nature is the bedrock of any political philosophy. Human beings are clearly distinguished from other species by the fact of self-consciousness. We are aware that we exist, and this gives our lives a sense of meaning or significance. We have been enjoined by the great Socrates to know ourselves—perhaps better than we have in the past. What is our nature? Do we have certain essential, unchanging qualities that make us human? If so, what are they? Are we primarily individualistic or communitarian? Is the human being by nature a "political animal" as Aristotle claims? Or are we wolves to our fellow human beings as Hobbes claims? Is our human nature changing or

[ix]Leo Strauss, *Liberalism: Ancient and Modern* (New York: Basic Books, 1968), p. 7.

unchanging over time? Are we naturally good and perfectible? Can we improve ourselves? Are we equal as human beings in a politically relevant sense? If so, in what ways? Do humans possess a certain dignity demanding respect and recognition? If so, what is that human dignity, and what rights are related to it?[x]

After considering the answers a particular political philosopher gives to some of these questions, we can begin to identify the comprehensive vision that emerges from his or her view of ultimate reality, human nature, the good society, politics, and the state. This text, which is an invitation to the study of political philosophy, uses the historical approach primarily to provoke you to consider the great importance of increasing the number of people in our democracy who can think critically and engage in reasoned argument about political issues.

Our text provides you with both guidance and key primary source selections. We offer well-crafted guides to some of the major political philosophers. You will be guided through their writings and issues as we discuss some of the great controversies of interpreting their texts, as well as questions for reflection and application of specific ideas to contemporary controversies. In each case we employ the following framework:

- The biographical, intellectual, and historical context of the political philosopher.
- Worldview and method of investigation: the theological, ontological, epistemological, and ethical foundations of the political philosopher's view of religion, reality, knowledge, and moral norms.
- The philosopher's views about the nature of politics and the role of the state.
- Problems of politics and the state, addressing controversial questions concerning freedom, equality, justice, public order, law, and ethics, and political change advocated by the political philosopher.
- The contribution and influence of the political philosopher regarding problems and case studies such as gender, just war, music, politics, biotechnology, and tyrannicide.
- The key concepts employed by the political philosopher.
- An annotated bibliography, including Web links.

CRITERIA FOR EVALUATING A POLITICAL PHILOSOPHER

This text examines a highly diverse group of political philosophers from Plato to Nietzsche who afford the reader various standards for justifying particular forms of politics and the state. The reader should look for the philosophers' reasons for these prescriptions. Political relationships and the use of state coercive power have far-reaching effects on human well-being or misery. How, then, can we evaluate the adequacy of a political philosophy?

How intelligible is the political philosopher's use of these key concepts in political or public discourse? Some background about how the political philosopher uses these concepts in the context of his or her time is needed. Recognition must also be given to

[x]For an excellent discussion of five images of human nature, see Elizabeth Monroe Drews and Leslie Lipson, *Values and Humanity* (New York: St. Martin's Press, 1971), Chapter 1.

the meaning a political philosopher assigns to a key concept posited as a norm. The concept is a communicative device. For example, when Thomas Hobbes employs the notion of the state of nature, he does so to prescribe an enlarged concept of state authority. When Karl Marx discusses his concept of equality, he advocates the abolition of economic and class differences. We must ask how each political philosopher's use of such concepts as equality and the state of nature can be justified. Are the terms clearly and coherently used by the political philosopher to communicate political teachings? Does empirical evidence or history justify for the philosopher's use of these concepts? Aristotle studied 158 constitutions of his time. Hobbes cites empirical data for his thesis of human egoism. Machiavelli studied historical and contemporary case studies of leadership in formulating his political advice. Rousseau cites anthropological and ethnographic studies. Although such empirical knowledge is necessary for the development of a comprehensive vision, it is far from sufficient.

Ultimately, we need to examine how soundly political philosophers reason about the truth or validity of their norms like justice, equality, and liberty. Are we capable of knowing which norms are true or valid and therefore which political concepts are appropriate in political communication and debate? Are we slaves of our passions? Or is reason capable of discerning the meaning of our existence, such as the meaning of human community? Are we capable of grasping objective moral principles? As we will see, political philosophers differ considerably about what role reason can play in justifying the validity of various political norms. They disagree sharply over which human beings can reason soundly and what role political education can play in cultivating or nurturing human rationality.

We invite you to begin the journey of considering these enduring issues and questions of political philosophy. We invite you to engage in dialogue with these epic thinkers. We expect that you will learn something from each of them and intellectually contend with all of them.

An Invitation to Political Thought

PLATO

CHAPTER I

By Carson Holloway *University of Nebraska*

PLATO'S HISTORICAL CONTEXT

Plato may be the single most important thinker in the long, distinguished tradition of Western political philosophy. His importance depends not only on the profundity of his thought but also on his key initiating role in the tradition in which he continues to hold an honored place. Plato may justly be credited as the cofounder of political philosophy.

Political philosophy emerged at an identifiable moment in history, about 400 B.C., in the Greek city of Athens as the activity of a particular man, **Socrates.** Socrates is commonly regarded as the initiator of political philosophy because he was the first philosopher to turn philosophy from inquiry into the whole order of nature to inquiry into human things. Pre-Socratic philosophers, like Thales and Empedocles, were concerned primarily with cosmology—with giving an account of the fundamental principles governing the universe. Although such thinkers had looked outward to the cosmos, Socrates looked inward to the human soul. That is, he was the first to concentrate on political and moral questions in which ordinary citizens might be, and commonly are, passionately interested in questions regarding the nature of justice and injustice, good and evil, nobility and baseness.

Although Socrates was the first known political philosopher, and although he began a tradition of rational reflection on politics that continues to the present, he cannot be considered the sole founder of political philosophy. Socrates did not commit his reflections to writing, opting instead to pursue his quest for knowledge solely through conversations with his fellow citizens. Socrates is, however, regarded as the founder of a dialectical approach to political inquiry, one that elicits common opinions about political and moral matters and then subjects them to rational scrutiny. But this achievement could not have given rise to a 2,500-year tradition of political philosophy unless some of those citizens had captured the character of Socratic dialectic in writing. Among these citizens, Plato succeeded most spectacularly, communicating Plato's explorations of political questions in the form of written **dialogues,** or fictitious philosophic conversations, that are still admired for the beauty of their composition and studied for the depth of their wisdom.

Beyond his writings, we know little about Plato's life. He was born into a prominent Athenian family, some of whose members were active in the oligarchic political faction that sought to overthrow the Athenian democratic regime. Late in his life he traveled to Sicily to try (unsuccessfully) to reform the rule of the Syracusan tyrant Dionysius II. At Athens he founded a school of philosophy known as the Academy; Aristotle was among his students. The pivotal events of Plato's life were his youthful turn to philosophy under the influence of Socrates and Socrates' subsequent execution by the city on charges of impiety and corruption of the youth. Plato usually makes Socrates the primary interlocutor in his dialogues, and the dialogues show an acute awareness of the problem of the philosopher's relationship to the political community of which he is a member: The philosopher's quest for the truth about political things often seems to threaten the community in which he lives, which depends for its stability on the uncritical acceptance of certain opinions about the nature and purposes of politics.

This theme is addressed in Plato's greatest dialogue, on which we will focus most of our attention here: the *Republic*. The *Republic* explores the problem of philosophy's relationship to the **city** (the ***polis*** in Greek) or the political community by constructing a

QUESTIONS FOR REFLECTION | *THE DIALOGUE VERSUS THE TREATISE*

Plato's political philosophy is expressed in a number of dialogues, in none of which Plato himself appears as a speaking character. In contrast, most other political philosophers have used treatises: straightforward arguments advanced in the author's own name and voice. What might be the strengths and weaknesses of each approach?

theoretical regime in which their interests might somehow be harmonized. Plato approaches these issues by depicting a dialogue involving Socrates and a number of younger men. Socrates descends to Piraeus, the port of Athens, with Glaucon, Plato's brother, to see a religious festival and pray to a goddess. Beginning to return to the city, they are detained by Polemarchus, who insists that they come to the home of his father, Cephalus, to talk.

THE ETHICS OF THE *REPUBLIC*

The *Republic* is addressed to an issue that must interest any serious human being. It is an inquiry into the nature of **justice**, seeking to clarify what justice is and why we should act justly. This issue arises in the context of Socrates' conversation with Cephalus. Socrates asks Cephalus, who is a very old and very rich man, about the difficulties of age and the benefits of wealth. Cephalus responds that possession of wealth saves people from being compelled to act unjustly and thus easing a key burden of age—fear that we will be punished after death for injustices we committed during our lives. Socrates turns the conversation to the question of the precise definition of justice, and in Book I he reveals the deficiencies of three opinions defended by three of his companions: Cephalus, Polemarchus, and Thrasymachus. Book I demonstrates the Socratic method of moral and political inquiry: Although Thrasymachus prefers **rhetoric** or speech making, passionately asserting a position for the others to take or leave, Socrates insists on **dialectic**—a process of asking and answering questions whereby we can rationally evaluate an opinion by seeing whether it can be defended as internally coherent and consistent with our experience.

Cephalus, in discussing the benefits of wealth, implies that justice is giving back what one has borrowed and telling the truth. Such actions may be just in most cases, but Socrates points out that they cannot by themselves simply define justice because at times it would not be just to do such things. One ought not, for example, give a borrowed weapon back or tell the truth to a person who has gone insane. Polemarchus then enters the conversation, both defending and revising his father's opinion. Justice, he says, is indeed giving what is owed; but this is to be understood as doing good to friends and harm to enemies. Socrates' questioning of Polemarchus reveals, however, that this view raises the following difficulty (among others): When harmed, human beings, like horses or dogs, appear to become worse with regard to their proper virtue, or their excellence or well-working. If justice is a human virtue, then Polemarchus' view would require us to believe that just men acting justly will make other men unjust. This Polemarchus takes to be impossible, so he agrees with Socrates that a just man will harm neither his friends nor anyone else—that it is never just to harm anyone. Thus in his discussion with Cephalus and Polemarchus, Socrates suggests that justice is somehow good for us and that the activity of justice in fact constitutes the proper functioning of the human being. Both of these notions are developed and clarified throughout the entire *Republic.*

Having eliminated two common but deficient notions of justice, Socrates proposes to Polemarchus a further inquiry into what justice is. They are interrupted, however, by Thrasymachus, who objects to their mode of inquiry, and to their presuppositions about justice, with a vehemence that leads Socrates to liken him to a wild beast. While the conversation thus far has depended to some extent on the decent assumption that justice involves a kind of principled concern with the good of others, Thrasymachus regards this as childish naiveté. Justice, he suggests, is a sham: It is merely "the advantage of the stronger," a human invention devised by some who seek to benefit at the expense of others. Specifically, political rulers invent justice as a means to exploit the ruled for the rulers' own profit. Moreover, injustice is more profitable than justice because in all undertakings the unjust person gets more than the just person. The full moral and political consequences of Thrasymachus' position are revealed by his willingness to invoke **tyranny** in the context of both arguments. What the tyrant sets down in a tyranny is just, and the tyrant is Thrasymachus' example of the great profitability of the greatest injustice!

While questioning Thrasymachus, Socrates brings to light the following difficulties with his understanding of justice and injustice. First, it has been set down in the argument that ruling is a kind of art—a provision that Thrasymachus does not dispute. Yet Socrates points out that it seems characteristic of all the arts that they seek the good of those they rule, rather than the good of the artist and ruler. Medicine, for example, seeks the health of the patient, not that of the physician. Although doctors may ask to be paid, this benefit is not intrinsic to their art. Indeed, their desire for payment shows that the art itself benefits someone else. In response to Thrasymachus' contention that injustice is more profitable than justice, Socrates observes that injustice leads to faction or conflict among human beings, so that they cannot then cooperate with a view to a common enterprise. Similarly, he argues, injustice causes such conflict even within a single human being that he or she will be unable to accomplish what is desired.

Socrates succeeds in subduing Thrasymachus. Nevertheless, it is evident that he has not yet adequately defended justice. His argument depends on the notion that ruling is a kind of art, a notion to which Thrasymachus agrees but that is not obviously true. Moreover, Thrasymachus insists throughout the argument that he is only answering as Socrates wishes in order to gratify him. Finally, Socrates himself admits that it is hardly possible to sufficiently defend justice when one has not yet said what it is! Despite its inconclusive ending, however, the dialogue of Book I need not be regarded as a loss. Socrates characterizes it as a "prelude" to the rest of the argument, and Book I introduces, among other key themes, the notion that it is possible for a human being to have factional conflict within himself. That idea, as we will see, is critical to Socrates' understanding of justice in the *Republic.*

Thus it falls to Glaucon and Adeimantus, the brothers of Plato, to offer a fuller and more powerful statement of Thrasymachus' understanding of justice and injustice, a view they associate with "the many," or the majority of merely ordinary human beings. The many contend, according to Glaucon, that justice is to be desired not for its own sake but only for the sake of its consequences. By itself it is a kind of drudgery that is practiced only for the sake of the benefits—such as wealth, power, and honor—that can be obtained through a just reputation. Glaucon insists that this is not his own view, but he nevertheless states it as completely as he can in the hope that Socrates will be able to refute it and show that justice is good in itself, that it alone has the power to make people happy.

According to Glaucon the many hold that justice is not directly rooted in human nature but is instead the product of a kind of agreement among people. By nature human beings are driven by greed—by a desire to get the better of their fellows. Thus by nature the best thing is to do injustice to others and get away with it. Most people, however, cannot succeed in doing this because they lack the strength or daring. Thus when all seek what is best by nature, many end up suffering what is worst: being treated unjustly and being unable to avenge it. Rather than suffer this, the many agree to treat each other justly—not because they believe justice is good in itself, but rather because they fear being treated unjustly by others. Thus justice is a form of drudgery that is practiced unwillingly. Accordingly, even those who seem just turn immediately to injustice the moment they think they can get away with it.

Socrates proposes to discover and defend justice by founding a **city in speech**, or a theoretical city, reasoning that when we see justice in the city we may be able to see it in the **soul.** The city, he contends, comes into being because people are needy rather than self-sufficient, and specifically because they need goods that can only be produced, or at least can best be produced, by other people. Thus Socrates contends that the human community requires a division of labor according to which people work only at the jobs for which they are best suited by nature, or for which they have the greatest aptitude. "One man, one art" and "minding one's own business" become fundamental principles of the *Republic*'s city in speech.

While the city requires a great variety of arts, the conversation suggests that ultimately these arts, and the corresponding human beings, can be arranged into three classes, each with its own specific virtue. Most obviously, the city will require a class of **artisans** or craftspeople to provide the goods necessary to the well-being of the body. These members of the city need the virtue of **moderation,** which enables them to govern their passions and submit to the commands of the city's rulers. If the city is to possess more than is necessary for mere subsistence living, however, it will need additional land, which may already be occupied, and which it therefore may need to take from its current occupants by force. Thus the city will require a class of soldiers or **guardians.** These citizens must have **courage** and therefore must possess **spiritedness,** that quality that includes the capacities—such as anger, love of distinction, and concern for one's own—that allow one to overcome fear of pain and death. More careful consideration reveals, however, that the soldiers, although their function is necessary to the city's good, do not necessarily know what that good is. Therefore a final class is required: a class of rulers who possess the **wisdom** about what is good for the city as a whole. These last, Socrates suggests, are the true guardians of the city, whereas the soldier class should be known as their **auxiliaries.**

Class	Defining Virtue
Artisans	Moderation
Guardians	Courage
Rulers	Wisdom

Justice in the city is secured, Socrates suggests, when each of these classes minds its own business or tends its own art, not meddling in each others' affairs or trying to take over each others' functions. Specifically, justice exists where the guardians, who possess wisdom, rule; the auxiliaries, who possess courage, defend the city and enforce the rule of the guardians; and the craftspeople obey and produce the things needed for the city. This justice in the city, moreover, corresponds to justice in the soul, which, again, is the ultimate object of Socrates and his companions' quest. The three classes in the city, they agree, correspond to the three elements of the human soul. That is, each soul possesses **reason,** capable of calculation; **spiritedness,** capable of anger, self-assertion, and moral indignation; and **desire,** concerned with the pleasures of the body. Justice in the soul is the proper ordering that exists when the rational element rules over the desires with the assistance of the spirited element. Conversely, injustice in the soul is the faction or discord that exists when the inferior elements in the soul seek to rule the whole—that is, when they do not mind their own business and obey reason, but seek to meddle with its rule.

The *Republic* suggests, then, that the city is the human soul writ large. Thus the order of the soul and that of the city do not simply mirror each other but in fact influence each other. Order in the soul fosters order in the city, and disorder in the soul tends to generate disorder in the city. For example, citizens who lack moderation, whose desires are excessively strong, will be unable to submit to the reasonable laws of the ruling guardian class but will instead seek to rule the city themselves, in the interests of the desires that dominate their own souls. We will take up this connection again in the next section's discussion of education.

Socrates suggests that the just order of the soul, whereby reason rules, is best insofar as reason is capable of foresight and therefore can tend to the needs of the whole soul. Indeed, Socrates insists that this ordering conforms to the **nature** of the soul and therefore amounts to a kind of health of soul. Just as there is a certain ordering of the parts of the body that we call physical health, a certain ordering of the parts of the soul ought to be understood as the natural health of the soul. With this view, we can see some reason why justice might be thought desirable for its own sake. As Glaucon asks, rhetorically, "If life doesn't seem livable with the body's nature corrupted . . . will it then be livable when the nature of that very thing [the soul] by which we live is confused and corrupted" (445a–b)?[1]

Despite Glaucon's laudable eagerness to agree to the intrinsic goodness of justice, some questions remain. The exact nature of reason's rule over the other parts of the soul is not yet clear. Why should we not allow reason to rule with a view to gratifying the desires of the body? Indeed, Glaucon's earlier description of the unjust person suggests that he or she is able to get away with injustice not only by force but also by cleverness. This could well be compatible with a kind of rule of reason in the soul—with reason carefully calculating the injustices necessary to the greatest possible gratification of the desires. Thus Socrates indicates later, at the beginning of Book VI, that there is still much to be learned to see the difference between just and unjust lives.

[1]Quotations used in the commentary in this chapter are taken from Allan Bloom's translation of the *Republic* (Basic Books, 1968). Passages are identified by the Stephanus numbers, which are uniform in all editions of Plato's works.

The *Republic* ultimately responds to this implicit challenge by suggesting that reason rules over the rest of the soul primarily for reason's own good and that reason's good is in truth the good of the whole soul. In Book VII Socrates introduces the *Republic*'s famous image of the **cave.** A good human life, Socrates suggests, can be likened to an ascent from a cave, in which confused people believe in the reality of shadows cast by artificial things, to the light of day, in which one who has made the ascent can delight in seeing real things in the light of the sun and even in seeing the sun itself. The cave, it seems, stands for the visible world in which we find our bodily selves, whereas the sunlit world outside the cave stands for the intelligible principles that inform the world's existence. Finally, the sun stands for what Socrates terms **the idea of the good:** the supreme and perfect cause of all being, intelligibility, and goodness that we see imperfectly reflected in the visible world. The rational element of the soul, the *Republic* indicates, is the part of us that is most akin to the idea of the good. Reason longs for the good and finds its happiness in contemplation of the good. Reason, however, is a distinctively human element, insofar as other animals possess bodily desire and even spiritedness. Thus reason is above all the human good. Ultimately, Socrates suggests, the good is "what every soul pursues and for the sake of which it does everything" (505e). The idea of the good is, the *Republic* suggests, the ultimate but imperfectly realizable standard for human life. As an intelligible essence that exists independent of this world of space and time, it provides measure of perfection in light of which we can judge between good and bad. At the same time, however, its transcendence of this world of limitations and imperfections makes it impossible for the good to be fully grasped or achieved in this life. Socrates states that the good itself is beyond being. Nevertheless, the *Republic* suggests that reason's imperfectly successful pursuit of the perfect good is productive of a greater happiness for the soul than the successful enjoyment of imperfect and inferior goods, like bodily pleasure and honor, sought by the lower parts of the soul—the desiring and spirited elements.

Those who are most earnest about seeking the good through rational contemplation, the *Republic* suggests, are both happiest, because they give their own soul what is most fitting for it, and also least inclined to injustice, because they are least interested in the bodily and spirited goods, such as gain and power, for the sake of which so much injustice is perpetrated. Thus the philosopher is the most just person, both in the internal organization of the soul and in dealings with others, and his or her justice is far from drudgery but is in fact intimately linked to supreme happiness.

The mirror image of the philosopher is the tyrant. Both are animated by a great love, although the objects of their loves are radically different. The philosopher loves and pursues wisdom, whereas the tyrant loves and pursues the gratification of bodily desires. As described in Book IX of the *Republic,* tyrants allow desires to rule their souls and accordingly subject their reason, their true and best selves, to slavery at the hands of their least dignified elements. Ruled by bodily passions, which are insatiable when ungoverned by reason, tyrants require more and more goods to feed their ravenous appetites. Thus they are led into the most obvious forms of injustice, taking the goods of others by force. Yet all this wealth and power cannot make them happy, both because their desires are insatiable and therefore always accompanied by the pain of inadequate satisfaction, and also because their reason is constantly stung by regret at its inability to enjoy its true good. Thus tyrants are the most unjust of people, both in the internal organization of their own souls and in their dealings with others, and their

QUESTIONS FOR REFLECTION

The Philosopher versus the Tyrant

While many think that power will ensure their happiness, Socrates teaches instead that true human happiness is found in wisdom or knowledge, especially knowledge of the highest things. In a sense, the most powerful person, the tyrant, is the weakest, because the disorder in his or her soul makes him or her powerless to be happy. Does Socrates' argument ring true? Would we count Saddam Hussein a happy man if he had been able to live out a complete life as ruler of Iraq?

injustice is far from profitable but is in fact the cause of ceaseless misery. Thus does the *Republic* refute the assertions of Thrasymachus and answer the demands of Glaucon and Adeimantus.

Despite the goodness, justice, and happiness of the philosophic life, the *Republic* does not teach that it is completely unproblematic, at least when we consider its relationship to other nonphilosophic lives. Rather, there is a tension between the life of the philosopher and that of the political community in which he or she must live. This tension is suggested by the fate of Socrates, who, we recall, was in the end executed by the city of Athens for impiety and corrupting the youth. This tension is also suggested by the *Republic*'s image of the cave. As mentioned before, Socrates presents the cave as a metaphor for the visible realm of material things, as opposed to the realm of intelligible principles. The cave may also be understood, however, as representing more particularly the city, the political community, and the realm of opinion in which it must exist. In this view, the shadows cast on the wall of the cave are understood as the opinions that citizens hold, while the artificial objects casting the shadows are the speeches of the sophists and rhetoricians who have the skill or cunning to influence their fellow citizens' opinions but who, as nonphilosophers, do not know the truth and therefore cannot lead others to it. However unfounded in nature their opinions may be, they appear as truth to the cave dwellers, and indeed as the only truth they have ever known. As a result, when the philosopher returns to the cave and tries to relate to fellow citizens what he or she has seen of the real beings that exist in the world outside, he or she is likely to be greeted not as a savior bringing truth but as a crazy person or evildoer whose own mind has been corrupted and who is now threatening to corrupt other minds.

THE NATURE OF POLITICS

For Plato, the purpose of the city or political community is to provide the citizens with an education in virtue. While certainly familiar to modern readers, both terms—*education* and *virtue*—require some clarification if we are fully to appreciate Plato's intention. For the Greeks, **education** (or ***paideia***) included not only the learning of information, but more especially the formation of character. Moreover, **virtue** (***arête***) signified not only the decent habits necessary to orderly living in society, but also the highest activities of the human soul. Thus for Plato the aim of the city is to provide the citizens with character formation that fosters civic and human excellence. It is in light of this understanding that Socrates, in *Gorgias*, claims that the great statesmen of Athens' past were really not statesmen at all, for they merely increased the power of the city without making the citizens better. Similarly, in the *Apology* Socrates goes so far

PRIMARY SOURCE 1.1

JUSTICE IN THE RING OF GYGES, FROM THE *REPUBLIC*, BOOK II[2]

[Glaucon:] They say that to do injustice is, by nature, good; to suffer injustice, evil; but that the evil is greater than the good. And so when men have both done and suffered injustice and have had experience of both, not being able to avoid the one and obtain the other, they think that they had better agree among themselves to have neither; hence there arise laws and mutual covenants; and that which is ordained by law is termed by them lawful and just. This they affirm to be the origin and nature of justice; it is a mean or compromise, between the best of all, which is to do injustice and not be punished, and the worst of all, which is to suffer injustice without the power of retaliation; and justice, being at a middle point between the two, is tolerated not as a good, but as the lesser evil, and honored by reason of the inability of men to do injustice. For no man who is worthy to be called a man would ever submit to such an agreement if he were able to resist; he would be mad if he did. Such is the received account, Socrates, of the nature and origin of justice.

Now that those who practice justice do so involuntarily and because they have not the power to be unjust will best appear if we imagine something of this kind: having given both to the just and the unjust power to do what they will, let us watch and see whither desire will lead them; then we shall discover in the very act the just and unjust man to be proceeding along the same road, following their interest, which all natures deem to be their good, and are only diverted into the path of justice by the force of law. The liberty which we are supposing may be most completely given to them in the form of such a power as is said to have been possessed by Gyges the ancestor of Croesus the Lydian. According to the tradition, Gyges was a shepherd in the service of the king of Lydia; there was a great storm, and an earthquake made an opening in the earth at the place where he was feeding his flock. Amazed at the sight, he descended into the opening, where, among other marvels, he beheld a hollow brazen horse, having doors, at which he stooping and looking in saw a dead body of stature, as appeared to him, more than human, and having nothing on but a gold ring; this he took from the finger of the dead and reascended. Now the shepherds met together, according to custom, that they might send their monthly report about the flocks to the king; into their assembly he came having the ring on his finger, and as he was sitting among them he chanced to turn the collet of the ring inside his hand, when instantly he became invisible to the rest of the company and they began to speak of him as if he were no longer present. He was astonished at this, and again touching the ring he turned the collet outwards and reappeared; he made several trials of the ring, and always with the same result—when he turned the collet inwards he became invisible, when outwards he reappeared. Whereupon he contrived to be chosen one of the messengers who were sent to the court; where as soon as he arrived he seduced the queen, and with her help conspired against the king and slew him, and took the kingdom. Suppose now that there were two such magic rings, and the just put on one of them and the unjust the other; no man can be imagined to be of such an iron nature that he would stand fast in justice. No man would keep his hands off what was not his own when he could safely take what he liked out of the market, or go into houses and lie with any one at his pleasure, or kill or release from prison whom he would, and in all respects be like a God among men. Then the actions of the just would be as the actions of the unjust; they would both come at last to the same point. And this we may truly affirm to be a great proof that a man is just, not willingly or because he thinks that justice is any good to him individually, but of necessity, for wherever any one thinks that he can safely be unjust, there he is unjust. For all men believe in their hearts that injustice is far more profitable to the individual than justice, and he who argues as I have been supposing, will say that they are

continued

[2]The primary source of excerpts in this chapter is the Benjamin Jowett translation of the *Republic*, which is available on MIT's Internet Classics Archive: http://classics.mit.edu/index.html.

PRIMARY SOURCE 1.1

Justice in the Ring of Gyges, from the *Republic*, Book II *continued*

right. If you could imagine any one obtaining this power of becoming invisible, and never doing any wrong or touching what was another's, he would be thought by the lookers-on to be a most wretched idiot, although they would praise him to one another's faces, and keep up appearances with one another from a fear that they too might suffer injustice.

http://classics.mit.edu/Plato/republic.html

as to contend that he is the only true statesman that Athens has ever had, for only he has taken care to lead his fellow citizens to virtue.

Plato's works do not merely advance this criticism of existing political practice, however, but also point the way toward its reform or improvement through the speeches and actions of philosophically educated citizens. In *Gorgias,* for example, Socrates spends much of his part in the conversation correcting the popular overestimation of the goodness of rhetoric by condemning it as a form of flattery rather than a science or art. While the sciences and arts lead to knowledge of what is good for the things that they study or produce, rhetoric is merely a knack by which the rhetorician gratifies his or her own passions by successfully flattering, and thereby manipulating, the passions of fellow citizens. Socrates finally suggests, however, that a political rhetoric informed by philosophy could be used to speak to the passions of citizens, not with a view to moving them to whatever end happens to suit the speaker, but with a view to drawing them toward the concern with virtue that is necessary to their own happiness and the well-being of the city as a whole. Thus a philosophically informed rhetoric could advance the cause of the true statesmanship of which Socrates speaks.

The *Apology,* Plato's account of Socrates' defense of himself at his trial, may be seen as an example of such a philosophically informed and public-spirited rhetoric and hence as an act of true statesmanship. In the *Apology* Socrates does what is rare for him and what he says he prefers not to do: He addresses a large group of people (the jury, which was made up of 500 of his fellow citizens) instead of conversing with a single individual. Thus his speech here is rhetorical rather than dialectical. Moreover, Socrates explicitly refuses to appeal to the sympathetic passions of the jurors to save himself and opts instead to undertake the more statesmanlike, and more challenging, mission of persuading his fellow citizens that his philosophic activity is not impious and corrupting but instead holy and virtuous. That is, he tries to improve his fellow citizens by awakening them to the importance of the virtue of their souls and to the role that philosophy plays in pursuing that virtue. Despite his conviction and execution, moreover, the *Apology* can be seen as demonstrating the possible effectiveness of such a philosophically informed rhetoric. Socrates nearly succeeds—he mentions that a switch of 30 votes would have won his acquittal—and the subsequent flourishing of philosophy in Athens, first at Plato's Academy and later at Aristotle's Lyceum, suggests that he may have succeeded in his broader aim even as he failed to save himself.

Nevertheless, Socrates' inability to persuade a majority of the jurors also demonstrates the limits of philosophic rhetoric. The difficulty, it seems, is that some souls are so ill-disposed toward virtue that even the most skillful rhetorician will be unable to

PRIMARY SOURCE 1.2 | THE CAVE ANALOGY, FROM THE *REPUBLIC*, BOOK VII

[Socrates, speaking to Glaucon:] AND now, I said, let me show in a figure how far our nature is enlightened or unenlightened: Behold! human beings living in a underground den, which has a mouth open towards the light and reaching all along the den; here they have been from their childhood, and have their legs and necks chained so that they cannot move, and can only see before them, being prevented by the chains from turning round their heads. Above and behind them a fire is blazing at a distance, and between the fire and the prisoners there is a raised way; and you will see, if you look, a low wall built along the way, like the screen which marionette players have in front of them, over which they show the puppets.

I see.

And do you see, I said, men passing along the wall carrying all sorts of vessels, and statues and figures of animals made of wood and stone and various materials, which appear over the wall? Some of them are talking, others silent.

You have shown me a strange image, and they are strange prisoners.

Like ourselves, I replied; and they see only their own shadows, or the shadows of one another, which the fire throws on the opposite wall of the cave?

True, he said; how could they see anything but the shadows if they were never allowed to move their heads?

And of the objects which are being carried in like manner they would only see the shadows?

Yes, he said.

And if they were able to converse with one another, would they not suppose that they were naming what was actually before them?

Very true.

And suppose further that the prison had an echo which came from the other side, would they not be sure to fancy when one of the passers-by spoke that the voice which they heard came from the passing shadow?

No question, he replied.

To them, I said, the truth would be literally nothing but the shadows of the images.

That is certain.

And now look again, and see what will naturally follow if the prisoners are released and disabused of their error. At first, when any of them is liberated and compelled suddenly to stand up and turn his neck round and walk and look towards the light, he will suffer sharp pains; the glare will distress him, and he will be unable to see the realities of which in his former state he had seen the shadows; and then conceive some one saying to him, that what he saw before was an illusion, but that now, when he is approaching nearer to being and his eye is turned towards more real existence, he has a clearer vision—what will be his reply?

And you may further imagine that his instructor is pointing to the objects as they pass and requiring him to name them,—will he not be perplexed? Will he not fancy that the shadows which he formerly saw are truer than the objects which are now shown to him?

Far truer.

And if he is compelled to look straight at the light, will he not have a pain in his eyes which will make him turn away to take and take in the objects of vision which he can see, and which he will conceive to be in reality clearer than the things which are now being shown to him?

True.

And suppose once more, that he is reluctantly dragged up a steep and rugged ascent, and held fast until he's forced into the presence of the sun himself, is he not likely to be pained and irritated? When he approaches the light his eyes will be dazzled, and he will not be able to see anything at all of what are now called realities.

Not all in a moment, he said.

He will require to grow accustomed to the sight of the upper world. And first he will see the shadows best, next the reflections of men and other objects in the water, and then the objects themselves; then he will gaze upon the light of the moon and the stars and the spangled heaven; and he will see the sky and the stars by night better than the sun or the light of the sun by day?

Certainly.

continued

PRIMARY SOURCE 1.2

The Cave Analogy, from the *Republic*, Book VII *continued*

Last of he will be able to see the sun, and not mere reflections of him in the water, but he will see him in his own proper place, and not in another; and he will contemplate him as he is.

Certainly.

He will then proceed to argue that this is he who gives the season and the years, and is the guardian of all that is in the visible world, and in a certain way the cause of all things which he and his fellows have been accustomed to behold?

Clearly, he said, he would first see the sun and then reason about him.

And when he remembered his old habitation, and the wisdom of the den and his fellow-prisoners, do you not suppose that he would felicitate himself on the change, and pity them?

Certainly, he would.

And if they were in the habit of conferring honors among themselves on those who were quickest to observe the passing shadows and to remark which of them went before, and which followed after, and which were together; and who were therefore best able to draw conclusions as to the future, do you think that he would care for such honors and glories, or envy the possessors of them?

Would he not say with Homer,

Better to be the poor servant of a poor master,

and to endure anything, rather than think as they do and live after their manner?

Yes, he said, I think that he would rather suffer anything than entertain these false notions and live in this miserable manner.

Imagine once more, I said, such a one coming suddenly out of the sun to be replaced in his old situation; would he not be certain to have his eyes full of darkness?

To be sure, he said.

And if there were a contest, and he had to compete in measuring the shadows with the prisoners who had never moved out of the den, while his sight was still weak, and before his eyes had become steady (and the time which would be needed to acquire this new habit of sight might be very considerable) would he not be ridiculous? Men would say of him that up he went and down he came without his eyes; and that it was better not even to think of ascending; and if any one tried to loose another and lead him up to the light, let them only catch the offender, and they would put him to death.

No question, he said.

SOCRATES–GLAUCON

persuade them. This question then arises: How can the dispositions of souls be so shaped that they will be open to virtue? Thus the most thoroughgoing philosophic statesmanship will be concerned with the education, understood as the character formation, of the young.

The *Republic* gives sustained attention to this concern. In their search for justice through the founding of the city in speech, Socrates and his companions find that they must consider what kind of education will produce a character capable of being a noble and good guardian of the city. The guardians, Socrates and his companions agree, present a problem. On the one hand, they must be spirited so they can be courageous in war. On the other hand, they need to be gentle with their fellow citizens. These qualities do not easily go together, so Socrates and his companions begin to consider the kind of education or rearing that could harmonize them in the same human being.

The traditional Greek education, which they take as the starting point of their discussion, includes gymnastic training—understood generally as physical conditioning—for the body and **music** education for the soul. Although Socrates and his friends discuss both music and gymnastic, they devote far more time to consideration of the former. In addition, they return to music repeatedly even in the midst of their discussion of gymnastic. Both to follow Plato's insinuation of the priority of music, then, and because of space limitations, we will confine ourselves to what the *Republic* says about music education.

The Greek understanding of music embraces but is not limited to what we mean by music today. Socrates thus defines it in terms of the familiar elements of **rhythm, harmony,** and melody, but also includes "speeches," or poetry and literature, as well. Beginning with a consideration of "tales" told to children, Socrates and Adeimantus agree that because the young are so impressionable, they should not be allowed to hear just any stories. In traditional Greek poetry—for example, in the works of Homer, the *Iliad* and the *Odyssey*—the gods are presented as being animated by unruly passions such as lust and anger and indeed are frequently at war with one another. Such stories, Socrates contends, are not fitting for those being reared to be guardians because those who believe that the gods do all manner of injustice to each other will not think such actions unworthy of themselves. And the aim of education, again, is to produce guardians who will not exploit their power over other citizens, who ought not believe that it is holy for fellow citizens to grow angry with each other. Such stories, Socrates concludes, should not be heard by the young. Although Socrates begins by considering what is fitting for children, at some points he notes that the speeches to which he objects are not suitable for guardians of any age. Thus he speaks of them not only as being excluded from education but in fact as being banished from the city itself. Both the formation of character in the young and the preservation of character in the mature, it seems, require that some things not be heard. Thus the city in speech, the just city, requires a regime of **censorship** or public control of speech and artistic expression.

Socrates makes no attempt to identify every element in the ancestral poetry that is corrosive of good character. Nor does he attempt what would be even more difficult: the composition of new stories suitable for the just city. Rather, in conversation with Adeimantus and Glaucon, he proposes a series of models or laws to govern the creative work of the poets. These models are to regulate both substance and style—both what is said and how it is said. We begin with the discussion of the substance or content of the tales, which can be divided into two broad considerations: the depiction of the gods and the afterlife, and the depiction of the heroic human beings of the past.

Socrates and Adeimantus together work out the models that are to guide the presentation of the gods and the afterlife. They agree, in the first place, that the city's stories must not depict the divine as the source of evil. The god must be shown as he really is, and he is in fact good and consequently cannot cause evil or harm. Thus the gods will not be depicted as the cause of all things but only of the good. This is not to say, however, that the gods must never be presented as inflicting some pain on human beings. Socrates adds the important qualification that if a poet attributes the sufferings of some human characters to the actions of a god, he must say that the god's actions were good and that the people in question benefited by being punished. Second, they agree that the gods must not be shown as changing their form or deceiving human beings by false appearances. The god, they reason, surely would not change his form as a result of external force because our experience suggests that those things that are in the best condition are most impervious to changes imposed from the outside. Nor would the god desire to transform himself. Insofar as he is in the best condition, any change would necessarily be a change for the worse. But no being would voluntarily alter himself for the worse. Nor do the gods falsely appear to change their form so as to deceive human beings. Socrates admits that there might be good reasons for some humans to deceive others—for example, when one needs to defend oneself from an enemy or protect a friend from his own foolishness or insanity. It would seem, however, that one cannot attribute such motives to a god. As Adeimantus agrees, fear of enemies, or friendship with the foolish or insane, do not seem characteristic of a god. Finally, they consider poetic depictions of the afterlife. Again, as warriors the guardians will need courage. They must fear defeat in battle more than they fear death, and consequently the afterlife must not be presented as a place of horrors. Here again Socrates adds an important qualification. He says that the poets must not "simply" disparage the next life, and he holds that the guardians will believe that "for the decent man . . . being dead is not a terrible thing" (387d). He therefore holds open the possibility that the poetry of the just city will depict the afterlife as something fearful for those who are bad.

Socrates and Adeimantus further consider how the city's poetry will depict heroic men. Such men, they hold, will not be shown as grieving excessively for their dead comrades, behavior that is evidently incompatible with the discipline of a good soldier, who must fight on in defense of the city even when his fellows fall in battle. This requirement also follows from what they have already established regarding teaching about the afterlife. After all, if what happens after death is not terrible for a good man, then the good man's friends need not lament excessively at his passing. Finally, this element of the just city's poetry also points to the ancient understanding of the self-sufficiency of virtue. Extreme grief is inappropriate to poetry, Socrates suggests, because a "good man is most of all sufficient unto himself for living well and, in contrast to others, has least need of another" (387d). Thus for him it is "least terrible" to lose a friend or kinsman to death. This is not to say that the good man will not grieve at all. Nevertheless, if the exercise of virtue is what makes life good, then the good man's life will not be radically impaired by the death of those he loves.

In addition, they agree, the guardians must be truthful. Again Socrates suggests that a falsehood may be useful to some human beings as a kind of remedy or medicine for their badness. Nevertheless, even if this is the case, it is for doctors, not patients, to prescribe remedies. Therefore, if anyone in the city is to lie, it will be the rulers, not the citizens, whether soldiers or craftspeople. For them lying is a great evil because it conceals from the rulers the true state of the city and the true condition of the citizens' souls. Lying to rulers, Socrates suggests, is as bad as a patient lying to a physician about his or her body or a sailor lying to the captain about the state of the ship. Modern readers will likely object to Socrates' suggestion that rulers may legitimately deceive the ruled—and perhaps more generally to the inequality Socrates establishes between rulers and ruled: The former are to enjoy the whole truth, whereas the latter are not. We can say in his defense, however, that his intention clearly is not that the rulers exploit the citizens through deception. Here Socrates once again speaks of ruling as an art comparable to other arts. We recall, then, his argument in Book I that political rule and other arts are exercised not for the benefit of the ruler but for the good of the ruled. For Socrates, the inequality in relation to truth that exists between ruler and ruled is analogous to the inequality in relation to truth that exists between doctor and patient: The good of a patient demands that he share the whole truth with his doctor, but it does not necessarily require that the doctor share the whole truth with her patient.

Indeed, it is commonly recognized that sometimes a patient's recovery may be assisted by a certain degree of ignorance about his own condition. These observations also point to a response to our unease with the *Republic*'s entire scheme of censorship. Whether or not it is defensible, it is organized not so much with a view to the defense of the position of a self-interested ruling class, but with a view to the common good understood as the flourishing of justice in the souls of the citizens.

Finally, the guardians of the best city will need moderation, understood on the one hand as mastery over their own bodily desires, and on the other as obedience to their rulers. Self-control with regard to eating, drinking, sleep, and sex is obviously essential to the soldier. The rigors of war call for some sacrifice of all these goods, and those who are self-indulgent in them will lack the strength of soul to endure war's hardships. Moreover, education through music is also intended, as we have seen, not only to make the guardians excellent in war, but also to make them gentle toward their fellow citizens. Yet immoderation fosters injustice. One who lacks self-control will be tempted to rob his fellow citizens to feed his insatiable bodily desires. Finally, deference to rulers is obviously essential to the good order of an army in particular and more generally to any organized society, including a political community. Thus the stories of the best city will depict the best people as self-controlled and obedient, and the common depictions of immoderation and arrogance in the Homeric heroes will have to be excluded.

As is suggested by the preceding discussion, Socrates' understanding of the proper content of the good city's poetry puts him in opposition to much of what is depicted by the greatest and most renowned of the Greek poets, Homer, whose works did more than any others to shape the minds of the ancient Greeks. This observation provides the basis for a correction of a common misunderstanding of ancient political philosophy in particular and the entire history of political philosophy more generally. It is often held that political philosophy does no more than rationalize the existing political and moral situation in which it finds itself, that it simply provides an intellectual justification for the practices and beliefs of the culture from which it emerges. Indeed, it is sometimes claimed that it is impossible for philosophy to do anything more because the human mind is incapable of rising above its immediate situation to discover truth that transcends particular cultures and historical periods. As our discussion shows, however, Plato, far from simply defending or explaining his culture's way of life, in fact engaged in a critical dialogue with—even a radical critique of—his own culture. The excessively spirited manliness of Homer's heroes is, the *Republic* suggests, a distortion of human nature incompatible with political or individual flourishing. A similarly self-critical posture is taken in all the great works of political philosophy, so it is erroneous to suggest that the Western tradition of political reflection was ever simply a justification of the political and moral status quo. Moreover, that political philosophers have been able to this extent to free themselves from the most deeply held beliefs of their own cultures suggests the possibility of a quest for a truth that transcends time and place.

Having considered the appropriate content of the stories to be told in the city in speech, Socrates and Adeimantus next investigate the style that will be suitable for such tales. This discussion further reveals the extent to which poetic expression may have to be controlled to provide a suitable rearing in virtue. Whereas the discussion of content indicates merely that bad actions will not be shown as being performed by

QUESTIONS FOR REFLECTION

Imitation and Narration

What would Plato likely think about the movies, television shows, and music produced by America's entertainment industry? Would he say that it is too willing to imitate excessive passions and wicked behaviors? Can a good story be told by narrating but not imitating such things? To what sort of moral standards, if any, should creative artists be held? Who, if anyone, should enforce those standards?

gods or famous men, the discussion of style suggests that such actions will not be shown at all in the poetry of the best city. Here a clarification is in order. This is not to say that the city in speech's poetry will simply avoid themes dealing with vice or evil. It is doubtful that any interesting story could be completely devoid of all less-than-virtuous actions. Rather, the kind of poetry Socrates proposes will relate the actions of bad men without actually depicting them. This can be achieved, Socrates suggests, by employing the proper combination of narration and imitation.

Poetry, Socrates explains to Adeimantus, sometimes takes the form of simple **narrative,** such as when an author relates the thrust of a character's speech or summarizes her actions. At other times poets use **imitation,** such as when they actually reproduce a character's words. Socrates clarifies his intention by referring to the poetic forms of his day—epic, drama, dithyramb; but we can more effectively clarify it for ourselves by seeking contemporary examples. For instance, a modern novel is typically a mixture of narration (the author describing the action and speeches) and imitation (the author actually quoting the words of the characters). Films, like the ancient drama, consist almost entirely of imitation, with actors not simply relating characters' deeds but speaking for and acting for—actually pretending to be—the characters themselves.

Imitation has moral consequences, however. More specifically, indiscriminate imitation is a moral hazard, especially for the young. The young are impressionable, and there is, Socrates holds, a real danger that they will "get a taste for the being"—that is, for the actual passions and deeds—from their "imitation" (395c–d). Thus it is essential that the guardians-in-training not take part in imitations of vice. The city in speech, then, will use only the narrative style of the "gentleman," or the noble and good man. It will allow imitation of the noble deeds and speeches of good men, whereas the disgraceful actions and speeches of bad men will merely be reported by simple narrative.

Socrates next turns to the more familiar parts of music, rhythm and harmony, with the more musical Glaucon taking Adeimantus' place in the conversation. Their handling of rhythm and harmony is guided by the same concerns that governed their discussion of poetry: For Socrates rhythm and harmony are just as imitative as poetry itself. That is, the various rhythms and harmonies are imitations or depictions of the various passions and states of character of which the human soul is capable. Thus certain rhythms and harmonies are appropriate to, or go with, certain kinds of speeches. Accordingly, because they have banished excessive grief from the city's poetry, the rhythm and harmony that communicate such feelings must be banished as well. Because immoderation is unsuitable for guardians, the rhythms and harmonies of symposia (drinking parties) must be excluded from the city's musical repertoire. Socrates seeks instead a music that will best represent the bearing and speech of the reasonable man in war and peace, one who endures the dangers of battle patiently and who holds his passions in check and listens to persuasion in peace.

It will no doubt at first seem strange to the modern reader that Plato should attribute such imitative powers to musical rhythm and harmony. Once again, a more careful definition of terms may clarify Plato's intention and reveal the reasonableness of his argument. For the ancient Greeks, the term *harmony* referred not, as it does for us, simply to a chord, but instead to a particular kind of mode or scale from which a melody could be constructed. More broadly, *mode* referred to a general style of music associated with a particular *harmonia* or scale. We still recognize, however, that different styles of music are suited to different emotions or actions—at the crudest level, for example, that major and minor musical keys tend to communicate different moods. Socrates' suggestion that rhythms can be ethically moderate or licentious is likewise confirmed by our own experience of music. We tend to recognize the stateliness of slow and even rhythms, on the one hand, and the frenzy of rapid and irregular ones, on the other.

Socrates' discussion of rhythm and harmony brings to light the ultimate aim of the good city's music education: gracefulness. That is, music—understood broadly again as poetry, stories, and tunes—aims to be graceful itself and to foster a graceful disposition in the souls of the citizens. There is, Socrates suggests, a reciprocal relationship between a graceful soul and graceful music. A graceful soul brings forth the orderly and dignified speeches and actions that are depicted in graceful music. Again, only certain forms of poetry and music adequately imitate the feelings, words, and deeds of good men. Conversely, exposure to a graceful poetic and musical presentation of the good speeches and deeds of good men tends to foster gracefulness in the souls of the audience. This occurs, Socrates argues, because music not only imitates the various moral dispositions of the characters but actually impresses them on the souls of the audience. The imitative arts not only depict characters; they also create sympathy for the characters and hence a willingness to be like them. This power is especially present in rhythm and harmony, Socrates contends, which have great emotional power and hence an ability to charm the soul. Thus the "rearing in music is most sovereign" because "rhythm and harmony most of all insinuate themselves into the inmost part of the soul and most vigorously lay hold of it in bringing grace with them; and they make a man most graceful if he is correctly reared, if not, the opposite" (401d).

This concern with gracefulness paves the way for Socrates' suggestion that music education culminates in love of the beautiful. The man properly reared in music, Socrates argues, will have the keenest appreciation of and affection for what is fine. He will praise and love what is beautiful and blame and hate what is ugly or disfigured. In particular, he will come to love the beauty of the well-ordered soul. If the "fine dispositions of the soul" should ever appear in anyone, Socrates notes, that would be "the fairest sight for him who is able to see," and the "musical man" would "most of all love such human beings" (402d). Once again Plato compels us to think beyond our own terminology to a new (to us) and different understanding of things. Music education, we recall, is moral education. Accordingly, for Plato moral education leads to, and is animated by a concern with, gracefulness of character or soul; and morality itself is somehow bound up with the beautiful. It is instructive to note in this connection that the Greeks typically used the same word—***kalon***—to signify both what is **noble** or morally dignified and what is **beautiful** or fine. Although we often seem to think of morality as being concerned with minimal standards of decency and

QUESTIONS FOR REFLECTION

Law and Character

Over the last 50 years or so, American law and culture have sought less and less to form character with a view to moderation. At the same time there has been an explosion of laws and regulations trying to govern the conduct of individuals and institutions. Would Plato see a connection between these two trends? Would he be correct?

orderliness, Plato's moral education and politics appear to aim at something higher, more difficult, and more refined.

The *Republic* suggests that the moral excellence of the musically educated citizens leads to a kind of civic health. Such citizens, while excelling mere decency and orderliness, will nonetheless be decent and orderly. Because of their musically induced love for moral beauty, they will be comparatively uninterested in the pleasures of the body. This moderation, in turn, fosters justice because human beings are commonly lead to unjust acts by the need to satisfy excessive desires. Thus Socrates suggests in Book IV that the regime's music education is a kind of lawful play that produces "law-abiding, good men" (424e). In contrast, cities that neglect music education will have citizens who are led by unruly or lawless desires to commit frequent injustices against each other. Unwilling to reform their characters, yet also unable to live with the conflicts caused by such injustice, these citizens, Socrates suggests, will try to remedy these clashes by setting down a multitude of rules governing the citizens' interactions with each other. This treats merely symptoms rather than the underlying disease, Socrates suggests, and such measures accomplish nothing other than to make the city's "illnesses more complicated and bigger" (426a). It is obvious to us, as modern readers, that the city founded by Socrates and his companions is, by reason of its scheme of censorship, radically unfree. Yet this political discipline over the arts is intended to secure a kind of freedom: freedom from the excessive legalism that tends to arise as an attempted remedy to the disorderly conduct of immoderate human beings.

Ultimately this musical education in moderation offers an even more important freedom. Again, Socrates contends, as we saw earlier, that the human soul finds its highest fulfillment in philosophic activity, in investigating and beholding the intelligible things, and above all the idea of the good. Yet he also compares the pleasures of the body and their "refinements" to "leaden weights" that turn the vision of the soul "downward," or away from the objects of philosophic contemplation (519a–b). The soul is prepared for philosophy, therefore, by proper rearing in music. That rearing fosters moderation, and immoderation of bodily desires is an impediment to philosophy. Thus the best city's music education frees both the city from conflict among its citizens and the soul for its highest happiness by calming the factionalism of the desires that impedes the activity of reason.

Although education in music is intended to prepare the soul for rule by reason, the *Republic* also suggests the insufficiency of such education, and indeed of reason itself, for fostering good citizenship. Ultimately the city must rely on myth to form citizens who will love each other and love the city, putting its well-being before their own. Thus Socrates introduces the **noble lie.** We must, he says, convince the members of the city that the period of their moral education was in fact a dream, that they were really being fashioned in the earth and were born of the land. Thus they will look upon the land as

PRIMARY SOURCE 1.3 | CENSORSHIP, FROM THE *REPUBLIC*, BOOK II

[Socrates, speaking to Adeimantus:] And shall we just carelessly allow children to hear any casual tales which may be devised by casual persons, and to receive into their minds ideas for the most part the very opposite of those which we should wish them to have when they are grown up?

We cannot.

Then the first thing will be to establish a censorship of the writers of fiction, and let the censors receive any tale of fiction which is good, and reject the bad; and we will desire mothers and nurses to tell their children the authorized ones only. Let them fashion the mind with such tales, even more fondly than they mould the body with their hands; but most of those which are now in use must be discarded.

Of what tales are you speaking? he said.

You may find a model of the lesser in the greater, I said; for they are necessarily of the same type, and there is the same spirit in both of them.

Very likely, he replied; but I do not as yet know what you would term the greater.

Those, I said, which are narrated by Homer and Hesiod, and the rest of the poets, who have ever been the great story-tellers of mankind.

But which stories do you mean, he said; and what fault do you find with them?

A fault which is most serious, I said; the fault of telling a lie, and, what is more, a bad lie.

But when is this fault committed?

Whenever an erroneous representation is made of the nature of gods and heroes, as when a painter paints a portrait not having the shadow of a likeness to the original.

Yes, he said, that sort of thing is certainly very blamable; but what are the stories which you mean?

First of all, I said, there was that greatest of all lies, in high places, which the poet told about Uranus, and which was a bad lie too—I mean what Hesiod says that Uranus did, and how Cronus retaliated on him. The doings of Cronus, and the sufferings which in turn his son inflicted upon him, even if they were true, ought certainly not to be lightly told to young and thoughtless persons; if possible, they had better be buried in silence. But if there is an absolute necessity for their mention, a chosen few might hear them in a mystery, and they should sacrifice not a common [Eleusinian] pig, but some huge and unprocurable victim; and then the number of the hearers will be very few indeed.

Why, yes, said he, those stories are extremely objectionable.

Yes, Adeimantus, they are stories not to be repeated in our State; the young man should not be told that in committing the worst of crimes he is far from doing anything outrageous; and that even if he chastises his father when he does wrong, in whatever manner, he will only be following the example of the first and greatest among the gods.

I entirely agree with you, he said; in my opinion those stories are quite unfit to be repeated.

Neither, if we mean our future guardians to regard the habit of quarrelling among themselves as of all things the basest, should any word be said to them of the wars in heaven, and of the plots and fightings of the gods against one another, for they are not true. No, we shall never mention the battles of the giants, or let them be embroidered on garments; and we shall be silent about the innumerable other quarrels of gods and heroes with their friends and relatives. If they would only believe us we would tell them that quarrelling is unholy, and that never up to this time has there been any quarrel between citizens; this is what old men and old women should begin by telling children; and when they grow up, the poets also should be told to compose for them in a similar spirit. But the narrative of Hephaestus binding Here his mother, or how on another occasion Zeus sent him flying for taking her part when she was being beaten, and all the battles of the gods in Homer—these tales must not be admitted into our State, whether they are supposed to have an allegorical meaning or not. For a young person cannot judge what is

continued

PRIMARY SOURCE 1.3 | CENSORSHIP, FROM THE *REPUBLIC*, BOOK II *continued*

allegorical and what is literal; anything that he receives into his mind at that age is likely to become indelible and unalterable; and therefore it is most important that the tales which the young first hear should be models of virtuous thoughts.

"a mother and nurse" and upon their fellow citizens as "brothers" also "born of the earth" (414d–e). The lie also includes an element intended to legitimize the political inequalities of the city in speech, to justify the rule by some over others. We will, Socrates says, teach the citizens that "the god, in fashioning those of you who are competent to rule mixed gold in at their birth; this is why they are most honored; in auxiliaries, silver; and iron and bronze in the farmers and the other craftsmen" (415a). Thus the city's myth must contain an element that provides a divine sanction for the political order and the authority of the ruling class. As with many institutions of the city in speech, it is not at all clear that Socrates expects it to be taken literally as a blueprint for real political reform. Socrates shows his awareness that such a lie would be very hard to swallow. Nevertheless, he brings it forward as a way of showing the limits of what reason can contribute to politics: All cities have such legitimizing myths, and the *Republic* suggests that even the most just city will require something like this.

PROBLEMS OF POLITICS AND THE STATE

The great and daunting problem confronted by the political teaching of the *Republic* is the massive gap between the theoretical city in speech that adequately supports justice, on the one hand, and on the other, the imperfectly just and often even corrupt character of existing cities. That is, the problem is the gulf between the "true" politics that philosophic reason can discover and the "real" politics of the ordinary regimes we encounter in practical political life. This problem is implicit even at the very beginning of Socrates and his companions' enterprise: After all, their search for justice through the founding of a city in speech indicates that justice is not to be found in actually existing cities. This problem grows more and more clear the further they pursue the argument, the more they seek to make their city in speech immune to injustice.

The problem of the gap between the best city and the politics with which almost all human beings are familiar, or the problem of the great cost of the pursuit of perfect justice, begins to come to light at the end of Book III of the *Republic*, after Socrates and his friends have completed their account of the music education of the guardians. As powerful as that education is, it seems that it is not yet an adequate safeguard for justice. Thus Socrates suggests that the difficulty that first pointed to the need for moral education—the possibility that the guardians would use their power to exploit the unarmed artisans—still remains. They will do so, he contends, if they are allowed to possess anything more than a bare minimum of personal property. "Whenever they'll possess private land, houses, and currency, they'll be householders and farmers instead of guardians, and they'll become masters and enemies instead of allies of the other citizens; hating and being hated, plotting and being plotted against" (417a). To forestall these dangers, the guardians must have their food and housing provided by the city, and

PRIMARY SOURCE 1.4 | MUSIC, FROM THE *REPUBLIC*, BOOK III

[Socrates, speaking with Glaucon:] But there is no difficulty in seeing that grace or the absence of grace is an effect of good or bad rhythm.

None at all.

And also that good and bad rhythm naturally assimilate to a good and bad style; and that harmony and discord in like manner follow style; for our principle is that rhythm and harmony are regulated by the words, and not the words by them.

Just so, he said, they should follow the words.

And will not the words and the character of the style depend on the temper of the soul?

Yes.

And everything else on the style?

Yes.

Then beauty of style and harmony and grace and good rhythm depend on simplicity—I mean the true simplicity of a rightly and nobly ordered mind and character, not that other simplicity which is only an euphemism for folly?

Very true, he replied.

And if our youth are to do their work in life, must they not make these graces and harmonies their perpetual aim?

They must.

And surely the art of the painter and every other creative and constructive art are full of them—weaving, embroidery, architecture, and every kind of manufacture; also nature, animal and vegetable—in all of them there is grace or the absence of grace. And ugliness and discord and inharmonious motion are nearly allied to ill words and ill nature, as grace and harmony are the twin sisters of goodness and virtue and bear their likeness.

That is quite true, he said.

But shall our superintendence go no further, and are the poets only to be required by us to express the image of the good in their works, on pain, if they do anything else, of expulsion from our State? Or is the same control to be extended to other artists, and are they also to be prohibited from exhibiting the opposite forms of vice and intemperance and meanness and indecency in sculpture and building and the other creative arts; and is he who cannot conform to this rule of ours to be prevented from practicing his art in our State, lest the taste of our citizens be corrupted by him? We would not have our guardians grow up amid images of moral deformity, as in some noxious pasture, and there browse and feed upon many a baneful herb and flower day by day, little by little, until they silently gather a festering mass of corruption in their own soul. Let our artists rather be those who are gifted to discern the true nature of the beautiful and graceful; then will our youth dwell in a land of health, amid fair sights and sounds, and receive the good in everything; and beauty, the effluence of fair works, shall flow into the eye and ear, like a health-giving breeze from a purer region, and insensibly draw the soul from earliest years into likeness and sympathy with the beauty of reason.

There can be no nobler training than that, he replied.

And therefore, I said, Glaucon, musical training is a more potent instrument than any other, because rhythm and harmony find their way into the inward places of the soul, on which they mightily fasten, imparting grace, and making the soul of him who is rightly educated graceful, or of him who is ill-educated ungraceful; and also because he who has received this true education of the inner being will most shrewdly perceive omissions or faults in art and nature, and with a true taste, while he praises and rejoices over and receives into his soul the good, and becomes noble and good, he will justly blame and hate the bad, now in the days of his youth, even before he is able to know the reason why; and when reason comes he will recognize and salute the friend with whom his education has made him long familiar.

Yes, he said, I quite agree with you in thinking that our youth should be trained in music and on the grounds which you mention.

Just as in learning to read, I said, we were satisfied when we knew the letters of the alphabet, which are very few, in all their recurring sizes and combinations; not slighting them as unimportant whether they occupy a space large

continued

PRIMARY SOURCE 1.4

Music, from the *Republic*, Book III *continued*

or small, but everywhere eager to make them out; and not thinking ourselves perfect in the art of reading until we recognize them wherever they are found:

True

Or, as we recognize the reflection of letters in the water, or in a mirror, only when we know the letters themselves; the same art and study giving us the knowledge of both:

Exactly—

Even so, as I maintain, neither we nor our guardians, whom we have to educate, can ever become musical until we and they know the essential forms, in all their combinations, and can recognize them and their images wherever they are found, not slighting them either in small things or great, but believing them all to be within the sphere of one art and study.

Most assuredly.

And when a beautiful soul harmonizes with a beautiful form, and the two are cast in one mould, that will be the fairest of sights to him who has an eye to see it?

The fairest indeed.

And the fairest is also the loveliest?

That may be assumed.

And the man who has the spirit of harmony will be most in love with the loveliest; but he will not love him who is of an inharmonious soul.

it must be enjoyed in common. They will share their meals together, and no one will possess a private home in which anyone who wishes cannot come. Thus the perfect security of justice appears to require, among the guardians, **communism** of property.

Such a proposal runs counter to actual political practice. Even in the communist societies of the 20th century most people had houses from which they could exclude most outsiders. It also seems to run counter to some deeply held human desires, as is indicated by Adeimantus' objection that this communistic arrangement will hardly make the guardians happy. To this charge Socrates offers a twofold response. He begins by noting that it would not be surprising if the guardians should in fact turn out to be the happiest of the citizens. After all, if, as the *Republic* suggests, human happiness is found more in the highest activities of the human soul than in the possession of large amounts of property, then the guardians, who have received a musical education in the beautiful, and some of whom will receive a philosophic education in addition, seem closer to true happiness than the artisans who can own as much property and gratify their desires as much as they like. In any case, Socrates continues, the city must be ordered with a view to the happiness of all the citizens and not just one class. And surely the happiness of the whole will be endangered if the class that can use military force is treated in such a way as to allow it to become greedy for property and possessions: It will have all the power it needs to take these from the subordinate class of craftspeople.

This argument seems to satisfy Adeimantus, but it contains the seeds of other, even bigger difficulties. In the context of his discussion of communism of property, Socrates suggests that the guardians will also hold their spouses and children according to the proverb that "friends have all things in common" (423e). This remark passes almost unnoticed at the time that it is made, and Socrates certainly attempts to pursue the argument without expanding on it. He is compelled to give an account of this apparently radical proposal, however, by the insistence of Polemarchus, Adeimantus, Glaucon, and Thrasymachus. Thus Socrates works through the famous **"three waves"** of Book V of the *Republic*: the three institutions, each more radical than the one

PRIMARY SOURCE 1.5 | THE NOBLE LIE, FROM THE *REPUBLIC*, BOOK III

[Socrates, speaking with Glaucon:] How then may we devise one of those needful falsehoods of which we lately spoke—just one royal lie which may deceive the rulers, if that be possible, and at any rate the rest of the city?

What sort of lie? he said.

Nothing new, I replied; only an old Phoenician tale of what has often occurred before now in other places (as the poets say, and have made the world believe), though not in our time, and I do not know whether such an event could ever happen again, or could now even be made probable, if it did.

How your words seem to hesitate on your lips!

You will not wonder, I replied, at my hesitation when you have heard.

Speak, he said, and fear not.

Well then, I will speak, although I really know not how to look you in the face, or in what words to utter the audacious fiction, which I propose to communicate gradually, first to the rulers, then to the soldiers, and lastly to the people. They are to be told that their youth was a dream, and the education and training which they received from us, an appearance only; in reality during all that time they were being formed and fed in the womb of the earth, where they themselves and their arms and appurtenances were manufactured; when they were completed, the earth, their mother, sent them up; and so, their country being their mother and also their nurse, they are bound to advise for her good, and to defend her against attacks, and her citizens they are to regard as children of the earth and their own brothers.

You had good reason, he said, to be ashamed of the lie which you were going to tell.

True, I replied, but there is more coming; I have only told you half. Citizens, we shall say to them in our tale, you are brothers, yet God has framed you differently. Some of you have the power of command, and in the composition of these he has mingled gold, wherefore also they have the greatest honour; others he has made of silver, to be auxiliaries; others again who are to be husbandmen and craftsmen he has composed of brass and iron; and the species will generally be preserved in the children. But as all are of the same original stock, a golden parent will sometimes have a silver son, or a silver parent a golden son. And God proclaims as a first principle to the rulers, and above all else, that there is nothing which should so anxiously guard, or of which they are to be such good guardians, as of the purity of the race. They should observe what elements mingle in their offspring; for if the son of a golden or silver parent has an admixture of brass and iron, then nature orders a transposition of ranks, and the eye of the ruler must not be pitiful towards the child because he has to descend in the scale and become a husbandman or artisan, just as there may be sons of artisans who having an admixture of gold or silver in them are raised to honour, and become guardians or auxiliaries. For an oracle says that when a man of brass or iron guards the State, it will be destroyed. Such is the tale . . .

before, that appear to be both essential to the perfectly just city and nearly impossible to imagine as existing in practice. As we will see, these institutions—and in particular the tension between the great care with which they are elaborated, on the one hand, and their extreme impracticability, on the other—have posed a serious challenge to interpreters of the *Republic*, who have been unable to agree on whether the three waves are to be taken as a literal political blueprint, as an ironic skewering of idealistic extremism, or as a way of educating the individual soul.

The first wave through which Socrates must struggle to swim is **equality of the sexes.** He and his companions agree that the women of the guardian class will share with the men in the work of guarding. If they are to share in the same tasks, however, they must also share in the same education as the men. This will appear a ridiculous

QUESTIONS FOR REFLECTION

Sex and Work

Many human societies have tended to assign different social functions to men and women. In recent generations, however, many developed nations have moved away from a sex-based division of labor toward opening all vocations to whoever can demonstrate an aptitude for them, regardless of whether they are men or women. That is, developed countries seem to be adopting notions of nature and justice similar to those advanced in Book V of the *Republic.* Other political philosophers, however, like Aristotle and Tocqueville, have defended a sexual division of labor as natural, arguing that men and women tend generally to have different emotional and moral dispositions that suit them for different tasks. Are there important natural differences between the sexes that have implications for how society should be organized?

conclusion to many, Socrates concedes, for it will result in something radically unheard of: a shared gymnastic education will require men and women to exercise naked together. Moreover, such a shared education, and generally the shared work that it serves, would appear to be not only ridiculous but also unreasonable because it seems to contradict a key principle on which the founders of the city in speech had earlier agreed. They had said at the outset of the creation of their city that its well-being would require different natures to perform different tasks. Yet it seems obvious that men and women have different natures and therefore should be assigned different jobs. Socrates answers this objection by suggesting a distinction between the nature of the body and the nature of the soul. While there are evident differences in the bodily natures of men and women, it is possible for their souls to be of a similar nature—for example, for a woman's soul to be equally capable as a man's of performing the doctor's art. Socrates and Glaucon then agree that with regard to the arts managed by the ruling guardian class, the appropriate natures are found in both men and women. We find some women who are spirited and some who are not, and some who are lovers of wisdom and some who are not. Thus some women are suited to the warlike and ruling functions assigned to the guardian class, and it would be unreasonable to assign such tasks exclusively to men. It is not, therefore, against nature to allow men and women to perform the same jobs. But if such things are not contrary to nature, they are surely not impossible. Nor can it be doubted that they are for the best. The education in music and gymnastic, after all, was designed to make the citizens as good as they can be. If, however, it has that effect on men, it must have a similar effect on the women who have the same kinds of souls as those men. Yet Socrates asks rhetorically what could be "better for the city than the coming into being in it of the best possible women and men." Finally, if such equality of the sexes is in harmony with nature and therefore good, then it cannot be truly ridiculous, no matter what jokes may be cracked by human beings whose minds have been formed by a traditional sexual division of labor that was contrary to nature.

Socrates must then confront the second wave of the argument: the **community of women and children,** or the abolition of the private family. "All these women" of the guardian class, Socrates states, will "belong to all these men in common, and no woman is to live privately with any man. And the children, in their turn, will be in common and neither will a parent know his own offspring, nor a child his parent" (547d). Training and working together, as the equality of the sexes demands, the men and women guardians will, Socrates observes, naturally be led to sexual coupling with each other. The laws of the city in speech, however, will not allow sexual permissiveness. Far from being a scheme of "free love," the community of women in the *Republic* actually involves the most stringent political regulation of the citizens' sexual behavior with a view to the good of the city, and specifically with a view to the breeding of the best possible class of guardians. Thus the rulers will allow frequent intercourse between the best men and best women, while not allowing it so often for inferior members of the guardian class. Moreover, given the resentments such a system is likely to cause, the rulers will devise a sexual lottery, elaborately fixed, so that those who are denied frequent sex will blame chance rather than the choice of the rulers. In addition to such deceptions, Socrates proposes something even darker. Because even the less-than-excellent guardians will not be completely denied access to sex, they will produce some children. These, and those who are born handicapped, Socrates says, will not be raised but instead will be hidden away and allowed to die. Thus the city in speech pursues its excellence even at the cost of embracing the evil of infanticide. Finally, children who are allowed to live will not be raised by their biological parents; they will be taken from their mothers and cared for in some common place, under the direction of citizens chosen for the task. When the mothers come to nurse the infants every care will be taken so that the actual mothers will not know their specific children.

It is difficult to see how the good of the city can be secured by the destruction of what the ordinary person usually takes to be the greatest good in life: his or her own particular family. Socrates, however, contends paradoxically that private families are in fact the source of much conflict in cities and therefore that their abolition will result in a certain harmony. Division, he argues, is the greatest evil for the city, while unity is the greatest good. The city is united by a community of pleasures and pains, when the same things please and pain all the members. It is divided, on the other hand, by the privacy of pleasures and pains, when some citizens are pained by the things that please the others. But the latter happens when people regard some fellow citizens as their own and some as not their own. Thus the most unified city, and hence the best city, is that in which each citizen regards all the rest as his or her own. Here, Socrates argues, the citizens will think of themselves as members of a single family and hence will be pleased and pained by the same things. Such a city will be free from factional conflict to the extent that human beings often do injustices to each other to advance the interests of their own relatives. The community of women and children, then, will be the cause of the greatest good for the city.

One might wonder whether abolition of the private family will really promote the unity of interests that Socrates seeks. That is, will the citizens of such a city actually feel and act as if they are all members of one family? This is the objection raised by Aristotle, who, in Book II of his *Politics*, criticizes the *Republic*'s communism on the grounds that when all are held to belong to each other, no one will feel any particularly strong attachment to anyone else. "Each of the citizens comes to have a thousand sons, though not as an individual, but each is in similar fashion the son of any of them; hence all will slight them in a similar fashion. . . . It is better, indeed, to have a cousin of one's own than a son in the sense indicated" in the *Republic*.[3]

---

[3]See Carnes Lord's translation of Aristotle's *Politics*, Book 2, Chapter 3 (University of Chicago Press, 1984).

QUESTIONS FOR REFLECTION

The Abolition of the Family

Is the private family an impediment to justice because it is a powerful source of partiality and conflict, as Book V of the *Republic* suggests? Or does the family serve the city well by fostering natural bonds of affection that can later be extended to the whole community, as Aristotle argues in the *Politics*? Can a plan to abolish the private family succeed, or will it necessarily cause so much frustration that sooner or later people will reject communal arrangements?

We might also wonder about the happiness of the guardians of such a city, who seem to have been stripped of every private pleasure. Socrates heads off such an inquiry, however, by suggesting that they will enjoy a certain happiness arising from the satisfaction of their spiritedness. After all, the guardians will be victors in the greatest competition, politics and war, and they will be honored by all citizens for the great victories they win. Surely, Socrates suggests, if the winners of the Olympic contests are happy in victory even after all the pleasures they have denied themselves in their training, the guardian class will be even more so, being awarded not mere medals for winning races, but the rule of the regime for preserving the city itself.

Is abolition of the private family and its replacement with a community of spouses and children possible? Is the greatest good for the city within our reach? The consideration of this question brings on the last and biggest wave of Book V, and the one that Socrates most tries to avoid. Glaucon, however, insists on hearing this final and most radical proposal, so Socrates again takes up the argument. Before continuing, however, he insists on the following qualification. We are seeking justice, he says, for the sake of a pattern or a standard by which we can judge our lives. That is, we are not out to prove that the justice we discover can come perfectly into being, but we are seeking it for the sake of showing that the person who most closely approaches it will be the happiest. This observation applies to justice in the city as well as justice in the soul. Indeed, they agree, things cannot simply be done as they are spoken. That is, there is a tension between political theory and political practice because the good that reason discovers cannot simply and directly be translated into action. Thus Socrates asks Glaucon to moderate his desire to be shown how the abolition of the family can be made possible. Glaucon consents, and Socrates proposes to show how something most approximating the arrangements they have discussed could come into being. According to Socrates, the single change that could transform the city in the direction of perfect justice would be for it to embrace the rule of philosophers. "Unless . . . the philosophers rule as kings or those now called kings and chiefs genuinely and adequately philosophize, and political power and philosophy coincide in the same place . . . there is no rest from ills for the cities, my dear Glaucon, nor I think for human kind, nor will the regime we have now described in speech ever come forth from nature, insofar as possible, and see the light of the sun" (473c–d).

Thus Socrates proposes the rule of **philosopher–kings** as the condition for the realization of the first two waves, sexual equality and community of women and children, and more generally for the realization of all that is good for the city. Of all the institutions proposed in Plato's *Republic*, the rule of philosopher–kings is probably the most famous—so famous, in fact, that it has almost become a commonplace. It may surprise the contemporary reader, then, to find that the *Republic* treats this institution as the most paradoxical and even outrageous, more controversial even than the aforementioned communism of property and family. Glaucon even indicates, perhaps in jest, that such a proposal is likely to provoke a violent response among Socrates' fellow citizens. Whether or not Glaucon is partly joking, Socrates himself thinks of this wave of the argument as the biggest and the most challenging. In fact, it is here that the *Republic* probably departs most radically from the Greek culture of Plato's day. The proposed abolition of the family, while radical, at least could be viewed as in harmony with the Greeks' extreme commitment to politics, which tended to view the family as radically subordinate to the public good, as merely a means to the breeding of a new generation of citizen–soldiers. That very commitment to political action as the highest human activity, however, also led most Greeks to look down on the pursuit of philosophy as a childish waste of time.

Socrates tries to defend the rule of philosophers by explaining what he means by a *philosopher*. The term is derived from the Greek words meaning "love" and "wisdom." The philosopher, then, is a lover of wisdom. When we speak of someone as a lover of something, however, we tend to mean that he or she loves *all* of that thing. For instance, lovers of food are not picky but like to eat whatever they can get their hands on. Or to take an example closer to political life, a lover of honor loves all honors, taking every distinction available, whether it is dignified or common. Such a person, Socrates says, is content to be praised by the competent or the ignorant, will be happy to be a general, but will take being a lieutenant if that is all that can be achieved. A philosopher, then, is a lover of *all* forms of learning and thus would appear to be uniquely fitted for ruling. Glaucon objects to Socrates' line of argument, noting that the lovers of all learning will surely include some strange characters, such as the lovers of sights and hearing, who are constantly in the theaters seeing every play and hearing every musical performance. These people do not seem particularly well equipped to govern the city.

In response to Glaucon's objection Socrates further clarifies what he means by a philosopher. He thereby returns us to the *Republic*'s concern with the transcendent good, which we earlier encountered in our discussion of the perfectly just person. The lovers of sights, Socrates argues, merely enjoy with their senses the various concrete things that to some extent participate in or give expression to beauty. In contrast, the philosopher loves to contemplate with the mind the nature of beauty itself. The beautiful and good things with which the lover of sights is preoccupied are not, after all, perfectly beautiful and good. They are all imperfect, all mixed with ugliness and evil. There is, after all, no perfectly beautiful human being, nor a perfectly just or good human being. All are in some way flawed. Yet in the excess of their love, the lovers of sights take these images of beauty and goodness to be the beautiful and the good themselves. Thus they are like people who are dreaming, who mistake images for realities. In contrast, the philosopher is fully awake, contemplating the natures of the beautiful and the good in themselves, and not the things of this world that give an imperfect impression of them. Thus in defining the philosopher as the lover of all wisdom, Socrates does not mean the person who is attracted to all things indiscriminately, but the person who is attracted to the highest, most perfect things that give the things of this world whatever goodness, beauty, and intelligibility it has.

Understood in this way, the true philosophers must be regarded as those who are best able to guard the city. In knowing the ultimate truth about things, they have "a clear pattern" of goodness "in the soul." "Looking off, as painters do, toward what is

QUESTIONS FOR REFLECTION

POLICY BLUEPRINT, CAUTIONARY TALE, OR THOUGHT EXPERIMENT?

Should the institutions discussed in Books V and VI of the *Republic* be understood as a program for political reform, as a way of illustrating the practical costs of an excessively idealistic commitment to justice, or as a way of revealing the proper ordering of the soul?

truest, and ever referring to it and contemplating it as precisely as possible," they can "give laws about what is fine, just, and good, if any need to be given, and as guardians" can "preserve those that are already established" (484c). The *Republic*'s theory of the best regime—and indeed that held by many of the classical political philosophers—can be summed up as follows: Because the aim of the city is to make the citizens as good as they can be, philosophers should rule because philosophers make it their business to know the nature of goodness.

Adeimantus objects to Socrates' defense of the rule of philosophers, and the objection appeals again to the apparent distance between speeches and actions, or between theory and practice. Most people, Adeimantus contends, will say that they cannot refute Socrates' argument that philosophers should rule. Nevertheless, they observe that in reality those who pursue philosophy over a lifetime become at worst very strange and perhaps even vicious, and at best simply useless to their political communities.

Socrates actually agrees that this is what typically happens. He argues, however, that this outcome results not because philosophy is a useless or wicked enterprise, but because the cities themselves are ignorant or corrupted. Bringing forth another of the great "images" of the *Republic*, Socrates compares the city to a disorderly ship. On this ship the sailors (politicians) take no concern for the art of navigation (statecraft) but instead spend all their time fighting over who will get to take the rudder (rule the city) and trying to dupe the ship owner (the people), who is powerful but knows nothing of navigation, into letting them steer. In such a situation, Socrates suggests, the true navigator (the philosopher) will indeed appear useless and a mere stargazer. He knows how to steer the ship on its proper course, but because he knows nothing about how to defeat those competing to get hold of the rudder, or about how to fool the ship owner into handing control over to him, he must appear worthless. Thus do decent philosophers appear useless in cities, through the fault not of the philosophers but of the cities themselves.

The prevailing political situation, Socrates continues, not only makes decent philosophers appear useless, but it also tends to corrupt any philosophic natures that might appear. When a young person appears who is capable of philosophy, who has a good mind and a desire for great things, his fellow citizens will sense his possible political usefulness. They will praise and cajole such a nature, doing everything they can to lead it into a political life and away from philosophy. Or to put it in terms of the image just described, when his fellow sailors see how clever the philosophic nature is, they will do all that they can to get him to leave off the study of the stars and join them in plotting to get the wheel. Intoxicated by the praise of the many, most such natures will leave philosophy for political competition and will turn away from the truly great things to the things, like power and rule, that are merely praised as great by ignorant and corrupted multitude. With the best natures drawn into politics, only unworthy

PRIMARY SOURCE 1.6 | GENDER EQUALITY, FROM THE *REPUBLIC*, BOOK V

[Socrates, speaking with Glaucon:] The part of the men has been played out, and now properly enough comes the turn of the women. Of them I will proceed to speak, and the more readily since I am invited by you. For men born and educated like our citizens, the only way, in my opinion, of arriving at a right conclusion about the possession and use of women and children is to follow the path on which we originally started, when we said that the men were to be the guardians and watchdogs of the herd.

True.

Let us further suppose the birth and education of our women to be subject to similar or nearly similar regulations; then we shall see whether the result accords with our design.

What do you mean?

What I mean may be put into the form of a question, I said: Are dogs divided into hes and shes, or do they both share equally in hunting and in keeping watch and in the other duties of dogs? Or do we entrust to the males the entire and exclusive care of the flocks, while we leave the females at home, under the idea that the bearing and suckling their puppies is labor enough for them?

No, he said, they share alike; the only difference between them is that the males are stronger and the females weaker.

But can you use different animals for the same purpose, unless they are bred and fed in the same way?

You cannot.

Then, if women are to have the same duties as men, they must have the same nurture and education?

Yes.

The education which was assigned to the men was music and gymnastic.

Yes.

Then women must be taught music and gymnastic and also the art of war, which they must practice like the men?

That is the inference, I suppose.

I should rather expect, I said, that several of our proposals, if they are carried out, being unusual, may appear ridiculous.

No doubt of it.

Yes, and the most ridiculous thing of all will be the sight of women naked in the palaestra, exercising with the men, especially when they are no longer young; they certainly will not be a vision of beauty, any more than the enthusiastic old men who in spite of wrinkles and ugliness continue to frequent the gymnasia.

Yes, indeed, he said: according to present notions the proposal would be thought ridiculous.

But then, I said, as we have determined to speak our minds, we must not fear the jests of the wits which will be directed against this sort of innovation; how they will talk of women's attainments both in music and gymnastic, and above all about their wearing armor and riding upon horseback!

Very true, he replied.

Yet having begun we must go forward to the rough places of the law; at the same time begging of these gentlemen.

---

characters remain to take up philosophy, which they do, giving it a bad name. Finally, if any decent philosophers remain, they stay clear of politics completely, seeing that it would be impossible to do any good among so many who are corrupt.

The chances of political reform, then, seem slight on the *Republic*'s account. All the reforms necessary to building the perfectly just city, or even an approximation to it, require the rule of philosophers. Yet in reality most human beings have contempt for philosophy, and politics tends to corrupt those capable of philosophy. Nevertheless, Socrates holds out the bare possibility that, though very hard, such reforms might come to pass. It is not, after all, impossible that by chance a true philosopher might be

CASE STUDY 1.1 | Plato's Contribution: The Critique of Democracy

Plato's contribution to political thought is so vast as to defy easy summarization. It has been well said by Alfred North Whitehead, and hence often repeated by many others, that the "history of Western philosophy" is a "series of footnotes to Plato." This is not to say that all subsequent political philosophers have accepted Plato's teaching and contented themselves with working out its details. However, Plato so clearly saw, and so vigorously articulated, the alternative answers to some of the deepest questions that all subsequent philosophers, even those most adamantly opposed to the tendencies of his thought, have found it necessary to engage Plato in one way or another, even if only in an effort to refute him. Here we will attend to just one aspect of Plato's thought that is as relevant now as it was in his own lifetime: his critique of **democracy**, which is laid out in Book VIII of the *Republic*.

We are tempted to deny the relevance of this critique because we suspect, quite understandably, that our way of life is so different from that known to Plato that his understanding of democracy must be vastly divergent from our own. To be sure, modern democracy is very different from that practiced in ancient Greece, both in scale—our authoritative political communities are nation–states, not cities—and in institutional organization—we legislate through elected legislatures, whereas the Greeks did so through an assembly of all the citizens. Nevertheless, Socrates' definition of democracy appears to include the core democratic principles that we still recognize and cherish today: equality of political power and individual liberty. Democracy, he suggests, is characterized by the citizens' sharing in "the regime and the ruling offices . . . on an equal basis" and by "full freedom" or a complete "license" to "do whatever one wants" (557a–b).

Socrates, as we will see, offers some rather pointed criticisms of democracy. He is not, however, insensitive to its beauties, which he praises in terms similar to those used by its contemporary defenders. Proponents of modern democracy often celebrate its pluralism, noting that its tolerance of diversity permits the flourishing of a variety of ways of life. Similarly, Socrates notes that unlike other regimes that use public authority to impose a certain way of life on the citizens, democracy, because of its emphasis on freedom, permits all sorts of human beings to appear. "Just like a many-colored cloak decorated in all hues," Socrates says, "this regime, decorated with all dispositions, would also look fairest" (557c). Moreover, because it permits all ways of life, democracy has the additional advantage of allowing philosophy. A democratic government will not actively prepare its best citizens for philosophic inquiry, as the *Republic*'s best regime seeks to do; but its respect for freedom at least opens a space in which those who are so disposed may pursue philosophy with minimal interference. Indeed, Socrates suggests that philosophy has a certain advantage in democracy, insofar as democratic diversity assists the philosopher in the quest for the best way of life. Because of its "license," democracy "contains all species of regimes"—that is, examples of all ways of life—so that "it is probably necessary for the man who wishes to organize a city" to go to a democracy, where he can examine all the alternatives and freely choose the best (557d).

Such praise, however, suggests a certain criticism of democracy. Insofar as Socrates holds that democracy is useful as a place in which one can seek the best regime, he implies that it is not itself the best. Indeed, Socrates offers a number of severe criticisms of democracy. Perhaps because of its ardent commitment to freedom, democracy tends to be soft, unwilling to impose standards of good behavior on its citizens. Democracy is noteworthy for its gentleness toward criminals. It is common there to see people who have been sentenced to death or exile nevertheless free and at large in the city. Perhaps because of its ardent commitment to equality, democracy is not particularly earnest about the moral quality, or even the public competence, of its leaders. The best regime, Socrates recalls, is convinced that its political health depends on the moral excellence of its citizens and especially its rulers. Thus it takes great pains to provide an education in nobility and goodness of soul. In contrast, Socrates holds, democracy disdains such education and "doesn't care at all from what kinds of practices a man goes to political action, but honors him if only he says he's well disposed toward the multitude" (558b). Indeed, democracy inclines to a certain injustice because its commitment to equality is so single-minded that it tends to desire to reward all equally regardless of their merit or achievement. Perhaps even here we can admit some

CASE STUDY 1.1 | PLATO'S CONTRIBUTION: THE CRITIQUE OF DEMOCRACY *continued*

relevance to the *Republic*'s critique of democracy. Although these criticisms may be somewhat exaggerated, we would be less than honest if we did not admit some truth to them. They are sometimes voiced by citizens of contemporary democracy.

According to Socrates, democracy tends to foster a certain lawlessness not only in the city but also within the soul of each citizen. The democratic person, he contends, is inclined toward immoderation because he or she refuses to distinguish necessary desires, those that are beneficial and just, from unnecessary ones, or those that bring nothing but pleasure. Again, this incapacity follows from democracy's commitment to its fundamental principles: freedom and equality. When embraced in an extreme form, such principles forbid not only that we assign different rights to different citizens, but even that we differently value different ways of life, actions, and passions. As Socrates notes, democratic people equally honor all desires and pursuits. They will not listen to the notion that "there are some pleasures belonging to fine and good desires and some belonging to bad desires, and that the ones must be practiced and honored and the others checked and enslaved. Rather they shake their heads at all this and say that all are alike and must be honored on an equal basis." Such a man thus tries all kinds of activities and ways of life indiscriminately, and "there is neither order nor necessity in his life" (561c–d).

Moreover, by infecting the soul of each citizen, democracy's excessive veneration of freedom and equality drives those principles beyond the political realm and into all areas of society, where they distort, as Socrates suggests, other human associations. Thus democratic citizens strive for equality even in relationships that make no sense except on the basis of a reasonable recognition of real inequalities in knowledge and experience. Parents and teachers, for example, not wishing to seem despotic, seek to be like their children and students, coming down to their level. On the other side, children and students seek to rise to the level of their parents and teachers, showing them no deference or respect, presuming to be their equals, because this is what adherence to democracy seems to require.

Ultimately, Socrates contends, democracy contains the seeds of its own demise—it paves the way for tyranny, the worst of all regimes. Democratic regimes, Socrates contends, give rise to three classes in the city. Democracy's commitment to freedom generally permits citizens to dispose of their property as they see fit. Free economic exchange results, which in turn gives rise to economic inequalities: The few who are orderly in character make sensible choices and grow wealthy, a larger number who are ruled by their passions squander their property and become poor, while a third class is sufficiently restrained to hold on to some small amount of property. This last group, Socrates says, is the largest and accordingly called "the people." Despite its numbers, however, this class does not dominate the politics of a democracy because its members are too preoccupied with keeping what they have earned and acquiring a bit more to pay much attention to public affairs. In contrast, the poor have every incentive to seek political influence because this is their sole remaining way to overcome their poverty. And because the wealthy are only few, and therefore in no position to control a process based on majority rule, the leadership in democracy tends to emerge from, and to advance the interests of, the poorest class.

Although the political dominance of the poor is natural to democracy, it is by no means healthy for democracy. According to Socrates, pursuing their own economic interests, the poor seek to use their political power to alleviate their poverty. Specifically, they try to pass laws taking property away from the wealthy and redistributing it among themselves. Because the wealthy are not sufficiently numerous to defend themselves within the democratic rules of the game, they, in order to defend their own interests, become enemies of democracy. That is, they become true oligarchs, those who desire rule by the wealthy and who therefore seek to overthrow the democratic regime. Perceiving this new threat to their interests and power, the poor, joined by the people generally, appoint some single person to be their leader and to exercise extraordinary powers in defense of their position. This person, however, will end up possessing power sufficient not only to preserve the democracy but in fact to rule it at his or her own discretion. Thus the people's leader becomes the city's tyrant; and the people, who had hoped to secure their freedom, end up being just as enslaved as the rich citizens whom they had begun by trying to oppress.

continued

CASE STUDY 1.1 PLATO'S CONTRIBUTION: THE CRITIQUE OF DEMOCRACY *continued*

We might be tempted to dismiss this account of democracy's fortunes as utterly irrelevant to us and indeed as disproved by our own experience. After all, American democracy has proved remarkably stable and has little class conflict—certainly none intense enough to threaten the life of the regime. Nevertheless, we would do well to consider that America's success in establishing a stable democracy may be in part attributable precisely to the influence of Plato's critique of democracy. Book VIII's account of democracy's suicidal tendencies is remarkably similar to that offered in *Federalist Papers* numbers 9 and 10, by Alexander Hamilton and James Madison, respectively. The American founders understood, both from study and experience, the inclination of democratic majorities, made up largely of the poor, to use their political power to take the property of the rich, thus provoking a factional conflict that could escalate into civil war. They accordingly devised institutions—like separation of powers, bicameralism, and representation—intended to permit majority rule while at the same time moderating it sufficiently to protect the rights, and particularly the property rights, of the wealthy. We must admit that taxation of the rich to benefit the poor and middle class remains a popular theme in American politics, and some Americans complain that our political institutions frustrate our ability to put such plans into effect. We would do well to consider, however, that these very institutions, precisely by protecting the property of the rich, allow them to remain loyal to our democracy without utterly sacrificing their own interests, and therefore foster a political stability that is rarely found in other democracies with less cleverly designed institutions. In other words, perhaps our democracy is so long-lived because its founders, under the influence of the Platonic critique of democracy, had the wisdom to moderate it.

thrust into power, or that a king might be attracted to true philosophy. Even here, however, he brings forth even more impediments to such politically saving philosophic rule. After all, being in love with the sight of the good itself, philosophers will be inclined to avoid political rule as a distraction from their truest happiness. And even a public spirited philosopher would likely demand that the slate be wiped clean before undertaking to reform the city, demanding that the young be turned over to his education while everyone over the age of 10 will be banished from the city. Such things are, to put it mildly, unlikely to come to pass.

Book V of Plato's *Republic* stands as a permanent problem and challenge to students of political philosophy. On the one hand, Socrates questions the possibility of these reforms and even leaves open the issue of their goodness. He hesitates to go through the waves, he says, out of fear that he might mislead his friends with regard to the greatest good. On the other hand, the institutions he describes appear to have a lasting appeal for the human political imagination, speaking to our longings for perfect equality, for a pure unity in commitment to the community, and for rule by wise leaders who will order things with a view to the ultimate good. Not surprisingly, then, Book V remains something of a puzzle to even the most famous and determined students of the *Republic*. Some, like Karl Popper, take it at face value as a sign of Plato's totalitarian utopianism, and so rank the author as an enemy of "open society." Others, like Leo Strauss, view Book V as intentionally ironic, a calculated effort to deflate utopian political aspirations by drawing out with a ruthless logic their extreme human costs, thus demonstrating the limits of politics and political reform. Still others, like Darrell Dobbs, argue that the institutions of Book V aim to reform not the city but the individual's soul by fostering a sense of responsible detachment from one's own particular goods on which both justice and philosophy depend.

Key Terms

Socrates
dialogues
city
polis
justice
rhetoric
dialectic
tyranny
city in speech
soul
artisans
moderation
guardians
courage
spiritedness
wisdom
auxiliaries
reason
desire
nature
cave
the idea of the good
education (*paideia)*
virtue (*arête)*
music
rhythm
harmony
censorship
narrative
imitation
kalon
noble
beautiful
noble lie
communism
three waves
equality of sexes
community of women and children
philosopher–kings
democracy

Sources and Resources

Key Texts

The *Republic*

The *Laws*

Four Texts on Socrates, translated by Thomas West and Grace Starry West (Cornell University Press, 1998). This book provides a fine and accessible introduction to Platonic political philosophy by offering four short works in which Socrates is a key figure: Plato's *Euthyphro, Apology*, and *Crito*, and Aristophanes' *The Clouds*. Especially instructive is the contrast between the critique of Socrates' influence on the city in *The Clouds* and his defense of his way of life in the *Apology*.

Secondary Texts

Karl Popper, *The Open Society and Its Enemies: Volume I, Plato* (Princeton University Press, 1971). Taking the city in speech of the *Republic* as an earnest blueprint for political reform, Popper criticizes Plato as a totalitarian.

Leo Strauss, *The City and Man* (University of Chicago Press, 1978). In this work's chapter about Plato, Strauss pioneers an interpretation that has proven very influential in recent decades: that the *Republic*'s city in speech is in fact intended to dissuade readers from utopian political aspirations by illustrating their extreme costs.

Darrell Dobbs, "Socratic Communism" (*The Journal of Politics*, May 2000). Dobbs offers an alternative to both Popper's and Strauss interpretations of the *Republic*. He argues that the communism of Book V is intended not as a political blueprint, nor simply as a debunking of the quest for political perfection, but as a way of teaching the reader a kind of responsible detachment from particular goods that fosters an orientation to human affairs that is congenial to Socratic philosophy.

Thomas Pangle and Peter Ahrensdorf, *Justice among Nations: On the Moral Basis of Power and Peace* (University Press of Kansas, 2002). Pangle and Ahrensdorf survey the various accounts of international politics that are offered by the great philosophers of the Western tradition, including Plato.

Carson Holloway, *All Shook Up: Music, Passion, and Politics* (Spence Publishing, 2001). Holloway traces the treatment of music and its political importance in the thought of several major figures in the history of political philosophy. The book includes a chapter about the *Republic*'s account of music and politics.

Eric Voegelin, *Order and History Volume Three: Plato and Aristotle* (Baton Rouge, Lousiana State University Press, 1957).

Robert E. Cushman, *Therapeia: Plato's Conception of Philosophy* (Westport, Greenwood Press, 1958).

Web Sites

The *Perseus Digital Library* (www.perseus.tufts.edu) contains the complete works of Plato, both in the original Greek and in English translation.

Introductory essays about Plato can be found in the *Internet Encyclopedia of Philosophy* (www.iep.utm.edu) and the *Stanford Encyclopedia of Philosophy* (http://plato.stanford.edu).

ARISTOTLE

CHAPTER **2**

By James Schall, S.J. *Georgetown University*

© Liz Michaud

LIFE, LEGACY, AND TIMES

The most famous ancient biographer Plutarch (45–125 A.D.) mentions Aristotle in his "Life of Alexander the Great." Aristotle's father was the court physician in Pella, the center of King Philip II of Macedon's empire. King Philip, who was Alexander the Great's father, wanted his son to receive the very best education. Thus "he sent for Aristotle, the most learned and the most celebrated philosopher of his time." When he was fighting in Asia, Alexander even sent Aristotle a letter in which he affirmed, with evident sincerity, that "I had rather excel others in the knowledge of what is excellent, than in the extent of my power and dominion."[1]

Notice in this passage that it is the future emperor who says these things to the philosopher, not the philosopher to the king. Generally, the ancient practice, from at least Plato, was the opposite: Usually the philosopher would provide a handbook to teach the young prince how to be virtuous and how to rule. This "educational" method was seen as the quickest way to reform a tyranny. Already here, however, we detect two of the greatest themes of political philosophy: the relation of the prince to the philosopher and the relation of knowledge to political power.

By all accounts Aristotle did not live a particularly exciting life, unless the life of the mind itself, seeking to understand *all that is,* constitutes its own fascination. One of Aristotle's abiding themes is that the political order is directly related to understanding the theoretical exploration of the purpose and end of being human. The great poet Dante called Aristotle simply "the master of all who know," a fitting description of a commanding thinker who earnestly sought not only to explain each thing in itself, in its actions and in its being, but to see how each thing related to all other things. It is the function of the wise man, Aristotle often said, to order things, to see how they relate to one another.

When Aristotle was 18, after his parents' death, he went to Athens to study in Plato's famous Academy. All who read both Plato and Aristotle (and indeed one has to read the teacher to understand the pupil) recognize a different spirit in Aristotle: more empirical, more concrete, and evidently more commonsensical. But even when he clearly disagreed with Plato, a point of agreement can always be found that is also based on something in Plato. For example, like Plato, Aristotle understands a thing's nature or essence in terms of its form. For both thinkers, the forms serve as the basis of formal causality (what the thing is). However, unlike Plato who located these forms outside of space and time, Aristotle located them in things within space and time.

Plato died in 347 B.C. when Aristotle was 37 years old. Somewhat surprisingly, Aristotle was not offered the chance to head the Platonic Academy. Instead he founded his own school known as the **Lycaeum.** Aristotle's teaching method seems to have been to "walk about" talking to students, hence the name ***peripatetics.*** As both Aristotle and Plato imply, philosophy ultimately exists in conversation so that at its heart are the need and occasion for individuals freely talking together, both in rigorous attention to truth and the ways it comes manifest to one another, particularly to students.

Aristotle was invited by King Philip of Macedon to tutor his son Alexander. Little is known about the relation of Alexander and Aristotle except that their political

[1] *Plutarch: The Lives of the Noble Grecians and Romans,* translated by John Dryden, and revised by Arthur Hugh Clough (New York: Modern Library, n.d.), 805.

outlooks were different. Alexander was something of a philosopher in his own right. But Aristotle did not think the great project of Alexander the Great to unite the whole world, Greek and barbarian, into one **cosmopolis**, one world state, under his effective leadership was feasible or wise. It was an idea, however, that often returned to political philosophy and keeps doing so even today. Indeed, Aristotle, on theoretical grounds thought the world state idea was dangerous. Its vague relationships undermined the very moral purpose of the Greek *polis*. Rather than making everyone friends and fellow citizens, it made them all impersonal and vague.

When he was 50, after Philip was murdered in 336 B.C. and Alexander went off to war in the East, Aristotle returned to Athens.

When Alexander died on the frontier in 323 B.C., anti-Macedonian revolts broke out in Athens. Aristotle was accused of impiety. Because Aristotle was associated with Macedon, he feared for his life. He thus fled to his mother's estate on the island of Euboea lest, as he is said to have exclaimed in a famous passage, "Athens commit the same crime twice"—namely that of again killing a philosopher as it did Socrates. Evidently Aristotle thought that if the Athenians did not get the point the first time with the death of Socrates, they would not get it in a second instance. Aristotle died the following year in 322 B.C.

Scholars dispute the exact nature of the Aristotelian works we do possess. Thirty entries, totaling some 2,000 pages, remain. He also wrote dialogues in the manner of Plato, though these were not preserved. His works were first published in 60 A.D. They seem, like his great book *Politics,* to be either his teaching lectures or notes compiled by his pupils. In general, they are well-ordered and clear. Aristotle's texts command careful attention. He gives examples of his points and tells the reader what he is about. To read him is to be taught by him. Any well-educated person should possess, read, and reread the basic works of Aristotle.

BACKGROUND TO POLITICAL TEACHINGS

The great medieval Christian thinker St. Thomas Aquinas referred to Aristotle as "the Philosopher," as if to say that he summed up in his work both how to be a philosopher and what a philosopher would hold or discover by using his rational faculty. He sought to know all there was to know in an orderly fashion. Aristotle himself, of course, was conscious of his philosophic and literary predecessors. He did not think he invented everything himself. He thought it proper for a philosopher to carefully consider what other people knew and proposed as true. His works are full of references to Greek places, poets, events, and thinkers. He did not disdain to state accurately what others held. Indeed, he thought it was the first step a philosopher had to take in the adventure of learning. There was nothing wrong in acknowledging a truth that someone else had already arrived at. That acknowledgment is itself a philosophical exercise—both to understand what someone else has said and to see for ourselves its objective truth and validity.

In the first book of his *Metaphysics,* Aristotle provides a brief history of philosophy up to his time. Here Aristotle tells us that the single most important impetus for us to think is a sense of "wonder" about the nature of things. Philosophizing thus begins with an experience of wonder. The single most important background to Aristotle's thought was his teacher Plato, who was himself a student of the first

Aristotle's Division of Three Sciences

Theoretical	Practical	Productive
Contemplation of things that are permanent and cannot be "otherwise." In the theoretical sciences, understanding is pursued for its own sake. Example: metaphysics, logic.	Knowledge of things that can be "otherwise" or variable given human freedom, choice, and circumstance. Example: politics, ethics.	Knowledge of rational production or the science of making, producing things. Example: technological know-how, carpentry, pottery. The productive sciences result in the making of some "product."

political philosopher—Socrates. In a famous passage, Aristotle advised us to "love Socrates, to love Plato, but to love truth more." No better advice has been given to young philosophers.

To understand Aristotle's political thought, we need to recall that he wrote about the **polis:** a small **city–state.** Unlike the modern nation–state, the city–state or polis did not acknowledge a separation between the state or the public sphere and society or the private sphere of the individual. Rather, the polis comprehended the private and the public spheres: The private was subject to public regulation. As a political form, the polis was on the verge of being absorbed into Alexander's larger empire. But that eventuality did not prevent its forming the grounds of our understanding the essential character and nature of political things, which are not dependent as such on the relative factor of size or numbers. Surprisingly, many everyday political terms we still use in English come from ancient Greek sources: democracy, politics, oligarchy, tyranny, aristocracy, monarchy, plutocracy, barbarian, and economy. As we already noted, Aristotle did not, for philosophic reasons, approve of the expansion to larger political entities like the cosmopolis (world state) because he thought that the practice of **arête** or virtue—excellent human qualities of moral character and intellect like wisdom, moderation, justice, and friendship—could take place only in small city–states, not in large, impersonal empires. However, Aristotle was able to see the general principles of most actual regimes from those of the barbarians to those of the tyrants and most everything in between.

PROBLEMS OF POLITICS AND THE STATE

For Aristotle, political things fall under what he calls "the practical sciences." Like ethics, poetry, and rhetoric, politics deals with things that can be otherwise because their subject matter is related to human freedom and to chance. The practical sciences exist only because human beings exist. This is why Aristotle cautions us not to expect too much certitude in political science as if it were a theoretical science of things that cannot be otherwise. The theoretical sciences are designed simply to know. The **practical sciences** are designed to do something. The cosmos is full of things that go on in a determined fashion. But it also contains things that can vary because of human **freedom.** This variability did not mean that no basic principles existed in politics. It

QUESTIONS FOR REFLECTION

What Is the Common Good?

Perhaps the common good of the political community can be illustrated by an analogy of a rowboat that develops a leak. The common good of all is served by making decisions, combining resources, and setting priorities to fix the leak before the boat sinks. The common good also dictates that anyone who attempts to undermine the enterprise must be prevented from doing so through coercion if necessary. (This is a view that both Aristotle and St. Thomas Aquinas share).

only meant that men did not always observe them—hence their variability. **Ethics,** a term that means moral habits, is the rule of ourselves over ourselves. Ethics is about "the good." It concerns what "ought" to be done and "why" we ought to do it. **Politics** is the rule of ourselves living in cities so that we might live well. Politics is concerned with the good of society as a whole. Ethics and politics are thus interrelated for Aristotle. Politics aims at the most comprehensive good of all—the common good. For Aristotle the **common good** is not merely the summation of individual subjective desire; rather, it is a shared life of objective perfection, of living well. The common good implies that which is truly good for human beings by nature, not something that is apparently good but in fact is harmful. It refers to the collective moral and intellectual flourishing of society as a whole measured by an objective standard of perfection. Indeed, the common good is a partnership in the ethical and virtuous life.

Aristotle's practical sciences—ethics, politics, and rhetoric—are designed to be not abstract descriptions of some vague subject but rather descriptions of general principles found guiding a subject matter wherever it occurs. These principles have to be put into effect by particular agents or political actors. Thus Aristotle's ethical and political works are intended not simply to be read but to be put into practice, to be acted upon, taking everything into account, including particulars of time, place, and circumstances. Ethics and politics live not in books but in reality, though they have a knowledge component that needs to be understood and addressed.

Aristotle did not know, for instance, what the Roman Empire, the medieval city, renaissance Florence, 18th-century France, the American Republic, Ming China, or the contemporary African states would do or look like in their particulars. He recognized that city–states of any area or time had to be set up and their particulars decided by those involved. Thus although he recognized differences in Sparta, Athens, and Thebes, he did not think these differences meant that human nature was radically different in different cities or times. In this sense his philosophy is universal. Aristotle would not accept the morally relativistic notion that there is somehow, say, a Chinese political science, or an Islamic political science, or a Latin American political science that is somehow immune from the analysis of philosophy.

But to set up and operate a city–state, we need to know what humans are, what other states have looked like, what principles ought to govern us, what can go wrong and why, and how to deal with both virtue and vice in their public manifestations. This analysis is what it means "to be a political animal by nature." The city–state must be founded, set up, governed, and preserved for humans to be what they are intended to be—to be "self-sufficient" and to live "well," to use Aristotle's terms. The "naturalness" of the state means not that it grows on trees, but that people use reason to set it up as a normal functioning of living with others in an orderly way. But this understanding of what is practical knowledge meant that Aristotle had a real insight into what actually happened, good and bad, among human beings in actual states. Reading Aristotle constantly surprises the perceptive student because what Aristotle says illuminates some real and perplexing problems in his own society.

Aristotle's concern with political science centers on moral evaluation, political actions, and decisions. He appeals to nature (**physis**) as a standard for judgment in his moral and political thought. Throughout his book the *Politics* he states that this or that exists "by nature." The nature of a thing refers to its essential characteristics that distinguish that thing from others. A thing's essential characteristics are grasped through the faculty of reason. As will be seen, the nature or essential characteristic of a human being is to exercise intellect and free choice. Possession of a rational soul and cognitive abilities distinguishes human beings from all other animals. Aristotle's understanding of nature not only includes a thing's essential characteristics but also its end (**telos**). That is, he understands the nature of a thing in terms of its terminal excellence, its objective perfection, its highest fulfillment or manifestation. For example, Aristotle famously explains that the nature of an oak tree is to be found not in the undeveloped acorn but rather in the healthy and fully developed oak tree that has flourished and realized its potential. Such a tree is tall and straight, with deep roots and full leaves. It provides the standard by which all other trees are to be judged as good or bad. Likewise, when speaking about the nature of a human being, Aristotle has in mind the person who most fully embodies moral and intellectual virtue or excellence: Socrates or Einstein. Aristotle's practical science of politics is therefore teleological—it explores the purpose and end of politics. Aristotle's conception of nature also implies a limitation of being. This means that the nature of a thing has particular limits and boundaries. In other words, by their nature or essence human beings are distinct from a beast or a god. Finally, the nature of a thing can be understood in contrast to convention or custom, which is the product of human agreement, will, or artifice and is therefore changeable or relative to time and place. In contrast, that which is nature is universal, timeless, and unchanging. It is not dependent on human will, custom, or agreement.

The essential nature of a human being is to possess **logos**—the capacity for reasoned speech that enables us to think, judge, and make moral decisions. Politics too has a nature. As noted, its essential characteristic is to provide for the common good, not the private interest or passions of individuals or groups in society. For Aristotle, politics is not to be understood as mere custom or convention. Legislators are bound to follow the standard of nature in discovering laws that promote the common good of society. Although the size of the legislature and the terms of the legislators can be a matter of convention, the substantive basis of the law must be grounded in the common good of society.

Perhaps the most significant and famous of Aristotle's statements is that "man by nature is a political animal." Indeed, this understanding of man's social political nature is foundational to Aristotle's political thought. The second most famous of Aristotle's statement is that one who lives outside of the city–state is either a beast or god. Human beings are social creatures dependent on their fellows for physical and intellectual development. We mature slowly, and nature does nothing in vain. For Aristotle, politics is a highly nurturing enterprise that enables human beings to cultivate what is highest in them—namely logos or reasoned speech. Politics, like

Aristotle's Understanding of Nature (Physis)

- *Essential characteristic:* The essence of something that makes it what it is. This essential characteristic is discovered by logos or reasoned speech.
  - For example, the essential characteristic of politics is that it serves the common good, not private interests or fantasies.
- *Terminal and peculiar excellence of a thing:* The developed form of that thing, its terminal excellence, the objective perfection of that thing's character—that is, its highest manifestation. The terminal and peculiar excellence of a thing is not necessarily what that thing actually is in its present condition, but how it ought to be in its perfected state.
  - For example, the peculiar excellence of politics is not any regime, but regimes that seriously strive to serve the general welfare of nations and are somewhat successful in doing so. Some individuals might cite the Democratic Socialist regimes of Scandinavia, whereas liberal capitalists might cite the United States at different moments in its history.
- *Limitation on being:* The limits or boundaries that distinguish one thing from another.
  - For example, our human nature is limited in that it cannot act in a divine manner. By nature we are more than the beasts and less than the gods. The limitation of being on politics prevents political coercion in areas that do not directly concern the common good. Politics does not enter the realm of private piety. The principle of the common good may require the state to intervene and regulate the actions or priests involved in sexual abuse of children; however, the same principles would prevent the use of state power to regulate sacramental practices of personal piety.
- *Universal:* Unchangeable, objective, timeless.
  - For example, by nature political principles like the best regime apply not only to Athens circa 5th century B.C. but to all political systems at all times and in all places.
- *Distinct from convention:* Not merely the product of custom or human will or prejudice.
  - For example, the nature of politics is to serve the common good, not to reflect the particular passions, opinions, mores, and prejudices that exist in various cultures. The function of politics must be separated from custom—human invention. The politics of the state must always struggle to serve the common good of that community. However, the way the common good is pursued in terms of the particular kinds of institutions and their size may be merely customary. We must therefore distinguish between aspects of politics that are universal by nature and those that are arbitrary and transient by custom or convention.

ethics, enables human beings to flourish. Though necessary, politics is not a sufficient enterprise for human beings. Politics ministers to a calling higher than itself: the life of the mind or philosophy that deals with the highest, unchanging, and eternal things.

NATURE OF POLITICS AND THE ROLE OF THE STATE

Aristotle's *Ethics* is an examination of a human being's capacity or incapacity for self-governance. To be "ethical" or "moral" means to rule ourselves according to an objective standard of right and wrong in each area where we have freedom to rule ourselves or fail to do so. Human happiness and flourishing require a high level of physical security, stable family life, friendships, education, and the enterprise of politics. This human flourishing can take place only in a regime—the constitution.

PRIMARY SOURCE 2.1

Man Is a Political Animal, from *Politics*, Book I, Chapter 2

Now, that man is more of a political animal than bees or any other gregarious animals is evident. Nature, as we often say, makes nothing in vain, and man is the only animal whom she has endowed with the gift of speech. And whereas mere voice is but an indication of pleasure or pain, and is therefore found in other animals (for their nature attains to the perception of pleasure and pain and the intimation of them to one another, and no further), the power of speech is intended to set forth the expedient and inexpedient, and therefore likewise the just and the unjust. And it is a characteristic of man that he alone has any sense of good and evil, of just and unjust, and the like, and the association of living beings who have this sense makes a family and a state.

Further, the state (polis) is by nature clearly prior to the family and to the individual, since the whole is of necessity prior to the part; for example, if the whole body be destroyed, there will be no foot or hand, except in an equivocal sense, as we might speak of a stone hand; for when destroyed the hand will be no better than that. But things are defined by their working and power; and we ought not to say that they are the same when they no longer have their proper quality, but only that they have the same name. The proof that the state is a creation of nature and prior to the individual is that the individual, when isolated, is not self-sufficing; and therefore he is like a part in relation to the whole. But he who is unable to live in society, or who has no need because he is sufficient for himself, must be either a beast or a god: he is no part of a state. A social instinct is implanted in all men by nature, and yet he who first founded the state was the greatest of benefactors. For man, when perfected, is the best of animals, but, when separated from law and justice, he is the worst of all; since armed injustice is the more dangerous, and he is equipped at birth with arms, meant to be used by intelligence and virtue, which he may use for the worst ends. Wherefore, if he have not virtue, he is the most unholy and the most savage of animals, and the most full of lust and gluttony. But justice is the bond of men in states, for the administration of justice, which is the determination of what is just, is the principle of order in political society.

In his own time, Aristotle had collected and classified 158 regimes or constitutions of various Greek and foreign city–states. This collection has been lost except for his description of the constitution of Athens. He knew what people did and how they variously organized themselves in terms of principles and institutions of rule. The term **regime** or constitution means how people organize themselves in terms of membership and offices according to which they rule and were ruled in their political order. Aristotle notices that cities more or less paralleled the ends for which individual citizens choose to rule their own lives. For instance, if the general purpose of the citizens of a polity was to create and keep wealth, the institutions of that polity were generally called an **oligarchy.** They were set up so that the rule would reflect this inner purpose in its distribution of honors and burdens. The Platonic notion that the city is the reflection of the inner order or disorder of the souls of its citizens is retained by Aristotle.

The first book of the *Politics* contains the second division of Aristotle's ethical–political tractate—namely the family or household. It is really "economics" in its classical sense: the rule and relationships within a household. Here are explained the relations of males and females with their purpose in relation to the begetting and rearing of their children and the temporal means needed to do so. Economics also deals with the necessary material goods needed for human living in a household—basically

QUESTIONS FOR REFLECTION

What is the American sense of the good life that is the basis of our regime and political organization of office? Does the American sense of the good life tend to promote or undermine the public interest?

the acquiring and management of needed goods, but especially training in virtue. Aristotle recognized that such goods were needed by human nature. He thought there could be too much or too little, but a sufficiency was certainly needed. But once these are present, we still need to address them to the primary task of the household in its relation to the condition of soul of its members.

Though all practical rule is the imposition of reason on what needs to be ruled, the purpose of rule in the household is different from the rule of oneself or rule in the polity. Ruling means knowing and deciding what must be done for the person, the family, or the polity. The natural authority of parents—**parental rule**—is needed because children lack the use of reason. This parental rule is designed ultimately to disappear when children reach an age to exercise their rational faculty and free choice as responsible adults. But Aristotle holds that all human beings, whether they have active use of reason or not, need to be ruled by reason. Hence parental rule substitutes parents' reason for the child's until the child can rule himself or herself. This is why in the nature of things, parental rule is both good and temporary.

Aristotle says that children are ruled with a **royal rule.** He means that the rule, the parental intention, is for the children's particular good, though within the context of the good of the family. As noted, under normal circumstances parental rule is designed to eventually disappear when the children can exercise their own rule over themselves. Obviously, it is a rule that gradually disappears over time. When a child leaves the household, he or she should be able to rule him- or herself and enter the polity capable of being ruled there according to active reason—that is, by being able to be persuaded, not coerced, to do reasonable actions required for the order of the polity.

Aristotle calls the relation of ruling between husband and wife a **constitutional-rule.** This becomes the paradigm for political rule: the rule of adults over adults according to the normal mode of human action, which is not force but persuasion and discussion. In the case of a household of husband and wife, Aristotle means that only two adult or fully rational citizens are found in the household, the husband and wife. He recognizes that there will have to be a principle of agreement about who decides in cases of disagreement about household matters. This decision-making authority, the "to rule," is a natural necessity and cannot be avoided in a two-adult institution. However, the husband (or the wife) cannot rule "despotically," as if the mind of the other need not be consulted, but must rule constitutionally. There must be two minds at work so that all decisions employ the wit of both members of the household, while both agree to abide by the choice of the one making the decision. The decision thus will contain something of the minds, freedom, and virtue of both.

Within the household there is also, in ancient cities, the much controverted question of slaves. Aristotle distinguishes between two kinds of slaves: 1) **slaves by law; 2) slaves by nature.** All sorts of terrible things have been attributed to Aristotle on the score that he maintained that there were "natural slaves." But to be fair to him, he must be read carefully. We should be slow to apply our ideas to his words. He did maintain that there

PRIMARY SOURCE 2.2 | THE POLIS AS THE MOST COMPREHENSIVE COMMUNITY, FROM *POLITICS*, BOOK I, CHAPTERS 1–4

Chapter 1

Every state is a community of some kind, and every community is established with a view to some good; for mankind always act in order to obtain that which they think good. But, if all communities aim at some good, the state or political community, which is the highest of all, and which embraces all the rest, aims at good in a greater degree than any other, and at the highest good.

Some people think that the qualifications of a statesman, king, householder, and master are the same, and that they differ, not in kind, but only in the number of their subjects. For example, the ruler over a few is called a master; over more, the manager of a household; over a still larger number, a statesman or king, as if there were no difference between a great household and a small state. The distinction which is made between the king and the statesman is as follows: When the government is personal, the ruler is a king; when, according to the rules of the political science, the citizens rule and are ruled in turn, then he is called a statesman.

But all this is a mistake; for governments differ in kind, as will be evident to any one who considers the matter according to the method which has hitherto guided us. As in other departments of science, so in politics, the compound should always be resolved into the simple elements or least parts of the whole. We must therefore look at the elements of which the state is composed, in order that we may see in what the different kinds of rule differ from one another, and whether any scientific result can be attained about each one of them.

Chapter 2

He who thus considers things in their first growth and origin, whether a state or anything else, will obtain the clearest view of them. In the first place there must be a union of those who cannot exist without each other; namely, of male and female, that the race may continue (and this is a union which is formed, not of deliberate purpose, but because, in common with other animals and with plants, mankind have a natural desire to leave behind them an image of themselves), and of natural ruler and subject, that both may be preserved. For that which can foresee by the exercise of mind is by nature intended to be lord and master, and that which can with its body give effect to such foresight is a subject, and by nature a slave; hence master and slave have the same interest. Now nature has distinguished between the female and the slave. For she is not niggardly, like the smith who fashions the Delphian knife for many uses; she makes each thing for a single use, and every instrument is best made when intended for one and not for many uses. But among barbarians no distinction is made between women and slaves, because there is no natural ruler among them: they are a community of slaves, male and female. Wherefore the poets say,

"It is meet that Hellenes should rule over barbarians;" as if they thought that the barbarian and the slave were by nature one.

Out of these two relationships between man and woman, master and slave, the first thing to arise is the family, and Hesiod is right when he says,

"First house and wife and an ox for the plough," for the ox is the poor man's slave. The family is the association established by nature for the supply of men's everyday wants, and the members of it are called by Charondas "companions of the cupboard," and by Epimenides the Cretan, "companions of the manger." But when several families are united, and the association aims at something more than the supply of daily needs, the first society to be formed is the village. And the most natural form of the village appears to be that of a colony from the family, composed of the children and grandchildren, who are said to be suckled "with the same milk." And this is the reason why Hellenic states were originally governed by kings; because the Hellenes were under royal rule before they came together, as the barbarians still are. Every family is ruled by the eldest, and therefore in the colonies of the family the kingly form of government prevailed because they were of the same blood. As Homer says:

PRIMARY SOURCE 2.2 | THE POLIS AS THE MOST COMPREHENSIVE COMMUNITY, FROM *POLITICS*, BOOK I, CHAPTERS 1–4 *continued*

"Each one gives law to his children and to his wives."

For they lived dispersedly, as was the manner in ancient times. Wherefore men say that the Gods have a king, because they themselves either are or were in ancient times under the rule of a king. For they imagine, not only the forms of the Gods, but their ways of life to be like their own.

When several villages are united in a single complete community, large enough to be nearly or quite self-sufficing, the state comes into existence, originating in the bare needs of life, and continuing in existence for the sake of a good life. And therefore, if the earlier forms of society are natural, so is the state, for it is the end of them, and the nature of a thing is its end. For what each thing is when fully developed, we call its nature, whether we are speaking of a man, a horse, or a family. Besides, the final cause and end of a thing is the best, and to be self-sufficing is the end and the best.

Hence it is evident that the state is a creation of nature, and that man is by nature a political animal. And he who by nature and not by mere accident is without a state, is either a bad man or above humanity; he is like the "Tribeless, lawless, hearthless one," whom Homer denounces—the natural outcast is forthwith a lover of war; he may be compared to an isolated piece at draughts.

* * * *

Chapter 3

Seeing then that the state is made up of households, before speaking of the state we must speak of the management of the household. The parts of household management correspond to the persons who compose the household, and a complete household consists of slaves and freemen. Now we should begin by examining everything in its fewest possible elements; and the first and fewest possible parts of a family are master and slave, husband and wife, father and children. We have therefore to consider what each of these three relations is and ought to be: I mean the relation of master and servant, the marriage relation (the conjunction of man and wife has no name of its own), and thirdly, the procreative relation (this also has no proper name). And there is another element of a household, the so-called art of getting wealth, which, according to some, is identical with household management, according to others, a principal part of it; the nature of this art will also have to be considered by us.

Let us first speak of master and slave, looking to the needs of practical life and also seeking to attain some better theory of their relation than exists at present. For some are of opinion that the rule of a master is a science, and that the management of a household, and the mastership of slaves, and the political and royal rule, as I was saying at the outset, are all the same. Others affirm that the rule of a master over slaves is contrary to nature, and that the distinction between slave and freeman exists by law only, and not by nature; and being an interference with nature is therefore unjust.

Chapter 4

Property is a part of the household, and the art of acquiring property is a part of the art of managing the household; for no man can live well, or indeed live at all, unless he be provided with necessaries. And as in the arts which have a definite sphere the workers must have their own proper instruments for the accomplishment of their work, so it is in the management of a household. Now instruments are of various sorts; some are living, others lifeless; in the rudder, the pilot of a ship has a lifeless, in the look-out man, a living instrument; for in the arts the servant is a kind of instrument. Thus, too, a possession is an instrument for maintaining life. And so, in the arrangement of the family, a slave is a living possession, and property a number of such instruments; and the servant is himself an instrument which takes precedence of all other instruments. For if every instrument could accomplish its own work, obeying or anticipating the will of others, like the statues of Daedalus, or the tripods of Hephaestus, which, says the poet, "of their own accord

continued

PRIMARY SOURCE 2.2

The Polis as the Most Comprehensive Community, from *Politics*, Book I, Chapters 1–4 *continued*

entered the assembly of the Gods"; if, in like manner, the shuttle would weave and the plectrum touch the lyre without a hand to guide them, chief workmen would not want servants, nor masters' slaves. Here, however, another distinction must be drawn; the instruments commonly so called are instruments of production, whilst a possession is an instrument of action. The shuttle, for example, is not only of use; but something else is made by it, whereas of a garment or of a bed there is only the use. Further, as production and action are different in kind, and both require instruments, the instruments which they employ must likewise differ in kind. But life is action and not production, and therefore the slave is the minister of action. Again, a possession is spoken of as a part is spoken of; for the part is not only a part of something else, but wholly belongs to it; and this is also true of a possession. The master is only the master of the slave; he does not belong to him, whereas the slave is not only the slave of his master, but wholly belongs to him. Hence we see what is the nature and office of a slave; he who is by nature not his own but another's man, is by nature a slave; and he may be said to be another's man who, being a human being, is also a possession. And a possession may be defined as an instrument of action, separable from the possessor.

were natural slaves, but it is important to see what he meant. First, a slave "by law" referred to someone who was, say, captured in battle and made or given the choice to work as the exchange for not being killed as a war hostage. Ironically, under this score, not a few college professors were slaves by law in the Greek and Roman worlds. There was nothing physically or mentally wrong with such slaves. This is why they are called "legal" not "natural" slaves. Things like amnesty, prison, or service are modern equivalents of this situation of what to do with those taken in war.

A "natural" slave, on the other hand, meant someone who was not a *causa sui*—that is, someone who because of injury, defect of birth, or other natural reasons could not objectively rule himself. Ironically, thus, a "natural" slave was someone whom some defect of nature or accident made incapable of ruling himself. Such people still exist in every society; they are human and need to be cared for. For his own good, such a person has to be "ruled" by others—that is, by someone else's reason. In the modern world such people are usually cared for in state or charitable institutions, though many are also cared for in families. In the ancient world they were taken care of almost exclusively by families.

But Aristotle also recognizes different degrees of inability to rule oneself, so that natural slaves, when possible, can do certain useful tasks for the family or the polity. Aristotle thinks any population will always have a certain percentage of its members who are permanently in this condition of needing to be ruled for their own good. This is as true today as in ancient times. Aristotle's judgment about who was in this condition was intended to be objective and accurate: Was or was not this particular person in need of authoritative guidance for his or her own good?

In the ancient world, moreover, slavery was not so much a question of the condition of the slave but of the dull and drudgery work that had to be done for a society to survive. A slave was someone who did this sort of work, which was so exhausting that no time was left for freer activities. Aristotle himself observes that if machines could be invented to do much of this drudge work, much of the need of

PRIMARY SOURCE 2.3

Aristotle on Slavery, from *Politics*, Book I, Chapters 5–6

Chapter 5

But is there anyone thus intended by nature to be a slave, and for whom such a condition is expedient and right, or rather is not all slavery a violation of nature?

There is no difficulty in answering this question, on grounds both of reason and of fact. For that some should rule and others be ruled is a thing not only necessary, but expedient; from the hour of their birth, some are marked out for subjection, others for rule.

And there are many kinds both of rulers and subjects (and that rule is the better which is exercised over better subjects—for example, to rule over men is better than to rule over wild beasts; for the work is better which is executed by better workmen, and where one man rules and another is ruled, they may be said to have a work); for in all things which form a composite whole and which are made up of parts, whether continuous or discrete, a distinction between the ruling and the subject element comes to fight. Such a duality exists in living creatures, but not in them only; it originates in the constitution of the universe; even in things which have no life there is a ruling principle, as in a musical mode.... At all events we may firstly observe in living creatures both a despotical and a constitutional rule; for the soul rules the body with a despotical rule, whereas the intellect rules the appetites with a constitutional and royal rule. And it is clear that the rule of the soul over the body, and of the mind and the rational element over the passionate, is natural and expedient; whereas the equality of the two or the rule of the inferior is always hurtful. The same holds good of animals in relation to men; for tame animals have a better nature than wild, and all tame animals are better off when they are ruled by man; for then they are preserved. Again, the male is by nature superior, and the female inferior; and the one rules, and the other is ruled; this principle, of necessity, extends to all mankind.

Where then there is such a difference as that between soul and body, or between men and animals (as in the case of those whose business is to use their body, and who can do nothing better), the lower sort are by nature slaves, and it is better for them as for all inferiors that they should be under the rule of a master. For he who can be, and therefore is, another's and he who participates in rational principle enough to apprehend, but not to have, such a principle, is a slave by nature. Whereas the lower animals cannot even apprehend a principle; they obey their instincts. And indeed the use made of slaves and of tame animals is not very different; for both with their bodies minister to the needs of life. Nature would like to distinguish between the bodies of freemen and slaves, making the one strong for servile labor, the other upright, and although useless for such services, useful for political life in the arts both of war and peace. But the opposite often happens—that some have the souls and others have the bodies of freemen. And doubtless if men differed from one another in the mere forms of their bodies as much as the statues of the gods do from men, all would acknowledge that the inferior class should be slaves of the superior. And if this is true of the body, how much more just that a similar distinction should exist in the soul? But the beauty of the body is seen, whereas the beauty of the soul is not seen. It is clear, then, that some men are by nature free, and others slaves, and that for these latter slavery is both expedient and right.

Chapter 6

But that those who take the opposite view have in a certain way right on their side, may be easily seen. For the words slavery and slave are used in two senses. There is a slave or slavery by law as well as by nature. The law of which I speak is a sort of convention—the law by which whatever is taken in war is supposed to belong to the victors. But this right many jurists impeach, as they would an orator who brought forward an unconstitutional measure: they detest the notion that, because one man has the power of doing violence and is superior in brute strength, another shall be his slave and subject. Even among philosophers there is a difference of opinion. The origin of the dispute, and what makes the views invade each other's territory, is as follows: in some sense

continued

PRIMARY SOURCE 2.3

ARISTOTLE ON SLAVERY, FROM *POLITICS*, BOOK I, CHAPTERS 5–6 *continued*

virtue, when furnished with means, has actually the greatest power of exercising force; and as superior power is only found where there is superior excellence of some kind, power seems to imply virtue, and the dispute to be simply one about justice (for it is due to one party identifying justice with goodwill while the other identifies it with the mere rule of the stronger). If these views are thus set out separately, the other views have no force or plausibility against the view that the superior in virtue ought to rule, or be master. Others, clinging, as they think, simply to a principle of justice (for law and custom are a sort of justice), assume that slavery in accordance with the custom of war is justified by law, but at the same moment they deny this. For what if the cause of the war be unjust? And again, no one would ever say he is a slave who is unworthy to be a slave. Were this the case, men of the highest rank would be slaves and the children of slaves if they or their parents chance to have been taken captive and sold. Wherefore Hellenes do not like to call Hellenes slaves, but confine the term to barbarians. Yet, in using this language, they really mean the natural slave of whom we spoke at first; for it must be admitted that some are slaves everywhere, others nowhere. The same principle applies to nobility. Hellenes regard themselves as noble everywhere, and not only in their own country, but they deem the barbarians noble only when at home, thereby implying that there are two sorts of nobility and freedom, the one absolute, the other relative. The Helen of Theodectes says:

"Who would presume to call me servant who am on both sides sprung from the stem of the gods?"

What does this mean but that they distinguish freedom and slavery, noble and humble birth, by the two principles of good and evil? They think that as men and animals beget men and animals, so from good men a good man springs. But this is what nature, though she may intend it, cannot always accomplish.

We see then that there is some foundation for this difference of opinion, and that all are not either slaves by nature or freemen by nature, and also that there is in some cases a marked distinction between the two classes, rendering it expedient and right for the one to be slaves and the others to be masters: the one practicing obedience, the others exercising the authority and lordship which nature intended them to have. The abuse of this authority is injurious to both; for the interests of part and whole, of body and soul, are the same, and the slave is a part of the master, a living but separated part of his bodily frame. Hence, where the relation of master and slave between them is natural they are friends and have a common interest, but where it rests merely on law and force the reverse is true.

slavery would be eliminated. In part this substitution is what subsequently happened. Aristotle was prophetic. We have replaced human slaves with mechanical and electronic ones, something that seems both wise and necessary for human worth.

The second book of Aristotle's *Politics* is an examination of theoretical regimes proposed by the philosophers, as well as actual regimes (constitutions) that he found in his time. Aristotle relied on both literary and experiential sources before he came to his own conclusions about political things. He begins his second book by consulting and analyzing the opinions of his predecessors about politics. Here we find his famous critique of his mentor Plato's two proposals for the best regime in the *Republic* and in the *Laws*. Aristotle did not think Plato's schemes of commonality of wives, children, and property, which Plato had proposed for the best state, would work. People care for what is their own in both children and property so that if everything were to be declared "common," Aristotle thought, nothing much would be properly cared for—the tragedy of the commons. Chaos and neglect would ensue.

QUESTIONS FOR REFLECTION

Does Aristotle's distinction between natural and conventional slaves cast doubt on the moral legitimacy of slavery as it was actually practiced in Athens? Has modern technology made the natural slave obsolete?

In Books III to VII of Aristotle's *Politics,* Aristotle discusses the forms of regimes and their principles. A **citizen** is someone who was an adult—that is, someone who has acquired virtue or vice in the family but now, having accomplished the purpose of parental rule, is ready to rule and be ruled. Notice that "to be ruled" is not a negative notion in Aristotle. It means that the citizen can understand and act on legitimate laws because he or she sees the reason for them. Citizens obey the law not because of its coercive power but because they see its reason, even if there might be other ways of doing something. That is, the laws too could be "otherwise."

In the final book of the *Ethics,* Aristotle said not only that man was by nature a political animal, but that he was at times, especially if he did not learn or practice virtue, a being who needed to be coerced because he was acting unreasonably to the detriment of himself and others. Law thus had a coercive element for the good of both the polity and the citizen who acted unjustly. It benefits both the polity and the individual citizen who is prevented from doing something wrong or is punished for so doing. Punishment, from Plato's *Gorgias,* carried the idea of the unjust man's recognizing his own wrongdoing and his willingness to accept the punishment as a sign of his renewed understanding of the requirements of public order. **Law** for Aristotle is simply "reason without passion"; in its essence, it was a statement of what was objectively right to be done. Both law and prudence were efforts to state and carry out what was right or just in the particular circumstances of civil life.

For Aristotle, justice is the virtue that defines our relations with others. It is an impersonal virtue in that it looks solely at the relationship of what is due no matter what the character of the people involved. Justice makes voluntary relationships of business or other agreements possible. It defines how we are to act toward others. Justice is involuntary when we are the cause of damage to others or they cause damage to us, say in accidents. In these senses we can enter into a chance relation of justice with anyone, whether a friend, relative, acquaintance, or stranger. Thus in justice we might even owe a debt to our enemies or to someone we do not like. It also requires that we treat equals equally and unequals unequally.

In Book V of the *Ethics* Aristotle observes that there are two kinds of justice: legal and special. *Legal justice* meant that any act of any virtue could affect others and hence could be a proper object of law. Drunken driving thus was not only an individual failure to rule oneself but also a danger to others. This latter fact is why it could properly become a matter of law. *Special justice* was divided into two parts: commutative (rectificatory) and distributive. **Commutative justice** simply meant "rendering what is due"—paying back what was agreed voluntarily, as in contracts and purchases. **Distributive justice** had to do with life in the community. Here the rendering what is due is proportional. In a group, more is distributed to those who contribute more or bear greater burdens.

CASE STUDY 2.1 | ARISTOTLE'S VIEW OF JUSTICE

When a decision has to be made about awarding a Stradivarius violin—the rarest and very best kind of Italian Renaissance violins—what would be a just basis for determining who should receive it? Should the decision be based on ability to pay? Family connections? Or talent alone? For Aristotle, what would it mean to treat equals equally and unequals unequally concerning talent for playing the violin? Using this principle, what do you think Aristotle's position would be concerning affirmative action in higher education, which justifies special preferences for historically discriminated-against minorities?

Although Aristotle thought that justice was the prime virtue of the polity, he did not think it the most important thing for the state. Aristotle devoted one book in the *Ethics* to justice but two to friendship. By this fact he indicated which relationship was more important. Indeed, he specifically remarks that polities need friendship more than justice. The purpose of justice is to allow something more than itself to come about. Thus in one sense, polities exist to make friendships possible. However, Aristotle believed that we could not have more than a few good friends and that Plato's ideas about being friends with everyone made friendship impossible. This position has ramifications for politics because it explains Aristotle's preference for small polities. One of the main questions behind theoretical questions of mixed regimes or federal regimes is related to this effort to connect the nature and limits of both justice and friendship—these are both high human goods. But Aristotle's tract on friendship in Books VIII and IX of the *Ethics* is one of the most insightful and moving discussions about actual human life ever written. It deserves study and reflection.

Once Aristotle tells us what a citizen is in Book III of the *Politics,* he classifies regimes based on the arrangements of ruling offices. A key question of political philosophy, memorably formulated by Plato, is always "What is the **best regime**?" This is the most penetrating question of political philosophy. The typical Aristotelian observations follow: Namely, if the best regime is not feasible, what regimes are the best possible? Which ones are the worst? Why? Is there an order of good and bad regimes?

THE SIX FORMS OF REGIMES

To answer these questions, Aristotle methodically sets down the six basic forms of regimes–constitutions. These differing regimes and the reasons for them need to be understood clearly. Each regime nonetheless has a range within itself. Differing kinds of oligarchy or monarchy exist and need to be described. Aristotle thinks that these differing actual regimes will usually be found over the range of existing political forms. Where does the best regime exist? Does it exist in fact or only in theory?

As noted, a regime or (constitution) is the principle of rule that organizes the polis and that determines who authoritatively makes the decisions for the whole. There are six simple regimes: monarchy, aristocracy, polity, democracy, oligarchy, and tyranny. The first three are what Aristotle considers the good forms of rule, and the last three are the bad or perverted forms of rule. In all good regimes the ruling part—one, few, or many—rules for the common good by enabling all goods to come forth; in the bad or perverted regimes, the ruling part or group rules for its own good at the expense of the good of others. Notice that there are two ways of classifying regimes. One is according

PRIMARY SOURCE 2.4

Aristotle's Critique of Plato, from *Politics*, Book II, Chapters 1–3

Chapter 1

Our purpose is to consider what form of political community is best of all for those who are most able to realize their ideal of life. We must therefore examine not only this but other constitutions, both such as actually exist in well-governed states, and any theoretical forms which are held in esteem; that what is good and useful may be brought to light. And let no one suppose that in seeking for something beyond them we are anxious to make a sophistical display at any cost; we only undertake this inquiry because all the constitutions with which we are acquainted are faulty.

We will begin with the natural beginning of the subject. Three alternatives are conceivable: The members of a state must either have (1) all things or (2) nothing in common, or (3) some things in common and some not. That they should have nothing in common is clearly impossible, for the constitution is a community, and must at any rate have a common place—one city will be in one place, and the citizens are those who share in that one city. But should a well ordered state have all things, as far as may be, in common, or some only and not others? For the citizens might conceivably have wives and children and property in common, as Socrates proposes in the Republic of Plato. Which is better, our present condition, or the proposed new order of society?

Chapter 2

There are many difficulties in the community of women. And the principle on which Socrates rests the necessity of such an institution evidently is not established by his arguments. Further, as a means to the end which he ascribes to the state, the scheme, taken literally is impracticable, and how we are to interpret it is nowhere precisely stated. I am speaking of the premise from which the argument of Socrates proceeds, "that the greater the unity of the state the better." Is it not obvious that a state may at length attain such a degree of unity as to be no longer a state? Since the nature of a state is to be a plurality, and in tending to greater unity, from being a state, it becomes a family, and from being a family, an individual; for the family may be said to be more than the state, and the individual than the family. So that we ought not to attain this greatest unity even if we could, for it would be the destruction of the state. Again, a state is not made up only of so many men, but of different kinds of men; for similars do not constitute a state. It is not like a military alliance. The usefulness of the latter depends upon its quantity even where there is no difference in quality (for mutual protection is the end aimed at), just as a greater weight of anything is more useful than a less (in like manner, a state differs from a nation, when the nation has not its population organized in villages, but lives an Arcadian sort of life); but the elements out of which a unity is to be formed differ in kind.... In like manner when they hold office there is a variety in the offices held. Hence it is evident that a city is not by nature one in that sense which some persons affirm; and that what is said to be the greatest good of cities is in reality their destruction; but surely the good of things must be that which preserves them. Again, in another point of view, this extreme unification of the state is clearly not good; for a family is more self-sufficing than an individual, and a city than a family, and a city only comes into being when the community is large enough to be self-sufficing. If then self-sufficiency is to be desired, the lesser degree of unity is more desirable than the greater.

Chapter 3

But, even supposing that it were best for the community to have the greatest degree of unity, this unity is by no means proved to follow from the fact "of all men saying 'mine' and 'not mine' at the same instant of time," which, according to Socrates, is the sign of perfect unity in a state. For the word "all" is ambiguous. If the meaning be that every individual says "mine" and "not mine" at the same time, then perhaps the result at which Socrates aims may be in some degree accomplished; each man will call the same person his own son and the

continued

PRIMARY SOURCE 2.4

Aristotle's Critique of Plato, from *Politics*, Book II, Chapters 1–3 *continued*

same person his wife, and so of his property and of all that falls to his lot. This, however, is not the way in which people would speak who had their had their wives and children in common; they would say "all" but not "each." In like manner their property would be described as belonging to them, not severally but collectively. There is an obvious fallacy in the term "all": like some other words, "both," "odd," "even," it is ambiguous, and even in abstract argument becomes a source of logical puzzles. That all persons call the same thing mine in the sense in which each does so may be a fine thing, but it is impracticable; or if the words are taken in the other sense, such a unity in no way conduces to harmony. And there is another objection to the proposal. For that which is common to the greatest number has the least care bestowed upon it. Every one thinks chiefly of his own, hardly at all of the common interest; and only when he is himself concerned as an individual. For besides other considerations, everybody is more inclined to neglect the duty which he expects another to fulfill; as in families many attendants are often less useful than a few. Each citizen will have a thousand sons who will not be his sons individually but anybody will be equally the son of anybody, and will therefore be neglected by all alike. Further, upon this principle, every one will use the word "mine" of one who is prospering or the reverse, however small a fraction he may himself be of the whole number; the same boy will be "so and so's son," the son of each of the thousand, or whatever be the number of the citizens; and even about this he will not be positive; for it is impossible to know who chanced to have a child, or whether, if one came into existence, it has survived. But which is better—for each to say "mine" in this way, making a man the same relation to two thousand or ten thousand citizens, or to use the word "mine" in the ordinary and more restricted sense? For usually the same person is called by one man his own son whom another calls his own brother or cousin or kinsman—blood relation or connection by marriage either of himself or of some relation of his, and yet another his clansman or tribesman; and how much better is it to be the real cousin of somebody than to be a son after Plato's fashion! Nor is there any way of preventing brothers and children and fathers and mothers from sometimes recognizing one another; for children are born like their parents, and they will necessarily be finding indications of their relationship to one another. Geographers declare such to be the fact; they say that in part of Upper Libya, where the women are common, nevertheless the children who are born are assigned to their respective fathers on the ground of their likeness. And some women, like the females of other animals—for example, mares and cows—have a strong tendency to produce offspring resembling their parents, as was the case with the Pharsalian mare called Honest.

to the number of people who compose the ruling part. Thus kingship (**monarchy**) and **tyranny** both are ruled by one person, **aristocracy** and **oligarchy** by a few, and **polity** and **democracy** by many.[2] In sum, Aristotle classifies regimes in terms of two criteria: the number of those who rule and the end to which the rule is directed—either the self-interest of the ruling class or the common good.

Because kingship and tyranny are rule by one person, what constitutes the difference between them? In a monarchy (the good regime) the king rules for the

[2]It should be noted that the good form of the rule of the many did not have a proper name in Greek. Usually modern commentators call it *polity,* as the rule of the many virtuous citizens for the good of the whole. But the word *polity* is also the Anglicized version of the political institution itself; we would say *state* or something like that.

PRIMARY SOURCE 2.5 | ON REGIMES, FROM *POLITICS*, BOOK III, CHAPTERS 6–7

Chapter 6

Having determined these questions, we have next to consider whether there is only one form of government or many, and if many, what they are, and how many, and what are the differences between them.

A constitution is the arrangement of magistracies in a state, especially of the highest of all. The government is everywhere sovereign in the state, and the constitution is in fact the government. For example, in democracies the people are supreme, but in oligarchies, the few; and, therefore, we say that these two forms of government also are different: and so in other cases.

First, let us consider what is the purpose of a state, and how many forms of government there are by which human society is regulated. We have already said, in the first part of this treatise, when discussing household management and the rule of a master, that man is by nature a political animal. And therefore, men, even when they do not require one another's help, desire to live together; not but that they are also brought together by their common interests in proportion as they severally attain to any measure of well-being. This is certainly the chief end, both of individuals and of states. And also for the sake of mere life (in which there is possibly some noble element so long as the evils of existence do not greatly overbalance the good) mankind meet together and maintain the political community. And we all see that men cling to life even at the cost of enduring great misfortune, seeming to find in life a natural sweetness and happiness.

There is no difficulty in distinguishing the various kinds of authority; they have been often defined already in discussions outside the school. The rule of a master, although the slave by nature and the master by nature have in reality the same interests, is nevertheless exercised primarily with a view to the interest of the master, but accidentally considers the slave, since, if the slave perish, the rule of the master perishes with him. On the other hand, the government of a wife and children and of a household, which we have called household management, is exercised in the first instance for the good of the governed or for the common good of both parties, but essentially for the good of the governed, as we see to be the case in medicine, gymnastic, and the arts in general, which are only accidentally concerned with the good of the artists themselves. For there is no reason why the trainer may not sometimes practice gymnastics, and the helmsman is always one of the crew. The trainer or the helmsman considers the good of those committed to his care. But, when he is one of the persons taken care of, he accidentally participates in the advantage, for the helmsman is also a sailor, and the trainer becomes one of those in training. And so in politics: when the state is framed upon the principle of equality and likeness, the citizens think that they ought to hold office by turns. Formerly, as is natural, every one would take his turn of service; and then again, somebody else would look after his interest, just as he, while in office, had looked after theirs. But nowadays, for the sake of the advantage which is to be gained from the public revenues and from office, men want to be always in office. One might imagine that the rulers, being sickly, were only kept in health while they continued in office; in that case we may be sure that they would be hunting after places. The conclusion is evident: that governments which have a regard to the common interest are constituted in accordance with strict principles of justice, and are therefore true forms; but those which regard only the interest of the rulers are all defective and perverted forms, for they are despotic, whereas a state is a community of freemen.

Chapter 7

Having determined these points, we have next to consider how many forms of government there are, and what they are; and in the first place what are the true forms, for when they are determined the perversions of them will at once be apparent. The words constitution and government have the same meaning, and the government, which is the supreme authority in states, must be in the hands of one, or of a few, or of the many. The true forms of government,

continued

PRIMARY SOURCE 2.5 | On Regimes, from *Politics*, Book III, Chapters 6–7 *continued*

therefore, are those in which the one, or the few, or the many, govern with a view to the common interest; but governments which rule with a view to the private interest, whether of the one or of the few, or of the many, are perversions. For the members of a state, if they are truly citizens, ought to participate in its advantages. Of forms of government in which one rules, we call that which regards the common interests, kingship or royalty; that in which more than one, but not many, rule, aristocracy; and it is so called, either because the rulers are the best men, or because they have at heart the best interests of the state and of the citizens. But when the citizens at large administer the state for the common interest, the government is called by the generic name—a constitution. And there is a reason for this use of language. One man or a few may excel in virtue; but as the number increases it becomes more difficult for them to attain perfection in every kind of virtue, though they may in military virtue, for this is found in the masses. Hence in a constitutional government the fighting-men have the supreme power, and those who possess arms are the citizens.

Of the above-mentioned forms, the perversions are as follows: of royalty, tyranny; of aristocracy, oligarchy; of constitutional government, democracy. For tyranny is a kind of monarchy which has in view the interest of the monarch only; oligarchy has in view the interest of the wealthy; democracy, of the needy: none of them the common good of all.

common good of all, and in a tyranny (the perverted regime) the tyrant rules for his selfish interest. An aristocracy is the rule of a few virtuous rulers for the common good, whereas an oligarchy is the rule of a few, usually rich people, for their selfish interest. A polity is the rule of the many for the good of all, whereas a democracy is the rule of the many for the many's selfish interest. Sometimes the Greek use of the word *democracy* is confusing to contemporary readers, who tend to think democracy must be synonymous with "the best regime," something to be applied always and everywhere. For Aristotle *democracy* meant specifically the rule of the many who rule according to a principle of liberty. But here the words *liberty* and *freedom* meant license—that is, not doing what was right or just or noble, but doing whatever one wanted to do. It implied no objective criterion of good or bad. Hence this democratic regime was for Aristotle a bad regime. Its opposite, usually called *polity,* is the good regime that rules for the good of all, not just for whatever some people want. Aristotle's use of the term *democracy* suggests rule by the mob.

Aristotle thought the best simple regime was a monarchy, the rule of the one best person. Why did he think this? Because it exemplifies unified decision making when the ruler (queen, monarch, president, or prime minister) has political prudence and rules wisely. It is always clear what the principles and rules are.

An aristocracy, for Aristotle, was the second best regime. It was weaker than monarchy because the ruling principal could be divided. Suppose, for instance, the

Number of Rulers	Rule Serving the Common Good	Rule Serving Private Interests of Those Who Rule
One	Kingship or monarchy	Tyranny
Few	Aristocracy	Oligarchy
Many	Polity	Democracy

ruling body is composed of 13 members. When we have a seven to six decision, it implies that the law is not so clear. People cannot easily agree on what is best.

The same problem is even more true of the polity, still a good form of rule, composed say of 50,001 members. What rules is 25,001. That is, the decision is not at all clear about what is the best way to act. This lack of clarity contributes to a weaker ruling principal. Obviously, even in the best of circumstances, if the vote on doing this or that is 25,001 to 25,000, the best choice is not at all clear. Aristotle recognizes implicitly the kinds of problems that would arise in regimes with such a situation.

Tyranny is the worst regime because the tyrant rules everything for personal good or interest. Plato had already intimated that the most likely source of political tyranny was democracy, where lack of a definite understanding of virtue and murky rule might let a powerful ruler take charge.

No doubt the most essential philosophical question for Aristotle is one he inherited from Plato: "What is the best regime?" This topic involved systematically knowing all imperfect regimes. Hence the cycle of regimes from monarchy to tyranny is accounted for. In Book II of the *Politics,* Aristotle criticized the descriptions of Plato's "best regime" in the *Republic* and *Laws*. Plato seemed to Aristotle an impractical visionary in some of his proposals. Aristotle doggedly examined and criticized each of Plato's famous institutions in his best regime. The exercise of reading these critiques by Aristotle is an excellent intellectual exercise for a student of politics. In almost every age of history, some form of this debate between Plato's visions and Aristotle's common sense has recurred.

Plato first proposed that the civic guardians, who were to run the best state, should have wives, children, and property in common. In Plato's view this communism or communality would free the guardians from the distracting burdens of family life and its demands. Hence he thought, rather naively Aristotle remarks, that they would be immune from personal corruption. Aristotle did not think the problem of political order could be solved by rearranging institutions.

Indeed, Aristotle maintained stoutly that such a system of common wives, children, and property simply would not work in practice. Calling everyone "father" or "son" or "daughter" or "mother" would solve nothing. Such diffuse love was no love. If property was in common, moreover, no one would take care of it. No one would have any guarantee of independent family life. Aristotle thought that Plato confused the kind of unity proper to a political society with the unity proper to an organic body. He thus ended up by having too much "unity" with no proper autonomy of the citizens to associate themselves reasonably and voluntarily with the good of the whole.

But Aristotle did not think the question of the best regime was silly. He thought that Plato's books tended to confuse and run together things that should be kept separate. Thus Aristotle wrote books about metaphysics, ethics, politics, and poetry, as if to say that this separation is the best way to understand them and to understand the whole of which they constitute parts: Separate them so that we can see how they belong together.

THE BEST POSSIBLE REGIME

Aristotle recognizes that historically many different kinds of regimes have existed. Each could be classified according to a principle of best, good, bad, worst. But Aristotle did not think the highest things were automatically associated with the best regime that he proposed—only that in such a regime it would be possible for the moral virtues to be practiced and the theoretical virtues, on their own, could be considered. The best regime for Aristotle was not "in speech or mind" but could be an actual regime, though it may rarely happen.

Aristotle thus could consider differing kinds of "best" regimes. That is, he talked about the best "actual" or "practical" regime for most people, which he called **polity**. The polity was a mixed regime that combined aristocratic and democratic elements. Notably, Aristotle uses the term *polity* in two senses to describe both the good regime that is based on majority rule and the mixed regime. This mixed regime (polity) combines the strengths and defects of the simple regimes so that they might counterbalance each other. For Aristotle, most societies will always include oligarchic and democratic factions. The art of politics is to avoid social control or dominance by either faction and to create political institutions that accommodate both these factions. When democrats gain too much control, accommodations need to be made to strengthen the oligarchic elements, and vice versa. Ironically, the combining of two perverted regimes—oligarchy and democracy—produces the best practical regime. It is as if the two negatives cancel each other out.

The best practical regime, polity, was not a regime of virtue per se but a regime that could counteract likely vices. The two most public vices are envy and greed. The many envy the riches of the few and the few are greedy. Aristotle thought that one could make a wider distribution of property to the many to solve the greed problem and give some participation in office to solve the envy problem. This solution did not automatically produce virtue, but it did mitigate the dangers of the extremes. Aristotle was willing to settle for such a solution as the best he could get in the circumstances. Aristotle also wrote about a "best" regime for a particular people with their peculiar habits, virtues, and vices—a solution that might not work for anyone else.

The **spoudaios**—the mature, scholarly statesman who is capable of advising future rulers—plays a crucial role in helping to maintain a balance of forces in the mixed regime. The spoudaios possesses the virtue of **prudence**—the ability to act well in practical matters by establishing policies and institutional arrangements that foster the common good under the circumstances.

In addition to the spoudaios, a healthy polity also requires the formation of a large **middle class**, which has a strong stake in fostering the political counterbalance between the oligarchic and democratic factions. Aristotle viewed the middle class as a golden mean between the extreme vices of oligarchy and democracy—greed and envy, respectively. This middle class mitigated the dangers of either extreme and was more inclined toward political prudence and moderation. The mixed regime may even include a monarchical element for decision making, an aristocratic element for deliberation, and a democratic element to choose people for these slots. In this manner ruling and being ruled could be combined with excellence and mediocrity within a large population. Through later writers like Cicero, Polybius, Aquinas, Montesquieu, and the American founders, this approach to rule became almost standard.

For Aristotle the best practical regime is designed for **leisure**—for things that are beyond politics, the life of contemplation, friendship, and virtue. Aristotle explains that "a state exists for the sake of a good life, and not for the sake of life only: if life only

PRIMARY SOURCE 2.6

Middle Class/Mixed Regime, from *Politics*, Book IV, Chapters 8–11

Chapter 8

I have yet to speak of the so-called polity and of tyranny. I put them in this order, not because a polity or constitutional government is to be regarded as a perversion any more than the above mentioned aristocracies. The truth is, that they fall short of the most perfect form of government, and so they are reckoned among perversions, and the really perverted forms are perversions of these, as I said in the original discussion. Last of all I will speak of tyranny, which I place last in the series because I am inquiring into the constitutions of states, and this is the very reverse of a constitution.

Having explained why I have adopted this order, I will proceed to consider constitutional government; of which the nature will be clearer now that oligarchy and democracy have been defined. For polity or constitutional government may be described generally as a fusion of oligarchy and democracy; but the term is usually applied to those forms of government which incline towards democracy, and the term aristocracy to those which incline towards oligarchy, because birth and education are commonly the accompaniments of wealth. Moreover, the rich already possess the external advantages the want of which is a temptation to crime, and hence they are called noblemen and gentlemen. And inasmuch as aristocracy seeks to give predominance to the best of the citizens, people say also of oligarchies that they are composed of noblemen and gentlemen. Now it appears to be an impossible thing that the state which is governed not by the best citizens but by the worst should be well-governed, and equally impossible that the state which is ill-governed should be governed by the best. But we must remember that good laws, if they are not obeyed, do not constitute good government. Hence there are two parts of good government; one is the actual obedience of citizens to the laws, the other part is the goodness of the laws which they obey; they may obey bad laws as well as good. And there may be a further subdivision; they may obey either the best laws which are attainable to them, or the best absolutely.

The distribution of offices according to merit is a special characteristic of aristocracy, for the principle of an aristocracy is virtue, as wealth is of an oligarchy, and freedom of a democracy. In all of them there of course exists the right of the majority, and whatever seems good to the majority of those who share in the government has authority. Now in most states the form called polity exists, for the fusion goes no further than the attempt to unite the freedom of the poor and the wealth of the rich, who commonly take the place of the noble. But as there are three grounds on which men claim an equal share in the government, freedom, wealth, and virtue (for the fourth or good birth is the result of the two last, being only ancient wealth and virtue), it is clear that the admixture of the two elements, that is to say, of the rich and poor, is to be called a polity or constitutional government; and the union of the three is to be called aristocracy or the government of the best, and more than any other form of government, except the true and ideal, has a right to this name.

Thus far I have shown the existence of forms of states other than monarchy, democracy, and oligarchy, and what they are, and in what aristocracies differ from one another, and polities from aristocracies—that the two latter are not very unlike is obvious.

Chapter 9

Next we have to consider how by the side of oligarchy and democracy the so-called polity or constitutional government springs up, and how it should be organized. The nature of it will be at once understood from a comparison of oligarchy and democracy; we must ascertain their different characteristics, and taking a portion from each, put the two together, like the parts of an indenture. Now there are three modes in which fusions of government may be affected. In the first mode we must combine the laws made by both governments, say concerning the administration of justice. In oligarchies they impose a fine on the rich if they do not serve as judges, and to the poor they give no pay; but in democracies they give

continued

PRIMARY SOURCE 2.6

Middle Class/Mixed Regime, from *Politics*, Book IV, Chapters 8–11 *continued*

pay to the poor and do not fine the rich. Now (1) the union of these two modes is a common or middle term between them, and is therefore characteristic of a constitutional government, for it is a combination of both. This is one mode of uniting the two elements. Or (2) a mean may be taken between the enactments of the two: thus democracies require no property qualification, or only a small one, from members of the assembly, oligarchies a high one; here neither of these is the common term, but a mean between them. (3) There is a third mode, in which something is borrowed from the oligarchical and something from the democratical principle. For example, the appointment of magistrates by lot is thought to be democratical, and the election of them oligarchical; democratical again when there is no property qualification, oligarchical when there is. In the aristocratical or constitutional state, one element will be taken from each—from oligarchy the principle of electing to offices, from democracy the disregard of qualification. Such are the various modes of combination.

There is a true union of oligarchy and democracy when the same state may be termed either a democracy or an oligarchy; those who use both names evidently feel that the fusion is complete. Such a fusion there is also in the mean; for both extremes appear in it. The Lacedaemonian constitution, for example, is often described as a democracy, because it has many democratical features. In the first place the youth receive a democratical education. For the sons of the poor are brought up with the sons of the rich, who are educated in such a manner as to make it possible for the sons of the poor to be educated by them. A similar equality prevails in the following period of life, and when the citizens are grown up to manhood the same rule is observed; there is no distinction between the rich and poor. In like manner they all have the same food at their public tables, and the rich wear only such clothing as any poor man can afford. Again, the people elect to one of the two greatest offices of state, and in the other they share; for they elect the Senators and share in the Ephoralty. By others the Spartan constitution is said to be an oligarchy, because it has many oligarchical elements. That all offices are filled by election and none by lot, is one of these oligarchical characteristics; that the power of inflicting death or banishment rests with a few persons is another; and there are others. In a well attempted polity there should appear to be both elements and yet neither; also the government should rely on itself, and not on foreign aid, and on itself not through the good will of a majority—they might be equally well-disposed when there is a vicious form of government—but through the general willingness of all classes in the state to maintain the constitution.

Enough of the manner in which a constitutional government, and in which the so-called aristocracies ought to be framed.

* * * *

Chapter 11

We have now to inquire what is the best constitution for most states, and the best life for most men, neither assuming a standard of virtue which is above ordinary persons, nor an education which is exceptionally favored by nature and circumstances, nor yet an ideal state which is an aspiration only, but having regard to the life in which the majority are able to share, and to the form of government which states in general can attain. As to those aristocracies, as they are called, of which we were just now speaking, they either lie beyond the possibilities of the greater number of states, or they approximate to the so-called constitutional government, and therefore need no separate discussion. And in fact the conclusion at which we arrive respecting all these forms rests upon the same grounds. For if what was said in the Ethics is true, that the happy life is the life according to virtue lived without impediment, and that virtue is a mean, then the life which is in a mean, and in a mean attainable by every one, must be the best. And the same the same principles of virtue and vice are characteristic of cities and of constitutions; for the constitution is in a figure the life of the city.

Now in all states there are three elements: one class is very rich, another very poor, and a third in a mean. It is admitted that moderation

PRIMARY SOURCE 2.6 | MIDDLE CLASS/MIXED REGIME, FROM *POLITICS*, BOOK IV, CHAPTERS 8–11 *continued*

and the mean are best, and therefore it will clearly be best to possess the gifts of fortune in moderation; for in that condition of life men are most ready to follow rational principle. But he who greatly excels in beauty, strength, birth, or wealth, or on the other hand who is very poor, or very weak, or very much disgraced, finds it difficult to follow rational principle. Of these two the one sort grow into violent and great criminals, the others into rogues and petty rascals. And two sorts of offenses correspond to them, the one committed from violence, the other from roguery. Again, the middle class is least likely to shrink from rule, or to be over-ambitious for it; both of which are injuries to the state. Again, those who have too much of the goods of fortune, strength, wealth, friends, and the like, are neither willing nor able to submit to authority. The evil begins at home; for when they are boys, by reason of the luxury in which they are brought up, they never learn, even at school, the habit of obedience. On the other hand, the very poor, who are in the opposite extreme, are too degraded. So that the one class cannot obey, and can only rule despotically; the other knows not how to command and must be ruled like slaves. Thus arises a city, not of freemen, but of masters and slaves, the one despising, the other envying; and nothing can be more fatal to friendship and good fellowship in states than this: for good fellowship springs from friendship; when men are at enmity with one another, they would rather not even share the same path. But a city ought to be composed, as far as possible, of equals and similars; and these are generally the middle classes. Wherefore the city which is composed of middle-class citizens is necessarily best constituted in respect of the elements of which we say the fabric of the state naturally consists. And this is the class of citizens which is most secure in a state, for they do not, like the poor, covet their neighbors' goods; nor do others covet theirs, as the poor covet the goods of the rich; and as they neither plot against others, nor are themselves plotted against, they pass through life safely. Wisely then did Phocylides pray—"Many things are best in the mean; I desire to be of a middle condition in my city."

Thus it is manifest that the best political community is formed by citizens of the middle class, and that those states are likely to be well-administered in which the middle class is large, and stronger if possible than both the other classes, or at any rate than either singly; for the addition of the middle class turns the scale, and prevents either of the extremes from being dominant. Great then is the good fortune of a state in which the citizens have a moderate and sufficient property; for where some possess much, and the others nothing, there may arise an extreme democracy, or a pure oligarchy; or a tyranny may grow out of either extreme—either out of the most rampant democracy, or out of an oligarchy; but it is not so likely to arise out of the middle constitutions and those akin to them. I will explain the reason of this hereafter, when I speak of the revolutions of states. The mean condition of states is clearly best, for no other is free from faction; and where the middle class is large, there are least likely to be factions and dissensions. For a similar reason large states are less liable to faction than small ones, because in them the middle class is large; whereas in small states it is easy to divide all the citizens into two classes who are either rich or poor, and to leave nothing in the middle. And democracies are safer and more permanent than oligarchies, because they have a middle class which is more numerous and has a greater share in the government; for when there is no middle class, and the poor greatly exceed in number, troubles arise, and the state soon comes to an end. A proof of the superiority of the middle class is that the best legislators have been of a middle condition; for example, Solon, as his own verses testify; and Lycurgus, for he was not a king; and Charondas, and almost all legislators.

These considerations will help us to understand why most governments are either democratical or oligarchical. The reason is that the middle class is seldom numerous in them, and

continued

PRIMARY SOURCE 2.6

Middle Class/Mixed Regime, from *Politics*, Book IV, Chapters 8–11 *continued*

whichever party, whether the rich or the common people, transgresses the mean and predominates, draws the constitution its own way, and thus arises either oligarchy or democracy. There is another reason—the poor and the rich quarrel with one another, and whichever side gets the better, instead of establishing a just or popular government, regards political supremacy as the prize of victory, and the one party sets up a democracy and the other an oligarchy. Further, both the parties which had the supremacy in Hellas looked only to the interest of their own form of government, and established in states, the one, democracies, and the other, oligarchies; they thought of their own advantage, of the public not at all. For these reasons the middle form of government has rarely, if ever, existed, and among a very few only. One man alone of all who ever ruled in Hellas was induced to give this middle constitution to states. But it has now become a habit among the citizens of states, not even to care about equality; all men are seeking for dominion, or, if conquered, are willing to submit.

What then is the best form of government, and what makes it the best, is evident; and of other constitutions, since we say that there are many kinds of democracy and many of oligarchy, it is not difficult to see which has the first and which the second or any other place in the order of excellence, now that we have determined which is the best. For that which is nearest to the best must of necessity be better, and that which is furthest from it worse, if we are judging absolutely and not relatively to given conditions: I say "relatively to given conditions," since a particular government may be preferable, but another form may be better for some people.

---

were the object, slaves and brute animals might form a state, but they cannot, for they have no share in happiness or in a life of free choice." Politics is designed to provide conditions of leisure whereby citizens can develop and fully realize their potential for moral and intellectual virtue or excellence. Politics ministers to a transpolitical end; that is, politics is for the sake of things that are beyond politics—namely the ethical and theoretical life of virtue. Aristotle judges the success or failure of politics in terms of how well it serves this transpolitical end. Indeed, once the political vocation was reasonably complete, men lived for things of beauty, truth, and the good. Aristotle's munificent man in Book IV of the *Ethics* saw to it that his wealth was used to enhance not himself but his community. The polity was supposed to provide for things beyond itself where the real questions of human nobility were pursued in beauty and some splendor.

It sometimes comes as a shock to realize that to Aristotle the highest things are not political things. By this affirmation, he does not intend to denigrate political life but rather to state exactly what it is and what can be expected of it. Politics has a definite place in the overall order of things and has its own legitimate intellectual fascination. Its specific subject matter must be studied in itself and not be confused with other legitimate objects of study and concern. Aristotle thinks that basically a political order, in its relation to virtue, both through habit and coercive law, makes it possible for men to be free to pursue things beyond politics. Here the theoretical virtues of wisdom, first principles, and science, discussed in Books VI and X of the *Ethics*, are pursued for their own sakes and to find the truth of things. Good habits are thus a condition of good thinking.

Book X of the *Ethics* discusses two kinds of human happiness, a theoretical one and a practical or political one. Both are necessary for a complete understanding of human flourishing. The political life, however, is an especially demanding one because so many things can go wrong and because of the instability caused by human freedom and natural chance. Aristotle's realism about political order takes into account chance, vice, and human freedom. Hurricanes and floods like Katrina have political consequences as much as greed, theft, or war. The prudent statesman seeks to minimize the evil things, promote political accommodation, and prevent revolution from taking place. But in most cases, he will have, in his personal life, little time for anything else but pressing, immediate, particular issues.

Aristotle does not doubt that a higher or immortal life exists, but this life is not the direct concern of politics. It is the concern of metaphysics and the theoretical sciences, to which polities are indirectly ordered. This **theoretical happiness** is what Aristotle considers the highest end of humanity. He sees it to be "higher" than human political life. But **political happiness** also exists as a second kind of happiness. It consists in the activities of all the moral virtues in a full life—that is, a life that includes all its normal changes from birth to death. The object of the **contemplative (or theoretic) life** is the truth of things. Politicians are not directly concerned with this life because they cannot change it. It is the direct concern of the philosopher. But it is important that a protected place be provided for intellectual life within the polity, or at least an attitude not antagonistic to it.

This latter concern is the context of the relation of the philosopher and the politician. The politician, as Plato was at pains to point out, can at any time, because he has the force, kill the philosopher in an attempt to control philosophy. The city and the philosopher thus must reach an agreement, in law, whereby the vocation of each can be fulfilled without destroying each other. However, some regimes, tyrannies in the classical sense, totalitarian governments in the modern sense, identify the theoretical and the practical in such a way as to allow nothing but what the prince or ruling principle or ideology wills.

In the last book of the *Politics* in particular, Aristotle distinguishes between amusement, work, relaxation, business, acting, and the theoretical activities. To understand the importance of these distinctions, we must realize that "leisure," a Greek word (*skole*) from which significantly derives our word "school," means the free activities of the human faculties in search of and in finding truth. It is toward this leisurely activity that all human political life, all friendship, and all theoretical life point as their purpose and context. This life presupposes the acquiring of the moral virtues and hence the political life. It also presupposes that the end of war, which is sometimes necessary, is peace. But peace is the order in which these higher virtues can be displayed.

Aristotle, practical and observant man that he was, knew that leisure would be a relatively rare thing, even in a well-ordered regime. The modern notion of "business," for instance, meant for Aristotle precisely an "unleisurely" life because it purpose was basically staying alive and producing the goods and conditions whereby "living well" was possible. Aristotle did not deny that such things were good and necessary—just that providing for them was not basically what the polis or friendship was ultimately about. We work and do business, in other words, to provide the conditions of the full human life. But once these are provided, it does not necessarily mean that we will actually enter into or even enjoy the leisurely life. Leisure does not mean here "free time" or "laziness" or "fooling around." And work can be exhausting, so that "relaxation," in Aristotle's sense, means not leisure but the time needed to recoup our losses so that we can go back to work. Work itself is for leisure.

Amusement and sport, moreover, were not looked down on by Aristotle. One of the definitions of man is not just "rational animal," or "political animal," or "mortal animal" but also *homo ludens,* the being that plays. He is also the "being who laughs." Aristotle in Book IV of his *Ethics* is quite aware of the difference between good humor and buffoonery, of sharp wit and wit that hurts. But he saw the dangers and sought to protect what it was, the very context of the highest things, of friendship and leisure. Sports too were important for Aristotle. He thought sports, both in playing and in watching good games, brought us very close to contemplation, to being fascinated with something that need not be, but in its working out, in its being played, brought us to wonder and dramas outside ourselves.

In all things political, it is important to understand Aristotle's teaching about pleasure. He devoted part of Book VII and part of Book X of the *Ethics* to a specific treatment of pleasure. It is a subject that is everywhere found in Aristotle because no human activity is without some relation to pleasure or its opposite. It is one of the four possible definitions of happiness in Book I of the *Ethics*. Pleasure is often said, with some exaggeration, to be the prime end or motive for human action. Basically Aristotle held that in activity there is manifest a proper pleasure. Indeed, education might be said to be learning to appreciate the proper pleasure of any act, be it in games, politics, craft, music, seeing, thinking, dining, or any real human activity. A thing was not, as such, good or bad because it had pleasure connected to it. What made the pleasure good or bad was the act in which it occurred and that act's objective purpose.

But it is possible, mentally at least, to separate the pleasure from the purpose of the act. We can concentrate on one, the pleasure, and ignore the other, the purpose. We can enjoy a stolen cake, but both the injustice of the act (stealing) and the pleasure (tasty cake) remain. So Aristotle was not against pleasure. No one accounted for it better than he did. Rather he advocated appreciating the proper pleasure that accompanied each act in what it was and was supposed to be. Aristotle was in fact the great defender of pleasure because he understood so clearly that pleasure is best when it reinforces the goodness and purpose of the acts in which it exists. One of the pleasures of pleasure, so to speak, is to understand what it is and why it is given to us.

It is important to say something more about Aristotle's notion of friendship and its relation to politics. The two chapters about friendship in *Ethics,* Books VIII and IX, are among the best and most powerful discussions of this topic ever written. Probably nothing in the whole corpus of Aristotle fascinates students more than these two insightful and moving chapters. Aristotle distinguishes friendships based on utility, pleasure, and the highest things. All three are good in themselves, though there is a principled difference among them.

The chapters about friendship are designed in part to mitigate the harshness of the virtue of justice (Book V, *Ethics*), which is concerned not with people but with the rightness of relationships among them. Aristotle recognizes that we cannot have many friends of the highest type—a question that itself leads to deep thought. But he also thinks that human polities, in part, exist so that such friendships can be possible and flourish. This view helps explain his preference for smaller states wherein everyone could know each other better. He thought that friendly exchanges of utility or business were good things. He thought friends of pleasure were good in themselves. But he recognized that if someone was in a friendship for utility or pleasure and the other partner thought it was for the highest things, it would corrupt the relationship—a common human experience.

The culmination of Aristotle's political thought, then, is not so much in the concord or civic friendship that, say, citizens of one nation have toward each other; rather, it is the exchange of the highest things. Of these latter, even tyrants are fearful or envious. Thus in not placing politics in a higher position than it belongs, Aristotle's political books allow us to see politics for what it is. Politics is not a substitute for philosophical life but requires it and leads to it. On the other hand, the service that a good politician gives to the common good of the given polity is of a high order. The politician's or statesman's service allows many things to flourish. These things could not exist if someone did not look to the interrelation of goods, citizens, and institutions that make up a polity. The proper virtue of the politician (Book VI, *Ethics*) is political prudence, the proper estimate of worthy ends and the means of attaining them. Nothing serves citizens better than truly prudential politicians.

One of the most important functions of the prudent ruler is preventing revolutions within the regime. Aristotle's famous Chapter 5 of *Politics* is his discussion of revolution or the reasons why regimes change. He thought they always changed, referring back to Book V of *Ethics*, because of differing concepts of justice. Those who think they are equal in some things tend to think they are equal in everything. This analysis explains the Greek problem with democracy. Those who are unequal in some things, moreover, think that they are unequal in everything. This latter assumption becomes the problem of oligarchy and aristocracy. All revolutions, though they begin in small things, are pursued in the name of some noble form of either commutative or distributive justice.

We should keep in mind the meanings of the various kinds of simple and mixed regimes that Aristotle depicted in the middle books of his *Politics:* monarchies, aristocracies, polities, democracies, oligarchies, and tyrannies with their practical combinations. These are the differing ways to configure the ruling group or party, who is to decide ruling norms and on what principles, and how this authority relates to the citizens. Some regimes combine oligarchical and democratic principles. Two types of tyranny exist: One concentrates all in itself, and the other imitates a king and has some limitations to itself. Within this schema, regimes can change from one form to another in an ordered, even at times predictable, fashion. They can change by custom, revolution, or conquest. We can see that the ability to accurately describe what a regime is in terms of the numbers and nature of its ruling principals, their relation to the citizens, and its moral purpose is both an intellectually necessary and often politically dangerous enterprise.

Tyrants exist in most ages, including today; but they rarely like to be called tyrants. They prefer to be called "democrats," "kings," "presidents," or "leaders." Oligarchs like to be called aristocrats. We sometimes underestimate the importance of calling things by their right names. We need to be aware of the political reality behind popular political words. Aristotle shows us how to not be too confused by politically charged words. He teaches us to learn what to expect, to look at the reality at hand so we know what it is no matter what words are used to depict it in public. He does not deny that words can be confusing. Deliberate efforts are often made to hide the reality behind them. Aristotle dealt with this issue in his *Rhetoric*.

As we noted, the word *democracy* in Aristotle's usage describes a weak and disordered regime. He meant specifically the rule of the many who have no internal principle of order in their souls. But it is not the worst regime and may, in fact, be the best regime under the circumstances of a certain people. Any change in regimes can produce something better or something worse. The statesman has to recognize this possibility of things becoming worse when he considers changing laws or customs. Change is not always in the direction of the better. What is bad can get worse. What is noble can become less noble. Likewise, what is terrible can become less bad. The Aristotelian politician is acutely aware of these alternatives. Moreover, those who instigate change, even if they are corrupt themselves, always do so in the name of the good. But there is a difference between intention and results that cannot be ignored. Good intentions (which most people think they have) are insufficient if circumstances, human perversity, and practical effects are ignored.

Many modern regimes that are called and call themselves "democracies" are clearly, by Aristotelian standards, tyrannies. And some regimes that call themselves "democracies" or "republics" are, to use the Roman word, "polities"—that is, good regimes in Aristotle's terms. The usefulness of studying Aristotle is that we find in him a guide to thinking about politics no matter what kind of actual regime we may happen to live in, in any time or place. There are in fact regimes that do not allow people to read Aristotle or Plato precisely because they do not want their regime to be questioned in the minds of their people. Aristotle, however, has good insight into the range of human possibilities and motives. He serves as a guide to the mind in analyzing and judging the situation before a polity and its citizens. Such consideration is aimed at action, not just at knowledge.

Aristotle was also perceptive about what tyrannical regimes are like, how they operate, and how they can be preserved. But first both Aristotle and Plato recognized that a "tyrant" was not necessarily an unattractive, ugly, or brutal man. Often he was handsome, polished, and suave. Aristotle thought, however, that we need thorough knowledge of bad regimes and how they operate to protect ourselves. Politics needs intelligence of itself. Tyrants must keep the population busy in war or construction so the people will not have the energy to conspire against the tyrannical ruler. Tyrants must prevent friendships from arising among citizens who could overthrow them. Everything has to be public, known to the tyrant. Aristotle was surprisingly perceptive here. He was quite aware of the disorders within the human soul and their dangers when they manifest themselves in political situations. He found a certain wickedness in human nature that the polity and the law were, in part, designed to counteract but that in principle had origins deeper than politics itself.

Aristotle was objective in describing actual regimes. He thought most regimes were oligarchies or democracies, or a combination of the two, sometimes with characteristics of other regimes. Aristotle did not think it wise to try to employ a constitutional form—that is, structure of offices of a good regime—if people in fact were unvirtuous in their actual lives. In this case, Aristotle advised preserving or gradually changing regimes. He thought that if we try to change things too quickly, they will likely get worse. The change from the worst to the best usually must pass through the less bad to the less good before reaching the better.

PRIMARY SOURCE 2.7

ON REVOLUTION, FROM *POLITICS*, BOOK V, CHAPTERS 1–2

Chapter 1

The design which we proposed to ourselves is now nearly completed. Next in order follow the causes of revolution in states, how many, and of what nature they are; what modes of destruction apply to particular states, and out of what, and into what they mostly change; also what are the modes of preservation in states generally, or in a particular state, and by what means each state may be best preserved: these questions remain to be considered.

In the first place we must assume as our starting-point that in the many forms of government which have sprung up there has always been an acknowledgment of justice and proportionate equality, although mankind fail attaining them, as I have already explained. Democracy, for example, arises out of the notion that those who are equal in any respect are equal in all respects; because men are equally free, they claim to be absolutely equal. Oligarchy is based on the notion that those who are unequal in one respect are in all respects unequal; being unequal, that is, in property, they suppose themselves to be unequal absolutely. The democrats think that as they are equal they ought to be equal in all things; while the oligarchs, under the idea that they are unequal, claim too much, which is one form of inequality. All these forms of government have a kind of justice, but, tried by an absolute standard, they are faulty; and, therefore, both parties, whenever their share in the government does not accord with their preconceived ideas, stir up revolution. Those who excel in virtue have the best right of all to rebel (for they alone can with reason be deemed absolutely unequal), but then they are of all men the least inclined to do so. There is also a superiority which is claimed by men of rank; for they are thought noble because they spring from wealthy and virtuous ancestors. Here then, so to speak, are opened the very springs and fountains of revolution; and hence arise two sorts of changes in governments; the one affecting the constitution, when men seek to change from an existing form into some other, for example, from democracy into oligarchy, and from oligarchy into democracy, or from either of them into constitutional government or aristocracy, and conversely; the other not affecting the constitution, when, without disturbing the form of government, whether oligarchy, or monarchy, or any other, they try to get the administration into their own hands. Further, there is a question of degree; an oligarchy, for example, may become more or less oligarchical, and a democracy more or less democratical; and in like manner the characteristics of the other forms of government may be more or less strictly maintained. Or the revolution may be directed against a portion of the constitution only, e.g., the establishment or overthrow of a particular office: as at Sparta it is said that Lysander attempted to overthrow the monarchy, and King Pausanias, the Ephoralty. At Epidamnus, too, the change was partial. For instead of phylarchs or heads of tribes, a council was appointed; but to this day the magistrates are the only members of the ruling class who are compelled to go to the Heliaea when an election takes place, and the office of the single archon was another oligarchical feature. Everywhere inequality is a cause of revolution, but an inequality in which there is no proportion—for instance, a perpetual monarchy among equals; and always it is the desire of equality which rises in rebellion.

Chapter 2

In considering how dissensions and political revolutions arise, we must first of all ascertain the beginnings and causes of them which affect constitutions generally. They may be said to be three in number; and we have now to give an outline of each. We want to know (1) what is the feeling? (2) what are the motives of those who make them? (3) whence arise political disturbances and quarrels? The universal and chief cause of this revolutionary feeling has been already mentioned; viz., the desire of equality, when men think that they are equal to others who have more than themselves; or, again, the desire of inequality and superiority, when conceiving themselves to be superior they think that they have not more but the same or less than their inferiors; pretensions

continued

PRIMARY SOURCE 2.7

On Revolution, from *Politics*, Book V, Chapters 1–2 *continued*

which may and may not be just. Inferiors revolt in order that they may be equal, and equals that they may be superior. Such is the state of mind which creates revolutions. The motives for making them are the desire of gain and honor, or the fear of dishonor and loss; the authors of them want to divert punishment or dishonor from themselves or their friends. The causes and reasons of revolutions, whereby men are themselves affected in the way described, and about the things which I have mentioned, viewed in one way may be regarded as seven, and in another as more than seven. Two of them have been already noticed; but they act in a different manner, for men are excited against one another by the love of gain and honor—not, as in the case which I have just supposed, in order to obtain them for themselves, but at seeing others, justly or unjustly, engrossing them. Other causes are insolence, fear, excessive predominance, contempt, disproportionate increase in some part of the state; causes of another sort are election intrigues, carelessness, neglect about trifles, dissimilarity of elements.

CONTRIBUTIONS AND INFLUENCE

We are fortunate that many of Aristotle's academic works were preserved and handed down to us from antiquity. We often do not understand how amazing it is that we have such texts despite the vicissitudes of history. We are not, of course, exactly sure about what more is missing. Aristotle has found careful and interested readers wherever he has been known in ancient, Muslim, medieval, modern, and contemporary settings. St. Thomas Aquinas had him translated into Latin from Spanish and Muslim sources in the 13th century. Aquinas commented on and explained many of Aristotle's works. German scholars in the 19th century managed to provide a critical edition of existing Aristotelian texts, a work that still goes on. Today reliable translations of Aristotle's Greek can be found in many languages.

Much of modern scientific thought was based, apparently, on the rejection of one or other of Aristotle's overall views, particularly his teleological approach to understanding things. However, as Henry Veatch has argued in his seminal *Aristotle: A Contemporary Appreciation*, many of the reasons once given for the rejection of Aristotle are themselves under suspicion and rejected. So perhaps, as Veatch maintained, it is indeed time to look again at Aristotle as if he were a contemporary philosopher. Indeed, Aristotle had an uncanny appreciation of the human mind and confronted, in his own terms, many ideas that were said to be the basis for rejecting his positions. Students will encounter few thinkers clearer than Aristotle or more instructive to read.

Perhaps the central thing to learn from Aristotle in political things is not his insightful description of political institutions but how they relate to the virtue of prudence (Book VI, *Ethics*). This is the virtue that applies principles to particular unrepeatable situations to guide one's actions or laws to a proper human end or good. This is but another way of saying that there are no automatic fixes in politics. There are insights and understandings, however, that explain how and why human beings act in the way they do. The raw material of politics is constituted by the character of a polity's citizens, what they consider vicious, what indifferent, what virtuous.

The Greek notion of history held that human situations were cyclic, as contrasted to the more linear view founded in scripture. This cyclic view was found elaborated in the great book of Thucydides about the Peloponnesian War between Athens and Sparta. This theory meant that we can expect to find today similar (not exact) situations that have happened before and can learn from them. Aristotle told us that most things had already been discovered. This is not so true in physical technology; however, much about the basic structure of matter itself remains the same. We must suspect as we read Aristotle's *Ethics, Rhetoric,* and *Politics* that what they explain, despite our different styles of political configurations, is fairly close to the truth, even in our own lives. It is no accident that in reading Aristotle's *Politics* we recognize what he is talking about because something similar happened according to yesterday afternoon's newspaper.

In the history of political thought, Thucydides, Augustine, Machiavelli, and Burke, among others, have been called "political realists." That is, they looked carefully at the record of what men actually did in political life and sought to account for it. Again and again the student should notice that Aristotle is quite blunt about what he expects most men to do or be capable of doing. He does not think it is likely that things will be perfect. Still, he thinks it is good and necessary to think in political things about the difference between good and best, between bad and worst. There are real differences between them that can and should be identified.

Aristotle too is thus a realist with common sense and also a touch of the ideal. He encourages any improvement—even a small one—and likewise advises, when possible, the prevention of something becoming worse. One soon has the impression that Aristotle has understood much about human nature as it exists and manifests itself in political societies. The fact that he lived some 2,300 years ago is irrelevant to whether he can still teach us. He can and does.

Aristotle acknowledges that there is much more to life than politics, but he conceives this knowledge not as a denigration of politics but as a proper appreciation of its place in reality. He simply insists on politics being what it is. We should expect politics to be a normal manifestation of what is necessary and good for humans, without being everything. But politics makes it possible for the higher things to exist and flourish. This is why politics is called the highest of the practical sciences but not the highest science or consideration in itself.

Aristotle observed politicians themselves very carefully. He specifically said that we do not need to be "rulers of earth and sea" to live a full and worthy life. In this sense the politician had a certain nobility of being a servant to the good of others. Aristotle also noted that if politicians themselves did not experience the pull and wonder of what is beyond politics, the pleasure of the higher things, they would likely try to substitute in their own personal lives less worthy pleasures for what they were lacking in theoretical insight.

Aristotle's theoretical preference for small city–states still perplexes residents of large nation–states with tens and hundreds of millions of population. Theories of federalism, with which Aristotle was not totally unfamiliar, often seek to accomplish the same effect within the larger states. Aristotle considered that it would take a "god" to rule large states, so complicated and morally unruly were they likely to be. He may have had a point. Moreover, because his "best" regime existed mostly in "prayer" or in hope, Aristotle was content to propose more practical goals and less than perfect regimes. Aristotle did distinguish between natural and civil justice. *Civil justice* referred to the particular laws that were set up in Thebes or Sparta that distinguished them: their taxing, penal, military, and economic laws. Aristotle thought that we needed to be just to everyone potentially. That is, if the occasion arose, we might have to be just even to someone from another polity if we did something unjust to him or made an agreement with him. We would have to "render to him what is due."

But Aristotle wrote that large impersonal societies would make the practice of virtue difficult. Whether he was wrong about this issue, as it sometimes appears, might be wondered. Aristotle, like Plato, spent a good deal of effort on education, especially on music and the arts. At first this emphasis might make us question the pertinence of music to politics. Plato had already remarked that a change in music or rules of games indicated a change in polity, in the spirit on which they were founded. We tend to think that sports rules and music have little or nothing to do with politics. But Aristotle thought that nothing indicated the internal life of the soul or affected it as much as the kind of music we listen to or play. Thus the discussion of music is no accident in a book about politics. It remains something each student should consider.

Aristotle, unlike Plato, did not think that the normal politician or statesman had time or even insight enough to be a philosopher. What is important for the statesman is to recognize the enormous role the spoudaios can play in the politician's sound or prudent decision making. Though Aristotle provided a place for both, he rejected the Platonic solution of identifying the philosopher and the politician. This separation left Aristotle with the problem of explaining how the politician could be open to the important things that the philosopher stood for without fully understanding them or devoting a lifetime to them. Even if a politician was not learned in the formal sense, he or she could be receptive to the advice of the philosopher or spoudaios. Politics for Aristotle never forgets its relation to the condition of the souls of its citizens and rulers. This understanding probably remains the best and most fruitful reason to continue to read Aristotle carefully and repeatedly. No matter how often we read him, he will always be new and provide fresh insight as our own experience of political things deepens enough for us to better understand him.

Key Terms

Lycaeum
peripatetics
cosmopolis
polis
city–state
arête
practical sciences
freedom
ethics
politics
common good
physis
telos
logos
regime
oligarchy
parental rule
royal rule
constitutional rule
slaves by law
slaves by nature
citizen
law
commutative justice
distributive justice
best regime
monarchy
tyranny
aristocracy
polity
democracy
spoudaios
prudence
middle class
leisure
theoretical happiness
political happiness
contemplative life

Sources and Resources

Key Texts

The Basic Works of Aristotle, edited with an introduction by Richard McKeon (New York: Random House, 1941).

The Loeb Classical Editions of the *Ethics, Rhetoric, Poetics,* and the *Politics* (Harvard) contain the Greek text on one page and the translation on the other.

Nicomachean Ethics, translated, introduction, notes, and glossary by Terence Irwin (Indianapolis: Hackett, 1985). The translations of the *Ethics* by Thompson (Penguin) is also good.

The *Politics,* translated with an introduction, notes, and glossary by Carnes Lord (Chicago: University of Chicago Press, 1984). The translations of the *Politics* by Jowett (Modern Library), Sinclair (Penguin), and Barker (Oxford) are likewise very good.

Secondary Texts

Arnhart, Larry. *Aristotle on Political Reasoning* (DeKalb: Northern Illinois University Press, 1981).

Jaffa, Harry V. "Aristotle," in *History of Political Philosophy,* 1st ed., edited by Leo Strauss and Joseph Cropsey (Chicago: Rand-McNally, 1961), pp. 64–129.

McCoy, Charles N.R. "Aristotle: Political Science and the Real World," *The Structure of Political Thought* (New York: McGraw-Hill, 1963), pp. 29–72.

Mulgan, R.G. *Aristotle's Political Theory: An Introduction for Students of Political Theory* (Oxford: Clarendon, 1977).

Nichols, Mary P. *Citizens and Statesmen: A Study of Aristotle's Politics* (Lanham, MD: Rowman & Littlefield, 1992).

Veatch, Henry B. *Rational Man: A Modern Interpretation of Aristotelian Ethics* (Bloomington: Indiana University Press, 1966).

Web Sites

Works by Aristotle: http://classics.mit.edu/Browse/browse-Aristotle.html

Aristotle's *Politics*: http://classics.mit.edu/Aristotle/politics.html

Summary of Aristotle's *Politics*: http://www.gradesaver.com/classicnotes/titles/politics/

St. Augustine

Chapter 3

By Joseph R. Fornieri *Rochester Institute of Technology*

© Liz Michaud

LIFE AND LEGACY

History records the rise, flourish, and fall of countless empires that boasted of divine favor. The Egyptians, the Assyrians, the Persians, the Macedonians—all claimed that destiny was on their side. All raised monuments to their own everlasting glory, built with the brick and mortar of countless human lives. Yet what remains of their splendor today? Their crumbled ruins are poignant reminders of the fleeting character of human glory. By the time of St. Augustine (A.D. 354–430), dominion had passed to the Romans. The auspicious reign of Caesar Augustus promised to usher in a ***pax romana***—a new era of peace, prosperity, and justice. Rome's claim to imperial glory was further buttressed through the construction of an imperial myth. Most notably, in the epic poem *Aeneid,* the poet Virgil captured the Roman imagination as a people uniquely destined to spread the benefits of civilization throughout the world. He portrayed the Romans as favored descendants of a surviving remnant of Trojan heroes fated to become masters of the known world. The Romans would preside over an "empire without end." Indeed, Virgil coined the motto that best defined Rome's imperial ambitions: "to spare the vanquished and to subdue the proud." And so by fire and sword Rome vanquished and subdued all those who stood in the way of its imperial designs.

In A.D. 410 the Roman dream of everlasting empire was shattered when the Visigoths sacked the "eternal city." Many blamed Christianity for the disaster. Only two decades earlier, the Emperor Theodosius had established Christianity as the official religion of the empire, thereby abolishing pagan worship. Pagan shrines were destroyed and the statue of Nike (the goddess of victory) was removed from the Senate, where it had presided since the beginning of the Republic. For Americans today, this act would be like tearing down the Lincoln Memorial. Despite Christianity's status as the official religion, paganism lingered. Pious Romans, still clinging to their ancestral beliefs, claimed that Christianity had provoked the wrath of their gods, causing them to withdraw their divine favor and protection from the eternal city. These traditionalists, many of whom were from the intelligentsia, further reviled Christianity for its otherworldly teachings of meekness, humility, "loving one's enemy," and "turning the other cheek." Such teachings were thought fit for women and slaves, not free men. Christianity, in their view, had sapped Rome of its manly, martial virtue—a claim Machiavelli would repeat more than a thousand years later.

When placed in its original context, the full title of St. Augustine's magnum opus (great work), *The City of God against the Pagans,* reveals the extent to which the book was a rebuttal to pagan charges that Christianity was responsible for the fall of Rome. Augustine defends his faith from this accusation through a counterindictment that probes the theological foundations of political order: He unmasks Rome's triumphalist history and founding myths as vainglorious delusions that obscure the true glory of God.[1] The root cause of Rome's decline was not its alleged failure to propitiate imaginary gods, but its own self-inflicted moral decadence and lust for power. To highlight the difference in orientation between the Roman longing for worldly glory and the Christian yearning for heavenly glory, Augustine contrasts the Roman motto

---

[1]Thomas W. Smith, "The Glory and Tragedy of Politics," pp. 187–216 in *Augustine and Politics,* eds. John Doody, Kevin L. Hughes, Kim Paffenroth (Oxford: Lexington Books, 2005).

"to spare the vanquished and to subdue the proud" to the Christian belief that "God is opposed to the proud, but gives grace to the humble."[2]

Augustine was truly an epochal figure who stood at the crossroad of classical civilization and medieval Christianity. He provided the first comprehensive integration of pagan philosophy and Christian revelation to date. In so doing, he both appropriated and modified classical concepts and ideas, placing them within a Christian framework. R.W. Dyson concisely summarizes his intellectual legacy: "In drawing upon the language and ideas of the pagan philosophical heritage, and in scrutinizing those ideas in the light of the Christian revelation, Augustine has effectively refashioned them into a Christian philosophy of politics."[3]

Augustine was born in A.D. 354 in the North African Roman province of Thagaste (now in Algeria). Ironically, scholars who claim that the ideas and culture of Western civilization were stolen from Africa ignore the profound influence of this African person of color on the development of the West. Augustine's father was a Roman public official who ensured that his son received a liberal education. This fortuitous decision, in part, accounts for the remarkable breadth and depth of classical learning displayed by Augustine. His mother Monica was a devout Catholic who served as a guiding spiritual presence. After a prolonged intellectual journey, Augustine the philosopher and theologian would return to the living faith of his illiterate mother.

Augustine reveals his quest for God in his ***Confessions***—a spiritual autobiography that bares his innermost yearnings. The experience of the hungry heart craving the fullness of God is a recurrent theme in the *Confessions:* "For you [God] have made us for you and our heart is restless until it rests in you."[4] Indeed, *Confessions* marks the beginning of a new literary genre in Western civilization, one that brings interiority and introspection to the fore of philosophical inquiry. It tells the story of a self-described lover in love with love. Indeed, the challenge of both individuals and societies to direct and properly order their love toward God and neighbor is a central motif in Augustine's social and political thought.

Augustine records several spiritual turning points in his life that culminated in his conversion to Catholic Christianity. Notably, this change of heart was prepared by years of intellectual reflection whereby he explored various philosophical and religious paths to wisdom. To appreciate Augustine's mature political thought, it is necessary to know something about these earlier teachings and their subsequent influence.

Augustine recalls that the reading of Cicero's book ***Hortensius***, an exhortation to philosophy, was the first defining moment of his intellectual life. "This book," he claimed, "transformed my affections . . . Suddenly every vain hope became worthless to me, and I longed with unbelievable warmth of the heart for the immortality of wisdom."[5] Cicero was a Roman philosopher, orator, and statesman during the late Republic. His thought reflected the teachings of the **Stoic school of philosophy,**

---

[2]James 4:6, New American Standard Translation.

[3]R.W. Dyson, *St. Augustine of Hippo: The Christian Transformation of Political Philosophy* (London: Continuum International Publishing Group, 2005), pp. 181–182.

[4]St. Augustine, *Confessions,* edited by R. S. Pine-Coffin (New York: Penguin Books, 1961), p. 21.

[5]Quoted in Dyson, p. 2.

a tradition that greatly influenced the fathers of the Church. Stoic beliefs were transmitted to Augustine both directly from original sources like Cicero and indirectly by way of the Christian fathers. More specifically, the Stoic teachings concerning (a) a law of nature based on right reason, (b) a lost Golden Age, and (c) a universal, common humanity influenced Augustine's respective Christian understanding of the law of nature, the fall from the Garden of Eden, and the spiritual dignity of all human beings created in the image of God.[6]

The next path on Augustine's spiritual journey led him to a religious sect known as **the Manicheans.** This philosophical–religious sect believed that the universe could be explained in terms of two equally powerful material forces of light (good) and darkness (evil), which were locked in an eternal struggle against each other. In sum, the Manicheans were both materialists and metaphysical dualists. They believed that over time the forces of light and darkness in the universe had become confused and mixed together. The goal of life was to distill and separate them into the purity of their original parts. Human liberation could be attained only by an elite few through **gnosis**—a secret knowledge of salvation involving techniques of ritualistic purity. Through gnosis, the elect would release the light particles in their souls from the prison of bodily darkness. Significantly, the Manicheans attributed evil not to themselves but to the alien force of darkness that actively penetrated and defiled the force of goodness within them. It thus followed that human beings were not responsible for evil.

Augustine's mature teaching on original sin would squarely reject the Manichean view that evil was to be attributed to an outside, alien force. On the contrary, he would argue that evil was something inherent to human beings. Though Augustine ultimately rejected Manicheanism, its dualistic legacy continued to influence his subsequent thought. As will be seen, something of this dualism is to be found in his crucial distinction between the two cities—the city of God and the city of man.

In A.D. 385 Augustine was appointed professor of rhetoric at Milan. There he met St. Ambrose, the famous bishop of Milan who had humbled the Emperor Theodosius, and whose multifaceted study of the Bible in terms of its wider allegorical meanings freed Augustine from a literalism that had been an obstacle to his faith. Indeed, Augustine's principle of interpretation for the Book of Genesis is still relevant to our contemporary debate over the compatibility between science and religion. "In matters that are so obscure and far beyond our vision," he explains, "we find in Holy Scripture passages which can be interpreted in very different ways without prejudice to the faith we have received. In such cases, we should not rush headlong and so firmly take our stand on one side that, if further progress in the search for truth justly undermines this position, we too fall with it."[7]

While in Milan, Augustine had a son with an unnamed concubine whom he abandoned to pursue an arranged marriage to an heiress from a more appropriate social class. Roman convention at the time frowned upon marriage below one's social rank. In *Confessions,* Augustine tells of his bereavement over the loss of his concubine. He refuses even to mention her name so as to spare her public humiliation. Despite

---

[6]Dyson.

[7]St. Augustine, *The Literal Meaning of Genesis,* translated by John Hammond Taylor, S.J. (New York: Newman Press, 1982), 1: 41. Also see: Francis S. Collins, *The Language of God: A Scientist Presents Evidence for Belief* (New York: Free Press, 2006).

leaving the mother of his son for a more suitable spouse, Augustine never married the heiress. And tragically, his son died young.

Augustine also explored the teachings of Plotinus and Porphyry—known as the neo-Platonists. Following their master Plato, the **neo-Platonists** envisioned the philosophical life as a process of participation in the divine life and ultimately as a path to divinization. They believed in an impersonal, intelligible, and immaterial divinity—the One. The One was the sustaining source of all that was good, true, and beautiful in the universe. The neo-Platonist cosmology was understood in terms of a hierarchical chain of being in which the One was at the apex. All things were drawn toward and sustained by the One. The soul's moral purity was a precondition for its ascent toward and communion with this divine source. Augustine would similarly argue that the purity of the human will was a precondition of wisdom, for both truly knowing and loving God.

Augustine credited the neo-Platonists with freeing him from the materialism and dualism of the Manicheans. Contrary to the Manicheans, the neo-Platonists denied that evil was an active, metaphysical force. Rather, they viewed it as a privation, a defect, a lapse, a falling away from the fullness of divine being toward the dissipation of lesser being. Indeed, Augustine's mature Christian thought would borrow from the neo-Platonic view of evil as a privation or the absence of the good. He attributes evil not to God but to free will. Evil is the consequence of the fall and original sin whereby our first parents freely chose privation over plenitude.

Augustine converted to Catholic Christianity around A.D. 385–386. He tells of this experience in *Confessions*. Though his intellect had assented to the truth of Christianity, his will or heart prevented him from taking the final leap. Augustine was tormented by the division within his own soul. He was powerlessness to break the force of bad habits that enchained him: "Oh God, make me chaste, but not yet." Frustrated by his own weakness and filled with despair, he retreated in solitude to a nearby garden. In the depths of his anguish, he heard the singing, consoling voice of a child say, "Take it and read, take it and read." He then picked up a nearby Bible and opened it. His eyes immediately seized upon the following passage from the Apostle Paul in his Letter to the Romans 13:13: "Not in reveling and drunkenness, not in lust and wantonness, not in quarrels and rivalries. Rather, clothe yourselves with the Lord Jesus Christ, spend no more thought on nature and nature's appetites."

This experience was interpreted as a response to his heartfelt prayers. In some ineffable manner, he believed that he had been touched and filled by the healing and uplifting power of **divine grace**—the unmerited, freely given divine love that assists, liberates, and saves human beings. A powerful lesson was drawn from this conversion experience: Human efforts alone are insufficient to break the chain of evil habits that holds the will captive. Just as the body's health is nourished by physical energy, so the soul's uplifting is elevated by the supernatural energy of divine grace.

The Apostle Paul's teaching in ***Romans 7:14–2*** further validated Augustine's experience of the will divided against itself: "I do not understand what I do. For what I want to do I do not do, but what I hate I do." Paul's teaching in Romans 7 challenges the superficial equation of virtue with knowledge that was orthodox to some pagan philosophers. Contrary to this, both the Apostle Paul and Augustine reject the view that evil can simply be attributed to one's ignorance of that which is good. Both emphasize the powerlessness of the human will in the face of evil and the disturbing fact that we choose evil with full knowledge that it is wrong.

Augustine further observed that human beings seem to take a perverse delight in sinning for its own sake, even when it brings no benefit. In *Confessions* he recalls how as a youth he delighted in the pointless sin of robbing a pear tree only to smash its fruits in a wanton act of destruction: "I stole them simply for the sake of stealing them; when I had stolen them, I threw them away. My only delight in them was my own sin."[8] Augustine develops his crucial doctrine of original sin to account for this perversity of the human will—a doctrine with enormous implications for his view of politics.

After his conversion, the gregarious Augustine established a philosophical retreat for friends and family in Italy. His life of leisure, however, was cut short by his call to the priesthood. Knowing the heavy burden of responsibility that this would entail, Augustine answered the call reluctantly. He was later appointed Bishop of Hippo in North Africa, where he would spend the rest of his life defending the faith from external foes and internal heretics.

Augustine died in A.D. 430 around the same time the Vandals were besieging the city of Hippo. His death coincided with the death of Roman Africa and the birth of the Dark Ages, a time marked by the collapse of Western civilization. Fortuitously his voluminous writings survived the fall of the Roman Empire and were preserved for posterity. He was so prolific that during the Middle Ages it was said that anyone who claimed to have read his entire life work was a liar!

AUGUSTINE'S THEOLOGY: THE WORD, CREATION, FALL, REDEMPTION, AND JUDGMENT

Because Augustine did not write a separate, unified treatise on politics apart from his theology, we must first consider how his Christian theology serves as the ultimate foundation of his politics. The doctrine of the Incarnation is central to Augustine's worldview: "In the beginning was the Word, and the Word was with God, and the Word was God. He was in the beginning with God. All things came into being through Him, and apart from Him nothing came into being that has come into being. In Him was life, and that life was the Light of men. The Light shines in the darkness, but the darkness did not comprehend it . . . the word became flesh dwelt among us."[9] Augustine maintained that **the Incarnation**—the belief that God took bodily form and entered history in the person of Jesus Christ—was the turning point of human history that divided time into a before and after.

The fullness of divinity revealed in the person of Jesus Christ profoundly challenged all worldly values about politics, ethics, success, power, and glory. The Incarnation made possible a greater intimacy and solidarity between human beings and the divine. The dignity of human nature was affirmed through the deity assuming human form. This Divine gift now extended friendship to human beings in the most personal manner. With the exception of sin, Jesus experienced everything we as humans experience, including pain and suffering. Paradoxically, although the Incarnation makes greater intimacy with God possible, it also heightens our awareness of

---

[8] *Confessins,* Book II, ch. vi, p. 49.

[9] John 1:1–5, 14.

our own sinful nature. Through the perfect example of Christ, which Augustine called a "pattern of purity," we become more acutely aware of the gulf separating ourselves and the divine and therefore more acutely aware of the need for saving grace.

Given the Incarnation as the pivotal event in history, politics must therefore take its bearings from the example of Christ, the God–man, who had come not to dominate but to serve. Through Christ, God provided a living example, "a pattern of purity," of how we ought to live and of the path to salvation. In radical contrast to all other earthly kings, Jesus Christ, the heavenly king and the long-anticipated **messiah**—the anointed one who would deliver the Jewish people from captivity—came not as a warrior prince but as a prince of peace. Unlike Caesar, he renounced the worldly empire. Remarkably, he even claimed that his kingdom was not of this world. Turning the values of the world upside down, Jesus taught that "the last would be first" and "the first last"; that we should "love our enemies"; and that we should "turn the other cheek." In his **Sermon on the Mount** he preached a radical ethics: The meek, the poor in spirit, the humble, the peacemakers, and the persecuted were blessed and would one day inherit His heavenly kingdom.[10] For Augustine, Christ's sacrificial love and humble service revealed human pretensions of glory as pale images at best and idolatrous perversions at worst of the true glory that belongs only to God.

While Augustine views God's revelation in the Bible as the authoritative source of wisdom and salvation, he also maintains that certain teachings of classical philosophy both anticipated and corresponded with Christian revelation. The relationship between faith and reason in Western civilization was shaped by the fact that the Christian revelation in the New Testament was written in Greek—the language of the philosophers. Christians thus borrowed Greek philosophical categories and forms of thought to communicate their experience of the divine. The theologian Jaroslav Pelikan goes so far as to say, "It remains one of the most momentous linguistic convergences in the entire history of the human mind and spirit that the New Testament happens to have been written in Greek."[11] In this regard, it is highly significant that the writer of St. John's Gospel identified Christ as the **divine logos or word**—a pregnant Greek term that signified divine wisdom or cosmic intelligence that ruled, ordered, and governed the universe. Indeed, the term *logos* had a long and distinguished philosophical lineage. Unfortunately, much of its original power and meaning are lost when it is translated into the blasé English term *word*.

The term *logos* carried a parallel meaning in Jewish revelation. In various related senses, it was used in the Jewish scriptures to describe God's word as an agent of creation, as law, and as a message to His prophets. In sum, *logos* constituted a symbolic bridge between the Hellenic and Judaic understandings of divinity. St. John used it to identify the Jewish God of Abraham, Isaac, and Jacob as the same God of the philosophers, further claiming that this same God was revealed in the flesh and person of Jesus Christ of Nazareth.

The identification of Jesus Christ as the *logos* or divine wisdom thus bears enormous implications for the relationship between reason (Athens) and faith (Jerusalem) in Western civilization. If God is divine wisdom itself (logos), then the love of God is

---

[10]Matthew 5:3–11.

[11]Jaroslav Pelikan, Christianity and Classic Culture: *The Metamorphosis of Natural Theology in the Christian Encounter with Hellenism,* translated by A. G. Hebert (New York: MacMillan, 1990), p. 3.

the love of wisdom. And if philosophy is the love of wisdom, then, argued Augustine, it followed that the true philosopher is a lover of God.[12] To be sure, the lines between philosophy and theology were not so distinctly drawn for Augustine as they are for us today in the modern era. Augustine even saw theology as a branch of philosophy.[13]

Given the meaning of *logos* as divine wisdom, Augustine rejected his Christian predecessor Tertullian's view of an antipathy or irreconcilable antagonism between the traditions of reason and revelation. Pointing to the incompatibility between classical philosophy and Christian revelation, **Tertullian**, the first Christian theologian to write in Latin (160–225), had rhetorically asked, "What has Athens to do with Jerusalem? Or what has the Academy in common with the Church?" He even went so far as to claim that faith recommended itself in proportion to its irrationality: "I believe because it is absurd." By contrast, Augustine's understanding of the relationship between faith and reason corresponded more closely with the second-century church father **Justin Martyr's** teaching of the **Logos Spermatikos**—the belief that the seeds of divine wisdom were sown throughout all creation and eternity, and thereby communicated in some form, even if inchoately, to all humanity. Testifying to the potential harmony between faith and reason, Augustine accepted the apocryphal story that upon traveling to Egypt, Plato had learned his most profound teachings from the prophet Jeremiah.[14] Given the experiential and symbolic parallels between the two wisdom traditions, Augustine credited Plato as the pagan philosopher who came closest to Christian understanding of God as *logos* or divine wisdom: "If Plato, therefore, has declared that the wise man imitates, knows and loves this God and is blessed through fellowship with him, why should we have to examine other philosophers? No school has come closer to us than the Platonists."[15]

As noted, Augustine's political theology was also informed by the Stoic and Christian teaching of a universal law of nature that is rationally accessible to all human beings. In Romans 1:20, the Apostle Paul explains that because of this law the invisible God may be known even to the pagans through the effects of His visible creation: "For since the creation of the world God's invisible qualities—his eternal powers and divine nature—have been clearly seen, being understood from what has been made...." Augustine likewise acknowledged the existence of an eternal law, a law of nature, and the law of conscience, terms he uses interchangeably. He likens the imprint of this universal law on our conscience to a ring that leaves its impression on wax:

> Where are these rules written in which even the unjust man recognizes what is just, and in which he perceives that he ought to have what he does not have? Where, then, are they written except in the book of that light which is called Truth? From thence every just law is transcribed and transferred to the heart of the man who works justice, not by wandering to it, but being as it were impressed upon it, just as the image from the ring passes over into the wax, and yet does not leave the ring.[16]

---

[12] *City of God* 8:1, 8:8.

[13] *City of God* 8:6.

[14] *City of God* 8:11.

[15] *City of God* 8:5.

[16] *De Trinitate* 14:15.

However, according to Augustine, humanity's ability to act in perfect conformity with this law was irrevocably damaged after the fall from the Garden of Eden. Augustine thus distinguishes between the perfect operation of the law of nature in a **prelapsarian state** (the condition of original innocence in the Garden of Eden before the fall) and humanity's rebellion against it in the **postlapsarian state** (the condition of original sin after the fall). In a postlapsarian state, human beings would forever be divided between the law of nature and the law of concupiscence or of the flesh, also described by the Apostle Paul as the "law of sin."[17]

Original sin vitiated but did not completely efface or obliterate human nature. Traces and vestiges of its original condition remain. Consequently, Augustine maintains that human reason, though darkened by a perverse will, still has a role to play in discerning the workings of God's eternal law and providential order: "Far be it from us to suppose that God abhors in us that by virtue of which He has made us superior to other animals. Far be it, I say, that we should believe such a way as to exclude the necessity either of accepting or requiring reason; since we could not even believe unless we possessed rational soul."[18] While necessary, human efforts alone are not sufficient to overcome the consequences of original sin. God's revelation and saving grace are needed to remedy this defect of fallen nature.

Because human striving alone is incapable of achieving salvation and wisdom, Augustine critiqued the limits of the pagan philosophers. Perhaps the greatest point of contention between Augustine and his pagan predecessors was their unwillingness to accept the incarnation as the living embodiment of God in the person of Jesus Christ. While they, accepted the discarnate word of the philosophers, they rejected the incarnate word. To classical philosophers like the neo-Platonists, it was utterly ridiculous for divine perfection to take on the limitations of finite human existence, not to mention suffering a humiliating death by crucifixion. Augustine contended that the pagan philosophers' denial of the incarnation actually stemmed from their prideful unwillingness to take up the cross and to follow Jesus' example of humility and self-sacrificial love.

Augustine also criticized the pagan philosophers of his time for their overconfidence in the ability of reason to attain wisdom. Without Christian insight into fallen human nature, they failed to appreciate the depths of human depravity and the bondage of human will. Consequently they erroneously believed that wisdom and salvation could be attained through their own unaided efforts without the assistance of divine grace.

Indeed, faith precedes wisdom for Augustine. He notes, "Unless you believe, you will not understand."[19] For Augustine, the philosophical enterprise itself presumes a kind of faith or trust that the cosmos is ordered and that the quest for wisdom is meaningful. Given the perversity of the will due to original sin, reason must be cleansed through the power of faith and through a purifying love. Following the Apostle Paul, Augustine contrasts the "wisdom of the world" with the "wisdom of

[17]Romans 7:7–25.

[18]Ep. 120, 13: quoted in Peter Brown, *Augustine of Hippo: A Biography* (Berkeley: University of California Press, 1967), p. 277.

[19]"nisi credideritis, non intelligetis." Enchiridion V. Robert E. Cushman, "Faith and Reason in the Thought of St. Augustine," *Faith Seeking Understanding* (Durham, NC: Duke, 1981).

God," maintaining that "the foolishness of God is wiser than men."[20] When Paul and Augustine speak of "the wisdom of the world" they are not rejecting wisdom per se. Instead they are referring to a prideful human knowledge that refuses to be purified by God's love and enlightened by God's grace. Without purification of the will through the charitable love of God, the human intellect will be held captive to perverse lusts. Reason will serve as the slave of desire. Given his understanding of the priority of faith, Augustine distinguishes wisdom (**sapienta**) from mere knowing (**scientia**). Sapienta (true wisdom) is made possible by loving rightly, whereas scientia (knowledge) without love and faith leads to vanity and pride.[21]

As validation of Augustine's teaching on the priority of faith to cleanse the will, one need only consider how throughout human history knowledge and advances in technology have been placed in the service of wicked ends. Moreover, it is undeniable that intelligent people have often used their gifts to satisfy their lusts with impunity.

Following Plato, Augustine maintained that the tyrannical and philosophical souls are not distinguished in terms of their intellectual capacities—both may be highly intelligent. Rather, the tyrant and the philosopher are distinguished primarily in terms of the character and orientation of their love. The tyrant loves himself; the philosopher loves wisdom. And for Augustine, wisdom is God.

To understand further the plight of the world as a consequence of original sin, we must now consider more specifically Augustine's theological teachings on creation, fall, redemption, and judgment.

For Augustine, revelation conveyed important truths and wisdom beyond the limited insights of the pagan philosophers. Jewish and Christian scriptures were unique in revealing a personal, transcendent God who created the universe ***ex-nihilio***—out of nothing. Augustine further rejected the classical Greek teaching of the eternity of the universe and its attendant **cyclical view of history** in which gold, silver, and bronze ages repeat themselves in an endless cycle of growth and decay. Instead, following *Genesis,* he held the Judaic view of a **linear history** in which creation had a definite beginning and will have a definite end with the final judgment.

This linear view of history presumes a corresponding trust in **providence**—the belief that a personal, creator God is overseeing the course of history and that He intervenes in it to bring about some ultimate good. The providential view of history views human beings as actors in a divine drama written and directed by God as both author and participant. Revelation may be seen as the script that provides the broad outlines of this drama. Through reason and revelation, humans may have a partial and limited access to the workings of providence. However, the particulars of God's design at any moment and the full knowledge of providence are not vouchsafed to finite and fallen human beings. The divine will is ultimately unfathomable. Augustine's theology distinguishes sharply between God the creator as a perfect, self-sufficient, and eternal being and his creatures as imperfect, dependent, and mutable beings.

God created all things good. In the Garden of Eden in the prelapsarian state, Adam and Eve lived in peace, harmony, and unity. As part of his providence, God endowed human beings with a free will and intellect, thereby elevating them above

---

[20] 1 Corinthians 1:25.

[21] 1 Corinthians 8:1 and *City of God* 9:20.

other sentient beings. Sin and evil entered the world when Adam and Eve disobeyed God. This loss of original innocence, this lapse from perfection whereby human nature was vitiated from its pristine condition by sin, death, and evil, is known as **the fall.**

The famous story from the book of Genesis narrates what happened. Not content with their status as dependent, created beings, Adam and Eve sought to become like God by eating from the tree of knowledge of good and evil in defiance of God's command. The serpent, or Satan, deceived humanity by saying, "You will not surely die. . . . For God knows that when you eat of it your eyes will be opened, and you will be like God, knowing good and evil." This original sin of pride was the archetype of all other sin. It was rooted in our original parents' rebellious longing for moral autonomy apart from the limits established by the creator. Adam and Eve aspired to be self-sufficient like God, rejecting the limits of their creaturely existence. Pope John Paul II clearly has explained "the tree of knowledge of good and evil" in the story of the fall. "The symbol is clear," he notes, "man was in no position to discern and decide for himself what was good and what was evil, but was constrained to appeal to a higher source. The blindness of pride deceived our first parents into thinking themselves sovereign and autonomous, and into thinking that they could ignore the knowledge which comes from God."[22]

As a consequence of the fall, human beings were divided against themselves (against their own bodily members), against nature and the natural world, and against others of their own kind. The peace and harmony once enjoyed in the prelapsarian state in the Garden was soon replaced by strife and discord. Death, slavery, suffering, disease, dominion, and war entered the world. Man's body turned against itself; his will became permanently divided; his desires went to war with his intellect. Augustine explains, "The soul, in fact, delighting now in its own freedom to do wickedness and scorning to serve God, was stripped of the former subjection of the body, and because it had willfully deserted in its own higher master, no longer kept its lower servant responsible to its will."[23] After the fall, the sin of pride necessarily perverted the freedom of the will, thereby tainting all human endeavors.

Augustine's interpretation of the fall led him to develop the doctrine of **original sin**—the belief that the sin of our original parents, Adam and Eve, was so great that it was transmitted to the entire human race as an inherent flaw of our nature. He states, "The whole mass of mankind was condemned, since he who first sinned was punished along with the stock that had its root in him, and from that just and merited punishment no one is freed except by merciful and unmerited grace."[24] As noted, due to this original sin, nature was **vitiated** or fundamentally altered from its pristine condition for the worse. Not only was the human intellect obscured by a perverse will, but politics as a whole was likewise infected by original sin. Augustine thus emphasizes the limits of politics in a fallen world, thereby disabusing his readers of any utopian expectations of perfection in this life.

---

[22]Pope John Paul II, *Fides and Ratio: On the Relationship between Faith and Reason* (Boston: Pauline Books, 1998), p. 34.

[23]*City of God,* Book XIII, ch. xiii, p. 179.

[24]*City of God* 21:12.

The condition of human beings in a postlapsarian state after the fall is perhaps best described by C.S. Lewis, who explains that we live in a "good world that has gone wrong but still retains the memory of what it ought to have been." Augustine similarly describes human nature in the postlapsarian fallen state as infirm and wounded, and therefore in need of healing and redemption. His related teaching of original sin and the fall squarely rejects the view that man is naturally good and can therefore be perfected. Evil, according to Augustine, resides within the human will. No amount of enlightened social engineering will remedy this defect. A realistic view of politics must account for this dark side of human nature.

God in his infinite mercy, however, did not leave human beings without hope of redemption. According to Augustine, the drama of providence further unfolds with the incarnation of Jesus Christ as a redeemer who atoned for the original sin of Adam and Eve. Jesus Christ is the ultimate example of God's grace. As the ultimate physician and healer of the soul, he cured humanity from its wounded condition of sin and death. As the God–man who was fully divine and fully human, Christ was seen as the mediator who reconciled God and man. As a human being, he shared our sufferings; as God, he conquered sin and death. Through his sacrifice, teaching, and example, he restored humanity and offered hope of eternal life for all people.

Jesus' example of humility and sacrificial love turned the values of the fallen world upside down. Finding conventional words inadequate to describe the selfless, sacrificial, and redemptive love of Christ, early Christians were inspired to invent a new word—**agape**, rendered in Latin as *caritas* and in English as *charity*. Throughout his writings, Augustine often points to the hymn of the early Church recorded by St. Paul in **Philippians 2:5–9** as the model of humble service and charitable love of God and humanity: "Your attitude should be the same as Jesus Christ: Who being, in very nature God, did not consider equality with God something to be grasped but made himself nothing, taking the very nature of a servant, being made in human likeness. And being found in appearance as a man, he humbled himself and became obedient to death—even death on a cross!"

The crucifixion, death, and resurrection of Jesus Christ did not establish a heavenly kingdom on earth. The redemption of the fallen world would not be fully completed until the second coming of Christ, which will end history through a final judgment of both the living and the dead. In the meantime, the followers of Christ must live by faith. In the words of the Apostle Paul, they "see through a glass darkly."[25] Augustine describes the time period on earth between the world's creation and its end as the *saeculum*.[26]

In sum, Augustine's political thought takes its descriptive and normative bearings from the foregoing Christian narrative of **creation, fall, redemption, and final judgment.** He diagnoses mankind's unredeemed, fallen condition in this world. And he prescribes the cure of divine grace and the hope for eternal life. Because all of creation will not be fully restored until the second coming and the final judgment at the end of

[25]1 Corinthians 13:12.

[26]Robert A. Markus, *Saeculum: History and Society in the Theology of St. Augustine* (New York: Columbia University Press, 1963).

time, Augustine's theology observes a dynamic tension between the fallen condition of this life and the promised perfection of the next.

Given this tension, it follows that in the saeculum—the remaining time until the end of the world and the final judgment—Christians will forever be divided by their allegiance to this world and the Kingdom of God. Augustine thus describes members of the city of God who live in the fallen world as "pilgrims," "sojourners," or "resident aliens" who are never completely at home in the world because their true homeland is heaven. Paradoxically, though true Christians may live in the world, they are not of it. This means that they are not conformed to, defined by, or absorbed by the worldly values of power, prestige, and pride, which are often placed before God. Their ultimate allegiance must be to God, not human idols.

Augustine heightens our awareness of the tension between this life and the next so that we may be able to maintain a better perspective of our status as dependent beings and sojourners in a fallen world. Augustine biographer Peter Brown thus explains, "So the *City of God,* far from being a book about flight from this world, is a book whose recurrent theme is 'our business within this common mortal life'; it is a book about being otherworldly in the world."[27] Subsequent thinkers like Karl Marx would seek to abolish this tension through the spurious promise of worldly utopia that could be achieved by human efforts in this life.[28] In effect, this means that man extends grace to himself. Augustine develops the concept of **the two cities—the city of God and the city of man** to explain more fully what it means to be "otherworldly in the world." What then are the political implications for Christians who live in the world, but are not of it?

THE CHARACTER AND HISTORY OF THE TWO CITIES

Augustine unmasked Roman claims to glory because they placed the "eternal city" at the center of history. Contrary to this triumphalist ideology, he redefined the history of humankind in terms of the two cities—the city of God and the city of man. Augustine borrowed the term *city of God* from the Psalms.[29] Christians of his day interpreted the city of God to have both a literal and figurative meaning. Literally it referred to the city of Jerusalem; figuratively it referred to the coming heavenly kingdom of Christ. Today we think of a city as an urban area in contrast to a suburb or rural area. In Augustine's time, however, the term *city* meant the broader association of the polis or the republic. It further carried the connotation of a sacred place of allegiance, identity, and belonging. In today's parlance, we often use the terms *country* and *homeland* to describe such a place.

Augustine defines the two cities in terms of two fundamental loves: the city of God by its love of God (*amor Dei*) and the city of man by the love of self (*amor sui*). Indeed, the power of love is absolutely crucial to Augustine's sociopolitical thought. He once profoundly noted, "My love is my weight; it carries me wherever I go."[30]

---

[27]Brown, p. 324.

[28]Eric Voegelin, *Science, Politics, and Gnosticism* (Chicago: Gateway, 1968).

[29]See Psalms 87, 46, 48.

[30]*Confessions* 13:9.

Augustine thus views love as the dominant force of attraction and repulsion in our lives. Today as a society obsessed with physical health, we often hear the cliché, "You are what you eat." If Augustine were alive today he would likely remind us instead, "You are what you love." Augustine further identifies the will with love. The two are synonymous. Loving is willing.

Most significantly, the characters of each person and society are best defined in terms of what they love. Augustine contends that we are actually transformed into what we love. A person becomes greedy through the love of money; a person becomes ambitious through love of honor; a person becomes gluttonous through love of food; a sensual person loves bodily pleasure; and a vain person loves admiration. At bottom, although different people love different things—money, honor, pleasure—these disparate loves are all rooted in the quintessential love of self or pride insofar as they are placed before the love of God. Augustine believes that ultimately there is room in the human to accommodate just one dominant love: either the love of God or the love of self. This decision to love God or oneself, in turn, profoundly affects our relationships with others.

According to Augustine, all things should thus be loved in reference to love of God and neighbor. The **love of God or amor Dei** that defines the city of God is none other than Christian charity. The rule of charity is expressed most clearly by Jesus in the **double commandment (Matthew 22:37),** "to love God with all your heart and with all your soul and with all your mind . . . and to love your neighbor as yourself."[31] Charity, in turn, is made possible by the gift of divine grace. Those who act out of an unconditional love of God and neighbor act charitably and therefore love in an ordered manner.

If amor Dei is the ordered and charitable love of God and neighbor, **amor sui or self-love** is its polar opposite: the love of self to the contempt of God and neighbor. The amor sui that defines the city of man is none other than pride. This prideful self-love is the root of all sin because it necessarily involves preferring the love of some worldly object, whatever it may be, above the love of God. We actually love ourselves in a selfish manner when we choose personal desire before our faithful love of God and neighbor. In loving this object of desire in such an inordinate manner we, in effect, love ourselves at the expense of God and neighbor.

Augustine uses the term *lust* to distinguish this disordered love of self from the ordered love of God and neighbor. In his political thought, lust refers to inordinate love in general, not simply sexual desire. Lust is the drive of greedy acquisitiveness, possessive selfishness, and obsessive accumulation that seeks fullness in the satisfaction of some worldly object of love. The original Latin words used by Augustine to describe this inordinate love or lust are revealing because they closely resemble in both spelling and meaning their English versions: *cupiditas* (cupidity or greed) and *concupiscentia* (concupiscence or disordered appetite).

As a consequence of the fall, human beings are dominated by their lusts. Tragically, we seek to fill the void within us through the gratification of a particular appetite or desire. We do this to no avail. The momentary thrill wears off and the

[31]Matthew 22:37.

gnawing emptiness returns. Even in our momentary satisfaction we are further plagued, Augustine argues, by the fear and certain knowledge that our contentment is only fleeting and that it will eventually come to an end. There is no everlasting enjoyment of goods in this life because everything perishes. Worldly objects can never fully satisfy what God was meant to satisfy. Friends die; beauty fades; pleasure surfeits; health deteriorates; life ends. Thus in this life we must learn to cope with dissatisfaction as a part of the human condition. Our heart's longings can never be fully satisfied until they are filled by God's loving presence in the next life. Augustine's diagnosis of the psychology of fallen man has profoundly shaped Western civilization. Indeed, both Hobbes and Rousseau offered secularized, modified versions of Augustine's account of human egocentrism.

Love is normative for Augustine: We ought to love those things that are truly worthy of love. God of course is the most worthy object of our love as the source, sustainer, and provider of our everlasting fullness. Augustine judges the character and quality of love in terms of the *ordo amoris*—the hierarchical order with God at the apex and the double commandment to love God and neighbor as the rule and measure of ordinate love. Indeed, the goodness or evil of human will depends on its object of love. Spiritual and eternal things are more worthy of our love than material and temporal things. Noble things are more worthy of love than base things. Human beings err both in loving the wrong things and in loving them in the wrong manner—that is, in an inordinate or disordered manner that seeks to find ultimate satisfaction in a finite, temporal object. It bears repeating that this love is tantamount to self-love or pride because it involves placing one's personal desire before the unconditional love of God and neighbor. The temporal goods of the world should not be loved as ends in themselves as if ultimate satisfaction and enjoyment can be found in them. Such love is futile because the goods of the world are ephemeral. The goods of this world are to be used in reference to the charitable love of God and neighbor.

Augustine's distinction between the two loves should not be misconstrued as an endorsement of self-hatred or self-loathing. Indeed, we may love ourselves, worldly goods, and others, provided we do so in reference to God. We love things in reference to God when we attribute the goods of this world to God as their creator and ultimate source, thereby giving praise and thanks to Him. When we love others charitably, in reference to God, we seek what is truly best for them. We respect them and love them unconditionally as beings created in the image of God. This means that we love them for who they are, not for what they are or what they possess. On the contrary, when we love others based on lust, we exploit them for our own selfish interests. We treat them as mere instruments to our own personal satisfaction. Amor dei or charitable love is the basis for true sharing in relationships. On the contrary, amor sui or selfish lust is the basis for exploitation, codependence, and domination in relationships.

Augustine redefined virtue and vice in terms of the normative order of love. We ought to love those things that are truly worthy of love and love them in an ordered manner. Because God is the most worthy object of our love, all things must be loved in reference to Him. Virtue thus refers to those acquired qualities or traits whereby we love the right things in an ordinate manner—that is, in an ordered way. Augustine understood the cardinal virtues of temperance, fortitude, prudence, and justice as four

QUESTIONS FOR REFLECTION

How do the views of both Aristotle and Augustine on happiness differ from the current belief that happiness consists in the satisfaction of subjective desire?

forms of love.[32] *Temperance* is the ability to love a thing in its proper measure; *fortitude* is the quality of holding steadfast to what one loves; *prudence* is the ability to direct one's love properly to a worthy object of love; and *justice* is "the love whereby a man loves God as he should be loved, and his neighbor as himself"—the double commandment.[33]

The ordered love of God and neighbor is a precondition of justice in the individual soul of man and in society as a whole. And as we have seen, amor dei or charity is a precondition of wisdom, without which the intellect becomes the slave of lusts. Augustine defines vice in terms of those habits and character traits whereby we love the wrong things inordinately—that is, in a disordered way. The vice of greed, for example, is the inordinate love of money; the vice of anger is the in ordinate desire for revenge.

Love and happiness are also linked in Augustine's political ethics. He observes that we are not always made happy by possessing what we desire. We are both corrupted and made unhappy by inordinate love. Augustine explains:

> Humans love many different things and when they seem to have all that they desire, we are accustomed to call them happy. But we can be happy only if we are loving what ought to be loved. Happiness does not consist simply in having what we happen to love. We sometimes are made more unhappy by having what we love than in not having it. When unhappy persons love something hurtful, they are made even more unhappy.[34]

Like Aristotle, Augustine views happiness in terms of objective perfection, not subjective desire. However, Augustine emphasizes that happiness consists primarily in the ordering of our love or will. Indeed, this proper ordering is a precondition of intellectual virtue and wisdom. Augustine's point that we are made unhappy by loving the wrong things calls to mind those who suffer from the many addictions that plague our society—power, pleasure, prestige, gambling, sex, alcohol, drugs. The addict satisfies his or her love in the short-term but at an awful price in the long-term.

Based on these two loves—the love of God and the love of self—Augustine traces the origin, course, and ends of the two cities. Christ is the eternal founder of the heavenly city from before creation to the end of time. The city of God—also called the heavenly city—is defined by its love of God even to the contempt of self. On the contrary, the city of man—also called the earthly city—is defined by its prideful love of earthly values to the contempt of God. By contempt of self, Augustine does not mean self-loathing. Rather, he means the contempt of one's base inclinations, selfish lusts, and sinful desires. These slavish desires must be disciplined and subordinated to the charitable love of God and neighbor.

---

[32]Herbert Deane, *The Political and Social Ideas of St. Augustine* (New York: Columbia University Press, 1963), p. 83.

[33]*City of God* 19:23.

[34]St. Augustine, *Commentary on Psalms,* p. 26.6

Augustine also uses the metaphors of flesh and spirit to differentiate the character of the two cities. The earthly city lives after the flesh, the heavenly city after the spirit. This terminology does not imply a Manichean dualism between the body and soul. Rather, flesh and spirit refer to the inner orientations of the human will. Flesh refers to the disordered, sinful desires of the self; spirit refers to the ordered love of God. To illustrate this point, Augustine notes that envy and jealousy, which are regarded as sins of the flesh, are actually defects of both the will and the intellect.

Augustine traces the origin of the two cities in time—in the saeculum—to Abel and Cain, the children of Adam and Eve. Abel and Cain are the symbolic representatives of the city of God and the city of man, respectively. After the fall, the consequences of Adam and Eve's prideful rebellion against God were manifested in Cain's murder of his brother Abel. This act foreshadowed the future character and destiny of the city of man, which originated with a fratricide motivated by jealousy and the lust for power. Hereinafter the city of man would be forever divided against itself. Augustine notes how Rome similarly began with a fratricide: its founder Romulus killed his brother Remus so he could exercise sole dominion. For Augustine the cities of Babylon and Rome epitomized the self-love and pride of the earthly city.

In the next generation Henoch, Cain's son, became the successor of the earthly city; Seth, Cain's second brother, became the representative of the heavenly city. According to Augustine, their names symbolize the character of the two cities. Henoch, which means "dedicated," symbolizes the city of man's dedication to earthly goods. Seth, which means "resurrection," symbolizes the heavenly city's promise of eternal life. Marked by their dedication to earthly goods, the citizens of the earthly city are at home in the world where they seek to enjoy possessions without limit to the contempt of God. By contrast, the members of the heavenly city are not at home in the world. They are pilgrims or sojourners who temporarily use the goods of this world with an eye toward their heavenly homeland.

One of the most telling illustrations of the earthly city's pride was Nimrod's effort to construct the Tower of Babel. In building the Tower of Babel, human beings sought to create a permanent home for themselves in the world. Like the first sin in the Garden of Eden, the construction of the tower was rooted in the prideful desire to become like God. God punished this rebellious endeavor by destroying the tower and scattering the once unified human race throughout the earth.

In the prelapsarian state, the possibility of unity was held out to human beings who would be joined through bonds of kinship and blood because all were to be descended from our original parents—Adam and Eve. The bonds of kinship were weakened, however, through original sin when members of the same family turned against each other. The destruction of the Tower of Babel further sapped these bonds by dispersing the human race throughout the world. The resulting differences in languages, customs, and tribes made communication between humans difficult, if not impossible at times. Augustine notes that the term *babel* is derived from the verbal confusion that resulted from the dispersion of the human race after the destruction of the tower. He describes God's punishment as particularly fitting:

> Since it is the tongue that is the usual way a person expresses a domineering command, this pride was punished in such a way that the man who refused to understand and obey the commands of God could not be understood by men when he tried to

PRIMARY SOURCE 3.1 | THE TWO CITIES, *CITY OF GOD*, BOOK XIV, CHAPTER xxviii

Accordingly, two cities have been formed by two loves: the earthly by the love of self, even to the contempt of God; the heavenly by the love of God, even to the contempt of self. The former, in a word, glories in itself, the latter in the Lord. For the one seeks glory from men; but the greatest glory of the other is God, the witness of conscience. The one lifts up its head in its own glory; the other says to its God, "You are my glory, and the lifter up of mine head." In the one, the princes and the nations it subdues are ruled by the love of ruling; in the other, the princes and the subjects serve one another in love, the latter obeying, while the former take thought for all. The one delights in its own strength, represented in the persons of its rulers; the other says to its God, "I will love You, O Lord, my strength." And therefore the wise men of the one city, living according to man, have sought for profit to their own bodies or souls, or both, and those who have known God "glorified Him not as God, neither were thankful, but became vain in their imaginations, and their foolish heart was darkened; professing themselves to be wise,"—that is, glorying in their own wisdom, and being possessed by pride,—"they became fools, and changed the glory of the incorruptible God into an image made like to corruptible man, and to birds, and four-footed beasts, and creeping things." For they were either leaders or followers of the people in adoring images, "and worshipped and served the creature more than the Creator, who is blessed for ever." Romans 1:21–25 But in the other city there is no human wisdom, but only godliness, which offers due worship to the true God, and looks for its reward in the society of the saints, of holy angels as well as holy men, "that God may be all in all." 1 Corinthians 15:28.

command them. Thus was the plot foiled. Since now no one could understand him, they abandoned him and he could associate only with those who would come to understand him. Thus were nations divided by language barriers and scattered over the earth.[35]

The two cities differ not only in their origins but also in their final destinations or ends. Members of the earthly city are destined for an eternity in hell, whereas those of the heavenly city are destined for eternity in paradise with God. Augustine refers to God's foreknowledge from the beginning of time of those who are saved and damned as **predestination.** He believes that only a remnant of the elect, those who are predestined by God's grace, would enjoy citizenship in the heavenly city. The members of the city of God sojourning on earth are vastly outnumbered. It is important to note that for Augustine God's foreknowledge does not cause people to be saved or damned. This feat is accomplished through their own free will, though their choice is known by God. Augustine's doctrine of predestination would greatly influence the subsequent political teaching of the theologian John Calvin.

Although Augustine distinguishes normatively between the two cities in terms of their respective objects of love, he also maintains that the inhabitants of the two cities are intermingled or mixed together in this earthly life during their sojourn on earth. That is, the citizens of the heavenly city coexist daily with those of the earthly city. In this life, they share a commonplace. Moreover, no one knows with certainty who is a

[35]*City of God* 16:4.

member of which city. Only God knows this. Finally, both cities include the community of the living and the dead. The membership of the city of God, for example, includes not only those saints who live on earth, but also the community of angels and saints who are already in heaven with God. Likewise, the membership of the city of man includes not only the wicked in this life, but also those fallen angels and damned already in hell. The citizens of the two cities will not be fully separated until the final judgment at the end of time.

It is also erroneous to identify the city of God with the visible church on earth. In his own time, Augustine recognized that the visible church was infiltrated by impostors—members of the city of man posing as citizens of the heavenly city. For this reason, among others, he rejected his predecessor Eusebius' belief that Rome was predestined as the carrier of a "Christian Empire" that heralded the establishment of the kingdom of heaven on earth. Eusebius and others had interpreted the Christian Emperor Thedosius' reign and his proclamation of Christianity as the official religion of the empire as ushering in a new era—a *pax Christiana* to replace the old *pax romana*. Though Augustine acknowledges that Christians may serve as emperors, he rejects the notion that a perfected and fully redeemed "Christian Empire" could be realized in the saeculum, within this world in time. This notion of a Christian empire was flawed because it mistakenly presumed that heavenly perfection could be attained on earth during the saeculum and because it further presumed that fallible human beings could know the workings of providence. Although the church is a divinely established institution that serves as a signpost toward God, the visible church in this life is composed of fallible human beings who are both saints and sinners.

AUGUSTINE'S CRITIQUE OF ROMAN GLORY AND THE *LIBIDO DOMINANDI*

Augustine treats Rome as a case study that epitomized the character of the earthly city. Rome serves as a cautionary tale of the inner contradictions and the plight of all earthly cities infected by pride.

Although the Romans possessed admirable virtue at the beginning of their republic, they descended into a downward spiral of decadence and corruption. This moral degeneration was observed by their own historians. By the time of Augustine, the empire had rotted from within. In what must have seemed impious to Roman traditionalists, Augustine demythologizes Rome's history, critiques its heroes, and rejects its gods as silly human inventions. The Romans credulously placed their faith in false divinities of their own making, rather than the true God. Augustine observes that they superstitiously invented a god for everything, as testified by their belief in Cluacina—the goddess of sewers.

The character of the Roman people is best understood in terms of what they loved—glory. More than anything else, the Romans coveted the praise of their fellow citizens, hoping to attain some share of immortality through the memory of their heroic deeds and reputation. So Augustine observes:

> This glory they most ardently loved. For its sake they chose to live and for its sake they did not hesitate to die. They suppressed all other desires in their boundless desire for

> this one thing. In short, since they held it shameful for their native land to be in servitude, and glorious for it to rule and command, their first passion to which they devoted all their energy was to maintain their independence; the second was to win dominion.[36]

Insofar as the Romans suppressed baser lusts and sacrificed their own private gain for the public good, their actions were still somewhat admirable and deserving of praise. Regulus, the legendary Roman hero, is a case in point. Regulus was captured by the Carthaginians, Rome's enemy during the Punic Wars. He was released temporarily to negotiate a truce and a prisoner exchange, being bound by an oath to return to his captors after terms were reached. Upon arriving in Rome, Regulus urged the senate to reject the treaty with Carthage and to take all measures necessary to defeat them. True to his oath, Regulus returned to Carthage, where he was tortured to death by an iron maiden-like device created especially for the occasion. Regulus was celebrated among Romans for his piety in keeping his oath and for his willingness to sacrifice his life for the greater good of the republic.

Though he does not consider such virtue perfect in comparison to the true virtue of the heavenly city, Augustine nonetheless praises Regulus' imperfect virtue. In fact, Augustine points to his example to spur Christians to sacrifice for their heavenly republic. If a pagan can keep his vow and sacrifice his life for the earthly city without the promise of immortality, then so much more should a Christian be willing to lay down his or her life for the heavenly city and its promise of immortality:

> Yes, it was through that empire, so far reaching in time and in space, so famous and glorious for the deeds of its heroes, that those men received the reward that they sought for their efforts, and that we have before us such models to remind us of our duty. If in serving the glorious city of God we do not cling to the virtues that they clung to in serving the glory of the earthly city, let us be pricked to our hearts with shame.[37]

Notwithstanding Regulus' heroic sacrifice, Augustine claims that all human virtue is still infected by the taint of pride and sin. He argues that Rome's heroes did not act out of the charitable love of god and neighbor. Rather they acted out of an inordinate pride and love of praise. This is vividly manifested by the Roman practice of suicide to uphold personal honor. The celebrated Lucretia and Cato provided examples of this practice. The Roman maiden Lucretia killed herself after being raped by Tarquin's son; the statesman Cato killed himself after his defeat by Caesar. Augustine contends that these suicides actually betray a prideful unwillingness to persevere humbly in the face of defeat and suffering. By contrast, suicide is not an option for pious Christians who are called to take up their cross and to bear their trials patiently as did their savior and role model, Jesus Christ.

Ironically, Augustine observes that the seeds of Rome's destruction were contained in the very qualities that enabled it to exercise dominion over others. Rome was conquered by its own lust for power! In the end, all earthly cities are conquered by idols of their own making. Augustine appeals to the testimony of Rome's own historians, who bore witness to the republic's steady corruption into an empire consumed by the lust for power and domination. In particular, he relies on the testimony of Sallust, who

---

[36] *City of God* 5:12.

[37] *City of God* 5:18.

noted that "after the destruction of Carthage, discord, avarice, ambition and others vices commonly arising from prosperity, particularly increased [in Rome]."[38]

As its own poets related, Rome was flawed in its very origins. The city began with a fratricide. Romulus, its namesake, murdered his brother Remus in competition for sole dominion. Speaking of Romulus' lust for dominion, Augustine states, "Since the goal was glory in domination, there would of course be less domination if power was limited by having to be shared. Accordingly, in order that all power might accrue to one single person, his fellow was removed; and what innocence would have kept smaller and better grew through crime into something larger and inferior."[39] Though Augustine does not explicitly pursue the implications of this statement, he suggests that in a fallen world marred by original sin no one can be entrusted with absolute power. If this train of thought is pursued further, it may lead to the proposed remedy or solution of constitutional checks and balances and limited government to prevent this single power from dominating all others.

C.S. Lewis unfolds the implications of Augustine's fallen view of human nature for democracy, equality, and constitutional government when he states,

> I am a democrat because I believe in the Fall of Man. I think most people are democrats for the opposite reason. A great deal of democratic enthusiasm descends from the ideas of people like Rousseau, who believed in democracy because they thought mankind so wise and good that everyone deserved a share in government. The real reason for democracy is just the reverse. Mankind is so fallen that no man can be trusted with unchecked power over his fellows. Aristotle said that some people were only fit to be slaves. I do not contradict him. But I reject slavery because I see no men fit to be masters.[40]

Reinhold Niebuhr, the 20th-century American theologian whose thought was profoundly influenced by Augustine, likewise observes that, "modern democracy requires a more realistic philosophical and religious basis, not only in order to anticipate and understand the perils to which it is exposed; but also to give it a more persuasive justification. Man's capacity for justice makes democracy possible; but man's inclination to injustice makes democracy necessary."[41]

In critiquing Rome's pretensions to virtue, Augustine further recounts the well-known stories of its brutal rape of the Sabine women; its relentless class warfare; its never-ending cycle of civil wars; its inhuman cruelty toward its enemies; and finally its corruption from a republic into an empire bent on dominion.

Roman ambition became unbounded. Rather than serving the public good, the love of praise began to serve the private lusts of those who sought notoriety at any price, no matter how shameful. Again Augustine appeals to Sallust, who observed that the republic "altering by slow degrees from being the first and best became the worst and most dissolute . . . [T]he morals of our ancestors were swept away, not by slow degrees, as hitherto, but in a headlong torrent, so greatly were the youth corrupted by

---

[38]*City of God* 2:18.

[39]*City of God* 15:5.

[40]C.S. Lewis, *Present Concerns*, ed. Walter Hooper (New York: Harcourt, 1986), p. 17.

[41]Reinhold Niebuhr: *Theologian of American Public Life*, edited by Larry Rasmussen (Minneapolis: Fortress Press), p. 253.

QUESTIONS FOR REFLECTION

In *Federalist No. 51* James Madison articulated the view of human nature that underlies the dynamisms of checks and balances: "Ambition must be made to counteract ambition. The interest of the man must be connected with the constitutional rights of the place. It may be a reflection of human nature that such devices should be necessary to control the abuses of government. But what is government itself but the greatest of all reflections of human nature? If men were angels, no government would be necessary. If angels were to govern men, neither external nor internal controls on government would be necessary. In framing a government which is to be administered by men over men, the great difficulty lies in this: you must first enable the government to control the governed; and in the next place oblige it to control itself. A dependence on the people is, no doubt, the primary control on the government; but experience has taught mankind the necessity of auxiliary precautions." And in *Federalist No. 55* Madison states, "In all very numerous assemblies, of whatever characters composed, passion never fails to wrest the scepter from reason. Had every Athenian citizen been a Socrates, every Athenian assembly would still have been a mob.... As there is a degree of depravity in mankind which requires a certain degree of circumspection and distrust, so there are other qualities in human nature which justify a certain portion of esteem and confidence. Republican government presupposes the existence of these qualities in a higher degree than any other form."

To what extent does Madison's view of human nature in the *Federalist* correspond with Augustine's?

high living and avarice." He then quotes Cicero's plaintive epitaph of the republic: "It is to our vices, not to any ill fortune, that we owe it that we preserve merely the name of a republic, having long since lost the reality."[42]

Eventually Rome's love of glory degenerated into a particularly vicious form of disordered love, which Augustine calls the ***libido dominandi***—the lust for power. We have already seen how according to Augustine Romulus' fratricide was rooted in this lust for dominion. The *libido dominandi* is perhaps the most wicked manifestation of pride because it exalts in lording over others for its own sake. Though it is rooted in the same acquisitiveness as greed, unlike those driven by the greed for material possessions and comforts, those in thrall to the *libido dominandi* will sacrifice comforts, pleasures, and all other appetites to gratify their ruling passion to dominate others.

The *libido dominandi* was likewise a consequence of the fall. Indeed, Augustine maintains that God created human beings as equals. Through their own sinful nature, humans replaced this original equality with dominion and slavery. Some developed a particular taste for lording over others. Quoting Augustine throughout, Herbert Deane explains the origin and effects of the *libido dominandi*:

> Men were created as equals, and God alone was the superior and the ruler of mankind. But the soul of fallen man, in "a reach of arrogance utterly intolerable," perversely seeks to ape God by aspiring "to lord it even over those who are by nature its equals—that is, its fellow men".... This lust for domination over other men is associated with the love of glory, honor, and fame, which men "with vain elation and pomp of arrogance seek to achieve by the subjection of others." Like avarice, this desire to exercise power and domination is not confined to a few men, although it is

[42] *City of God* 2:21.

QUESTIONS FOR REFLECTION

What does Augustine's diagnosis of the *libido dominandi* mean for politics? Is the lust for power intrinsic or can it be cured through proper social conditioning? Can we appease those who are driven by its tyrannical longings?

particularly strong in the ambitious and the arrogant; "there is hardly any one who is free from the love of rule, and craves not human glory."[43]

Augustine's diagnosis of the lust for power—*libido dominandi*—forces us to come to terms with some of the darkest and most diabolical manifestations of human pride. Put another way, it refers to the lust for absolute power, dominion, and control over others for its own sake. This is the most tyrannical form of greed. Whether or not he had Augustine in mind, former Secretary of State Henry Kissinger bore witness to the *libido dominandi* when he said, "Power is the ultimate aphrodisiac." Human beings will seek to control and dominate their fellows even when there is a fair share of resources for all. The existence of the *libido dominandi* means that extraordinary tyrants among us will sacrifice everything and endure all kinds of personal deprivation to quench their longing to dominate others and to shape the world according to their own image.

In sum, Augustine contends that Rome was corrupt far before the advent of Christianity. He further argues that its worship of cruel and vicious ancestral gods—like its founder Romulus—aided and abetted its corruption. The Romans thus had no one to blame but themselves.

In contrast to all worldly pretensions of glory, Augustine emphasizes that "true justice exists only in that republic whose founder and ruler is Christ."[44] Throughout the *City of God* he uses the qualifier "true" to distinguish the "true justice" of the heavenly city from the sham or faux justice of the earthly city. Indeed, what passes for justice in the city of man is often nothing other than tyranny, self-interest, or the "will of the stronger" disguised as right. Augustine explodes the founding myths of all states by likening them to bands of robbers. (See Primary Source 3.2).

Augustine's devastating critique of the earthly city as a band of robbers should be understood in the context of the Roman Empire's pretensions to glory and in response to claims that a perfectly just order can be realized in this life. The vanity and hollowness of these claims must be exposed because they threaten to obscure the true glory that belongs to the heavenly city of God—the true standard for measuring claims of justice by the city of man. As a political realist who emphasizes the limits of politics and the gulf between the real and ideal, Augustine has the sobering effect of curbing our expectations of what can be achieved politically in a fallen world.

Greek philosophers like Plato and Aristotle grasped at perfection when they spoke of an ideal "city in speech" that served as a pattern for judging politics. Augustine concedes that the Greeks were able to gain intimations of the heavenly city. However, as seen, they were overconfident in their estimation of human reason and in the ability

---

[43]Deane, p. 49.

[44]*City of God* 2:21.

PRIMARY SOURCE 3.2

KINGDOMS AS DENS OF ROBBER BARONS, *CITY OF GOD*, BOOK IV, CHAPTER iv

Justice being taken away, then, what are kingdoms but great robberies? For what are robberies themselves, but little kingdoms? The band itself is made up of men; it is ruled by the authority of a prince, it is knit together by the pact of the confederacy; the booty is divided by the law agreed on. If, by the admittance of abandoned men, this evil increases to such a degree that it holds places, fixes abodes, takes possession of cities, and subdues peoples, it assumes the more plainly the name of a kingdom, because the reality is now manifestly conferred on it, not by the removal of covetousness, but by the addition of impunity. Indeed, that was an apt and true reply which was given to Alexander the Great by a pirate who had been seized. For when that king had asked the man what he meant by keeping hostile possession of the sea, he answered with bold pride, "What you mean by seizing the whole earth; but because I do it with a petty ship, I am called a robber, while you who does it with a great fleet are styled emperor."

of human initiative without the assistance of divine grace. Despite their longings for this city in speech, it was never realized. Moreover, the Greek philosophers themselves admitted its implausibility by claiming that its actualization depended on the convergence of incredible circumstances and good fortune. For Augustine this admission meant that in effect, the Greeks themselves tacitly conceded the impossibility of realizing perfect justice in this life. Significantly, the Greek word *utopia* means "no place." Augustine's critique of the vast gulf separating the ideal and real in Greek thought forces his ancient predecessors Plato, Aristotle, and Cicero to admit that their celebrated city of speech was much more a matter of wishful thinking than a reality. To dispel the illusion that perfect justice ever existed on earth and to highlight the difference between the true justice that exists only in the heavenly city and the injustice or faux justice of all earthly cities, he thus compares states to bands of robbers.

Following Plato, Cicero had likewise defined the Roman republic in terms of an ideal of "true justice" that never existed. Speaking through the character Scipio, Cicero described a republic as a "multitude united in fellowship by a common sense of right and a community of interest." Augustine critiqued this definition and revised it in terms of what truly binds a people together—not some imaginary justice, but a common object of love.

Augustine's critique begins by assuming Cicero's definition of a people as united "by a common sense of right." According to this definition, "a republic cannot be administered without justice; therefore where there is no true justice there can be no right." Indeed, Cicero himself acknowledged that "there was no people's estate. . .when a tyrant or a party took over the republic, nor was the people itself any longer a people, if it was unjust, since in that case it was not a multitude united in fellowship by a common sense of right and a community of interest, as specified in the definition."[45]

Taking Cicero at his word then, Augustine draws the absurd conclusion that because true justice never existed in Rome, as Cicero and their own historians admit, it follows that the Roman people and the republic never existed. Obviously this

[45] *City of God* 2:21.

conclusion is counterfactual: At least in name, a people and a republic did indeed exist in Rome.

Thus, because true justice has never existed on earth, it cannot serve as the defining characteristic of a republic. Something else must serve as the basis. Augustine therefore revises Scipio's definition to correspond with reality. People are best defined not in terms of a common sense of right but in terms of a common object of love.

Though a society is a collection of many different individuals with different loves, it is defined primarily by the predominant love in society. The state upholds and affirms this predominant love by privileging it through laws and by suppressing, even punishing, interests and desires that challenge its preeminence. For example, a society that loves money and wealth is defined in terms of laws and penalties that sanction this end. By contrast, a society that loves beauty and art will have different laws and penalties that promote aesthetics. In sum, for Augustine, the end (telos) or final cause of any society is defined in terms of what that society ultimately loves, thrills to, and looks up to.

THE ROLE OF THE STATE

Given Augustine's pessimistic view of human nature riddled by sin and the impossibility of ever establishing a perfectly just regime on earth, what role does the state play in his political thought? R.W. Dyson observes that the state is the product of human artifice whose primary purpose is to maintain some degree of order in a chaotic world fractured by sin and evil. "The State has come into being," he explains, "and continues in being, for three reasons. It is a consequence and an expression of sin; it is a means of reducing or containing the material harm that the behavior of fallen men produces; and it is a disciplinary order, by which sinners are chastised and the righteous made ready for their eternal reward."[46] In a fallen world, authority and social hierarchies are maintained primarily through fear and force, rather than charitable obedience. Augustine has been described as a Christian realist given his unvarnished view of politics as the interplay of power, force, and self-interest.

Regardless of whether or not the state would have existed in the Garden of Eden had the fall not occurred—and scholars disagree over this—all agree that the coercive and punitive dimensions of the state are both a consequence of original sin and a necessary instrument to repress the wickedness and vice of fallen human beings. Just as the law of nature was perfectly followed before the fall, Augustine maintained that originally all human beings were created equal by God. Following the Stoics, and anticipating Rousseau, he observed that freedom and equality were part of the natural order (*naturalis ordo*) of human beings before the fall. Tragically, this original condition of equality is now irrevocably lost as a consequence of sin:

> For he [God] did not wish a rational creature, made in his own image, to have dominion save over irrational creatures: not man over man, but man over the beasts. So it was that the first just men were established as shepherds of flocks, rather than kings of men, so that even so the principle of gradation among his creatures, and what the guilt of sinners demands . . .[47]

---

[46]Dyson, p. 48.

[47]*City of God* 19:15.

CASE STUDY 3.1 | AUGUSTINE AND AMERICAN EXCEPTIONALISM

Americans have always considered themselves an exceptional people called to a higher purpose. Our Puritan forefathers described their new colony in Massachusetts Bay as a "city upon the hill" (Matthew 5:14)—a nation set apart. Borrowing from Virgil, the founders likewise proclaimed that they had established a *novus ordo seclorum*—a new order for the ages (eternity). Indeed, this motto, along with "In God we trust" and *annuit coeptis* ("God smiles upon us"), is stamped on our currency. Consonant with this exceptionalist strain in American history, Ronald Reagan referred to the United States as "a shining city upon the hill." Indeed, throughout their history, Americans have understood their national destiny in terms of a mission—or a special calling—to serve as an exemplar or model of democracy to the world.

If men were intended by God to be equal, then it follows that all forms of dominion of one human being over another are purely conventional and against the natural order. This is particularly the case with slavery, which Augustine condemns as unjust. Slavery is yet another painful consequence of original sin:

> But by nature (*autem natura*), in which God first created man, no man is the slave either of another man or of sin. Yet slavery as a punishment is also ordained by that law which bids us to preserve the natural order and forbids us to disturb it; for if nothing had been done contrary to that law, there would have been nothing requiring the check of punishment by slavery.[48]

Though Augustine claims that both slavery and tyranny were against the natural order as God intended, he does not provide a theory of resistance to the state. All authorities, no matter how wicked, must be obeyed, provided they do not command beliefs and actions contrary to conscience. In the event that they do so, the Christian is obliged to resist passively by refusing to obey the law and to suffer willingly the consequences, even death and martyrdom.

If Augustine saw slavery and tyranny as something against the natural order, why did he fail to recognize the possibility of legitimate resistance or a right to revolution? This is because he saw all powers as ordained of God, no matter how wicked.[49] In His providence, God grants power to both good and evil. Those in power may ultimately serve some divine purpose known only to God. Thus in persecuting Christians, a tyrant may be testing the faith of true believers and may be punishing sinners who are

QUESTIONS FOR REFLECTION

Is American exceptionalism any different from Rome's founding myth? Does it inevitably lead to national arrogance and imperialism? Did Abraham Lincoln introduce an important qualification to this belief when he referred to Americans as God's "almost chosen people?" What would Augustine think of American exceptionalism?

---

[48] *City of God* 19:15.

[49] Romans 13.

PRIMARY SOURCE 3.3

A People Are Defined in Terms of the Object of Their Love, from *City of God*, Book XIX, Chapter xxiii–xxiv

But if we discard this definition of a people, and, assuming another, say that a people is an assemblage of reasonable beings bound together by a common agreement as to the objects of their love, then, in order to discover the character of any people, we have only to observe what they love. Yet whatever it loves, if only it is an assemblage of reasonable beings and not of beasts, and is bound together by an agreement as to the objects of love, it is reasonably called a people; and it will be a superior people in proportion as it is bound together by higher interests, inferior in proportion as it is bound together by lower. According to this definition of ours, the Roman people is a people, and its weal is without doubt a commonwealth or republic. But what its tastes were in its early and subsequent days, and how it declined into sanguinary seditions and then to social and civil wars, and so burst asunder or rotted off the bond of concord in which the health of a people consists, history shows, and in the preceding books I have related at large. And yet I would not on this account say either that it was not a people, or that its administration was not a republic, so long as there remains an assemblage of reasonable beings bound together by a common agreement as to the objects of love. But what I say of this people and of this republic I must be understood to think and say of the Athenians or any Greek state, of the Egyptians, of the early Assyrian Babylon, and of every other nation, great or small, which had a public government. For, in general, the city of the ungodly, which did not obey the command of God that it should offer no sacrifice save to Him alone, and which, therefore, could not give to the soul its proper command over the body, nor to the reason its just authority over the vices, is void of true justice.

false believers. Furthermore, given his emphasis on human depravity, Augustine did not sanction a right to resistance because of the possible chaos that would likely ensue. Although his critique of all human institutions as deficient was profoundly radical, his defense of the status quo given the anarchic tendencies of human beings was highly conservative. In a word, Augustine's motto for politics seems to be, "Things can always get worse." Finally, because he viewed life on earth as a pilgrimage, Augustine would likely regard the desire for revolution as betraying too great a preoccupation with the things of this world.

Though imperfect, a partial justice or likeness of true justice may nonetheless be attained in this life. For this reason, Augustine acknowledged that pagan states can be well ordered (*bene ordinate*) and well constituted (*bene constituta*).[50] Although every state is imperfect, there are varying degrees of depravity, from better to worse. With this principle in mind, Augustine taught that Christians are called to strive to attain the measure of partial justice that is possible in this world without making an idol of the state.

This tension between striving to attain a partial justice within the limits of a fallen world leads us to St. Augustine's political prescription. What should Christian pilgrims expect from politics? What should they strive to attain in this life? It is clear that for Augustine the utopian aspiration to build a perfect world in this life is doomed to failure. Yet it is possible to attain some degree of order, justice, and peace in our

[50] Dyson, p. 66.

QUESTIONS FOR REFLECTION

How does Augustine's Christian realism differ from the political realism of Machiavelli and Hobbes?

sojourn on earth. According to Augustine, Christians have a duty to serve the state. They must not "abandon the field" to the wicked. In the saeculum, politics secures a necessary temporal peace that is shared between the members of the two cities but used for different ends. The city of God uses this temporal peace to worship, serve, and love God and neighbor. The city of man uses it for material well-being. Indeed, the concept of peace is foundational to Augustine's political teaching and an area of common interest from the perspective of the two cities. This is corroborated by the fact that he used the term *pax* or peace more than 2,500 times in his writings!

Augustine thought that all living beings possess an intrinsic and natural yearning for peace, which he understood as an internal law that governs living creatures in their self-preservation: "All physical things, since they exist and have therefore their own rank, design and, as it were, internal law of peace, are surely good. And when they are in places where they should be according to the natural order, they keep their own beings safe and in such measure as they have received it."[51] Each creature is naturally ordered by God toward a certain kind of peace that is distinctive to its own being. For example, the peace that is proper to the body is physical health.

Peace may also be understood as a concord or harmony of parts as they relate to the whole. Thus physical peace may be attained when each part of the body functions properly and performs its unique task in serving the whole. In sum, Augustine describes peace in two related ways: negatively as the cessation of strife; and positively as the satisfaction or fullness of desire.

After describing peace in general, Augustine considered more specifically the domestic peace of the household. This particular kind of peace consists in an orderly relation and harmony between members of the family. Today we use the term *dysfunctional* to describe a family that lacks such peace and concord. In such a family, relations are marked by emotional or physical abuse, disrespect, betrayal, infidelity, neglect, or disobedience. Domestic peace is clearly absent where children do not honor their mother or father; where spouses betray each other; and where parents neglect their children for their own selfish pursuits. Significantly, Augustine understood society as a whole in terms of a collection of families or households. This means that the absence or existence of domestic peace of the household will radiate outward, affecting the peace of society as a whole. Thus Augustine would be deeply concerned with "family values" that maintain familial peace and stability.

The human will accepts peace through love or fear. Augustine notes that concord can be maintained in the household through the fear of the paterfamilias (the father figure) or through a love that humbly accepts obedience and filial obligation. As it is with families, so it is with both societies and states. Peace—the cessation of strife and a degree of tranquility—may be accepted through love or coerced through fear of punishment.

---

[51] *City of God,* Book XII, ch. vi, p. 23.

QUESTIONS FOR REFLECTION

Does Augustine's teaching on slavery as a punishment for sin and his related teaching on obedience to tyrants lead to a political quietism that passively resigns us to the evils of this world rather than confronting them?

After its civil wars ended with the crowning of Caesar Augustus as emperor, the Romans boasted of a new era, a *pax romana*—a promised reign of peace for a thousand years. Despite their savagery and brutality in maintaining domestic tranquility, Augustine concedes that the Romans did maintain a kind of peace. The Romans waged war not for its own sake but for the sake of a glorious peace, which they thought would bring them everlasting fame. In truth, this peace was brutally imposed on others through fear and conquest.

Thus, for Augustine, each state and society therefore maintains a kind of peace, concord, or temporal tranquility that enables its citizens to pursue the satisfaction of the objects of their love. For the citizens of the earthly city the temporal peace is a cessation of hostilities, a fragile truce so each can gratify his or her perverse lusts. Indeed, if the two cities are defined in terms of the objects of their love, they are also defined in terms of the corresponding peace they maintain to satisfy these lusts.

However, like true justice, true peace will forever elude human beings in this life. Augustine therefore distinguishes between the true peace of the city of God and the temporal peace of the city of man. Augustine calls the temporal peace shared between the members of the two cities the **Peace of Babylon.** As noted, the imperfect peace of Babylon is shared by the two cities though it is used for different ends: Citizens of the city of man use it to satisfy their lusts with impunity; citizens of the heavenly city use it to worship and serve God until their pilgrimage on earth is over.

Given that the Peace of Babylon is an area of common concern between the citizens of both cities, Augustine maintains that the state serves a primarily negative purpose in maintaining this fragile Peace of Babylon. This goal should not be disparaged. To maintain even an imperfect peace is no easy task given original sin in a fallen world where society may be seen as a collection of individuals pursuing their own passions and desires at the expense of each other. The state must necessarily impose some kind of concord or peace upon clashing interests and lusts. By so doing, it will necessarily privilege the satisfaction of the lusts of the majority or the stronger in society over the minority and the weaker. It follows that those who are more successful in satisfying their particular objects of love will be honored and rewarded: their peculiar love and peace will define society.

Christians have an obligation to do their part in maintaining the Peace of Babylon. Indeed, Jesus himself acknowledged the legitimate claims of political authority over citizens in this world, as when he taught, "Render unto Caesar that which is Caesar's and unto God's that which is God's."[52] Henceforth Western civilization would face the vexing problem of distinguishing between the things of God and the things of Caesar (the state). In distinguishing between the things of God and the things of Caesar, Christ

[52]Matthew 22:21.

PRIMARY SOURCE 3.4 | The Peace of Babylon, *City of God*, Book XIX, Chapter XXVI

Chapter 26—Of the Peace Which Is Enjoyed by the People That Are Alienated from God, and the Use Made of It by the People of God in the Time of Its Pilgrimage.

Wherefore, as the life of the flesh is the soul, so the blessed life of man is God, of whom the sacred writings of the Hebrews say, "Blessed is the people whose God is the Lord." Miserable, therefore, is the people which is alienated from God. Yet even this people has a peace of its own which is not to be lightly esteemed, though, indeed, it shall not in the end enjoy it, because it makes no good use of it before the end. But it is our interest that it enjoy this peace meanwhile in this life; for as long as the two cities are commingled, we also enjoy the peace of Babylon. For from Babylon the people of God is so freed that it meanwhile sojourns in its company. And therefore the apostle also admonished the Church to pray for kings and those in authority, assigning as the reason, "that we may live a quiet and tranquil life in all godliness and love." And the prophet Jeremiah, when predicting the captivity that was to befall the ancient people of God, and giving them the divine command to go obediently to Babylonia, and thus serve their God, counseled them also to pray for Babylonia, saying, "In the peace thereof shall you have peace,"—the temporal peace which the good and the wicked together enjoy.

recognized a division between spiritual and temporal authority. This division would subsequently serve as the basis of the modern separation of church and state.

According to Augustine, Christians are bound to obey the temporal authorities, provided these powers do not command them to act against conscience. This also means that they are obliged to serve in the army and to fight wars. Augustine rejected the pacifism of his Christian predecessors. And he articulated one of the first Christian theories of just war, which was developed further by St. Thomas Aquinas in the Middle Ages (see the next chapter). War, though lamentable, will always be inevitable in a fallen world.

Augustine's theory of just war is based on the related concepts of ***jus ad bellum*** (right reasons for going to war) and ***jus in bello*** (right actions in waging war). He discusses the criteria to determine a just war in the following passage:

> A great deal depends on the reasons why humans undertake wars and on the authority to begin a war. The natural order of the universe which seeks peace among humans must allow the king the power to enter into a war if he thinks it necessary. That same natural order commands that the soldiers should then perform their duty, protecting the peace and safety of the political community. When war is undertaken in accord with the will of God (the God who wishes to rebuke, humble, and crush malicious human beings), it must be just to wage it.[53]

Augustine sees war, like slavery, as both a consequence and an expression of our fallen nature. God may use war to chastise sinners and to test the righteous.

Although Augustine rejects the notion of a divinely ordained Christian empire on earth during the *saeculum,* he does allow for the possibility of a Christian prince.

---

[53] *Contra Faustum* 22:75.

PRIMARY SOURCE 3.5 | "MIRROR OF A CHRISTIAN PRINCE," *CITY OF GOD*, BOOK V, CHAPTER xxiv

For neither do we say that certain Christian emperors were therefore happy because they ruled a long time, or, dying a peaceful death, left their sons to succeed them in the empire, or subdued the enemies of the republic, or were able both to guard against and to suppress the attempt of hostile citizens rising against them. These and other gifts or comforts of this sorrowful life even certain worshippers of demons have merited to receive, who do not belong to the kingdom of God to which these belong; and this is to be traced to the mercy of God, who would not have those who believe in Him desire such things as the highest good. But we say that they are happy if they rule justly; if they are not lifted up amid the praises of those who pay them sublime honors, and the obsequiousness of those who salute them with an excessive humility, but remember that they are men; if they make their power the handmaid of His majesty by using it for the greatest possible extension of His worship; if they fear, love, worship God; if more than their own they love that kingdom in which they are not afraid to have partners; if they are slow to punish, ready to pardon; if they apply that punishment as necessary to government and defense of the republic, and not in order to gratify their own enmity; if they grant pardon, not that iniquity may go unpunished, but with the hope that the transgressor may amend his ways; if they compensate with the lenity of mercy and the liberality of benevolence for whatever severity they may be compelled to decree; if their luxury is as much restrained as it might have been unrestrained; if they prefer to govern depraved desires rather than any nation whatever; and if they do all these things, not through ardent desire of empty glory, but through love of eternal felicity, not neglecting to offer to the true God, who is their God, for their sins, the sacrifices of humility, contrition, and prayer. Such Christian emperors, we say, are happy in the present time by hope, and are destined to be so in the enjoyment of the reality itself, when that which we wait for shall have arrived.

As seen, political leadership may be a legitimate vocation for Christians in a fallen world who must strive to attain the partial justice that is possible in this life. This is attained first and foremost by securing the Peace of Babylon, which is precondition for any higher aspirations. In the *City of God,* Augustine provided a normative description of the qualities that ought to define a Christian prince. In offering this portrait of a Christian prince, Augustine reworked the traditional pagan genre known as the "Mirror of Princes."

Though Augustine allowed for the possibility of a Christian emperor, he did not believe that this state of affairs would bring about perfection or purity on earth. As noted, the first responsibility of a Christian prince must be to maintain the fragile Peace of Babylon. In a fallen world, all leaders, including Christian leaders, will inevitably confront tragic moral dilemmas in which there is no clear choice between good and evil, but only the lesser of two evils. The moral ambiguity of a fallen world does not

QUESTIONS FOR REFLECTION

What are the necessary qualities that define a Christian emperor for Augustine? How do Augustine and Machiavelli differ in their understanding of these qualities?

CASE STUDY 3.2 | REINHOLD NIEBUHR: A 20TH-CENTURY AUGUSTINIAN ON THE IRONIES OF AMERICAN HISTORY

In his book the *Ironies of American History*, the Christian realist and Augustinian scholar Reinhold Niebuhr warned of the perils confronting American global hegemony in the postwar era. Most notably, he warned that liberal democracies are just as prone to utopian temptations as totalitarian regimes. In a fallen world, America's idealism and self-righteousness may lead to well-intended policies that have the unintended consequence of producing greater evil. It may lead to a hubristic overreaching that is blind to the limits of politics. According to Niebuhr, Americans must seek "a tolerable justice" in international affairs without expecting too much. Echoing Augustine, he explains,

> Such a measured judgment upon the virtues and perils of America's position in the world community accurately describes the hazards of our position in the world. Our moral perils are not those of conscious malice or the explicit lust for power. They are perils which can be understood only if we realize the ironic tendency of virtues to turn into vices when too complacently relied upon; and of power to become vexatious if the wisdom which directs it is trusted too confidently. The ironic elements in American history can be overcome, in short, only if American idealism comes to terms with the limits of all human striving, the fragmentariness of all human wisdom, the precariousness of all historic configurations of power, and the mixture of good and evil in all human virtue.

To what extent does Niebuhr's diagnosis of the ironies of American history apply to current American foreign policy?

disappear once Christians attain power. So-called Christian leaders must therefore resist the temptation of self-righteousness and triumphalism. They must confront the depravity of human nature in themselves and in the world without illusion.

CONCLUSION

In conclusion, Augustine's teachings on God, man, and society emphasizes the limits of politics. He unmasks the selfish interests beneath the surface of all claims to absolute value. And he warns that the effort to achieve perfection in this life through one's own efforts is doomed to failure. This dangerous illusion tempts us to forget our own weakness, dependence, and need for redemption. All too often, the human heart's craving for fullness is lavished upon self-made idols to replace God. Indeed, the 20th century, perhaps the worst century in human history, reveals the demonic consequences of what can occur when the state is used as a vehicle for secular salvation in this world. Nazism and communism were both *ersatz* (pseudo) religions that promised transfiguration in this life through the triumph of the master race or the classless society respectively. As Augustine may have predicted, their utopian dreams ended in the nightmare of world war, the Holocaust, and the gulag. The utopian temptation to create a kingdom of God on earth, however, is by no means unique to totalitarian regimes. Liberal democracies are not immune to this spiritual sickness, particularly in their effort to master, perfect, and emancipate human nature through technology. A brave new world of designer babies, material comfort, perpetual health, beauty, longevity, liberation, and freedom from pain and suffering is promised on the horizon. Will the wonders of technology and empire fill the void within the human heart? Augustine's answer to this question is clear.

Key Terms

pax romana
Confessions
Hortensius
Stoic school of philosophy
the Manicheans
gnosis
neo-Platonists
divine grace
Romans 7:14–2
the Incarnation
messiah
Sermon on the Mount
divine logos or word
Tertullian
Justin Martyr
Logos Spermatikos
prelapsarian state
postlapsarian state
sapienta
scientia
exnihilio
cyclical view of history
linear history
providence
the fall
original sin
vitiated
agape
Philippians 2:5–9
saeculum
creation, fall, redemption, and final judgment
the two cities—the city of God and the city of man
love of God or amor Dei
double commandment (Matthew 22:37)
amor sui or self-love
cupiditas
concupiscentia
ordo amoris
predestination
libido dominandi
Peace of Babylon
jus ad bellum
jus in bello

Sources and Resources

Key Texts

City of God
Confessions

Secondary Texts

Brown, Peter. *Augustine of Hippo: A Biography* (Berkeley: University of California Press, 1967).

Burt, Donald X. *Friendship and Society: An Introduction to Augustine's Practical Philosophy* (Grand Rapids: Eerdmans, 1999).

Deane, Herbert. *The Political and Social Ideas of St. Augustine* (New York: Columbia University Press, 1963).

Dyson, R.W. *St Augustine of Hippo: The Christian Transformation of Political Philosophy* (London: Continuum International Publishing Group, 2005).

Fortin, Ernest L. *Political Idealism and Christianity in the Thought of St. Augustine* (Villanova, PA: Villanova University Press, 1972).

Markus, Robert A. *Saeculum: History and Society in the Theology of St. Augustine* (Cambridge: Cambridge University Press, 1970).

Von Heyking, John. *Augustine and Politics as Longing in the World*) Columbia, MO: University of Missouri Press, 2001).

Web Sites

Stanford Encyclopedia of Philosophy entry online: http://plato.stanford.edu/entries/augustine/

Texts, translations, introductions, and commentaries online: http://ccat.sas.upenn.edu/jod/augustine/

Reference site for Augustine and the Order of Saint Augustine online: http://www.augnet.org

St. Thomas Aquinas

CHAPTER 4

By Kenneth L. Deutsch *SUNY Geneseo*

LIFE AND TIMES

St. Thomas Aquinas (1224–1274) ranks among the most influential thinkers in Western civilization. Aquinas was born around 1224 into the noble Aquino family near Naples. He received his early education at the Benedictine monastery of Monte Cassino and his later training at the University of Naples. To the disgust of his family, he entered the Dominican order and was sent to Paris to study theology under Albert the Great, an early leader in the Aristotelian revival. His family expected him to inherit and eventually manage the family home and estate. Aquinas' decision to take the habit of a new religious order created a sensation among the young people of Naples as well as in his family. His father died just a few months before this decision. His mother was completely opposed to this choice. Traditionally, the eldest son of a noble family took over the estate or became a powerful abbot—and definitely did not enter a radically new religious order such as the Dominicans, who were mostly known for their absolute vow of poverty. His mother directed her other sons to kidnap Thomas and place him in a forced residence for about a year to break his will. A chronicle of the time even claims that the brothers attempted to employ a prostitute's seduction! None of this worked. Legend claims Aquinas used a hot poker to drive her away. During the summer of 1245 he regained his freedom, went back to Naples, reentered Dominican religious life, and then returned to study in Paris. He studied with Albert the Great, one of the leading scholars of the time, until he was 25. The study of **Aristotle (the Philosopher)** along with Augustine most shaped Aquinas' thought. After finishing his study, he became a professor at the University of Naples. He served as adviser to the rector and during the last years of his life he was given the task to reorganize the university. He died in 1274 at the age of 49. He was canonized (sainted) in 1323; the hot poker incident was used by the Church as one of the miracles—including his chaste night with the prostitute—to justify his canonization. The second required miracle took place at Aquinas' deathbed, when he asked his nurse to get him some herring even though the herring were not running during the summer. The nurse could not find the requested herring at the market. However, when she returned home she saw a fishing boat, and there was herring on board. Though these miracles may be mundane, a truly great miracle to ascribe to Thomas Aquinas would be the great writings such as the Summas that this doctor of the Roman Catholic Church produced for over 25 years of his life as teacher, scholar, and university reformer.

ULTIMATE REALITY

Thomas Aquinas was primarily a Christian theologian rather than a political philosopher. He sought to show that the whole of human wisdom is a vast pattern of thought with the sciences of ethics and politics found at the base, philosophy above them, and theology at the apex. His scholastic method taught that reason and faith cooperate in the discovery of truth. Divine revelation and natural (unaided) human reason are not contradictory; biblical revelation and faith complete the pattern of knowledge of which science and reason provide the beginning. Theology's faith and philosophy's reason are each valid in their own realm; faith actually complements reason. Aquinas' scholastic method claimed that reason can illuminate faith: It can correct or complete fallible or erring reason.

The world is a rational order, created by divine will and made so by the teleological principle, which is to say that the divine creation is composed of various things with particular natures or purposes, each of which is fitted for existence and also for ideal development. God's order operates according to laws of nature. Aquinas would agree with Aristotle that "nature does nothing in vain." The difference between them is that Aquinas sees the purposiveness of everything in nature as due to the divine will or plan. God moves all things to realize their end. For humans their end is to act in ways that fulfill the moral and political inclinations of their nature, which will lead to an eternal life and the beatific vision to see God face to face. The natural order or harmony of nature is the result of rule by divine providence and governance of divine reason in which each thing, including humans, seeks its proper end and full potential. Aquinas' scholastic method, then, integrates Aristotle's teleological view of nature into the biblical theology of creation and Christian salvation.

HUMAN NATURE AND THE COMMON GOOD AND THE NECESSITY OF GOVERNMENT

The political condition is a **natural condition** of human beings as part of creation. The act of creating is the unfolding of a multiplication of existences. Aquinas notes that in Genesis it states that "God created man in his image, in the image of God he created him" (I:27). Because God cannot be sufficiently well represented by one finite creature, the diverse multiplication of human creatures compensates for their individual deficiencies. Diverse human beings reflect both the multiple beauty of God and the mutual limitations and dependencies on other human beings. Aquinas states,

> God has produced things in the human being in order to communicate his goodness to the created things and to represent his goodness in them. And because his goodness cannot be represented efficiently in one single creature, he created multiple and diverse things in such a way that whatever is lacking in one creature in representing the divine goodness may be made up for by another. Thus the goodness which in God is simple and unique is found in countless and differentiated creatures. Consequently it is the entire universe which shares perfectly the goodness of God and represents it more than one creature by itself.[1]

Human beings are partners with God in the divine plan in the building up of the world. The mutual dependence between human beings is a sacred and natural ordering of creation where humans have a special vocation—the humanization of the world and eternal salvation in which organizing different people with different talents builds up the world. Humans need politics! And this would be true even in the Garden of Eden before the "fall."

Aquinas argues,

> Every human being is naturally endowed with the light of reason, which is used to direct actions to their ends. If it were fitting to live without others, as many animals do, there would be no need for anyone else to direct actions to human ends; each man would be his own monarch, directing his own actions under the rule of God, the

[1]*Summa Theologica* I, Q. 22, Art. 4.

> supreme monarch who gave man the light of reason. But that humans are naturally social and political animals, more so than any other animals, is proved by the things which are necessary to human life.[2]

Aquinas continues his reflections about human mutual dependence by presenting the following empirical evidence:

1. Nonhuman animals have specific natural defenses (such as claws), whereas humans must rely on reason for their survival.
2. Human co-creation requires human cooperation and cannot be done by single individuals with their limited talents.
3. The power of human speech shows that solitary existence is inappropriate ("nature does nothing in vain"); speech and language provide the means for interpersonal projects.

Humans have a nature created by God. Humans cannot normally or ordinarily survive and thrive and reach their end (salvation or eternal communion with God) without sound cooperation. Human cooperation means our natural potential to be rational—to pursue our proper end by thinking about ends and means. To accomplish the humanization of the world and eternal salvation, Aquinas further argues that there must be a principle of government within society:

> If it is natural for human beings to live in society, then it follows that there must be regulation of that society. For no human group can long endure if each person sought only his individual ends. One of them would have to provide for the common interest, just as an organism would break apart unless it had some controlling power in it which worked for the good of all the bodily parts . . . As individual interests differ, so the common interest unites. Things which differ have differing causes responsible for them. It must be the case, then, and above that which moves us to our individual ends, there be some factor which moves the group to a common end.[3]

Humans require political rule for social survival. We have a political obligation to the survival of the group, which is related to our own survival. Aquinas' argument is not merely hypothetical: If you wish to survive, you must accept these arrangements. We are naturally political in the sense that it is normal and necessary to be placed under the political rule of those who "would provide for the common interest" or **common good.** Humans must try to do that which is right and reasonable in reference to the common interest. The king or government exists as political rule to prevent the chaos of human conflicting interests grounded in original sin and the irrational use of power for selfish gain when these interests are opposed to the common interest. Aquinas denies that our human nature is vitiated or corrupted by original sin. Rather, original sin leads to human woundedness, fallibility, and frailty. Government and the common good exist to foster or guarantee peace. As part of the divine plan, political institutions must also foster the pursuit of knowledge, the virtuous life, and the cultural conditions that permit humans to seek their ultimate end, which is the enjoyment of God. We should reflect on what Aquinas means by his view that the state exists by nature.

---

[2]A.P.D. Entreves (ed.), *Aquinas: Selected Political Writings*, trans. J.G. Dawson (Oxford: Basil Blackwell, 1959), Book I, Ch. 1.

[3]Ibid., 12 Q. 22, Art. 4.

QUESTIONS FOR REFLECTION

Do you agree that there is a moving principle or internal compulsion that generally inclines human society to a political unity and consequently forms and organizes the individual parts into a social whole?

Aquinas claims that the "ordering" of the social whole reasonably implies a directing authority. See the accompanying box with an excerpt from *On Kingship*.

"Just as the soul rules the body, a ruler rules the body politic." As one person or a few people are superior to the multitude in knowledge and justice, it is good that he or they rule over others for their own benefit. Rulership is a trust for the entire community. "Among men an order is found to exist inasmuch as those who are superior by intellect are by nature rulers."[4] Some have a capacity to rule; others have the aptitude to carry out tasks under a supervisor; and still others have only the ability to follow. Wisdom and the order of nature are demonstrated here for Aquinas. If all human beings were by nature born leaders (or for that matter born followers), an integrated social and political order would be all but impossible. A ruler's direction of free people would have existed even in the Garden of Eden. Even in the original state of paradise, God made people with different (or unequal) natural abilities, thereby requiring some guidance and direction in the community. If the state's proper task is to provide for the common good in earthly terms, the final and ultimate end of humanity is beyond the political ruler's natural capacities. The church is given the task of caring for human souls. The two, though separate, are ultimately complementary. Spiritual goods are preeminent but cannot be realized without the fulfillment of the secular goods of peace, order, justice, protection of the family, and the freedom to practice the Catholic faith. So, too, revelation completes the pursuit of reason, divine grace helps us realize our natural capacities, and the church must guide the state. The kind of guidance the church should provide was not presented in any detail by Aquinas.

Political authority is derived from God. The best rulers follow not only natural reason as the basis of just rule but also the divine law of love and mercy. Rulers are called on to be magnanimous and prudent.

A **magnanimous** (or great-souled) person recognizes that whatever talents to rule he or she possesses must be grounded in the desire to do great things on behalf of the mutually dependent people who comprise the community, as well as the glorification of God—the creator and sustainer of those talents. A magnanimous person recognizes not only the gifts that God has given him or her but also that he or she has limitations as a human being in terms of many weaknesses and sinful tendencies. Such a ruler should reflect on how the pursuer of political honors or status can become irrational in three ways:

> First, when a man desires recognition of an excellence he has not; this is to desire more than his share of honor. Secondly, when a man desires honor for himself without referring to God. Thirdly, when a man's appetite rests in honor itself, without referring it to the profit of others.[5]

---

[4] *Summa Contra Gentiles II,* 81.

[5] *Summa Theologica,* Ia, Iiae, cxxix, Art. 3, ad 4.

PRIMARY SOURCE 4.1 | ON KINGSHIP

[6] Moreover, all other animals are able to discern, by inborn skill, what is useful and what is injurious, even as the sheep naturally regards the wolf as his enemy. Some animals also recognize by natural skill certain medicinal herbs and other things necessary for their life. Man, on the contrary, has a natural knowledge of the things which are essential for his life only in a general fashion, inasmuch as he is able to attain knowledge of the particular things necessary for human life by reasoning from natural principles. But it is not possible for one man to arrive at a knowledge of all these things by his own individual reason. It is therefore necessary for man to live in a multitude so that each one may assist his fellows, and different men may be occupied in seeking, by their reason, to make different discoveries—one, for example, in medicine, one in this and another in that.

[7] This point is further and most plainly evidenced by the fact that the use of speech is a prerogative proper to man. By this means, one man is able fully to express his conceptions to others. Other animals, it is true, express their feelings to one another in a general way, as a dog may express anger by barking and other animals give vent to other feelings in various fashions. But man communicates with his kind more completely than any other animal known to be gregarious, such as the crane, the ant, or the bee. With this in mind, Solomon says, "It is better that there be two than one; for they have the advantage of their company."

[8] If, then, it is natural for man to live in the society of many, it is necessary that there exist among men some means by which the group may be governed. For where there are many men together and each one is looking after his own interest, the multitude would be broken up and scattered unless there were also an agency to take care of what appertains to the common weal. In like manner, the body of a man or any other animal would disintegrate unless there were a general ruling force within the body which watches over the common good of all members. With this in mind Solomon says, "Where there is no governor, the people shall fall."

[9] Indeed it is reasonable that this should happen, for what is proper and what is common are not identical. Thing differ by what is proper to each: they are united by what they have in common. But diversity of effects is due to diversity of causes. Consequently, there must exist something which impels toward the common good of the many, over and above that which impels toward the particular good of each individual. Wherefore also in all things that are ordained toward one end, one thing is found to rule the rest. Thus in the corporeal universe, by the first body, i.e. the celestial body, the other bodies are regulated according to the order of Divine Providence; and all bodies are ruled by a rational creature. So, too, in the individual man, the soul rules the body; and among the parts of the soul, the irascible in the concupiscible parts are ruled by reason. Likewise, among the members of a body, one, such as the heart or the head, is the principal and moves all the others. Therefore in every multitude there must be some governing power.

[10] Now it happens in certain things which are ordained toward an end that one may proceed in a right way and also in a wrong way. So, too, in the government of a multitude there is a distinction between right and wrong. A thing is rightly directed when it is led toward a befitting end; wrongly when it is led toward an unbefitting end. Now the end which befits a multitude of free men is different from that which befits a multitude of slaves, for the free man is one who exists for his own sake, while the slave, as such, exists for the sake of another. If, therefore, a multitude of free men is ordered by the ruler toward the common good of the multitude, that rulership will be right and just, as is suitable to free men. If, on the other hand, a rulership aims, not at the common good of the multitude but at the private good of the ruler, it will be an unjust and perverted rulership. The Lord, therefore, threatens such rulers, saying by the mouth of Ezekiel, "Woe to the shepherds that feed themselves (seeking, that is, their own interest): should not the flocks be fed by the shepherd?" Shepherds indeed should seek the good of their flocks,

PRIMARY SOURCE 4.1 | ON KINGSHIP *continued*

and every ruler, the good of the multitude subject to him.

[11] If an unjust government is carried on by one man alone, who seeks his own benefit from his rule and not the good of the multitude subject to him, such a ruler is called a "tyrant"—a word derived from "strength"—because he oppresses by might instead of ruling by justice. Thus among the ancients all powerful men were called tyrants. If an unjust government is carried on, not by one but by several, and if they be few, it is called an "oligarchy," that is, the rule of a few. This occurs when a few, who differ from the tyrant only by the fact that they are more than one, oppress the people by means of their wealth. If, finally, the bad government is carried on by the multitude, it is called a "democracy," i.e., control by the populace, which comes about when the plebian people by force of numbers oppress the rich. In this way the whole people will be as one tyrant.

[12] In like manner we must divide just governments. If the government is administered by many, it is given the name common to all forms of government, viz., "polity," as for instance when a group of warriors exercises dominion over a city or province. If it is administered by a few men of virtue, this kind of government is called an "aristocracy," i.e., noble governance, or governance by noble men, who for this reason are called the "Optimates." And if a just government is in the hands of one man alone, he is properly called a "king." Wherefore the Lord says by the mouth of Ezekiel: "My servant, David, shall be king over them and all of them shall have one shepherd."

[13] From this it is clearly shown that the idea of king implies that he be one man who is chief and that he be a shepherd seeking the common good of the multitude and not his own.

[14] Now since man must live in a group, because he is not sufficient unto himself to procure the necessities of life were he to remain solitary, it follows that a society will be the more perfect the more it is sufficient unto itself to procure the necessities of life. There is, to some extent, sufficiency for life in one *family of one household,* namely insofar as pertains to the natural acts of nourishment and the begetting of offspring and other things of this kind. Self sufficiency exists furthermore, in one street with regard to those things which belong to the trade of one guild. In a *city* which is a perfect community, it exists with regard to all the necessities of life. Still more self sufficiency is found in a province because of the need of fighting together and of mutual help against enemies. Hence the man ruling a perfect community, i.e. a city or a province, is antonomastically called the king. The ruler of a household is called father, not king, although he bears a certain resemblance to the king, for which reason kings are sometimes called the fathers of their peoples.

[15] It is plain therefore, from what has been said, that a king is one who rules the people of one city or province, and rules them for the common good. Wherefore Solomon says, "The king ruleth over all the land subject to him."

Chapter II: Whether It Is More Expedient for a City or Province to Be Ruled by One Man or by Many

[16] Having set forth these preliminary points we must now inquire what is better for a province or a city: whether to be ruled by one man or by many.

[17] This question may be considered first from the viewpoint of the purpose of government. The aim of any ruler should be directed toward securing the welfare of that which he undertakes to rule. The duty of the pilot, for instance, is to preserve his ship amidst the perils of the sea and to bring it unharmed to the port of safety. Now the welfare and safety of a multitude formed into a society lies in the preservation of its unity, which is called peace. If this is removed, the benefit of social life is lost and, moreover, the multitude in its disagreement becomes a burden to itself. The chief concern of the ruler of a multitude, therefore, is to procure the unity of peace. It is not even legitimate for him to deliberate whether he shall establish peace in the multitude subject to him, just as a physician does not deliberate whether he shall heal the sick man encharged to him, for no one

continued

PRIMARY SOURCE 4.1 | ON KINGSHIP *continued*

should deliberate about an end which he is obliged to seek, but only about the means to attain that end. Wherefore the Apostle, having commended the unity of the faithful people, says, "Be ye careful to keep the unity of the spirit in the bond of peace." Thus, the more efficacious a government is in keeping the unity of peace, the more useful it will be. For we call that more useful which leads more directly to the end. Now it is manifest that what is itself one can more efficaciously bring about unity than several—just as the most efficacious cause of heat is that which is by its nature hot. Therefore the rule of one man is more useful than the rule of many.

[18] Furthermore, it is evident that several persons could by no means preserve the stability of the community if they totally disagreed. For union is necessary among them if they are to rule at all; several men, for instance, could not pull a ship in one direction unless joined together in some fashion. Now several are said to be united according as they come closer to being one. So one man rules better than several who come near being one.

[19] Again, whatever is in accord with nature is best, for in all things nature does what is best. Now every natural governance is governance by one. In the multitude of bodily members there is one which is the principal mover, namely, the heart; and among the powers of the soul one power presides as chief, namely, the reason. Among bees there is one king bee, and in the whole universe there is One God, Maker, and Ruler of all things. And there is a reason for this. Every multitude is derived from unity. Wherefore, if artificial things are an imitation of natural things and a work of art is better according as it attains a closer likeness to what is in nature, it follows that it is best for a human multitude to be ruled by one person.

[20] This is also evident from experience. For provinces or cities which are not ruled by one person are torn with dissentions and tossed about without peace, so that the complaint seems to be fulfilled which the Lord uttered through the Prophet: "Many pastors have destroyed my vineyard." On the other hand, provinces and cities which are ruled under one king enjoy peace, flourish in justice, and delight in prosperity. Hence, the Lord by His prophets promises to His people as a great reward that He will give them one head and that "one Prince will be in the midst of them."

This statement about the magnanimous person is a good example of Aquinas' **scholastic method** of harmonizing or synthesizing **faith and reason**, whereby rational cognition and spiritual humility are integrated. Honor and glory must not be the sole motives of the magnanimous ruler (or statesman) who creates or manages a polity for the common good. Although such rulers in high positions of public trust cannot be indifferent about their reputations, they should secure their reputations by performing the duties of their positions in such a way as to merit honor and glory.

Such rulers must possess the intellectual and moral virtues. This rulership must not be despotic or arrogant. Rather, political rule must be prudent as well as magnanimous. **Prudence** or practical wisdom rarely overpowers the activities of others in society. Excellent rulership is not dictatorship—not even benevolent dictatorship. It must appeal to citizens in terms of their own culture, history, traditions, or problems to do what leads to the best possible response to serve the common good.

Prudence is central to Aquinas' political philosophy. The human being acts best when he or she acts according to the measure of practical wisdom that comes to the person, whether by divine inspiration or by human industry. Prudence is the master virtue that affects all the rest. Aquinas clearly distinguishes the use of the term *prudence* as cleverness (*astutia*) from moral prudence (*prudentia*), which is the virtue of practical wisdom. Thomas Gilby, a great scholar of Aquinas' political philosophy, characterizes his view of moral prudence as

> ... a good habit or settled quality, of the practical reason giving an active bent toward right doing as an individual act; it ranges from our pondering over what should be done through our judgment of what we should choose to do, and is completed in that being an effective command.[6]

A prudent ruler conducts his or her discussions in the full light of the general precepts of the natural law through the light of reason and in consultation with others who are wise (that is, who have a good track record of prudence). Being prudent means not only knowing these general precepts, and supporting the common good, but also knowing through experience how to apply them in particular material circumstances in a way that fully respects the right order of means to ends. In effect, for Aquinas, political prudence requires that (1) the ends of one's actions be morally right and (2) the means be morally suited to those same ends. Perhaps an obvious example would include national security as a legitimate moral end under the natural law: Only certain means are morally suitable and workable under particular conditions. Prudence as *prudentia* must be present in the highest degree in the rulers of the state. Such rulers must

- Assiduously investigate alternative courses of conduct together with the means for accomplishing a moral end.
- Know how to make practical judgments about possible courses of action.
- Possess a good memory to draw from the storehouse of past experience.
- Possess circumspection, which involves close attention to the attendant circumstances of a political decision.
- Consult those with a strong reputation for practical wisdom and service in the public interest.
- Possess foresight to reasonably project into the future the consequences of a given line of action.

The ruler who is prudent is capable of apprehending the general precepts of the moral law and displays a deep sense of political balance and common sense. Ultimately, prudent decisions produce a just society (though imperfect) society. Such rulership requires the tough virtues of discipline and focus with the finesse of courtesy and charity.

Aquinas repeatedly cautions rulers about their attitude toward honors, which suggests that he was concerned with a ruler's excessive preoccupation with honors and recognition. It is far better for the ruler to approach governance as a public trust that should not dissolve into tyranny. As Aquinas put it,

> First it is necessary that the man who raised up to be king by those whom it concerns should be of such condition that it is improbable that he should become a tyrant.... Then, once the king is established, the government of the kingdom must be so arranged that the opportunity for tyranny is removed. At the same time his power should be so tempered that he cannot easily fall into tyranny.[7]

[6]Thomas Gilby (ed.) St. Blackfriersed., vol. 36, appendix 4, p. 183.

[7]*On Kingship*, I. Th. Eschwann (ed.) (Toronto: Pontifical Institute, 1949), p. 24.

A decent society requires a ruler capable of tempering "bodily" or "sexual" powers or desires by rational faculties. Thus

> ...the [power of] reason rules the irascible [easily provoked by anger] and concupiscible powers by a political rule, such as that which by free men are ruled, who in some respect have a free will of their own.[8]

So a person's bodily functions and desires should be ruled by intellect or reason—in civil society the proper "order among men." The good ruler rarely overpowers the activities of others in civil society in the manner of political manipulation, but rather channels these activities into a prudent mode of response for the common good.

TYPES OF LAWS

Political rulership must be under the law. Even if there is no institutional means available to pass sentence on the ruler or rulers, the ruler is obliged in conscience to follow the law of the realm: "whatever law a man makes for another, he should keep for himself."[9] As human beings we deliberate about and judge what we do. There is no point to rulers persuading, punishing, threatening, or rewarding the public if we deny that in this life humans are obliged by reason. It is because of Aquinas' moral commitment to social harmony and limited rulership that he developed his theory of law, which involves a consideration of the essence, kinds, and effects of law. He justified his political teachings by providing a detailed exploration of the nature of law. What is the essence of law? It is, he says, reason: **Law** is grounded in a life of deliberation, action, and judgment:

> Law is a rule and measure of acts whereby man is induced to act or is restrained from acting: for *lex* (law) is derived from *ligare* (to bind), because it binds one to act. Now the rule and measure of human acts, as is evident from what has been stated above, since it belongs to the reason to direct the end, which is the first principle in all matters of action according to the Philosopher (Aristotle).[10]

To claim that the essence of law is reason means that law is not merely or arbitrarily whatever the sovereign ruler commands. A command is true law provided that it is reasonable. There are various kinds of reason, so there are various types of law. The four kinds of law that correspond to the different kinds of reason include eternal law, natural law, human law, and divine law:

> **Eternal law**: Divine reason and wisdom comprise an eternal law—a law governing the whole of creation, a law not made but eternally existing and therefore unknowable to humans entirely, yet the source of all true law on earth. It is the government of things in God to the realization of their end. Ultimately, right and wrong in the practical field of human ethical and political action depend on whether these actions conform "to the eternal plan

[8]*Summa Theologica,* I–II, Q. 56a, ad 3.

[9]*Summa Theologica,* I–II Q. 96a. 5, 3.

[10]Ibid., Q. 90.

of government in the Chief governor" from which "all the plans of the lesser governors must be defined."[11]

Natural law: Natural law is the "rational creature's participation in the eternal law." This sharing in eternal reason is a practical reflection in human beings of divine intuition. This practical reflection or sharing in "eternal reason" provides humans with objective, changeless, universal rules or general principles of action for ethical and political life. We have natural inclinations that direct humans to goods that enable us to sustain a truly human existence, such as "conserve life and protect health." These natural inclinations are apprehended by reason. We will discuss these general precepts of natural law next.

Human law: Human law is true law that is derived from natural law. Such a true law is binding in conscience. A rule of the state that is inconsistent with the natural law is not law at all. It loses its legitimacy because no law can exist without justice; just laws conform to natural law and made known by "right reason" and deliberation.

Divine law: This is a derivation of eternal law that proceeds from God as divine legislator through revelation to humanity. It supplements and corrects the limitations (fallibility and frailty) of human reason and consists of rules made known to humanity at different periods in history. These rules are contained in the Bible, such as the Ten Commandments or the Sermon on the Mount. Divine law directs human beings to their eternal happiness. Natural law demands justice and a well-ordered, decent society. Divine law calls for mercy and charity.

RULERSHIP AND THE NATURAL LAW

The major concern of rulership is the relationship between the natural law and human law. The reasonableness of human law involves its consistency with the natural law, which means that its formal promulgation (made public) and its direction at the common good ensure the peace and the welfare of the community. The ruler's purpose is to discover the natural law by reason and practically apply the natural law to existing conditions. By **nature**—that is, by an intrinsic **inclination** or direction within the ruler's mind—the ruler seeks practical ethical and political knowledge about human well-being.

Laws, for Aquinas, are discovered not made. How are the general precepts of natural law discovered? When the ruler has a political problem requiring a decision to be made, he or she has an obligation through **synderesis** to do good and avoid evil. Aquinas states this obligation in these terms: "... good is to be done and promoted and evil is to be avoided." Our practical reason is then moved or enabled: It apprehends the objective principles of natural law, such as human self-preservation and the wrongness of murder, which require society to punish murder in the interest of peace and order. This process is what Aquinas means when he says that humans (in this case rulers) participate in eternal law when they apprehend these objective principles of natural law. Now the actual punishments for the crime are prudently determined.

[11]*Summa Theologica,* I, II, Q. 96, a. 3.

PRIMARY SOURCE 4.2 "NATURAL LAW AND JUSTICE," FROM THE *SUMMA THEOLOGICA*

Whether the Law Is Always Something Directed to the Common Good

I answer that, As stated above (Article [1]), the law belongs to that which is a principle of human acts, because it is their rule and measure. Now as reason is a principle of human acts, so in reason itself there is something which is the principle in respect of all the rest: wherefore to this principle chiefly and mainly law must needs be referred. Now the first principle in practical matters, which are the object of the practical reason, is the last end: and the last end of human life is bliss or happiness, as stated above (Question [2], Article [7]; Question [3], Article [1]). Consequently the law must needs regard principally the relationship to happiness. Moreover, since every part is ordained to the whole, as imperfect to perfect; and since one man is a part of the perfect community, the law must needs regard properly the relationship to universal happiness. Wherefore the Philosopher, in the above definition of legal matters mentions both happiness and the body politic: for he says (Ethic. v, 1) that we call those legal matters "just, which are adapted to produce and preserve happiness and its parts for the body politic": since the state is a perfect community, as he says in Polit. i, 1.

Now in every genus, that which belongs to it chiefly is the principle of the others, and the others belong to that genus in subordination to that thing: thus fire, which is chief among hot things, is the cause of heat in mixed bodies, and these are said to be hot in so far as they have a share of fire. Consequently, since the law is chiefly ordained to the common good, any other precept in regard to some individual work, must needs be devoid of the nature of a law, save in so far as it regards the common good. Therefore every law is ordained to the common good.

Whether the Reason of Any Man Is Competent to Make Laws

I answer that, A law, properly speaking, regards first and foremost the order to the common good. Now to order anything to the common good, belongs either to the whole people, or to someone who is the viceregent of the whole people. And therefore the making of a law belongs either to the whole people or to a public personage who has care of the whole people: since in all other matters the directing of anything to the end concerns him to whom the end belongs.

Whether Promulgation Is Essential to a Law

Objection 1: It would seem that promulgation is not essential to a law. For the natural law above all has the character of law. But the natural law needs no promulgation. Therefore it is not essential to a law that it be promulgated.

Objection 2: Further, it belongs properly to a law to bind one to do or not to do something. But the obligation of fulfilling a law touches not only those in whose presence it is promulgated, but also others. Therefore promulgation is not essential to a law.

On the contrary, It is laid down in the Decretals, dist. 4, that "laws are established when they are promulgated."

I answer that, As stated above (Article [1]), a law is imposed on others by way of a rule and measure. Now a rule or measure is imposed by being applied to those who are to be ruled and measured by it. Wherefore, in order that a law obtain the binding force which is proper to a law, it must needs be applied to the men who have to be ruled by it. Such application is made by its being notified to them by promulgation. Wherefore promulgation is necessary for the law to obtain its force.

Thus from the four preceding articles, the definition of law may be gathered; and it is nothing else than an ordinance of reason for the common good, made by him who has care of the community, and promulgated.

Reply to Objection 1: The natural law is promulgated by the very fact that God instilled it into man's mind so as to be known by him naturally.

Reply to Objection 2: Those who are not present when a law is promulgated, are bound to observe the law, in so far as it is notified or

PRIMARY SOURCE 4.2 | "NATURAL LAW AND JUSTICE," FROM THE *SUMMA THEOLOGICA* *continued*

can be notified to them by others, after it has been promulgated.

Whether the Natural Law Is a Habit

Objection 1: It would seem that the natural law is a habit. Because, as the Philosopher says (Ethic. ii, 5), "there are three things in the soul: power, habit, and passion." But the natural law is not one of the soul's powers: nor is it one of the passions; as we may see by going through them one by one. Therefore the natural law is a habit.

Objection 2: Further, Basil [*Damascene, De Fide Orth. iv, 22] says that the conscience or "synderesis is the law of our mind"; which can only apply to the natural law. But the "synderesis" is a habit, as was shown in the FP, Question [79], Article [12]. Therefore the natural law is a habit.

On the contrary, Augustine says (De Bono Conjug. xxi) that "a habit is that whereby something is done when necessary." But such is not the natural law: since it is in infants and in the damned who cannot act by it. Therefore the natural law is not a habit.

I answer that, A thing may be called a habit in two ways. First, properly and essentially: and thus the natural law is not a habit. For it has been stated above (Question [90], Article [1], ad 2) that the natural law is something appointed by reason, just as a proposition is a work of reason. Now that which a man does is not the same as that whereby he does it: for he makes a becoming speech by the habit of grammar. Since then a habit is that by which we act, a law cannot be a habit properly and essentially.

Secondly, the term habit may be applied to that which we hold by a habit: thus faith may mean that which we hold by faith. And accordingly, since the precepts of the natural law are sometimes considered by reason actually, while sometimes they are in the reason only habitually, in this way the natural law may be called a habit. Thus, in speculative matters, the indemonstrable principles are not the habit itself whereby we hold those principles, but are the principles the habit of which we possess.

Reply to Objection 1: The Philosopher proposes there to discover the genus of virtue; and since it is evident that virtue is a principle of action, he mentions only those things which are principles of human acts, viz. powers, habits and passions. But there are other things in the soul besides these three: there are acts; thus "to will" is in the one that wills; again, things known are in the knower; moreover its own natural properties are in the soul, such as immortality and the like.

Reply to Objection 2: "Synderesis" is said to be the law of our mind, because it is a habit containing the precepts of the natural law, which are the first principles of human actions.

Whether the Natural Law Contains Several Precepts, or Only One

Objection 1: It would seem that the natural law contains, not several precepts, but one only. For law is a kind of precept, as stated above (Question [92], Article [2]). If therefore there were many precepts of the natural law, it would follow that there are also many natural laws.

Objection 2: Further, the natural law is consequent to human nature. But human nature, as a whole, is one; though, as to its parts, it is manifold. Therefore, either there is but one precept of the law of nature, on account of the unity of nature as a whole; or there are many, by reason of the number of parts of human nature. The result would be that even things relating to the inclination of the concupiscible faculty belong to the natural law.

Objection 3: Further, law is something pertaining to reason, as stated above (Question [90], Article [1]). Now reason is but one in man. Therefore there is only one precept of the natural law.

On the contrary, The precepts of the natural law in man stand in relation to practical matters, as the first principles to matters of demonstration. But there are several first indemonstrable principles. Therefore there are also several precepts of the natural law.

I answer that, As stated above (Question [91], Article [3]), the precepts of the natural

continued

PRIMARY SOURCE 4.2 "NATURAL LAW AND JUSTICE," FROM THE *SUMMA THEOLOGICA* *continued*

law are to the practical reason, what the first principles of demonstrations are to the speculative reason; because both are self-evident principles. Now a thing is said to be self-evident in two ways: first, in itself; secondly, in relation to us. Any proposition is said to be self-evident in itself, if its predicate is contained in the notion of the subject: although, to one who knows not the definition of the subject, it happens that such a proposition is not self-evident. For instance, this proposition, "Man is a rational being," is, in its very nature, self-evident, since who says "man," says "a rational being": and yet to one who knows not what a man is, this proposition is not self-evident. Hence it is that, as Boethius says (De Hebdom.), certain axioms or propositions are universally self-evident to all; and such are those propositions whose terms are known to all, as, "Every whole is greater than its part," and, "Things equal to one and the same are equal to one another." But some propositions are self-evident only to the wise, who understand the meaning of the terms of such propositions: thus to one who understands that an angel is not a body, it is self-evident that an angel is not circumscriptively in a place: but this is not evident to the unlearned, for they cannot grasp it.

Now a certain order is to be found in those things that are apprehended universally. For that which, before aught else, falls under apprehension, is "being," the notion of which is included in all things whatsoever a man apprehends. Wherefore the first indemonstrable principle is that "the same thing cannot be affirmed and denied at the same time," which is based on the notion of "being" and "not-being": and on this principle all others are based, as is stated in Metaph. iv, text. 9. Now as "being" is the first thing that falls under the apprehension simply, so "good" is the first thing that falls under the apprehension of the practical reason, which is directed to action: since every agent acts for an end under the aspect of good. Consequently the first principle of practical reason is one founded on the notion of good, viz. that "good is that which all things seek after." Hence this is the first precept of law, that "good is to be done and pursued, and evil is to be avoided." All other precepts of the natural law are based upon this: so that whatever the practical reason naturally apprehends as man's good (or evil) belongs to the precepts of the natural law as something to be done or avoided.

Since, however, good has the nature of an end, and evil, the nature of a contrary, hence it is that all those things to which man has a natural inclination, are naturally apprehended by reason as being good, and consequently as objects of pursuit, and their contraries as evil, and objects of avoidance. Wherefore according to the order of natural inclinations, is the order of the precepts of the natural law. Because in man there is first of all an inclination to good in accordance with the nature which he has in common with all substances: inasmuch as every substance seeks the preservation of its own being, according to its nature: and by reason of this inclination, whatever is a means of preserving human life, and of warding off its obstacles, belongs to the natural law. Secondly, there is in man an inclination to things that pertain to him more specially, according to that nature which he has in common with other animals: and in virtue of this inclination, those things are said to belong to the natural law, "which nature has taught to all animals" [*Pandect. Just. I, tit. i], such as sexual intercourse, education of offspring, and so forth. Thirdly, there is in man an inclination to good, according to the nature of his reason, which nature is proper to him: thus man has a natural inclination to know the truth about God, and to live in society: and in this respect, whatever pertains to this inclination belongs to the natural law; for instance, to shun ignorance, to avoid offending those among whom one has to live, and other such things regarding the above inclination.

Reply to Objection 1: All these precepts of the law of nature have the character of one natural law, inasmuch as they flow from one first precept.

Reply to Objection 2: All the inclinations of any parts whatsoever of human nature, e.g. of

PRIMARY SOURCE 4.2 | "NATURAL LAW AND JUSTICE," FROM THE *SUMMA THEOLOGICA* *continued*

the concupiscible and irascible parts, in so far as they are ruled by reason, belong to the natural law, and are reduced to one first precept, as stated above: so that the precepts of the natural law are many in themselves, but are based on one common foundation.

Reply to Objection 3: Although reason is one in itself, yet it directs all things regarding man; so that whatever can be ruled by reason, is contained under the law of reason.

Whether All Acts of Virtue Are Prescribed by the Natural Law

Objection 1: It would seem that not all acts of virtue are prescribed by the natural law. Because, as stated above (Question [90], Article [2]) it is essential to a law that it be ordained to the common good. But some acts of virtue are ordained to the private good of the individual, as is evident especially in regards to acts of temperance. Therefore not all acts of virtue are the subject of natural law.

Objection 2: Further, every sin is opposed to some virtuous act. If therefore all acts of virtue are prescribed by the natural law, it seems to follow that all sins are against nature: whereas this applies to certain special sins.

Objection 3: Further, those things which are according to nature are common to all. But acts of virtue are not common to all: since a thing is virtuous in one, and vicious in another. Therefore not all acts of virtue are prescribed by the natural law.

On the contrary, Damascene says (De Fide Orth. iii, 4) that "virtues are natural." Therefore virtuous acts also are a subject of the natural law.

I answer that, We may speak of virtuous acts in two ways: first, under the aspect of virtuous; secondly, as such and such acts considered in their proper species. If then we speak of acts of virtue, considered as virtuous, thus all virtuous acts belong to the natural law. For it has been stated (Article [2]) that to the natural law belongs everything to which a man is inclined according to his nature. Now each thing is inclined naturally to an operation that is suitable to it according to its form: thus fire is inclined to give heat. Wherefore, since the rational soul is the proper form of man, there is in every man a natural inclination to act according to reason: and this is to act according to virtue. Consequently, considered thus, all acts of virtue are prescribed by the natural law: since each one's reason naturally dictates to him to act virtuously. But if we speak of virtuous acts, considered in themselves, i.e. in their proper species, thus not all virtuous acts are prescribed by the natural law: for many things are done virtuously, to which nature does not incline at first; but which, through the inquiry of reason, have been found by men to be conducive to well-living.

Reply to Objection 1: Temperance is about the natural concupiscences of food, drink, and sexual matters, which are indeed ordained to the natural common good, just as other matters of law are ordained to the moral common good.

Reply to Objection 2: By human nature we may mean either that which is proper to man—and in this sense all sins, as being against reason, are also against nature, as Damascene states (De Fide Orth. ii, 30): or we may mean that nature which is common to man and other animals; and in this sense, certain special sins are said to be against nature; thus contrary to sexual intercourse, which is natural to all animals, is unisexual lust, which has received the special name of the unnatural crime.

Reply to Objection 3: This argument considers acts in themselves. For it is owing to the various conditions of men, that certain acts are virtuous for some, as being proportionate and becoming to them, while they are vicious for others, as being out of proportion to them.

Whether the Natural Law Is the Same in All Men

Objection 1: It would seem that the natural law is not the same in all. For it is stated in the Decretals (Dist. i) that "the natural law is that which is contained in the Law and the Gospel." But this is not common to all men; because, as it is written (Rm. 10:16), "all do not obey the

continued

gospel." Therefore the natural law is not the same in all men.

Objection 2: Further, "Things which are according to the law are said to be just," as stated in Ethic. v. But it is stated in the same book that nothing is so universally just as not to be subject to change in regard to some men. Therefore even the natural law is not the same in all men.

Objection 3: Further, as stated above (Articles [2], 3), to the natural law belongs everything to which a man is inclined according to his nature. Now different men are naturally inclined to different things; some to the desire of pleasures, others to the desire of honors, and other men to other things. Therefore there is not one natural law for all.

On the contrary, Isidore says (Etym. v, 4), "The natural law is common to all nations."

I answer that, As stated above (Articles [2], 3), to the natural law belongs those things to which a man is inclined naturally: and among these it is proper to man to be inclined to act according to reason. Now the process of reason is from the common to the proper, as stated in Phys. i. The speculative reason, however, is differently situated in this matter, from the practical reason. For, since the speculative reason is busied chiefly with the necessary things, which cannot be otherwise than they are, its proper conclusions, like the universal principles, contain the truth without fail. The practical reason, on the other hand, is busied with contingent matters, about which human actions are concerned: and consequently, although there is necessity in the general principles, the more we descend to matters of detail, the more frequently we encounter defects. Accordingly then in speculative matters truth is the same in all men, both as to principles and as to conclusions: although the truth is not known to all as regards the conclusions, but only as regards the principles which are called common notions. But in matters of action, truth, or practical rectitude is not the same for all, as to matters of detail, but only as to the general principles: and where there is the same rectitude in matters of detail, it is not equally known to all.

It is therefore evident that, as regards the general principles whether of speculative or of practical reason, truth or rectitude is the same for all, and is equally known by all. As to the proper conclusions of the speculative reason, the truth is the same for all, but is not equally known to all: thus it is true for all that the three angles of a triangle are together equal to two right angles, although it is not known to all. But as to the proper conclusions of the practical reason, neither is the truth or rectitude the same for all, nor, where it is the same, is it equally known by all. Thus it is right and true for all to act according to reason: and from this principle it follows as a proper conclusion, that goods entrusted to another should be restored to their owner. Now this is true for the majority of cases: but it may happen in a particular case that it would be injurious, and therefore unreasonable, to restore goods held in trust; for instance, if they are claimed for the purpose of fighting against one's country. And this principle will be found to fail the more, according as we descend further into detail, e.g. if one were to say that goods held in trust should be restored with such and such a guarantee, or in such and such a way; because the greater the number of conditions added, the greater the number of ways in which the principle may fail, so that it be not right to restore or not to restore.

Consequently we must say that the natural law, as to general principles, is the same for all, both as to rectitude and as to knowledge. But as to certain matters of detail, which are conclusions, as it were, of those general principles, it is the same for all in the majority of cases, both as to rectitude and as to knowledge; and yet in some few cases it may fail, both as to rectitude, by reason of certain obstacles (just as natures subject to generation and corruption fail in some few cases on account of some obstacle), and as to knowledge, since in some the reason is perverted by passion, or evil habit, or an evil disposition of nature; thus formerly, theft, although it is expressly contrary to the natural law, was not considered wrong among the Germans, as Julius Caesar relates (De Bello Gall. vi).

PRIMARY SOURCE 4.2 | "NATURAL LAW AND JUSTICE," FROM THE *SUMMA THEOLOGICA* *continued*

Reply to Objection 1: The meaning of the sentence quoted is not that whatever is contained in the Law and the Gospel belongs to the natural law, since they contain many things that are above nature; but that whatever belongs to the natural law is fully contained in them. Wherefore Gratian, after saying that "the natural law is what is contained in the Law and the Gospel," adds at once, by way of example, "by which everyone is commanded to do to others as he would be done by."

Reply to Objection 2: The saying of the Philosopher is to be understood of things that are naturally just, not as general principles, but as conclusions drawn from them, having rectitude in the majority of cases, but failing in a few.

Reply to Objection 3: As, in man, reason rules and commands the other powers, so all the natural inclinations belonging to the other powers must needs be directed according to reason. Wherefore it is universally right for all men, that all their inclinations should be directed according to reason.

Whether the Natural Law Can Be Changed

Objection 1: It would seem that the natural law can be changed. Because on Ecclus. 17:9, "He gave them instructions, and the law of life," the gloss says, "He wished the law of the letter to be written, in order to correct the law of nature." But that which is corrected is changed. Therefore the natural law can be changed.

Objection 2: Further, the slaying of the innocent, adultery, and theft are against the natural law. But we find these things changed by God: as when God commanded Abraham to slay his innocent son (Gn. 22:2); and when he ordered the Jews to borrow and purloin the vessels of the Egyptians (Ex. 12:35); and when He commanded Osee to take to himself "a wife of fornications" (Osee 1:2). Therefore the natural law can be changed.

Objection 3: Further, Isidore says (Etym. 5:4) that "the possession of all things in common, and universal freedom, are matters of natural law." But these things are seen to be changed by human laws. Therefore it seems that the natural law is subject to change.

On the contrary, It is said in the Decretals (Dist. v), "The natural law dates from the creation of the rational creature. It does not vary according to time, but remains unchangeable."

I answer that, A change in the natural law may be understood in two ways. First, by way of addition. In this sense nothing hinders the natural law from being changed: since many things for the benefit of human life have been added over and above the natural law, both by the Divine law and by human laws.

Secondly, a change in the natural law may be understood by way of subtraction, so that what previously was according to the natural law, ceases to be so. In this sense, the natural law is altogether unchangeable in its first principles: but in its secondary principles, which, as we have said (Article [4]), are certain detailed proximate conclusions drawn from the first principles, the natural law is not changed so that what it prescribes be not right in most cases. But it may be changed in some particular cases of rare occurrence, through some special causes hindering the observance of such precepts, as stated above (Article [4]).

Reply to Objection 1: The written law is said to be given for the correction of the natural law, either because it supplies what was wanting to the natural law; or because the natural law was perverted in the hearts of some men, as to certain matters, so that they esteemed those things good which are naturally evil; which perversion stood in need of correction.

Reply to Objection 2: All men alike, both guilty and innocent, die the death of nature: which death of nature is inflicted by the power of God on account of original sin, according to 1 Kgs. 2:6: "The Lord killeth and maketh alive." Consequently, by the command of God, death can be inflicted on any man, guilty or innocent, without any injustice whatever. In like manner adultery is intercourse with another's wife; who is allotted to him by the law emanating from God. Consequently intercourse with any woman, by the command of God, is neither adultery nor

continued

fornication. The same applies to theft, which is the taking of another's property. For whatever is taken by the command of God, to Whom all things belong, is not taken against the will of its owner, whereas it is in this that theft consists. Nor is it only in human things, that whatever is commanded by God is right; but also in natural things, whatever is done by God, is, in some way, natural, as stated in the FP, Question [105], Article [6], ad 1.

Reply to Objection 3: A thing is said to belong to the natural law in two ways. First, because nature inclines thereto: e.g. that one should not do harm to another. Secondly, because nature did not bring in the contrary: thus we might say that for man to be naked is of the natural law, because nature did not give him clothes, but art invented them. In this sense, "the possession of all things in common and universal freedom" are said to be of the natural law, because, to wit, the distinction of possessions and slavery were not brought in by nature, but devised by human reason for the benefit of human life. Accordingly the law of nature was not changed in this respect, except by addition.

Whether the Law of Nature Can Be Abolished from the Heart of Man

Objection 1: It would seem that the natural law can be abolished from the heart of man. Because on Rm. 2:14, "When the Gentiles who have not the law," etc. a gloss says that "the law of righteousness, which sin had blotted out, is graven on the heart of man when he is restored by grace." But the law of righteousness is the law of nature. Therefore the law of nature can be blotted out.

Objection 2: Further, the law of grace is more efficacious than the law of nature. But the law of grace is blotted out by sin. Much more therefore can the law of nature be blotted out.

Objection 3: Further, that which is established by law is made just. But many things are enacted by men, which are contrary to the law of nature. Therefore the law of nature can be abolished from the heart of man.

On the contrary, Augustine says (Confess. ii): "Thy law is written in the hearts of men, which iniquity itself effaces not." But the law which is written in men's hearts is the natural law. Therefore the natural law cannot be blotted out.

I answer that, As stated above (Articles [4], 5), there belong to the natural law, first, certain most general precepts, that are known to all; and secondly, certain secondary and more detailed precepts, which are, as it were, conclusions following closely from first principles. As to those general principles, the natural law, in the abstract, can be blotted out from men's hearts. But it is blotted out in the case of a particular action, in so far as reason is hindered from applying the general principle to a particular point of practice, on account of concupiscence or some other passion, as stated above (Question [77], Article [2]). But as to the other, i.e. the secondary precepts, the natural law can be blotted out from the human heart, either by evil persuasions, just as in speculative matters errors occur in respect of necessary conclusions; or by vicious customs and corrupt habits, as among some men, theft, and even unnatural vices, as the Apostle states (Rm. i), were not esteemed sinful.

Reply to Objection 1: Sin blots out the law of nature in particular cases, not universally, except perchance in regard to the secondary precepts of the natural law, in the way stated above.

Reply to Objection 2: Although grace is more efficacious than nature, yet nature is more essential to man, and therefore more enduring.

Reply to Objection 3: This argument is true of the secondary precepts of the natural law, against which some legislators have framed certain enactments which are unjust.

Whether It Was Useful for Laws to Be Framed by Men

Objection 1: It would seem that it was not useful for laws to be framed by men. Because the purpose of every law is that man be made good

PRIMARY SOURCE 4.2 | "NATURAL LAW AND JUSTICE," FROM THE *SUMMA THEOLOGICA* *continued*

thereby, as stated above (Question [92], Article [1]). But men are more to be induced to be good willingly by means of admonitions, than against their will, by means of laws. Therefore there was no need to frame laws.

Objection 2: Further, as the Philosopher says (Ethic. v, 4), "men have recourse to a judge as to animate justice." But animate justice is better than inanimate justice, which is contained in laws. Therefore it would have been better for the execution of justice to be entrusted to the decision of judges, than to frame laws in addition.

Objection 3: Further, every law is framed for the direction of human actions, as is evident from what has been stated above (Question [90], Articles [1], 2). But since human actions are about singulars, which are infinite in number, matter pertaining to the direction of human actions cannot be taken into sufficient consideration except by a wise man, who looks into each one of them. Therefore it would have been better for human acts to be directed by the judgment of wise men, than by the framing of laws. Therefore there was no need of human laws.

On the contrary, Isidore says (Etym. v, 20), "Laws were made that in fear thereof human audacity might be held in check, that innocence might be safeguarded in the midst of wickedness, and that the dread of punishment might prevent the wicked from doing harm." But these things are most necessary to mankind. Therefore it was necessary that human laws should be made.

I answer that, As stated above (Question [63], Article [1]; Question [94], Article [3]), man has a natural aptitude for virtue; but the perfection of virtue must be acquired by man by means of some kind of training. Thus we observe that man is helped by industry in his necessities, for instance, in food and clothing. Certain beginnings of these he has from nature, viz. his reason and his hands; but he has not the full complement, as other animals have, to whom nature has given sufficiency of clothing and food. Now it is difficult to see how man could suffice for himself in the matter of this training: since the perfection of virtue consists chiefly in withdrawing man from undue pleasures, to which above all man is inclined, and especially the young, who are more capable of being trained. Consequently a man needs to receive this training from another, whereby to arrive at the perfection of virtue. And as to those young people who are inclined to acts of virtue, by their good natural disposition, or by custom, or rather by the gift of God, paternal training suffices, which is by admonitions. But since some are found to be depraved, and prone to vice, and not easily amenable to words, it was necessary for such to be restrained from evil by force and fear, in order that, at least, they might desist from evil-doing, and leave others in peace, and that they themselves, by being habituated in this way, might be brought to do willingly what hitherto they did from fear, and thus become virtuous. Now this kind of training, which compels through fear of punishment, is the discipline of laws. Therefore in order that man might have peace and virtue, it was necessary for laws to be framed: for, as the Philosopher says (Polit. i, 2), "as man is the most noble of animals if he be perfect in virtue, so is he the lowest of all, if he be severed from law and righteousness"; because man can use his reason to devise means of satisfying his lusts and evil passions, which other animals are unable to do.

Reply to Objection 1: Men who are well disposed are led willingly to virtue by being admonished better than by coercion: but men who are evilly disposed are not led to virtue unless they are compelled.

Reply to Objection 2: As the Philosopher says (Rhet. i, 1), "it is better that all things be regulated by law, than left to be decided by judges": and this for three reasons. First, because it is easier to find a few wise men competent to frame right laws, than to find the many who would be necessary to judge a right of each single case. Secondly, because those who make laws consider long beforehand what laws to make; whereas judgment on each single case has to be pronounced as soon as it arises: and it is easier for man to see what is right, by taking many instances into consideration, than by

continued

PRIMARY SOURCE 4.2

"Natural Law and Justice," from the *Summa Theologica* *continued*

considering one solitary fact. Thirdly, because lawgivers judge in the abstract and of future events; whereas those who sit in judgment of things present, toward which they are affected by love, hatred, or some kind of cupidity; wherefore their judgment is perverted.

Since then the animated justice of the judge is not found in every man, and since it can be deflected, therefore it was necessary, whenever possible, for the law to determine how to judge, and for very few matters to be left to the decision of men.

Reply to Objection 3: Certain individual facts which cannot be covered by the law "have necessarily to be committed to judges," as the Philosopher says in the same passage: for instance, "concerning something that has happened or not happened," and the like.

Whether Every Human Law Is Derived from the Natural Law

Objection 1: It would seem that not every human law is derived from the natural law. For the Philosopher says (Ethic. v, 7) that "the legal just is that which originally was a matter of indifference." But those things which arise from the natural law are not matters of indifference. Therefore the enactments of human laws are not derived from the natural law.

Objection 2: Further, positive law is contrasted with natural law, as stated by Isidore (Etym. v, 4) and the Philosopher (Ethic. v, 7). But those things which flow as conclusions from the general principles of the natural law belong to the natural law, as stated above (Question [94], Article [4]). Therefore that which is established by human law does not belong to the natural law.

Objection 3: Further, the law of nature is the same for all; since the Philosopher says (Ethic. v, 7) that "the natural just is that which is equally valid everywhere." If therefore human laws were derived from the natural law, it would follow that they too are the same for all: which is clearly false.

Objection 4: Further, it is possible to give a reason for things which are derived from the natural law. But "it is not possible to give the reason for all the legal enactments of the lawgivers," as the jurist says [*Pandect. Justin. lib. i, ff, tit. iii, v; De Leg. et Senat.]. Therefore not all human laws are derived from the natural law.

On the contrary, Tully says (Rhet. ii), "Things which emanated from nature and were approved by custom, were sanctioned by fear and reverence for the laws."

I answer that, As Augustine says (De Lib. Arb. i, 5), "that which is not just seems to be no law at all": wherefore the force of a law depends on the extent of its justice. Now in human affairs a thing is said to be just, from being right, according to the rule of reason. But the first rule of reason is the law of nature, as is clear from what has been stated above (Question [91], Article [2], ad 2). Consequently every human law has just so much of the nature of law, as it is derived from the law of nature. But if in any point it deflects from the law of nature, it is no longer a law but a perversion of law.

But it must be noted that something may be derived from the natural law in two ways: first, as a conclusion from premises, secondly, by way of determination of certain generalities. The first way is like to that by which, in sciences, demonstrated conclusions are drawn from the principles: while the second mode is likened to that whereby, in the arts, general forms are particularized as to details: thus the craftsman needs to determine the general form of a house to some particular shape. Some things are therefore derived from the general principles of the natural law, by way of conclusions; e.g. that "one must not kill" may be derived as a conclusion from the principle that "one should do harm to no man": while some are derived therefrom by way of determination; e.g. the law of nature has it that the evil-doer should be punished; but that he be punished in this or that way, is a determination of the law of nature.

Accordingly both modes of derivation are found in the human law. But those things which are derived in the first way, are

PRIMARY SOURCE 4.2 | "NATURAL LAW AND JUSTICE," FROM THE *SUMMA THEOLOGICA* *continued*

contained in human law not as emanating therefrom exclusively, but have some force from the natural law also. But those things which are derived in the second way, have no other force than that of human law.

Reply to Objection 1: The Philosopher is speaking of those enactments which are by way of determination or specification of the precepts of the natural law.

Reply to Objection 2: This argument avails for those things that are derived from the natural law, by way of conclusions.

Reply to Objection 3: The general principles of the natural law cannot be applied to all men in the same way on account of the great variety of human affairs: and hence arises the diversity of positive laws among various people.

Reply to Objection 4: These words of the Jurist are to be understood as referring to decisions of rulers in determining particular points of the natural law: on which determinations the judgment of expert and prudent men is based as on its principles; in so far, to wit, as they see at once what is the best thing to decide.

Hence the Philosopher says (Ethic. vi, 11) that in such matters, "we ought to pay as much attention to the undemonstrated sayings and opinions of persons who surpass us in experience, age and prudence, as to their demonstrations."

Whether Human Law Should Be Framed for the Community Rather Than for the Individual

I answer that, Whatever is for an end should be proportionate to that end. Now the end of law is the common good; because, as Isidore says (Etym. v, 21) that "law should be framed, not for any private benefit, but for the common good of all the citizens." Hence human laws should be proportionate to the common good. Now the common good comprises many things. Wherefore law should take account of many things, as to persons, as to matters, and as to times. Because the community of the state is composed of many persons; and its good is procured by many actions; nor is it established to endure for only a short time, but to last for all time by the citizens succeeding one another, as Augustine says (De Civ. Dei ii, 21; xxii, 6).

Whether It Belongs to the Human Law to Repress All Vices

Objection 1: It would seem that it belongs to human law to repress all vices. For Isidore says (Etym. v, 20) that "laws were made in order that, in fear thereof, man's audacity might be held in check." But it would not be held in check sufficiently, unless all evils were repressed by law. Therefore human laws should repress all evils.

Objection 2: Further, the intention of the lawgiver is to make the citizens virtuous. But a man cannot be virtuous unless he forbear from all kinds of vice. Therefore it belongs to human law to repress all vices.

Objection 3: Further, human law is derived from the natural law, as stated above (Question [95], Article [2]). But all vices are contrary to the law of nature. Therefore human law should repress all vices.

On the contrary, We read in De Lib. Arb. i, 5: "It seems to me that the law which is written for the governing of the people rightly permits these things, and that Divine providence punishes them." But Divine providence punishes nothing but vices. Therefore human law rightly allows some vices, by not repressing them.

I answer that, As stated above (Question [90], Articles [1], 2), law is framed as a rule or measure of human acts. Now a measure should be homogeneous with that which it measures, as stated in Metaph. x, text. 3,4, since different things are measured by different measures. Wherefore laws imposed on men should also be in keeping with their condition, for, as Isidore says (Etym. v, 21), law should be "possible both according to nature, and according to the customs of the country." Now possibility or faculty of action is due to an interior habit or disposition: since the same thing is not possible to one who has not a virtuous habit, as is possible to one who has. Thus the same is not

continued

possible to a child as to a full-grown man: for which reason the law for children is not the same as for adults, since many things are permitted to children, which in an adult are punished by law or at any rate are open to blame. In like manner many things are permissible to men not perfect in virtue, which would be intolerable in a virtuous man.

Now human law is framed for a number of human beings, the majority of whom are not perfect in virtue. Wherefore human laws do not forbid all vices, from which the virtuous abstain, but only the more grievous vices, from which it is possible for the majority to abstain; and chiefly those that are to the hurt of others, without the prohibition of which human society could not be maintained: thus human law prohibits murder, theft, and such like.

Reply to Objection 1: Audacity seems to refer to the assailing of others. Consequently it belongs to those sins chiefly whereby one's neighbor is injured: and these sins are forbidden by human law, as stated.

Reply to Objection 2: The purpose of human law is to lead men to virtue, not suddenly, but gradually. Wherefore it does not lay upon the multitude of imperfect men the burdens of those who are already virtuous, viz. that they should abstain from all evil. Otherwise these imperfect ones, being unable to bear such precepts, would break out into yet greater evils: thus it is written (Pr. 30:33): "He that violently bloweth his nose, bringeth out blood"; and (Mt. 9:17) that if "new wine," i.e. precepts of a perfect life, "is put into old bottles," i.e. into imperfect men, "the bottles break, and the wine runneth out," i.e. the precepts are despised, and those men, from contempt, break into evils worse still.

Reply to Objection 3: The natural law is a participation in us of the eternal law: while human law falls short of the eternal law. Now Augustine says (De Lib. Arb. i, 5), "The law which is framed for the government of states, allows and leaves unpunished many things that are punished by Divine providence. Nor, if this law does not attempt to do everything, is this a reason why it should be blamed for what it does." Wherefore, too, human law does not prohibit everything that is forbidden by the natural law.

Whether Human Law Binds a Man in Conscience

Objection 1: It would seem that human law does not bind man in conscience. For an inferior power has no jurisdiction in a court of higher power. But the power of man, which frames human law, is beneath the Divine power. Therefore human law cannot impose its precept in a Divine court, such as is the court of conscience.

Objection 2: Further, the judgment of conscience depends chiefly on the commandments of God. But sometimes God's commandments are made void by human laws, according to Mt. 15:6: "You have made void the commandment of God for your tradition." Therefore human law does not bind a man in conscience.

Objection 3: Further, human laws often bring loss of character and injury on man, according to Is. 10:1 et seq.: "Woe to them that make wicked laws, and when they write, write injustice; to oppress the poor in judgment, and do violence to the cause of the humble of My people." But it is lawful for anyone to avoid oppression and violence. Therefore human laws do not bind man in conscience.

On the contrary, It is written (1 Pt. 2:19), "This is thankworthy, if the conscience . . . a man endure sorrows, suffering wrongfully."

I answer that, Laws framed by man are either just or unjust. If they be just, they have the power of binding in conscience, from the eternal law whence they are derived, according to Prov. 8:15: "By Me kings reign, and lawgivers decree just things." Now laws are said to be just, both from the end, when, to wit, they are ordained to the common good—and from their author, that is to say, when the law that is made does not exceed the power of the lawgiver—and from their form, when, to wit, burdens are laid on the subjects, according to an equality of proportion and with a view to the common good.

PRIMARY SOURCE 4.2 | "NATURAL LAW AND JUSTICE," FROM THE *SUMMA THEOLOGICA* *continued*

For, since one man is a part of the community, each man in all that he is and has, belongs to the community; just as a part, in all that it is, belongs to the whole; wherefore nature inflicts a loss on the part, in order to save the whole: so that on this account, such laws as these, which impose proportionate burdens, are just and binding in conscience, and are legal laws.

On the other hand laws may be unjust in two ways: first, by being contrary to human good, through being opposed to the things mentioned above—either in respect of the end, as when an authority imposes on his subjects burdensome laws, conducive, not to the common good, but rather to his own cupidity or vainglory—or in respect of the author, as when a man makes a law that goes beyond the power committed to him—or in respect of the form, as when burdens are imposed unequally on the community, although with a view to the common good. The like are acts of violence rather than laws; because, as Augustine says (De Lib. Arb. i, 5), "a law that is not just, seems to be no law at all." Wherefore such laws do not bind in conscience, except perhaps in order to avoid scandal or disturbance, for which cause a man should even yield his right, according to Mt. 5:40,41: "If a man . . . take away thy coat, let go thy cloak also unto him; and whosoever will force thee one mile, go with him other two."

Secondly, laws may be unjust through being opposed to the Divine good: such are the laws of tyrants inducing to idolatry, or to anything else contrary to the Divine law: and laws of this kind must nowise be observed, because, as stated in Acts 5:29, "we ought to obey God rather than man."

Reply to Objection 1: As the Apostle says (Rm. 13:1,2), all human power is from God . . . "therefore he that resisteth the power," in matters that are within its scope, "resisteth the ordinance of God"; so that he becomes guilty according to his conscience.

Reply to Objection 2: This argument is true of laws that are contrary to the commandments of God, which is beyond the scope of (human) power. Wherefore in such matters human law should not be obeyed.

Reply to Objection 3: This argument is true of a law that inflicts unjust hurt on its subjects. The power that man holds from God does not extend to this: wherefore neither in such matters is man bound to obey the law, provided he avoid giving scandal or inflicting a more grievous hurt.

The ruler must be experienced; familiar with the relevant facts of the social, economic, and political problem of crime in a particular society; and teachable in terms of the complexity of the problem in order to establish a just or reasonable set of laws of punishment. For example, the best or most reasonable law of punishment of wrongdoers should include an analysis of the efficacy of various types of sanctions, the impact of certain kinds of punishments on the larger community, any extenuating circumstances that may be present in a particular case, and so forth. Murder is always objectively wrong; the proper punishment requires practical decision making. This whole process is what Aquinas means by *law*.

Aquinas did not view natural law as a comprehensive and specific code of rules and regulations; it sets forth only general precepts to guide human moral and political action. Their application may vary as changing conditions require. Although natural law is unchangeable, its practical application varies to some degree in concrete circumstances. We recall that the most general principle of natural law is the principle of synderesis: "Good is to be done, and evil is to be avoided." We must reflect on what the human good is, how we can flourish, and how it is realized in each particular moral and political situation of natural law in which we find ourselves.

PRIMARY SOURCE 4.3

17 Essentials of The Political Philosophy of Aquinas

James V. Schall

Thomas Aquinas put things succinctly. He found numberless things about which to think. He could, with few words, illuminate the whole of what is in logical form. He wrote little about political things. He discussed other topics normally called "political"—property, rebellion, prudence, justice, virtue, and common good. In commenting on the Gospels of Matthew and John, he spoke of the death of Christ and the things of Caesar.

Here, in propositional form, is what Aquinas held about political things. Presenting them this way gives, I hope, some overall view of where Aquinas' thought leads.

(1) A human being, body and soul, is a single person, created for his own sake, with a destiny that transcends and therefore limits any political order. (2) Man is and remains naturally a political animal. (3) A state (polity) is an established relationship existing among real human beings, outlining the order of action, especially free actions, toward one another. (4) The highest end of man is thus not political. The political can and should provide "happiness," usually called "temporal." No actual polity is perfect. Often it contains laws or customs militating against the human good.

(5) Human happiness consists in the activities of the virtues, the objects of which are our fears, pleasures, relation to others, property, wit, anger, and speech. Each person is responsible for his own self-rule. (6) Every action has an accompanying proper pleasure. Pleasure as such is never wrong, only its experience when out of order. It is designed to foster and enhance the goods that are given to us. (7) The forms of rule correspond to the order or disorder of souls. Polities reflect the habitual choices of the citizens, their self-definition of what they consider to be virtue or vice. Modern notions that the soul is only formed by the polity deny the basis and origin of vitality and action in the public order. (8) Law, defined as "the ordination of reason, for the common good, by the proper authority, and promulgated," is the context in which Aquinas discusses most political things. An unreasonable law is no law, as Aquinas cites from Augustine; it lacks one or more elements of this definition.

(9) A thing can be an end that itself becomes a means to a further end. Thus, the polity is an end, but it ordains those within it to a higher purpose. The polity does not itself define this higher purpose, but only recognizes it. (10) A polity needs to contain within itself at least some who are wholly oriented to what is beyond politics. All members of any existing polity are intended for a transcendent destiny. The presence of contemplatives and philosophers within any society is necessary for its well-being. (11) The life of politics is worthy but dangerous. The Fall is a factor in each individual life, including that of the politician. His virtues are prudence and justice; however, legal justice brings all virtues under the purview of the polity.

(12) The majority of men are not perfect. Therefore the law should not be more strict than the majority of ordinary men can observe. (13) Law ought to be a standard of what is right or wrong even if it is not fully observed. (14) Virtue is not simply following the letter of the law; it is normally more strict or noble than what the law defines. (15) Aquinas holds that private property is the best way to meet the purposes for which the world is given—i.e., that the generality of men can provide for themselves.

(16) Revelation is given so that ordinary men can do what is right and necessary both for their own salvation and, indirectly, for the good of the polity. (17) Revelation addresses reason. Reason will only recognize this address provided reason has already formulated genuine questions that it has asked itself and attempted to answer.

Aquinas presents several examples of the **general precepts** that flow from or are based on the principle of synderesis. Rational reflection and deliberations on our human fulfillment include the following:

- Human well-being is such that humans tend toward self-preservation. Our tendencies to protect ourselves require the protections of national security or housing, which are general precepts of natural law.
- Humans are inclined to propagate the species, so family life must be protected.
- Humans as rational beings naturally desire or tend to obtain knowledge. Here the natural law general precept is that humans should seek education.
- Humans are naturally inclined to be socially or communally dependent. We should live in societies based on the division of labor as a general precept of natural law.
- Caring for and protecting children forms the natural law general precept of monogamy.

Legitimate rulers must act prudently in effecting particular determinations or positive laws based on the general precepts of natural law.

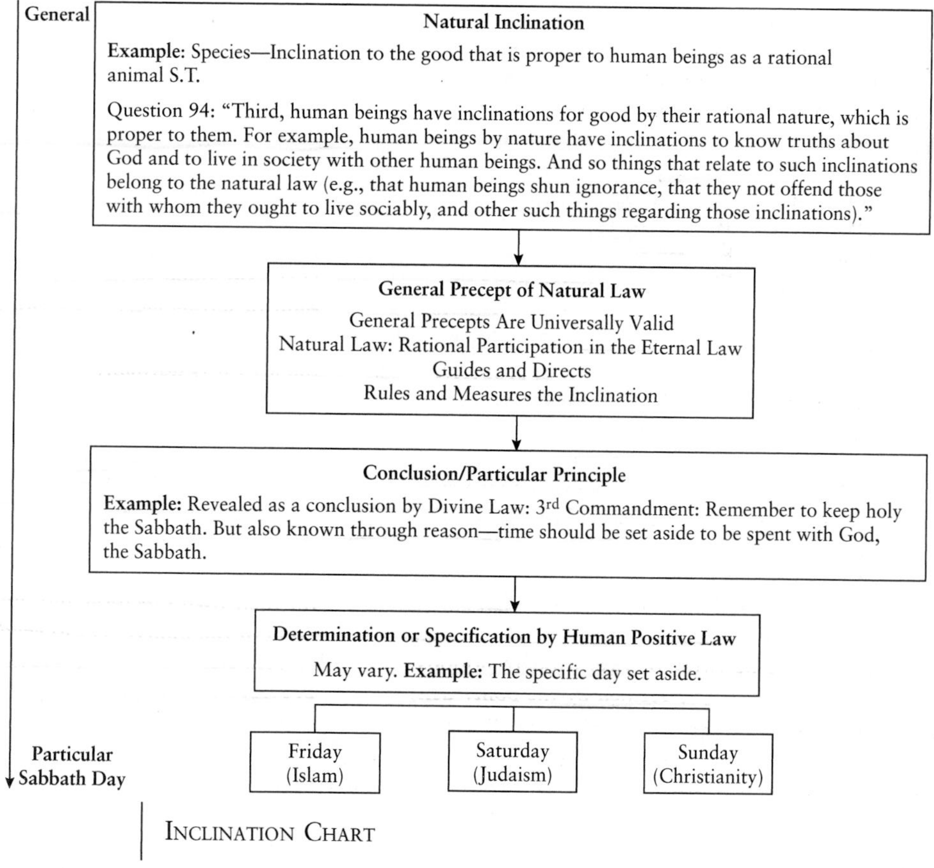

INCLINATION CHART

QUESTIONS FOR REFLECTION

When Martin Luther King was arrested in 1963 during his protests in Birmingham, Alabama, against its segregated social system, he found himself in jail reflecting on the question of how one knows when a law is just or unjust. All of the major clergy in Birmingham urged him to oppose the laws but not break them. The result of his reflections was his letter to the Birmingham clergy known as the "Letter from a Birmingham City Jail." He used Aquinas' teaching to justify civil disobedience:

> How does one determine when a law is just or unjust? A just law is a man-made code that squares with the moral law or the law of God. An unjust law is a code that is out of harmony with the moral law. To put it in the terms of St. Thomas Aquinas, an unjust law is a human law that is not rooted in eternal and natural law. Any law that uplifts human personality is just. Any law that degrades human personality is unjust. I think that we all have moral obligations to obey just laws. On the other hand, I think that we have moral obligations to disobey unjust laws because noncooperation with evil is just as much moral obligation as cooperation with good.[12]

Do you think that all or most human beings are capable of knowing these transcendent moral laws? Is a magnanimous and prudent leader like Dr. King absolutely necessary for principled civil disobedience to take place?

[12]Cited in Michael P. Smith and Kenneth L. Deutsch (eds.), *Political Obligation and Civil Disobedience* (New York: Crowell), pp. 56–57.

Apprehending and applying the Natural Law in the case of Sabbath observance: From Natural Inclination, to General Precept, to Conclusion, to Determination by Human Law.

In summary of Aquinas, then, human law is just and reasonable only if it meets five criteria:

1. It must be promulgated (or ordained) by a legitimate ruler for the common good—lawmaking must be transparent.
2. It must not exceed the authorized power of the lawgiver in a particular society.
3. It must lay only reasonable burdens on subjects according to the equality of proportion (such as a graduated income tax based on the ability to pay).
4. It must be consistent with the principles of **subsidiarity**: The lowest unit of society that is capable of accomplishing a needed social function in an adequate manner should be permitted to perform that function (from the family, to the local community, up to the centralized state). This preserves the vitality of the family, private groups, and local communities as well as the centralized state.
5. It must not be opposed to eternal law.

Any statute or rule that violates any of these criteria is unjust and does not "bind one in conscience." Rulers enacting statutes or rules must know and apply the general criteria for just laws, be experienced and practical concerning the difficulties of determining the efficacy of particular rules or regulations for a particular society, and serve as a committed pursuer of justice for the rest of society.

In his magnum opus the *Summa Theologica*, Aquinas reflects on the question of what is the best form of government:

> The best form of government is in a State or Kingdom wherein one is given the power to preside over all, while under him are others having governing powers. Yet a government of this kind is shared by all, because all are eligible to govern, and because the rulers are chosen by all. This is the best form of polity, being partly kingdom since there is

one at the head of all; partly aristocracy, insofar as a number of persons are set in authority; partly democracy, that is, government by the people, insofar as the rulers can be chosen from the people, and the people have the right to choose their rulers.[13]

No single person can determine the common interest or common good between people with private interests. Rulers must take care of what pertains toward the common good. It is most appropriate, therefore, for the rulers to call themselves their subjects' servants. Although in Aquinas' judgment the best form of government is one-person monarchical rule, he allows that no one form of government is best in any absolute sense. A form of government can merely be the best possible under particular conditions of time, place, and culture as long as the rule serves justice and the common good and is tempered by mercy. No particular form of government, however, is ordained by God. Aquinas concludes that a mixed regime of monarchy, aristocracy, and democracy is worthy of consideration.

Finally, the ruler or rulers must protect human "spiritual equality." Aquinas recognizes that humans are unequal in physical powers or intellect yet are spiritually equal. In what pertains to the interior motion of the will, states Aquinas, man is bound to obey only God, not man. Man is obligated under the precepts of natural law to obey man in external bodily actions; but even to such as these that refer to the nourishment of the body and the generation of offspring, "man is not bound to obey man but God alone, for all men are by nature equal."[14] No ruler has authority to abridge the equal right to spiritual freedom; these rights are taken to be inalienable, whether proprietary, personal, or marital. Within this sacred sphere, no human artifice or organization should intrude. This human right, for Aquinas, is to be found in all strata of society—"a serf is his master's property in matters superadded to the natural, but in matters concerning nature all are equal."[15] Although humans are spiritually equal, they are politically unequal. The state must have rulers who respect equal rights to spiritual freedom and the common good. A healthy polity cannot be sustained by mediocrity, imprudence, or incompetence. Human law cannot prohibit and seek to remove all evils. Trying to do so might take away resources necessary for the common good. Law should regulate only acts of vice from which the majority are able to abstain, which are injurious to others, and which are necessary to prohibit for social order. Politics and law cannot produce perfect justice, perfect peace, or salvation.

TYRANNY AND TYRANNICIDE

It is quite clear that a legitimate ruler is just power according to law, which is in conformity with natural law. A tyrant is one who pursues his or her own private interests and seeks to impose those private interests by force. Tyranny is a perversion of rulership. The welfare of the community is based on peace, moral enhancement, and a sufficient distribution of material goods. Tyrannical actions do not fulfill these objective political principles, and to seek the removal of such governance is not, strictly speaking, sedition. Actually Aquinas considers the tyrant to be guilty of

---

[13] *Summa Theologica* I–II, 105.1, Vol. II,

[14] *Summa Theologica* II–II, Q. 104 and 5.

[15] *Summa Theologica* I–II, Q. 97, a.1c.

sedition by initiating discord and strife among subjects. In Aquinas' own words, "When government is unjustly exercised by one man who seeks personal profit from his position instead of the good of the community subject to him, such a ruler is called a tyrant."[16] Because a unitary power lacking internal friction or checks is more efficient, the tyrant is more efficiently evil. The unjust laws of tyrants must be opposed, and political arrangements must be pursued to resist them. Even if the law is unjust, the disobedience must be proportional to the problem; and those who resist must consider the problems of scandal contributing to the sins of others and public disturbance.

Aquinas feared the corruption of unified rulership. Consequently he established a number of conditions whereby a ruler could lose claim to legitimacy. A monarch could lose claim to obedience because of a procedurally defective way in which authority has been obtained, such as usurping power by violence or stealing an election. In addition, there are two ways in which a defect may arise due to substantive misuse of power. First, the law ordered by those in authority may be inconsistent with the precepts of natural law. An example would be a ruler's order of genocide within the community rather than promoting the safety or economic well-being of subjects. Second, those in authority may command acts that exceed the competence of their authority, such as taxing excessively or establishing disproportionate burdens in terms of the ability to pay taxes.

Aquinas states the dangers of tyranny in these terms:

> Those who rule have awesome responsibilities. If ordinary men and women are rightly praised for helping the needy or settling disputes, or rescuing the oppressed, how much more, does the ruler deserve praise who gladdens a whole country with peace, restrains the violent, and establishes and secures justice. It is because of their responsibilities heaped upon legitimate rulers that tyrants are held to be guilty not only for their own wrongdoing or sins but also for the wrongdoing and sins they encourage in their subjects.

Before we examine Aquinas' teachings on political resistance to tyranny, we need to consider his penchant for political order. Political harmony allows justice to take place, the common good to be served, and the church to perform its divine mandate. Sometimes it is better to suffer some injustices than to undermine that order and stability. Aquinas, though, was no friend of tyranny and realized that tyrannical government may oppress the human spirit.

The remedy for dealing with tyranny must be grounded in reason and faith. Rulers who ordain a public policy opposed to the divine good must not be obeyed. When dealing with governmental rules that are inconsistent with the precepts of natural law, one should act in a politically proportionate manner—first noncompliance; then political opposition; and finally, if necessary, civil disobedience. As tyrannical acts become habitual and excessive, the political acts just listed become reasonable and appropriate. Aquinas, though, does not support violent revolution except under the most stringent conditions. Revolutionary violence can produce conditions far worse than the original grievances.

Aquinas was convinced that it would harm civil order if private individuals could assume the right to murder their rulers, even when they believe them to be habitual

---

[16] *On Rulership*, trans. Gerald B. Philan (1949), II, p. 118.

PRIMARY SOURCE 4.4 "TYRANTS, TYRANNICIDE AND A LEGITIMATE REVOLUTION," FROM *ON KINGSHIP*

Part II: That the Dominion of a Tyrant is the Worst

[21] Just as the government of a king is the best, so the government of a tyrant is the worst.

[22] For democracy stands in contrary opposition to polity, since both are governments carried on by many persons, as is clear from what has already been said; while oligarchy is the opposite of aristocracy, since both are governments carried on by a few persons; and kingship is the opposite of tyranny, since both are carried on by one person. Now, as has been shown above, monarchy is the best government. If, therefore, "it is the contrary of the best that is worst," it follows that tyranny is the worst kind of government.

[23] Further, a united force is more efficacious in producing its effect than a force which is scattered or divided. Many persons together can pull a load which could not be pulled by each one taking his part separately and acting individually. Therefore, just as it is more useful for a force operating for a good to be more united, in order that it may work good more effectively, so a force operating for evil is more harmful when it is one than when it is divided. Now, the power of one who rules unjustly works to the detriment of the multitude, in that he diverts the common good of the multitude to his own benefit. Therefore, for the same reason that, in a just government, the government is better in proportion as the ruling power is one—thus monarchy is better than aristocracy, and aristocracy better than polity—so the contrary will be true of an unjust government, namely, that the ruling power will be more harmful in proportion as it is more unitary. Consequently, tyranny is more harmful than oligarchy and oligarchy more harmful than democracy.

[24] Moreover, a government becomes unjust by the fact that the ruler, paying no heed to the common good, seeks his own private good. Wherefore the further he departs from the common good the more unjust will his government be ruled. But there is a greater departure from the common good in an oligarchy, in which the advantage of a few is sought, than in a democracy, in which the advantage of many is sought; and there is a still greater departure from the common good in a tyranny, where the advantage of only one man is sought. For a large number is closer to the totality than a small number, and a small number than only one. Thus, the government of a tyrant is the most unjust.

[25] The same conclusion is made clear to those who consider the order of divine providence, which disposes everything in the best way. In all things, good ensues from one perfect cause, i.e., from the totality of the conditions favorable to the production of the effect, while evil results from any one partial defect. There is beauty in a body when all its members are fittingly disposed; ugliness, on the other hand, arises when any one member is not fittingly disposed. Thus ugliness results in different ways from many causes, beauty in one way from one perfect cause. It is thus with all good and evil things, as if God so provided that good, arising from one cause, be stronger, and evil, arising from many causes, be weaker. It is expedient therefore that a just government be that of one man only in order that it may be stronger; however, if the government should turn away from justice, it is more expedient that it be a government by many, so that it may be weaker and the many may mutually hinder one another. Among unjust governments, therefore, democracy is the most tolerable, but the worst is tyranny.

[26] This same conclusion is also apparent if one considers the evils which come from tyrants. Since a tyrant, despising the common good, seeks his private interest, it follows that he will oppress his subjects in different ways according as he is dominated by different passions to acquire certain goods. The one who is enthralled by the passion of cupidity seizes the goods of his subjects; whence Solomon says, "A just king setteth up the land; a covetous man shall destroy it." If he is dominated by the passion of anger, he sheds blood for nothing; whence it is said by

continued

PRIMARY SOURCE 4.4

"TYRANTS, TYRANNICIDE AND A LEGITIMATE REVOLUTION," FROM *ON KINGSHIP* *continued*

Ezekiel, "Her princes in the midst of her are like wolves ravening the prey to shed blood." Therefore this kind of government is to be avoided as the Wise man admonishes: "Keep thee far from the man who has the power to kill," because, forsooth, he kills not for justice' sake but by his power, for the lust of his will. Thus there can be no safety. Everything is uncertain when there is a departure from justice. Nobody will be able firmly to state: This thing is such and such, when it depends upon the will of another, not to say upon his caprice. Nor does the tyrant merely oppress his subjects in corporal things but he also hinders their spiritual good. Those who seek more to use than to be of use to their subjects prevent all progress, suspecting all excellence in their subjects to be prejudicial to their own evil domination. For tyrants hold the good in greater suspicion than the wicked, and to them the valor of others is always fraught with danger.

[27] So the above-mentioned tyrants strive to prevent those of their subjects who have become virtuous from acquiring valor and high spirit in order that they may not want to cast off their iniquitous domination. They also see to it that there be no friendly relations among these so that they may not enjoy the benefits resulting from being on good terms with one another, for as long as one has no confidence in the other, no plot will be set up against the tyrant's domination. Wherefore they sow discords among the people, foster any that have arisen, and forbid anything which furthers society and cooperation among men, such as marriage, company at table, and anything of like character, through which familiarity and confidence are engendered among men. They moreover strive to prevent their subjects from becoming powerful and rich since, suspecting these to be as wicked as themselves, they fear their power and wealth; for the subjects might become harmful to them even as they are accustomed to use power and wealth to harm others. Whence in the Book of Job it said of the tyrant, "The sound of dread is always in his ears, and when there is peace (that is, when there is no one to harm him) he always suspects treason."

[28] It thus results that when rulers, who ought to induce their subjects to virtue, are wickedly jealous of the virtue of their subjects and hinder it as much as they can, few virtuous men are found under the rule of tyrants. For, according to Aristotle's sentence brave men are found where brave men are honored. And as Cicero says, "Those who are despised by everybody are disheartened and flourish but little." It is also natural that men brought up in fear should become mean of spirit and discouraged in the face of any strenuous and manly task. This is shown by experience in provinces that have long been under tyrants. Hence the Apostle says to the Colossians, "Fathers, provoke not your children to indignation, lest they be discouraged."

[29] So, considering these evil effects of tyranny, King Solomon says, "When the wicked reign, men are ruined," because, forsooth, through the wickedness of tyrants, subjects fall away from the perfection of virtue. And again he says, "When the wicked shall bear rule the people shall mourn, as though led into slavery." And again, "When the wicked rise up men shall hide themselves," that they may escape the cruelty of the tyrant. It is no wonder, for a man governing without reason, according to the lust of his soul, in no way differs from the beast. Whence Solomon says, "As a roaring lion and a hungry bear, so is a wicked prince over the poor people." Therefore men hide from tyrants as from cruel beasts, and it seems that to be subject to a tyrant is the same thing as to lie prostrate beneath a raging beast.

* * * *

Chapter VI: How Provision Might Be Made That the King May Not Fall into Tyranny

[41] Therefore, since the rule of one man, which is the best, is to be preferred, and since it may happen that it be changed into a tyranny, which is the worst (all this is clear from what has been said), a scheme should be carefully worked out which would prevent the multitude ruled by a king from falling into the hands of a tyrant.

PRIMARY SOURCE 4.4 | "TYRANTS, TYRANNICIDE AND A LEGITIMATE REVOLUTION," FROM *ON KINGSHIP* *continued*

[42] First, it is necessary that the man who is raised up to be king by those whom it concerns should be of such condition that it is improbable that he should become a tyrant. Wherefore Daniel, commending the providence of God with respect to the institution of the king says, "The Lord hath sought him a man according to his own heart, and the Lord hath appointed him to be prince over his people." Then, once the king is established, the government of the kingdom must be so arranged that opportunity to tyrannize is removed. At the same time his power should be so tempered that he cannot easily fall into tyranny. How these things may be done we must consider in what follows.

[43] Finally, provision must be made for facing the situation should the king stray into tyranny.

[44] Indeed, if there be not an excess of tyranny it is more expedient to tolerate the milder tyranny for a while than, by acting against the tyrant, to become involved in many perils more grievous that the tyranny itself. For it may happen that those who act against the tyrant are unable to prevail and the tyrant then will rage the more. But should one be able to prevail against the tyrant, from this fact itself very grave dissensions among the people frequently ensue: the multitude may be broken up into factions either during their revolt against the tyrant or in process of the organization of the government, after the tyrant has been overthrown. Moreover, it sometimes happens that while the multitude is driving out the tyrant by the help of some man, the latter, having received the power, thereupon seizes the tyranny. Then, fearing to suffer from another what he did to his predecessor, he oppresses his subjects with an even more grievous slavery. This is wont to happen in tyranny, namely, that the second becomes more grievous than the one preceding, inasmuch as, without abandoning the previous oppressions, he himself thinks up fresh ones from the malice of his heart. When in Syracuse, at a time when everyone desired the death of Dionysius, a certain old woman kept constantly praying that he might be unharmed and that he might survive her. When the tyrant learned this he ask why she did it. She then said, "When I was a girl we had a harsh tyrant and I wished for his death; when he was killed, there succeeded him one who was a little harsher. I was very eager to see the end of his dominion also, and we began to have a third ruler still more harsh—that was you. So if you should be taken away, a worse would succeed in your place."

[45] If the excess of tyranny is unbearable, some have been of the opinion that it would be and act of virtue for strong men to slay the tyrant and to expose themselves to the danger of death in order to set the multitude free. An example of this occurs even in the Old Testament, for a certain Aioth slew Eglon, King of Moab, who was oppressing the people of God under harsh slavery, thrusting a dagger into his thigh; and he was made a judge of the people.

[46] But this opinion is not in accord with apostolic teaching. For Peter admonishes us to be reverently subject to our masters, no only to the good and gentle but also the forward: "For if one who suffers unjustly bear his trouble for conscience' sake, this is grace." Wherefore, when many emperors of the Romans tyrannically persecuted the faith of Christ, a great number both of the nobility and the common people were converted to the faith and were praised for patiently bearing death for Christ. They did not resist although they were armed, and this is plainly manifested in the case of the holy Theban legion. Aioth, then, must be considered rather as having slain a foe that assassinated a ruler, however tyrannical, of the people. Hence in the Old Testament we also read that they who killed Joas, the King of Juda, who had fallen away from the worship of God, were slain and their children spared according to the precept of the law.

[47] Should private persons attempt on their own private presumption to kill the rulers, even though tyrants, this would be dangerous for the multitude as well as for their rulers. This is because the wicked usually expose themselves to

continued

PRIMARY SOURCE 4.4 "TYRANTS, TYRANNICIDE AND A LEGITIMATE REVOLUTION," FROM *ON KINGSHIP* *continued*

dangers of this kind more than the good, for the rule of a king, no less than that of a tyrant, is burdensome to them, since, according to the words of Solomon, "A wise king scattereth the wicked." Consequently, by presumption of this kind, danger to the people from the loss of a good king would be more probable than relief through the removal of a tyrant.

[48] Furthermore, it seems that to proceed against the cruelty of tyrants is an action to be undertaken, not through the private presumption of a few, but rather by public authority.

[49] If to provide itself with a king belongs to the right of a given multitude, it is not unjust that the king be deposed or have his power restricted by that same multitude if, becoming a tyrant, he abuses the royal power. It must not be thought that such a multitude is acting unfaithfully in deposing the tyrant, even though it had previously subjected itself to him in perpetuity, because he himself has deserved that the covenant with his subjects should not be kept, since, in ruling the multitude, he did not act faithfully as the office of a king demands. Thus did the Romans, who had accepted Tarquin the Proud as their king, cast him out from the kingship on account of his tyranny and the tyranny of his sons; and they set up in their place a lesser power, namely, the consular power. Similarly Domitian, who had succeeded those most moderate emperors, Vespasian, his father, and Titus, his brother, was slain by the Roman senate when he exercised tyranny, and all his wicked deeds were justly and profitably declared null and void by a decree of the senate. Thus it came about that Blessed John the Evangelist, the beloved disciple of God, who had been exiled to the island of Patmos by that very Domitian, was sent back to Ephesus by a decree of the senate.

[50] If, on the other hand, it pertains to the right of a higher authority to provide a king for a certain multitude, a remedy against the wickedness of a tyrant is to be looked for from him. Thus when Archelaus, who had already begun to reign in Judaea in the place of Herod, his father, was imitating his father's wickedness, a complaint against him having been laid before Caesar Augustus by the Jews, his power was at first diminished by depriving him of his title of king and by dividing one-half of his kingdom between his two brothers. Later, since he was not restrained from tyranny even by this means, Tiberius Caesar sent him into exile to Lugdunum, a city in Gaul.

[51] Should no human aid whatsoever against a tyrant be forthcoming, recourse must be had to God, the King of all, Who is a helper in due time in tribulation. For it lies in his power to turn the cruel heart of the tyrant to mildness. According to Solomon, "The heart of the king is in the hand of the Lord, withersoever He will He shall turn it." He it was who turned into mildness the cruelty of King Assuerus, who was preparing death for the Jews. He it was who so filled the cruel king Nabuchodonosor with piety that he became a proclaimer of the divine power. "Therefore," he said, "I, Nabuchodonosor do now praise and magnify and glorify the King of Heaven; because all His works are true and His ways judgments, and they that walk in pride He is able to abase." Those tyrants, however, whom He deems unworthy of conversion He is able to put out of the way or to degrade, according to the words of the Wise Man: "God hath overturned the thrones of proud princes and hath set up the meek in their stead." He it was who, seeing the affliction of his people in Egypt and hearing their cry, hurled Pharaoh, a tyrant over God's people, with all his army into the sea. He it was who not only banished from his kingly throne the above-mentioned Nabuchondonosor, because of his former pride, but also cast him from the fellowship of men and changed him into the likeness of a beast. Indeed, his hand is not shortened that He cannot free his people from tyrants. For by Isaias He promised to give his people rest from their labors and lashings and harsh slavery in which they had formerly served; and by Ezekiel He says, "I will deliver my flock from their mouth," i.e., from the mouth of shepherds who feed themselves.

[52] But to deserve to secure this benefit from God, the people must desist from sin, for

PRIMARY SOURCE 4.4

"Tyrants, Tyrannicide and a Legitimate Revolution," from *On Kingship* *continued*

it is by divine permission that wicked men receive power to rule as a punishment for sin, as the Lord says by the Prophet Osee: "I will give thee a king in my wrath," and it is said in Job that he "maketh a man that is a hypocrite to reign for the sins of the people." Sin must therefore be done away with in order that the scourge of tyrants may cease.

tyrants. Tyrants who usurp political power or are persistently unjust in their actions should be removed by public authorities, such as through the impeachment process in the United States or a parliamentary vote of no confidence in the British political system. If there is no recourse to public authorities, the last resort is to pray for divine intervention, which Aquinas believed could turn the cruel heart to gentleness.

There are, however, certain extreme situations under which violent rebellion or **tyrannicide** might be justified. The ruler can lose the right to rule by a long train of repressive behavior; sovereignty then reverts to the people. In a number of Aquinas' writings he set up prudential norms that must be seriously considered before a legitimate revolution begins.

Aquinas prudently considers the following extreme preconditions that would justify resistance to a tyrant who either usurps power (seizes power without a legal right) or abuses power properly acquired (commands unjust things):

1. The tyranny must be excessive; otherwise using coercion to move against a tyrant may bring about greater dangers if the violent resistance should fail and the tyrant becomes even more vicious.
2. Great care must be given that the effort to overthrow the tyrant does not produce greater social factionalism and dissent among the people.
3. The leadership in removing the tyrant must support the common good and not private interests or passions, making every reasonable effort not to substitute a new tyrant for the old one.
4. Private judgment must not to determine whether a tyrant who refuses to surrender should be slain, thereby emphasizing the principle of a public body representing the national good as a whole.

Aquinas' "legitimate revolution" can be cobbled from his various texts, which include these four themes and are set down not as absolute imperatives but as prudential norms: The ruler has become habitually or excessively tyrannical, without a prospect of a change for the better within a reasonable time; all legal and peaceful means to recall the ruler to a sense of duty have been exhausted; there is a reasonable expectation that the revolution will succeed; and the revolutionaries are not a movement of only a single faction, social class, or geographic district, but have significant backing of the people as a whole.

For Aquinas, the political system (or the state) does not arise as a result of divine action. This cause is to be found in the social and political inclination in humanity that reveals human gregariousness and human rationality grounded in free and conscious activity. As moral beings, humans have a basic obligation to establish an order of right and justice, as well as the common good. The fall of humanity in the Garden of Eden

CASE STUDY 4.1 | Resistance to Tyranny

Toward the end of World War II, Count Klaus von Stauffenberg, a devout Roman Catholic German colonel, sought to organize an act of violent resistance against Adolf Hitler on July 20, 1944. He concluded that Hitler's brutal tyranny and the well-developed military resistance organization against Hitler justified a bombing attempt on Hitler's life in terms of Aquinas' prudential norms for a legitimate revolution. The resistance failed. After doing some research on the July 20, 1944, resistance movement, would you conclude that Colonel von Stauffenberg's attempted tyrannicide was reasonable in Aquinas' terms? One could ask this question in reference to the American Revolution or to the coalition that sought the removal of Saddam Hussein from power.

has not eclipsed the natural reality embodied in natural law or the purpose of the state. Our cognitive powers have not been vitiated by original sin. Rather, these cognitive powers are sometimes fallible and frail. Therefore, state power must be limited and subject to law and rational scrutiny. For Christians, it is crucial to follow God's will in the face of fallible cognitive powers. It is thus necessary to seek divine grace and the divine law of revelation to fully realize one's obligations to one's fellow human beings and to God as one pursues one's spiritual destination. Aquinas' most fundamental teaching is that divine grace and divine revelation do not destroy human nature; they perfect it. Such grace helps human beings achieve their natural end and, most important, their spiritual end. The limited state subject to law is necessary but not sufficient for humans who choose to pursue their supernatural destiny. The guidance of the church is also crucial.

JUST WAR

One way for us to explore the role of church and state, faith and reason, in Aquinas' political thought is to present his teachings concerning **just war**, in which both institutions struggle in every generation to make judgments about this volatile question.

True happiness is not to be found in the never-ending pursuit of power, wealth, and glory; it comes in loving and following God. For Aquinas, nations must state and defend their intention to go to war. Power, wealth, and glory are not just causes. A moral demand for just intentions tempers human competitiveness and aggressiveness. Keeping in mind what we already discussed concerning just law and a just or legitimate revolution, here are Aquinas' criteria for a just war:

1. *Just cause:* This is the most fundamental criterion for resorting to war. Without meeting this criterion, the others do not even matter. Just cause can involve (1) protecting people from aggression—a defensive war; (2) restoring rights that have wrongly been taken away—a war to protect the victimized of other nations; or (3) reestablishing a just political order.
2. *Just authority:* A decision to go to war must serve the common good and not merely private interests and passions. This decision must be made by those who are given the responsibility to declare war and decide for the people. The legitimate authorities must give an appropriate account of their reasons to go to war.

PRIMARY SOURCE 4.5 | JUST WAR, FROM THE SUMMA

Whether It Is Always Sinful to Wage War

Objection 1: It would seem that it is always sinful to wage war. Because punishment is not inflicted except for sin. Now those who wage war are threatened by Our Lord with punishment, according to Mt. 26:52: "All that take the sword shall perish with the sword." Therefore all wars are unlawful.

Objection 2: Further, whatever is contrary to a Divine precept is a sin. But war is contrary to a Divine precept, for it is written (Mt. 5:39), "But I say to you not to resist evil"; and (Rm. 12:19), "Not revenging yourselves, my dearly beloved, but give place unto wrath." Therefore war is always sinful.

Objection 3: Further, nothing, except sin, is contrary to an act of virtue. But war is contrary to peace. Therefore war is always a sin.

Objection 4: Further, the exercise of a lawful thing is itself lawful, as is evident in scientific exercises. But warlike exercises which take place in tournaments are forbidden by the Church, since those who are slain in these trials are deprived of ecclesiastical burial. Therefore it seems that war is a sin in itself.

On the contrary, Augustine says in a sermon on the son of the centurion [*Ep. ad Marcel. cxxxviii]: "If the Christian Religion forbade war altogether, those who sought salutary advice in the Gospel would rather have been counseled to cast aside their arms, and to give up soldiering altogether. On the contrary, they were told, 'Do violence to no man . . . and be content with your pay' [*Lk. 3:14]. If he commanded them to be content with their pay, he did not forbid soldiering."

I answer that, In order for a war to be just, three things are necessary. First, the authority of the sovereign by whose command the war is to be waged. For it is not the business of a private individual to declare war, because he can seek for redress of his rights from the tribunal of his superior. Moreover it is not the business of a private individual to summon together the people, which has to be done in wartime. And as the care of the common weal is committed to those who are in authority, it is their business to watch over the common weal of the city, kingdom or province subject to them. And just as it is lawful for them to have recourse to the sword in defending that common weal against internal disturbances, when they punish evil-doers, according to the words of the Apostle (Rm. 13:4), "He beareth not the sword in vain: for he is God's minister, an avenger to execute wrath upon him that doth evil"; so too, it is their business to have recourse to the sword of war in defending the common weal against external enemies. Hence it is said to those who are in authority (Ps. 81:4), "Rescue the poor: and deliver the needy out of the hand of the sinner"; and for this reason Augustine says (Contra Faust. xxii, 75), "The natural order conducive to peace among mortals demands that the power to declare and counsel war should be in the hands of those who hold the supreme authority."

Secondly, a just cause is required, namely that those who are attacked, should be attacked because they deserve it on account of some fault. Wherefore Augustine says (Questions. in Hept., qu. x, super Jos.), "A just war is wont to be described as one that avenges wrongs, when a nation or state has to be punished, for refusing to make amends for the wrongs inflicted by its subjects, or to restore what it has seized unjustly."

Thirdly, it is necessary that the belligerents should have a rightful intention, so that they intend the advancement of good, or the avoidance of evil. Hence Augustine says (De Verb. Dom. [*The words quoted are to be found not in St. Augustine's works, but Can. Apud. Caus. xxiii, qu. 1]), "True religion looks upon as peaceful those wars that are waged not for motives of aggrandizement, or cruelty, but with the object of securing peace, of punishing evildoers, and of uplifting the good." For it may happen that the war is declared by the legitimate authority, and for a just cause, and yet be rendered unlawful through a wicked intention. Hence Augustine says (Contra Faust. xxii, 74), "The passion for inflicting harm, the cruel thirst for vengeance, an unpacific and relentless spirit, the fever of revolt, the lust of power, and

continued

PRIMARY SOURCE 4.5 | **JUST WAR, FROM THE SUMMA** *continued*

such like things, all these are rightly condemned in war."

Reply to Objection 1: As Augustine says (Contra Faust. xxii, 70), "To take the sword is to arm oneself in order to take the life of anyone, without the command or permission of superior or lawful authority." On the other hand, to have recourse to the sword (as a private person) by the authority of the sovereign or judge, or (as a public person) through zeal for justice, and by the authority, so to speak, of God, is not to "take the sword," but to use it as commissioned by another, wherefore it does not deserve punishment. And yet even those who make sinful use of the sword are not always slain with the sword, yet they always perish with their own sword, because, unless they repent, they are punished eternally for their sinful use of the sword.

Reply to Objection 2: Such like precepts, as Augustine observes (De Serm. Dom. in Monte i, 19), should always be borne in readiness of mind, so that we be ready to obey them, and, if necessary, to refrain from resistance or self-defense. Nevertheless it is necessary sometimes for a man to act otherwise for the common good, or for the good of those with whom he is fighting. Hence Augustine says (Ep. ad Marcellin. cxxxviii), "Those whom we have to punish with a kindly severity, it is necessary to handle in many ways against their will. For when we are stripping a man of the lawlessness of sin, it is good for him to be vanquished, since nothing is more hopeless than the happiness of sinners, whence arises a guilty impunity, and an evil will, like an internal enemy."

Reply to Objection 3: Those who wage war justly aim at peace, and so they are not opposed to peace, except to the evil peace, which Our Lord "came not to send upon earth" (Mt. 10:34). Hence Augustine says (Ep. ad Bonif. clxxxix), "We do not seek peace in order to be at war, but we go to war that we may have peace. Be peaceful, therefore, in warring, so that you may vanquish those whom you war against, and bring them to the prosperity of peace."

Reply to Objection 4: Manly exercises in warlike feats of arms are not all forbidden, but those which are inordinate and perilous, and end in slaying or plundering. In olden times warlike exercises presented no such danger, and hence they were called "exercises of arms" or "bloodless wars," as Jerome states in an epistle (*Reference incorrect: cf. Veget., De Re Milit. i).

3. *Last resort:* It is only justifiable to resort to war after all peaceful alternatives have been exhausted without success. A war policy should not be pursued if there is a reasonable chance of obtaining just objectives by less violent means.
4. *Proportionality:* Resort to war is not just if the destructive effects of the war will be greater than the good to be attained. There must be some assessment of the consequences, even though this is always difficult. It is still better to try as carefully as possible to calculate the costs.
5. *Reasonable chance of success:* It is just to resort to war if there is a reasonable chance of attaining one of the justifiable objectives. Declaring military victory is not an adequate basis for declaring success.
6. *Right intention:* This refers to the proper motives for the war policy. There must be no drumbeat of hatred, demonization of the enemy, or desire for revenge. For Christians to go to a just war, it must be done out of love—service and sacrifice for one's enemies as well as for the victimized. If the war is to be just, it must be a means to restoring a just peace.

QUESTIONS FOR REFLECTION

During the past generation, we have witnessed two Iraqi wars waged by the United States and its allies against Saddam Hussein: the Gulf War (1991) and Iraq's War of Liberation (2003). After some research and reflection, do you think Aquinas' criteria for a just war would lead you to conclude that either one or both of these wars should be considered just?

Aquinas' political vision argues for an approach to political rulers that emphasizes their public servant role in providing for the common good of peace and justice. Political institutions promote the imperfect happiness of human life by suppressing the most egregious of human vices, and by fostering an environment in which moral virtues may be formed and the church may be free to pursue its work. He summarizes his political vision in these terms:

> ...to establish a virtuous living in a multitude, three things are necessary. First of all, the multitude be established in the unity of peace. Second that the multitude thus united in the bond of peace be directed to acting well... In the third place, it is necessary that there be at hand in sufficient supply of things required for proper living, procured by the ruler's efforts.

Aquinas' view of the purpose of the state or political rulership is a robust, albeit limited one showing enormous support for statesmanship and the role special circumstances play in the world of politics. Political prudence requires a reasonable balance between the pursuit of justice and the common good, the recognition that human laws cannot demand perfect virtue, and the understanding that moral and political perfection is only attainable in heaven.

Key Terms

Aristotle as the Philosopher	scholastic method	natural law	synderesis
natural condition	faith and reason	human law	general precepts
common good	prudence	divine law	subsidiarity
magnanimous	law	nature	tyrannicide
	eternal law	inclination	just war

Sources and Resources

Key Texts

Summa Theologica
On Kingship to the King of Cyprus

Secondary Texts

Copleston, Frederick. *Thomas Aquinas* (New York: Barnes & Noble Imports, 1976).

Finnis, John. *Aquinas: Moral, Political, and Legal Theory* (New York: Oxford University Press, 1998).

Jaffa, Harry V. *Thomism and Aristotelianism: A Study of the Commentary by Thomas Aquinas on the Nicomachean Ethics* (Westport Conn.: Greenwood Press, 1971).

Maritain, Jacques. *Man and the State* (New York: Catholic University of America Press, 1998).

Schall, Rev. James V. "The Political Philosophy of Aquinas," *S.J. Crisis Magazine*, July/August 2006: www.crisismagazine.com/julaug2006/sense.htm.

Sigmund, Paul E. *Natural Law in Political Thought* (New York: University Press of America, 1981).

Web Sites

Stanford Encyclopedia of Philosophy entry online at http://plato.stanford.edu/entries/aquinas/

Summa Theologica online at www.newadvent.org/summa/

Summa Contra Gentiles online at www2.nd.edu/Departments/Maritain/etext/gc.htm

News and newsletter devoted to the academic study of Aquinas online at http://thomistica.net/

Luther and Calvin

CHAPTER 5

By Ralph C. Hancock *Brigham Young University*

CHRISTIANITY AND THE PROBLEM OF TWO WORLDS

Jean-Jacques Rousseau, in the last chapter of *The Social Contract*, forcefully describes Christianity's fundamental transformation of the political problem. Before Christianity, he observes, there was no separation between the political and the religious; every religion was "attached solely to the laws of the State which prescribed it." It was Jesus who, by introducing "the new idea of a kingdom of the other world," separated "the theological from the political" and destroyed the unity of the pagan state.

We need not share Rousseau's nostalgia for pagan unity to recognize the seriousness of the challenge Christianity poses for political philosophy. We modern beneficiaries of a liberal democratic regime that many take to establish "the separation of church and state" may imagine that the spiritual and secular realms can be neatly divided and insulated from each other. But a moment's study of the actual politics of the United States, for example, would suffice to show that the very meaning and the terms of such a separation remain contentious political and philosophical questions.

Christianity thus opens up the possibility of another, spiritual world, distinct from our present world, from the world determined by the exercise of human power within the limits set by nature. But whatever their ultimate spiritual destiny, humans remain natural and political beings; and their orientation toward another world, their sense of possibilities beyond the limits of the human condition must somehow be reconciled with the requirements of political order in the here and now. The spiritual and the secular may be distinct, but they are far from simply separate; they must be ordered with respect to each other in some way. This is the inescapability of political thinking.

The difficulty of this ordering is clearly visible in St. Augustine's *City of God*. Augustine honors the New Testament's separation between the spiritual and political kingdoms, and in fact he structures his entire account of the human condition and of history around the distinction and the rivalry between the city of God and the city of man. Accordingly, in terms that seem to anticipate a modern liberal restriction of the scope of politics, the Bishop of Hippo limits the purposes of secular authority to the securing of a "compromise between human wills in respect of the provisions relevant to the mortal nature of man. . . ." The heavenly city grants the legitimacy of the earthly city for these limited purposes, and it does not prescribe any single vision of the political community: "She takes no account of any difference in customs, laws, and institutions by which earthly peace is achieved or preserved." But even as Augustine acknowledges the necessities of politics, he clearly subordinates them to humans' ultimate purposes, with which the church is charged. After all, heavenly peace is "the only peace deserving of the name," and the heavenly city (of which the church is the visible anticipation) "makes use" of the peace secured by the temporal authority. Earthly peace is seen as ministerial to heavenly peace; so the church defends the lower, defective peace only "so far as may be permitted without detriment to true religion and piety" (*City of God* XIX.17). The spiritual and the secular are distinct, but the latter is clearly answerable to the higher purposes and thus the higher authority of the former.

This distinction, colored by a clear sense of the superiority of spiritual to secular purposes, may be called the central feature of medieval political thought. But medieval theory did not arrive at any final and authoritative understanding of the institutional implications of humanity's spiritual destiny in relation to those of its political condition. Although the distinctness and legitimacy of political authority were unmistakably affirmed already in the New Testament—"Render therefore unto Caesar..." (Matthew 22:21) "...the powers that be are ordained of God..." (Romans 13:1)—the church's responsibility for humans' higher purpose inevitably implied claims to "make use of" the political arm.

By the end of the Middle Ages such religious claims over the political realm had been formalized in the clearest and most extreme fashion in the idea of absolute papal supremacy. This idea was proclaimed in Boniface's 1302 bull *Unam Sanctum,* ghostwritten by Giles of Rome (d. 1316, Archbishop of Bourges and prolific scholar). Giles' logic was impeccable (if we admit his terms and premises) and can be seen as the culmination of a tendency inherent in the medieval Christian understanding of the subordination of body to soul, temporal to spiritual: The Pope governs souls; political authorities govern bodies. But the soul is more important than the body; so the Pope's authority trumps any secular ruler's. Giles was working within an Augustinian framework, but his argument can just as well be seen as the culmination of Thomas Aquinas' Christian appropriation of Aristotle. If "**grace** perfects nature," as Aquinas so influentially taught, then it would seem to follow that those who claim natural political authority must finally defer to those endowed with the means of grace.

Giles' argument was of course by no means universally accepted; in fact it represented a rather late and desperate attempt to stem the rising tide of secular power, as European kings asserted increasing powers against the authority of Rome. By the late Middle Ages the claims of "grace" over "nature," of the heavenly city over the city of man, were meeting resistance on many fronts as the crisis that was to become the Protestant Reformation approached.

Martin Luther and John Calvin, destined to emerge as the most important makers of this Reformation, were thus seized in the most fundamental way by the problem of the relationship between the two worlds—between the spiritual and secular realms. While their primary concerns were theological, their reconfigurations of the relationship between these realms could not help but have momentous political implications.

MARTIN LUTHER: CRISIS AND CONVERSION

Martin Luther was born of peasant stock to a pious and newly prosperous family of the town of Eisleben in Saxony in 1883. Luther's fateful break with Rome began as a personal crisis, an intense individual struggle concerning the meaning of salvation. Martin Luther did not set out to start the Protestant Reformation or to fracture the unity of Western Christianity; but when such consequences began to emerge from his denunciations of certain teachings and practices of the Roman Church, he did not shrink from them.

The tyranny against which he revolted was in the first instance what he came to understand as a tyranny over his soul that was the effect of a fundamental theological error. Young Martin Luther had experienced anxiety concerning his identity and purpose in life from an early age—partly, it seems, as a result of a difficult relationship with his parents, who had groomed him for the study of law. In the midst of a terrifying thunderstorm in the summer of his 23rd year, Luther made a sacred vow to enter a monastery, a vow he fulfilled shortly thereafter. But the discipline and teaching of the Augustinian order (first in Erfurt, then in Wittenberg) brought the young monk no peace of mind, in fact driving him to an unbearable sense of his own sinfulness.

Here is how Luther later (in the preface to the 1545 edition of his Latin works) described his crisis and the scriptural insight by which he resolved it:

> But I, blameless monk that I was, felt that before God I was a sinner with an extremely troubled conscience. I couldn't be sure that God was appeased by my satisfaction. I did not love, no, rather I hated the just God who punishes sinners. In silence, if I did not blaspheme, then certainly I grumbled vehemently and got angry at God. I said, "Isn't it enough that we miserable sinners, lost for all eternity because of original sin, are oppressed by every kind of calamity through the Ten Commandments? Why does God heap sorrow upon sorrow through the Gospel and through the Gospel threaten us with his justice and his wrath?" This was how I was raging with wild and disturbed conscience. I constantly badgered St. Paul about that spot in Romans 1 and anxiously wanted to know what he meant.
>
> I meditated night and day on those words until at last, by the mercy of God, I paid attention to their context: "The justice of God is revealed in it, as it is written: 'The just person lives by **faith**.'" I began to understand that in this verse the justice of God is that by which the just person lives by a gift of God, that is, by faith. I began to understand that this verse means that the justice of God is revealed through the Gospel, but it is a passive justice, i.e., that by which the merciful God justifies us by faith, as it is written: "The just person lives by faith." All at once I felt that I had been born again and entered into paradise itself through open gates. . . .
>
> I exalted this sweetest word of mine, "the justice of God," with as much love as before I had hated it with hate. This phrase of Paul was for me the very gate of paradise.

Luther's intolerable malaise had resulted, he now believed, from a misunderstanding of the righteousness that God requires of us. He had believed that God demanded a transformation of his, Luther's, nature, to some divine purity; but Luther was vividly aware of his gross impurity, despite his best efforts to conform to the monastic discipline of poverty, chastity, and the like. It was Luther's rereading of Paul's letter to the Romans that finally allowed him to see that the righteousness required was a righteousness of faith, one that was not and could not be possessed by the penitent sinner through some transformation of his nature; what was promised was rather God's righteousness imputed to the sinner by faith (an inward assent and trusting acceptance of Christ) and the grace (that is, unmerited gift) of God. (Though Luther later reported this insight as having come to him suddenly in the *cloaca*—probably the tower library of the monastery—his early lectures on the Bible show him arriving more gradually at this distinctive understanding of **justification** by faith.)

MARTIN LUTHER: THE LIBERTY OF FAITH VERSUS ROMAN "WORKS"

Luther blames scholastic theology for perverting the biblical meaning of *justification*, and he locates none other than Aristotle as the pagan fountainhead of this perversion. The 41st thesis of his *Disputation against Scholastic Theology* (1517) could not be clearer on this point: "The whole of Aristotle's *Ethics* is the worst enemy of grace." The scholastic appropriation of Aristotle corrupted Christianity, according to Luther, by attributing to human nature the power to cultivate a certain measure of virtue or righteousness. By practicing the moral virtues, Aristotle had taught, people can fulfill their natural potential and in fact become virtuous. Theologians from Aquinas down to Ockham and Gabriel Biel had adapted this teaching in various ways to limit the biblical teaching concerning the fallenness of human nature and thereby to define a role in the economy of salvation for the moral efforts of human beings.

But this apparent boon to humanity was in fact, according to Luther, the source of the harshest tyranny over people's souls. By requiring of human beings an inner rectitude that was in fact impossible for fallen human nature, the Roman church terrorized souls and exploited this terror to gain earthly power. The instance of this exploitation that Luther, like many of his contemporaries, found most shocking was the Church's practice of offering "indulgences" to sinners seeking remission of the pains of purgatory in consideration of "gifts" made to the Church. Apologetic theologians avoided formulating this transaction as a direct commercial exchange, but in practice it was hard not to see the indulgence as the selling of exemptions from divine punishment. Here was the plainest case of the Church's wielding worldly power by exploiting the broadly Aristotelian belief in the spiritual efficacy of outward acts.

Luther posted his protest against the theory and practice of indulgences on the door of the Castle of Wittenberg (as was common practice for announcements of academic disputations) on October 31, 1517, in the form of the now famous *95 Theses*. At this point in his quarrel with church practices, Luther seems still to have considered himself loyal to the Pope, and he endeavored to put the best face on Rome's intentions. But church authorities immediately identified Luther's views as heretical, and a breach opened up that was never to be closed. Branded as a heretic, Luther turned to a study of the history of the papacy, and by 1520 he was ready to affirm that John Huss of Bohemia, burned at the stake a century earlier, had been right to deny the infallibility of the church, whether represented by the Pope or by a council. Martin Luther, and the many who were ready to follow him (for material as well as spiritual reasons), were no longer Roman Catholics.

A plain, early statement of the basic premises of Luther's break with the Roman church is his *Concerning Christian Liberty* of 1520. Here he sharply divides man's "spiritual" nature from his "bodily" nature, the inner from the outer man, to show that justification comes by faith alone, which is therefore radically free from dependence upon works or upon anything external:

The righteousness that God commands, especially and in the first instance the pure and absolute loving worship of God, Luther argues, is something of which no human being is capable. By nature we are enemies of God. Only God himself in the person of Jesus Christ can reconcile us to Him by covering our sins with his righteousness. This is grace, and faith or belief is the spiritual act by which we receive God's righteousness.

Luther does not, of course, deny that good works are commanded and ought to be done; he only insists that they have no saving efficacy in themselves. At the same time, the very meaning of *good works* shifts from an emphasis on sacramental performances, dependent upon the authority of ordained priests, to ordinary service addressing the mundane needs of one's neighbor:

> From all this it is easy to perceive on what principle good works are to be cast aside or embraced, and by what rule all teachings put forth concerning works are to be understood. For if works are brought forward as grounds of justification, and are done under the false persuasion that we can pretend to be justified by them, they lay on us the yoke of necessity, and extinguish liberty along with faith, and by this very addition

PRIMARY SOURCE 5.1 | *Concerning Christian Liberty*

A Christian man is the most free lord of all, and subject to none; a Christian man is the most dutiful servant of all, and subject to every one.

Although these statements appear contradictory, yet, when they are found to agree together, they will make excellently for my purpose. They are both the statements of Paul himself, who says, "Though I be free from all men, yet have I made myself servant unto all" (1 Cor. ix. 19), and "Owe no man anything, but to love one another" (Rom. xiii. 8). Now love is by its own nature dutiful and obedient to the beloved object. Thus even Christ, though Lord of all things, was yet made of a woman; made under the law; at once free and a servant; at once in the form of God and in the form of a servant.

Let us examine the subject on a deeper and less simple principle. Man is composed of a twofold nature, a spiritual and a bodily. As regards the spiritual nature, which they name the soul, he is called the spiritual, inward, new man; as regards the bodily nature, which they name the flesh, he is called the fleshly, outward, old man. The Apostle speaks of this: "Though our outward man perish, yet the inward man is renewed day by day" (2 Cor. iv. 16)....

We first approach the subject of the inward man, that we may see by what means a man becomes justified, free, and a true Christian; that is, a spiritual, new, and inward man. It is certain that absolutely none among outward things, under whatever name they may be reckoned, has any influence in producing Christian righteousness or liberty, nor, on the other hand, unrighteousness or slavery. This can be shown by an easy argument.

What can it profit the soul that the body should be in good condition, free, and full of life; that it should eat, drink, and act according to its pleasure; when even the most impious slaves of every kind of vice are prosperous in these matters? Again, what harm can ill health, bondage, hunger, thirst, or any other outward evil, do to the soul, when even the most pious of men and the freest in the purity of their conscience, are harassed by these things? Neither of these states of things has to do with the liberty or the slavery of the soul.

And so it will profit nothing that the body should be adorned with sacred vestments, or dwell in holy places, or be occupied in sacred offices, or pray, fast, and abstain from certain meats, or do whatever works can be done through the body and in the body. Something widely different will be necessary for the justification and liberty of the soul, since the things I have spoken of can be done by any impious person, and only hypocrites are produced by devotion to these things. On the other hand, it will not at all injure the soul that the body should be clothed in profane raiment, should dwell in profane places, should eat and drink in the ordinary fashion, should not pray aloud, and should leave undone all the things above mentioned, which may be done by hypocrites.

And, to cast everything aside, even speculation, meditations, and whatever things can be performed by the exertions of the soul itself, are of no profit. One thing, and one alone, is necessary for life, justification, and Christian liberty; and that is the most holy word of God, the Gospel of Christ, as He says, "I am the resurrection and the life; he that believeth in Me shall not die eternally" (John xi. 25), and also, "If the Son shall make you free, ye shall be free indeed" (John viii. 36), and, "Man shall not live by bread alone, but by every word that proceedeth out of the mouth of God" (Matt. iv. 4).

Let us therefore hold it for certain and firmly established that the soul can do without everything except the word of God, without which none at all of its wants are provided for. But, having the word, it is rich and wants for nothing, since that is the word of life, of truth, of light, of peace, of justification, of salvation, of joy, of liberty, of wisdom, of virtue, of grace, of glory, and of every good thing....

* * * *

Meanwhile it is to be noted that the whole Scripture of God is divided into two parts:

PRIMARY SOURCE 5.1 | *CONCERNING CHRISTIAN LIBERTY continued*

precepts and promises. The precepts certainly teach us what is good, but what they teach is not forthwith done. For they show us what we ought to do, but do not give us the power to do it. They were ordained, however, for the purpose of showing man to himself, that through them he may learn his own impotence for good and may despair of his own strength. For this reason they are called the Old Testament, and are so.

* * * *

Now when a man has through the precepts been taught his own impotence, and become anxious by what means he may satisfy the law—for the law must be satisfied, so that no jot or tittle of it may pass away, otherwise he must be hopelessly condemned—then, being truly humbled and brought to nothing in his own eyes, he finds in himself no resource for justification and salvation.

Then comes in that other part of Scripture, the promises of God, which declare the glory of God, and say, "If you wish to fulfill the law, and, as the law requires, not to covet, lo! believe in Christ, in whom are promised to you grace, justification, peace, and liberty." All these things you shall have, if you believe, and shall be without them if you do not believe. For what is impossible for you by all the works of the law, which are many and yet useless, you shall fulfill in an easy and summary way through faith, because God the Father has made everything to depend on faith, so that whosoever has it has all things, and he who has it not has nothing. "For God hath concluded them all in unbelief, that He might have mercy upon all" (Rom. xi. 32). Thus the promises of God give that which the precepts exact, and fulfill what the law commands; so that all is of God alone, both the precepts and their fulfillment. He alone commands; He alone also fulfills. Hence the promises of God belong to the New Testament; nay, are the New Testament.

* * * *

From all this it is easy to understand why faith has such great power, and why no good works, nor even all good works put together, can compare with it, since no work can cleave to the word of God or be in the soul. Faith alone and the word reign in it; and such as is the word, such is the soul made by it, just as iron exposed to fire glows like fire, on account of its union with the fire. It is clear then that to a Christian man his faith suffices for everything, and that he has no need of works for justification. But if he has no need of works, neither has he need of the law; and if he has no need of the law, he is certainly free from the law, and the saying is true, "The law is not made for a righteous man" (1 Tim. i. 9). This is that Christian liberty, our faith, the effect of which is, not that we should be careless or lead a bad life, but that no one should need the law or works for justification and salvation.

* * * *

From all this you will again understand why so much importance is attributed to faith, so that it alone can fulfill the law and justify without any works. For you see that the First Commandment, which says, "Thou shalt worship one God only," is fulfilled by faith alone. If you were nothing but good works from the soles of your feet to the crown of your head, you would not be worshipping God, nor fulfilling the First Commandment, since it is impossible to worship God without ascribing to Him the glory of truth and of universal goodness, as it ought in truth to be ascribed. Now this is not done by works, but only by faith of heart. It is not by working, but by believing, that we glorify God, and confess Him to be true. On this ground faith alone is the righteousness of a Christian man, and the fulfilling of all the commandments. For to him who fulfills the first the task of fulfilling all the rest is easy.

Works, since they are irrational things, cannot glorify God, although they may be done to the glory of God, if faith be present...

QUESTIONS FOR REFLECTION

How are our inward selves related to our outward behaviors and our externally perceived character traits? Can these be wholly separated?

to their use they become no longer good, but really worthy of condemnation. For such works are not free, but blaspheme the grace of God, to which alone it belongs to justify and save through faith. Works cannot accomplish this, and yet, with impious presumption, through our folly, they take it on themselves to do so; and thus break in with violence upon the office and glory of grace.

We do not then reject good works; nay, we embrace them and teach them in the highest degree. It is not on their own account that we condemn them, but on account of this impious addition to them and the perverse notion of seeking justification by them. These things cause them to be only good in outward show, but in reality not good, since by them men are deceived and deceive others, like ravening wolves in sheep's clothing.

* * * *

Yet a Christian has need of none of these things for justification and salvation, but in all his works he ought to entertain this view and look only to this object—that he may serve and be useful to others in all that he does; having nothing before his eyes but the necessities and the advantage of his neighbor. Thus the Apostle commands us to work with our own hands, that we may have to give to those that need. He might have said, that we may support ourselves; but he tells us to give to those that need. It is the part of a Christian to take care of his own body for the very purpose that, by its soundness and well-being, he may be enabled to labor, and to acquire and preserve property, for the aid of those who are in want, that thus the stronger member may serve the weaker member, and we may be children of God, thoughtful and busy one for another, bearing one another's burdens, and so fulfilling the law of Christ.

Here is the truly Christian life, here is faith really working by love, when a man applies himself with joy and love to the works of that freest servitude in which he serves others voluntarily and for nought, himself abundantly satisfied in the fullness and riches of his own faith.

MARTIN LUTHER: POLITICAL AUTHORITY RECONCEIVED

Luther's radical understanding of justification by faith alone, with the sharp distinction it involves between the spiritual and temporal realms, has revolutionary implications for conceptions of authority, both ecclesiastical and political. Though Luther accepts the utility of distinct ecclesiastical offices, he radically narrows the meaning of ecclesiastical authority by proclaiming the **priesthood of all believers**:

These two things stand thus. First, as regards kingship, every Christian is by faith so exalted above all things that, in spiritual power, he is completely lord of all things, so that nothing whatever can do him any hurt; yea, all things are subject to him, and are compelled to be subservient to his salvation. Thus Paul says, "All things work together for good to them who are the called" (Rom. viii. 28), and also, "Whether life, or death, or things present, or things to come, all are yours;

QUESTIONS FOR REFLECTION

Can spiritual and temporal authority be completely separated?

and ye are Christ's" (1 Cor. iii. 22, 23). Not that in the sense of corporeal power any one among Christians has been appointed to possess and rule all things, according to the mad and senseless idea of certain ecclesiastics. That is the office of kings, princes, and men upon earth. In the experience of life we see that we are subjected to all things, and suffer many things, even death. Yea, the more of a Christian any man is, to so many the more evils, sufferings, and deaths is he subject, as we see in the first place in Christ the First-born, and in all His holy brethren. This is a spiritual power, which rules in the midst of enemies, and is powerful in the midst of distresses. And this is nothing else than that strength is made perfect in my weakness, and that I can turn all things to the profit of my salvation; so that even the cross and death are compelled to serve me and to work together for my salvation. This is a lofty and eminent dignity, a true and almighty dominion, a spiritual empire, in which there is nothing so good, nothing so bad, as not to work together for my good, if only I believe. And yet there is nothing of which I have need—for faith alone suffices for my salvation—unless that in it faith may exercise the power and empire of its liberty. This is the inestimable power and liberty of Christians. Nor are we only kings and the freest of all men, but also priests forever, a dignity far higher than kingship, because by that priesthood we are worthy to appear before God, to pray for others, and to teach one another mutually the things which are of God. For these are the duties of priests, and they cannot possibly be permitted to any unbeliever. Christ has obtained for us this favor, if we believe in Him: that just as we are His brethren and co-heirs and fellow-kings with Him, so we should be also fellow-priests with Him...

* * * *

Here you will ask, "If all who are in the Church are priests, by what character are those whom we now call priests to be distinguished from the laity?" I reply, By the use of these words, "priest," "clergy," "spiritual person," "ecclesiastic," an injustice has been done, since they have been transferred from the remaining body of Christians to those few who are now, by hurtful custom, called ecclesiastics. For Holy Scripture makes no distinction between them, except that those who are now boastfully called popes, bishops, and lords, it calls ministers, servants, and stewards, who are to serve the rest in the ministry of the word, for teaching the faith of Christ and the liberty of believers. For though it is true that we are all equally priests, yet we cannot, nor, if we could, ought we all to minister and teach publicly. Thus Paul says, "Let a man so account of us as of the ministers of Christ and stewards of the mysteries of God" (1 Cor. iv. 1).

This bad system has now issued in such a pompous display of power and such a terrible tyranny that no earthly government can be compared to it, as if the laity were something else than Christians. Through this perversion of things it has happened that the knowledge of Christian grace, of faith, of liberty, and altogether of Christ, has utterly perished, and has been succeeded by an intolerable bondage to human works and laws; and, according to the Lamentations of Jeremiah, we have become the slaves of the vilest men on earth, who abuse our misery to all the disgraceful and ignominious purposes of their own will.

Similarly, political authority is severed from all concern for the good of the soul, and obedience is reconceived as an expression of service for the temporal needs of others:

> Christ also, when His disciples were asked for the tribute money, asked of Peter whether the children of a king were not free from taxes. Peter agreed to this; yet Jesus commanded him to go to the sea, saying, "Lest we should offend them, go thou to the sea, and cast a hook, and take up the fish that first cometh up; and when thou hast opened his mouth thou shalt find a piece of money; that take, and give unto them for Me and thee" (Matt. xvii. 27).
>
> This example is very much to our purpose; for here Christ calls Himself and His disciples free men and children of a King, in want of nothing; and yet He voluntarily submits and pays the tax. Just as far, then, as this work was necessary or useful to Christ for justification or salvation, so far do all His other works or those of His disciples avail for justification. They are really free and subsequent to justification, and only done to serve others and set them an example.
>
> Such are the works which Paul inculcated, that Christians should be subject to principalities and powers and ready to every good work (Titus iii. 1), not that they may be justified by these things—for they are already justified by faith—but that in liberty of spirit they may thus be the servants of others and subject to powers, obeying their will out of gratuitous love.

MARTIN LUTHER: MILITANT REFORM

As the storm gathered that was to be the Protestant Reformation, Luther was hardly in command, either theoretically or practically, of the various possible implications of his rejection of traditional understandings of authority. Forced by events to grope toward a consistent and coherent political teaching, his separate pronouncements often appear to be determined more by the exigencies of rapidly changing circumstances than by a logic flowing from his theological premises.

Perhaps Luther's most momentous polemic, the *Open Letter to the Christian Nobility of the German Nation,* was a direct appeal to secular rulers to take up the cause of reforming the church by dismantling the instruments of Rome's worldly powers. This bold action he justifies by the doctrine of the priesthood of all believers, or the spiritual equality of all Christians: In an emergency like the present, Luther argues, any Christian who can is authorized, indeed obligated, to use his power to serve the faith.

MARTIN LUTHER: THE LIMITS OF SECULAR AUTHORITY

Very striking in this text is Luther's complete collapsing of the traditional hierarchy between spiritual and secular functions: The policeman and the cobbler are no less priests than those who happen to be charged "with the administration of the word of God and the sacraments." This leveling is possible only because the dignity of such functions has been severed from any humanly accessible evaluation of higher or lower purposes—that is, from the teleological or purpose-oriented reasoning of the classical (especially Aristotelian) tradition of political reflection.

The appeal to the Christian nobility of Germany obviously makes no attempt at a general theory of politics; as a response to what Luther understood to be an

PRIMARY SOURCE 5.2

"Three Walls of the Romanists," from *An Open Letter to the Christian Nobility of the German Nation Concerning Reform to the Christian Estate*

The Three Walls of the Romanists

The Romanists [1], with great adroitness, have built three walls about them, behind which they have hitherto defended themselves in such wise that no one has been able to reform them; and this has been the cause of terrible corruption throughout all Christendom.

First, when pressed by the temporal power, they have made decrees and said that the temporal power has no jurisdiction over them, but, on the other hand, that the spiritual is above the temporal power. Second, when the attempt is made to reprove them out of the Scriptures, they raise the objection that the interpretation of the Scriptures belongs to no one except the pope. Third, if threatened with a council, they answer with the fable that no one can call a council but the pope.

* * * *

Against the first wall we will direct our first attack.

It is pure invention that pope, bishops, priests, and monks are to be called the "spiritual estate"; princes, lords, artisans, and farmers the "temporal estate." That is indeed a fine bit of lying and hypocrisy. Yet no one should be frightened by it; and for this reason—viz., that all Christians are truly of the "spiritual estate," and there is among them no difference at all but that of office, as Paul says in I Corinthians 12:12, We are all one body, yet every member has its own work, where by it serves every other, all because we have one baptism, one Gospel, one faith, and are all alike Christians; for baptism, Gospel, and faith alone make us "spiritual" and a Christian people.

But that a pope or a bishop anoints, confers tonsures; ordains, consecrates, or prescribes dress unlike that of the laity, this may make hypocrites and graven images,[4] but it never makes a Christian or "spiritual" man. Through baptism all of us are consecrated to the priesthood, as St. Peter says in I Peter 2:9, "Ye are a royal priesthood, a priestly kingdom," and the book of Revelation says, Rev. 5:10 "Thou hast made us by Thy blood to be priests and kings." For if we had no higher consecration than pope or bishop gives, the consecration by pope or bishop would never make a priest, nor might anyone either say mass or preach a sermon or give absolution. Therefore when the bishop consecrates it is the same thing as if he, in the place and stead of the whole congregation, all of whom have like power, were to take one out of their number and charge him to use this power for the others; just as though ten brothers, all king's sons and equal heirs, were to choose one of themselves to rule the inheritance for them all—they would all be kings and equal in power, though one of them would be charged with the duty of ruling.

* * * *

Since, then, the temporal authorities are baptized with the same baptism and have the same faith and Gospel as we, we must grant that they are priests and bishops, and count their office one which has a proper and a useful place in the Christian community. For whoever comes out the water of baptism [10] can boast that he is already consecrated priest, bishop, and pope, though it is not seemly that every one should exercise the office.

* * * *

From all this it follows that there is really no difference between laymen and priests, princes and bishops, "spirituals" and "temporals," as they call them, except that of office and work, but not of "estate"; for they are all of the same estate, [12]—true priests, bishops, and popes—though they are not all engaged in the same work, just as all priests and monks have not the same work. This is the teaching of St. Paul in Romans 12:4 and I Corinthians 12:12, and of St. Peter in I Peter 2:9, as I have said above, viz., that we are all one body of Christ, the Head, all members one of another. Christ has not two different bodies, one "temporal," the other "spiritual." He is one Head, and He has One body.

Therefore, just as Those who are now called "spiritual"—priests, bishops, or popes—are neither different from other Christians nor superior to them, except that they

continued

PRIMARY SOURCE 5.2

"Three Walls of the Romanists," from *An Open Letter to the Christian Nobility of the German Nation Concerning Reform to the Christian Estate* continued

are charged with the administration of the Word of God and the sacraments, which is their work and office, so it is with the temporal authorities—they bear sword and rod with which to punish the evil and to protect the good. A cobbler, a smith, a farmer, each has the work and office of his trade, and yet they are all alike consecrated priests and bishops, and every one by means of his own work or office must benefit and serve every other, that in this way many kinds of work may be done for the bodily and spiritual welfare of the community, even as all the members of the body serve one another.

* * * *

Therefore, when necessity demands, and the pope is an offense to Christendom, the first man who is able should, a faithful member of the whole body, do what he can to bring about a truly free council. [29] No one can do this so well as the temporal authorities, especially since now they also are fellow-Christians, fellow-priests, "fellow-spirituals," [30] fellow-lords over all things, and whenever it is needful or profitable, they should give free course to office and work in which God has put them above every man. Would it not be an unnatural thing, if a fire broke out in a city, and everybody were to stand by and it burn on and on and consume everything that could burn, for the sole reason that nobody had the authority of the burgomaster, or because, perhaps, the fire broke in the burgomaster's house? In such case is it not the duty of every citizen to arouse and call the rest? How much more should this be done in the spiritual city of Christ, if a fire of offense breaks out, whether in the papal government, or anywhere else? In the same way, if the enemy attacks a city, he who first rouses the others deserves honor and thanks; why then should he not deserve honor who makes known the presence of the enemy from hell, awakens the Christians, and calls them together?

emergency—Rome's effort to kill the Reformation in its cradle—the author's main theoretical intention was in a way negative: to knock down theological barriers to immediate action on behalf of reform. This is the limited purpose of Luther's attack on the Roman conception of the special, higher dignity of the "spiritual," or priestly, office in favor of the idea of "the priesthood of all believers." But it was no doubt inevitable, especially in the unsettled, tumultuous religious and political circumstances of Luther's Germany, that some leaders attempted to exploit a more general, radically egalitarian, and populist potential of the critique of hierarchy. Thus radical preachers such as the apocalyptic genius Thomas Muntzer (1489–1525) would soon rouse peasants to violent revolution against all masters. The title of Luther's most virulent response to the peasant revolts is sufficient to indicate his disposition on the question: *Against the Murdering and Thieving Hordes of Peasants* (1525). But he had already given a more measured and complete answer to the radicals in a tract of 1523, *On Secular Authority: How Far Does the Obedience Owed to It Extend?*

This tract is perhaps the most complete single statement on politics that Luther has left us. In it he returns to what he regards as the fundamental Biblical distinction between the kingdom of God and the kingdom of the world, the spiritual and temporal realms, and on this basis constructs a remarkable account of the source and meaning of political authority.

PRIMARY SOURCE 5.3 — *On the Secular Authority: How Far Does the Obedience Owed to It Extend?*

1. Our first task is [to find] a firm grounding for secular law and the Sword, in order to remove any possible doubt about their being in the world as a result of God's will and ordinance. The passages [of Scripture] which provide that foundation are these: Romans, 12 [in fact 13.1–2]: "Let every soul be subject to power and superiority. For there is no power but from God and the power that exists everywhere is ordained by God. And whoever resists the power, resists God's ordinance. But whosoever resists God's ordinance shall receive condemnation on himself." And again 1 Peter 2 [13–14]: "Be subject to every kind of human order, whether it be to the king as the foremost, or governors as sent by him, as a vengeance on the wicked and a reward to the just." The Sword and its law have existed from the beginning of the world.... How the secular Sword and law are to be employed according to God's will is thus clear and certain enough: to punish the wicked and protect the just.
2. But what Christ says in Matthew 5 [38 & 9] sounds as if it were emphatically opposed to this: "You have heard what was said to your ancestors: an eye for an eye, a tooth for a tooth. But I say to you: resist no evil. Rather, if anyone strikes you on the right cheek, turn him the other cheek. And if someone will dispute with you at law, to take your coat, let him have your cloak also. And if a man should compel you to go with him one mile, go two miles etc." To the same effect, Paul in Romans 12 [19]: "Dearly beloved, do not defend yourselves, but rather give place unto the wrath of God. For it is written: Vengeance is mine; I will repay, says the Lord." And again, Matthew 5 [44]: "Love your enemies. Do good unto them that hate you." And 1 Peter 2 [error for 3:9]: "No one shall render evil for evil, or insults for insults etc." These and others of the same sort are hard sayings, and sound as if Christians in the New Covenant were to have no secular Sword. This is why the sophists say that Christ has abolished the Law of Moses, and why they make [mere] "counsels of perfection" out of such commands. They then divide up Christian doctrine and the Christian estate into two parts. The one part they call "those who are perfect," and to this they allot the "counsels," the other part they term "the imperfect" and to them they allot the commands. But this is pure effrontery and willfulness, without any warrant from Scripture. They fail to notice that in that very place Christ imposes his teachings so emphatically, that he will not have the slightest thing removed from it, and condemns to hell those who do not love their enemies [Matt. 5:22ff]. We must therefore interpret him in another way, so that his words continue to apply to all, be they "perfect" or "imperfect." For perfection and imperfection do not inhere in works, and do not establish any distinction in outward condition or status between Christians; rather, they inhere in the heart, in faith, in love, so that whoever believes more [firmly] and loves more, that person is perfect, irrespective of whether it be a man or a woman, a prince or a peasant, monk or layman. For love and faith create no factions and no outward distinctions.
3. Here we must divide Adam's children, all mankind, into two parts: the first belong to the kingdom of God, the second to the kingdom of the world. All those who truly believe in Christ belong to God's kingdom, for Christ is king and lord in God's kingdom, as the second Psalm [v. 6] and the whole of Scripture proclaims. And Christ came in order to begin the kingdom of God and to establish it in the world.... And indeed he calls the Gospel a gospel of the kingdom of God, in that it teaches, governs, and preserves the kingdom of God. Now: these people need neither secular [*weltlich*] Sword nor law. And if all the world [*Welt*] were true Christians, that is, if everyone truly believed, there would be neither need nor use for princes, kings, lords, the Sword or law. What would there be for them to do.' Seeing that [true Christians] have the Holy Spirit in their hearts, which teaches and moves them to love everyone, wrong no one, and suffer wrongs gladly, even unto death. Where all wrongs are endured willingly and what is right' is done freely, there is

continued

PRIMARY SOURCE 5.3 | *On the Secular Authority: How Far Does the Obedience Owed to It Extend? continued*

no place for quarrelling, disputes, courts, punishments, laws, or the Sword. And therefore laws and the secular Sword cannot possibly find any work to do among Christians, especially since they of themselves do much more than any laws or teachings might demand.... But since no man is by nature a Christian or just, but all are sinners and evil, God hinders them all, by means of the law, from doing as they please and expressing their wickedness outwardly in actions....

4. All those who are not Christians [in the above sense] belong to the kingdom of the world or [in other words] are under the law. There are few who believe, and even fewer who behave like Christians and refrain from doing evil [themselves], let alone not resisting evil [done to them]. And for the rest God has established another government, outside the Christian estate and the kingdom of God, and has cast them into subjection to the Sword. So that, however much they would like to do evil, they are unable to act in accordance with their inclinations, or, if they do, they cannot do so without fear, or enjoy peace and good fortune. In the same way, a wicked, fierce animal is chained and bound so that it cannot bite or tear, as its nature would prompt it to do, however much it wants to; whereas a tame, gentle animal needs nothing like chains or bonds and is harmless even without them. If there were [no law and government], then seeing that all the world is evil and that scarcely one human being in a thousand is a true Christian, people would devour each other and no one would be able to support his wife and children, feed himself, and serve God. The world [*Welt*] would become a desert. And so God has ordained the two governments, the spiritual [government] which fashions true Christians and just persons through the Holy Spirit under Christ, and the secular [*weltlich*] government which holds the Unchristian and wicked in check and forces them to keep the peace outwardly and be still, like it or not.... If someone wanted to have the world ruled according to the Gospel, and to abolish all secular law and the Sword, on the ground that all are baptized and Christians and that the Gospel will have no law or sword used among Christians, who have no need of them [in any case], what do you imagine the effect would be? He would let loose the wild animals from their bonds and chains, and let them maul and tear everyone to pieces, saying all the while that really they are just fine, tame, gentle, little things. But my wounds would tell me different. And so the wicked under cover of the name of Christians, would misuse the freedom of the Gospel, would work their wickedness and would claim that they are Christians and [therefore] subject to no law and no Sword.... Therefore care must be taken to keep these two governments distinct, and both must be allowed to continue [their work], the one to make [people] just, the other to create outward peace and prevent evildoing. Neither is enough for the world without the other. Without the spiritual government of Christ, no one can be made just in the sight of God by the secular government [alone]. However, Christ's spiritual government does not extend to everyone; on the contrary, Christians are at all times the fewest in number and live in the midst of the Unchristian. Conversely, where the secular government or law rules on its own, pure hypocrisy must prevail, even if it were God's own commandments [that were being enforced]. For no one becomes truly just without the Holy Spirit in his heart, however good his works. And equally where the spiritual government rules over a country and its people unaided, every sort of wickedness is let loose and every sort of knavery has free play. For the world in general is incapable of accepting it or understanding it [i.e. the spiritual government]. You can now see the implication of the words of Christ which we cited earlier from Matthew 5[39], that Christians are not to go to law or use the secular Sword amongst themselves....

5. You will object here: seeing that Christians need neither the secular Sword nor law, why does Paul in Romans 13 [1] say to all

PRIMARY SOURCE 5.3 | *On the Secular Authority: How Far Does the Obedience Owed to It Extend?* *continued*

Christians, "Let every soul be subject to power" and superiority! And St. Peter [1 Pet. 2:13]: "Be subject to every human ordinance etc." as cited above. My answer is, I have already said that Christians among themselves and for themselves need no law and no Sword, for they have no use for them. But because a true Christian, while he is on the earth, lives for and serves his neighbor and not himself, he does things that are of no benefit to himself, but of which his neighbor stands in need. Such is the nature of the Christian's spirit. Now the Sword is indispensable for the whole world, to preserve peace, punish sin, and restrain the wicked. And therefore Christians readily submit themselves to be governed by the Sword, they pay taxes, honor those in authority, serve and help them, and do what they can to uphold their power, so that they may continue their work, and that honor and fear of authority may be maintained. [All this] even though Christians do not need it for themselves, but they attend to what others need, as Paul teaches in Ephesians 5[21]. In the same way, the Christian performs every other work of love that he does not require for himself. He visits the sick, but not in order to become well himself. He does not feed others because he needs food for himself. And neither does he serve authority because he himself stands in need of it, but because others do, in order that they might enjoy protection, and so that the wicked might not grow even worse. [...]

6. You ask whether a Christian can even wield the secular Sword and punish the wicked [himself], seeing that Christ's words "Do not resist evil" seem so peremptory and clear that the sophists have to water them down into a mere "counsel." Answer, "You have now heard two [conflicting] things. One is that there can be no Sword amongst Christians. And therefore you cannot bear the Sword over or among Christians. So the question is irrelevant in that context and must instead be asked in connection with the other group [the Unchristian]: Can a Christian use be made of it with regard to them? This is where the second part [of what I have said] applies, the one that says that you owe the Sword your service and support, by whatever means are available to you, be it with your body, goods, honor, or soul. For this is a work of which you yourself have no need, but your neighbor and the whole world most certainly do. And therefore if you see that there is a lack of hangmen, court officials, judges, lords, or princes, and you find that you have the necessary skills, then you should offer your services and seek office, so that authority, which is so greatly needed, will never come to be held in contempt, become powerless, or perish. The world cannot get by without it. How does this resolve the difficulty? In this way: all such actions would be devoted wholly to the service of others; they would benefit only your neighbor and not you or your possessions and honor. You would not be aiming at revenge [for yourself], at repaying evil with evil, but rather at the good of your neighbors, the preservation, protection, and peace of others. As far as you yourself and your possessions are concerned, you keep to the Gospel and act according to Christ's word; you would gladly turn the other cheek and give up your cloak as well as your coat, when it is you and your possessions that are involved. And so the two are nicely reconciled: you satisfy the demands of God's kingdom and the world's at one and the same time, outwardly and inwardly; you both suffer evil and injustice and yet punish them; you do not resist evil and yet you do resist it. For you attend to yourself and what is yours in one way, and to your neighbor and what is his in another. As to you and yours, you keep to the Gospel and suffer injustice as a true Christian. But where the next man and what is his are concerned, you act in accordance with the [command to] love and you tolerate no injustice against him [...]

MARTIN LUTHER: "SPIRITUAL" AND "SECULAR" RECONFIGURED

Luther in this text effects an ingenious and surprising breakthrough in Christian political theory, one that is rich in implications for modern thought. He accepts and in fact radicalizes the basic Christian dichotomy between the two kingdoms, the spiritual and the temporal. In the earlier tradition of Christian political thought, from Augustine forward, the drawing of this dichotomy had always implied a depreciation of the affairs of this world and thus redounded finally to the benefit of the spiritual power. The logic that had constrained political theorizing in the earlier Christian tradition in fact appears inescapable: If spiritual and secular concerns are considered distinct, and spiritual concerns are acknowledged to be of ultimate importance and therefore superior, then clearly these higher concerns must always trump those that are merely political. If the secular realm has any dignity, then it can only be derived from and considered subservient to the superior, spiritual realm. In a word, as long as humanity's ultimate purpose is understood as distinctly spiritual or otherworldly, as a Christian can hardly deny, then it seems inevitable that secular authority be subordinated to spiritual or priestly authority.

Luther cuts through this Gordian knot of medieval Christian thought by radicalizing the basic Christian dichotomy and in a way liberating the secular from the spiritual. Salvation, or the spiritual kingdom, is radically inward, a matter of conscience, a secret, spiritual, hidden region dependent on no human power but entirely on the word of Scripture. The kingdom of this world is wholly external; it deals with mortal life and with property. So complete is Luther's removal of the kingdom of God from the kingdom of the world that he proclaims the absolute uselessness of politics for true believers: The righteous do of themselves more than the law commands, attach no intrinsic importance to the things of this world, and have no need of compulsion. (Thomas Aquinas, by contrast, taught that political authority was essential to our humanity, even our uncorrupted humanity prior to the Fall.) Luther is confident, on the other hand, that the individual's conscience is immune from external force: "Faith is free, and no one can be compelled to believe."

Now, one would expect this radical separation to imply a radical depreciation of the political realm. But Luther avoids this consequence by shifting the account of the purpose of politics entirely to the needs of the non-Christian neighbor. Politics contributes in no way to the spiritual purposes of Christians, but only to the secular needs of their neighbors. Secular needs become authoritative for Christians *as someone else's needs*. By this remarkable displacement of the question of purpose, Luther bypasses the logic that seemed, in Christendom, to necessitate the subordination, direct or indirect, of political to spiritual authorities.

Luther thus insulates the political realm from any higher purposes and thereby from the authority of priests. He refounds politics on material necessity, yet does so in such a way that this secularization does not amount to a depreciation. The key to Luther's ingenious rethinking is that the worldly or material necessity of politics is not left to rely on its own dignity but is considered as enjoined by the Christian duty of love. Thus Luther accomplishes what seems impossible: securing at once the dignity of the political realm and its separation from any more authoritative spiritual ends. The linking of love to a material political necessity and the severing of any direct ties between this dutiful love and the authority of higher, specifically religious purposes is evident in Luther's uncompromising examples: "The world needs a hangman? Offer your services!" Or further, in the case of war: "It is a Christian act, and an act of love, to kill enemies without scruple, to rob and to burn, and to do whatever damages the enemy, according to the usages of war, until he is defeated" (*On Secular Authority*, Part 3).

MARTIN LUTHER: FREEDOM OF CONSCIENCE

Further in this treatise *On Secular Authority*, Luther draws from his radical distinction between the spiritual and temporal realms a strikingly modern understanding of the inviolability of the individual conscience, and he concludes against the use of force to suppress heresy:

> Another important point is this. However stupid they are, they must admit that they have no power over the soul. For no human being can kill the soul or bring it to life, or lead it to heaven or to hell. And if they will not believe us, then Christ will show it clearly enough when he says in Matthew 10[28], "Do not be afraid of those that kill the body and after that can do nothing more. Fear rather him who, after he kills the body, has the power to condemn to hell." Surely that is clear enough: the soul is taken out of the hands of any human being whatsoever, and is placed exclusively under the power of God. Now tell me this: would anyone in his right mind give orders where he has no authority? [. . .]
>
> Each must decide at his own peril what he is to believe, and must see to it that he believes rightly. Other people cannot go to heaven or hell on my behalf, or open or close [the gates to either] for me. And just as little can they believe or not believe on my behalf, or force my faith or unbelief. How he believes is a matter for each individual's conscience, and this does not diminish [the authority of] secular governments. They ought therefore to content themselves with attending to their own business, and allow people to believe what they can, and what they want, and they must use no coercion in this matter against anyone. Faith is free, and no one can be compelled to believe. More precisely, so far from being something secular authority ought to create and enforce, faith is something that God works in the spirit. Hence that common saying which also occurs in Augustine: no one can or ought to be forced to believe anything against his will. Those blind and wretched people do not realize what a pointless and impossible thing they are attempting. However strict their orders, and however much they rage, they cannot force people to do more than obey by word and [outward] deed; they cannot compel the heart, even if they were to tear themselves apart trying. There is truth in the saying: Thought is free. What is the effect of their trying to force people to believe in their hearts! All they achieve is to force people with weak consciences to lie, to perjure themselves, saying one thing while in their hearts they believe another. . . For my ungracious lords, the pope and bishops, should be [real] bishops and preach the Word of God; but they have left off doing so and have become secular princes, ruling by means of laws that concern only life and goods. They have managed to turn everything upside down: they ought to rule souls with God's Word, inwardly, and instead they rule castles, towns, countries, and peoples, outwardly, and torment souls with unspeakable murders. And the secular lords, who should rule countries and peoples outwardly, do not do so either; instead, the only thing they know how to do is to poll and fleece, heap one tax on another, let loose a bear here, a wolf there. There is no good faith or honesty to be found amongst them; thieves and

QUESTIONS FOR REFLECTION

Is thought free from external influences?

> villains behave better than they do, and secular government is sunk as low as the government of the spiritual tyrants. God has made them to be of perverse minds and has deprived them of their senses, so that they want to rule spiritually over souls, just as the spiritual authorities want to rule in a worldly manner. [...]

Luther is convinced that, by radically separating the two spheres, he has finally reconciled them, or ordered them properly with respect to each other, satisfying "at the same time God's kingdom inwardly and the kingdom of the world outwardly." Both the spiritual and the secular are given their due, without one impinging on the other. The "powers that be are ordained of God," part of "God's work and creation," and therefore are "good." Given the fallenness of human nature ("no one is by nature Christian or pious, but every one sinful and evil . . ."), these powers must be ample and energetic. "The world is too wicked to deserve princes much wiser and more just than this. Frogs must have storks."

MARTIN LUTHER: OBEDIENCE AND RESISTANCE

But we have seen that rulers' powers are not unlimited. "We must obey God rather than men" (Acts 5:29). Luther's perfectly characteristic example (in this same text) of an exception to secular powers over external things concerns the human artifact most closely associated with the inward spiritual life: "If you do not resist [the secular ruler] and let him take away your faith or your books, then you will truly have denied God." (A certain prince had in fact attempted to confiscate copies of Luther's German translation of the New Testament.) Luther immediately takes a step back here and teaches the reader not to resist violently, but to let books be taken only by force, and to offer no assistance to such wickedness. Further on, though, he does not shrink here from warning rulers and at least implicitly encouraging popular resistance: "The common man is becoming knowledgeable. . . . People will not put up with your tyranny and arbitrariness any longer."

Like other early reformers, Luther would not countenance revolution or regicide, but only passive resistance to rulers who overstepped the bounds of their authority. He did give preachers full reign to reprimand and instruct secular rulers, but never to encourage disobedience.

Luther would never achieve a consistent theoretical position on the question of a "right of resistance" to established authority. He was aware that he was sitting on a powder keg of social unrest bound up with the religious question—and he had indeed done much to light the fuse. As much as he distrusted established authorities, he had learned from the peasant revolts the danger of a destructive response. Human nature is not to be trusted; the civil sword is an insuperable necessity. Frogs, as we have seen, need storks.

But defining the limit between secular authority and spiritual freedom proved difficult in practice. We have seen that Luther was not reluctant in 1520 to call upon

QUESTIONS FOR REFLECTION

Does it make sense to urge obedience and at the same time to denounce the injustice of rulers?

the "the Christian nobility of the German nation" to use their power to reform the church by force. In doing so he did not of course mean to grant them authority to *decide* how the church should be reformed (its structure, sacraments, etc.), but assumed rather that the Bible was sufficiently clear to direct reform, and that tradition might hold sway where the Bible was silent. (In this Luther tended to defer more to Catholic traditions than did later, and in particular Calvinist, reformers.) When some princes had their own ideas about reform and in fact persecuted Lutherans, then Luther insisted on the strict limitation of secular authority to "external" matters. But then again, when the Emperor Charles of Hapsburg attempted to reassert Roman authority at the Diet of Augsburg in 1530, Luther reluctantly endorsed the right of German princes to active resistance against the emperor. This stand was based on already developed juridical arguments concerning the constitutional limitation of the emperor's power and the responsibilities of inferior magistrates. (We will see John Calvin drawing upon the same kinds of arguments.) It is notable, however, that Luther never explicitly attributes the same right of active resistance to "private" persons—that is, to the people generally.

Likewise, although, as we have seen, Luther argues against the right, indeed the possibility, of using "external" power to punish or eliminate heresy, in practice he finds it necessary to countenance the secular princes' authority in settling matters of religion in their domains. Here as elsewhere it was left to Luther's followers, including John Calvin, to work out arguments on behalf of the state's role with respect to religious practices and institutions.

MARTIN LUTHER: RATIONAL ADVICE TO PRINCES

In the last part of the treatise *On Secular Authority*, Luther permits himself to give advice on "how a prince should go about exercising" this authority. Along with much wholesome and generally unsurprising advice on governing, he offers some very interesting observations on the superiority of reason to law:

> Therefore the prince must keep the laws as firmly under his own control as he does the Sword, and use his own reason to judge when and where the law should be applied in its full rigor, and when it should be moderated. So that reason remains the ruler at all times, the supreme law and master of all the laws.

At the very end of the treatise, in an addendum on the question of the restitution of wrongfully acquired goods, Luther remarks that "there is no law to be found for this, except the law of love.... For nature teaches the same as love: I ought to do what I would have done unto me." Thus, he concludes, "unfettered reason ... is greater than all the laws in books."

Luther's political teaching is, then, open to the authority of reason; but reason is now understood as restricted to the purely secular realm of "needs," a realm Luther has insulated from all philosophical or priestly claims to higher purposes.

CASE STUDY 5.1 | **LUTHER, CALVIN, AND THE RIGHT TO RESISTANCE**

The Christian thinkers St. Paul and St. Augustine both counseled obedience to the state, except in cases where conscience was violated. By contrast, certain teachings of the Protestant Reformation allow for the possibility of resistance to the state. Indeed, during the Revolutionary War, American Protestants invoked the right to resistance against Great Britain, citing the authority of both John Locke and divine revelation. During World War II, Karl Barth, a Swiss German theologian from Calvin's Geneva, supported resistance to Hitler and the Nazis. In Luther's Germany, however, Protestant leadership generally supported obedience to authority and did not advocate resistance to the Nazis. Is there anything in the content of Luther's and Calvin's teachings that would lead to these different approaches to resistance to the state?

MARTIN LUTHER: THE MUTUAL EMANCIPATION OF THE "SPIRITUAL" AND THE "SECULAR"

We have seen that Martin Luther breaks decisively with the medieval Christian political tradition by a twofold strategy. First, he emancipates the spiritual and secular realms from each other by a radicalization of the Christian distinction between spiritual and inward things on the one hand and secular and external things on the other. Next, having severed secular, political matters from higher spiritual purposes, he nonetheless secures the dignity and binding character of political authority by recourse to the Christian duty of love for the other. It is fair to call this duty of love operative in politics "secularized" because it concerns only external necessities, thus preserving the essential separation from concern for the good of the soul. My neighbor's material–political need is in no way intrinsically ordered with respect to my spiritual destiny; my duty to love my neighbor is commanded by God but in no intelligible way ordered by His love. This duty is commanded by God, but it aims at nothing divine, except insofar as everything is God's creation. My Christian love has no other object, at least as far as politics is concerned, than the fallen needs of my non-Christian neighbor.

Beneath the now familiar dichotomy between the spiritual and the secular, or the internal and the external, this abstraction of duty from purpose is the lynchpin of Luther's remarkable attempt to do full justice at once to the claims of the soul and those of the body—spiritual transcendence and material necessity. The question Luther bequeaths to the future of political theory is whether the secular realm, now grounded in its own needs, can avoid encroaching on concerns of the spirit. Luther seems not to envision a situation in which a person's duty to the needs of humanity might appear to be in tension with, or might even claim to trump, the calling to some inward perfection.

JOHN CALVIN: LIFE AND LEGACY

A short generation younger than Luther, John Calvin (1509–1564) was just eight years old when the German reformer posted the *95 Theses* that unleashed forces that soon became the Protestant Reformation. By the time Calvin reached maturity, this Reformation was already a growing concern, and the young Frenchman was to

QUESTIONS FOR REFLECTION

Can spiritual and the secular interests be neatly divided and kept separate in practice?

become its most brilliant exponent and most powerful organizer. Calvin would eventually find himself at odds with Lutherans in a number of controversies (particularly surrounding the understanding of the Eucharist, or the sacrament of the Last Supper), convinced that they had retained too much of Roman superstition; he would impart a distinctly austere, disciplined, and independent cast to what became the Calvinist version of the Reformation. But it is beyond question that the first premises of Calvin's break with Rome were learned from Luther or his followers: namely, that human works are corrupted to the core by sin and have no saving power, and consequently that salvation is by faith in Christ alone.

In many ways the two men could hardly be more different: Luther warm and courageous, but also impetuous, sometimes carried to extremes by the brute force of his own dominant insight; Calvin much more restrained, nuanced, and ready and equipped to refute his opponents with painstaking, even exhaustive logical argument. Luther unleashed a movement he soon despaired of controlling; Calvin was the consummate organizer and institutionalizer. Unlike Luther, Calvin produced (in successively larger Latin editions, from 1536 to 1559, and in French translations that did much to shape the evolution of that language) a systematic, comprehensive treatise of his Christian teaching, fittingly titled *Institutes of the Christian Religion*. This work has been called the great Protestant Summa, and Calvin is thus a kind of Protestant answer to the great synthesizer of medieval Catholicism, Thomas Aquinas.

Calvin was born in Noyon, in northern France, and was sent as a youth to study Latin and theology in Paris until his father, alert to the financial advantages of the study of law, diverted him to that field and thus to the city of Orleans and later to Bourges. Before leaving Paris he was already associating with an emerging school of literary humanists on the model of Erasmus, including men such as Guillaume Budé. Calvin himself in fact authored a commentary in the humanist style on Seneca's *De Clementia*. Calvin's literary education would leave significant traces on his later religious writings; but his association with the humanist movement ended with his conversion, which, like Luther, he later remembered as a sudden and overwhelming event. This conversion seems to have occurred sometime in late 1533 or early 1534.

Less than three years later, Calvin had published his first edition of the *Institutes* and was already being looked to for leadership in the Protestant cause. Fleeing persecution in France, he found refuge for a time in Basel and then just happened to pass through Geneva, the city that he would make the home base of an international Calvinist movement. Geneva did not take immediately to Calvin's reforming efforts; in fact he fell into disfavor with the Genevan authorities and was exiled from that city from 1538 to 1541. Even after his return, it would be a gross exaggeration to suggest that Calvin completely had his way with the city of Geneva. But from 1541 until his death, Calvin's teaching was a dominant force in all the affairs of the city, which was made over to a considerable degree by his reforming efforts.

During his exile from Geneva, Calvin met a widow, Idelette de Bure, whom he converted from Anabaptism and married. She became, as he said, "the excellent companion of my life." More than two decades after being welcomed back to Geneva, following a long and painful illness, the great reformer died in the arms of his trusted friend and successor in the leadership of Calvinism, Theodore Beza.

JOHN CALVIN: DISTINGUISHING SPIRITUAL AND TEMPORAL

John Calvin's most fully developed political teaching is embedded in the magisterial, comprehensive interpretation of Christianity in his *Institutes of the Christian Religion.* Calvin in fact devotes the entire final chapter (xx) of the final book (IV) of his great treatise to the subject of civil government. Granting that "this topic seems by nature alien to the spiritual doctrine of faith" (IV.xx.1; 1485), Calvin introduces his political teaching with a defense of the subject matter itself ("which pertains only to the establishment of civil justice and outward morality") as part of a treatise on spiritual and inward matters. Like Luther, Calvin thus based his teaching on a rigorous dichotomy between the spiritual and the temporal.

Calvin most fully develops this dichotomy in a chapter whose very title echoes Luther's seminal treatise on **Christian freedom** (Book III, Chapter xix). Calvin is aware that this "freedom" is a very sensitive and controversial topic, a topic fraught with political implications, because many "wanton spirits" (referring no doubt to radicals such as Thomas Muntzer) had abused it as a pretext to "shake off all obedience toward God and break out into unbridled license" (III.xix.1; 834). Thus Calvin takes great pains to explain just what Christian freedom means and how it has been misunderstood, where it applies and where it does not. Following Luther, he grounds this freedom directly in the doctrine of justification by faith in Christ alone, and a rejection of the efficacy of works for salvation. Christian freedom is freedom from the impossible burden of the righteousness of works:

> 2. Christian liberty seems to me to consist of three parts. First, the consciences of believers, while seeking the assurance of their justification before God, must rise above the law, and think no more of obtaining justification by it. For while the law, as has already been demonstrated, (supra, chap. 17, sec. 1,) leaves not one man righteous, we are either excluded from all hope of justification, or we must be loosed from the law, and so loosed as that no account at all shall be taken of works. For he who imagines that in order to obtain justification he must bring any degree of works whatever, cannot fix any mode or limit, but makes himself debtor to the whole law. Therefore, laying aside all mention of the law, and all idea of works, we must in the matter of justification have recourse to the mercy of God only; turning away our regard from ourselves, we must look only to Christ. For the question is, not how we may be righteous, but how, though unworthy and unrighteous, we may be regarded as righteous. If consciences would obtain any assurance of this, they must give no place to the law. Still it cannot be rightly inferred from this that believers have no need of the law. It ceases not to teach, exhort, and urge them to good, although it is not recognized by their consciences before the judgment-seat of God. The two things are very different, and should be well and carefully distinguished. The whole lives of Christians ought to be a kind of aspiration after piety, seeing they are called unto holiness (Eph. 1:4; 1 Thess. 4:5). The office of the law is to excite them to the study of purity and

QUESTIONS FOR REFLECTION

Is pure, disinterested love (of God or of another person) impossible? Are human motives inevitably tainted or even polluted?

holiness, by reminding them of their duty. For when the conscience feels anxious as to how it may have the favor of God, as to the answer it could give, and the confidence it would feel, if brought to his judgment-seat, in such a case the requirements of the law are not to be brought forward, but Christ, who surpasses all the perfection of the law, is alone to be held forth for righteousness.

In the second part of Calvin's exposition of Christian freedom, he argues that this freedom from works liberates the believer to obey God voluntarily:

> 4. Another point which depends on the former is, that consciences obey the law, not as if compelled by legal necessity; but being free from the yoke of the law itself, voluntarily obey the will of God. Being constantly in terror so long as they are under the dominion of the law, they are never disposed promptly to obey God, unless they have previously obtained this liberty. Our meaning shall be explained more briefly and clearly by an example. The command of the law is, "Thou shalt love the Lord thy God with all thine heart, and with all thy soul, and with all thy might" (Deut. 6:5). To accomplish this, the soul must previously be divested of every other thought and feeling, the heart purified from all its desires, all its powers collected and united on this one object. Those who, in comparison of others, have made much progress in the way of the Lord, are still very far from this goal. For although they love God in their mind, and with a sincere affection of heart, yet both are still in a great measure occupied with the lusts of the flesh, by which they are retarded and prevented from proceeding with quickened pace toward God. They indeed make many efforts, but the flesh partly enfeebles their strength, and partly binds them to itself. What can they do while they thus feel that there is nothing of which they are less capable than to fulfill the law? They wish, aspire, endeavor; but do nothing with the requisite perfection. If they look to the law, they see that every work which they attempt or design is accursed. Nor can any one deceive himself by inferring that the work is not altogether bad, merely because it is imperfect, and, therefore, that any good which is in it is still accepted of God. For the law demanding perfect love condemns all imperfection, unless its rigor is mitigated. Let any man therefore consider his work which he wishes to be thought partly good, and he will find that it is a transgression of the law by the very circumstance of its being imperfect.
>
> 5. See how our works lie under the curse of the law if they are tested by the standard of the law. But how can unhappy souls set themselves with alacrity to a work from which they cannot hope to gain any thing in return but cursing? On the other hand, if freed from this severe exaction, or rather from the whole rigor of the law, they hear themselves invited by God with paternal levity, they will cheerfully and alertly obey the call, and follow his guidance...

The third and final part of Calvin's argument concerning Christian freedom is that "we are not bound before God to any observance of external things which are in themselves indifferent (*adiafora*), but that we are now at full liberty either to use or omit them." As long as we do not recognize this complete liberty regarding "external things," Calvin explains, we are easy prey to superstitions. He recognizes that charity requires that we avoid giving unnecessary offense to others in our use of this liberty, but he insists that we must also be careful not to give any ground to superstitious belief in the effectiveness of "works."

Toward the end of this chapter about Christian freedom, Calvin acknowledges the danger of misconstruing this teaching that believers' "consciences are exempted from all human authority." The danger is that "the moment the abolition of human constitutions is mentioned, the greatest disturbances are excited, partly by the seditious, and partly by calumniators, as if obedience of every kind were at the same time abolished and overthrown." To address this danger, Calvin carefully lays out his understanding of the distinction between spiritual and political government:

> 15. Therefore, lest this prove a stumbling-block to any, let us observe that in man government is twofold: the one spiritual, by which the conscience is trained to piety and divine worship; the other civil, by which the individual is instructed in those duties which, as men and citizens, we are bold to perform (see Book 4, chap. 10, sec. 3–6). To these two forms are commonly given the not inappropriate names of spiritual and temporal jurisdiction, intimating that the former species has reference to the life of the soul, while the latter relates to matters of the present life, not only to food and clothing, but to the enacting of laws which require a man to live among his fellows purely, honorably, and modestly. The former has its seat within the soul, the latter only regulates the external conduct. We may call the one the spiritual, the other the civil kingdom. Now, these two, as we have divided them, are always to be viewed apart from each other. When the one is considered, we should call off our minds, and not allow them to think of the other. For there exists in man a kind of two worlds, over which different kings and different laws can preside. By attending to this distinction, we will not erroneously transfer the doctrine of the gospel concerning spiritual liberty to civil order, as if in regard to external government Christians were less subject to human laws, because their consciences are unbound before God, as if they were exempted from all carnal service, because in regard to the Spirit they are free. Again because even in those constitutions which seem to relate to the spiritual kingdom, there may be some delusion, it is necessary to distinguish between those which are to be held legitimate as being agreeable to the Word of God, and those, on the other hand, which ought to have no place among the pious. We shall elsewhere have an opportunity of speaking of civil government (see Book 4, chap. 20)....

Calvin thus distinguishes very sharply—even more radically than Luther—between the spiritual and the temporal, a dichotomy he equates with that between soul and body, or between inner mind and outward behavior. This radical severing of inner spirituality from external works is necessary, Calvin believes, in order to combat the "savage tyranny and butchery" (IV.x.1179) of popes and priests, who wield power over souls by claiming to know what works are necessary to salvation.

JOHN CALVIN: HUMAN DEPRAVITY

It is important to note here that for John Calvin the term "external works" does not refer exclusively, or even mainly, to ordinarily observable behaviors. To liberate souls from Roman tyranny, Calvin must deny the soul's capacity to produce any good from itself. Calvin rejects as presumptuous and impious the teaching of "sophists" (his name for scholastic philosophers, in the tradition of Thomas Aquinas), learned from

Aristotle, that human laws can and ought to contribute to the forming of the human soul to virtues understood to be intrinsically good.

Calvin's rejection of the intrinsic goodness of virtue and therefore of the politics of virtue formation is associated with his very radical understanding of the Fall. Calvin insists upon the absolute inability of human beings to contribute to the good of their own souls or those of their fellows, or even to grasp intellectually in the slightest degree the nature of the good. Calvin rejects Aquinas' partial exemption of the rational faculty from the effects of the Fall; he insists that "the whole man is flesh," and that "the soul . . . is utterly devoid of all good" (II.iii.1&2).

Institutes II.i. 9

I have said, therefore, that all the parts of the soul were possessed by sin, ever since Adam revolted from the fountain of righteousness. For not only did the inferior appetites entice him, but abominable impiety seized upon the very citadel of the mind, and pride penetrated to his inmost heart (Rom. 7:12; Book 4, chap. 15, sec. 10–12), so that it is foolish and unmeaning to confine the corruption thence proceeding to what are called sensual motions, or to call it an excitement, which allures, excites, and drags the single part which they call sensuality into sin. Here Peter Lombard has displayed gross ignorance (Lomb., lib. 2 Dist. 31). When investigating the seat of corruption, he says it is in the flesh (as Paul declares), not properly, indeed, but as being more apparent in the flesh. As if Paul had meant that only a part of the soul, and not the whole nature, was opposed to supernatural grace. Paul himself leaves no room for doubt, when he says, that corruption does not dwell in one part only, but that no part is free from its deadly taint. For, speaking of corrupt nature, he not only condemns the inordinate nature of the appetites, but, in particular, declares that the understanding is subjected to blindness, and the heart to depravity (Eph. 4:17, 18). The third chapter of the Epistle to the Romans is nothing but a description of original sin; the same thing appears more clearly from the mode of renovation. For the spirit, which is contrasted with the old man, and the flesh, denotes not only the grace by which the sensual or inferior part of the soul is corrected, but includes a complete reformation of all its parts (Eph. 4:23). And, accordingly, Paul enjoins not only that gross appetites be suppressed, but that we be renewed in the spirit of our mind (Eph. 4:23), as he elsewhere tells us to be transformed by the renewing of our mind (Rom. 12:2). Hence it follows, that that part in which the dignity and excellence of the soul are most conspicuous, has not only been wounded, but so corrupted, that mere cure is not sufficient. There must be a new nature. How far sin has seized both on the mind and heart, we shall shortly see. Here I only wished briefly to observe, that the whole man, from the crown of the head to the sole of the foot, is so deluged, as it were, that no part remains exempt from sin, and, therefore, everything which proceeds from him is imputed as sin. Thus Paul says, that all carnal thoughts and affections are enmity against God, and consequently death (Rom. 8:7).

Having affirmed the **total depravity** of human nature, Calvin goes on (in II.ii.26 & 27) to spell out the implications for the idea of freedom of the will: There is no such thing. Humans may desire some good, he argues, but this desire is merely instinctive and shared with the brute beasts; it is not a rational choice of some higher good. "The natural desire of happiness in man no more proves the freedom of the will, than the tendency of metals and stones to attain the perfection of their nature . . ." Against the tradition of "the schoolmen" and even "certain of the ancient Fathers," Calvin

QUESTIONS FOR REFLECTION

Can there be freedom without some knowledge of a higher good, a good transcending material incentives?

vigorously denies that "the soul has in itself a power of aspiring to good." Not by nature, but only by a "regeneration" that depends wholly upon God, does the spirit of man oppose the flesh. It cannot, then, be admitted, "that men, without grace, have any motions to good, however feeble. . . ."

JOHN CALVIN: PREDESTINATION

The term "works" thus refers to anything within human power, or producible by human effort, whereas the "spirit" is totally subject to the imponderable will of God, who dispenses grace according to a plan beyond human comprehension. Christian freedom has nothing to do with a humanistic affirmation of free will; free will would imply the capacity to will what is good, but humans are free from human power precisely because the only thing that matters—the salvation of the soul—is not available to human choice but is determined by God's inscrutable election, his **predestination,** before the foundation of the world, of certain souls to salvation and others to damnation:

> We shall never feel persuaded as we ought that our salvation flows from the free mercy of God as its fountain, until we are made acquainted with his eternal election, the grace of God being illustrated by the contrast, viz., that he does not adopt all promiscuously to the hope of salvation, but gives to some what he denies to others. It is plain how greatly ignorance of this principle detracts from the glory of God, and impairs true humility. But though thus necessary to be known, Paul declares that it cannot be known unless God, throwing works entirely out of view, elect those whom he has predestined. (III.xxi.1)

The doctrine that God predestines a few to salvation and the rest to eternal damnation is thus a strict correlate of the Christian's freedom from the tyranny of works. Calvin is aware that reason must find such a teaching (which came to be called "double predestination") appalling; but unlike Luther's great successor Melanchthon, for example, he does not believe that this severe doctrine, a necessary implication of the rejection of works in favor of the pure teaching of justification by faith, ought to be left in the shadows or swept under the rug. In his zeal for rigor and clarity, the Genevan reformer goes even beyond his teacher St. Augustine, who had affirmed the predestination of the elect but considered the damned to have been abandoned to their sins rather than explicitly preassigned to hell.

JOHN CALVIN: THE DIGNITY OF THE POLITICAL

It would seem to follow from Calvin's radical separation of the spiritual from the temporal, and from his consequent denial of the efficacy of human choice, that politics is a low and sordid business without spiritual significance. But this is far from Calvin's teaching. In fact, like Luther, but more emphatically and systematically, Calvin radically separates the two realms only to prepare to join them in a new way:

> Calvin clearly grants politics a much higher status than did St. Augustine: For . . . it is not owing to human perverseness that supreme power on earth is lodged in kings and other governors, but by Divine Providence, and the holy decree of Him to whom it has seemed good so to govern the affairs of men . . . Wherefore no man can doubt that civil authority is in the sight of God, not only sacred and lawful, but the most sacred and by far the most honorable, of all stations in mortal life. (IV.xx.4)

Calvin does not follow Luther's argument that government is necessary only for those who are not true Christians. Rather, he holds that government is directly ordained of God and, in apparent agreement with Aquinas, that it is essential to our humanity:

> [I]ts use among men being not less than that of bread and water, light and air, while its dignity is much more excellent. Its object is not merely, like those things, to enable men to breathe, eat, drink, and be warmed (though it certainly includes all these, while it enables them to live together); this, I say, is not its only object, but it is that no idolatry, no blasphemy against the name of God, no calumnies against his truth, nor other offences to religion, break out and be disseminated among the people; that the public quiet be not disturbed, that every man's property be kept secure, that men may carry on innocent commerce with each other, that honesty and modesty be cultivated; in short, that a public form of religion may exist among Christians, and humanity among men. (IV.xx.3)

How is it possible for Calvin to combine such a low view of human nature—the doctrine of total depravity—with such a high view of the political function? If everything human, including, notably, the faculty of reason, is utterly corrupt, then how can politics be not only necessary but excellent?

JOHN CALVIN: REASON AND NATURAL LAW

Recall that Luther's strategy for grounding political obligation, after denying the direct relevance of politics to the Christian soul, is to embrace it under the duty to one's non-Christian neighbor. Calvin's strategy is more thoroughgoing and perhaps more satisfactory. It consists essentially in including political order immediately under God's providential order, allowing it to exhibit His glory as does the rest of natural creation. But how is this possible given the corruption of human nature? To understand this will require a review of Calvin's teaching concerning **natural law.** The fact is that Calvin's radical understanding of the fall of humanity does not preclude a robust, if nontraditional, natural law teaching.

In the very chapters in which Calvin insists on humanity's total depravity, he also develops an apparently contradictory argument that the soul retains certain traces of a love of truth that lifts humanity above the irrational creation (II.ii.12). Thus, just as we seem ready to conclude that human reason is entirely incompetent to govern human action, Calvin explicitly rejects this inference. Instead he recurs to a more traditional Christian distinction between supernatural gifts, which were stripped from humans by the Fall, and natural gifts, which, though corrupted, remain partly intact. The latter

Calvin considers inseparable from human nature, and he argues therefore that they cannot have been entirely eliminated (II.ii.12). Fallen reason is, therefore, not entirely worthless, especially when his attention is directed to "inferior objects"—that is, to "earthly things":

> By earthly things, I mean those which relate not to God and his kingdom, to true righteousness and future blessedness, but have some connection with the present life, and are in a manner confined within its boundaries. By heavenly things, I mean the pure knowledge of God, the method of true righteousness, and the mysteries of the heavenly kingdom.... As to the former, the view to be taken is this: Since man is by nature a social animal, he is disposed, from natural instinct, to cherish and preserve society; and accordingly we see that the minds of all men have impressions of civil order and honesty. Hence it is that every individual understands how human societies must be regulated by laws, and also is able to comprehend the principles of those laws. Hence the universal agreement in regard to such subjects, both among nations and individuals, the seeds of them being implanted in the breasts of all without a teacher or lawgiver.... For while men dispute with each other as to particular enactments, their ideas of equity agree in substance. This, no doubt, proves the weakness of the human mind, which, even when it seems on the right path, halts and hesitates. Still, however, it is true, that some principle of civil order is impressed on all. And this is ample proof that, in regard to the constitution of the present life, no man is devoid of the light of reason. (II.ii.13)

Calvin thus grants natural reason considerable competence when applied to things confined to the present life. It is essential to Calvin thus to maintain this rigorous confinement of secular things, to deny any linkage or continuity between natural desires and divine goodness. Thus, although Calvin once allows that humans' sense of shame, or "regard for what is honorable," proves that human beings are made for some higher purpose (II.xv.6), he later insists that this openness to the divine remains an empty possibility:

> In every age there have been some who, under the guidance of nature, were all their lives devoted to virtue.... Such examples, then, seem to warn us against supposing that the nature of man is utterly vicious, since, under its guidance, some have not only excelled in illustrious deeds, but conducted themselves most honorably through the whole course of their lives. But we ought to consider, that, notwithstanding of the corruption of our nature, there is some room for divine grace, such grace as, without purifying it, may lay it under internal restraint... [God] lays [the non-elect] under such restraint as may prevent them from breaking forth to a degree incompatible with the preservation of the established order of things. Hence, how much soever men may disguise their impurity, some are restrained only by shame, others by a fear of the laws, from breaking out into many kinds of wickedness. Some aspire to an honest life, as deeming it most conducive to their interest, while others are raised above the vulgar lot, that, by the dignity of their station, they may keep inferiors to their duty. Thus God, by his providence, curbs the perverseness of nature, preventing it from breaking forth into action, yet without rendering it inwardly pure. (II.iii.3)

What we call "virtue," the control of behavior through the motives of shame and honor, serves to check the consequences of human depravity but in no way transforms or elevates it internally, spiritually. Human virtue does not improve the condition of the soul or bring it closer to God. There is no continuity between what people by nature praise and the righteousness God requires:

> But as those endowed with the greatest talents were always impelled by the greatest ambitions (a stain which defiles all virtues and makes them lose all favor in the sight of God), so we cannot set any value on anything that seems praiseworthy in ungodly men. We may add, that the principal part of rectitude is wanting, when there is no zeal for the glory of God, and there is no such zeal in those whom he has not regenerated by his Spirit.... The virtues which deceive us by an empty show may have their praise in civil society and the common intercourse of life, but before the judgment-seat of God they will be of no value to establish a claim of righteousness. (II.iii.4)

It is precisely because human virtue and true righteousness have nothing in common that Calvin considers natural reason to be competent within its rigorously confined sphere. Severed from any intrinsic connection with the divine, this sphere can now be defined, as we have seen above (II.ii.13) in terms of the natural instinct of self-preservation. Calvin's natural law thus operates without any reference to "higher purposes"; in fact, it explicitly rejects the prideful appeal to some more elevated justice. In the following passage Calvin discusses the powers of reason as they apply to the Second Table of the Ten Commandments, which deals with our duties to our fellow human beings:

> As to the precepts of the Second Table, there is considerably more knowledge of them, inasmuch as they are more closely connected with the preservation of civil society. Even here, however, there is something defective. Every man of understanding deems it most absurd to submit to unjust and tyrannical domination, provided it can by any means be thrown off, and there is but one opinion among men, that it is the part of an abject and servile mind to bear it patiently, the part of an honorable and high-spirited mind to rise up against it. Indeed, the revenge of injuries is not regarded by philosophers as a vice. But the Lord condemning this too lofty spirit, prescribes to his people that patience which mankind deems infamous. In regard to the general observance of the law, concupiscence altogether escapes our animadversion. For the natural man cannot bear to recognize diseases in his lusts. The light of nature is stifled sooner than take the first step into this profound abyss. (II.ii.24)

Note that here the will of God and the rational recognition of the common instinct of preservation make a common front against the proud "man of understanding" or the "honorable and high-spirited" minds. The light of nature, which God has given to all humans in the form of rational instinct, opposes "the natural man's" lustful and haughty appeal to justice, honor, or freedom. Thus Calvin defends nature as the social instinct of self-preservation against nature as lustful ambition, and reason as the rational acknowledgement of this instinct against reason as the presumptuous assertor of standards above this instinct. Calvin's doctrine is not opposed to reason as such—as long as reason is strictly confined to the needs of preservation—but only to reason's claim to intrinsic goodness.[1]

Calvin thus helps to prepare a modern understanding of natural law divorced from a reflection on nature's higher purposes. Precisely because he conceives of godliness as altogether above, or rather beyond, natural human desires, he must

---

[1]This discussion of natural law in Calvin is adapted from the author's *Calvin and the Foundations of Modern Politics* (Ithaca, NY: Cornell University Press, 1989), pp. 100–119.

conceive reason as governing those desires without reference to anything higher. But this is not to say that Calvin regards natural reason as self-sufficient, even in the secular world to which it is confined. On the contrary, it is precisely because of natural reason's propensity to violate the limitations of preservation, disguising its lust with appeals to some higher purpose, that revealed authority is necessary to the order of society. Apart from the fear of God, men do not preserve equity and love among themselves. The rational instinct of self-preservation cannot hold its own against the presumption of reason without the help of revealed authority.

We have already noticed that in this chapter Calvin first sharply distinguishes spiritual from civil government and then justifies joining these topics together; and we have seen that he goes on to defend the high dignity of politics and to describe its purposes as the securing of "a public form of religion . . . among Christians" and of "humanity among men." We now see that his understanding of humanity excludes any traditional (Aristotelian or Thomistic, as in St. Thomas Aquinas) reference to a hierarchy of the soul's purposes, which would culminate in some intrinsic good of reason. Calvin's appreciation of order rests upon what might be called a humbler understanding of the human condition, one that sees a certain holiness in the blameless and diligent care of the more mundane necessities of life. Since we are not to seek proudly for some higher, rational purpose for human activities beyond God's will, all honest human callings may be considered equally honorable. No task is so sordid and base that, considered as a calling, "it will not shine and be reckoned very precious in God's sight" (III.xi.6).

JOHN CALVIN: THE CHRISTIAN COMMONWEALTH

We must not, however, neglect the first purpose Calvin ascribes to politics: the securing of "a public form of religion among Christians." For Calvin goes far beyond Luther in addressing the question of the proper role of political power in establishing true religion. Although Luther had occasion to call upon secular authorities friendly to the Reformation to counter the power of the papists, he never developed the idea of a Christian commonwealth that we find in Calvin. Since "the church does not have the power to coerce," Calvin writes, "it is the duty of godly kings and princes to sustain religion by laws, edicts, and judgments" (IV.xi.16). Thus does Calvin seem to join, without embarrassment, the spiritual and secular functions, the inward and external agencies that have previously radically distinguished. Calvin has thus often been understood to have taken a kind of step back toward a medieval, even Thomistic view of the religious purposes of political order. However, while it is fair to note a formal parallel between Calvinist order and medieval hierarchy, a key distinction must not be neglected: Calvinist order is not structured according to a hierarchy of purposes. Since human beings have no natural access to higher purposes, coercive political power cannot be directed toward a substantive good of the soul. Instead the discipline of human power, what Calvin calls "the sting" of the law, serves only to awaken people to the fear of God. Humans can know no higher natural purposes leading to God, but it appears that the fear of God and the fear of humans have enough in common that external human means (the discipline of coercive law) may be used to remind people of God's power. The link between political power and God's holiness is not a direct analogy of purpose, but an indirect effect of fear. This link is what allows Calvin, much more than Luther, to present political order as integral to God's general government of the universe, as reflective of the glory of God.

Whereas Luther's attack on the Roman hierarchy created a void of power that tended be filled by secular powers, each with its own interest in and ideas about the meaning of "reformation," Calvin addresses this gap by developing a definite (if still quite general) ecclesiology, or theory of church government. The key for Calvin is the authority of scripture, but because "we see it to be necessary in all companies of men that there should be some police to keep peace and concord between them," given "such great contrarieties of mind and of judgment between men," "certain forms" are necessary to govern the association of Christians (IV.x.27). The control of interpretation of scripture and therefore of church government Calvin confides to a collegial ministry, in part self-sustaining though allowing some participation by a limited church electorate. It has been noted that here, as in the political realm, Calvin's preferences tend toward a mixed form of government, eschewing extremes of monarchy and democracy.

JOHN CALVIN: FORMS OF GOVERNMENT

With this background in Calvin's theology and ecclesiology, let us now return to his thematic discussion of politics in the last book of the *Institutes*. This book contains 32 sections. In Section III he divides the subject of his chapter into three parts: "The Magistrate, who is president and guardian of the laws; the Laws, according to which he governs; and the People, who are governed by the laws, and obey the magistrate." Much of the burden of the sections devoted to "the magistrate" is to defend and amplify Paul's teaching to the Romans 13 view that "There is no power but of God; the powers that be are ordained of God." But Calvin also includes, almost despite himself, a very notable chapter (8) about the classic question of forms of government:

> 8. And certainly it were a very idle occupation for private men to discuss what would be the best form of polity in the place where they live, seeing these deliberations cannot have any influence in determining any public matter. Then the thing itself could not be defined absolutely without rashness, since the nature of the discussion depends on circumstances. And if you compare the different states with each other, without regard to circumstances, it is not easy to determine which of these has the advantage in point of utility; so equal are the terms on which they meet. Monarchy is prone to tyranny. In an aristocracy, again, the tendency is not less to the faction of a few, while in popular ascendancy there is the strongest tendency to sedition. When these three forms of government, of which philosophers treat, are considered in themselves, I, for my part, am far from denying that the form which greatly surpasses the others is aristocracy, either pure or modified by popular government, not indeed in itself, but because it very rarely happens that kings so rule themselves as never to dissent from what is just and right, or are possessed of so much acuteness and prudence as always to see correctly. Owing, therefore, to the vices or defects of men, it is safer and more tolerable when several bear rule, that they may thus mutually assist, instruct, and admonish each other, and should any one be disposed to go too far, the others are censors and masters to curb his excess. This has already been proved by experience, and confirmed also by the authority of the Lord himself, when he established an aristocracy bordering on popular government among the Israelites, keeping them under that as the best form, until he exhibited an image of the Messiah in David. And as I willingly

QUESTIONS FOR REFLECTION

Is there a best form of government? A form most in accord with the Christian faith?

admit that there is no kind of government happier than where liberty is framed with becoming moderation, and duly constituted so as to be durable, so I deem those very happy who are permitted to enjoy that form, and I admit that they do nothing at variance with their duty when they strenuously and constantly labor to preserve and maintain it. Nay, even magistrates ought to do their utmost to prevent the liberty, of which they have been appointed guardians from being impaired, far less violated. If in this they are sluggish or little careful, they are perfidious traitors to their office and their country. But should those to whom the Lord has assigned one form of government, take it upon them anxiously to long for a change, the wish would not only be foolish and superfluous, but very pernicious. If you fix your eyes not on one state merely, but look around the world, or at least direct your view to regions widely separated from each other, you will perceive that divine Providence has not, without good cause, arranged that different countries should be governed by different forms of polity. For as only elements of unequal temperature adhere together, so in different regions a similar inequality in the form of government is best. All this, however, is said unnecessarily to those to whom the will of God is a sufficient reason. For if it has pleased him to appoint kings over kingdoms and senates or burgomasters over free states, whatever be the form which he has appointed in the places in which we live, our duty is to obey and submit.

Clearly a tension exists within Calvin's treatment of forms of government: On one hand, the will of God as manifest in the actual existence of regimes is sufficient; on the other hand, deliberation is competent to judge a certain kind of regime—some moderate blending of aristocratic and popular elements, in a manner friendly to ordered liberty—as superior to others. This tension reflects a deeper strain well described long ago by Pierre Mesnard: Two basic postulates underlie Calvin's political teaching, and they do not obviously or necessarily converge: "all power comes from God," and "power exists only to lead men according to God." Mesnard cogently explains that Calvin attempts to hold these principles together, but "according to circumstances and especially the necessities of practical action, Protestants will have a tendency, sometimes to be aware of one postulate, sometimes of the other" (*L'essor de la philosophie politique au XVIe siecle*, p. 281). The close identification of God with political power, "the powers that be," can seem either to bolster existing powers or to call attention to a gap between those powers and God's authority.

JOHN CALVIN: OBEDIENCE AND RESISTANCE

This tension works its way to the surface of Calvin's teaching when he turns to the delicate question of duties of obedience and resistance to established authorities, which is the central concern of the last sections (IV.xx.22–32) of the *Institutes*.

PRIMARY SOURCE 5.4

FROM *OF CIVIL GOVERNMENT*, BOOK IV, CHAPTER 20

22. The first duty of subjects toward their rulers, is to entertain the most honorable views of their office, recognizing it as a delegated jurisdiction from God, and on that account receiving and reverencing them as the ministers and ambassadors of God.... We have also the remarkable injunction of Paul, "Be subject not only for wrath, but also for conscience sake" (Rom. 13:5). By this he means that subjects, in submitting to princes and governors, are not to be influenced merely by fear (just as those submit to an armed enemy who see vengeance ready to be executed if they resist), but because the obedience which they yield is rendered to God himself, inasmuch as their power is from God. Speak not of the men as if the mask of dignity could cloak folly, or cowardice, or cruelty, or wicked and flagitious manners, and thus acquire for vice the praise of virtue; but I say that the station itself is deserving of honor and reverence, and that those who rule should, in respect of their office, be held by us in esteem and veneration.

23. From this, a second consequence is, that we must with ready minds prove our obedience to them, whether in complying with edicts, or in paying tribute, or in undertaking public offices and burdens which relate to the common defense, or in executing any other orders. "Let every soul," says Paul, "be subject unto the higher powers." "Whosoever, therefore, resisteth the power, resisteth the ordinance of God" (Rom. 13:1, 2)... Let no man here deceive himself, since we cannot resist the magistrate without resisting God. For although an unarmed magistrate may seem to be despised with impunity, yet God is armed, and will signally avenge this contempt. Under this obedience, I comprehend the restraint which private men ought to impose on themselves in public, not interfering with public business, or rashly encroaching on the province of the magistrate, or attempting any thing at all of a public nature. If it is proper that any thing in a public ordinance should be corrected, let them not act tumultuously, or put their hands to a work where they ought to feel that their hands are tied, but let them leave it to the cognizance of the magistrate, whose hand alone here is free. My meaning is, let them not dare to do it without being ordered. For when the command of the magistrate is given, they too are invested with public authority. For as, according to the common saying, the eyes and ears of the prince are his counselors, so one may not improperly say that those who, by his command, have the charge of managing affairs, are his hands.

* * * *

25. But if we have respect to the word of God, it will lead us farther, and make us subject not only to the authority of those princes who honestly and faithfully perform their duty toward us, but all princes, by whatever means they have so become, although there is nothing they less perform than the duty of princes. For though the Lord declares that ruler to maintain our safety is the highest gift of his beneficence, and prescribes to rulers themselves their proper sphere, he at the same time declares, that of whatever description they may be, they derive their power from none but him. Those, indeed, who rule for the public good, are true examples and specimens of his beneficence, while those who domineer unjustly and tyrannically are raised up by him to punish the people for their iniquity. Still all alike possess that sacred majesty with which he has invested lawful power....

* * * *

27....If we constantly keep before our eyes and minds the fact, that even the most iniquitous kings are appointed by the same decree which establishes all regal authority, we will never entertain the seditious thought, that a king is to be treated according to his deserts, and that we are not bound to act the part of good subjects to him who does not in his turn act the part of a king to us.

28. It is vain to object, that that command was specially given to the Israelites. For we must attend to the ground on which the Lord places it—"I have given the kingdom to Nebuchadnezzar; therefore serve him and live." Let us doubt not that on whomsoever the kingdom has been

continued

PRIMARY SOURCE 5.4 | FROM *OF CIVIL GOVERNMENT*, BOOK IV, CHAPTER 20 *continued*

conferred, him we are bound to serve. Whenever God raises any one to royal honor, he declares it to be his pleasure that he should reign.

29. This feeling of reverence, and even of piety, we owe to the utmost to all our rulers, be their characters what they may. This I repeat the softener, that we may learn not to consider the individuals themselves, but hold it to be enough that by the will of the Lord they sustain a character on which he has impressed and engraven inviolable majesty. But rulers, you will say, owe mutual duties to those under them. This I have already confessed. But if from this you conclude that obedience is to be returned to none but just governors, you reason absurdly. Husbands are bound by mutual duties to their wives, and parents to their children. Should husbands and parents neglect their duty; should the latter be harsh and severe to the children whom they are enjoined not to provoke to anger, and by their severity harass them beyond measure; should the former treat with the greatest contumely the wives whom they are enjoined to love and to spare as the weaker vessels; would children be less bound in duty to their parents, and wives to their husbands? They are made subject to the forward and undutiful. Nay, since the duty of all is not to look behind them, that is, not to inquire into the duties of one another but to submit each to his own duty, this ought especially to be exemplified in the case of those who are placed under the power of others. Wherefore, if we are cruelly tormented by a savage, if we are rapaciously pillaged by an avaricious or luxurious, if we are neglected by a sluggish, if, in short, we are persecuted for righteousness' sake by an impious and sacrilegious prince, let us first call up the remembrance of our faults, which doubtless the Lord is chastising by such scourges. In this way humility will curb our impatience. And let us reflect that it belongs not to us to cure these evils, that all that remains for us is to implore the help of the Lord, in whose hands are the hearts of kings, and inclinations of kingdoms. "God standeth in the congregation of the mighty; he judgeth among the gods." Before his face shall fall and be crushed all kings and judges of the earth, who have not kissed his anointed, who have enacted unjust laws to oppress the poor in judgment, and do violence to the cause of the humble, to make widows a prey, and plunder the fatherless.

30. Herein is the goodness, power, and providence of God wondrously displayed. At one time he raises up manifest avengers from among his own servants and gives them his command to punish accursed tyranny and deliver his people from calamity when they are unjustly oppressed; at another time he employs, for this purpose, the fury of men who have other thoughts and other aims. Thus he rescued his people Israel from the tyranny of Pharaoh by Moses; from the violence of Chusa, king of Syria, by Othniel; and from other bondage by other kings or judges. Thus he tamed the pride of Tyre by the Egyptians; the insolence of the Egyptians by the Assyrians; the ferocity of the Assyrians by the Chaldeans; the confidence of Babylon by the Medes and Persians—Cyrus having previously subdued the Medes, while the ingratitude of the kings of Judah and Israel, and their impious contumacy after all his kindness, he subdued and punished—at one time by the Assyrians, at another by the Babylonians. All these things however were not done in the same way. The former class of deliverers being brought forward by the lawful call of God to perform such deeds, when they took up arms against kings, did not at all violate that majesty with which kings are invested by divine appointment, but armed from heaven, they, by a greater power, curbed a less, just as kings may lawfully punish their own satraps. The latter class, though they were directed by the hand of God, as seemed to him good, and did his work without knowing it, had naught but evil in their thoughts.

31. But whatever may be thought of the acts of the men themselves, the Lord by their means equally executed his own work, when he broke the bloody scepters of insolent kings, and

PRIMARY SOURCE 5.4

From *Of Civil Government*, Book IV, Chapter 20 *continued*

overthrew their intolerable dominations. Let princes hear and be afraid; but let us at the same time guard most carefully against spurning or violating the venerable and majestic authority of rulers, an authority which God has sanctioned by the surest edicts, although those invested with it should be most unworthy of it, and, as far as in them lies, pollute it by their iniquity. Although the Lord takes vengeance on unbridled domination, let us not therefore suppose that that vengeance is committed to us, to whom no command has been given but to obey and suffer. I speak only of private men. For when popular magistrates have been appointed to curb the tyranny of kings (as the Ephori, who were opposed to kings among the Spartans, or Tribunes of the people to consuls among the Romans, or Demarchs to the senate among the Athenians; and, perhaps, there is something similar to this in the power exercised in each kingdom by the three orders, when they hold their primary diets). So far am I from forbidding these officially to check the undue license of kings, that if they connive at kings when they tyrannize and insult over the humbler of the people, I affirm that their dissimulation is not free from nefarious perfidy, because they fraudulently betray the liberty of the people, while knowing that, by the ordinance of God, they are its appointed guardians.

32. But in that obedience which we hold to be due to the commands of rulers, we must always make the exception, nay, must be particularly careful that it is not incompatible with obedience to Him to whose will the wishes of all kings should be subject, to whose decrees their commands must yield, to whose majesty their scepters must bow. And, indeed, how preposterous were it, in pleasing men, to incur the offense of Him for whose sake you obey men! The Lord, therefore, is King of kings. When he opens his sacred mouth, he alone is to be heard, instead of all and above all. We are subject to the men who rule over us, but subject only in the Lord. If they command any thing against Him, let us not pay the least regard to it, nor be moved by all the dignity which they possess as magistrates—a dignity to which, no injury is done when it is subordinated to the special and truly supreme power of God. On this ground Daniel denies that he had sinned in any respect against the king when he refused to obey his impious decree (Dan. 6: 22), because the king had exceeded his limits, and not only been injurious to men, but, by raising his horn against God, had virtually abrogated his own power. On the other hand, the Israelites are condemned for having too readily obeyed the impious edict of the king. For, when Jeroboam made the golden calf, they forsook the temple of God, and, in submissiveness to him, revolted to new superstitions, (1 Kings 12:28). With the same facility posterity had bowed before the decrees of their kings. For this they are severely upbraided by the Prophet (Hosea 5:11). So far is the praise of modesty from being due to that pretense by which flattering courtiers cloak themselves, and deceive the simple, when they deny the lawfulness of declining any thing imposed by their kings, as if the Lord had resigned his own rights to mortals by appointing them to rule over their fellows or as if earthly power were diminished when it is subjected to its author, before whom even the principalities of heaven tremble as suppliants. I know the imminent peril to which subjects expose themselves by this firmness, kings being most indignant when they are condemned. As Solomon says, "The wrath of a king is as messengers of death" (Prov. 16:14). But since Peter, one of heaven's heralds, has published the edict, "We ought to obey God rather than men" (Acts 5: 29), let us console ourselves with the thought, that we are rendering the obedience which the Lord requires when we endure anything rather than turn aside from piety. And that our courage may not fail, Paul stimulates us by the additional considerations (1 Cor. 7: 23) that we were redeemed by Christ at the great price which our redemption cost him, in order that we might not yield a slavish obedience to the depraved wishes of men, far less do homage to their impiety.

THE RIGHT OF RESISTANCE IN LUTHERANISM AND CALVINISM

Clearly Calvin's dominant theme in these last pages of his great *Institutes of the Christian Religion* is the duty of obedience Christians owe to rulers. Yet at the same time, the ultimate subordination of secular powers to God is affirmed very boldly, even in the direct language of warning to princes. Calvin goes so far as to appeal (in the next to last section) to certain "popular magistrates" to "curb the tyranny of kings" in defense of "the liberty of the people." And in the last section he seems to open the door to a right of resistance by ordinary subjects when he justifies Daniel's refusal to obey the king's "impious decree" and refers to the king having "exceeded his limits."

These statements are somewhat equivocal, and Calvin never does us the service of addressing apparent contradictions with his dominant emphasis on the duty to obey God's appointed rulers. It should be noted that *Institutes* was Calvin's most public and therefore probably most cautious statement, in which he was most at pains to distance himself from the more radical and disreputable Anabaptists. Later, in the posthumously published *Sermons on the Last Eight Chapters of the Book of Daniel,* Calvin took the momentous step of arguing that private persons are permitted to resist an unjust prince.

As Quentin Skinner has noted,[2] Calvin here again insists that Daniel "committed no sin when he disobeyed the king" because impious rulers "are no longer worthy to be counted as princes." But now Calvin not only denies the authority of such rulers but adds, more clearly than in the earlier discussions of Daniel, that "when they raise themselves up against God ... *it is necessary that they should in turn be laid low*" (author's emphasis). Only by the use of the passive voice does the Genevan reformer stop short here of explicitly authorizing subjects to take up arms in order to "lay low" an unrighteous prince.

Already in Calvin's lifetime English Calvinists such as John Ponet (1514–1556) and Christopher Goodman (1520–1603) were directly affirming the limited character of monarchical authority and (in Goodman's case, at least) the lawfulness of forcible resistance.[3] And in the century following Calvin's death, the doors he set ajar for defenses of resistance to established authorities would be opened wider and wider by Calvinist activists, and the emphasis on duties of obedience would tend to recede.[4] Some interpreters thus attribute an important role to Calvinism in the development of more modern views espousing popular liberty against the claims of kings and nobles. Others point out the gap between a religious *duty* to resist, which may be developed on the basis of Calvin's premises, and a natural, human, and moral *right* to resist, which appears to be a quite different thing.[5]

Calvin, like Luther, seems to hesitate to the end of his life between a traditional Augustinian affirmation of the divine authority of established political power and various somewhat muted invitations to armed resistance. And many of the bolder arguments for resistance put forward by Calvinists in the middle 16th century were

---

[2]Quentin Skinner, *The Foundations of Modern Political Thought, vol. II: The Age of Reformation* (New York: Cambridge University Press, 1978) p. 220.

[3]Skinner, pp. 221–224.

[4]Skinner, pp. 225–238.

[5]Skinner (p. 240) argues that this right "was first fully articulated by the Huguenots during the French religious wars in the second half of the sixteenth century."

borrowed from an earlier generation of Lutheran writers, who themselves drew upon previous debates within the Roman church. Thus the fact that the more radical side of the argument soon came to the fore among Calvinist militants, first in Britain and then on the continent, may appear to owe as much to circumstance as to any basic theological difference between Calvinism and Lutheranism.

Still, there are good reasons for crediting Calvinist theology with a more dynamic role than that of Lutheranism in the development of a modern, rights-based understanding of political authority. First, as we have already noted, Calvin opens the door, in the final chapter of the final Latin edition of his magisterial *Institutes of the Christian Religion,* to the idea that not only "inferior magistrates" but any person might be justified in resisting unrighteous authority—a door the reformer in fact seemed to walk through in his *Sermons on... Daniel.* Second, and perhaps more importantly, Calvin's discussions (again at the end of the *Institutes*) of lesser magistrates tend much more than those of Luther or his followers to emphasize the *popular* source of these officers' authority. Calvin even directly cites the contemporary example of the gathering of the three estates of a kingdom, which everyone knew required the election of certain magistrates by the people. Thus Calvin's argument clearly involves a kind of constitutionalist appeal to powers elected by the people.[6]

A third and most theologically significant reason for the greater influence of Calvinism than Lutheranism on the development of a modern idea of political authority concerns the concept of the covenant. Luther understands the "covenant of Grace" as a matter of individual conversion and baptism, as the promise of the New Testament that superseded the old law. Calvin, by contrast, understands the language of covenant in terms of an actual covenanting community, and he situates the communal oath sworn by the citizens of Geneva in 1537 in the lineage of a sequence of covenants with God that culminated in Christ's sacrifice but also extended back to Adam and the history of Israel.[7]

This difference points us to the most fundamental theological difference between Luther and Calvin. Calvin's understanding of Christianity is based on the same doctrine of salvation by faith from which Luther launched the Protestant Reformation. Calvin follows Luther in declaring works, including the cultivation of the intellectual soul, to be completely impotent to produce salvation. But Calvin may be said to have taken this doctrine a subtle but decisive step further than Luther. Whereas Luther's doctrine of faith tends to focus the believer's attention on the joyful inward state of belief, Calvin's doctrine eschews all inwardness and converts the energy of faith into outward activity, including political and economic energy. While embracing the Lutheran motto "by faith alone" (*sola fides)*, Calvin puts new emphasis on the theme "to the Glory of God" (*ad gloria Dei*), and his rigorously anti-Aristotelian and antiteleological understanding of God's world tends, much more than within Lutheranism, to convert spiritual fervor into worldly energy[8]

[6]See Skinner, pp. 230–233.

[7]Skinner, p. 236.

[8]This is a central theme of my *Calvin and the Foundations of Modern Politics* (Ithaca, New York: Cornell University Press, 1989).

QUESTIONS FOR REFLECTION

Is constitutional liberty best understood as moral liberty, as liberty under God, or as natural liberty, unlimited in principle by moral or religious prejudices?

THE LEGACY OF THE REFORMATION

The question of the historical influence of Reformation political thought is a vast and rich one, inseparable from the larger question of the critical role played by the Protestant Reformation in shaping the modern age in general. It would be a mistake to assume that this question can be separated from a reflection on the meaning of modernity itself, for in fact the question of what modernity *is* must be prior to, or at least intimately bound up with, that of how it came to be, or of what influences contributed to it.

Let us nevertheless venture some suggestions about influence, or rather, survey some of the enduring suggestions that others have made. We have already noticed the unmistakably modern ring of Luther's emancipation of the individual conscience, which resonates clearly, for example, in Jefferson's and Madison's invocations of the inviolability of freedom of the human mind. The difference, of course, is that the Reformers liberated the individual's conscience from what they regarded as Roman tyranny only by binding it to God's will as available in Holy Scripture. The freedom they proclaimed, it must not be forgotten, was to its core a Christian freedom. Moreover, it is at least arguable that in practice Luther's liberation from Roman Catholic institutions contributed at least as much to the rising power of national states as to the freedom of autonomous individuals. Calvin, for his part, did much to secure the independence of the church (as defined by Scripture, he was convinced), but only by acknowledging the legitimacy of civil coercion on behalf of public religious order. This hardly seems consistent with modern ideas of freedom and equality under nonsectarian law.

Some have argued, though, that it is precisely a broadly Calvinist idea of ordered liberty, liberty under law, the individual conscience acknowledging God's ultimate sovereignty, that has under girded the development of the most successful free regime in the modern world. On this argument, the Puritan immigrants to America, heirs of Calvinism, were the true founders of American republicanism. Notable in this connection is the distinction drawn by John Winthrop, first governor of the Massachusetts Bay Colony, between unlimited natural liberty, which people share with beasts, and higher civil or moral liberty. Alexis de Tocqueville, author of *Democracy in America* (1835 and 1840), is only the most famous of those to argue (though with more nuance and even irony than is often appreciated) that the success of American democracy is grounded in the survival, beyond the eclipse of Puritanism, of a sense of moral freedom inherited from Christianity. Whether these limits should now be seen as an accidental residue in what has happily evolved to be a purely secular order, or as still essential to the very meaning of American freedom, is obviously a live question.

This debate over the historical influence of Reformation political argument has the virtue of pointing us to a deeper problem. What is at stake, ultimately, is less a question of the development of particular doctrines concerning forms of government or the rights of authority and of resistance than of our basic understanding of the dichotomy between religious and secular. The Reformers engaged this distinction in a fundamental way that allows us to see that the very notion of a secular world, which we now take so much for granted, may be the product of a certain theological strategy for categorizing and separating natural human concerns. There was no secular world before such a world was defined by its opposition to the other world posited by Christianity. But this opposition or separation has always been problematic. At this level, the great themes of the Protestant Reformation, articulated most powerfully and authoritatively by Martin Luther and John Calvin, remain living challenges for contemporary thinkers.

Key Terms

grace
faith
justification
priesthood of all believers
Christian freedom
total depravity
predestination
natural law

Sources and Resources

Key Texts

Calvin: *Institutes*
Luther: *Concerning Christian Liberty*

Secondary Texts

Chadwick, Owen. *The Reformation* (New York: Penguin, 1972).

Hancock, Ralph C. *Calvin and the Foundations of Modern Politics* (Ithaca, NY: Cornell University Press, 1989).

Ozment, Steven. *The Age of Reform, 1250–1550* (New Haven: Yale University Press, 1980).

Stevenson, William R. *Sovereign Grace: The Place and Significance of Christian Freedom in John Calvin's Political Thought* (New York: Oxford University Press, 1999).

Wendel, Francois. *Calvin* (New York: Harper & Row, 1963).

Web Sites

Internet *Encyclopedia of Philosophy* entry on Calvin online at www.iep.utm.edu/c/calvin.htm

Free, full-text works by John Calvin online at www.ccel.org/c/calvin/

Internet *Encyclopedia of Philosophy* entry on Luther online at www.iep.utm.edu/l/luther.htm

Luther Electronic Archive online at www.ctsfw.edu/etext/luther/

MACHIAVELLI

CHAPTER 6

By Andrea Rubery *SUNY Brockport*

© Liz Michaud

LIFE AND LEGACY

In the history of political thought, no name seems to engender greater response than that of Niccolo Machiavelli. One does not have to be a student of either politics or history to have heard of Machiavelli and to know of his infamous reputation. In our own time, the term "Machiavellian" is commonly applied to a person or action that is ruthless and cruel—someone who is willing to break all rules to get what he or she wants. This reputation is largely the result of Machiavelli's most famous work, *The Prince,* a work that sets him apart from other political thinkers by its brutal candor and realism. Although a true supporter of republican government, Machiavelli seems to have masked this in *The Prince,* where his efforts focus largely on a prince's ability to attain and maintain power. Although this effort seems to have forever cast him into disrepute as the "father of realpolitik," one cannot help but wonder whether such a reputation is deserved. Did this man of modest Florentine origins deliberately redirect the entire course of political discourse in a manner that has irreversibly damaged the political environment of our own day? Is he responsible for the creation of the "modern" world, with its focus on materialism, individualism, and power? While many scholars remain divided over whether Machiavelli's teachings are intentionally corrupt, they are unified in their view that his teachings have had a lasting impact on the world.

Why such controversy? Why such impact? In part, Machiavelli's fame (or infamy) comes because of the content of his teaching and its place within the context of ancient political thought. As you may recall, ancient Greek and Roman political philosophers devoted much care to the study of human actions and their impact upon the well-being of the state. Both Plato and Aristotle believed in the superiority of the state over individual interests. The state was seen not as a vehicle for furthering a private agenda, but instead as a type of organic whole, whose parts, when working well, better all its members. To this end, rulers were obliged (at least in theory) to create and nurture an environment whereby laws, institutions, and education might further the interests of the whole. Ideally rulers were deemed either good or perverted based on whose interests they served and how well they served the common good of all.

This effort was assisted by the ancient belief in a fixed moral order, whereby virtues and vices were identifiable and knowable. Such virtues as courage and moderation were always worthy and good; such vices as cowardice and dishonesty were always deemed wrong. The presence of these virtues and vices could be witnessed in the excessive or deficient behaviors of rulers and subjects alike. For someone like Plato, excessive or deficient behaviors were the direct result of an internal imbalance within the soul. People's internal state or nature was thus determined by the overall relationship between the three parts of their souls: reason, spirit, and emotion. Reason was supposed to control emotion with the help of spirit. How well reason ruled the other parts determined the frequency of excessive or deficient behavior. Thus our internal balance directly affected our external actions and visa versa.

Placing Machiavelli within this context reveals the divergent nature of his teachings from the ancients. Without concern for the souls or the moral well-being of subjects, Machiavelli puts forth an unapologetic instruction that presumes the worst about human nature. Assuming that such baseness will manifest itself in all human activities, Machiavelli reveals the brutal world of "real" politics, with its duplicity, cruelty, and savagery. However, unlike the ancients, who were well aware of how horridly people can behave, Machiavelli makes little effort to change such misbehavior. Instead he celebrates its existence by teaching others to accept its presence and to maximize its use in every situation. Only from effective use of human cruelty can humans, and especially rulers, begin to manipulate and control the world to their purpose.

How could this seemingly good and dutiful citizen prescribe such revolutionary teaching? In part, Machiavelli was the product of his time. Born on May 3, 1469, in the city of Florence, Machiavelli lived through a tumultuous period, with his beloved city undergoing a radical change from a quasi-Medici rule to republicanism and back to Medici control. During the latter part of the 14th century, Florence had attained "... unprecedented happiness and greatness" as a republic under the guidance of such leaders as Maso degli Albizzi; but the good fortune quickly ended with the Medici ascent to power.[1] The Medici, under the direction of Cosimo de'Medici, were members of a leading Florentine family whose fame and influence emerged during the 15th century from a banking empire. Because much of Florence's world stature came from its successful wool and silk guilds, along with other specialized artistry skills, financial support to promote trade was necessary. The monetary role played by the Medici met this need and allowed the family to maximize its political influence in the city.

Interestingly, the Medici family members did not hold public office. Instead, during the first several decades of their rule, they governed covertly, showing outward compliance to the various Florentine procedures for elected and rotational office holding. This, according to the famous Machiavelli biographer Roberto Ridolfi, allowed the Medici to attain great gains: Their compliance held the semblance of republicanism while they in fact operated in anything but a republican manner. Their control was skillfully maintained by making sure that favored citizens aligned with the Medici were elected to certain governing bodies. This effort guaranteed that governmental decisions would be made in their favor. Moreover, through delicate combinations of gift giving, special favors, artistic contributions, endowments, and arranged marriages, the Medici kept an iron hold on a city and reaped the benefits of such self-serving generosity.[2]

Machiavelli's formative years were spent under the reign of Lorenzo the Magnificent, Cosimo's grandson, the great patron of the arts who championed the humanistic movement within Florence. Although not born to nobility, Machiavelli was the product of a respectable but struggling middle-class family. His father was a doctor of law but made little money, finding it necessary to take on additional work, such as collecting and organizing names and places for Titus Livy's history of Rome. This work would be of lasting influence on Machiavelli, prompting the creation of his other famous work, *The Discourses on Livy*. Machiavelli's study of Latin would allow him to study Livy's history, but there is little evidence to suggest that he studied Greek.[3] In fact, we know little about his formative years.

---

[1]Roberto Ridolfi, *The Life of Niccolo Machiavelli* (Chicago: University of Chicago Press, 1963), p. 4.

[2]Ridolfi, pp. 5–6.

[3]Ridolfi, p. 3.

Ridolfi notes, however, that certain events surrounding Machiavelli's childhood must have made a lasting impression on the young boy. For example, the attempt to murder Lorenzo and Giuliano Medici in 1478 by such rivals as the Archbishop of Pisa and some relatives of Pope Sixtus IV likely impacted the young Florentine: Giuliano was murdered in the cathedral while taking communion. Ridolfi is convinced that the brutal irony of receiving the sacrament of communion while being murdered on the altar could not have escaped the keen young mind of Machiavelli. Moreover, the cruel retribution taken by the Medici against the conspirators, culminating in the hanging of the archbishop from the Medici Palazzo, must have served as an early lesson on the usefulness of spectacle within the political realm. Lorenzo survived and went on to rule Florence well, but not without restricting Florentine liberties and increasing his own personal power. Ridolfi notes that under the reign of Lorenzo, the Florentine tendency toward vice and corruption increased dramatically for both laypeople and clerics.[4] Not until the pious and visionary priest Savonarola appeared on the scene in 1490 and challenged the Medici policies did their hold on power begin to weaken. By 1494 the Medici were gone, Florence had become a republic, and the young Machiavelli would find himself at the center of its policy-making.

In events that are still unclear for many historians, Machiavelli was made the second chancellor of the Florentine republic in June 1498. Untitled and inexperienced, he was most likely chosen for this post because of a past teacher, Marcello Virgilio Adriani, who was the head of the first chancery. As Ridolfi notes, the office of the first chancery dealt with foreign matters and the second with domestic issues and matters of conflict. Under the new republic, however, the boundaries of these functions loosened, and the secretaries of both the first and second chanceries found themselves handling matters of both foreign and domestic importance. In part, this loosening was the result of the inexperience and insecurities of the new Florentine republic. As the unintended result of France's incursion into Italy in 1494, Florence faced continual economic insecurities and the constant threat by states more powerful than itself to the north.[5] Its political leaders and diplomatic corps often had to improvise when dealing with formidable powers as France and Spain, which were thought to be waiting for any opportunity to exploit the weaknesses of the Italian city–states. The presence of these foreign powers in Italy, along with the occupation by their mercenary and auxiliary troops, would lead Machiavelli to his lifelong preoccupation with their foreign and "barbaric" domination of Italy. Thus, until the Medici returned to power, Machiavelli would play an integral role in shaping these volatile and dangerous political threats facing the new republic. During this time he witnessed some of the most lasting political lessons of his life, upon which he assiduously reflects in his *The Prince* and *The Discourses*.

Unfortunately Machiavelli's days of political participation came to an abrupt end in 1512 with the return of the Medici at the hands of Pope Julius II. Realizing that the republic was over, its good leader and close friend to Machiavelli, Piero Soderini, *gonfalonieri* for life, left in the night for safe passage to Siena. Machiavelli remained in his job for a short time but was soon dismissed as secretary of the second chancery.

---

[4]Ridolfi, p. 8.

[5]Hanna Fenichel Pitkin, *Fortune Is a Woman* (Berkeley: University of California Press, 1984), p. 15.

If losing his job was not bad enough, Machiavelli would soon be fined and then implicated in a plot to overthrow the Medici. In an ill-thought, ill-structured plan to kill Cardinal Giuliano de' Medici, Agostino Capponi and several other prominent Florentines wrote a list of names of men "likely" to be interested in such a scheme, on which Machiavelli's name appeared. Ironically, he knew nothing of this plot; but the Medici nonetheless had him arrested and tortured, ending with his release and banishment from Florence political life. For Machiavelli, this forced retreat to a desolate, rural existence outside Florence was viewed as a cruel, undeserved twist of fate. To future generations, however, this banishment would prove to be the fortuitous environment in which *The Prince* and *The Discourses* would be conceived, by which they would recognize the enormous impact of his teaching. We now turn to Machiavelli's political philosophy.

THE CONSISTENCY OF REPUBLICS AND PRINCIPALITIES

Discerning Machiavelli's worldview and methodology is no less controversial than figuring out his place in political thought. While most agree that the effects of his teaching have been tremendous, few can agree on its meaning and intent. Machiavelli is largely to blame for this controversy. His two most famous political works, *The Prince* and *The Discourses,* deal with the different subjects of principalities and republics, respectively. Moreover, *The Prince* was written under the duress of banishment, aimed at regaining political favor with the Medici. *The Discourses,* however, were written for like-minded republican friends who shared the same realistic political sentiments as Machiavelli. Thus some have argued that because of the differences in subject matter and audience, Machiavelli either must be aligned with only one of these works or must have presented an inconsistent teaching: How can a true lover of republicanism write such harsh maxims for princely rule?

Fortunately, Machiavelli is not so black and white. The case can be made that although these two books are different on the surface, there is a methodological consistency in their structure, purpose, and teaching. What that teaching might mean will be discussed throughout this chapter; but first we must establish the structure and consistency of this singular teaching. Despite the fact that one text deals with the nature of principalities and the other republics, they both begin with a similar "dedicatory letter" that reflects a single-minded purpose: the offering of a new and serious view of politics. A closer look at both letters is necessary.

While both books are directed to different audiences, they share similar themes and concerns. Machiavelli is troubled by the worthiness of rule; he concludes that not all those who hold power deserve it and conversely that not all those who are denied it should be. There is clearly a sense in both dedicatory letters that power is a deserved entity, worthy of the most grand souls. In *The Discourses* there can be no doubt that he feels his friends deserve such power, while in *The Prince* there is some doubt whether he thinks Lorenzo worthy of his station. Nonetheless, the issue of deserved power appears in both letters and thus reflects Machiavelli's concern with the present worth of political actors. In addition, both letters discuss the nature of gifts and the intentions of the gift givers. In both letters and with almost exact language, Machiavelli writes that these two works are the product of his personal experience, hardship, and close reading of past actions. Thus the gift is a teaching that is based on his life's hard work

PRIMARY SOURCE 6.1 | FROM *THE PRINCE*

Dedicatory Letter—*The Prince*

Niccolo Machiavelli to the Magnificent Lorenzo de' Medici:

It is customary most of the time for those who desire to acquire favor with a Prince to come to meet him with things that they care most for among their own or with things that they see please him most. Thus, one sees them many times being presented with horses, arms, cloth of gold, precious stones, and similar ornaments worthy of their greatness. Thus, since I desire to offer myself to your Magnificence with some testimony of my homage to you, I have found nothing in my belongings that I care so much for and esteem so greatly as the knowledge of the actions of great men, learned by me from long experience with modern things and a continuous reading of ancient ones. Having thought out and examined these things with great diligence for a long time, and now reduced them to one small volume, I send it to your Magnificence.

And although I judge this work undeserving of your presence, yet I have much confidence that through your humanity it may be accepted, considering that no greater gift could be made by me than to give you the capacity to be able to understand in a very short time all that I have learned and understood in so many years and with so many hardships and dangers for myself. I have not ornamented this work, nor filled it with fulsome phrases nor with pompous superfluous ornament whatever, with which it is customary for many to describe and adorn their things. For I wanted it either not to be honored for anything or to please solely for the variety of the matter and the gravity of the subject. Nor do I want it to be thought presumption if a man from a low and mean state dares to discuss and give rules for the governments of princes. For just as those who sketch landscapes place themselves down in the plain to consider the nature of mountains and high places and to consider the nature of low places place themselves high atop mountains, similarly, to know well the nature of peoples one needs to be prince, and to know well the nature of princes one needs to be of the people.

Therefore, your Magnificence, take this small gift in the spirit with which I sent it. If your Magnificence considers and reads it diligently, you will learn from it my extreme desire that you arrive at the greatness that fortune and your other qualities promise you. And if your Magnificence will at some time turn your eyes from the summit of your height to these low places, you will learn how undeservedly I endure a great and continuous malignity of fortune.

---

and observations regarding the nature of humanity, both in and out of the political realm. Moreover, he establishes the seriousness of both works by distancing himself from the common likes of other gift givers. His gift is not materialistic or ostentatious. Its value is greater than those given commonly by flatterers for its serious, useful, and novel nature.

We can see these thematic and structural similarities when comparing the dedicatory letter and Chapter 15 of *The Prince* with the preface from the first book of *The Discourses*. In both works Machiavelli repeats the claim that he is taking a path "...untrodden by anyone" (*The Discourses*, Preface, Book I), suggesting a consistent and comprehensive view of human nature that does not vary by regime type. Thus it does not seem to matter that Machiavelli is talking about princes in one work and republics in another. What does matter is his consistent, realistic conclusions about human nature. To express this colloquially, Machiavelli is announcing that he, better than others, "gets" human beings and that because he "gets" us as we truly are and not as we ought to be, he alone can discuss politics realistically

PRIMARY SOURCE 6.2 | FROM *THE DISCOURSES*

Dedicatory Letter—*The Discourses*
Niccolo Machiavelli to Zanobi Buondelmonti and Cosimo Rucellai, Greetings:

I send you a present that, if it does not correspond to the obligations I have to you, is without doubt the greatest Niccolo Machiavelli has been able to send you. For in it I have expressed as much as I know and have learned through a long practice and a continual reading in worldly things. And since neither you nor others can desire more of me, you cannot complain if I have not given you more. You can well regret the poverty of my talent, if these narrations of mine are poor; and the fallaciousness of my judgment, if in many parts I deceive myself while discoursing. That being so, I do not know which of us has to be less obligated to the other: whether I to you, who have forced me to write what I would never have written for myself; or you to me, if in writing I have not satisfied you. So take this in the mode that all things from friends are taken, where one always considers the intention of the sender more than the qualities of the thing sent. And believe that in this my only satisfaction is that I think that even if I have deceived myself in many of its circumstances, in this one only I know that I have not made an error, in choosing you above all others to address these discourses to: whether because in doing this it appears to me I have shown some gratitude for benefits received, or because it appears to me I have gone outside the common usage of those who write, who are accustomed always to address their works to some prince and, blinded by ambition and avarice, praise him for all virtuous qualities whey they should blame him for every part worthy of reproach. Hence, so as not to incur this error, I have chosen not those who are princes but those who for their infinite good parts deserve to be; not those who could load me with ranks, honors, and riches but those who, though unable, would wish to do so. For men wishing to judge rightly have to esteem those who are liberal, not those who can be; and likewise those who know, not those who can govern a kingdom without knowing. Writers praise Hiero the Syracusan when he was a private individual more than Perseus the Macedonian when he was a king, for Hiero lacked nothing other than the principality to be a prince while the other had no part of a king other than a kingdom. Enjoy, therefore, the good or the ill that you yourselves have wished for; and if you persist in the error that these opinions of mine gratify you, I shall not fail to follow with the rest of the history, as I promised you in the beginning. Farewell.

---

and thus effectively. There is no idealism or hype. We are what we are; and no matter what regime we find ourselves in, whether a principality or republic, no leadership will keep its power without this realistic understanding of human motivations and behavior. Again, a comparison of parts of the preface to Book I of *The Discourses* and Chapter 15 of *The Prince* demonstrates this singular view of human nature and political purpose.

Thus the singularity of purpose and consistency of worldview are apparent in both of these excerpts. Note that Machiavelli states in both that he is doing something new and that it is a course not taken by other thinkers. Moreover, nowhere does he say that his new teaching is for only one regime or another but instead reveals it to his readers within the context of both works: "In ordering republics, maintaining states . . . neither prince nor republic may be found" (*The Discourses,* Preface, Book I) and "And many have imagined republics and principalities that have never been seen or known to exist in truth . . . " (*The Prince,* Chapter 15). Because Machiavelli groups republics and principalities together in a general discussion of the novelty and purpose

PRIMARY SOURCE 6.3 | FROM *THE DISCOURSES*, BOOK I

Preface—First Book, *The Discourses*

Although the envious nature of men has always made it no less dangerous to find new modes and orders than to seek unknown waters and lands, because men are more ready to blame than to praise the actions of others, nonetheless, driven by that natural desire that has always been in me to work, without any respect, for those things I believe will bring common benefit to everyone, I have decided to take a path as yet untrodden by anyone, and if it brings me trouble and difficulty, it could also bring me reward through those who consider humanely the end of these labors of mine. If poor talent, little experience of present things, and weak knowledge of ancient things make this attempt of mine defective and not of much utility, it will at least show the path to someone who with more virtue, more discourse and judgment, will be able to fulfill this intention of mine, which, if it will not bring me praise, ought not to incur blame.

Considering thus how much honor is awarded to antiquity, and how many times—letting pass infinite other examples—a fragment of an ancient statue has been bought at a high price because someone wants to have it near oneself, to honor his house with it, and to be able to have it imitated by those who delight in that art, and how the latter then strive with all industry to present it in all their works; and seeing, on the other hand, that the most virtuous works the histories show us, which have been done by ancient kingdoms and republics, by kings, captains, citizens, legislators, and others who have labored for their fatherland, are rather admired than imitated—indeed they are so much shunned by everyone in every least thing that no sign of the ancient virtue remains with us—I can do no other than marvel and grieve. And so much the more when I see that in the differences that arise between citizens in civil affairs or in the sicknesses that men incur; they always have recourse to those judgments or those remedies that were judged or ordered by the ancients. For the civil laws are nothing other than verdicts given by ancient jurists, which, reduced to order, teach our present jurists to judge. Nor is medicine other than the experiments performed by ancient physicians, on which present physicians found their judgments. Nonetheless, in ordering republics, maintaining states, governing kingdoms, ordering the military and administering war, judging subjects, and increasing empire, neither prince nor republic may be found that has recourse to the examples of the ancients. This arises, I believe, not so much from the weakness into which the present religion has led the world, or from the evil that an ambitious idleness has done to many Christian provinces and cities, as from not having a true knowledge of histories, through not getting from reading them that sense nor tasting that flavor that they have in themselves. From this arises that the infinite number who read them take pleasure in hearing of the variety of accidents contained in them without thinking of imitating them, judging that imitation is not only difficult but impossible—as if heaven, sun, elements, and men had varied in motion, order, and power from what they were in antiquity. Wishing, therefore, to turn men from this error, I have judged it necessary to write on all those books of Titus Livy that have not been intercepted by the malignity of the times whatever I shall judge necessary for their greater understanding, according to knowledge of ancient and modern things, so that those who read these statements of mine can more easily draw from them that utility for which one should seek knowledge of histories. Although this enterprise may be difficult, nonetheless, aided by those who have encouraged me to accept this burden, I believe I can carry it far enough so that a short road will remain for another to bring it to the destined place.

PRIMARY SOURCE 6.4 | FROM *THE PRINCE,* CHAPTER 15

"OF THOSE THINGS FOR WHICH MEN AND ESPECIALLY PRINCES ARE PRAISED OR BLAMED"

It remains now to see what the modes and government of a prince should be with subjects and with friends. And because I know that many have written of this, I fear that in writing of it again, I may be held presumptuous, especially since in disputing this matter I depart from the orders of others. But since my intent is to write something useful to whoever understands it, it has appeared to me more fitting to go directly to the effectual truth of the thing than to the imagination of it. And many have imagined republics and principalities that have never been seen or known to exist in truth; for it is so far from how one lives to how one should live that he who lets go of what is done for what should be done learns his ruin rather than his preservation. For a man who wants to make a profession of good in all regards must come to ruin among so many who are not good. Hence it is necessary to a prince, if he wants to maintain himself, to learn to be able not to be good, and to use this and not use it according to necessity.

Thus, leaving out what is imagined about a prince and discussing what is true, I say that all men, whenever one speaks of them, and especially princes, since they are placed higher, are noted for some of the qualities that bring them either blame or praise. And this is why someone is considered liberal, someone mean [using the Tuscan term because *avaro* (greedy) in our language is still one who desires to have something by violence, *misero* (mean) we call one who refrains too much from using what is his]; someone is considered a giver, someone rapacious; someone cruel, someone merciful; the one a breaker of faith, the other faithful; the one effeminate and pusillanimous, the other fierce and spirited; the one humane, the other proud; the one lascivious, the other chaste; the one honest, the other clever; the one hard, the other agreeable; the one grave, the other light; the one religious, the other unbelieving; and the like. And I know that everyone will confess that it would be a very laudable thing to find in a prince all of the above-mentioned qualities that are held good. But because he cannot have them, nor wholly observe them, since human conditions do not permit it, it is necessary for him to be so prudent as to know how to avoid the infamy of those vices against those that do not, if that is possible; but if one cannot, one can let them go on with less hesitation. And furthermore one should not care about incurring the reputation of those vices without which it is difficult to save one's state; for if one considers everything well, one will find something appears to be virtue, which if pursued would be one's ruin, and something else appears to be vice, which if pursued results in one's security and well-being.

---

of his efforts, readers soon realize that his central teaching is fundamentally the same in both works. Finally, Machiavelli states in both excerpts that his purpose is to write something useful to those who understand the truth of the matter. Clearly political utility is at the core of these works, and its attainment will be had by learning from the mistakes and successes of the ancients and not by the guidelines of an ideal regime.

In the final analysis, Machiavelli offers a practical, useful, and candid teaching that differs from those that came before; it is predicated upon the truth of things, determined by the successes and failures of past and present actions, and applicable to all regimes and purposes. Indeed, a republic and a principality may look very different on the surface and may have to be governed differently in terms of participation, policies, and so forth. However, both regimes want stability, order, and the means for promoting the well-being of citizens and subjects. To accomplish this, Machiavelli recognized the need for a realistic political understanding of human nature and human action within the political realm, with its promise of power and glory. To this end, he developed consistent maxims that provide the means for attaining and maintaining power, all of which are predicated upon a simple belief about human nature: "... it is necessary to whoever disposes a republic and orders laws in it to presuppose that all men are bad, and that they always have to use the malignity of their spirit whenever they have a free opportunity for it" (*The Discourses*, I, 3).

MEANING AND WORLDVIEW

Although Machiavelli's teaching may be consistent, the question of its meaning has been the subject of much debate among scholars for centuries. Several reasons can be considered as the cause of these divergent interpretations. First, the inconsistencies of Machiavelli's own life have allowed divided interpretations of his work to evolve. As a theorist, Machiavelli prescribes such things as duplicity, breaking one's word, "well-used" cruelty, and murdering whole families, all in the name of political power. However, in his own life he was a loyal friend, a trusted ally, a loving parent, and a passionate patriot and defender of his city. We cannot help but wonder how such a decent man could prescribe such brutal teachings. Some, like contemporary scholar Sebastian de Grazia, see Machiavelli as a loyal citizen and friend, taking a more apologetic tone and asserting Machiavelli's republicanism. De Grazia says that Machiavelli's ruthless maxims are nothing more than the desire to better the political order of his native land. Moreover, his cruelty is not a true evil because it was prescribed only to attain the common good; rather, it is seen as a temporary evil designed to bring about a higher good for all.[6] One need only look to Machiavelli's famous letter of April 16, 1527, to Francesco Vettori, in which he writes, "I love my native city more than my own soul," for proof of this interpretation.[7]

Scholars who pay less attention to the man and his life and more to his written prescriptions often level harsh judgment against the Florentine. For example, contemporary theorist Leo Strauss sees Machiavelli as a "teacher of evil": "... what other description would fit a man who teaches lessons like these: princes ought to exterminate the families of rulers whose territory they wish to possess securely; ... true liberality consists in being stingy with one's own property and in being generous with what belongs to others; not virtue but the prudent use of virtue and vice leads to happiness...."[8] Strauss is unwilling to justify such cruelties; he sees Machiavelli's "patriotism" as nothing more than "collective selfishness," whereby the state acts only in self-promotion, independent of any consideration of good and evil. This, according to Strauss, is both erroneous and dangerous because it places patriotism as the highest good and the ultimate justification for the prescription of evil.[9]

While the inconsistencies between Machiavelli's life and his teachings have made it difficult to discern his true message, his own peculiar admissions and odd comments to friends have complicated things further. For example, on May 17, 1521, Machiavelli

---

[6]Sebastian de Grazia, *Machiavelli in Hell* (Princeton, New Jersey: Princeton University Press, 1989), pp. 316–317.

[7]Niccolo Machiavelli, *The Letters of Machiavelli*, ed. Allan Gilbert (Chicago: University of Chicago Press, 1988), p. 249.

[8]Leo Strauss, *Thoughts on Machiavelli* (Chicago: University of Chicago Press, 1984), p. 9.

[9]Strauss, p. 11.

wrote to his friend Francesco Guicciardini regarding the way in which humans could best reach heaven—a way in which he later admits is best traveled via hell. Nonetheless, it is here that he concedes the following: "... for a long time I have not said what I believed, nor do I ever believe what I say, and if indeed sometimes I do happen to tell the truth, I hide it among so many lies that it is hard to find."[10] What is to be made of such a comment? Is Machiavelli being serious? Does such an admission cast doubt on the truthfulness of his teaching? Because this letter was addressed to a close friend, are we to assume a level of honesty beyond other writings? If so, how can we feel confident about the truthfulness of any of his work?

The question of whether Machiavelli tells the truth is further obfuscated within his political writings as he seems to contradict himself within the confines of the same chapter. For example, in Chapter 8 of *The Prince,* Machiavelli talks about Agathocles the Sicilian and the "... actions and virtue of this man ..." while in the same chapter implying that his cruel actions could never be seen as virtuous. Moreover, in Chapter 25 of *The Prince,* Machiavelli tells his readers that "... fortune is arbiter of half of our actions, but also she leaves the other half, or close to it, for us to govern," implying that we can, at best, shape only half of the events around us. However, within that same chapter, he invites his readers to take control of their lives and prepare so that when changes occur, their fortunes will not have to change. Again, what are we to make of this mixed message? Do we have only partial control over the events of our lives? Or given adequate preparations, do we have total control? Is Machiavelli merely trying to motivate his readers to believe they can control all things, in order to better approach each task with energy and enthusiasm? But is this not naive and overly optimistic? Does Machiavelli not wish to inject a dose of realism into politics, thereby "lowering the sights" and expectations of political actors?

If at this point you are confused about how to interpret and make sense of this clever thinker, you are in good company. For centuries, the confusion that has arisen from the different subject matter of his works, the disparity of his life from the prescriptions of his work, the inconsistencies of his verbiage within the same works, and finally, the differences in his own admissions and purposes have made Machiavelli one of the most confusing and intriguing thinkers in human history. Nonetheless, such complexity must not stand in the way of our figuring out Machiavelli's intent; as he says, he is writing for those who "understand." The challenge at hand, then, is to read his texts closely.

THE NATURE OF POLITICS AND THE ROLE OF THE STATE

Machiavelli's political teaching reveals itself largely through such works as *The Prince* and *The Discourses.* Although these works are not the exclusive source of his political thought (such works as *The History of Florence, The Exhortation to Penitence, The Mandragola,* and others also show his instruction), they are the most substantive and direct sources of his message. If we look closely at these works and put aside the controversy surrounding his different subject matter, different audiences, and different

[10]Niccolo Machiavelli, *The Letters of Machiavelli*, ed. Allan Gilbert (Chicago: University of Chicago Press, 1988), p. 200.

interpretive meanings, we can see a consistent and original teaching. The congruous nature of repeated themes, along with his periodic admissions of certain intentions, demonstrate that Machiavelli's works are truly novel.

One of the best ways to study the intention of an author is to pay attention to what he or she says directly to the reader. In his two most famous works, Machiavelli states repeatedly that he is doing something new—something untried by others. How is his political teaching new? *The Prince* best answers this question.

Not surprisingly, Machiavelli begins this famous work in a conventional manner, telling his readers that all regimes are either principalities or republics and that the purpose of this work is to examine principalities. The first fourteen chapters of the work seem traditional, discussing various types of principalities and similar subjects. However, not until the pivotal Chapter 15 is the radical nature of Machiavelli's teaching fully revealed. In fact, we might argue that the novelty of the entire work first becomes apparent in this chapter, which sheds light on the true objective of Machiavelli's teaching.

The bold and novel nature of Chapter 15, titled "Of Those Things for Which Men and Especially Princes Are Praised or Blamed," has been the subject of much analysis. Commonly referred to as "the lowering of the sights" because of its reduced expectations of human behavior, Machiavelli revolutionizes the way in which his readers are to think about politics, forcing them to confront the realities of human nature within the political realm. As he tells us (an excerpt was included earlier in this chapter), many people before him have written about principalities; but unlike their efforts, he will "... depart from the orders of others ..." because he will examine the behavior of princes and subjects from a realistic perspective. Machiavelli could not be more straightforward on this issue: His work will be different, useful, and realistic. Those who have come before have made the mistake of assuming that people can be made good or shown how to behave. This is a foundational error for Machiavelli. If a political order is based on the assumption or hope of virtuous human acts, failure is guaranteed, "... for it is so far from how one lives to how one should live that he who lets go of what is done for what should be done learns his ruin rather than his preservation" (Chapter 15). Machiavelli's realism presumes that people are selfish, cruel, and always ready to deceive.

HUMAN NATURE

As Machiavelli tells his readers throughout *The Prince,* the main task of any leader is to get and keep power. Recognizing humans' depraved nature is the first step in attaining power and creating a realistic political structure. A second step in forming and ultimately maintaining such a structure is to possess a willingness "... not to be good" (Chapter 15). "Among so many who are not good," a prince must himself be bad in order to preserve his reign. Machiavelli could not be clearer on this issue: He tells us that good men cannot attain or maintain power in a world filled with deceit. He admits that such a prescription would not be beneficial if people were in fact good; but they are not, so a prince must follow this realistic prescription to survive.

For modern people, such lessons may not seem shocking. As we watch daily news reports of school hostage situations, drug-related killings, and genocide, Machiavelli's pronouncement regarding the evil of human nature seems ordinary. However, we must not let the events of our day blur the true significance of his teaching. Arguably, Machiavelli writes nothing that ancient Greeks and Romans did not observe in human nature. People were equally as cruel and selfish in their world as they were in Machiavelli's and as they are today. What makes Machiavelli's teaching so unique is his willingness to acknowledge human selfishness, make no effort to change it, and exploit it for maximum political benefit. In fact, we might even say that he embraces what others are disinclined to recognize and accept. For this realistic Florentine, people's refusal to accept human depravity and their optimistic adherence to the possibility of moral improvement has created a political world that is unworkable and wrought with failure. Only by embracing Machiavelli's dim view of human beings can a prince (or anyone in power) begin to shape and control the world in a realistic fashion.

Being a shrewd student of human nature, Machiavelli is aware of people's desires to be honored and loved; thus he seems to recognize that his shocking prescription might conflict with our vain tendencies. How can we not be made into virtuous beings? How can we just stop trying? To answer these questions, Machiavelli reassuringly acknowledges our desires to be "humane," "chaste," "agreeable," and "faithful" with the words "And I know that everyone will confess that it would be a very laudable thing to find in a prince all of the above-mentioned qualities that are held good" (Chapter 15). This must not, however, mislead the reader. These comments play to our vanity while reinforcing the earlier teaching. If one looks closely at his words, Machiavelli does not actually call such traits "good," but rather things "held good." What is the difference? If he pronounced chastity, faithfulness, and other traits as good, he would be admitting to a fixed moral order in the world where there are permanent virtues and vices, and thus he would once again be ascribing to the tenets of ancient thinkers. Their adherence to the ideas of right and wrong ultimately led to their inability to carry out the requisite tasks of attaining and maintaining power. These traits may be held good by many, but in fact they may not be good at all. For Machiavelli, such traits possess no inherent goodness. Their goodness depends on circumstance and outcome: "... for if one considers everything well, one will find something appears to be virtue, which if pursued would be one's ruin, and something else appears to be vice, which if pursued results in one's security and well-being" (Chapter 15). Note the word "appears." It is used in the same context that "held" was used earlier. Both reflect Machiavelli's rejection of a transcendent moral order, suggesting instead a willingness to judge the goodness of an act wholly by its political outcome. This we might call **situational ethics**—goodness is not intrinsic but is relative to success.

What are we to make of such a revolutionary chapter and teaching? Are humans incapable of goodness? Is there no moral standard by which we can be judged? Are outcomes the determinants of everything? As with most questions asked about Machiavelli's works, the answers are both yes and no. If we return to what Machiavelli said in the dedications to *The Prince* and *The Discourses,* we see that he writes these works for the few who "understand." In short, he writes for a small group of individuals who, because they recognize the harsh reality of politics, will be able to understand the realism and nuances of his teaching. They recognize that to stabilize power, all traditional means of rule must be reconsidered. Thus what Machiavelli begins in Chapter 15 and carries out throughout *The Prince* is the semblance of a **dual-layered** moral code that appears different on the surface, but is, at its core, the same. In his view, the world is split between those who rule and those who are ruled. Those who rule must do whatever is necessary to promote the stability of the state. This is especially critical in a principality, where the state is the prince himself. The success of such an effort requires a willingness to impose situational ethics, whereby traditional notions of right and wrong are discarded for actions that work. However, Machiavelli recognizes that it would be highly disadvantageous for citizens or subjects at large to practice such situational ethics: This would make the prince's job almost impossible. A ruler needs subjects or citizens to be virtuous, dutiful, God-fearing, and so forth because such people are likely to be obedient and thus easy to rule. For this reason, traditional moral standards (such as the Christian standards of his day) should be held and practiced by the people.

We cannot help but wonder about this double standard. While this dual-layered morality appears at odds, it is inherently the same. In both instances, morality is never examined from the perspective of its inherent value or goodness. Rather, it is judged only by its usefulness in a situation. Thus virtue is not good in and of itself, and vice is not inherently bad. Machiavelli's prince must adopt situational ethics because it is useful to him, while subjects and citizens must adhere to traditional morality for the benefit of the state. Machiavelli pays no heed to the transcendent values of either classical or Christian virtues. What matters ultimately is political value, so what appears on the surface to be a contradictory moral prescription is a consistent assumption that the value of all things is determined by their usefulness in success or failure in politics.

A WORLD OF NEW MODES AND ORDERS

In many ways, studying Chapter 15 first prepares the reader to understand the radical nature of this book. As already noted, Chapters 1–14 are viewed by many as traditional in their theme and approach. On the surface, this is true. Machiavelli discusses the various types of principalities, including hereditary and mixed types and those that were once free states. His aim here is simple—to look at the difficulties of attaining and maintaining these various states, presenting all of the challenges that come to a prince en route to power. This may not seem like anything out of the ordinary; but when examined closely, it is anything but ordinary. Machiavelli cleverly introduces his readers to the traditional topic of principalities, listing all of the challenges inherent to their rule, only to ease the readers into recognizing that the success of any of these regimes falls largely upon the wherewithal of the prince. His innate ability to assess a situation, accommodate to that situation, and carry out the necessary tasks to bring about order will determine how well he can seize and hold power. It is with these "necessary tasks" that we again begin to see the novel and radical teaching of Machiavelli; he calls these necessary tasks "new modes and orders"—techniques that will be anything but ordinary.

But first Machiavelli must introduce these **mixed regimes,** and soon the reader realizes that Machiavelli has little interest in hereditary regimes because they are easy both to attain and to hold. The means of succession are already in place; those who come to power have few challenges to maintain it, for all the prince must do is "...not to depart from the order of his ancestors..." (*The Prince*, Chapter 2). Machiavelli's real interest lies in newly acquired principalities that are challenging to get and keep. The precarious nature of "mixed principalities" are most interesting because they are difficult in all ways, thus providing an opportunity to show a prince's acumen. Here Machiavelli tells his readers that mixed principalities are largely "added members" to a state or empire; they can be near or far, and they may or may not have the same customs and language. Both scenarios present challenges. In the first instance, in which a prince adds neighbors to his reign, the challenges are less daunting because the customs and languages of the two states are similar. However, there will be difficulties with people who benefited by the old regime. Even citizens who enlisted the help of this prince and encouraged his entry into their state cannot be satisfied easily, as Machiavelli notes:

> [M]en willingly change their masters in the belief that they will fare better: this belief makes them take up arms against him, in which they are deceived because they see later by experience that they have done worse.... So you have as enemies all those whom you have offended in seizing that principality and you cannot keep as friends those who have put you there because you cannot satisfy them in the mode they had presumed and because you cannot use strong medicines against them, since you are obligated to them. (*The Prince,* Chapter 3)

In this troublesome scenario, Machiavelli suggests that a prince must eliminate the bloodline of the former ruling family and preserve as many past customs as possible. This will likely appease the people and make maintenance of his rule easy.

Real difficulties are found with the second example of a mixed regime, in which the state acquired has different customs and language. Machiavelli suggests that a prince must show great "industry": He must either go to the newly acquired state and live there himself or send his citizens there to set up colonies. This latter suggestion is Machiavelli's favorite because it costs the prince little and allows a constant presence of the prince's "eyes and ears" in the form of his own subjects. The first alternative is also good, but it is less desirable for a prince because he must leave his own land and move to one of different habits and tongue. Nonetheless, both offer a valuable means to maintain rule that is far superior in result and cost-effectiveness than the alternative of a standing military presence. As Machiavelli notes,

> I conclude that such colonies are not costly, are more faithful, and less offensive; and those who are offended can do no hurt, since they are poor and dispersed as was said. For this has to be noted: that men should either be caressed or eliminated, because they avenge themselves for slight offenses but cannot do so for grave ones; so the offense one does to a man should be such that one does not fear revenge for it. (*The Prince,* Chapter 3)

Here the ordinary topics of mixed principalities and the difficulties they present are cleverly overshadowed by the extraordinary means necessary to order the state. Note the importance of two simple lines from the preceding passage: First, "men should either be caressed or eliminated," and second, "the offense one does to a man should be such that one does not fear revenge for it." Machiavelli here is recommending that a prince either coddle new subjects or destroy them in a way that guarantees no retribution. In the latter scenario, this implies a complete and speedy removal of enemies.

Already by Chapter 3, we can see that Machiavelli's teaching is anything but conventional. Readers soon realize that even when the subject matter is traditional and the examples are classical, the underlying teaching is still radical. Although

Machiavelli may cite the Romans as an example to follow in how to establish colonies, he nonetheless turns their acts into a bold and unabashed prescription for how to keep power. What others may have quietly known or did, he prescribes openly. In this example, his prescriptive order is the unsentimental, calculating elimination of anyone who poses a threat to the prince. Guilt or innocence, right or wrong have no place here. Only the effective use of either flattery or murder is prescribed as a means to secure power.

This same unsentimental teaching is present in Machiavelli's description of the difficulties that befall a prince who takes control of a formerly free city–state. Here again his message is simple, realistic, and harsh: "When those states that are acquired, as has been said, are accustomed to living by their own laws and in liberty, there are three modes for those who want to hold them: first, ruin them; second, go there to live personally; third, let them live by their laws . . . " (*The Prince,* Chapter 5). Machiavelli concedes that free cities are most easily held by their own citizens and with the continuation of their established habits, but still he concludes on a harsh note: "For in truth there is no secure mode to possess them other than to ruin them . . . " because " . . . in republics there is greater life, greater hatred, more desire for revenge . . . " (*The Prince,* Chapter 5). In these words we see an indifference to life and freedom. What matters is power, and he has provided his readers with some simple rules to attain it.

Machiavelli's favorite regime is the regime acquired by one's own arms and one's own virtue. Here Machiavelli introduces the figure of the **new founder:** the extraordinary man who breaks away from all traditional boundaries and limitations and, by his own acumen, founds and orders a state to his liking. By Machiavelli's estimate, this is the most difficult state to found because it depends wholly on the skills and ***virtu*** of the founder. What does Machiavelli mean by *virtu?* In part this is a kind of manly energy that directs its attention to doing great things here on earth. Such great things would include setting up new orders and creating new laws and institutions with the use of one's own arms, all for dominion and glory. Even though Machiavelli retains the ancient word *virtu,* its meaning is fully different because its qualities speak of earthly success, not moral order. Thus, Machiavelli redefines the traditional meaning of virtue to include qualities that were formerly considered vicious, like cruelty and fraud. Unlike other men, Machiavelli's new founder is not hesitant or reticent in his rule. He is not hesitant in his use of unscrupulous means or methods that are traditionally considered evil and vicious, provided they will attain the desirable political result or end.

The new founder does not suffer from the ***ozio*** or idleness from which so many Italian princes suffer. He sees the world as it is; identifies opportunities where others see nothing; and by his own devices fully orders a situation to his benefit, without the help of fortune. He succeeds in this with the aid of both ***prudenzia*** and ***astuzia.*** By *prudenzia* Machiavelli means a type of foresight and agility that allow a ruler to make the most of a situation, assessing and acting upon proper measures to guarantee success. *Astuzia* is a type of clever perceptiveness that allows the new founder to identify such situations. The possession of these great traits makes the new founder a wholly unique and innovative individual whom most others, at best, can merely imitate to come near to his achievements. Machiavelli cites the likes of " . . . Moses, Cyrus, Romulus, Theseus . . . " as examples of new founders who had no advantage of fortune, other than their innate *virtu* to seize the opportunities before them.

As we can see, the list of new founders is short because so few people in Machiavelli's estimation deserve such a title. These extraordinary leaders face innumerable challenges that never seem to cease:

> Those like these men, who become princes by the paths of virtue, acquire their principality with difficulty but hold it with ease; and the difficulties they have in acquiring their principality arise in part from the new orders and modes that they are forced to introduce so as to found their state and their security. And it should be considered that nothing is more difficult to handle, more doubtful of success, nor more dangerous to manage, than to put oneself at the head of introducing new orders. For the introducer has all those who benefit from the old order as enemies, and he has lukewarm defenders in all those who might benefit from the new orders. This lukewarmness arises partly from fear of adversaries who have the laws on their side and partly from the incredulity of men, who do not truly believe in new things unless they come to have a firm experience of them. (*The Prince,* Chapter 6)

The rewards of a new founder's willingness to implement "new orders and modes" that promote security and thus advance his agenda are innumerable. Machiavelli may see this situation as the most dire, but in the end it is the most noble. This conclusion is expressed not only in *The Prince* but in *The Discourses* as well, as Machiavelli again admits,

> And truly, if a prince seeks the glory of the world, he ought to desire to possess a corrupt city—not to spoil it entirely as did Caesar but to reorder it as did Romulus. And truly the heavens cannot give to men a greater opportunity for glory, nor can men desire any greater. If one who wishes to order a city well had of necessity to lay down the principate, he would deserve some excuse if he did not order it so as not to fall from that rank; but if he is able to hold the principate and order it, he does not merit any excuse. In sum, those to whom the heavens give such an opportunity may consider that two ways have been placed before them: one that makes them live secure and after death renders them glorious; the other that makes them live in continual anxieties and after death leaves them eternal infamy. (*The Discourses,* I, 10)

Indeed, Machiavelli's list of new founders is both short and ancient; but he discusses the modern example of Brother Girolamo Savonarola, who began to implement new religious modes and orders within Florence. The inclusion of Savonarola in a discussion of new founders seems to serve a dual purpose. First, it shows the problems of attempting to implement new modes and orders without the use of arms. This dynamic friar challenged Florentines to examine their sumptuous lifestyles and follow a more pious existence. The people were quite persuaded by Savonarola's new ordering, but as Machiavelli points out, such new modes and orders are useless without the backing of arms. He notes that there came a time when the people no longer believed in Savonarola's prescriptions and "... he had no mode for holding firm those who had believed nor for making unbelievers believe" (*The Prince,* Chapter 6).

Second (and more interesting), Savonarola's failure allows Machiavelli to engage in a somewhat philosophical discussion of unarmed prophets. According to Machiavelli, a new founder will likely meet with success when he can make use of his own arms because "... when they depend on their own and are able to use force, then it is that they are rarely in peril. From this it arises that all the armed prophets conquered and the unarmed ones were ruined" (*The Prince,* Chapter 6). On the surface, this may not look like a radical pronouncement; history provides ample examples. However, we must think critically about this statement and return to Machiavelli's curious admission of his propensity to lie and hide the truth. Is Machiavelli being forthright here? Has there never been a prophet who succeeded without arms? What about the historic figure of Jesus Christ? Is it possible that Machiavelli merely forgot this man of peace? Whether or not we believe in the message of Christ, we cannot dispute its impact over the past 2,000 years. It seems unlikely that the astute mind of Machiavelli would make such an omission. The question then remains: Why such an omission? The answer may lie with Machiavelli himself.

There can be little doubt that *The Prince* and *The Discourses* offer a radical teaching, filled with new modes and orders designed to control the political arena to one's own design. Machiavelli has no arms, but he is a prophet of new and subversive ideas. If he truly believed that all unarmed prophets fail, then why bother to reveal his new teaching, even to those who understand? The fact is that he knew unarmed prophets can succeed: Christ's message had forever changed the world in which he lived. While Machiavelli may have wondered whether his message would impact the political world, he may also have wondered whether Lorenzo was thinking the same. Would Machiavelli, the brilliant yet exiled author of *The Prince*, be so risky as to expose the successes of unarmed prophets to a Medici? Maybe not.

CESARE BORGIA: CASE STUDY OF A NEW FOUNDER AND VIRTU

While Machiavelli clearly attempts to conceal some of his more subversive teachings, he reveals others quite openly. This can be seen in Chapter 7 of *The Prince,* where he introduces readers to the infamous **Cesare Borgia,** a man most admired by Machiavelli for his ruthlessness and duplicity. Although Cesare did not fully conform to Machiavelli's idea of a true new founder who both acquires and maintains his state by his own virtue, Cesare was a modern example that came close. Acquiring his state with the help of his father, Pope Alexander VI, Cesare proved capable of maintaining it by his own talents. Up to this point, Machiavelli's new modes and orders have been somewhat shocking, calling for a rejection of traditional morality replaced by situational ethics, a willingness to ruin whole states in an effort to reduce them to order and the elimination of enemy bloodlines. However, the modes and orders revealed in the actions of Cesare take this teaching to a new level that forever alters one's impression of Machiavelli.

Machiavelli begins by telling his readers that when a new prince is given his power by fortune, he is likely to face many difficulties in holding his regime, for he has yet to prove whether he possesses the virtue necessary for successful rule. This was the beginning scenario for Cesare Borgia, whose father gave him the Romagna region to order and rule. Cesare, who commonly went by the name Duke Valentino, captured Machiavelli's attention because of his understanding of political realities and his willingness to do what is necessary to hold power. Machiavelli writes,

> ...he [Cesare] made use of every deed and did all those things that should be done by a prudent and virtuous man to put his roots in the states that the arms and fortune of others had given him. For, as was said above, whoever does not lay his foundations

> at first might be able, with great virtue, to lay them later, although they might have to be laid with hardship for the architect and with danger to the building. Thus, if one considers all the steps of the duke, one will see that he had laid for himself great foundations for future power, which I do not judge superfluous to discuss; for I do not know what better teaching I could give to a new prince than the example of his actions. And if his orders did not bring profit to him, it was not his fault, because this arose from an extraordinary and extreme malignity of fortune. (*The Prince,* Chapter 7)

For Machiavelli, all regimes require good **foundations**—structural institutions and laws that produce a stable and prosperous state. Although such institutions and laws may vary between principality and republic, they are needed in both regimes and require the same "modes and orders" to bring them about. Cesare seemed to understand this as he took on the enormous task of breaking down the Romagna's corrupt edifices and replacing them with good laws and institutions. In both works, Machiavelli suggests that stability often requires carrying out things "thought to be cruel" because the foundations must be firm and lasting, and this cannot occur until all disruptive and unnecessary elements of society are eliminated. The unique feature of Cesare Borgia, however, was his ability to recognize not only the need for things thought to be cruel but also the implications of perceived cruelties among the people. Because he understood the implications of the latter, Cesare carried out his cruelties in a most unique and clever manner.

The artistry of Cesare's rule so caught Machiavelli's attention that he gives the following account:

> And because this point is deserving of notice and of being imitated by others, I do not want to leave it out. Once the duke had taken over Romagna, he found it had been commanded by impotent lords who had been readier to despoil their subjects than to correct them, and had given their subjects matter for disunion, not for union. Since that province was quite full of robberies, quarrels, and every other kind of insolence, he judged it necessary to give it good government, if he wanted to reduce it to peace and obedience to a kingly arm. So he put there Messer Remirro de Orco, a cruel and ready man, to whom he gave the fullest power. In a short time Remirro reduced it to peace and unity, with the very greatest reputation for himself. Then the duke judged that such excessive authority was not necessary, because he feared that it might become hateful; and he set up a civil court in the middle of the province, with a most excellent president, where each city had its advocate. And because he knew that past rigors had generated some hatred for Remirro, to purge the spirits of that people and to gain them entirely to himself, he wished to show that if any cruelty had been committed, this had not come from him but from the harsh nature of his minister. And having seized the opportunity, he had him placed one morning in the piazza at Cesena in two pieces, with a piece of wood and a bloody knife beside him. The ferocity of this spectacle left the people at once satisfied and stupefied. (*The Prince,* Chapter 7)

The opening line of this passage sets the stage for one of Machiavelli's greatest teaching examples, as he directly tells his readers that the actions of Cesare are "...deserving of notice and of being imitated by others." There can be little doubt that Machiavelli wants other leaders to copy what Cesare, a true innovator, was able to do by his own accord. Next he reveals the difficulties faced in assuming control of the Romagna: Its leadership was inept, its people disunited, and its leading patricians bent on "despoiling" their fellow citizens. Recognizing that any changes imposed on this rotting state would be for naught, Cesare set out to reduce the Romagna to its foundations. However, he understood that such acts would likely engender great hatred by the people because what was necessary to ensure stability would mandate the harshest modes and orders. Thus he hired Remirro de Orco, "a cruel and ready man," to do the dirty work. Cesare knew his vicious nature, hired him for that reason, and gave him full control to carry out whatever was necessary to reduce the people to submission.

What happened next is the most interesting part of the story. Hatred among the people began to develop; so in order that it not come in his direction, Cesare had his minister arrested with the seeming intention to have him tried. Appointing a man of excellent repute to head the trial, Cesare asked for each city in the region to send an advocate to attest to the crimes of his minister. These efforts gave the semblance of justice, with Cesare posturing as a man of reason and fairness and ultimately one who was willing to listen to and act upon the sufferings of his people. However, Cesare had no intention of ever holding such a trial—he could never risk his minister being brought before the public. What if Remirro talked and blamed Cesare for his actions? To avoid this, Borgia had Remirro secretly killed and "... placed one morning in the piazza at Cesena in two pieces, with a piece of wood and a bloody knife beside him." For Machiavelli, the brilliance and reward for this act seem without limit. First, Cesare got rid of a minister who did the necessary cruel acts to stabilize the state, without any negative repercussions being leveled in his direction. Second, the ruse of a trial made Cesare look like a friend of justice and a man of the people. Third, the method of Remirro de Orco's murder would prove of immense value, bringing to a new art form the **political use of spectacle.** Although Cesare might have chosen to have Remirro hung or strangled publicly, he chose instead to have him cut in half privately, with a knife and piece of wood placed by his side. Moreover, he had him placed in the public square during the morning hours. What are the purpose and value of such acts? Imagine yourself witnessing this scene and someone asks you, What role did the wood play? Was this the knife that cut him in half? Were the two weapons used in consort? In all likelihood, you have no better idea than did the people who were witness to the actual scene hundreds of years ago! What is certain, however, is that the uncertainty of the murderous event would lead to hours, weeks, and maybe months of speculation and theories. This likely scenario would be enhanced further by the fact that the body was present in the piazza in the early morning hours, when most townspeople were out doing their marketing. The equation then is quite simple: A brutal and mysterious act plus high visibility equals "... the people at once satisfied and stupefied." Justice was served, the cruel minister was removed, and Cesare looked like the hero. However, he was not a kindly hero. The brutality of the act also sent the message that Cesare was not a man to be toyed with. He was capable of being just as brutal as his minister.

Why is the story of Remirro de Orco so important? Machiavelli tells us that Cesare's actions are worthy of both our attention and our imitation. He is serious in his call for imitation because Italy's corrupt regimes will require a return to their foundations, which will likely engender great hatred toward any prince who carries out this effort. What Machiavelli respects in Cesare is his realism in recognizing what needs to be done but also his cleverness in recognizing that such acts might be better carried out by someone else. This result is maximal political benefit with minimal political risk. In terms of new modes and orders, Machiavelli here demonstrates the enormous power of political spectacle. The brutality of the act, along with the secrecy of its method, would likely spur on much debate and consternation about the minister's death as well as about the brutal acumen of the new leader. Cesare seemed to understand the opportunity presented by this scenario; and as Machiavelli suggests, most would see nothing here but concern, whereas new founders like Cesare see only the possibilities.

Machiavelli's respect for Cesare does not end with this story. He tells us that Cesare did what all great new founders almost instinctively know to do: prepare constantly for future adversity. Cesare seemed to understand that fortune is forever changing and thus, if one could prepare well and change one's self to accommodate fortune, then fortune would always work to one's advantage. Because his father had given him the Romagna, Cesare recognized the need to prepare for the possibility that the next pope might want it back. To this effort, "He thought he might secure himself against this in four modes: first, to eliminate the bloodlines of all those lords he had despoiled, so as to take that opportunity away from the pope; second, to win over to himself all the gentlemen in Rome, as was said, so as to be able to hold the pope in check with them; third, to make the College of Cardinals as much his as he could; and fourth, to acquire so much empire before the pope died that he could resist a first attack on his own" (*The Prince,* Chapter 7). As Machiavelli recalls, Cesare largely accomplished these tasks but did not anticipate that he too would be dying at the same time as his father. What proves most interesting, however, is Machiavelli's final analysis of this great innovator. He praises Cesare's extraordinary ability to assess and respond to the most difficult of situations:

> But Alexander died five years after he had begun to draw his sword. He left the duke with only the state of Romagna consolidated, with all the others in the air, between two very powerful enemy armies, and sick to death. And there was such ferocity and such virtue in the duke, and he knew so well how men have to be won over or lost, and so sound were the foundations that he had laid in so little time, that if he had not had these armies on his back or if he had been healthy, he would have been equal to every difficulty. And that his foundations were good one may see: Romagna waited for him for more than a month; in Rome, though he was half-alive, he remained secure; and although the Baglioni, Vitelli, and Orsini came to Rome, none followed them against him; if he could not make pope whomever he wanted, at least it would not be someone he did not want.
>
> Thus, if I summed up all the actions of the duke, I would not know how to reproach him; on the contrary, it seems to me he should be put forward, as I have done, to be imitated by all those who have risen to empire through fortune and by the arms of others. For with his great spirit and high intention, he could not have conducted himself otherwise, and the only things in the way of his designs were the brevity of Alexander's life and his own sickness. (*The Prince,* Chapter 7)

Although Machiavelli tells us that he "... does not know how to reproach him ...," he nonetheless manages to do just that at the end of his analysis. The worst thing Cesare could have done was to have allowed Julius II to become pope—this was someone whom Cesare had offended in the past, and "... whoever believes that among great personages new benefits will make old injuries be forgotten deceives himself" (*The Prince,* Chapter 7). Cesare made a gross miscalculation in thinking that Julius' exalted position would render him more magnanimous toward a former nemesis like himself. If Cesare erred in allowing Julius to come to power, did he err

QUESTIONS FOR REFLECTION

1. How have extremist groups today used Machiavelli's example of grand spectacle as a means of furthering their political agendas?
2. Cesare gained tremendous political mileage out of one man's murder. How have groups like Al Qaeda and the Chechen rebels either succeeded or failed in their implementation of Machiavelli's use of fear through spectacle? What makes such acts succeed or fail? Are there limits to Machiavelli's teachings about spectacle?
3. What have been the political effects or fallout from such media attention to violent spectacle in places like Iraq? How has this subsequently affected U.S. foreign policy regarding terrorism worldwide? In the Middle East?

in allowing *anyone* come to power? Machiavelli writes these curious words: "... for, as was said, though he could not make a pope to suit himself, he could have kept anyone from being pope" (*The Prince,* Chapter 7). Critics have wondered what the Florentine means by these ambiguous words. Does he mean that Cesare could have prevented any particular person from being pope? Or does he mean that he could have prevented anyone from being pope, thus doing away with the papacy completely? While no answer can be given with certainty, phrases such as these have forever cast Machiavelli's piety into question.

Machiavelli contends that a ruler can maintain a state only with an accurate understanding of human nature, a willingness to do what is necessary to hold one's power, and the agility to change one's nature to conform to fluid circumstances. Of course this requires the possession of virtue (properly understood), along with the implementation of new modes and orders. Cesare understood this; and while he was given much of his power, his keen understanding of human nature and willingness to put aside moral constraints and do what was necessary allowed him to keep his power until his death. However, the uniqueness of such a person, along with the challenges of rule, makes politics one of the most difficult challenges. For this reason, Machiavelli sets out in his *The Prince, The Discourses, The History of Florence,* and other works to inform his readers about the many difficulties that present themselves in the political world and the strategies necessary to surmount these difficulties. In doing so, his list of new modes and orders grows.

GOOD LAWS AND GOOD ARMS

During his career, Machiavelli realized that no power can be attained or maintained without the use of one's own arms. The division of Italy into small city–states left many unable to defend themselves against each other, making it necessary either to enlist the help of more powerful, unified states like France and Spain or to hire mercenary soldiers to fight their cause. Whatever the choice, the outcome was the same: disaster. Machiavelli's concern for the use of one's own or native troops permeates all of his works; he labels this lack of native soldiers as the cause of the present disarray in Italy. Without the love of one's own land as a motive for fighting, mercenary troops prove useless in their battle efforts. More often than not, these fee for service soldiers bring about total ruin to a region, for as Machiavelli suggests,

". . . they are disunited, ambitious, without discipline, unfaithful; bold among friends, among enemies cowardly; no fear of God, no faith with men, ruin is postponed only as long as attack is postponed; and in peace you are despoiled by them, in war by the enemy" (*The Prince,* Chapter 12).

While the ineptitude of mercenaries is great and their potential damage significant, nothing is more dangerous than the use of "auxiliary" troops. Borrowed from a more powerful neighbor, these troops speak the same language, have at their helm a competent leader, and are unified in purpose. Ironically, their danger comes with this unity; as Machiavelli warns, any state that uses them has brought a cohesive military force upon its soil:

> These arms can be useful and good in themselves, but for whoever calls them in, they are almost always harmful, because when they lose you are undone; when they win, you are left their prisoner. (*The Prince,* Chapter 13)

Again, if you win or lose with their service, you have still lost because now within your boundaries is present a formidable army, to which you are indebted. Either way, no good can come of this situation, so it must be avoided at all costs. In the end, the leader of any regime must make every attempt to employ his own arms, made up of loyal and dedicated native citizens. This effort, coupled with a commitment to think and plan for nothing but war, will result in a successful and secure state.

THE CHALLENGES OF NECESSITY

Machiavelli demonstrates repeatedly the need to change one's self to fit with new circumstances. This implies not only flexibility with military plans or political policies, but also flexibility in moral behavior. Situations may require a harsh response by the prince that in turn may cause shock and dismay among the people. Machiavelli understood this well; he recognized the likelihood and necessity for the people to maintain traditional morality. They will see only the action and not the political necessity behind the action. For this reason, Machiavelli writes that all rulers must engage in what might be called the art of political appearance—a new mode and order to be employed in the maintenance of one's state. How well one uses appearance to accommodate necessity will determine how well one masters *fortuna* or **fortune.**

In his famous chapter "In What Mode Faith Should Be Kept by Princes," Machiavelli outlines how a ruler must adapt his nature to fit circumstances, all the while appearing to be steadfast in his word and moral conduct. He begins this section with his usual appeasement of the reader:

> How laudable it is for a prince to keep his faith, and to live with honesty and not by astuteness, everyone understands. Nonetheless one sees by experience in our times that the princes who have done great things are those who have taken little account of faith and have known how to get around men's brains with their astuteness; and in the end they have overcome those who have founded themselves on loyalty. Thus, you must know that there are two kinds of combat: one with laws, the other with force. The first is proper to man, the second to beasts; but because the first is often not enough, one must have recourse to the second. Therefore it is necessary for a prince to know well how to use the beast and the man. This role was taught covertly to

> princes by ancient writers, who wrote that Achilles, and many other ancient princes, were given to Chiron the centaur to be raised, so that he would look after them with his discipline. To have as teacher a half-beast, half-man means nothing other than that a prince needs to know how to use both natures; and the one without the other is not lasting. (*The Prince,* Chapter 18)

Almost as if speaking in platitudes, Machiavelli tells us how laudable it would be if princes could keep all their promises and carry out their commitments. But the implication here is that in doing so, a prince would lose everything because keeping one's word proves dangerous in an ever-changing world. Instead a prince must employ a kind of harsh realism. As Machiavelli alerts his readers, people have the capabilities to both act and think their way out of problems. One method employs the internal beast—calling upon human strength and warlike qualities. The second method, which is most natural to humans, employs cunning and deception. We are capable of both, so we must employ both to ensure our survival; and as Machiavelli points out, one without the other is not sufficient. The prince's virtue will help determine which nature is most appropriate in certain circumstances. In choosing the animals to model ourselves after, the lion and the fox prove most beneficial: ". . . the lion does not defend itself from snares and the fox does not defend itself from wolves. So one needs to be a fox to recognize snares and a lion to frighten the wolves" (*The Prince,* Chapter 18). *Virtu* and *astuzia* aid in this process.

In the end, cleverness and force prove necessary to maintain one's power; but how does this occur without offending citizens? The answer lies in the art of political appearance. Machiavelli writes,

> A prudent lord, therefore, cannot observe faith, nor should he, when such observance turns against him, and the causes that made him promise have been eliminated. And if all men were good, this teaching would not be good; but because they are wicked and do not observe faith with you, you also do not have to observe it with them. Nor does a prince ever lack legitimate causes to color his failure to observe faith. One could give infinite modern examples of this, and show how many peace treaties and promises have been rendered invalid and vain through the infidelity of princes; and the one who has known best how to use the fox has come out best. But it is necessary to know well how to color this nature, and to be a great pretender and dissembler; and men are so simple and so obedient to present necessities that he who deceives will always find someone who will let himself be deceived. (*The Prince,* Chapter 18)

Because men are vicious and corrupt, a prince should not feel compelled to keep promises when situations change. In fact, it is often to his benefit to break a promise in order to maximize his success. As Machiavelli notes, such changes bring no harm to a prince when he is able to be a "pretender and dissembler," masking his actions with false words and acts that give the impression of faithfulness. No one did this better than Machiavelli's contemporary, Pope Alexander VI, who did nothing but trick people by making promises that he always intended to break. His duplicity worked to his advantage, however, because of his appearance of sincerity.

Why does this work? Because people are easily fooled by appearances. Machiavelli does not hesitate to suggest that most people can be readily duped by the clever use of false appearances. In fact, Machiavelli implies that following this course of appearances will lead to successful political endeavors, especially if one is adept in appearing virtuous. For example, Machiavelli claims that Cesare Borgia's father, Alexander VI, "...never did anything, nor ever thought of anything, but how to deceive men, and he always found a subject to whom he could do it. And there never was a man with greater efficacy in asserting a thing, and in affirming it with greater oaths, who observed it less; nonetheless, his deceits succeeded at his will, because he well knew this aspect of the world" (*The Prince,* Chapter 18). The "aspect of the world" that Alexander VI understood was that most people judge things by how they appear, and thus a ruler must appear to be what his subjects want. Because Machiavelli lived in Christian Europe, he understood that Christian mores would be the expected norm of most people; thus his prince needed to co-opt the appearance of such moral habits:

> Thus, it is not necessary for a prince to have all the above-mentioned qualities in fact, but it is indeed necessary to appear to have them. Nay, I dare say this, that by having them and always observing them, they are harmful; and by appearing to have them, they are useful, as it is to appear merciful, faithful, humane, honest, and religious, and to be so; but to remain with a spirit built so that, if you need not to be those things, you are able and know how to change to the contrary. This has to be understood: that a prince, and especially a new prince, cannot observe all those things for which men are held good since he is often under a necessity, to maintain his state, of acting against faith, against charity, against humanity, against religion. And so he needs to have a spirit disposed to change as the winds of fortune and variations of things command him, and as I said above, not depart from good, when possible, but know how to enter into evil, when forced by necessity.
>
> A prince should thus take great care that nothing escape his mouth that is not full of the above-mentioned five qualities and that, to see him and hear him, he should appear all mercy, all faith, all honesty, all humanity, all religion. And nothing is more necessary to appear to have than this last quality. Men in general judge more by their eyes than by their hands, because seeing is given to everyone, touching to a few. Everyone sees how you appear, few touch what you are; and these few dare not oppose the opinion of many, who have the majesty of the state to defend them; and in the actions of all men, and especially of princes, where there is no court to appeal to, one looks to the end. So let a prince win and maintain his state: the means will always be judged honorable, and will be praised by everyone. For the vulgar are taken in by the appearance and the outcome of a thing, and in the world there is no one but the vulgar. (*The Prince,* Chapter 18)

As Machiavelli points out, the implementation of traditional virtues by a prince would lead to his ruin, for habits of goodness and virtue are often counterindicated in politics. Instead, unfaithfulness, deception, and cruelty are commonly required to maintain the state. All a prince needs to do is to appear to possess such virtues, easily fooling his subjects into believing him a good and generous ruler. Machiavelli does note that a prince should try to follow virtue when applicable; but again, this is not virtue for virtue's sake, but virtue for necessity's sake. Machiavelli remains consistent in his belief that the necessity of circumstance dictates all actions and that a prince should be willing and able to do whatever is necessary to keep order and security. In the end, Machiavelli reassures his readers that his teaching on appearance will be carried out easily: Most men see only appearances, and the few who are perceptive enough to see through the ruse will dare say nothing against the champion of the many.

THE PROBLEMS OF CRUELTY AND HATRED

One of the most shocking modes and orders introduced by Machiavelli is his call for the use of cruelty. In Chapter 8 of *The Prince,* Machiavelli tells the story of Agathocles the Sicilian, who came from severe poverty but through the most cruel actions rose through the military ranks and made himself praetor of Syracuse. Desiring to be prince, Agathocles devised a plan to seize power:

> Having given intelligence of his design to Hamilcar the Carthaginian, who was with his armies fighting in Sicily, one morning he assembled the people and Senate of Syracuse as if he had to decide things pertinent to the republic. At a signal he had ordered, he had all the senators and the richest of the people killed by his soldiers. Once they were dead, he seized and held the principate of that city without any civil controversy.... Thus, whoever might consider the actions and virtue of this man will see nothing or little that can be attributed to fortune. For as was said above, not through anyone's support but through the ranks of the military, which he had gained for himself with a thousand hardships and dangers, he came to the principate and afterwards he maintained it with many spirited and dangerous policies. (*The Prince,* Chapter 8)

Machiavelli does little to hide his admiration for Agathocles and his cruel acts. To him, Agathocles understood the nature of politics and its occasional need for cruel measures. Instead of avoiding such supposed bad acts, Agothacles embraced these tactics, using them to stabilize himself at each stage of his rise to power. Machiavelli not only respected his willingness to carry out such cruelty but also his implementation of cruelty, writing that he knew how to use it "well."

What did Machiavelli mean by ***well-used cruelty***? In the case of **Agathocles,** Machiavelli tells us that Agathocles knew that the implementation of cruelty could easily turn into popular hatred toward the prince, and thus he always acted "speedily" in his delivery of cruelty. Machiavelli explains:

> Some could question how it happened that Agathocles and anyone like him, after infinite betrayals and cruelties, could live for a long time secure in his fatherland, defend himself against external enemies, and never be conspired against by his citizens, inasmuch as many others have not been able to maintain their states through cruelty even in peaceful times, not to mention uncertain times of war. I believe that this comes from cruelties badly used or well used. Those can be called well used (if it is permissible to speak well of evil) that are done at a stroke, out of the necessity to secure oneself, and then are not persisted in but are turned to as much utility for the subjects as one can. Those cruelties are badly used which, though few in the beginning, rather grow with time than are eliminated. Those who observe the first mode can have some remedy for their state with God and with men, as had Agathocles; as for the others it is impossible for them to maintain themselves. (*The Prince*, Chapter 8)

As Machiavelli understood, the reality of certain situations requires harsh deeds that will cause much damage to property and human life but will nonetheless bring order to a region. So long as the cruel acts are directed toward stability and are carried out in an expeditious manner, they will be forgiven by the people. It is only when the cruelty is protracted and perceived as pointless that it becomes dangerous to the prince. As Machiavelli notes, the longer the cruel acts continue, the greater the diminishment on one's return in terms of both the stability of the state and popular sentiments toward the prince.

Interestingly, although Agathocles understood how to use cruelty well, Machiavelli notes that he never attained glory, for "... his savage cruelty and inhumanity, together with his infinite crimes, do not allow him to be celebrated among the most excellent men" (*The Prince,* Chapter 8). While Agathocles delivered order, stabilized his state, and did all the things necessary for a new founder to do, he did not prove worthy of Machiavelli's honored title of "new founder." The reason for this can be found in the way in which Agathocles carried out his endeavors. Unlike Cesare Borgia, Agathocles did all the dirty work himself. There was no doubt among the people who was behind every harsh directive and at whose hands such directives were being carried out. Cesare, on the other hand, understood how the game of appearances needed to be played, getting others to carry out the necessary cruelties. For Machiavelli, Cesare's elevated understanding about the political repercussions of cruelty, even cruelty well used, makes him a more admirable figure and one closer to his prototype of a new founder.

THE PROBLEMS OF GLORY, COURTIERS, AND FLATTERERS

The figure of Agathocles brings to our attention the problematic relationship between cruelty and glory. Machiavelli reminds his readers of the need to carry out harsh and violent acts to stabilize one's state. This proves especially true for a new founder who faces innumerable challenges throughout his endeavor to power. So long as the cruelty is directed toward bringing about order, and is not cruelty without purpose, the people will not hate their ruler. However, as we saw with Agathocles, the ability to attain security for one's state is quite different than the ability to attain glory for one's self. This is an art unto itself and one that Cesare seemed to understand because unlike Agathocles, he was more a fox than a lion. Glory requires grand and mystifying acts that are dazzling and awe-inspiring. Ferdinand of Spain captured Machiavelli's attention because of his understanding of this delicate art:

> Nothing makes a prince so much esteemed as to carry on great enterprises and to give rare examples of himself. In our times we have Ferdinand of Aragon, the present king of Spain. This man can be called an almost new prince because from being a weak king he has become by fame and by glory the first king among the Christians; and, if you consider his actions, you will find them all very great and some of them extraordinary. (*The Prince,* Chapter 21)

As Machiavelli notes, Ferdinand would go on to transform his rule into a most powerful state, whereby his constant engagement in extraordinary actions left the people bedazzled, providing little time to ponder the nature and ramifications of his actions. In part, Ferdinand's brilliance was due to his ability to seek out or conjure up adversity in order to respond with the most splendid of deeds. The mark of a new founder is often shown by precisely this phenomenon: Arduous circumstances, either real or artificial, provide the opportunity to showcase the extraordinary talents of a leader. Glory results, and the prince's reputation soars.

For Machiavelli, the most extraordinary men seem naturally capable of discerning the nuances of glory. While these men seem to need little assistance in their pursuit of grandeur, some may reach this same end with the help of aides or advisers. Much like our own world, Machiavelli's complex political arena required the presence of

QUESTIONS FOR REFLECTION

Machiavelli clearly understood the difficult nature of attaining glory through one's political actions; he writes that a leader must demonstrate an unmatched agility of mind and body in understanding human nature, an ability to assess situations accurately, and a willingness to act in the necessary manner to attain and maintain power—and do so all in a way that allows such activities to gain earthly glory. To this end, a leader and especially a new founder can employ advisers to assist in this effort. How then must Machiavelli be viewed in relationship to the role of an adviser? Is he not assuming such a role with Lorenzo de' Medici? To what end does he advise? To what end does Lorenzo listen? What conclusions can be drawn about Machiavelli's worth as an adviser? Is there another audience for whom Machiavelli advises?

such people, and thus Machiavelli thought it critical to discuss the nature and role of the people who advise princes. Like all things in politics, the presence of such advisers can be both dangerous and beneficial. On one hand, an adviser may bring experience and problem-solving skills to the job. On the other, he may be nothing more than a flatterer, seeking his own grandeur at the cost of the prince's. For this reason, Machiavelli warns, "The choice of ministers is of no small importance to a prince; they are good or not according to the prudence of the prince. And the first conjecture that is to be made of the brain of the lord is to see the men he has around him; and when they are capable and faithful, he can always be reputed wise . . . " (*The Prince,* Chapter 22). Thus the mind of a prince may be judged by the wisdom of his advisers; but is this not in some way dangerous? What if the adviser posseses a keener mind and better judgment than the prince? Could he not imagine himself in the place of the prince? To such questions, Machiavelli offers the following advice: Seek out a wise but selfless minister whose purpose should be only the advancement of the prince's well-being. Second, the prince should avoid flatterers and seek candid and forthright advisers, but only within the context of the prince seeking their advice. As Machiavelli warns, an adviser who feels free to tell the prince his thoughts at any time, without the prince's beckoning, is of no value. Such a man sees his own worth as equal or superior to that of the prince and thus is dangerous.

THE CHALLENGES OF RELIGION

Machiavelli's view of religion remains one of the most contentious and debated subjects within his works. For centuries, scholars have come to no resolution regarding his view of Christianity. While not contesting the critical nature of his views, many are divided over whether his views are anticlerical or impious. For scholars like Sebastian de Grazia and Dante Germino, Machiavelli's works are indeed scathing in their representation of the church and its activities within the political realm; but they do not see Machiavelli as an unbeliever. Instead they see him as a privately pious man who viewed the development of the 16th-century Roman Church as corrosive and damaging to the stability of all Italy. Here the fault lies not with the faith but with its earthly implementation through the pursuits of corrupt clerics. Machiavelli makes this point most clearly in Book I, Chapter 12, of *The Discourses:*

> [T]he evil example of the Court of Rome has destroyed all piety and religion in Italy, which brings in its train infinite improprieties and disorders; for as we may presuppose

> all good where religion prevails, so where it is wanting we have the right to suppose the very opposite. We Italians then owe to the Church of Rome and to her priests our having become irreligious and bad.

While Machiavelli speaks here to the corruptive influence of priests' poor behavior upon Christians throughout the world, their political actions seem to follow suit. In another revealing passage from the same chapter, Machiavelli writes,

> Thus, since the church has not been powerful enough to be able to seize Italy, nor permitted another to seize it, it has been the cause that [Italy] has not been able to come under one head but has been under many princes and lords, from whom so much weakness has arisen that it has been led to be the prey not only of barbarian powers but of whoever assaults it. For this we other Italians have an obligation to the church and not to others. (*The Discourses*, Book I, Chapter 12)

For Machiavelli, it appears that these clerics are not only morally bankrupt, and thus a bad influence on others whom they should inspire, but also politically inept and thus the cause of Italy's present state of disorder. The church's unwillingness to hold a standing army of its own has rendered it incapable of maintaining its power effectively. Instead it has opted to use mercenaries and auxiliaries, both of whom prove incapable of rendering any real security. In the end, these clerics function in the worlds of heaven and earth, muddling through with poor moral behavior and political ineptitude in both. Machiavelli seems to imply that the church needs to choose one realm or the other, but not both, because the requirements of a heavenly kingdom are far different than that of an earthly kingdom.

The charge of anticlericism finds other support within Machiavelli's writings. Though not nearly as scathing as his descriptions of the church and its prelates in *The Prince* and *The Discourses,* Machiavelli's comedy *The Mandragola* offers a comical depiction of a cleric, Frate Timoteo, whose scandalous behavior is not only memorable but consistent with everything Machiavelli suggests in his political works. In this comedy, Frate Timoteo is involved with a bed-switching plot that helps a brilliant but amoral nobleman bed down the woman of his desires. Unfortunately this woman, Lucrezia, is both just and married. To gain her participation in this bed-switching plot, of which her foolish husband is a part, the young nobleman Callimaco must enlist the help of the good priest Timoteo. Machiavelli's anticlericism becomes apparent as those complicit in the plot immediately think to enlist his help without any doubt of his willingness to participate. Tempted by money, Timoteo will agree to just about anything, as the conspirators test his willingness with another proposition:

TIMOTEO: What do you want from me?

LIGURIO: Messer Nicia here and another good man, whom you'll hear about later, are going to have several hundred ducats distributed in alms.

NICIA: Bloody shit!

LIGURIO: (Be quiet, damn you, it won't be much.) Don't marvel at anything he says, Padre, because he doesn't hear, and sometimes it seems to him that he hears, but he doesn't respond to the purpose.

TIMOTEO: Continue then, and let him say whatever he wants.

LIGURIO: I have part of that money with me, and they have designated that you be the one to distribute it.

TIMOTEO: Very willingly . . .

LIGURIO: A year ago, this man went to France on some business of his, and, not having a wife—for she had died—he left his one marriageable daughter in the care of a convent, the name of which I don't have to tell you now.

TIMOTEO: What followed?

LIGURIO: It followed that, either through the carelessness of the nuns, or the brainlessness of the girl, she finds herself four months pregnant; so that if the situation's not repaired with prudence, the Dottore, the nuns, the girl, Cammillo, and the house of Calfucci will be disgraced; and the Dottore regards this shame as so great that he has vowed, if it's not disclosed, to give three hundred ducats for the love of God. . . . And he will give them through your hands; and only you and the abbess can remedy this.

TIMOTEO: How?

LIGURIO: By persuading the abbess to give the girl a potion to make her miscarry.

TIMOTEO: This is something to be thought about.

LIGURIO: Keep in mind, in doing this, how many goods will result from it; you maintain the honor of the convent, of the girl, of her relatives; you restore a daughter to her father; you satisfy Messer here, and so many of his relatives; you do as much charity as you can with these three hundred ducats; and on the other side, you don't offend anything but a piece of unborn flesh, without sense, which could be dispersed in a thousand ways; and I believe that good is that which does good to the most, and that by which the most are contented.

TIMOTEO: So be it in the name of God. I'll do what you want, and may everything be done for God and for charity. Tell me the convent, give me the potion, and if you like, this money, with which I can begin to do some good. (*The Mandragola,* Act 3, Scene 4)

In this comic exchange, the audience witnesses a priest who is willing to administer a potion designed to cause a miscarriage for a young, noble, unwed mother. While the priest's complicity may seem outrageous to a modern audience, one must remember that *The Mandragola* is a comedy, designed to amuse the audience with familiar subjects. Machiavelli is counting on his audience's familiarity with the well-known corruption of both clerics and nuns. Moreover, he is counting on the popular assumption regarding the clergy and their love of material goods to rouse laughter and amusement with the audience. The irony of all of this, of course, is not only that Fr. Timoteo agrees to assist in an abortion for money, but that he does so in the name of God. For Timoteo, God's name is invoked when the greatest number engage in the greatest shared pleasures. Even though he says the greatest good will be brought to many by carrying out this act, it is clear that his "good" is nothing more than material pleasure.

For many, Machiavelli's irreligious reputation is largely the product of his anticlericism. However, does such anticlericism indicate the author's impiety? Is he just a man who is fed up with the way in which Christianity is implemented on earth, with all of its corruption and military ineptitude? Not surprisingly, theorists are again in disagreement. Some, like Sebastian de Grazia, believe that there are two levels to Machiavelli's criticisms of the church: first (and already noted), the vicious and corrupt habits of church prelates, and second, the way in which the actual doctrines of the faith have been interpreted by princes. We need only look at Book II, Chapter 2 of *The Discourses* to witness this view:

> Thinking then whence it can arise that in those ancient times peoples were more lovers of freedom than in these, I believe it arises from the same cause that makes men less strong now, which I believe is the difference between our education and the ancient, founded on the difference between our religion and the ancients. For our religion,

> having shown the truth and the true way, makes us esteem less the honor of the world, whereas the Gentiles, esteeming it very much and having placed the highest good in it, were more ferocious in their actions.... Our religion has glorified humble and contemplative more than active men. It has then placed the highest good in humility, abjectness, and contempt of things human; the other placed it in greatness of spirit, strength of body, and all other things capable of making men very strong.

For de Grazia and others, Machiavelli's problem with the church is not just its materialism and greed, but the way in which the church has interpreted Christ's doctrinal teachings. Somehow the church has come to view the Christian message as one that places greater emphasis on our salvation in the next world and not our accomplishments in this world. This shift in focus from the ancients has left this world neglected, as princes pay less focus to their actions here and more on what passive measures might deliver them to the next. Interestingly, de Grazia does not view this as Machiavelli's rejection of the Christian message. Instead he believes that Machiavelli wishes to right the present interpretation of Christ's words. Within Machiavelli's teaching we witness many calls for courageous actions within this world. All that needs to be done is to turn our attention to great events, like Christ's crucifixion, and reinterpret them with the same ferocity and gruesomeness of ancient ceremonies. It is with such religious spectacle that people's focus can be redirected to this world and energized to do spectacular things here on earth.

Not all theorists, however, share de Grazia's view that Machiavelli wishes to merely reinterpret Christianity, not do away with it. Some, like Vickie Sullivan, believe that the facility of such a reinterpretation is impossible without a full rejection of the doctrine itself. For example, Sullivan cannot imagine how Christ's Sermon on the Mount speech, with its plea for man to endure earthly sufferings with the promise of true life in heaven, can ever be reinterpreted to mean anything other than the superiority of heaven over earth. The meek, not the strong, are rewarded with the final blessing; and those who are too focused on this world and not the next are the ultimate losers. For Sullivan, Christ's teachings could not be more clear, leaving little room for creative reinterpretation to suit one's political needs.[11]

The question of Machiavelli's piety remains one of the more troubling aspects in understanding the Florentine's teachings. While most of his contemporaries would have had little trouble with his anticlericism, there would be many concerned with a charge of impiety. If his teachings were written by the hand of an unbeliever, then his message proves more troubling because we cannot presume that it functions within the realm of the Judaic–Christian tradition. If the Old and New Testaments offer no moral boundaries for his teachings, and neither do the Greek and Roman ethical traditions, then by what moral constraint does Machiavelli prescribe?

In answering this difficult question, some look to Machiavelli's little-known piece, *The Exhortation to Penitence,* for possible answers. Here, in this overtly Christian piece, Machiavelli writes a sermon to be delivered before the Company of Charity, a Florentine lay confraternity. Little is known about this piece, but Roberto Ridolfi believes that Machiavelli wrote and delivered this small work as an invited speaker,

---

[11]Vickie B. Sullivan, "Neither Christian nor Pagan: Machiavelli's Treatment of Religion in The *Discourses,*" *Polity* 26 (1993):264.

before the membership of the Company, sometime late in his life.[12] The Company of Charity was a *disciplinati* organization, so its members would engage in acts of self-flagellation or whipping to share in Christ's suffering and humiliation. To accomplish this, they would have to first be brought to a point of emotional upheaval—often the result of an energized speech about penitence. It is believed that Machiavelli served this function with his *The Exhortation to Penitence.*

On its surface, *The Exhortation* meets all the traditional criteria of a work revolving around the sinful and penitential nature of man. For example, Machiavelli invokes the image of David, a true penitent whose contrite heart begs God for forgiveness for his adulterous and murderous acts. He reassures his audience that God not only forgave both David and Peter for their acts of murder and denial, respectively, but rewarded them for their expressions of true penitence, as he asks, "What sin will God not forgive you, my brothers, if you sincerely resort to penitence, since he forgave these to them?" (*The Exhortation to Penitence*). For Machiavelli, man is forever cursed with ingratitude toward God and a lack of charity toward his fellow human beings. What we need to become are beings that show gratitude to God for his immeasurable gifts and friendliness toward neighbors with whom we share God's bounty. As many scholars have noted, these two calls for improvement are likely to remind audiences of God's two great commandments: to love thy God and thy neighbor. This, along with traditional themes of man's depravity, tendencies toward sin, and repentant nature, all conform to traditional 16th-century penitential sermons.

For many scholars, this work demonstrates the depth of Machiavelli's piety, viewing it as a "manifestation of an overtly Christian commitment by Machiavelli."[13] However, not all see it as an expression of a true believer; some see an overall irreverent and impious attitude toward the whole penitential process.[14] For example, while David and Peter are indeed forgiven for their sins, they were truly contrite and determined to commit themselves to a faithful life. But Machiavelli's recap of events seems too positive and simplistic, giving the impression that no matter what is done by man, God will forgive. Machiavelli suggests that this is the only way for man to move beyond his sins; but in fact there is another way that Machiavelli does not mention—following the way of Christ. In reality, penitence is only one route to salvation; the other is the more difficult dedication to the habits and teachings of Jesus Christ. As with most of Machiavelli's silences, we can assume that he knows about this other option but deems it inconvenient. Moreover, some have even argued that his modification of the two great commandments is really a reduction of God's moral demands upon mankind. Being grateful to God and friendly to neighbors is much easier than loving either one. We need only to have read a few chapters of *The Prince* to realize that this commandment is in direct odds with much of what Machiavelli deems necessary to attain and maintain power.

Whether we think that *The Exhortation to Penitence* proves or disproves Machiavelli's piety, there is little doubt that this overtly religious piece adds further

---

[12]Ridolfi, p. 253.

[13]Dante Germino, "Second Thoughts on Leo Strauss's Machiavelli," *Journal of Politics* 28 (1966): 800.

[14]Andrea Ciliotta-Rubery, *Piety and Humanity: Essays on Religion and Early Modern Political Philosophy* (Lanham, MD: Rowman & Littlefield Publishers), 1997, pp. 11–44.

controversy to the piety debate. In the end, all we can do to understand this controversy is to return to his works and see whether there is a consistent position on religion. In doing this, we see routine anticlericism, political teachings that are contrary to the message of Christ, a genuine desire for the church of Rome to either fully engage or disengage from politics, and an overall desire to reinvigorate Christian ceremony to mirror the ancients. To these observations, we must add Machiavelli's consistent willingness to judge the presence of Christianity from the perspective of its political usefulness. We cannot help but notice that Machiavelli prescribes actions for a prince that would be disastrous if carried out by all citizens. His often amoral teachings are intended for princes alone, and not the general public, whose actions must remain within the traditional boundaries of Christian morality. To ease the job of the prince, his people must fear God, abide by just rules of behavior, and fear punishment in the afterlife for earthly wrongdoings. This cannot be achieved without a steadfast adherence to traditional 16th-century Christian morality. Machiavelli thus recognizes its usefulness and prescribes that the people conform to it while princes ignore it. Compliance to such traditional morality would render a prince ineffective in his pursuit of power and endanger his attempts to maintain the state.

The one caveat, however, is the need for princes to appear religious. Because the people believe in God, he must appear to do the same. No God-fearing people would follow a nonbeliever, and thus Machiavelli goes to great lengths in reinforcing the need for princes to appear religious. The passage quoted earlier bears repeating in this context:

> A prince should thus take great care that nothing escape his mouth that is not full of the above-mentioned five qualities and that, to see him and hear him, he should appear all mercy, all faith, all honesty, all humanity, all religion. And nothing is more necessary to appear to have than this last quality. Men in general judge more by their eyes than by their hands, because seeing is given to everyone, touching to few. Everyone sees how you appear, few touch what you are; and these few dare not oppose the opinion of many, who have the majesty of the state to defend them; and in the actions of all men, and especially of princes, where there is no court to appeal to, one looks to the end. So let a prince win and maintain his state: the means will always be judged honorable, and will be praised by everyone. For the vulgar are taken in by the appearance and the outcome of a thing, and in the world there is no one but the vulgar. (*The Prince,* Chapter 18)

Machiavelli's message could not be more straightforward: Princes must do whatever is necessary to maintain their power, but since their people are faithful, they too must appear faithful to Christian morality to guarantee the people's support. Nonetheless, princes should not worry about this duplicity because most people are easily deceived, and the few who see the falsehood of the prince will not dare challenge the many who support and believe in him. The prince has numbers on his side, as well as the recognition that most people judge the world by appearances and nothing more. As Machiavelli notes, "... the vulgar are taken in by the appearance and the outcome of a thing, and in the world there is no one but the vulgar...." So long as the outcome or end is in their favor, most people will care little about the means used by a prince or the duplicitous nature employed to carry out his endeavors. The prescription here is to placate the people by appearing to be the faithful prince they want, all the while employing the necessary acts to gain and maintain one's power.

Machiavelli backs up this prescription with two contemporary examples of **princes who used religion effectively** to either manipulate or placate the people. First, and not surprisingly, is **Pope Alexander VI,** who Machiavelli claims "... never did anything, nor ever thought of anything, but how to deceive men... (*The Prince,* Chapter 18). Machiavelli clearly respects Alexander VI for his ability to use his religious position to appease people while pursuing his own power-driven agenda: "... there never was a man with greater efficacy in asserting a thing, and in affirming it with greater oaths, who observed it less; nonetheless, his deceits succeeded at his will, because he well knew this aspect of the world" (*The Prince,* Chapter 18). What did he know? He realized that human beings are easily deceived and are likely to take a powerful man (especially a pope) at his word. Alexander VI exploited this, all the while proceeding with whatever was necessary to keep power.

A second example can be seen in **King Ferdinand of Spain,** who used religion as both a battle cry and an excuse for some of the most politically motivated cruelty. Machiavelli praises Ferdinand for his keen understanding of popular sentiments toward religion, as well as his willingness to exploit them for political purposes:

> Nothing makes a prince so much esteemed as to carry out great enterprises and to give rare examples of himself. In our times we have Ferdinand of Aragon, the present king of Spain. This man can be called an almost new prince because from being a weak king he has become by fame and by glory the first king among the Christians; and, if you consider his actions, you will find them all very great and some of them extraordinary. In the beginning of his reign he attacked Granada, and that enterprise was the foundation of his state.... He was able to sustain armies with money from the Church and the people, and with that long war to lay a foundation for his own military, which later brought him honor. Besides this, in order to undertake greater enterprises, always making use of religion, he turned to an act of pious cruelty, expelling the Marranos from his kingdom and despoiling them; nor could there be an example more wretched and rarer than this. He attacked Africa under this same cloak, made his campaign in Italy, and has lately attacked France; and so he has always done and ordered great things, which have always kept the minds of his subjects in suspense and admiration, and occupied with their outcome. And his actions have followed upon one another in such a mode that he has never allowed an interval between them for men to be able to work quietly against him. (*The Prince,* Chapter 21)

In the person of King Ferdinand, Machiavelli observes some of the most astute political actions, worthy of imitation. Ferdinand made himself the "... first king among the Christians,..." cloaking himself in the garb of the faith, to sanctify his political ambitions. Believing that Ferdinand was carrying out God's work, the people soon followed with awe and devotion. Their allegiance to Ferdinand was enhanced by his continual procurement of "great enterprises." For Machiavelli, such great enterprises were those unthinkable acts of "pious cruelty," such as expelling the Moors from Spain, seizing their property, and then doing similar things in Italy and France. Even though Machiavelli uses such phrases as "pious cruelty" and "wretched" to describe Ferdinand's actions, he does so with underlying approval. The nature, scope, and frequency of these "rare" acts make Ferdinand most extraordinary among men; as Machiavelli concludes, "he always kept the minds of his subjects in suspense and admiration...." Such accomplishments would not have been possible without Ferdinand's co-option of Christianity, using it as an excuse to carry out the most

QUESTIONS FOR REFLECTION

1. How has religion been used in the 20th and 21st centuries to advance political causes?
2. How have recent actions by Al Qaeda mirrored the actions of Ferdinand?
3. From a political perspective, how would Machiavelli view their acts?
4. How does the Western and/or Middle Eastern perspective influence our evaluation of events and their use of religion as a motivating cause?

brutal acts. Both Ferdinand and Machiavelli realized that men would not only allow but take part in great atrocities in the name of God. In reality, religion was used as nothing more than a tool to foster Ferdinand's love of power. He amassed great territory, great wealth, and many fearful subjects, all under the assumed guise of God's will and not his own.

Machiavelli's approval of Ferdinand is based largely on the king's recognition of the combined power of religion and politics. Moreover, he had the internal strength or *virtu* to carry out these acts. Others may think of them, but few have the wherewithal to do such horrific deeds. Ferdinand did them with speed and frequency. Most cleverly, he did them in a way that prevented the people from catching on to his real motives of expanding and solidifying his earthly power base. In the end, the real Ferdinand remained hidden by the public demigod.

THE ROLE OF FORTUNE

Machiavelli's willingness to use religion as a political tool presents a strong challenge to the view that Machiavelli is pious. In part, his willingness to do this, along with most other unconventional things, reflects his belief in the superiority of this world. Nowhere is this more vivid than in Machiavelli's discussion of fortune. Throughout his writings, Machiavelli seems preoccupied with man's ability to shape his environment in accordance to his vision. Unfortunately, as many in the medieval and Renaissance world believed, certain events occurred beyond human control, happening without people's approval and resulting in unforeseen consequences. Such phenomena were seen as the result of *fortuna,* a force within the world that controls accidental events.[15] According to Anthony J. Parel, Machiavelli sees the world as a complex cosmos, where predictable and patterned events are the result of God's ordering while unpredictable daily events are shaped by *fortuna*. Describing Fortuna as a woman, Machiavelli likens her to something or someone who needs to be controlled through forceful and audacious acts. Make no mistake: He sees her as a formidable rival who, when presenting herself, offers a great opportunity for the truly extraordinary man to demonstrate his *virtu* through her mastery. She can be won, but only by the most innovative and creative means. Machiavelli looks upon such circumstances with favor because they offer a unique opportunity to shape one's world in accordance to one's liking as well as demonstrate one's true acumen.

[15]Anthony J. Parel, *The Machiavellian Cosmos* (New Haven: Yale University Press, 1992), p. 63.

Unfortunately, contemporary Italian princes were not of this mindset; more often than not they seemed inclined to run away from such difficulties rather than stay and face the challenges. The result was quite bad, with control of the state being lost and sorrowful princes in exile. Blaming *fortuna* for their adverse circumstances instead of themselves, these Italian princes remained inactive, hoping that the fickle goddess would again change her course and alter circumstances for the better. We can imagine Machiavelli clenching his fists as he observed such a weak course of action. He concedes that this might be an acceptable course if all other plans fail but generally speaking, such inaction should be avoided at all costs. For Machiavelli, Fortune is a formidable opponent—but not so formidable that man must cower in her presence. Instead he must rise to meet her challenges; and when he does so, she rewards his strength with favorable circumstances.

To prove this point, Machiavelli describes Fortune as a river whose destructive power is most pronounced upon lands with no provisions:

> And I liken her to one of these violent rivers which, when they become enraged, flood the plains, ruin the trees and the buildings, lift earth from this part, drop it in another; each person flees before them, everyone yields to their impetus without being able to hinder them in any regard. And although they are like this, it is not as if men, when times are quiet, could not provide for them with dikes and dams so that when they rise later, either they do by a can or their impetus is neither so wanton nor so damaging. It happens similarly with fortune, which shows her power where virtue has not been put in order to resist her and therefore turns her impetus where she knows that dams and dikes have not been made to contain her. And if you consider Italy, which is the seat of these variations and that which has given them motion, you will see a country without dams and without any dike. If it had been diked by suitable virtue, like Germany, Spain, and France, either this flood would not have caused the great variations that it has, or it would not have come here. (*The Prince,* Chapter 25)

The lack of preparation by Italian princes has left Italy in ruin, allowing fortune to command circumstances without any opposition. Machiavelli's emotional battle cry is meant to awaken these princes to the opportunities before them, challenging them to stand their ground, to think and prepare for the most adverse political situations and take action. Adversity is not to be avoided but seized, turning it around to reflect one's will. Ironically, scholars have debated the degree to which Machiavelli truly believes we can fully control fortune. While he admits that "... fortune is the arbiter of half of our actions, ..." and we, the other, he suggests that with the best of preparations, adverse fortune "... need not have come here" (*The Prince,* Chapter 25). Given that his name appeared on a list of would-be Medici conspirators without his knowledge, we can only wonder!

WOMEN

Machiavelli's likeness of fortune to a woman invites discussion of the role of women within his works. Generally speaking, Machiavelli makes little mention of women in his political writings, with a bit more notice in his comedies and literary works. This lack of attention is somewhat to be expected, given that the medieval and Renaissance world of politics was largely controlled by men. However, when he does mention women, the picture presented is often unflattering. In the most comprehensive work done on the topic of gender within Machiavelli's writings, Hanna Pitkin's *Fortune Is a Woman* offers a provocative look at Machiavelli's male-centered world, where masculine autonomy drives contemporary events. According to Pitkin, with the passing of the medieval period with its reliance on social orderings and relationships, the Renaissance man found himself very much an independent actor whose ability to shape his life depended largely on his cleverness and energy. In many ways, it was a new and open world by which the most enterprising of men could carve out their own sphere of influence. To this purpose, Machiavelli's concern rested largely with those men who were effective in these efforts. The world was dominated by such men as they became and took on the male-centered "parentage" of new states. This domination by a male ethos left little room for women. As Pitkin argues, even some of the most traditional functions of women, such as birth mothers, were co-opted by a male view of the world that saw the birthing of nations as a male function.[16]

But women do occasionally appear in Machiavelli's works with a mixed presentation. For example, the matron Lucrezia in *The Mandragola* appears first as a beautiful, dutiful, and virtuous wife. Bothered by lecherous priests and a foolish husband, she is depicted as one of the most grounded figures in the play. However, her beauty distracts young men, causing the shrewd Callimaco to leave France and set upon a whirlwind of duplicitous events in order to sexually conquer this good woman. Ironically, she is the only character whose virtue is never questioned in the play; and yet in a short time and with little prodding, her goodness is corrupted. She becomes a willing participant in the bed-switching plot, in part because she recognizes that the world around her is forever scheming and she will not be subject to its effects without some say in the matter. She proclaims, "Since your astuteness, my husband's stupidity, my mother's simplicity, and my confessor's wickedness have led me to do what I never would have done by myself, I'm determined to judge that it comes from a heavenly disposition which has so willed; and I don't have it in me to reject what Heaven wills me to accept" (*The Mandragola*, Act 5, Scene 4).

With one female character as an unknowing temptress whose virtue is easily compromised, another woman is presented, Sostrata, whose age and cleverness make her a formidable player in a male-dominated world. Throughout the play, audiences witness Sostrata's complicity in the entire scheme to bed her daughter down with the young Callimaco. While modern audiences might think that this mother should protect her daughter against such schemes, Sostrata is complicit at every stage of the planning, with her male counterparts confident of her participation. For example, when the husband Nicia fears that his wife will have nothing to do with this scheme, Ligurio, the assistant in the plot, suggests that her confessor be brought in to help convince her to carry out this scheme. Both Callimaco and her husband Nicia are not convinced that she will do it; yet Ligurio reassures them that with the aid of her mother, she will be brought to the priest and all will be well, as he states, "And I know that her mother is of our opinion. Come on, we're letting time go by, it's getting on towards evening. Callimaco, get going, and make sure that at eight o'clock we find you at the house with the potion in order. We'll go to her mother's house, the Dottore and I, to prepare her, because I'm acquainted with her. Then we'll go to the Frate, and we'll

[16]Pitkin, pp. 241–243.

report to you what we have done" (*The Mandragola,* Act 2, Scene 6). The implication here is that Ligurio knows the mother's nature and that she will be willing to aid in the whole process of having her daughter sleep with the clever Callimaco. Clearly her nature is as duplicitous as the others.

What is to be made of these two women, especially in light of what Machiavelli says regarding Fortuna? Pitkin suggests that Machiavelli views women in either one of two ways: first as a young and beautiful temptress who cause young men to be both distracted and foolish in pursuit of her beauty. For this reason women must be conquered and controlled, like Fortuna. Otherwise they will preoccupy these young men to the point of ruin. On the other hand, Machiavelli seems to present women as clever old matrons who are capable of carrying out the most duplicitous acts, comparable to men. Pitkin writes,

> Older women constitute an even greater political danger than seductive girls. For one thing, these women can be as ambitious as men, particularly for their families or for their marriageable daughters, thus in ways that privatize and tend to fragment the community. Their power to exploit the divisive effect of sexual concerns take on legendary proportions.... The older women in Machiavelli's fiction are very different from their daughters. They are not sexually attractive or seductive, but they often control access to the young women; either by blocking or facilitating the men's desires. The mother in *The Mandragola* is presented from the outset as worldly wise and knowledgeable, and corrupt.[17]

Pitkin believes that Machiavelli's dichotomous depiction of women holds true throughout his fictional writing. Even within such plays as *Clizia* and *Belfagor*, we again see young temptresses who have no real depth or purpose other than to be possessed by men, along with their corrupt matrons or mothers, who have "...a distinct personality and is indeed capable of action, but she is filled with fury, and more dangerous to her husband than the devil himself."[18] Machiavelli seems to find proof of this later depiction in the real-life person of Caterina Sforza, who after the murder of her husband, Count Girolamo, and the seizure of her castle by his enemies, realizes that she can never regain her security without having to retake the castle. In a clever manner, she proposes to her enemies that she be allowed to reenter her home and gather some personal things, as Machiavelli notes:

> "(she)...promised the conspirators that if they let her enter it, she would deliver it to them and they might keep her children with them as hostages. Under this faith they let her enter it. As soon as she was inside, she reproved them from the walls for the death of her husband and threatened them with every kind of revenge. And to show that she did not care for her children, she showed them her genital parts, saying that she still had the mode for making more of them. So, short of counsel and late to perceive their error, they suffered the penalty of their lack of prudence with perpetual exile. (*The Discourses,* Book III, Chapter 6)

Imagine the treachery of a mother who would abandon her children to her husband's murderers to get back her castle! One can almost hear Machiavelli's dual

---

[17]Pitkin, p. 119.

[18]Pitkin, p. 121.

reaction of approval and disdain: This type of emboldened act is what Italian princes need to do in order to secure their states, while at the same time this is the type of treacherous act that clever matrons are willing and able to do.

MACHIAVELLI'S CONTRIBUTION AS A POLITICAL PHILOSOPHER

Recognizing the significance of Machiavelli's teachings proves easier than establishing his place in political philosophy. No matter where he is located within the time line of political thought, his positioning engenders controversy. Generally speaking, there seem to be three views regarding Machiavelli's placement within the framework of political thought. First, and for many, Machiavelli is the beginning of modern political thought. Machiavelli is largely the cause of this view because he pronounces throughout both *The Prince* and *The Discourses* that he is "... depart[ing] from the orders of others" (*Prince*, Chapter 15) and "... tak[ing] a path yet untrodden by anyone" (*Discourses,* Preface, Book I). As he says in both works, he will abandon traditional approaches to statecraft and replace them with a radical, useful teaching "... to whoever understands it" (*The Prince,* Chapter 15). What is this extreme teaching, why is it so different from anything else, and who are the people who understand it? In varying degrees, Machiavelli uses *The Prince* and *The Discourses* as vehicles to impart realism into politics—a realism that awakens the audience to see that politics is about nothing more than power. It is about getting power and keeping power, however it is defined. Theorists such as Leo Strauss and Harvey Mansfield, who see Machiavelli as a modern, contend that never before him had there been such a brash pronouncement and celebration of power and the acts that gain it. Mansfield sums up this position as he writes, "The renown of *The Prince* is precisely to have been the first and the best book to argue that politics has and should have its own rules and should not accept rules of any kind or from any source where the object is not to win or prevail over others."[19] Unbridled by Christian morality or the ethical considerations of the ancients, Machiavelli's teachings focus on manly actions that bring about earthly success. Such actions are viewed not within any moral context but rather within the sole political context of whether the end result was fortuitous to the actor involved. Success alone matters; thus Machiavelli's political teaching demands a mindset that is unencumbered by idealistic visions of a perfectly just state. There is no idealism of Plato, no discussion of perfect justice. All that exists is the reality of a circumstance by which a shrewd leader should determine what must be done to get or keep power—and then proceed with whatever actions are necessary to accomplish such goals. In the end, theorists like Mansfield and Strauss cannot help but place Machiavelli at the beginning of the modern world because his novel teachings "... contain a fundamental assault on all morality and political science, both Christian and classical, as understood in Machiavelli's time."[20]

Not all historians see Machiavelli as a diabolical thinker who has given us the realism and brutality of the modern world. Others, like the Italian historian and

---

[19]Harvey Mansfield, Introduction, *The Prince* (Chicago: University of Chicago Press, 1985), p. vii.

[20]Mansfield, p. x.

theorist Maurizio Viroli, see Machiavelli as a refiner of the ancient world and its teachings.[21] Unlike the first modern view discussed, this second view sees Machiavelli as a type of restorer of the ancient world's love of the political realm and its view of man as an active, patriotic citizen. We need only look at Machiavelli's *The Discourses* to see the Florentine's respect for Roman institutions, political practices, and rhetoric. This ancient civilization viewed man as a being capable of doing great things, thinking great things, and expressing himself in great ways. Machiavelli did not turn his back on such presumptions but instead embraced them and modified them to improve upon the circumstances of his own world. For Machiavelli, the ancients had much to teach, and the modern world has much to learn. This can be accomplished not only by examining closely the acts of great Roman leaders but by studying their words and determining how their artful rhetorical skills could shape a political debate and motivate people to great things. Thus, for those in this second school of thought, Machiavelli's place in political theory is alongside the ancients: He is the standard-bearer of all classical notions of political action, virtue, honor, patriotism, republicanism, and rhetoric, albeit with an Italian, more modern twist.[22]

Finally, a third position in this debate suggests that Machiavelli's teachings fall somewhere between the modern and ancient worlds. Theorists like Vickie Sullivan argue that Machiavelli admires ancient Romans because they understood and carried out politics far better than his 16th-century contemporaries. Nonetheless, she believes Machiavelli is critical of the ancient world for its complicity, intended or unintended, in the ascent of Christianity. While the political actors of his modern world may be inept, the ancient world was not perfect either. Machiavelli's recognition of the ancients' brilliance did not prevent him from recognizing their error in allowing Christianity to become a strong and dominant force throughout the Middle Ages. Thus, according to Sullivan, Machiavelli chose the best elements and teachings from the ancient world, and he adapted them with some of his own novel ideas to fit the circumstances of a Christian, modern world.[23] He recognized that the political realities of his day could never allow him to fully embrace the modes and orders of the ancient world.

So who is the real Machiavelli? A ground-breaking modern? An imitator of the ancients? Or someone who is perhaps a little bit of both? The world may never be in agreement with the categorization of this Renaissance thinker; but almost everyone agrees that his teachings have had enormous impact. For better or worse, Machiavelli's realism has shaped our world around the notion of power, with its unbridled pursuit, its eventual attainment, and its ultimate preservation. Today many people recognize the impolitic nature of some of his harshest teachings and thus dismiss them as an obsolete and dangerous course of action no longer to be followed by heads of state. This is good. However, some of his most brutal prescriptions are now being carried out by extremist groups, who perform these acts under the cover of freedom and religion. While we can only speculate about whether Machiavelli would be concerned with how his teachings are being implemented, we can be sure he would

---

[21]Maurizio Viroli, *Machiavelli* (New York: Oxford University Press, 1998), p. 4.

[22]Viroli, Introduction, pp. 1–10.

[23]Vickie B. Sullivan, *Machiavelli's Three Romes* (Dekalb, Illinois: Northern Illinois University Press, 1996).

never be fooled by their appearance of freedom and religious motivation. To him, all political actions are induced by the desire for power and glory—and little else. We in the modern world would be foolish to overlook this important teaching.

Key Terms

situational ethics
dual-layered
mixed regimes
new founder
virtu
ozio
prudenzia
astuzia
Cesare Borgia
foundations
political use of spectacle
fortune
well-used cruelty
Agathocles
princes who uses religion effectively
Pope Alexander VI
King Ferdinand of Spain

Sources and Resources

Key Texts

The Prince
The Discourses

Secondary Texts

Berlin, Isaiah. "The Originality of Machiavelli," in his *Against the Current: Essays in the History of Ideas*, ed. H. Hardy (London: Hogarth Press, 1979).

Butterfield, Herbert. *The Statecraft of Machiavelli* (London: G. Bell and Sons, 1940).

Skinner, Quentin. *Machiavelli* (Oxford: Oxford University Press, 1981).

Strauss, Leo. *Thoughts on Machiavelli* (Chicago: University of Chicago Press, 1958).

Viroli, Maurizio. *Machiavelli* (Oxford: Oxford University Press, 1998).

Web Sites

Stanford Encyclopedia of Philosophy entry online at http://plato.stanford.edu/entries/machiavelli/

Full text works of Machiavelli online at www.intratext.com/Catalogo/Autori/Aut242.HTM

Machiavelli webliography online at www.timoroso.com/philosophy/machiavelli/

Thomas Hobbes

CHAPTER 7

By Sean D. Sutton *Rochester Institute of Technology*

THE LIFE AND TIMES OF THOMAS HOBBES

Thomas Hobbes was born on April 5, 1588, near Malmesbury in Wiltshire, England. We are told that the news of the approaching Spanish Armada induced his mother into early labor. Hobbes would later joke that his mother brought forth that day "twins at once, both me and fear."[1] Shortly after his birth, his father, the vicar of Charlton and Westport, was forced to leave town for brawling outside his own church, leaving his three children in the care of a wealthy uncle.

At the age of 14, Hobbes entered Oxford and completed his degree in five years. Upon his graduation, William Cavendish, the Earl of Devonshire, employed Hobbes to tutor his son William. This association with the Cavendish family, which was to last almost a lifetime, allowed Hobbes to continue his studies and to meet many leading thinkers of his day. In 1610, Hobbes and the younger William embarked on a three-year tour of France, Italy, and Germany. While on tour, Hobbes began to work on the first English translation of Thucydides' *History of the Peloponnesian War* (1629) and began to study Euclidean geometry along with the new physics of Copernicus and Galileo.

The development of modern science, especially physics, was controversial. In 1632 Galileo published the *Dialogue Concerning the Two Chief World Systems,* a defense of the Copernican heliocentric theory of the solar system. The Roman church condemned the theories of Copernicus and Galileo for contradicting the scriptural account of the motion of the planets and for undermining belief in divine providence.[2] The church argued that modern physics depicted the world as a mechanism governed by cause and effect that did not need a divine caretaker to oversee its operation. The Inquisition confiscated the existing copies of Galileo's book, forced him to recant his position, and prohibited him from publishing again. Not deterred by the controversy, Hobbes visited Galileo in Florence and in Paris. Convinced that the methods of the new physics were the foundations of knowledge, Hobbes began his three-part *Elementa Philosophiae,* which would include a materialistic metaphysics, *De Corpore* (1655); a materialistic account of man, *De Homine* (1658); and a work on the rights and duties of citizens, *De Cive* (1642). In 1637 Hobbes returned to England, where a religious civil war was brewing.

In April 1640, after 11 years of absolute rule, Charles I recalled Parliament to raise taxes to underwrite the imposition of his religious reforms on Scotland. One month later, Charles I dissolved Parliament when it began to debate the abuses of his rule. In the midst of this rancor, Hobbes completed his first work of political philosophy, *The Elements of Law,* where he developed the core theme of his political science, the necessity of an absolute and undivided sovereignty for securing peace. When civil war erupted in 1642 between the king and Parliament, Hobbes escaped to Paris, where he published *De Cive*. Historical circumstances and "experience, known to all men and denied by none," he wrote, confirmed his thinking that civil war begins when there are

---

[1]See Thomas Hobbes, *Leviathan,* (ed.) Edwin Curley (Indianapolis, IN: Hackett Publishing Co., 1994), "Editor's Introduction," p. liv.

[2]Consider Psalms 93 and 104 and Ecclesiastes 1:5.

conflicting opinions "concerning the rights of dominion and obedience due from subjects" and there is no absolute authority to settle such disputes.[3]

The English Civil War ended in 1646 with a defeat for the royalists. Hobbes began to write *Leviathan, or the Matter, Form, and Power of a Commonwealth, Ecclesiastical and Civil* (1651). King Charles I was imprisoned, but his son, Charles II, fled to Paris, where Hobbes tutored him in mathematics. In 1647, to Parliament's surprise, Charles I escaped from custody and enlisted the Scots to subdue England and restore the monarchy. Oliver Cromwell defeated the army of Scots at Preston. In 1649 Charles I was tried and executed. Within the year Parliament abolished both the monarchy and the House of Lords and instituted the Commonwealth.

In 1651 Charles II, with an army of Scots, invaded England to reclaim his father's throne. Shortly after Cromwell defeated the invaders at Worcester, Hobbes presented Charles II with a copy of *Leviathan*. He was forced to flee to England because those around Charles II accused him of justifying Cromwell's revolution. It was not until 1660, when the English monarchy was restored, that Hobbes regained his former student's favor. But trouble was not far away. In 1666 the House of Commons introduced a bill against atheism and blasphemy, singling out Hobbes' *Leviathan*. Two years later, Hobbes suffered Galileo's fate and was forbidden from publishing his history of the English Civil War, *Behemoth* (1670). In October 1679, at the age of 92, Hobbes died of a stroke and was buried in the churchyard of Ault Hucknall in Derbyshire, England. Four years after his death, Oxford condemned and burned his books *De Cive* and *Leviathan* for heresy.

HOBBES—THE FIRST POLITICAL SCIENTIST

Traditionally Socrates is considered the founder of political philosophy. Yet Thomas Hobbes called himself the first true political philosopher. Hobbes believed he had discovered the principles underlying political order and the means to securing civil peace, where Socrates, Plato, Aristotle, Plutarch, and Cicero had all failed. He accuses his predecessors of errors that fomented sedition, anarchy, and civil war. The distinction between virtue and vice, a distinction thought to be grounded in nature rather than in positive law, Hobbes argues, teaches men to judge privately the actions of others and to conduct their affairs according to a standard outside the confines of civil law. Hobbes observes that this teaching justifies the distinction between monarchy and tyranny and allows citizens to pass judgment on whether the sovereign was fit to rule, which encourages civil disobedience and justified tyrannicide. Hobbes also rejects Aristotle's physics and metaphysics because they presuppose the existence of incorporeal substances or essences that support the notion of an incorporeal soul. He contends that the doctrine of the soul—and with it the conscience—encourages the belief that divine punishments are to be feared before the punishments of civil authorities.[4]

---

[3]See Thomas Hobbes, *De Cive,* "Preface."

[4]See Thomas Hobbes, *Elements of Law,* "Epistle Dedicatory"; *De Cive,* "Epistle Dedicatory" and "Preface"; *Leviathan,* pp. 7, 19, 46–47, 243, 460 ff.

Hobbes accepts Machiavelli's criticism that classical political philosophy is useless because it takes its bearings by how people ought to live and not how people actually live.[5] He also agrees with Machiavelli that people are by nature asocial. He even goes so far as to assert that speech is an acquired attribute and not a natural endowment. But Hobbes does not fully accept Machiavelli's shocking teaching. Instead he grounds his political science in a moral or **natural law,** and today Hobbes is considered the founder of the modern doctrine of **natural right.**

The modern doctrine of natural right culminates in the idea that individuals construct government to secure their natural rights. Hobbes identifies natural right with the desire for self-preservation, the rational expression of the fear of death. From this passion Hobbes deduces the laws of nature, which willed peace and the preservation of mankind. The task of government, then, is to enforce these rational precepts or laws of nature and secure the natural rights of the individual.

We can grasp Hobbes' claim to originality by considering the introduction to *Leviathan*. Hobbes intends to "create" the Leviathan or commonwealth, which is an artificial man "of greater stature and strength" than the original work of nature, man. To do this Hobbes will imitate "the art whereby God has made and governs the world." This art imparts to the world mechanical motion so that it moves according to the laws of motion. By imitating this art man can make an "artificial animal" that resembles all *automata* or mechanical engines. Hobbes' intention is to create the "great Leviathan" or commonwealth by incorporating into it the soul, joints, nerves, strength, business, memory, reason, and will in the same way that the parts of a watch collectively give it motion. Hobbes' claim to originality is that he was the first political philosopher to ground political science in the physical sciences, or what he called **natural philosophy.**

Hobbes invites this further conclusion: If physics can make the natural world intelligible because it imitates the art whereby God has made and governs the world, man as part of that creation can also be understood through physics. If the material universe is composed of material bodies and their motions, man cannot be thought of in terms of a purpose or an end, but only in terms of motion. Hobbes' use of the methods of physics coincides with his rejection of classical political philosophy's teaching of a teleological understanding of nature.

Hobbes makes a second argument in the introduction that strengthens his claim to originality by reformulating the Socratic exhortation to "know thyself" as to know and study the passions, such as desire, fear, and hope. Hobbes argues that the passions are the same in all men, but their objects differ from one man to the next. He adds that "to govern a whole nation" one must consider these passions in the abstract—that is, separate from their objects. While this may be "harder than to learn any language or science," Hobbes claims that he has set down an orderly reading of the passions, leaving readers the task of considering whether their experience coincides with his account. The readers then are left with two sides to Hobbes' argument: the scientific and mechanistic argument and the humanist argument.

HOBBESIAN NOMINALISM AND THE MECHANICAL PSYCHOLOGY OF MAN

Hobbes recognized that if man is subject to the laws of mechanical motion, the manner of man's thinking must coincide with the principles of mechanics and the laws of physics. The first step in grounding political science in the physical sciences is

[5]See Niccolo Machiavelli, *The Prince,* trans. Leo Paul S. de Alvarez (Prospect Heights, IL: Waveland Press, 1989), pp. 17–18.

PRIMARY SOURCE 7.1 | FROM *LEVIATHAN*

Introduction

NATURE (the art whereby God hath made and governs the world) is by the *art* of man, as in many other things, so in this also imitated, that it can make an artificial animal. For seeing life is but a motion of limbs, the beginning whereof is in some principal part within, why may we not say that all *automata* (engines that move themselves by springs and wheels as doth a watch) have an artificial life? For what is the *heart,* but a *spring;* and the *nerves,* but so many *strings*; and the *joints,* but so many *wheels,* giving motion to the whole body, such as was intended by the Artificer? *Art* goes yet further, imitating that rational and most excellent work of Nature, man. For by art is created that great LEVIATHAN called a COMMONWEALTH, or STATE (in Latin, CIVITAS), which is but an artificial man, though of greater stature and strength than the natural, for whose protection and defense it was intended; and in which the *sovereignty* is an artificial soul, as giving life and motion to the whole body; the *magistrates* and other *officers* of judicature and execution, artificial *joints; reward* and *punishment* (by which fastened to the seat of the sovereignty, every joint and member is moved to perform his duty) are the *nerves,* that do the same in the body natural; the *wealth* and *riches* of all the particular members are the *strength; salus populi* (the people's safety) its *business; counselors,* by whom all things needful for it to know are suggested unto it, are the *memory; equity* and *laws,* an artificial *reason* and *will; concord, health; sedition, sickness*; and *civil war, death*. Lastly, the *pacts* and *covenants,* by which the parts of this body politic were at first made, set together, and united, resemble that *fiat,* or the *Let us make man,* pronounced by God in the Creation...

[T]here is a saying much usurped of late, that wisdom is acquired, not by reading of books, but of men. Consequently whereunto, those persons, that for the most part can give no other proof of being wise, take great delight to show what they think they have read in men, by uncharitable censures of one another behind their backs. But there is another saying not of late understood, by which they might learn truly to read one another, if they would take the pains; and that is, *Nosce teipsum,* Read thyself: which was not meant, as it is now used, to countenance either the barbarous state of men in power toward their inferiors, or to encourage men of low degree to a saucy behavior toward their betters; but to teach us that for the similitude of the thoughts and passions of one man, to the thoughts and passions of another, whosoever looks into himself and considers what he doth when he does think, opine, reason, hope, fear, etc., and upon what grounds; he shall thereby read and know what are the thoughts and passions of all other men upon the like occasions. I say the similitude of passions, which are the same in all men, *desire, fear, hope, etc.*; not the similitude of the objects of the passions, which are the things *desired, feared, hoped, etc.;* for these the constitution individual, and particular education, do so vary, and they are so easy to be kept from our knowledge, that the characters of man's heart, blotted and confounded as they are with dissembling, lying, counterfeiting, and erroneous doctrines, are legible only to him that searches hearts. And though by men's actions we do discover their design sometimes; yet to do it without comparing them with our own, and distinguishing all circumstances by which the case may come to be altered, is to decipher without a key, and be for the most part deceived, by too much trust or by too much diffidence, as he that reads is himself a good or evil man.

But let one man read another by his actions never so perfectly, it serves him only with his acquaintance, which are but few. He that is to govern a whole nation must read in himself, not this, or that particular man; but mankind: which though it be hard to do, harder than to learn any language or science; yet, when I shall have set down my own reading orderly and perspicuously, the pains left another will be only to consider if he also find not the same in himself. For this kind of doctrine admits no other demonstration.

QUESTIONS FOR REFLECTION

Does Hobbes's materialistic account of sense experience reduce all sense experience to a matter of touch?

to elaborate a mechanical psychology of man. To do this Hobbes begins in the manner of all scientists by defining his terms, and from these terms he derives their consequences.

For Hobbes the beginning of human thought is **sense experience.** Originally, without the use of speech, man's thoughts were images of external bodies. According to physics, because all things are reducible to matter and motion, the generating cause of sense experience must relate to the motions of corporeal bodies, which press the organ proper to each sense, as in taste, touch, sight, hearing, or smell. This pressure causes a motion that ripples through the nerves and membranes of the body, traveling inward to the brain and the heart, causing a resistance or counterpressure, and leaving behind an image of the external body.[6] Hobbes concludes that sense experience is deceptive and subjective because the image of an object is merely the consequence of motions of the material world and resides within the perceiver. The qualities of an object, such as "good" and "useful," also must be subjective because they reside not in the thing but in the individual. As such, there can be nothing good in this world, but only that which is pleasurable or painful, which also turns out to be subjective. Morally, this means that the good and the just are indistinguishable from pleasure and pain, or what we would call today *preferences.* For Hobbes, this is crucial for his political science because it allows him to claim there are no standards of justice or the good by which we can judge the conduct of government. Consequently, government is free to define the good and the just in a way that is useful for providing order and security.

Hobbes' mechanistic account of sense perception is inseparable from a corporealism or **materialism** that restricts human knowledge to knowledge of the material world. But Hobbes' materialistic account of the senses means that knowledge is not possible through sense experience. What is required is a method to overcome the unreliability of the senses.

Mental discourse, as the succession of one thought to another, is also understood mechanically. Hobbes assumes that speech is not natural to man, which means mental discourse originally was limited to the images and representations of causes and effects associated with corporeal bodies. Mental discourse therefore depends on and is limited by sense experience. According to Hobbes, the desires of the body both guide and prompt mental discourse. Whenever desire arises, it causes the thought of the means to satisfy the desire and further, the thoughts respecting the means to that means, until we have within our grasp or power the means to satisfy our desire. Due to material necessity people seek by reason the cause and the means that will satisfy their desires. Both man and beast exhibit this rudimentary form of mental discourse. The peculiarity that Hobbes found in man was that when man imagines anything whatsoever, he seeks all the possible effects that it can produce. Man can imagine, hypothesize, or speculate what he can do with a thing when he has it within his power

[6] *Leviathan,* p. 7.

or under his command. Man's ability is, therefore, the power to locate the origin of his desire and the means to satisfy it.[7]

Hobbes' account of mental discourse treats human reason as instrumental. "For the thoughts are to the desires as scouts and spies, to range abroad and find the way to the things desired."[8] Hobbes rejects Aristotle's account of reason as the ruling and architectonic element of the human soul. For Hobbes the desires of the body, as articulated by the passions, are primary and establish the ends of man, while the task for reason is to satisfy these desires. Hobbes goes even further. For Aristotle reason and speech, or reasoned speech (*logos*), are naturally linked, supporting the conclusion that man is by nature political. Aristotle argues that reasoned speech reveals the advantageous, the harmful, and also the just and the unjust, the foundations of political life.[9] Man's natural endowment of reasoned speech indicates the naturalness of politics. While Hobbes admits that reason is natural, he claims that speech had to be acquired or invented because man was not by nature fit for communal living. Hobbes calls speech "the most noble and profitable" invention of man because without speech there could neither be "commonwealth, nor society, nor contract, nor peace, no more than amongst lions, beasts and wolves."[10] Without the use of speech, man could not invent science.

Nominalism is the doctrine that nothing is general or universal but names. To illustrate, the name *man* or horse represents in its generality nothing real because there are only particular men and particular horses. Universal names are mere conveniences for speaking and necessities of human thought. All universal knowledge is illusionary. Or alternatively, whatever we know of this world is an artificial creation of our minds; that is, our understanding of the world must rely on models or intellectual constructs.

Science is necessary to overcome the deceptiveness of sense experience and is linked by Hobbes to "the right definitions of names," or what is called **nominalism.** Science stands or falls according to the precision of its definitions because imprecise definitions are, according to Hobbes, an abuse of speech "as truth consists in the right ordering of names."[11] The archetype of science is Euclidean geometry. As science requires the correct use of names, Hobbes reduces the diversity of names to four categories that reflect the harmony between science and the internal workings of the human mind.

To retrace our steps, Hobbes argues that physics is the basis for understanding man and nature. Physics reduces all of nature to the constituent elements of matter and motion. This allows Hobbes to explain sense experience in terms of the generation of an image caused by the motion of corporeal bodies. The gulf between the image and the perceived object means that sense experience is deceptive and subjective. To overcome this obstacle man must invent speech and science, which Hobbes calls the art of the correct use of names. The progress of the argument indicates that Hobbes could reduce the number of names to four: Names of matter, names of motion, names of images, and a fourth category of names, "names given to names themselves" or scientific terms modeled after Euclidean geometry (see Primary Source 7.2).

The first category of names signifies particular bodies and matter. The second category, "names abstract," enables us to name the perceived qualities of bodies. Hobbes calls these "names abstract" because "they are severed (not from matter, but) from the account of matter." For example, from something living, we invent the

[7] *Leviathan,* pp. 12–13.

[8] *Leviathan,* p. 41.

[9] Aristotle, *Politics,* p. 1253a.

[10] *Leviathan,* p. 16.

[11] *Leviathan,* p. 19.

name *life;* from something moved, *motion;* from something hot, *heat.* Names abstract are the names of motions or the accidental properties by which one external body is distinguished from another. The third category of names relates to the sensible qualities of a material object caused by its peculiar motion. These are "names of fancies," or names of images. Fourth, there are "names given to names" themselves by virtue of which we reason and understand. These names are scientific or technical definitions.[12]

For the development of science, the second and fourth categories of names are most significant. Hobbes illustrates the importance of the correct use of names through an example drawn from geometry: If a man who "has no use of speech at all" is shown a triangle and two right angles, he may by meditation find that the three angles of that triangle are equal to the two right angles. When shown another triangle, different in shape from the former, Hobbes argues, the same man "cannot know without a new labor, whether the three angles of that [triangle] also be equal to the same." This is not true for the man who has the use of words. Such a man, when he observes a triangle, can by "mental reckoning" conclude universally from the fact that it was named *triangle,* and not from any particular thing in the triangle observed, but because "the sides were straight and the angles three," that its three angles equal two right angles. The man who has the use of words and knows why a triangle is so named is thought by Hobbes to know the definition of a triangle, which presupposes the definitions of "figure," "straight line," and "point."

"Point" is the first definition in Euclid's *Elements:* "A point is that which has no part." Euclid's second definition is of line: "breadthless length." As defined, line or point and therefore figure cannot be drawn, but when drawn they never appear to have the properties for which they are named. The perceived figure, the triangle, according to Hobbes, is "seeming or fancy," and the name given to that figure would belong to the third category of names—unless by use of names the abstract quality is severed, not from the particular triangular body, but from the account of that particular body, by being incorporated into a definition that is universally agreed or settled upon. In this way scientific definitions are independent of sense experience, though ideas are originally aroused by sense experience. This illustrates the proper use and end of reason, which for Hobbes "is not the finding of the sum and truth of one or a few consequences of names, remote from the first definitions and settled significations of names, but to begin at these, and proceed from one consequence to another." He adds that there can be no certainty of the last conclusion, without a certainty in all the preceding definitions and conclusions on which the final conclusion is grounded and inferred.[13]

Hobbesian nominalism shows how man through the use of technical definitions can overcome the subjectivity of sense perception. Hobbes' nominalism allows him to speak of the passions, pleasures, and pains of man, which are subjective according to his account of sense experience, as though they are objective motions, in the same way, we speak of gravity as an objective and measurable force.

---

[12]*Leviathan,* pp. 19–20.

[13]*Leviathan,* pp. 18, 23. Compare also Euclid, *The Thirteen Books of Euclid's Elements,* trans. Sir Thomas L. Heath (New York: Dover Publications, 1956), p. 159.

PRIMARY SOURCE 7.2 | OF SPEECH, FROM *LEVIATHAN*, CHAPTER 4

... [T]he most noble and profitable invention of all ... was that of SPEECH, consisting of *names* or *appellations,* and their connection; whereby men register their thoughts, recall them when they are past, and also declare them one to another for mutual utility and conversation; without which there had been amongst men neither Commonwealth, nor society, nor contract, nor peace, no more than amongst lions, bears, and wolves....

The general use of speech is to transfer our mental discourse into verbal, or the train of our thoughts into a train of words, and that for two commodities; whereof one is the registering of the consequences of our thoughts, which being apt to slip out of our memory and put us to a new labor, may again be recalled by such words as they were marked by. So that the first use of names is to serve for *marks* or *notes* of remembrance. Another is when many use the same words to signify, by their connection and order one to another, what they conceive or think of each matter; and also what they desire, fear, or have any other passion for. And for this use they are called *signs.* Special uses of speech are these: first, to register what by cogitation we find to be the cause of anything, present or past; and what we find things present or past may produce, or effect; which, in sum, is acquiring of arts. Secondly, to show to others that knowledge which we have attained; which is to counsel and teach one another. Thirdly, to make known to others our wills and purposes that we may have the mutual help of one another. Fourthly, to please and delight ourselves, and others, by playing with our words, for pleasure or ornament, innocently.

To these uses, there are also four correspondent abuses. First, when men register their thoughts wrong by the inconstancy of the signification of their words; by which they register for their conceptions that which they never conceived, and so deceive themselves. Secondly, when they use words metaphorically; that is, in other sense than that they are ordained for, and thereby deceive others. Thirdly, when by words they declare that to be their will which is not. Fourthly, when they use them to grieve one another: for seeing nature hath armed living creatures, some with teeth, some with horns, and some with hands, to grieve an enemy, it is but an abuse of speech to grieve him with the tongue, unless it be one whom we are obliged to govern; and then it is not to grieve, but to correct and amend.

The manner how speech serveth to the remembrance of the consequence of causes and effects consisteth in the imposing of *names,* and the *connection* of them....

By this imposition of names, some of larger, some of stricter signification, we turn the reckoning of the consequences of things imagined in the mind into a reckoning of the consequences of appellations. For example, a man that hath no use of speech at all (such as is born and remains perfectly deaf and dumb), if he set before his eyes a triangle, and by it two right angles (such as are the corners of a square figure), he may by meditation compare and find that the three angles of that triangle are equal to those two right angles that stand by it. But if another triangle be shown him different in shape from the former, he cannot know without a new labor whether the three angles of that also be equal to the same. But he that hath the use of words, when he observes that such equality was consequent, not to the length of the sides, nor to any other particular thing in his triangle; but only to this, that the sides were straight, and the angles three, and that that was all, for which he named it a triangle; will boldly conclude universally that such equality of angles is in all triangles whatsoever, and register his invention in these general terms: *Every triangle hath its three angles equal to two right angles* [Euclid *Elements,* I, 32]. And thus the consequence found in one particular comes to be registered and remembered as a universal rule; and discharges our mental reckoning of time and place, and delivers us from all labor of the mind, saving the first; and makes that which was found true *here,* and *now,* to be true in *all times* and *places....*

continued

PRIMARY SOURCE 7.2 | OF SPEECH, FROM *LEVIATHAN*, CHAPTER 4 *continued*

Seeing then that *truth* consisteth in the right ordering of names in our affirmations, a man that seeketh precise *truth* had need to remember what every name he uses stands for, and to place it accordingly; or else he will find himself entangled in words, as a bird in lime twigs; the more he struggles, the more belimed. And therefore in geometry (which is the only science that it hath pleased God hitherto to bestow on mankind), men begin at settling the significations of their words; which settling of significations, they call *definitions,* and place them in the beginning of their reckoning.

By this it appears how necessary it is for any man that aspires to true knowledge to examine the definitions of former authors; and either to correct them, where they are negligently set down, or to make them himself. For the errors of definitions multiply themselves, according as the reckoning proceeds, and lead men into absurdities, which at last they see, but cannot avoid, without reckoning anew from the beginning; in which lies the foundation of their errors.... So that in the right definition of names lies the first use of speech; which is the acquisition of science: and in wrong, or no definitions, lies the first abuse; from which proceed all false and senseless tenets; which make those men that take their instruction from the authority of books, and not from their own meditation, to be as much below the condition of ignorant men as men endued with true science are above it. For between true science and erroneous doctrines, ignorance is in the middle. Natural sense and imagination are not subject to absurdity. Nature itself cannot err: and as men abound in copiousness of language; so they become more wise, or more mad, than ordinary. Nor is it possible without letters for any man to become either excellently wise or (unless his memory be hurt by disease, or ill constitution of organs) excellently foolish. For words are wise men's counters; they do but reckon by them: but they are the money of fools, that value them by the authority of an *Aristotle,* a *Cicero,* or a *Thomas,* or any other doctor whatsoever, if but a man.

Subject to names is whatsoever can enter into or be considered in an account, and be added one to another to make a sum, or subtracted one from another and leave a remainder.... This diversity of names may be reduced to four general heads.

First, a thing may enter into account for *matter,* or *body*; as *living, sensible, rational, hot, cold, moved, quiet*; with all which names the word *matter,* or *body,* is understood; all such being names of matter.

Secondly, it may enter into account, or be considered, for some accident or quality which we conceive to be in it; as for *being moved,* for *being so long,* for *being hot,* etc.; and then, of the name of the thing itself, by a little change or wresting, we make a name for that accident which we consider; and for *living* put into the account *life*; for *moved, motion*; for *hot, heat*; for *long, length,* and the like: and all such names are the names of the accidents and properties by which one matter and body is distinguished from another. These are called *names abstract,* because severed, not from matter, but from the account of matter.

Thirdly, we bring into account the properties of our own bodies, whereby we make such distinction: as when anything is *seen* by us, we reckon not the thing itself, but the *sight,* the *color,* the *idea* of it in the *fancy*; and when anything is heard, we reckon it not, but the hearing or sound only, which is our fancy or conception of it by the ear: and such are *names of fancies.*

Fourthly, we bring into account, consider, and give names, to *names* themselves, and to *speeches*: for, *general, universal, special, equivocal,* are names of names. And *affirmation, interrogation, commandment, narration, syllogism, sermon, oration,* and many other such are names of speeches. And this is all the variety of names *positive;* which are put to mark somewhat which is in nature, or may be feigned by the mind of man, as bodies that are, or may be conceived to be; or of bodies, the properties that are, or may be feigned to be; or words and speech....

THE MOTIONS OF MAN AND THE STATE OF NATURE

Once Hobbes conceived his mechanical psychology of man, he was left with the task of distinguishing man from other living matter by identifying his peculiar motion. If motion begets motion, the cause of this motion must itself be a motion. The beginnings of motion within the human body, before they produce action, Hobbes calls **endeavor.** When endeavor moves toward its cause, it is called *appetite* or *desire*; and when the endeavor is away from its cause, it is called *aversion.* From endeavor, the motion toward or away, Hobbes formulates his understanding of **deliberation** as a weighing of appetites against aversions, hopes against fears, or pleasures against pains, until the thing is done or thought impossible. The will to choose or pursue an action is the last appetite in the process of deliberation.

Hobbes' scientific account of deliberation is a calculus of pleasure and pain, or what could be called *deliberative hedonism*. If the universe is nothing but bodies and their motions, then living creatures like man can be understood as being moved by the motions of pleasure and pain. The political significance of Hobbes' notion of deliberation is that it denies the possibility of making qualitative distinctions, such as the distinction between good and bad, not to mention the distinctions between the just and the unjust and between prudence and mean expediency. By limiting human deliberation to a calculus of quantities of pleasure and pain, Hobbesian deliberation denies that individuals are capable of making moral distinctions, leaving the way for the sovereign power to define authoritatively the moral terms that make political life possible.

The continual success in obtaining those things that satisfy our desires is called **felicity.** According to Hobbes, felicity consists not in the repose of a satisfied mind because there can be no final good in this world, "as is spoken of in the books of the old moral philosophers." If life is a motion of the body, then to remain still or at rest means that the body dies: There can be no rest or repose in this world. It follows, therefore, that felicity is "a continual progress of the desire, from one object to another, the attaining of the former being still but the way to the latter." The cause of the fleeting character of felicity is that man's desire is not to enjoy something for a moment or an instant, "but to assure forever the way of his future desire."[14]

Endeavor is consistent with felicity, which consists of the continual motion from one desire to the next and from aversion to aversion. Together they suggest that man is characterized by restlessness, which can also be thought of as a reflection of the principle of inertia. If, as Hobbes argues, all pleasures, desires, hopes, and fears are motions, the law of inertia governs them. Just as the ripples on a lake that meet the resistance of the surface of water begin to dissipate when the breeze ceases, so too do the motions of pleasure and pain begin to dissipate. Consequently, man's motion is a restless search to acquire power or command over those things conducive to a contented life.

Hobbes' account of endeavor and felicity allows him to characterize the general inclination or motion of mankind as "a perpetual and restless desire for power after power, that ceases only in death."[15] Success in attaining felicity in this life is

---

[14]*Leviathan,* pp. 27–28, 33, 34, 57.

[15]*Leviathan,* p. 58.

PRIMARY SOURCE 7.3

Of the Interior Beginning of Voluntary Motions, Commonly Called the Passions; and the Speeches by Which They Are Expressed, from *Leviathan*, Chapter 6

THERE be in animals two sorts of *motions* peculiar to them: One called *vital,* begun in generation, and continued without interruption through their whole life; such as are the *course* of the *blood,* the *pulse,* the *breathing,* the *concoction, nutrition, excretion,* etc.; to which motions there needs no help of imagination: the other is *animal motion,* otherwise called *voluntary motion;* as to *go,* to *speak,* to move any of our limbs, in such manner as is first fancied in our minds. That sense is motion in the organs and interior parts of man's body, caused by the action of the things we see, hear, etc., and that fancy is but the relics of the same motion, remaining after sense, has been already said in the first and second chapters. And because *going, speaking,* and the like voluntary motions depend always upon a precedent thought of *whither, which way,* and *what,* it is evident that the imagination is the first internal beginning of all voluntary motion. And although unstudied men do not conceive any motion at all to be there, where the thing moved is invisible, or the space it is moved in is, for the shortness of it, insensible; yet that doth not hinder but that such motions are. For let a space be never so little, that which is moved over a greater space, whereof that little one is part, must first be moved over that. These small beginnings of motion within the body of man, before they appear in walking, speaking, striking, and other visible actions, are commonly called ENDEAVOR.

This endeavor, when it is toward something which causes it, is called APPETITE, or DESIRE, the latter being the general name, and the other oftentimes restrained to signify the desire of food, namely *hunger* and *thirst.* And when the endeavor is from ward something, it is generally called AVERSION....

...[W]hatsoever is the object of any man's appetite or desire, that is it which he for his part calleth *good;* and the object of his hate and aversion, *evil;* and of his contempt, *vile* and *inconsiderable.* For these words of good, evil, and contemptible are ever used with relation to the person that useth them: there being nothing simply and absolutely so; nor any common rule of good and evil to be taken from the nature of the objects themselves; but from the person of the man, where there is no Commonwealth; or, in a Commonwealth, from the person that representeth it; or from an arbitrator or judge, whom men disagreeing shall by consent set up and make his sentence the rule thereof....

As in sense that which is really within us is, as I have said before, only motion, caused by the action of external objects but in appearance; to the sight, light and color; to the ear, sound; to the nostril, odor, etc.: so, when the action of the same object is continued from the eyes, ears, and other organs to the heart, the real effect there is nothing but motion, or endeavor; which consisteth in appetite or aversion to or from the object moving. But the appearance or sense of that motion is that we either call DELIGHT or TROUBLE OF MIND.

This motion, which is called appetite, and for the appearance of it *delight* and *pleasure,* seemeth to be a corroboration of vital motion, and a help thereunto; and therefore such things as caused delight were not improperly called *jucunda* (*a juvando*), from helping or fortifying; and the contrary, molesta, offensive, from hindering and troubling the motion vital.

Pleasure therefore, or *delight,* is the appearance or sense of good; and *molestation* or *displeasure,* the appearance or sense of evil. And consequently all appetite, desire, and love is accompanied with some delight more or less; and all hatred and aversion with more or less displeasure and offence....

When in the mind of man appetites and aversions, hopes and fears, concerning one and the same thing, arise alternately; and diverse good and evil consequences of the doing or omitting the thing propounded come

PRIMARY SOURCE 7.3

Of the Interior Beginning of Voluntary Motions, Commonly Called the Passions; and the Speeches by Which They Are Expressed, from *Leviathan*, Chapter 6 *continued*

successively into our thoughts; so that sometimes we have an appetite to it, sometimes an aversion from it; sometimes hope to be able to do it, sometimes despair, or fear to attempt it; the whole sum of desires, aversions, hopes and fears, continued till the thing be either done, or thought impossible, is that we call DELIBERATION....

In deliberation, the last appetite, or aversion, immediately adhering to the action, or to the omission thereof, is that we call the WILL; the act, not the faculty, of *willing*. And beasts that have *deliberation* must necessarily also have *will*. The definition of the *will*, given commonly by the Schools, that it is a *rational appetite*, is not good. For if it were, then could there be no voluntary act against reason. For a *voluntary act* is that which proceedeth from the will, and no other. But if instead of a rational appetite, we shall say an appetite resulting from a precedent deliberation, then the definition is the same that I have given here. *Will*, therefore, *is the last appetite in deliberating*. And though we say in common discourse, a man had a will once to do a thing, that nevertheless he forbore to do; yet that is properly but an inclination, which makes no action *voluntary;* because the action depends not of it, but of the last inclination, or appetite. For if the intervenient appetites make any action voluntary, then by the same reason all intervenient aversions should make the same action involuntary; and so one and the same action should be both voluntary and involuntary.

By this it is manifest that, not only actions that have their beginning from covetousness, ambition, lust, or other appetites to the thing propounded, but also those that have their beginning from aversion, or fear of those consequences that follow the omission, are *voluntary actions*....

And because in deliberation the appetites and aversions are raised by foresight of the good and evil consequences, and sequels of the action whereof we deliberate, the good or evil effect thereof dependeth on the foresight of a long chain of consequences, of which very seldom any man is able to see to the end. But for so far as a man seeth, if the good in those consequences be greater than the evil, the whole chain is that which writers call *apparent* or *seeming good*. And contrarily, when the evil exceedeth the good, the whole is apparent or seeming evil: so that he who hath by experience, or reason, the greatest and surest prospect of consequences, deliberates best himself; and is able, when he will, to give the best counsel unto others.

Continual success in obtaining those things which a man from time to time desireth, that is to say, continual prospering, is that men call FELICITY; I mean the felicity of this life. For there is no such thing as perpetual tranquility of mind, while we live here; because life itself is but motion, and can never be without desire, nor without fear, no more than without sense. What kind of felicity God hath ordained to them that devoutly honor him, a man shall no sooner know than enjoy; being joys that now are as incomprehensible as the word of Schoolmen, *beautifical vision*, is unintelligible....

momentary and depends on the acquisition of power or command over those things necessary for life. Man's general inclination is a reflection of his tenuous grasp over the necessary things of life, which points to the malevolence of nature toward man. The inference can be drawn that nature sanctions man's selfishness and egocentric character. This view of nature supports the conclusion that man is by nature not fit for civil society: "Man is a wolf to his fellow man."[16] If man is by nature apolitical,

[16]*De Cive,* "Epistle Dedicatory."

QUESTIONS FOR REFLECTION

John Locke distinguishes between the state of nature and a state of war. Yet he depicts the state of nature as inconvenient and something from which man must escape. Does Locke in the end agree with Hobbes' depiction of the state of nature as a war of all against all?

Hobbes argues, he must originally have lived in a prepolitical state or what he calls the **state of nature.** Hobbes understands that if the inclination of man were a ceaseless desire for power, the original condition of man would be a state of war.

While the ceaseless desire for power is common to all mankind, Hobbes argues that the ability to acquire power is more or less evenly distributed. In the state of nature men are equal in the faculties of body and mind where no man can claim to himself any benefit to which another may aspire. The consequence is that even "the weakest has strength enough to kill the strongest, either by secret machination, or by confederacy with others that are in the same danger with himself."[17] The equal ability to kill reveals that man is burdened by a natural fragility of the human frame. Men are by nature equally vulnerable to death at the hands of their fellows. This natural fragility of the human frame, in a way similar to the unreliability of our natural senses, reflects nature's indifference toward man. As to the faculties of the mind, Hobbes finds a greater equality among men than that of strength. For if prudence is experience, with time all men will have an equal allotment with respect to those things they equally apply themselves to. The equality of bodily strength and of mind implies that no man is by nature superior to another—and especially no man is the natural ruler of another.[18]

The political significance of Hobbes' teaching on **equality** should not be overlooked. First, the equality of men in terms of strength, mind, and vulnerability to death means that there is no natural claim to political rule as Aristotle argues in his *Politics*. This means that politics is fundamentally conventional. Second, Hobbes' teaching on equality implies that individuals have an equal right or claim to consent to a government that would secure their rights. Hobbes is the originator of modern **social contract theory.**

From this equality of ability to kill each other, Hobbes derives three principle causes of quarrels among men: **competition, diffidence,** and **glory.** The most frequent reason men desire to hurt each other arises from the equal hope of attaining their ends, where the chief end is self-preservation. Due to the economy of nature the situation arises frequently that two or more men desire and compete for the same things that cannot be held in common or shared. The competition for the scarce means of survival justifies acquisition through war and makes men mutual enemies. Further, the enmity between men means that they cannot "plant, sow, build, or possess a convenient seat" without the fear that another will attempt to seize through force or fraud the fruits of their labor or destroy their life and liberty. Competition for the means of survival provokes diffidence or a mutual distrust between men. This distrust prompts men to

[17] *Leviathan*, p. 74.

[18] *Leviathan*, pp. 74–75.

anticipate and to preempt the threats of other men and to imagine the possibility of subjugating other men for the sake of self-preservation.[19]

The final cause of quarrels among men is the **love of glory,** which is based on comparisons with others. The lover of glory demands that all men honor him, but when that honor is not forthcoming, he prepares for war. The love of glory is related to the preceding causes of quarrels in the following way: Although the equal ability of hope, which underlies the warlike competition among men, is primarily aimed at the conservation of life, Hobbes admits that competition sometimes arises out of delight. Moreover, because of the distrust among men arising from the slim grasp we have on those things we enjoy, Hobbes argues, it is not unreasonable to anticipate the warlike intention of others and "by force or wiles to master the person of all men he can, so long till he see no other power great enough to endanger him." That this is no more than his conservation requires is generally allowed. Hobbes notes, however, that there is a certain pleasure or delight men take in contemplating their power in the act of conquest, which they pursue further than their security requires. If we are to trace the rise of the love of glory as a cause of quarrels to the natural inclination of man, the desire for power after power, we must admit that often the desire for power is associated with a delight in exercising that power.[20]

Hobbes argues that the beginning of all motion within man is endeavor, where every man desires what is good and shuns what is evil. The greatest of natural evils is death, which man shuns as if "by a certain impulsion of nature, no less than that whereby a stone moves downward."[21] Therefore, the most powerful of all passions, the force of gravity within the human heart, is the fear of violent death. The reflex of the fear of violent death is the desire for self-preservation and by inference is the greatest good. Starting with this most powerful of passions, Hobbes builds his science of politics and deduces the purpose of political society as the remedy for the defects of man's natural conditions.

Without a common power to govern them, Hobbes argues, men naturally resort to war in the blameless pursuit of self-preservation. This natural condition of mutual animosity ensures that men live with only the degree of security that their own strength and their own invention can furnish. The cardinal virtues of such a state are force and fraud. Consequently, each man is obliged to stand alone: No man can trust another because each is consumed with his own preservation. Hence there are no natural obligations or duties to other men. "In such condition there is no place for industry, because the fruit thereof is uncertain" and consequently "no knowledge of the earth, no account of time, no art, no letters, no society, and which is worst of all, continual fear and danger of violent death, and the life of man, solitary, poor, nasty, brutish, and short." In short, the state of nature prohibits civilization. It is a state of misery from which every man should endeavor to escape.[22]

Hobbes concedes that it may seem strange to those men who have not reflected adequately upon these things "that nature should thus dissociate, and render men apt

---

[19] *Leviathan,* p. 75.

[20] *Leviathan,* p. 75.

[21] *De Cive,* p. 115.

[22] *Leviathan,* pp. 76, 78, 159 ff.

PRIMARY SOURCE 7.4

Of the Natural Condition of Mankind as Concerning Their Felicity and Misery, from *Leviathan*, Chapter 13

NATURE hath made men so equal in the faculties of body and mind as that, though there be found one man sometimes manifestly stronger in body or of quicker mind than another, yet when all is reckoned together the difference between man and man is not so considerable as that one man can thereupon claim to himself any benefit to which another may not pretend as well as he. For as to the strength of body, the weakest has strength enough to kill the strongest, either by secret machination or by confederacy with others that are in the same danger with himself.

And as to the faculties of the mind, setting aside the arts grounded upon words, and especially that skill of proceeding upon general and infallible rules, called science, which very few have and but in few things, as being not a native faculty born with us, nor attained, as prudence, while we look after somewhat else, I find yet a greater equality amongst men than that of strength. For prudence is but experience, which equal time equally bestows on all men in those things they equally apply themselves unto. That which may perhaps make such equality incredible is but a vain conceit of one's own wisdom, which almost all men think they have in a greater degree than the vulgar; that is, than all men but themselves, and a few others, whom by fame, or for concurring with themselves, they approve. For such is the nature of men that howsoever they may acknowledge many others to be more witty, or more eloquent or more learned, yet they will hardly believe there be many so wise as themselves; for they see their own wit at hand, and other men's at a distance. But this proveth rather that men are in that point equal, than unequal. For there is not ordinarily a greater sign of the equal distribution of anything than that every man is contented with his share.

From this equality of ability ariseth equality of hope in the attaining of our ends. And therefore if any two men desire the same thing, which nevertheless they cannot both enjoy, they become enemies; and in the way to their end (which is principally their own conservation, and sometimes their delectation only) endeavor to destroy or subdue one another. And from hence it comes to pass that where an invader hath no more to fear than another man's single power, if one plant, sow, build, or possess a convenient seat, others may probably be expected to come prepared with forces united to dispossess and deprive him, not only of the fruit of his labor, but also of his life or liberty. And the invader again is in the like danger of another.

And from this diffidence of one another, there is no way for any man to secure himself so reasonable as anticipation; that is, by force, or wiles, to master the persons of all men he can so long till he see no other power great enough to endanger him: and this is no more than his own conservation requireth, and is generally allowed. Also, because there be some that, taking pleasure in contemplating their own power in the acts of conquest, which they pursue farther than their security requires, if others, that otherwise would be glad to be at ease within modest bounds, should not by invasion increase their power, they would not be able, long time, by standing only on their defense, to subsist. And by consequence, such augmentation of dominion over men being necessary to a man's conservation, it ought to be allowed him.

Again, men have no pleasure (but on the contrary a great deal of grief) in keeping company where there is no power able to overawe them all. For every man looketh that his companion should value him at the same rate he sets upon himself, and upon all signs of contempt or undervaluing naturally endeavors, as far as he dares (which amongst them that have no common power to keep them in quiet is far enough to make them destroy each other), to extort a greater value from his contemners, by damage; and from others, by the example.

PRIMARY SOURCE 7.4

Of the Natural Condition of Mankind as Concerning Their Felicity and Misery, from *Leviathan*, Chapter 13 *continued*

So that in the nature of man, we find three principal causes of quarrel. First, competition; secondly, diffidence; thirdly, glory.

The first maketh men invade for gain; the second, for safety; and the third, for reputation. The first use violence, to make themselves masters of other men's persons, wives, children, and cattle; the second, to defend them; the third, for trifles, as a word, a smile, a different opinion, and any other sign of undervalue, either direct in their persons or by reflection in their kindred, their friends, their nation, their profession, or their name.

Hereby it is manifest that during the time men live without a common power to keep them all in awe, they are in that condition which is called war; and such a war as is of every man against every man. For WAR consisteth not in battle only, or the act of fighting, but in a tract of *time*, wherein the will to contend by battle is sufficiently known: and therefore the notion of time is to be considered in the nature of war, as it is in the nature of weather. For as the nature of foul weather lieth not in a shower or two of rain, but in an inclination thereto of many days together: so the nature of war consisteth not in actual fighting, but in the known disposition thereto during all the time there is no assurance to the contrary. All other time is PEACE.

Whatsoever therefore is consequent to a time of war, where every man is enemy to every man, the same consequent to the time wherein men live without other security than what their own strength and their own invention shall furnish them withal. In such condition there is no place for industry, because the fruit thereof is uncertain: and consequently no culture of the earth; no navigation, nor use of the commodities that may be imported by sea; no commodious building; no instruments of moving and removing such things as require much force; no knowledge of the face of the earth; no account of time; no arts; no letters; no society; and which is worst of all, continual fear, and danger of violent death; and the life of man, solitary, poor, nasty, brutish, and short.

It may seem strange to some man that has not well weighed these things that Nature should thus dissociate and render men apt to invade and destroy one another: and he may therefore, not trusting to this inference, made from the passions, desire perhaps to have the same confirmed by experience. Let him therefore consider with himself: when taking a journey, he arms himself and seeks to go well accompanied; when going to sleep, he locks his doors; when even in his house he locks his chests; and this when he knows there be laws and public officers, armed, to revenge all injuries shall be done him; what opinion he has of his fellow subjects, when he rides armed; of his fellow citizens, when he locks his doors; and of his children, and servants, when he locks his chests. Does he not there as much accuse mankind by his actions as I do by my words? But neither of us accuse man's nature in it. The desires, and other passions of man, are in themselves no sin. No more are the actions that proceed from those passions till they know a law that forbids them; which till laws be made they cannot know, nor can any law be made till they have agreed upon the person that shall make it.

It may peradventure be thought there was never such a time nor condition of war as this; and I believe it was never generally so, over all the world: but there are many places where they live so now. For the savage people in many places of *America*, except the government of small families, the concord whereof dependeth on natural lust, have no government at all, and live at this day in that brutish manner, as I said before. Howsoever, it may be perceived what manner of life there would be, where there were no common power to fear, by the manner of life which men that have formerly lived under a peaceful government use to degenerate into a civil war.

continued

PRIMARY SOURCE 7.4

Of the Natural Condition of Mankind as Concerning Their Felicity and Misery, from *Leviathan*, Chapter 13 *continued*

But though there had never been any time wherein particular men were in a condition of war one against another, yet in all times kings and persons of sovereign authority, because of their independency, are in continual jealousies, and in the state and posture of gladiators, having their weapons pointing, and their eyes fixed on one another; that is, their forts, garrisons, and guns upon the frontiers of their kingdoms, and continual spies upon their neighbors, which is a posture of war. But because they uphold thereby the industry of their subjects, there does not follow from it that misery which accompanies the liberty of particular men.

To this war of every man against every man, this also is consequent; that nothing can be unjust. The notions of right and wrong, justice and injustice, have there no place. Where there is no common power, there is no law; where no law, no injustice. Force and fraud are in war the two cardinal virtues. Justice and injustice are none of the faculties neither of the body nor mind. If they were, they might be in a man that were alone in the world, as well as his senses and passions. They are qualities that relate to men in society, not in solitude. It is consequent also to the same condition that there be no propriety, no dominion, no mine and thine distinct; but only that to be every man's that he can get, and for so long as he can keep it. And thus much for the ill condition which man by mere nature is actually placed in; though with a possibility to come out of it, consisting partly in the passions, partly in his reason.

The passions that incline men to peace are: fear of death; desire of such things as are necessary to commodious living; and a hope by their industry to obtain them. And reason suggesteth convenient articles of peace upon which men may be drawn to agreement. These articles are they which otherwise are called the Laws of Nature, whereof I shall speak more particularly in the two following chapters.

---

to invade and destroy one another." The "inference made from the passions," he argues, is confirmed by experience. For example, when taking a journey we arm ourselves and travel well accompanied; when going to sleep we lock our doors; and even in our homes we lock our chests because we mistrust our family and our servants. It is natural for men to distrust each other, even in a society where there are laws and an authority to enforce them. Hobbes concludes that our actions and our experience accuse mankind as much as his words.[23] He indicates the change in moral outlook as follows: "The desires and other passions of man are in themselves no sin. No more are the actions that proceed from those passions, till they know a law that forbids them—which till laws be made they cannot know. Nor can any law be made, till they have agreed upon the person that shall make it." In such a state, "nothing can be unjust. The notions of right and wrong, justice and injustice, have there no place. Where there is no common power, there is no law, where no law, no injustice."[24] It is only within the context of civil society that there can be justice.

Hobbes' natural philosophy poses an important challenge for his political philosophy. If natural necessity compels man to acquire speech and eventually invent science, why wouldn't it compel man to seek the security of the political community?

---

[23] *Leviathan*, pp. 76–77.

[24] *Leviathan*, p. 77.

QUESTIONS FOR REFLECTION

What if the state of nature did not exist historically? Would this undermine Hobbes' political teaching?

If this were so, should we not conclude that man is by nature compelled to associate with others and form political communities? Does this not imply that politics is somehow natural? Hobbes was aware of this difficulty and was forced to distinguish his natural philosophy from his political philosophy by claiming that politics is based on its own principles that can be discovered by looking inward—that is, by attempting to "know thyself." But Hobbes' scientific account of sense experience and experience seems to undermine the turn inward to "knowing thyself."

What then is the role of Hobbes' natural philosophy? It seems that Hobbes' natural philosophy provides theoretical support for his political philosophy in much the same way that theological apologetics attends theological dogmatics.[25] For example, Hobbes' natural science, which is fundamentally materialistic, implies that there are no goods of the soul, indeed that there is no soul, thereby elevating the importance of this life and therefore the desire for self-preservation, the linchpin of his political science. Further, Hobbes' natural science buries the notion of teleology and Aristotle's doctrine of essences, posing a seemingly insurmountable obstacle to what Hobbes calls the private judgment of virtue and vice, which can be leveled against the sovereign. By eliminating private moral judgments, Hobbes hoped to secure political peace. His mechanical account of deliberation, a calculus of pleasure and pain, also shows that individuals are incapable of making qualitative judgments and moral distinctions.

NATURAL RIGHT, THE LAWS OF NATURE, AND THE POLITICAL

The original condition of man, the state of nature, is a state of war of all against all. In such a state there can be no civilization—just continual fear and the persistent danger of violent death. The natural concern of man in the state of nature is self-preservation. There is no appeal in such a state to justice because there can be nothing unjust if self-preservation is the highest end. Hobbes identifies the blameless liberty of each man to use his own power for the preservation of his own nature as the right of nature. Thus the first foundation of natural right is that every man must preserve himself. Hobbes notes that the right to an end implies a right to the means to the end; otherwise it would be vain. Consequently, Hobbes extends the natural right to self-preservation to include the means to self-preservation. Men have a right to preserve themselves by any means. The consequence of Hobbes' notion of natural right, which in effect is a natural liberty, is that the natural state of man cannot be anything other than a state of war. From here Hobbes derives the laws of nature that point to the necessity to seek peace and establish the social compact—the state.[26]

---

[25]See Leo Strauss, "On the Basis of Hobbes's Political Philosophy" in *What Is Political Philosophy? And Other Studies* (Chicago: The University of Chicago Press, 1988), p. 180.

[26]*Leviathan*, pp. 79–80.

QUESTIONS FOR REFLECTION

Is Hobbes' account of natural right the beginning of our notion of entitlement?

Hobbes views nature as a negative standard rather than an end, as traditionally understood. Nature understood in this way is to be conquered, overcome, or escaped from. The state of nature presents man with a grave problem that he must of necessity solve. The solution consists partly in the passions and partly in man's reason. The fear of violent death and its more rational expression, the desire for self-preservation, begin the mental discourse whereby man's reason seeks the means to satisfy the desire: The passions set the ends of man, while reason scouts out the means to satisfy the passions.

Hobbes writes, "The passions that incline men to peace are fear of death, desire of such things as are necessary to commodious living, and a hope by their industry to obtain them."[27] When compared to the principal causes of quarrels among men, namely competition, diffidence, and vain glory, it is found that fear of death and desire for comfort are both among the inclinations to peace and war; vanity is the odd man out. But it is the fear of violent death that is "the passion to be reckoned upon," suggesting that perhaps the desire for a comfortable life and hope are somehow secondary, or at least subservient, to the necessity of preservation.[28] The task of Hobbes' reason or political science is, therefore, to use the fear of violent death to overcome man's vanity and his inclination to war. This task is made all the more possible by Hobbes' mechanical psychology of man, which not only reveals those motions or passions, which can be relied upon to construct civil society, but also holds out the possibility of manipulating human nature for the sake of the political order, security, and peace.

Reason's assignment is to conceive the "convenient articles of peace upon which men may be drawn to agreement."[29] Hobbes names these articles the laws of nature. The laws of nature are derivative and subordinate to the fundamental natural right of self-preservation, which is derived from the most powerful passion within man, the fear of violent death. This fundamental natural right, Hobbes writes, is "the liberty each man hath to use his own power, as he will himself, for the preservation of his own nature, of his own life." Since nature makes no distinctions between men, all men are equally obligated to preserve themselves and have a right to whatever means they discern will preserve their lives. Everything is permitted by nature. Hobbes notes that having the right to the end, but not the means to the end, is to have no right to the end in the first place. "And therefore, as long as this natural right of every man to everything endureth, there can be no security to any man (how strong or wise soever he be) of living out the time which nature ordinarily alloweth men to live."[30] To end the mutual slaughter and secure our natural right, one must choose to give up the unrestricted

---

[27] *Leviathan*, p. 78.

[28] *Leviathan*, pp. 87–88.

[29] *Leviathan*, p. 78.

[30] *Leviathan*, p. 80.

QUESTIONS FOR REFLECTION

Do Hobbes and Aquinas agree about the content and the character of natural law?

right to the means—that is, the right to everything, including the liberty of private judgment regarding those means.

The laws of nature are deduced from the fundamental natural right to self-preservation as follows: The state of nature as a state of war means no man's natural right of self-preservation is secure. If all men exercise their natural right, no man is secure. Every man ought to seek peace; and when peace cannot be secured, he ought to pursue war. This "precept, or general rule, of reason" is the fundamental law of nature. All the subsequent laws of nature intend the same end—namely the peace and preservation of all mankind. From the first law of nature, Hobbes derives the second law of nature: that when a man is willing, when others are too, for the sake of peace and security, he should lay down his weapons, his claim to the right to every means for the sake of preservation, including the right to judge the means by which they intend to preserve themselves.

"The mutual transferring of right" is accomplished by what we call the *social contract* but what Hobbes calls the **covenant.** What is transferred is the right to all the means necessary for self-preservation—a right that prevents men living in peace. When a man renounces or transfers a right, he is bound not to hinder those to whom he has granted that right from exercising it. From this Hobbes derives the third law of nature, that men perform their covenants, which is the origin of justice. "For where no covenant hath preceded, there hath no right been transferred, and every man has right to everything; and consequently, no action can be unjust." To break the covenant is to be unjust, which is to exercise a right that one no longer possesses. Justice accordingly is contractual. Political society is fundamentally artificial and therefore must be constructed.[31]

The conclusion of reason is that individuals must renounce their right to judge the means by which they are to preserve themselves. Questions of justice, right, and wrong are to be determined by the civil authority. The thrust of Hobbes' argument is clear: The civil authority must be the supreme arbitrator and authority of what is good and evil, just and unjust, and a power to be fully obeyed. Hobbes' teaching on natural law culminates in the **absolute sovereign,** or absolute government.

Hobbes' doctrine of absolute sovereignty amounts to the absolute authority of government to define the just and the unjust. Similar to the scientist or geometrician who begins with definitions universally agreed upon, Hobbes' doctrine of natural right culminates in the teaching that the sovereign secure universal agreement to the lawful, just, and true. The sovereign can be said to proceed like a "political geometer"; but unlike actual geometers, the sovereign does not rely on good-natured scientific inquiry to secure agreement, but force and fear. Hobbes' teaching on natural law culminates in government determining the meaning of justice through its law, or what we would call today *legal positivism*.

---

[31]*Leviathan,* p. 89.

QUESTIONS FOR REFLECTION

Is Hobbes correct that civil peace depends on an agreement on the political terms and principles that govern a people? Abraham Lincoln's Speech at the Sanitary Fair, Baltimore, Maryland, April 18, 1864, shows that the American Civil War can be understood as the consequence of a disagreement concerning the terms *equality* and *liberty*. Do Lincoln and Hobbes agree on the meaning of equality and liberty and their implications for government?

The full meaning of Hobbes' state of nature can now be stated: The state of nature, as a replacement of the biblical account of man's beginnings, is intended to deflate man's vanity or pride and reveal his true plight. The antitheological character of the state of nature entails that man stands alone in a world not of his creation that is hostile or at the very least indifferent to his survival. According to Hobbes, to assume that nature cares for man, that there is divine support for humanity, that there is a providential God, is vanity. By the necessity forced upon him by nature, man is driven to save himself and to construct an artificial order, conducive to his survival. The salvation of humanity depends not upon divine providence or the grace of God, but upon human industry and labor.

The state of nature establishes the primacy of the fear of violent death and therefore the natural right to self-preservation. It is the fear of violent death, Hobbes says, that compels men to sue for peace. Peace can be secured only if man escapes his natural condition and constructs the political order. The state of nature reveals that the political order is radically artificial or conventional. The key to constructing an artificial political order is to reflect on the meaning of the passions and in particular the meaning of the fear of violent death. Reason is no longer sovereign because the passions determine the ends of government—namely peace and preservation—but reason does discern the full meaning of the passions.

If justice is contractual, it is effective only if men are obliged to fulfill their contracts. According to Hobbes, however, contracts and covenants of mutual trust where there is no fear of nonperformance by either party are invalid.[32] "Therefore, before the names of just and unjust can have place, there must be some coercive power to compel men equally to the performance of their covenants, by the terror of some punishment greater than the benefit they expect by the breach of their covenant."[33] The essential defect of the laws of nature is, therefore, that they are ineffective in the absence of a common power set over men to ensure with right and sufficient force that covenants are fulfilled. Covenants not supported by the sword are merely words without "strength to secure a man at all." When there is no power to force the observation of the laws of nature, no man can afford to be the first to obey those dictates of reason. "For he that performeth first has no assurance the other will perform after, because the bonds of words are too weak to bridle men's ambition, avarice, anger and other passions, without the fear of some coercive power," a power that is absent in "the condition of mere nature."[34] Hobbes' political remedy to the

[32] *Leviathan*, pp. 84–85.

[33] *Leviathan*, p. 89 ff.

[34] *Leviathan*, pp. 84, 87–88, 106–107.

QUESTIONS FOR REFLECTION

Does Hobbes make the same argument regarding the rule of law that Machiavelli does when he says in *The Prince* that good laws depend on good arms?

difficulty posed by the asociality of man is the absolute sovereign, who must see to it that terror of punishment is a greater force than the anticipated benefits that could be derived from breaching covenants. No moral pressure is relied on to establish the conditions of trust—fear of violent death is to be relied on. Calculated self-interest is the only basis of justice and morality.

ABSOLUTE SOVEREIGNTY, LIBERTY, AND THE RIGHTS OF SUBJECTS

According to Hobbes, men introduced the constraints of government upon themselves for the sake of self-preservation and a peaceful life. While the laws of nature deduced from the natural right to self-preservation dictate peace and the keeping of promises, they are ineffective without some coercive power to enforce them. Hobbes separates himself from the traditional teaching of natural law by looking to the passions rather than reason to determine its content and by claiming that natural law is not effective without an external visible force to enforce it.

If government is necessary to make the laws of nature effective, it must be powerful enough to keep men in awe and stop them from acting on their mutual fear. While men's mutual fear of each other characterizes life in the state of nature, the fear of government characterizes civil society. Civil society, as Hobbes conceives it, depends on government providing the only object to fear—which men should pay serious attention to. Hobbes does not promise a transformation of human nature; the political is configured to accommodate the natural motions or passions of men.

The remedy for the state of nature is absolute government. Hobbes rejects our notion of limited government in favor of absolute sovereignty. Limited government fails to secure the individual's natural right to self-preservation, returning him back into the state of nature. When government is weak, he argues, every man may rely rightly on his own strength and guile to protect himself from the actions of others. To secure the natural rights of each individual, Hobbes' sovereign must retain the full natural right, including the right to every means available for survival. Hobbes' sovereign is to be absolute in the same way that every individual is absolute in the state of nature. The horrors and terrors of the state of nature justify absolute government because they are far worse than an absolute sovereign. Only under absolute government are peace and commodious living possible.

Absolute sovereignty is established when men confer all their power and strength on one man or an assembly of men through a contract or a covenant.[35] The covenant entails relinquishing the natural right to use and judge the means

[35] *Leviathan,* p. 109 ff.

PRIMARY SOURCE 7.5

OF THE FIRST AND SECOND NATURAL LAWS, AND OF CONTRACTS, FROM *LEVIATHAN,* CHAPTER 15

THE Right of Nature, which writers commonly call *jus naturale,* is the liberty each man hath to use his own power as he will himself for the preservation of his own nature; that is to say, of his own life; and consequently, of doing anything which, in his own judgment and reason, he shall conceive to be the aptest means thereunto.

By LIBERTY is understood, according to the proper signification of the word, the absence of external impediments; which impediments may oft take away part of a man's power to do what he would, but cannot hinder him from using the power left him according as his judgment and reason shall dictate to him.

A LAW OF NATURE, *lex naturalis,* is a precept, or general rule, found out by reason, by which a man is forbidden to do that which is destructive of his life, or taketh away the means of preserving the same, and to omit that by which he thinketh it may be best preserved. For though they that speak of this subject use to confound *jus* and *lex* (*right* and *law*), yet they ought to be distinguished, because RIGHT consisteth in liberty to do, or to forbear; whereas LAW determineth and bindeth to one of them: so that law and right differ as much as obligation and liberty, which in one and the same matter are inconsistent.

And because the condition of man (as hath been declared in the precedent chapter) is a condition of war of every one against every one, in which case every one is governed by his own reason, and there is nothing he can make use of that may not be a help unto him in preserving his life against his enemies; it followeth that in such a condition every man has a right to every thing, even to one another's body. And therefore, as long as this natural right of every man to every thing endureth, there can be no security to any man, how strong or wise soever he be, of living out the time which nature ordinarily alloweth men to live. And consequently it is a precept, or general rule of reason: *that every man ought to endeavor peace, as far as he has hope of obtaining it; and when he cannot obtain it, that he may seek and use all helps and advantages of war.* The first branch of which rule containeth the first and fundamental law of nature, which is: *to seek peace and follow it.* The second, the sum of the right of nature, which is: *by all means we can to defend ourselves.*

From this fundamental law of nature, by which men are commanded to endeavor peace, is derived this second law: *that a man be willing, when others are so too, as far forth as for peace and defense of himself he shall think it necessary, to lay down this right to all things; and be contented with so much liberty against other men as he would allow other men against himself.* For as long as every man holdeth this right, of doing anything he liketh; so long are all men in the condition of war. But if other men will not lay down their right, as well as he, then there is no reason for anyone to divest himself of his: for that were to expose himself to prey, which no man is bound to, rather than to dispose himself to peace. This is that law of the gospel: Whatsoever you require that others should do to you, that do ye to them. And that law of all men, *quod tibi fieri non vis, alteri ne feceris.*

To *lay down* a *man's right* to anything is to *divest* himself of the *liberty* of hindering another of the benefit of his own right to the same. For he that renounceth or passeth away his right giveth not to any other man a right which he had not before, because there is nothing to which every man had not right by nature, but only standeth out of his way that he may enjoy his own original right without hindrance from him, not without hindrance from another. So that the effect which redoundeth to one man by another man's defect of right is but so much diminution of impediments to the use of his own right original.

Right is laid aside, either by simply renouncing it, or by transferring it to another. By *simply* RENOUNCING, when he cares not to whom the benefit thereof redoundeth. By TRANSFERRING, when he intendeth the benefit thereof to some certain person or persons. And when a man hath in either manner abandoned or granted away his right, then is he said

PRIMARY SOURCE 7.5 | OF THE FIRST AND SECOND NATURAL LAWS, AND OF CONTRACTS, FROM *LEVIATHAN,* CHAPTER 15 *continued*

to be OBLIGED, or BOUND, not to hinder those to whom such right is granted, or abandoned, from the benefit of it: and that he *ought,* and it is DUTY, not to make void that voluntary act of his own: and that such hindrance is INJUSTICE, and injury, as being *sine jure;* the right being before renounced or transferred. So that *injury* or *injustice,* in the controversies of the world, is somewhat like to that which in the disputations of scholars is called absurdity. For as it is there called an *absurdity* to contradict what one maintained in the beginning; so in the world it is called injustice, and injury voluntarily to undo that which from the beginning he had voluntarily done.

The way by which a man either simply renounceth or transferreth his right is a declaration, or signification, by some voluntary and sufficient sign, or signs, that he doth so renounce or transfer, or hath so renounced or transferred the same, to him that accepteth it. And these signs are either words only, or actions only; or, as it happeneth most often, both words and actions. And the same are the bonds, by which men are bound and obliged: BONDS that have their strength, not from their own nature (for nothing is more easily broken than a man's word), but from fear of some evil consequence upon the rupture.

Whensoever a man transferreth his right, or renounceth it, it is either in consideration of some right reciprocally transferred to himself, or for some other good he hopeth for thereby. For it is a voluntary act: and of the voluntary acts of every man, the object is some *good to himself.* And therefore there be some rights which no man can be understood by any words, or other signs, to have abandoned or transferred. As first a man cannot lay down the right of resisting them that assault him by force to take away his life, because he cannot be understood to aim thereby at any good to himself. The same may be said of wounds, and chains, and imprisonment, both because there is no benefit consequent to such patience, as there is to the patience of suffering another to be wounded or imprisoned, as also because a man cannot tell when he seeth men proceed against him by violence whether they intend his death or not. And lastly the motive and end for which this renouncing and transferring of right is introduced is nothing else but the security of a man's person, in his life, and in the means of so preserving life as not to be weary of it. And therefore if a man by words, or other signs, seem to despoil himself of the end for which those signs were intended, he is not to be understood as if he meant it, or that it was his will, but that he was ignorant of how such words and actions were to be interpreted.

The mutual transferring of right is that which men call CONTRACT....

...If a covenant be made wherein neither of the parties perform presently, but trust one another, in the condition of mere nature (which is a condition of war of every man against every man) upon any reasonable suspicion, it is void: but if there be a common power set over them both, with right and force sufficient to compel performance, it is not void. For he that performeth first has no assurance the other will perform after, because the bonds of words are too weak to bridle men's ambition, avarice, anger, and other passions, without the fear of some coercive power; which in the condition of mere nature, where all men are equal, and judges of the justness of their own fears, cannot possibly be supposed. And therefore he which performeth first does but betray himself to his enemy, contrary to the right he can never abandon of defending his life and means of living....

...Men are freed of their covenants two ways: by performing, or by being forgiven. For performance is the natural end of obligation, and forgiveness the restitution of liberty, as being a retransferring of that right in which the obligation consisted.

Covenants entered into by fear, in the condition of mere nature, are obligatory. For example, if I covenant to pay a ransom, or service for my life, to an enemy, I am bound by it. For it is a contract, wherein one receiveth the benefit of life; the other is to receive money, or service for

continued

PRIMARY SOURCE 7.5 | OF THE FIRST AND SECOND NATURAL LAWS, AND OF CONTRACTS, FROM *LEVIATHAN*, CHAPTER 15 *continued*

it, and consequently, where no other law (as in the condition of mere nature) forbiddeth the performance, the covenant is valid. Therefore prisoners of war, if trusted with the payment of their ransom, are obliged to pay it: and if a weaker prince make a disadvantageous peace with a stronger, for fear, he is bound to keep it; unless (as hath been said before) there ariseth some new and just cause of fear to renew the war. And even in Commonwealths, if I be forced to redeem myself from a thief by promising him money, I am bound to pay it, till the civil law discharge me. For whatsoever I may lawfully do without obligation, the same I may lawfully covenant to do through fear: and what I lawfully covenant, I cannot lawfully break.

A former covenant makes void a later. For a man that hath passed away his right to one man today hath it not to pass tomorrow to another: and therefore the later promise passeth no right, but is null.

A covenant not to defend myself from force, by force, is always void. For (as I have shown before) no man can transfer or lay down his right to save himself from death, wounds, and imprisonment, the avoiding whereof is the only end of laying down any right; and therefore the promise of not resisting force, in no covenant transferreth any right, nor is obliging. For though a man may covenant thus, *unless I do so, or so, kill me;* he cannot covenant thus, *unless I do so, or so, I will not resist you when you come to kill me.* For man by nature chooseth the lesser evil, which is danger of death in resisting, rather than the greater, which is certain and present death in not resisting. And this is granted to be true by all men, in that they lead criminals to execution, and prison, with armed men, notwithstanding that such criminals have consented to the law by which they are condemned.

A covenant to accuse oneself, without assurance of pardon, is likewise invalid. For in the condition of nature where every man is judge, there is no place for accusation: and in the civil state the accusation is followed with punishment, which, being force, a man is not obliged not to resist. The same is also true of the accusation of those by whose condemnation a man falls into misery; as of a father, wife, or benefactor. For the testimony of such an accuser, if it be not willingly given, is presumed to be corrupted by nature, and therefore not to be received: and where a man's testimony is not to be credited, he is not bound to give it. Also accusations upon torture are not to be reputed as testimonies. For torture is to be used but as means of conjecture, and light, in the further examination and search of truth: and what is in that case confessed tendeth to the ease of him that is tortured, not to the informing of the torturers, and therefore ought not to have the credit of a sufficient testimony: for whether he deliver himself by true or false accusation, he does it by the right of preserving his own life.

The force of words being (as I have formerly noted) too weak to hold men to the performance of their covenants, there are in man's nature but two imaginable helps to strengthen it. And those are either a fear of the consequence of breaking their word, or a glory or pride in appearing not to need to break it. This latter is a generosity too rarely found to be presumed on, especially in the pursuers of wealth, command, or sensual pleasure, which are the greatest part of mankind. The passion to be reckoned upon is fear; whereof there be two very general objects: one, the power of spirits invisible; the other, the power of those men they shall therein offend. Of these two, though the former be the greater power, yet the fear of the latter is commonly the greater fear. The fear of the former is in every man his own religion, which hath place in the nature of man before civil society. The latter hath not so; at least not place enough to keep men to their promises, because in the condition of mere nature, the inequality of power is not discerned, but by the event of battle. . . .

Chapter 15 *Of Other Laws of Nature*

FROM that law of nature by which we are obliged to transfer to another such rights as, being retained, hinder the peace of mankind,

PRIMARY SOURCE 7.5 | **OF THE FIRST AND SECOND NATURAL LAWS, AND OF CONTRACTS, FROM *LEVIATHAN*, CHAPTER 15** *continued*

there followeth a third; which is this: *that men perform their covenants made;* without which covenants are in vain, and but empty words; and the right of all men to all things remaining, we are still in the condition of war.

And in this law of nature consisteth the fountain and original of JUSTICE. For where no covenant hath preceded, there hath no right been transferred, and every man has right to everything and consequently, no action can be *unjust.* But when a covenant is made, then to break it is unjust and the definition of INJUSTICE is no other than *the not performance of covenant.* And whatsoever is not unjust is *just.*

But because covenants of mutual trust, where there is a fear of not performance on either part (as hath been said in the former chapter), are invalid, though the original of justice be the making of covenants, yet injustice actually there can be none till the cause of such fear be taken away; which, while men are in the natural condition of war, cannot be done. Therefore before the names of just and unjust can have place, there must be some coercive power to compel men equally to the performance of their covenants, by the terror of some punishment greater than the benefit they expect by the breach of their covenant, and to make good that propriety which by mutual contract men acquire in recompense of the universal right they abandon: and such power there is none before the erection of a Commonwealth. And this is also to be gathered out of the ordinary definition of justice in the Schools, for they say that *justice is the constant will of giving to every man his own.* And therefore where there is no own, that is, no propriety, there is no injustice; and where there is no coercive power erected, that is, where there is no Commonwealth, there is no propriety, all men having right to all things: therefore where there is no Commonwealth, there nothing is unjust. So that the nature of justice consisteth in keeping of valid covenants, but the validity of covenants begins not but with the constitution of a civil power sufficient to compel men to keep them: and then it is also that propriety begins,...

For the question is not of promises mutual, where there is no security of performance on either side, as when there is no civil power erected over the parties promising; for such promises are no covenants: but either where one of the parties has performed already, or where there is a power to make him perform, there is the question whether it be against reason; that is, against the benefit of the other to perform, or not. And I say it is not against reason. For the manifestation whereof we are to consider; first, that when a man doth a thing, which notwithstanding anything can be foreseen and reckoned on tendeth to his own destruction, howsoever some accident, which he could not expect, arriving may turn it to his benefit; yet such events do not make it reasonably or wisely done. Secondly, that in a condition of war, wherein every man to every man, for want of a common power to keep them all in awe, is an enemy, there is no man can hope by his own strength, or wit, to himself from destruction without the help of confederates; where every one expects the same defense by the confederation that any one else does: and therefore he which declares he thinks it reason to deceive those that help him can in reason expect no other means of safety than what can be had from his own single power. He, therefore, that breaketh his covenant, and consequently declareth that he thinks he may with reason do so, cannot be received into any society that unite themselves for peace and defense but by the error of them that receive him; nor when he is received be retained in it without seeing the danger of their error; which errors a man cannot reasonably reckon upon as the means of his security: and therefore if he be left, or cast out of society, he perisheth; and if he live in society, it is by the errors of other men, which he could not foresee nor reckon upon, and consequently against the reason of his preservation; and so, as all men that contribute not to his destruction forbear him only out of ignorance of what is good for themselves...

And for the other instance of attaining sovereignty by rebellion; it is manifest that, though

continued

PRIMARY SOURCE 7.5

Of the First and Second Natural Laws, and of Contracts, from *Leviathan*, Chapter 15 *continued*

the event follow, yet because it cannot reasonably be expected, but rather the contrary, and because by gaining it so, others are taught to gain the same in like manner, the attempt thereof is against reason. Justice therefore, that is to say, keeping of covenant, is a rule of reason by which we are forbidden to do anything destructive to our life, and consequently a law of nature.

There be some that proceed further and will not have the law of nature to be those rules which conduce to the preservation of man's life on earth, but to the attaining of an eternal felicity after death; to which they think the breach of covenant may conduce, and consequently be just and reasonable; such are they that think it a work of merit to kill, or depose, or rebel against the sovereign power constituted over them by their own consent. But because there is no natural knowledge of man's estate after death, much less of the reward that is then to be given to breach of faith, but only a belief grounded upon other men's saying that they know it supernaturally or that they know those that knew them that knew others that knew it supernaturally, breach of faith cannot be called a precept of reason or nature....

The names of just and unjust when they are attributed to men, signify one thing, and when they are attributed to actions, another. When they are attributed to men, they signify conformity, or inconformity of manners, to reason. But when they are attributed to action they signify the conformity, or inconformity to reason, not of manners, or manner of life, but of particular actions. A just man therefore is he that taketh all the care he can that his actions may be all just; and an unjust man is he that neglecteth it. And such men are more often in our language styled by the names of righteous and unrighteous than just and unjust though the meaning be the same. Therefore a righteous man does not lose that title by one or a few unjust actions that proceed from sudden passion, or mistake of things or persons, nor does an unrighteous man lose his character for such actions as he does, or forbears to do, for fear: because his will is not framed by the justice, but by the apparent benefit of what he is to do. That which gives to human actions the relish of justice is a certain nobleness or gallantness of courage, rarely found, by which a man scorns to be beholding for the contentment of his life to fraud, or breach of promise. This justice of the manners is that which is meant where justice is called a virtue; and injustice, a vice.

But the justice of actions denominates men, not just, but guiltless: and the injustice of the same (which is also called injury) gives them but the name of guilty....

Justice of actions is by writers divided into *commutative* and *distributive:* and the former they say consisteth in proportion arithmetical; the latter in proportion geometrical. Commutative, therefore, they place in the equality of value of the things contracted for; and distributive, in the distribution of equal benefit to men of equal merit. As if it were injustice to sell dearer than we buy, or to give more to a man than he merits. The value of all things contracted for is measured by the appetite of the contractors, and therefore the just value is that which they be contented to give. And merit (besides that which is by covenant, where the performance on one part meriteth the performance of the other part, and falls under justice commutative, not distributive) is not due by justice, but is rewarded of grace only. And therefore this distinction, in the sense wherein it useth to be expounded, is not right. To speak properly, commutative justice is the justice of a contractor; that is, a performance of covenant in buying and selling, hiring and letting to hire, lending and borrowing, exchanging, bartering, and other acts of contract.

And distributive justice, the justice of an arbitrator; that is to say, the act of defining what is just. Wherein, being trusted by them that make him arbitrator, if he perform his trust, he is said to distribute to every man his own: and this is indeed just distribution, and may be called, though improperly, distributive justice, but more properly equity, which also is a law of nature, as shall be shown in due place.

PRIMARY SOURCE 7.5 | OF THE FIRST AND SECOND NATURAL LAWS, AND OF CONTRACTS, FROM *LEVIATHAN*, CHAPTER 15 *continued*

As justice dependeth on antecedent covenant; so does GRATITUDE depend on antecedent grace; that is to say, antecedent free gift; and is the fourth law of nature, which may be conceived in this form: *that a man which receiveth benefit from another of mere grace endeavor that he which giveth it have no reasonable cause to repent him of his good will.* For no man giveth but with intention of good to himself, because gift is voluntary; and of all voluntary acts, the object is to every man his own good; of which if men see they shall be frustrated, there will be no beginning of benevolence or trust, nor consequently of mutual help, nor of reconciliation of one man to another; and therefore they are to remain still in the condition of war, which is contrary to the first and fundamental law of nature which commandeth men to *seek peace.* The breach of this law is called *ingratitude,* and hath the same relation to grace that injustice hath to obligation by covenant.

A fifth law of nature is COMPLAISANCE; that is to say, *that every man strive to accommodate himself to the rest.* For the understanding whereof we may consider that there is in men's aptness to society a diversity of nature, rising from their diversity of affections, not unlike to that we see in stones brought together for building of an edifice. For as that stone which by the asperity and irregularity of figure takes more room from others than itself fills, and for hardness cannot be easily made plain, and thereby hindereth the building, is by the builders cast away as unprofitable and troublesome: so also, a man that by asperity of nature will strive to retain those things which to himself are superfluous, and to others necessary, and for the stubbornness of his passions cannot be corrected, is to be left or cast out of society as cumbersome thereunto. For seeing every man, not only by right, but also by necessity of nature, is supposed to endeavor all he can to obtain that which is necessary for his conservation, he that shall oppose himself against it for things superfluous is guilty of the war that thereupon is to follow, and therefore doth that which is contrary to the fundamental law of nature, which commandeth to *seek peace.* The observers of this law may be called SOCIABLE (the Latins call them *commodi*); the contrary, *stubborn, insociable, forward, intractable.*

A sixth law of nature is this: *that upon caution of the future time, a man ought to pardon the offences past of them that, repenting, desire it.* For PARDON is nothing but granting of peace; which though granted to them that persevere in their hostility, be not peace, but fear; yet not granted to them that give caution of the future time is sign of an aversion to peace, and therefore contrary to the law of nature.

A seventh is: *that in revenges* (that is, retribution of evil for evil), *men look not at the greatness of the evil past, but the greatness of the good to follow.* Whereby we are forbidden to inflict punishment with any other design than for correction of the offender, or direction of others. For this law is consequent to the next before it, that commandeth pardon upon security of the future time. Besides, revenge without respect to the example and profit to come is a triumph, or glorying in the hurt of another, tending to no end (for the end is always somewhat to come); and glorying to no end is vain-glory, and contrary to reason; and to hurt without reason tendeth to the introduction of war, which is against the law of nature, and is commonly styled by the name of *cruelty.*

And because all signs of hatred, or contempt, provoke to fight; insomuch as most men choose rather to hazard their life than not to be revenged, we may in the eighth place, for a law of nature, set down this precept: *that no man by deed, word, countenance, or gesture, declare hatred or contempt of another.* The breach of which law is commonly called *contumely.*

The question who is the better man has no place in the condition of mere nature, where (as has been shown before) all men are equal. The inequality that now is has been introduced by the laws civil. I know that Aristotle in the first book of his *Politics,* for a foundation of his doctrine, maketh men by nature, some more worthy to command, meaning the wiser sort,

continued

PRIMARY SOURCE 7.5 | OF THE FIRST AND SECOND NATURAL LAWS, AND OF CONTRACTS, FROM *LEVIATHAN*, CHAPTER 15 *continued*

such as he thought himself to be for his philosophy; others to serve, meaning those that had strong bodies, but were not philosophers as he; as master and servant were not introduced by consent of men, but by difference of wit: which is not only against reason, but also against experience. For there are very few so foolish that had not rather govern themselves than be governed by others: nor when the wise, in their own conceit, contend by force with them who distrust their own wisdom, do they always, or often, or almost at any time, get the victory. If nature therefore have made men equal, that equality is to be acknowledged: or if nature have made men unequal, yet because men that think themselves equal will not enter into conditions of peace, but upon equal terms, such equality must be admitted. And therefore for the ninth law of nature, I put this: *that every man acknowledge another for his equal by nature.* The breach of this precept is *pride.*

On this law dependeth another: *that at the entrance into conditions of peace, no man require to reserve to himself any right which he is not content should be reserved to every one of the rest.* As it is necessary for all men that seek peace to lay down certain rights of nature; that is to say, not to have liberty to do all they list, so is it necessary for man's life to retain some: as right to govern their own bodies; enjoy air, water, motion, ways to go from place to place; and all things else without which a man cannot live, or not live well. If in this case, at the making of peace, men require for themselves that which they would not have to be granted to others, they do contrary to the precedent law that commandeth the acknowledgement of natural equality, and therefore also against the law of nature. The observers of this law are those we call *modest,* and the breakers *arrogant* men. The Greeks call the violation of this law *pleonexia;* that is, a desire of more than their share.

Also, *if a man be trusted to judge between man and man,* it is a precept of the law of nature that he *deal equally between them.* For without that, the controversies of men cannot be determined but by war. He therefore that is partial in judgment, doth what in him lies to deter men from the use of judges and arbitrators, and consequently, against the fundamental law of nature, is the cause of war.

The observance of this law, from the equal distribution to each man of that which in reason belonged to him, is called EQUITY, and (as I have said before) distributive justice: the violation, *acception of persons, prosopolepsia.*

And from this followeth another law: *that such things as cannot be divided be enjoyed in common, if it can be; and if the quantity of the thing permit, without stint; otherwise proportionably to the number of them that have right.* For otherwise the distribution is unequal, and contrary to equity.

But some things there be that can neither be divided nor enjoyed in common. Then, the law of nature which prescribeth equity requireth: *that the entire right, or else (making the use alternate) the first possession, be determined by lot.* For equal distribution is of the law of nature; and other means of equal distribution cannot be imagined.

Of lots there be two sorts, *arbitrary* and *natural.* Arbitrary is that which is agreed on by the competitors; natural is either *primogeniture* (which the Greek calls *kleronomia,* which signifies, *given by lot*), or *first seizure.*

And therefore those things which cannot be enjoyed in common, nor divided, ought to be adjudged to the first possessor; and in some cases to the first born, as acquired by lot.

It is also a law of nature: *that all men that mediate peace be allowed safe conduct.* For the law that commandeth peace, as the end, commandeth intercession, as the *means;* and to intercession the means is safe conduct.

And because, though men be never so willing to observe these laws, there may nevertheless arise questions concerning a man's action; first, whether it were done, or not done; secondly, if done, whether against the law, or not against the law; the former whereof is called a question *of fact,* the latter a question *of right;* therefore unless the parties to the question covenant mutually to stand to the sentence of

PRIMARY SOURCE 7.5

Of the First and Second Natural Laws, and of Contracts, from *Leviathan*, Chapter 15 *continued*

another, they are as far from peace as ever. This other, to whose sentence they submit, is called an ARBITRATOR. And therefore it is of the law of nature *that they that are at controversy submit their right to the judgment of an arbitrator.*

And seeing every man is presumed to do all things in order to his own benefit, *no man is a fit arbitrator in his own cause:* and if he were never so fit, yet equity allowing to each party equal benefit, if one be admitted to be judge, the other is to be admitted also; and so the controversy, that is, the cause of war, remains, against the law of nature.

For the same reason no man in any cause ought to be received for arbitrator to whom greater profit, or honor, or pleasure apparently ariseth out of the victory of one party than of the other: for he hath taken, though an unavoidable bribe, yet a bribe; and no man can be obliged to trust him. And thus also the controversy and the condition of war remaineth, contrary to the law of nature.

And in a controversy of *fact,* the judge being to give no more credit to one than to the other, if there be no other arguments, must give credit to a third; or to a third and fourth; or more: for else the question is undecided, and left to force, contrary to the law of nature.

These are the laws of nature, dictating peace, for a means of the conservation of men in multitudes; and which only concern the doctrine of civil society. There be other things tending to the destruction of particular men; as drunkenness, and all other parts of intemperance, which may therefore also be reckoned amongst those things which the law of nature hath forbidden, but are not necessary to be mentioned, nor are pertinent enough to this place.

And though this may seem too subtle a deduction of the laws of nature to be taken notice of by all men, whereof the most part are too busy in getting food, and the rest too negligent to understand; yet to leave all men inexcusable, they have been contracted into one easy sum, intelligible even to the meanest capacity; and that is: *Do not that to another which thou wouldest not have done to thyself,* which showeth him that he has no more to do in learning the laws of nature but, when weighing the actions of other men with his own they seem too heavy, to put them into the other part of the balance, and his own into their place, that his own passions and self-love may add nothing to the weight; and then there is none of these laws of nature that will not appear unto him very reasonable. . . .

The laws of nature are immutable and eternal; for injustice, ingratitude, arrogance, pride, iniquity, acception of persons, and the rest can never be made lawful. For it can never be that war shall preserve life, and peace destroy it.

The same laws, because they oblige only to a desire and endeavor, mean an unfeigned and constant endeavor, are easy to be observed. For in that they require nothing but endeavor, he that endeavoreth their performance fulfilleth them; and he that fulfilleth the law is just.

And the science of them is the true and only moral philosophy. For moral philosophy is nothing else but the science of what is *good* and *evil* in the conversation and society of mankind. *Good* and *evil* are names that signify our appetites and aversions, which in different tempers, customs, and doctrines of men are different: and diverse men differ not only in their judgment on the senses of what is pleasant and unpleasant to the taste, smell, hearing, touch, and sight; but also of what is conformable or disagreeable to reason in the actions of common life. Nay, the same man, in diverse times, differs from himself; and one time praiseth, that is, calleth good, what another time he dispraiseth, and calleth evil: from whence arise disputes, controversies, and at last war. And therefore so long as a man is in the condition of mere nature, which is a condition of war, private appetite is the measure of good and evil: and consequently all men agree on this, that peace is good, and therefore also the way or means of peace, which (as I have shown before) are *justice, gratitude, modesty, equity, mercy,* and the rest of the laws of nature, are

continued

PRIMARY SOURCE 7.5

OF THE FIRST AND SECOND NATURAL LAWS, AND OF CONTRACTS, FROM *LEVIATHAN*, CHAPTER 15 *continued*

good; that is to say, *moral virtues;* and their contrary vices, evil.

Now the science of virtue and vice is moral philosophy; and therefore the true doctrine of the laws of nature is the true moral philosophy. But the writers of moral philosophy, though they acknowledge the same virtues and vices; yet, not seeing wherein consisted their goodness, nor that they come to be praised as the means of peaceable, sociable, and comfortable living, place them in a mediocrity of passions: as if not the cause, but the degree of daring, made fortitude; or not the cause, but the quantity of a gift, made liberality.

These dictates of reason men used to call by the name of laws, but improperly: for they are but conclusions or theorems concerning what conduceth to the conservation and defense of themselves; whereas law, properly, is the word of him that by right hath command over others. But yet if we consider the same theorems as delivered in the word of God that by right commandeth all things, then are they properly called laws.

necessary for self-preservation by transferring this right into the hands of the absolute sovereign. Hobbes adds that everyone must acknowledge that they are the authors of this sovereign power and that they have authorized the actions of the sovereign for the sake of peace and their preservation. The absolute sovereign is not representative of the wills of the citizens, but a separate will authorized to secure the natural right of the citizens. Consequently, the absolute sovereign is not subject to or limited by the covenant because it was not party to the covenant—it was the outcome of the covenant. Accordingly, all legislation of the sovereign can be viewed as self-legislation. Further, no citizen can rightfully resist the will of the sovereign or judge the actions of the sovereign because the sovereign has been empowered to accomplish what individuals fought for in the state of nature: peace and security. To accuse the sovereign of any crime or injury, for example, is to accuse oneself of wrongdoing—and by Hobbes' logic, to do injustice to oneself is impossible. Obedience, therefore, is exchanged for protection. The security of the citizenry rests in the comforting knowledge that any man who seeks to harm another has more to fear from the sovereign than he can contemplate benefiting from any crime.

> Thomas Hobbes' approach to law and crime is the precursor to the economic or rational choice approach to crime, which treats crime like any activity in that it has benefits and costs. That is, criminals can be depicted as going through a calculation in the manner of Hobbes' notion of deliberation, weighing the costs and benefits of breaking the law. Rational choice theorists and Hobbes agree that the incidence of crime can be decreased by increasing the costs of breaking the law and by increasing the probability of getting caught. See, for example, Gary S. Becker, "Crime and Punishment: An Economic Approach to Crime," *Journal of Political Economy* 76:2 (1968): 169–217.

The sovereign has the right to wage war and to negotiate peace, to levy taxes, to coin money, to regulate commerce, and to establish property rights. The absolute sovereign must possess the legislative, executive, and judicial powers of government. Hobbes' reasoning is clear: No one will obey the laws, commands, or judgments of someone they have no reason to fear. Hobbes rejects the modern doctrine of separation of powers, today considered the cornerstone of individual liberty, because it limits and hinders the power of government to secure peace and security; divided sovereignty is no remedy to the state of nature. Hobbes' sovereign also possesses the power to censure opinions and doctrines according to whether they are conducive to peace. For the actions of men proceed from their opinions; and to govern men well while securing peace and concord, Hobbes argues that both opinions and actions must be regulated. Although Hobbes admits that the truth of the doctrine ought to be the criteria, he argues that any doctrine that is not conducive to peace cannot be considered true and must be a violation of the laws of nature. Religious liberty is similarly questioned. Hobbes understands religious obedience or piety as he does all forms of obedience,

QUESTIONS FOR REFLECTION

Do Aristotle and Thomas Hobbes agree that the political authority must be architectonic and authoritative? Do they agree on the essential nature of politics?

dependent on fear. This is why he describes religion as the fear of "powers invisible." Understood in this way, religious belief is a competitor to the fear of the sovereign. The Hobbesian solution is to subject religion to political regulation to make it compatible with the ends of government.

Some critics of Hobbes question his political solution by asking, If the government is to be absolutely sovereign, how can individuals be assured of their preservation, if the means to peaceful preservation of property is not secure? Returning to Hobbesian first principles: All men in the state of nature had a right to all things that could secure their preservation, and consequently no man's property was secure. Indeed, the right to all things meant that all men were in a state of war, and private property could not exist. Because men renounced the right to the means to everything by forming the covenant, Hobbes would argue that the right to determine the kinds of property rights individuals can possess and how things are to be exchanged resides with the absolute sovereign. Only under these conditions would property be secure from the transgression of others because the absolute sovereign would not be limited by claims to property rights. Moreover, if the full meaning of what Hobbes means by *felicity* is considered, the role of commerce within Hobbes' schema can be appreciated. The continual success in obtaining those things that satisfy our desire is called *felicity*. Because pleasures, like all motions, are subject to the principle of inertia, the feeling of felicity is temporary. Hence men have a concern to acquire power after power over things that ensure their survival. On the one hand, felicity can be associated with warlike acquisition; but on the other, it could be compatible with the peaceful acquisition of commerce. Hobbes' sovereign would be determined to ensure that commerce remain free enough to channel the passions of men toward peace. While the sovereign may have a comprehensive power to regulate commerce and property, it may not be conducive to peace if he is too heavy-handed in his regulation. In other words, property rights would be secure under Hobbes' absolute sovereign because the peace of the commonwealth demands it, but property rights cannot be considered absolute because this would limit and undermine the sovereign's authority.

Some critics of Hobbes question whether there can be any **liberty** under an absolute government. Hobbes understands *liberty* as the absence of external impediments of motion, which can be applied to both rational and irrational creatures and inanimate objects. Liberty so understood is a freedom from, rather than a freedom for the sake of, something such as virtue. Liberty can be applied only to bodies because what is not subject to motion is not subject to impediment. So a man is said to be free if he finds nothing to stop him from doing what he has a will, desire, or inclination to do. Hobbes also argues that liberty and fear are consistent. For example, if a man obeys the laws out of fear, he is still free because he has the liberty to disobey the law.

Civil laws can thus be viewed as artificial chains that by their nature are weak and hold only while men fear breaking them. The other source of liberty then depends on the silence of the laws. What the law does not forbid, individuals are permitted to

PRIMARY SOURCE 7.6 | OF THE CAUSES, GENERATION, AND DEFINITION OF A COMMONWEALTH, FROM *LEVIATHAN*, CHAPTER 17–18

THE final cause, end, or design of men (who naturally love liberty, and dominion over others) in the introduction of that restraint upon themselves, in which we see them live in Commonwealths, is the foresight of their own preservation, and of a more contented life thereby; that is to say, of getting themselves out from that miserable condition of war which is necessarily consequent, as hath been shown, to the natural passions of men when there is no visible power to keep them in awe, and tie them by fear of punishment to the performance of their covenants, and observation of those laws of nature set down in the fourteenth and fifteenth chapters.

For the laws of nature, as *justice, equity, modesty, mercy,* and, in sum, *doing to others as we would be done to,* of themselves, without the terror of some power to cause them to be observed, are contrary to our natural passions, that carry us to partiality, pride, revenge, and the like. And covenants, without the sword, are but words and of no strength to secure a man at all. Therefore, notwithstanding the laws of nature (which every one hath then kept, when he has the will to keep them, when he can do it safely), if there be no power erected, or not great enough for our security, every man will and may lawfully rely on his own strength and art for caution against all other men. . . .

The only way to erect such a common power, as may be able to defend them from the invasion of foreigners, and the injuries of one another, and thereby to secure them in such sort as that by their own industry and by the fruits of the earth they may nourish themselves and live contentedly, is to confer all their power and strength upon one man, or upon one assembly of men, that may reduce all their wills, by plurality of voices, unto one will: which is as much as to say, to appoint one man, or assembly of men, to bear their person; and every one to own and acknowledge himself to be author of whatsoever he that so beareth their person shall act, or cause to be acted, in those things which concern the common peace and safety; and therein to submit their wills, every one to his will, and their judgments to his judgment. This is more than consent, or concord; it is a real unity of them all in one and the same person, made by covenant of every man with every man, in such manner as if every man should say to every man: *I authorize and give up my right of governing myself to this man, or to this assembly of men, on this condition; that thou give up, thy right to him, and authorize all his actions in like manner.* This done, the multitude so united in one person is called a COMMONWEALTH; in Latin, CIVITAS. This is the generation of that great LEVIATHAN, or rather, to speak more reverently, of that *mortal God* to which we owe, under the *immortal God,* our peace and defense. For by this authority, given him by every particular man in the Commonwealth, he hath the use of so much power and strength conferred on him that, by terror thereof, he is enabled to form the wills of them all, to peace at home, and mutual aid against their enemies abroad. And in him consisteth the essence of the Commonwealth; which, to define it, is: *one person, of whose acts a great multitude, by mutual covenants one with another, have made themselves every one the author, to the end he may use the strength and means of them all as he shall think expedient for their peace and common defense.*

And he that carryeth this person is called SOVEREIGN, and said to have *Sovereign Power;* and every one besides, his SUBJECT.

The attaining to this sovereign power is by two ways. One, by natural force: as when a man maketh his children to submit themselves, and their children, to his government, as being able to destroy them if they refuse; or by war subdueth his enemies to his will, giving them their lives on that condition. The other, is when men agree amongst themselves to submit to some man, or assembly of men, voluntarily, on confidence to be protected by him against all others. This latter may be called a political Commonwealth, or Commonwealth by *Institution;* and the former, a Commonwealth by *acquisition.* And first, I shall speak of a Commonwealth by institution.

PRIMARY SOURCE 7.6

Of the Causes, Generation, and Definition of a Commonwealth, from *Leviathan,* Chapter 17–18

continued

Chapter 18 Of the Rights of Sovereigns by Institution

A COMMONWEALTH is said to be *instituted* when a multitude of men do agree, and *covenant, every one with every one,* that to whatsoever *man,* or *assembly of men,* shall be given by the major part the *right* to *present* the person of them all, that is to say, to be their representative; every one, as well he that voted for it as he that voted against it, shall authorize all the actions and judgments of that man, or assembly of men, in the same manner as if they were his own, to the end to live peaceably amongst themselves, and be protected against other men.

From this institution of a Commonwealth are derived all the rights and faculties of him, or them, on whom the sovereign power is conferred by the consent of the people assembled.

First, because they covenant, it is to be understood they are not obliged by former covenant to anything repugnant hereunto. And consequently they that have already instituted a Commonwealth, being thereby bound by covenant to own the actions and judgments of one, cannot lawfully make a new covenant amongst themselves to be obedient to any other, in anything whatsoever, without his permission. And therefore, they that are subjects to a monarch cannot without his leave cast off monarchy and return to the confusion of a disunited multitude; nor transfer their person from him that beareth it to another man, other assembly of men: for they are bound, every man to every man, to own and be reputed author of all that already is their sovereign shall do and judge fit to be done; so that any one man dissenting, all the rest should break their covenant made to that man, which is injustice: and they have also every man given the sovereignty to him that beareth their person; and therefore if they depose him, they take from him that which is his own, and so again it is injustice. Besides, if he that attempteth to depose his sovereign be killed or punished by him for such attempt, he is author of his own punishment, as being, by the institution, author of all his sovereign shall do; and because it is injustice for a man to do anything for which he may be punished by his own authority, he is also upon that title unjust....

Secondly, because the right of bearing the person of them all is given to him they make sovereign, by covenant only of one to another, and not of him to any of them, there can happen no breach of covenant on the part of the sovereign; and consequently none of his subjects, by any pretense of forfeiture, can be freed from his subjection. That he which is made sovereign maketh no covenant with his subjects before hand is manifest; because either he must make it with the whole multitude, as one party to the covenant, or he must make a several covenant with every man. With the whole, as one party, it is impossible, because as they are not one person: and if he make so many several covenants as there be men, those covenants after he hath the sovereignty are void; because what act soever can be pretended by any one of them for breach thereof is the act both of himself, and of all the rest, because done in the person, and by the right of every one of them in particular. Besides, if any one or more of them pretend a breach of the covenant made by the sovereign at his institution, and others or one other of his subjects, or himself alone, pretend there was no such breach, there is in this case no judge to decide the controversy: it returns therefore to the sword again; and every man recovereth the right of protecting himself by his own strength, contrary to the design they had in the institution....

Thirdly, because the major part hath by consenting voices declared a sovereign, he that dissented must now consent with the rest; that is, be contented to avow all the actions he shall do, or else justly be destroyed by the rest. For if he voluntarily entered into the congregation of them that were assembled, he sufficiently declared thereby his will, and therefore tacitly covenanted, to stand to what the major part should ordain: and therefore if he refuse to stand thereto, or make protestation against any

continued

PRIMARY SOURCE 7.6

Of the Causes, Generation, and Definition of a Commonwealth, from *Leviathan*, Chapter 17–18

continued

of their decrees, he does contrary to his covenant, and therefore unjustly. And whether he be of the congregation or not, and whether his consent be asked or not, he must either submit to their decrees or be left in the condition of war he was in before; wherein he might without injustice be destroyed by any man whatsoever.

Fourthly, because every subject is by this institution author of all the actions and judgments of the sovereign instituted, it follows that whatsoever he doth, can be no injury to any of his subjects; nor ought he to be by any of them accused of injustice. For he that doth anything by authority from another doth therein no injury to him by whose authority he acteth: but by this institution of a Commonwealth every particular man is author of all the sovereign doth; and consequently he that complaineth of injury from his sovereign complaineth of that whereof he himself is author, and therefore ought not to accuse any man but himself; no, nor himself of injury, because to do injury to oneself is impossible. It is true that they that have sovereign power may commit iniquity, but not injustice or injury in the proper signification.

Fifthly, and consequently to that which was said last, no man that hath sovereign power can justly be put to death, or otherwise in any manner by his subjects punished. For seeing every subject is author of the actions of his sovereign, he punisheth another for the actions committed by himself.

And because the end of this institution is the peace and defense of them all, and whosoever has right to the end has right to the means, it belonged of right to whatsoever man or assembly that hath the sovereignty to be judge both of the means of peace and defense, and also of the hindrances and disturbances of the same; and to do whatsoever he shall think necessary to be done, both beforehand, for the preserving of peace and security, by prevention of discord at home, and hostility from abroad; and when peace and security are lost, for the recovery of the same. And therefore, . . .

Sixthly, it is annexed to the sovereignty to be judge of what opinions and doctrines are averse, and what conducing to peace; and consequently, on what occasions, how far, and what men are to be trusted withal in speaking to multitudes of people; and who shall examine the doctrines of all books before they be published. For the actions of men proceed from their opinions, and in the well governing of opinions consisteth the well governing of men's actions in order to their peace and concord. And though in matter of doctrine nothing to be regarded but the truth, yet this is not repugnant to regulating of the same by peace. For doctrine repugnant to peace can no more be true, than peace and concord can be against the law of nature. It is true that in a Commonwealth, where by the negligence or unskillfulness of governors and teachers false doctrines are by time generally received, the contrary truths may be generally offensive: yet the most sudden and rough bustling in of a new truth that can be does never break the peace, but only sometimes awake the war. For those men that are so remissly governed that they dare take up arms to defend or introduce an opinion are still in war; and their condition, not peace, but only a cessation of arms for fear of one another; and they live, as it were, in the procincts of battle continually. It belonged therefore to him that hath the sovereign power to be judge, or constitute all judges of opinions and doctrines, as a thing necessary to peace; thereby to prevent discord and civil war.

Seventhly, is annexed to the sovereignty the whole power of prescribing the rules whereby every man may know what goods he may enjoy, and what actions he may do, without being molested by any of his fellow subjects: and this is it men call propriety. For before constitution of sovereign power, as hath already been shown, all men had right to all things, which necessarily causeth war: and therefore this propriety, being necessary to peace, and depending on sovereign power, is the act of that power, in order to the public peace. These rules of propriety (or *meum* and *tuum*) and of good,

PRIMARY SOURCE 7.6

Of the Causes, Generation, and Definition of a Commonwealth, from *Leviathan*, Chapter 17–18

continued

evil, lawful, and unlawful in the actions of subjects are the civil laws; that is to say, the laws of each Commonwealth in particular. . . .

Eighthly, is annexed to the sovereignty the right of judicature; that is to say, of hearing and deciding all controversies which may arise concerning law, either civil or natural, or concerning fact. For without the decision of controversies, there is no protection of one subject against the injuries of another; the laws concerning *meum* and *tuum* are in vain, and to every man remaineth, from the natural and necessary appetite of his own conservation, the right of protecting himself by his private strength, which is the condition of war, and contrary to the end for which every Commonwealth is instituted.

Ninthly, is annexed to the sovereignty the right of making war and peace with other nations and Commonwealths; that is to say, of judging when it is for the public good, and how great forces are to be assembled, armed, and paid for that end, and to levy money upon the subjects to defray the expenses thereof. For the power by which the people are to be defended consisteth in their armies, and the strength of an army in the union of their strength under one command; which command the sovereign instituted, therefore hath, because the command of the militia, without other institution, maketh him that hath it sovereign. And therefore, whosoever is made general of an army, he that hath the sovereign power is always generalissimo.

Tenthly, is annexed to the sovereignty the choosing of all counselors, ministers, magistrates, and officers, both in peace and war. For seeing the sovereign is charged with the end, which is the common peace and defense, he is understood to have power to use such means as he shall think most fit for his discharge.

Eleventhly, to the sovereign is committed the power of rewarding with riches or honor; and of punishing with corporal or pecuniary punishment, or with ignominy, every subject according to the law he hath formerly made; or if there be no law made, according as he shall judge most to conduce to the encouraging of men to serve the Commonwealth, or deterring of them from doing disservice to the same.

Lastly, considering what values men are naturally apt to set upon themselves, what respect they look for from others, and how little they value other men; from whence continually arise amongst them, emulation, quarrels, factions, and at last war, to the destroying of one another, and diminution of their strength against a common enemy; it is necessary that there be laws of honor, and a public rate of the worth of such men as have deserved or are able to deserve well of the Commonwealth, and that there be force in the hands of some or other to put those laws in execution. . . . To the sovereign therefore it belonged also to give titles of honor, and to appoint what order of place and dignity each man shall hold, and what signs of respect in public or private meetings they shall give to one another.

These are the rights which make the essence of sovereignty, and which are the marks whereby a man may discern in what man, or assembly of men, the sovereign power is placed and resideth. For these are incommunicable and inseparable. The power to coin money, to dispose of the estate and persons of infant heirs, to have preemption in markets, and all other statute prerogatives may be transferred by the sovereign, and yet the power to protect his subjects be retained. But if he transfer the militia, he retains the judicature in vain, for want of execution of the laws; or if he grant away the power of raising money, the militia is in vain; or if he give away the government of doctrines, men will be frighted into rebellion with the fear of spirits. And so if we consider any one of the said rights, we shall presently see that the holding of all the rest will produce no effect in the conservation of peace and justice, the end for which all Commonwealths are instituted. And this division is it whereof it is said, a kingdom divided in itself cannot stand: for unless this division precede, division into

continued

PRIMARY SOURCE 7.6

Of the Causes, Generation, and Definition of a Commonwealth, from *Leviathan*, Chapter 17–18

continued

opposite armies can never happen. If there had not first been an opinion received of the greatest part of England that these powers were divided between the King and the Lords and the House of Commons, the people had never been divided and fallen into this Civil War; first between those that disagreed in politics, and after between the dissenters about the liberty of religion, which have so instructed men in this point of sovereign right that there be few now in England that do not see that these rights are inseparable, and will be so generally acknowledged at the next return of peace; and so continue, till their miseries are forgotten, and no longer, except the vulgar be better taught than they have hitherto been. . . .

But a man may here object that the condition of subjects is very miserable, as being obnoxious to the lusts and other irregular passions of him or them that have so unlimited a power in their hands. And commonly they that live under a monarch think it the fault of monarchy; and they that live under the government of democracy, or other sovereign assembly, attribute all the inconvenience to that form of Commonwealth; whereas the power in all forms, if they be perfect enough to protect them, is the same: not considering that the estate of man can never be without some incommodity or other; and that the greatest that in any form of government can possibly happen to the people in general is scarce sensible, in respect of the miseries and horrible calamities that accompany a civil war, or that dissolute condition of masterless men without subjection to laws and a coercive power to tie their hands from rapine and revenge: nor considering that the greatest pressure of sovereign governors proceedeth, not from any delight or profit they can expect in the damage weakening of their subjects, in whose vigor consisteth their own strength and glory, but in the restiveness of themselves that, unwillingly contributing to their own defense, make it necessary for their governors to draw from them what they can in time of peace that they may have means on any emergent occasion, or sudden need, to resist or take advantage on their enemies. For all men are by nature provided of notable multiplying glasses (that is their passions and self-love) through which every little payment appeareth a great grievance, but are destitute of those prospective glasses (namely moral and civil science) to see afar off the miseries that hang over them and cannot without such payments be avoided.

---

pursue. Hobbes provides several examples to illustrate this point: Because the laws cannot cover every human endeavor, individuals are left free to buy and sell those things that can be lawfully bought and sold; contract with others; choose where they live, their own diet, and their own trade; and bring up their children as they see fit. Hobbes would say that far from eliminating liberty, he is more permissive than the ancient political philosophers. Within the confines of the commonwealth the individual is largely left free to do as he pleases. But he is not free to disturb and disrupt the concord of society. If we consider what Hobbes' account implies for the meaning of the political, we find that what the government does is establish the conditions that make it safe to obey the law and fulfill contracts. This is achieved through the use of laws that act as hedges keeping men within the bounds of "peaceful motion."

Still we may raise the issue of whether subjects retain any rights under Hobbes' absolute sovereign. That is, does the subject have inalienable rights—rights that cannot be transferred by the covenant? The covenant of course was established to secure individuals' natural right to self-preservation; so the covenant cannot be incompatible

QUESTIONS FOR REFLECTION

Can the commonwealth grounded in Hobbesian principles establish any obligation on behalf of its citizens? Does Hobbes' understanding of natural rights imply civic duty?

with this natural right—self-preservation and the means to securing our lives. The right to self-preservation is inalienable, although the means to securing it are limited by the confines established by the government. Hobbes would recognize in addition that the individual is bound to defend his own life, and that he is not bound to kill himself at the demand of the sovereign, or incriminate himself, or even go peacefully to the gallows. Consistently, the individual is not bound to die for his country and may in fact flee the battlefield. While this is cowardly, Hobbes admits, it is not unjust. But he suggests that the way to secure obedience on the battlefield is to ensure that the fear of disobeying the sovereign exceeds the fear of the battlefield.

Two further problems with Hobbes' argument seem to arise. If there are inalienable rights, is there not some standard by which we can judge the conduct of the sovereign or the government? Could we say that there is a right to revolution or even grounds for civil disobedience? Hobbes denies that any such rights exist: They would plunge the country into civil war and return it to the state of nature. Hobbes argues that an oppressive government is preferable to the state of nature. Recall also that the covenant does not apply to the sovereign; that is, while the government is to secure peace and security, it is not party to the covenant that put it into place. As we have said, the government is also the source of what is lawful and what is just, and as such the citizens cannot judge the actions of the government. But more than that—if we return to Hobbes' account of deliberation, which is little more than a calculus of pleasure and pain, the distinction between good and evil is transformed accordingly; that is, Hobbesian natural philosophy rules out the possibility of making these moral distinctions. When subjects complain about their government and when they accuse the sovereign of being a tyrant, Hobbes accuses them of merely saying that the government does not satisfy their personal preferences. Hobbes rejects, therefore, Aristotle's distinction between good and bad regimes according to whether rulers rule for the common good or for their own selfish ends. These distinctions are false because they merely reflect the subjective preferences of individual subjects. To call a monarch a tyrant, an aristocrat, an oligarch, a democrat, or an anarchist is meaningless for Hobbes. Because all subjects, including the sovereign, benefit from the peace and security of the government, these distinctions lose their meaning, reflecting merely the subjective feelings of the disgruntled and disaffected. The distinctions collapse therefore into monarchy, aristocracy, and democracy.

CONCLUDING THOUGHTS

Hobbes' teaching concerning natural right culminates in his doctrine of the absolute sovereign, who is authorized to use any means available to secure peace and the safety of his subjects. Unfortunately, if the sovereign is too oppressive or too weak, civil war will likely erupt, putting his life at risk. Presumably the fear of violent death will

QUESTIONS FOR REFLECTION

What prevents Hobbes' absolute sovereign from abusing absolute power? Is the fear of violent death to be relied upon? Does this not suggest that implicit in Hobbes' teaching there is a right to revolution? Could the nature of political life point beyond itself to universal standards by which citizens can judge the laws, policies, and conduct of their governments?

motivate the sovereign to refrain from abusing his power, but poor judgment is harder to avoid.

The general thrust of Hobbes' *Leviathan* understates the problem. His teaching on the laws of nature suggests that making, maintaining, and governing a Commonwealth consists in following certain rules, just as we do in arithmetic and geometry—and not, to use Hobbes' example, as we do in tennis, where success depends on practice and experience. But Hobbes declares that he was the first to discover the true principles of politics. It seems there is no necessity in political life that makes these rules manifest. However, Hobbes also writes that oppression proceeds from "the unskilfullness of the governors, ignorant of the true rules of politics." He additionally acknowledges that the sovereign may from time to time require the counsel of experts. Yet Hobbes suggests that there are certain rules of politics, similar to those of mechanics, civil engineering, and geometry, that are better than experience if one knows them. Unfortunately, he notes, where there are no rules, the one with the most experience is the best judge and therefore is the best counselor. Hobbes concedes further that he who looks to those who know best acts properly in the manner as he who "uses able seconds at tennis play, placed in the proper stations." Governing a commonwealth looks more like playing tennis than geometry because it requires judgment and experience. The surprising implication is that the laws of nature, which are rational precepts, are not sufficient guides for the sovereign but must serve as general guidelines for his judgment, rather than absolute and infallible rules. In other words, the laws of nature do not necessarily bind the sovereign, who may have to rely on his judgment or the counsel of others rather than obeying rational precepts. Hobbes acknowledges this in drawing the distinction between prudence and science by observing that a man gifted with a natural dexterity in handling arms will more than likely lose to one who augments his dexterity with the science of the use of arms. The sovereign's judgment must be supplemented with Hobbes' principles of politics.[36]

We may wonder, given the power of the passions described by Hobbes, whether any sovereign, individual, or assembly can judge well or distinguish the prudent course of action from momentary passion. We may wonder whether Hobbes has discovered the final answer to these political questions. We may also wonder whether Hobbesian political science is exposed to the same difficulty that allowed Socrates to silence Thrasymachus in the *Republic*.[37]

---

[36]*Leviathan,* pp. 26, 126, 135, 170, 171–172. Cf. Harvey C. Mansfield, Jr., *Taming of the Prince: The Ambivalence of Modern Executive Power* (New York: Free Press, 1989), pp. 176–178.

[37]See Larry Arnhart, *Political Questions: Political Philosophy from Plato to Rawls* (Long Grove, IL: Waveland Press, Inc., 2003), pp. 164, 172–173.

PRIMARY SOURCE 7.7

Of the Liberty of Subjects, from *Leviathan*, Chapter 21

LIBERTY, or FREEDOM, signifieth properly the absence of opposition (by opposition, I mean external impediments of motion); and may be applied no less to irrational and inanimate creatures than to rational. For whatsoever is so tied, or environed, as it cannot move but within a certain space, which space is determined by the opposition of some external body, we say it hath not liberty to go further. And so of all living creatures, whilst they are imprisoned, or restrained with walls or chains; and of the water whilst it is kept in by banks or vessels that otherwise would spread itself into a larger space; we use to say they are not at liberty to move in such manner as without those external impediments they would. But when the impediment of motion is in the constitution of the thing itself, we use not to say it wants the liberty, but the power, to move; as when a stone lieth still, or a man is fastened to his bed by sickness.

And according to this proper and generally received meaning of the word, a FREE-MAN is *he that, in those things which by his strength and wit he is able to do, is not hindered to do what he has a will to.* But when the words *free* and *liberty* are applied to anything but bodies, they are abused; for that which is not subject to motion is not to subject to impediment: and therefore, when it is said, for example, the way is free, no liberty of the way is signified, but of those that walk in it without stop. And when we say a gift is free, there is not meant any liberty of the gift, but of the giver, that was not bound by any law or covenant to give it. So when we *speak freely,* it is not the liberty of voice, or pronunciation, but of the man, whom no law hath obliged to speak otherwise than he did. Lastly, from the use of the words *free will,* no liberty can be inferred of the will, desire, or inclination, but the liberty of the man; which consisteth in this, that he finds no stop in doing what he has the will, desire, or inclination to do.

Fear and liberty are consistent: as when a man throweth his goods into the sea for *fear* the ship should sink, he doth it nevertheless very willingly, and may refuse to do it if he will; it is therefore the action of one that was *free:* so a man sometimes pays his debt, only for fear of imprisonment, which, because no body hindered him from detaining, was the action of a man at *liberty.* And generally all actions which men do in Commonwealths, for fear of the law, are actions which the doers had *liberty* to omit.

Liberty and *necessity* are consistent: as in the water that hath not only *liberty,* but a *necessity* of descending by the channel; so, likewise in the actions which men voluntarily do, which, because they proceed their will, proceed from *liberty,* and yet because every act of man's will and every desire and inclination proceedeth from some cause, and that from another cause, in a continual chain (whose first link is in the hand of God, the first of all causes), proceed from *necessity.* So that to him that could see the connection of those causes, the necessity of all men's voluntary actions would appear manifest. And therefore God, that seeth and disposeth all things, seeth also that the *liberty* of man in doing what he will is accompanied with the *necessity* of doing that which God will and no more, nor less. For though men may do many things which God does not command, nor is therefore author of them; yet they can have no passion, nor appetite to anything, of which appetite God's will is not the cause. And did not His will assure the *necessity* of man's will, and consequently of all that on man's will dependeth, the *liberty* of men would be a contradiction and impediment to the omnipotence and *liberty* of God. And this shall suffice, as to the matter in hand, of that natural *liberty,* which only is properly called *liberty.*

But as men, for the attaining of peace and conservation of themselves thereby, have made an artificial man, which we call a Commonwealth; so also have they made artificial chains, called *civil laws,* which they themselves, by mutual covenants, have fastened at one end to the

continued

PRIMARY SOURCE 7.7 | OF THE LIBERTY OF SUBJECTS, FROM *LEVIATHAN*, CHAPTER 21 *continued*

lips of that man, or assembly, to whom they have given the sovereign power, and at the other to their own ears. These bonds, in their own nature but weak, may nevertheless be made to hold, by the danger, though not by the difficulty of breaking them.

In relation to these bonds only it is that I am to speak now of the liberty of subjects. For seeing there is no Commonwealth in the world wherein there be rules enough set down for the regulating of all the actions and words of men (as being a thing impossible): it followeth necessarily that in all kinds of actions, by the laws pretermitted, men have the liberty of doing what their own reasons shall suggest for the most profitable to themselves. For if we take liberty in the proper sense, for corporal liberty; that is to say, freedom from chains and prison, it were very absurd for men to clamor as they do for the liberty they so manifestly enjoy. Again, if we take liberty for an exemption from laws, it is no less absurd for men to demand as they do that liberty by which all other men may be masters of their lives. And yet as absurd as it is, this is it they demand, not knowing that the laws are of no power to protect them without a sword in the hands of a man, or men, to cause those laws to be put in execution. The liberty of a subject lieth therefore only in those things which, in regulating their actions, the sovereign hath pretermitted: such as is the liberty to buy, and sell, and otherwise contract with one another; to choose their own abode, their own diet, their own trade of life, and institute their children as they themselves think fit; and the like.

Nevertheless we are not to understand that by such liberty the sovereign power of life and death is either abolished or limited. For it has been already shown that nothing the sovereign representative can do to a subject, on what pretense soever, can properly be called injustice or injury; because every subject is author of every act the sovereign doth, so that he never wanteth right to any thing, otherwise than as he himself is the subject of God, and bound thereby to observe the laws of nature. And therefore it may and doth often happen in Commonwealths that a subject may be put to death by the command of the sovereign power, and yet neither do the other wrong. . . .

To come now to the particulars of the true liberty of a subject; that is to say, what are the things which, though commanded by the sovereign, he may nevertheless without injustice refuse to do; we are to consider what rights we pass away when we make a Commonwealth; or, which is all one, what liberty we deny ourselves by owning all the actions, without exception, of the man or assembly we make our sovereign. For in the act of our *submission* consisteth both our *obligation* and our *liberty;* which must therefore be inferred by arguments taken from thence; there being no obligation on any man which ariseth not from some act of his own; for all men equally are by nature free. And because such arguments must either be drawn from the express words, *I authorize all his actions,* or from the intention of him that submitteth himself to his power (which intention is to be understood by the end for which he so submitteth), the obligation and liberty of the subject is to be derived either from those words, or others equivalent, or else from the end of the institution of sovereignty; namely, the peace of the subjects within themselves, and their defense against a common enemy.

First therefore, seeing sovereignty by institution is by covenant of every one to every one; and sovereignty by acquisition, by covenants of the vanquished to the victor, or child to the parent; it is manifest that every subject has liberty in all those things the right whereof cannot by covenant be transferred. I have shown before, in the fourteenth chapter, that covenants not to defend a man's own body are void. Therefore,

If the sovereign command a man, though justly condemned, to kill, wound, or maim himself; or not to resist those that assault him; or to abstain from the use of food, air, medicine, or any other thing without which he cannot live; yet hath that man the liberty to disobey.

PRIMARY SOURCE 7.7 | OF THE LIBERTY OF SUBJECTS, FROM *LEVIATHAN*, CHAPTER 21 *continued*

If a man be interrogated by the sovereign, or his authority, concerning a crime done by himself, he is not bound (without assurance of pardon) to confess it; because no man, as I have shown in the same chapter, can be obliged by covenant to accuse himself.

Again, the consent of a subject to sovereign power is contained in these words, *I authorize, or take upon me, all his actions;* in which there is no restriction at all of his own former natural liberty: for by allowing him to kill me, I am not bound to kill myself when he commands me. It is one thing to say, *Kill me, or my fellow, if you please;* another thing to say, *I will kill myself, or my fellow.* It followeth, therefore, that

No man is bound by the words themselves, either to kill himself or any other man; and consequently, that the obligation a man may sometimes have, upon the command of the sovereign, to execute any dangerous or dishonorable office, dependeth not on the words of our submission, but on the intention; which is to be understood by the end thereof. When therefore our refusal to obey frustrates the end for which the sovereignty was ordained, then there is no liberty to refuse; otherwise, there is.

Upon this ground a man that is commanded as a soldier to fight against the enemy, though his sovereign have right enough to punish his refusal with death, may nevertheless in many cases refuse, without injustice; as when he substituteth a sufficient soldier in his place: for in this case he deserteth not the service of the Commonwealth. And there is allowance to be made for natural timorousness, not only to women (of whom no such dangerous duty is expected), but also to men of feminine courage. When armies fight, there is on one side, or both, a running away; yet when they do it not out of treachery, but fear, they are not esteemed to do it unjustly, but dishonorably. For the same reason, to avoid battle is not injustice, but cowardice. But he that enrolleth himself a soldier, or taketh impressed money, taketh away the excuse of a timorous nature, and is obliged, not only to go to the battle, but also not to run from it without his captain's leave. And when the defense of the Commonwealth requireth at once the help of all that are able to bear arms, every one is obliged; because otherwise the institution of the Commonwealth, which they have not the purpose or courage to preserve, was in vain.

To resist the sword of the Commonwealth in defense of another man, guilty or innocent, no man hath liberty; because such liberty takes away from the sovereign the means of protecting us, and is therefore destructive of the very essence of government. But in case a great many men together have already resisted the sovereign power unjustly, or committed some capital crime for which every one of them expecteth death, whether have they not the liberty then to join together, and assist, and defend one another? Certainly they have: for they but defend their lives, which the guilty man may as well do as the innocent. There was indeed injustice in the first breach of their duty: their bearing of arms subsequent to it, though it be to maintain what they have done, is no new unjust act. And if it be only to defend their persons, it is not unjust at all. But the offer of pardon taketh from them to whom it is offered the plea of self-defense, and maketh their perseverance in assisting or defending the rest unlawful.

As for other liberties, they depend on the silence of the law. In cases where the sovereign has prescribed no rule, there the subject hath the liberty to do, or forbear, according to his own discretion. And therefore such liberty is in some places more, and in some less; and in some times more, in other times less, according as they that have the sovereignty shall think most convenient. As for example, there was a time when in *England* a man might enter into his own land, and dispossess such as wrongfully possessed it, by force. But in after times that liberty of forcible entry was taken away by a statute made by the king in Parliament. And in some places of the world men have the liberty of many wives: in other places, such liberty is not allowed. . . .

CASE STUDY 7.1 | HOBBES AND THE MODERN LIBERAL STATE

Is Hobbes relevant for understanding the practice of the modern liberal state? Let us consider for a moment property and property rights. *Federalist* 10 suggests that "the most common and durable source of factions has been the various and unequal distribution of property." Publius goes so far as to say that "[t]he regulation of these various and interfering interests forms the principal task of modern legislation and involves the spirit of partisanship and faction in the necessary and ordinary operations of government." Congress under the Constitution of 1787 has the power "to regulate Commerce with foreign nations, and among the several States, and with the Indian tribes." Simply reading the commerce clause points to the general power Publius spoke of in *Federalist* 10. Today, however, we read the clause as though *among* means *between* the states. We assume that there is a strict constitutional distinction between interstate and intrastate commerce. It seems we have adopted a Lockean notion that with respect to property and commerce, the government ought to adopt the principles of laissez-faire. Does the government have to be as powerful as Hobbes conceives it to ensure that property does not become a source of faction?

More recently, in *Kelo v. London* (2004), a bitterly divided U.S. Supreme Court upheld the constitutionality of local and state governments taking private property via the power of eminent domain for economic development projects. Would Hobbes agree that the distribution of private property and the determination of private property rights belong to the sovereign power? Would Hobbes' sovereign recognize that there may exist limits to the regulation of property?

CASE STUDY 7.2 | HOBBES AND INTERNATIONAL RELATIONS

Hobbesian political thought is sometimes taken to be an example of the realistic approach to international relations. Hobbes argues that, internationally, countries stand opposed to each other in a state of nature, where every country is striving for its own survival. To survive, the sovereign must be concerned with keeping the country strong and in a state of concord. Because nothing is unjust in the state of nature, Hobbes concludes that no principles rule and measure international politics. Do you agree? How does Thomas Aquinas differ on this issue? Is there any ground for agreement between Hobbes and Aquinas on war and the conduct of foreign relations?

Consider also the "War on Terror." In response to the terrorist attacks of September 11, 2001, the Bush administration reformulated U.S. foreign policy to include the option of preemptive strikes. In his graduation speech at West Point on June 1, 2002, President Bush argued that the United States faces a threat without precedent, "where our enemies no longer need great armies or great industrial capabilities to harm the American people." He noted that the chaos and suffering of September 11 were purchased for much less than the cost of a single tank. "The gravest danger to freedom lies at the perilous crossroads of radicalism and technology." Even weak states and small groups, he noted, can purchase biological nuclear weapons "to strike great nations." The president concluded, "New threats require new thinking." The Cold War strategies of "deterrence—the promise of massive retaliation against nations—mean nothing against shadowy terrorist networks with no nation or citizens to defend." Moreover, "containment is not possible when unbalanced dictators with weapons of mass destruction can deliver those weapons on missiles or secretly provide them to terrorist allies." It is for these reasons that the United States must go on the offensive and "disrupt the plans of the enemy and confront the worst threats before they emerge."[38]

Would Hobbes agree with this reasoning? Does Hobbes believe that the sovereign retains the right to preemptively strike enemies of the commonwealth?

Consider also the anti-Hobbesian argument of *Federalist* 8, wherein Publius argues that while "safety from external danger is the most powerful director of national conduct," eventually "even the ardent love of liberty will, after a time, give way to its dictates" and adopt policies and institutions "which have a tendency to destroy their civil and political rights." Is Publius correct in his reasoning? How would Hobbes respond?

---

[38]President George W. Bush, Graduation Speech, West Point, June 1, 2002 (www.whitehouse.gov/news/release/2002).

Key Terms

natural law
natural right
natural philosophy
sense experience
materialism
mental discourse
nominalism
endeavor
deliberation
felicity
state of nature
equality
social contract theory
competition
diffidence
glory
love of glory
convenant
absolute sovereign
liberty

Sources and Resources

Key Texts

Leviathan
On the Citizen

Secondary Texts

Coleman, Frank M. *Hobbes and America: Exploring the Constitutional Framework* (Toronto: University of Toronto Press, 1977).

Dietz, Mary G. (ed.) *Thomas Hobbes and Political Theory* (Lawrence, KS: University Press of Kansas, 1990).

Gauthier, David. *The Logic of Leviathan* (London: Oxford University Press, 1969).

Goldsmith, M. M. *Hobbes' Science of Politics* (New York: Columbia University Press, 1966).

Herbert, Gary B. *Thomas Hobbes: The Unity of Scientific and Moral Wisdom* (Vancouver: University of British Columbia Press, 1989).

Johnson, David. *The Rhetoric of Leviathan* (Princeton: Princeton University Press, 1986).

Kraynak, Robert P. *History and Modernity in the Thought of Thomas Hobbes* (Ithaca, NY: Cornell University Press, 1990).

Mace, George. *Locke, Hobbes, and the Federalist Papers: An Essay on the Genesis of the American Political Heritage* (Carbondale and Edwardsville, IL: Southern Illinois Press, 1979).

Oakshott, Michael. *Hobbes on Civil Association* (Indianapolis, IN: Liberty Fund Books, 2000).

Spragens, Thomas A. Jr. *The Politics of Motion: The World of Thomas Hobbes* (London: Croom Helm, 1973).

Strauss, Leo. *The Political Philosophy of Hobbes*, trans. Elsa M. Sinclair (Chicago: University of Chicago Press, 1952).

Web Sites

"Thomas Hobbes (1588–1679): Moral and Political Philosophy": www.iep.utm.edu/h/hobmoral.htm

"Thomas Hobbes (1588–1679)—The Natural Law Philosopher": http://cepa.newschool.edu/het/profiles/hobbes.htm

LOCKE

CHAPTER 8

By David Walsh *The Catholic University of America*

© Liz Michaud

LIFE AND LEGACY: THE ELUSIVE LOCKE

John Locke (1632–1704) is arguably the most influential of all political theorists. The type of liberal democracy that is now the global political paradigm may be traced to his *Second Treatise of Government.* This is not to suggest that all contemporary states have embraced the Lockean model; it is simply to recognize that no alternatives are seriously proposed. Even states that are neither liberal nor democratic, such as Communist China or the Kingdom of Saudi Arabia, have conceded the need to evolve in the liberal democratic direction. With the collapse of Marxism as the remaining alternative, there is no longer any serious competitor on the world scene. Many nations may still fall short of the liberal democratic standard, but none present a serious challenge to its normative authority. The battle of ideas is essentially over once the Lockean conception reigns as the indisputably successful modern political form. This is why understanding John Locke is now more vital than ever. Far from constituting an item of merely historical interest, his thought has become the means by which we understand ourselves today.

It was different when Locke's political thought was viewed as a mere way station on the road of ideological revolution. Then little hinged on getting him right—the inexorable march of history had already passed him by. But now that Locke has proved so durable, the stakes in his interpretation have risen considerably. It matters a great deal that we understand what Locke has bequeathed to us, as is evident not only from the great attention to his work but also from the intense debates surrounding it. The comfortably familiar picture of Locke as the author of an atomistic liberal politics, the defender of "possessive individualism," has begun to dissolve. In its place emerges a far more complex figure who is not as fully modern as he appears but has an unerring sense of the world that was already emerging within his time. Locke is thus a more elusive figure than we thought. His affinities with the medieval Christian world are far stronger than might be suspected at first glance, while his anticipation of developments that have become fully apparent in our own time demonstrate the impressive reach of his thought. The quality of elasticity most characterizes his mind; this quality enabled him to build a thoroughly modern political form, liberal democracy, while retaining within it the substance of the medieval Christian past. Scholars today are gaining a new appreciation of the bridge that Locke erected where previously we had been conscious only of a gap. Locke's piety used to be viewed as an obsolete remnant contradicted by the rationalism of his analysis, but now we are inclined to view the uneasy tensions within his thought as the core of Locke's philosophical and political achievement. We ourselves have not been able to resolve these tensions between faith and reason, religion and politics.

It is not simply the unavoidable ambiguity of his situation that renders Locke so elusive. He made ambiguity a virtue and thereby found the means of shaping a consensus within a time of great theological and political fracture. Defying the odds of reaching an agreement between opposing factions, he showed that they were nevertheless capable of being reconciled by what they still held in common. Locke's genius consisted in finding a formulation that evoked the essentials in such a way that no one could disagree with him. Both in politics and in theology he rigorously stripped away what he regarded as inessential to arrive at the bedrock on which a new conception of community could be built. In the practical nature of his enterprise he provided a less theoretically comprehensive account of politics, but he achieved a far more rhetorically powerful evocation of the future that at the time was only dimly visible. Locke did not write merely to analyze the political situation in which he found himself. He wrote to persuade people of the direction in which it should go. His work is driven by a moral purpose and draws much of its authority from that inspiration. This helps to explain the power it still exercises on us today. Reading Locke is in many respects like looking into a mirror. Like Jefferson in *The Declaration of Independence,* we find ourselves admitting that "we hold these truths to be self-evident": We can think of no other way of founding political society than on the recognition of the inalienable rights of human beings that Locke has taught us. An extended philosophical defense of the self-evident truths may remain desirable, but the convictions themselves are indispensable. In clothing our deepest intuitions in the language of rights, Locke has shaped the world in which we live.

The effort to understand the horizon that contains our political life is a continuing task that must always begin with understanding Locke himself. His own words within their historical context provide our starting point. Although we may recognize ourselves in Locke, it is important not to read ourselves into him. The elusiveness of Locke as a man between the medieval and the modern worlds must be fully appreciated. The categories we are inclined to retrospectively apply do not work: The terms *liberal* and *democratic* had not yet been invested with the meanings we attach to them. All that Locke himself could have said was that he sided with the party that opposed royal absolutism. Throughout the 17th century this was the overriding constitutional struggle within English politics. It had already instigated the wrenching civil war that had culminated in the execution of Charles I in 1649. At the time Locke was attending a nearby school. His education continued at Oxford University, where he studied medicine and eventually met his most famous patient, the Earl of Shaftesbury. Having performed a lifesaving operation on the earl (draining his liver abscess), Locke was welcomed into the household of the prominent aristocrat who would become the leader of the parliamentary resistance to the encroachments of the monarchy. That placed Locke at the center of the great political events of his day as the struggle between king and Parliament continued, following the restoration of the monarchy with Charles II in 1660. Suspicion and mistrust were rife as the prospect of the king forming an alliance with the absolutist French monarch Louis XIV hung like a sword over parliamentary independence. If Charles II were to receive a subsidy from the French king, he could dispense with the need for Parliament to provide any subvention. His rule would be absolute. What brought the situation to a boiling point, however, was the efforts of Charles II to secure the succession of his brother, the Catholic James of Scotland, to the English throne. It was during this succession crisis of 1681 that Locke was most politically active, especially by writing the *Two Treatises of Government.* Given the nearly total defeat of the king's opponents, however, he decided not to publish the manuscripts but to place them in a trunk for future use. Locke spent much of the remainder of the decade in Holland, returning to England only after the crisis had finally broken out. When James succeeded his brother, opposition grew to the point that armed conflict was inevitable. It was at this point that Parliament offered the throne to William of Orange and his wife Mary, who was also the daughter of James. William's acceptance of this offer is known as **The Glorious Revolution of 1688.** James and his supporters

QUESTIONS FOR REFLECTION

Can we imagine a better political regime than a self-governing society based on respect for the rights of all? To the extent that we have difficulty coming up with superior alternatives, we live in a Lockean political universe.

were pursued to Ireland, where a decisive battle, the Battle of the Boyne, resulted in his defeat in 1690.

By that time the constitutional crisis had been resolved: A Protestant monarch would restore the role of Parliament as the bulwark of English rights. This was the point at which Locke published his *Two Treatises of Government* (anonymously) in 1689. For a long time it was thought that he wrote them to provide a rationale for the constitutional revolution of the previous year; but more recent scholarship has demonstrated their earlier origin. It is less likely therefore that Locke sought to defend what had happened than that he intended to influence its unfolding and interpretation. Events had in many ways overtaken his reflection on them, and it is unlikely that Locke exercised any significant influence. Yet his interpretation, with its far more radical assertion of the principle of consent of the governed, has often been taken as definitive of what was more ambiguously played out within the Glorious Revolution itself. The pivotal character of that constitutional settlement cannot be underestimated within his work—almost everything he did in the remaining 15 years of his life may be seen as an effort to sustain its underpinnings. This is particularly the case in the area of religion, which Locke saw as not only a potential source of conflict but, more importantly, as the wellspring of the moral consensus that could alone guarantee political harmony. As preparation for this great project of tackling the foundations of morality and religion, he published his philosophical masterpiece, *An Essay Concerning Human Understanding,* in his own name in 1690. This work established Locke as a leading intellectual light in his own time, and it has remained a principal text within the history of modern philosophy. It was preceded by a far shorter tract that penetrated to the core of the religious disputes of the day, *A Letter Concerning Toleration* (1689), which Locke followed with his own outline of a purely scriptural Christianity, *On The Reasonableness of Christianity* (1695). He continued to labor over the method of scriptural interpretation that he hoped might yield a broad or "Latitudinarian" Christianity that could provide a basis for consensus bridging denominational differences. The last fruit of these efforts was his final work, *Notes and Paraphrase of the Epistles of Saint Paul.*

PRIORITY OF COMMUNITY

The guiding intuition that prompted Locke's search for consensus was that the community of human beings came before and remained despite their disagreements. One of the curious aspects of the conventional interpretation of Locke is that he is seen as promoting individual self-interest as the basis for civil society. A closer examination reveals that the individual on whom he focuses is firmly embedded in community. Much of the contemporary debate between libertarians and communitarians, with both sides appealing to Locke, could be resolved if closer attention were paid to what he actually said. While it may be argued that we have subsequently created a society of possessive individualists, Locke himself had a far more profound vision. His individual emerges precisely at the point at which he begins to act socially. This is not an individual absorbed in the cares and pleasures of his private world but a human being who steps forward in the name of the bond with others that he already carries within him. We might say that he becomes an individual through his assumption of civic responsibility. In this sense, it is not the individual who sustains the political community but rather the political community that sustains the individual. This may seem a surprising suggestion in light of the emphasis that from Locke onward has been placed on the preservation of private rights; but it is less surprising once we recognize that no such conception of rights can survive unless it relies on a common responsibility for sustaining them. Rights are meaningless without a community that is prepared to defend them. The individual who sets himself outside the community is the principal threat to an order of rights.

Many readers of Locke have taken his forceful defense of rights as an indication that he has introduced a far-reaching revision in the idea of natural law. He can indeed sound as if rights are prior to obligations. But this is hearing Locke with ears attuned to our own more anarchic social reality, in which individuals feel entitled to pursue their subjective claims against one another without reference to any order of justice that ought to unite them. Locke's own context was one in which the medieval idea of natural law had in many respects been reinforced by the scientific discovery of a **law of nature.** The latter term Locke generally uses because he wishes to invest moral law with the authority emerging with the scientific discovery of law. There is no suggestion that the moral law operates blindly or automatically; it is precisely to persuade people to recognize their obligations to support civil society that he wrote the *Two Treatises*. The mere assertion of rights, he argues, is bound to remain ineffectual so long as it is not sustained by an order of mutual obligation authorized to defend them. Far from juxtaposing natural rights against natural law, Locke understood that they were reciprocal. There could be no enjoyment of rights without law, and there could be no law without respect for rights. In the 18th century the language of **natural rights** became widespread while (not coincidentally) there was also a flourishing renewal of interest in natural law. Only later was the concept of nature dropped, and then the status of rights became more attenuated. For Locke, however, the situation remained clear. The danger of an unlimited assertion of rights arose from monarchical claims of standing outside community law.

Resistance to **royal absolutism** was not simply the overriding issue of Locke's day. It was the central principle of his political thought. In this respect he differs from Hobbes, who made the absolute authority of the sovereign the linchpin of his political construction. Where Hobbes sees the sovereign as outside the covenant by which civil society is instituted, Locke insists that the sovereign must ultimately be subordinate to the social compact. For Hobbes there can be no agreement without an absolute power capable of enforcing it; for Locke only an agreement that includes the absolute power is worthy of the consent of free people. Yet despite the apparent sharp differences between Hobbes and Locke, these differences are more apparent than real. Hobbes' sovereign is not as absolute as he appears: His power ultimately derives from the free consent of the majority. Conversely, Locke cannot dispense altogether with a power whose imposition must settle many issues to which we have neither consented nor discussed. Perhaps the differences between them boil down to emphasis. Hobbes places power firmly in the foreground, whereas Locke's more constitutionalist leanings prefer power to recede into the background. Above all Locke is concerned with making government responsible, not with the question of the existence of a government. This means that he must bring before us the **priority of the moral community** from which government emerges and by which it can be checked.

The question of the origin of government, to which Locke's *Two Treatises of Government* are addressed, is not therefore a factual inquiry. His purpose is to establish the moral source of the authority that **civil society** exercises over its members, especially with a view to articulating the principles by which such power might be restrained. This is why the *Two Treatises* form a unity. Even though the *First Treatise* is less widely read than its successor, it performs the important function of eliminating the main competing argument to the one Locke expounds in the *Second Treatise*. That alternative position was generally referred to as the **divine right of kings.** Locke critiques its exposition in Robert Filmer's *Patriarcha*. Against Filmer's contention that political authority derives from God through the descent of authority given to Adam, being passed along the royal line in each generation up to the present, Locke argues that such a derivation is inherently unworkable. Whether the means of transmission is biological, through primogeniture, or legal, by inheritance, there is no reliable way of deciding between the many potential claimants of the Adamic authority. Instead Locke emphasizes that each human being is born into the world with the same authority that Adam had—namely authority over his own person and over his children until they are old enough to become responsible for themselves. No group of human beings is entitled by God or nature to rule over others because we all have the same God-given authority over ourselves. This means that the authority of kings and princes must be derived from the consent of individuals, all of whom are free and equal. Government is based on **consent of the governed.** Of course none of us can recall the point at which we gave such consent because we were born into an existing commonwealth and can at best exercise what Locke refers to as our **"tacit consent."** Locke states:

> *Every Man* being, as had been shown, *naturally free,* and nothing being able to put him into subjection to any Earthly Power, but only his own Consent; it is to be considered, what shall be understood to be *a sufficient Declaration of a Man's Consent, to make him subject* to the Laws of any Government. There is a common distinction of an express and a tacit consent, which will concern our present Case. No body doubts but an *express Consent,* of any Man, entering into any Society, makes him a perfect Member of that Society, a Subject of that Government. The difficulty is, what ought to be look'd upon as a *tacit Consent,* and how far it binds, i.e. how far any one shall be looked on to have consented, and thereby submitted to any Government, where he has made no Expressions of it at all. And to this I say, that every Man, that hath any Possession, or Enjoyment, of any part of the Dominions of any Government, doth thereby give his *tacit Consent,* and is as far forth obliged to Obedience to the Laws of that Government. . . . (*Second Treatise,* par. 119)

To explain the principle of free and equal consent it was necessary for Locke, like Hobbes and Rousseau, to have recourse to a fictional **state of nature** from which civil society emerged. *The Second Treatise of Government* begins with such a description of the state of nature, which for Locke is essentially the condition of human beings without any superior to settle their differences. It is a state of neither anarchy nor war, although conflict can erupt within it, because the Lockean state of nature is not primarily defined by individual self-interest. Instead the state of nature is essentially a state of community without government to act on its behalf. This means that the state of nature is unreliable, filled with the **inconveniences** of ineffective administration of justice. Everyone must be a judge in his own case, and no one can call on effective means of punishing wrongdoers. But Locke's state of nature is not without justice and consensus concerning its meaning. The problem is that the law has no institutional carrier and therefore devolves to the initiative and responsibility of every individual. In the state of nature, according to Locke, we are all responsible for prosecuting the law of nature both in cases that affect ourselves and in those that affect others. The community of humans who live together may not have a political representation in the form of a government, but it is not for that reason any less real. Bonds of mutual obligation remain even in the absence of an effective means of enforcing them. This **prepolitical community** that lacks any visible manifestation is carried within each individual member, and from that mutual trust and recognition the compact to form civil society eventually emerges. For Locke there really is no problem in accounting for the transition from an individual to a communal perspective because individuals carry the sense of common obligation toward one another from the beginning. They can enter civil society because they are already bound up with its moral premises.

STATE OF NATURE

This contrasts markedly with Hobbes' more radically individualistic depiction of the state of nature. He famously describes the state of nature as a state of war that, if it is not always overt, constantly simmers as the threat each must remain prepared to confront. Whereas Locke emphasizes the degree to which trust can be reliably placed in others, Hobbes forces us to contemplate what must be done when that trust breaks down. These are not mutually exclusive positions, but they do point in different directions. This difference in direction gives Locke's thought a far more communitarian bent, in contrast to the bleakly individualist outlook provided by Hobbes. In each case, however, some appeal to a moral community must be made; otherwise it would be impossible to erect governmental authority on the basis of consent. Both thinkers recognize that the consent given is only as good as the moral reliability of the giver. Even when Hobbes insists on the need for a sovereign to act as the ultimate enforcer of agreements, he is aware that the enforcer remains dependent on the voluntary support of the majority. If he has to compel everyone, he lacks the power to compel anyone. The difference between Hobbes and Locke is centered in the extent of the moral community they presuppose in the state of nature. Hobbes is prepared to count on only a narrowly defined sense of right, while Locke assumes that human beings are more broadly oriented toward the good. Both recognize the impossibility of basing government on simple self-interest, which is why they each studiously avoid the term "social contract." Hobbes insists that the basic agreement is a "covenant," a term full of theological overtones that imply its solemn and eternal character. Locke consistently uses the term **compact** to suggest the enduring

QUESTIONS FOR REFLECTION

Is Aristotle right that man is by nature a political animal? That we cannot really be human without living in community with others? To what extent does Locke confirm this by asking us to think about what life would be like without government, in the state of nature?

relationship of trust that does not depend on a purely individualist calculation of returns.

Indeed Locke goes to considerable lengths to rebut the presumption that liberal democracy is rooted in the vagaries of individual whim. This is why his account of the state of nature dwells so heavily on the moral obligations that define it, and why those obligations are traced to their source in the obligations we owe toward God. The state of nature may be a state of freedom, but it is not a state of license. Absent a government we are still subject to law—namely the law of nature that comes to us from the divine lawgiver. Locke states:

> The *State of Nature* has a Law of Nature to govern it, which obliges every one: And Reason, which is that Law, teaches all Mankind, who will but consult it, that being all equal and independent, no one ought to harm another in his Life, Health, Liberty, or Possessions. For Men being all the Workmanship of one Omnipotent, and infinitely wise Maker; All the Servants of one Sovereign Master, sent into the World by his order and about his business, they are his Property, whose Workmanship they are, made to last during his, not one anothers Pleasure." (*Second Treatise,* par. 6)

God's government of the whole of reality constitutes the boundary within which we exist. Locke's theological anchoring of our moral obligations has often been read as a concession to the conventional piety of his time, while the thrust of his thought pointed toward the emergence of an autonomously secular order. This is a view that has become harder to defend as we become more aware of the concerns that animated Locke's efforts. Although he possessed a healthy respect for convention, he was also cognizant of the inability of convention to stand on its own. A morality that was subscribed to simply because society dictated it was a morality vulnerable to the shifting winds of fashion. Only a morality rooted in the eternal could withstand the endlessly compromising pressures that buffeted it. If human beings create their own morality, they can alter it at will. This is why Locke insisted that even our rights have their source in the obligations we ultimately owe toward God. So while we possess the right to preserve ourselves in the state of nature, the rationale is derived from the duty we owe to God. By implication, the same responsibility extends toward the preservation of others who are equally God's property. The most comprehensive statement of the law of nature is therefore that we are obliged to preserve ourselves and, when it is not in conflict with that, to preserve others. "Every one as he is *bound to preserve himself,* and not to quit his station willfully; so by the like reason when his own Preservation comes not in competition, ought he, as much as he can, *to preserve the rest of Mankind*" (*Second Treatise,* par. 6). Upholding this complex of rights and responsibilities is the chief task of humanity in the state of nature and, as we shall see, by extension the state of civil society.

PRIMARY SOURCE 8.1

Of the State of Nature, from *Second Treatise*, Chapter 2

Sect. 4. TO understand political power right, and derive it from its original, we must consider, what state all men are naturally in, and that is, a *state of perfect freedom* to order their actions, and dispose of their possessions and persons, as they think fit, within the bounds of the law of nature, without asking leave, or depending upon the will of any other man.

A *state* also of *equality* wherein all the power and jurisdiction is reciprocal, no one having more than another; there being nothing more evident, than that the creatures of the same species and rank, promiscuously born to all the same advantages of nature, and the use of the same faculties, should also be equal one amongst another without subordination or subjection, unless the lord and master of them all should, by any manifest declaration of his will, set one above another, and confer on him, by an evident and clear appointment, an undoubted right to dominion and sovereignty.

Sect. 5. This *equality* of men by nature, the judicious Hooker looks upon as so evident in itself, and beyond all question, that he makes it the foundation of that obligation to mutual love amongst men, on which he builds the duties they owe one another, and from whence he derives the great maxims of justice and charity. His words are,

—*The like natural inducement hath brought men to know that it is no less their duty, to love others than themselves; for seeing those things which are equal, must needs all have one measure; if I cannot but wish to receive good, even as much at every man's hands, as any man can wish unto his own soul, how should I look to have any part of my desire herein satisfied, unless myself be careful to satisfy the like desire, which is undoubtedly in other men, being of one and the same nature? To have any thing offered them repugnant to this desire, must needs in all respects grieve them as much as me; so that if I do harm, I must look to suffer, there being no reason that others should show greater measure of love to me, than they have by me showed unto them: my desire therefore to be loved of my equals in nature as much as possible may be, imposeth upon me a natural duty of bearing to them-ward fully the like affection; from which relation of equality between ourselves and them that are as ourselves, what several rules and canons natural reason hath drawn, for direction of life, no man is ignorant.* Eccl. Pol. Lib. 1.

Sect. 6. But though this be a *state of liberty,* yet it is *not a state of license:* though man in that state have an uncontrollable liberty to dispose of his person or possessions, yet he has not liberty to destroy himself, or so much as any creature in his possession, but where some nobler use than its bare preservation calls for it. The *state of nature* has a law of nature to govern it, which obliges every one: and reason, which is that law, teaches all mankind, who will but consult it, that being all *equal and independent,* no one ought to harm another in his life, health, liberty, or possessions: for men being all the workmanship of one omnipotent, and infinitely wise maker; all the servants of one sovereign master, sent into the world by his order, and about his business; they are his property, whose workmanship they are, made to last during his, not one another's pleasure: and being furnished with like faculties, sharing all in one community of nature, there cannot be supposed any such *subordination* among us, that may authorize us to destroy one another, as if we were made for one another's uses, as the inferior ranks of creatures are for ours. Every one, as he is *bound to preserve himself,* and not to quit his station willfully, so by the like reason, when his own preservation comes not in competition, ought he, as much as he can, *to preserve the rest of mankind,* and may not, unless it be to do justice on an offender, take away, or impair the life, or what tends to the preservation of the life, the liberty, health, limb, or goods of another.

Sect. 7. And that all men may be restrained from invading others rights, and from doing hurt to one another, and the law of nature be observed, which willeth the peace and

continued

PRIMARY SOURCE 8.1

OF THE STATE OF NATURE, FROM *SECOND TREATISE,* CHAPTER 2 *continued*

preservation of all mankind, the *execution* of the *law of nature* is, in that state, put into every man's hands, whereby every one has a right to punish the transgressors of that law to such a degree, as may hinder its violation: for the *law of nature* would, as all other laws that concern men in this world be in vain, if there were no body that in the state of nature had a *power to execute* that law, and thereby preserve the innocent and restrain offenders. And if any one in the state of nature may punish another for any evil he has done, every one may do so: for in that *state of perfect equality,* where naturally there is no superiority or jurisdiction of one over another, what any may do in prosecution of that law, every one must needs have a right to do.

Sect. 8. And thus, in the state of nature, *one man comes by a power over another;* but yet no absolute or arbitrary power, to use a criminal, when he has got him in his hands, according to the passionate heats, or boundless extravagancy of his own will; but only to retribute to him, so far as calm reason and conscience dictate, what is proportionate to his transgression, which is so much as may serve for *reparation* and *restraint:* for these two are the only reasons, why one man may lawfully do harm to another, which is that we call *punishment.* In transgressing the law of nature, the offender declares himself to live by another rule than that of reason and common equity, which is that measure God has set to the actions of men, for their mutual security; and so he becomes dangerous to mankind, the tye, which is to secure them from injury and violence, being slighted and broken by him. Which being a trespass against the whole species, and the peace and safety of it, provided for by the law of nature, every man upon this score, by the right he hath to preserve mankind in general, may restrain, or where it is necessary, destroy things noxious to them, and so may bring such evil on any one, who hath transgressed that law, as may make him repent the doing of it, and thereby deter him, and by his example others, from doing the like mischief. And in the case, and upon this ground, *every man hath a right to punish the offender, and be executioner of the law of nature.*

Sect. 9. I doubt not but this will seem a very strange doctrine to some men: but before they condemn it, I desire them to resolve me, by what right any prince or state can put to death, or *punish an alien,* for any crime he commits in their country. It is certain their laws, by virtue of any sanction they receive from the promulgated will of the legislative, reach not a stranger: they speak not to him, nor, if they did, is he bound to hearken to them. The legislative authority, by which they are in force over the subjects of that commonwealth, hath no power over him. Those who have the supreme power of making laws in *England, France* or *Holland,* are to an *Indian,* but like the rest of the world, men without authority: and therefore, if by the law of nature every man hath not a power to punish offenses against it, as he soberly judges the case to require, I see not how the magistrates of any community can punish an alien of another country; since, in reference to him, they can have no more power than what every man naturally may have over another.

Sect. 10. Besides the crime which consists in violating the law, and varying from the right rule of reason, whereby a man so far becomes degenerate, and declares himself to quit the principles of human nature, and to be a noxious creature, there is commonly *injury* done to some person or other, and some other man receives damage by his transgression: in which case he who hath received any damage, has, besides the right of punishment common to him with other men, a particular right to seek *reparation* from him that has done it: and any other person, who finds it just, may also join with him that is injured, and assist him in recovering from the offender so much as may make satisfaction for the harm he has suffered.

Sect. 11. From these *two distinct rights,* the one of *punishing* the crime *for restraint,* and preventing the like offense, which right of punishing is in every body; the other of taking *reparation,* which belongs only to the injured party,

PRIMARY SOURCE 8.1 | OF THE STATE OF NATURE, FROM *SECOND TREATISE,* CHAPTER 2 *continued*

comes it to pass that the magistrate, who by being magistrate hath the common right of punishing put into his hands, can often, where the public good demands not the execution of the law, *remit* the punishment of criminal offenses by his own authority, but yet cannot *remit* the satisfaction due to any private man for the damage he has received. That, he who has suffered the damage has a right to demand in his own name, and he alone can remit: the damnified person has this power of appropriating to himself the goods or service of the offender, *by right of self-preservation,* as every man has a power to punish the crime, to prevent its being committed again, *by the right he has of preserving all mankind,* and doing all reasonable things he can in order to that end: and thus it is, that every man, in the state of nature, has a power to kill a murderer, both *to deter* others from doing the like injury, which no reparation can compensate, by the example of the punishment that attends it from every body, and also to secure men from the attempts of a criminal, who having renounced reason, the common rule and measure God hath given to mankind, hath, by the unjust violence and slaughter he hath committed upon one, declared war against all mankind, and therefore may be destroyed as a *lion* or a *tiger,* one of those wild savage beasts, with whom men can have no society nor security: and upon this is grounded that great law of nature, *Whoso sheddeth man's blood, by man shall his blood be shed.* And *Cain* was so fully convinced, that every one had a right to destroy such a criminal, that after the murder of his brother, he cried out, *Every one that findeth me, shall slay me;* so plain was it writ in the hearts of all mankind.

Sect. 12. By the same reason may a man in the state of nature *punish the lesser breaches* of that law. It will perhaps be demanded, with death? I answer, each transgression may be *punished* to that *degree,* and with so much *severity,* as will suffice to make it an ill bargain to the offender, give him cause to repent, and terrify others from doing the like. Every offense, that can be committed in the state of nature, may in the state of nature be also punished equally, and as far forth as it may, in a commonwealth: for though it would be besides my present purpose, to enter here into the particulars of the law of nature, or its *measures of punishment;* yet, it is certain there is such a law, and that too, as intelligible and plain to a rational creature, and a studier of that law, as the positive laws of commonwealths; nay, possibly plainer; as much as reason is easier to be understood, than the fancies and intricate contrivances of men, following contrary and hidden interests put into words; for so truly are a great part of the *municipal laws* of countries, which are only so far right, as they are founded on the law of nature, by which they are to be regulated and interpreted.

Sect. 13. To this strange doctrine, viz. That *in the state of nature every one has the executive power* of the law of nature, I doubt not but it will be objected, that it is unreasonable for men to be judges in their own cases, that self-love will make men partial to themselves and their friends: and on the other side, that ill nature, passion, and revenge will carry them too far in punishing others; and hence nothing but confusion and disorder will follow, and that therefore God hath certainly appointed government to restrain the partiality and violence of men. I easily grant, that *civil government* is the proper remedy for the inconveniencies of the state of nature, which must certainly be great, where men may be judges in their own case, since it is easy to be imagined, that he who was so unjust as to do his brother an injury, will scarce be so just as to condemn himself for it: but I shall desire those who make this objection, to remember, that *absolute monarchs* are but men; and if government is to be the remedy of those evils, which necessarily follow from men's being judges in their own cases, and the state of nature is therefore not to how much better it is than the state of nature, where one man, commanding a multitude, has the liberty to be judge in his own case, and may do to all his subjects

continued

PRIMARY SOURCE 8.1 | OF THE STATE OF NATURE, FROM *SECOND TREATISE*, CHAPTER 2 *continued*

whatever he pleases, without the least liberty to any one to question or control those who execute his pleasure? and in whatsoever he doth, whether led by reason, mistake or passion, must be submitted to? much better it is in the state of nature, wherein men are not bound to submit to the unjust will of another: and if he that judges, judges amiss in his own, or any other case, he is answerable for it to the rest of mankind.

Sect. 14. It is often asked as a mighty objection, *where are,* or ever were there any *men in such a state of nature?* To which it may suffice as an answer at present, that since all princes and rulers of *independent* governments all through the world, are in a state of nature, it is plain the world never was, nor ever will be, without numbers of men in that state. I have named all governors of *independent communities,* whether they are, or are not, in league with others: for it is not every compact that puts an end to the state of nature between men, but only this one of agreeing together mutually to enter into one community, and make one body politic; other promises, and compacts, men may make one with another, and yet still be in the state of nature. The promises and bargains for truck, etc. between the two men in the desert island, mentioned by *Garcilasso de la Vega,* in his history of *Peru;* or between a *Swiss* and an *Indian,* in the woods of *America,* are binding to them, though they are perfectly in a state of nature, in reference to one another: for truth and keeping of faith belongs to men, as men, and not as members of society.

Sect. 15. To those that say, there were never any men in the state of nature, I will not only oppose the authority of the judicious *Hooker, Eccl. Pol. lib. i. sect.* 10, where he says, *The laws which have been hitherto mentioned, i.e. the laws of nature, do bind men absolutely, even as they are men, although they have never any settled fellowship, never any solemn agreement amongst themselves what to do, or not to do: but forasmuch as we are not by ourselves sufficient to furnish ourselves with competent store of things, needful for such a life as our nature doth desire, a life fit for the dignity of man; therefore to supply those defects and imperfections which are in us, as living single and solely by ourselves, we are naturally induced to seek communion and fellowship with others: this was the cause of men's uniting themselves at first in politic societies.* But I moreover affirm, that all men are naturally in that state, and remain so, till by their own consents they make themselves members of some politic society; and I doubt not in the sequel of this discourse, to make it very clear.

PROPERTY

The mutual preservation of rights that constitutes the purpose of civil society is for Locke principally accomplished through the security of property. The singular preeminence he attaches to property may strike us today as somewhat eccentric—we are far more concerned with the rights of personal liberty and much more tolerant of restrictions on the enjoyment of our property. A large part of the reason for Locke's emphasis on property rights is that encroachments on property by, for example, assertions of the royal prerogative were experienced by him as the principal threat to liberty. It is testament to the success of his argument that we no longer experience the same level of anxiety about property. But it is even more important to understand how the term *property* functions within Locke's political vocabulary. He should not be read as a narrow defender of the interests of the propertied class. **Property** is for him the nexus through which all of our other rights are exercised. The **right to life** depends on the secure acquisition of the means of living; the right to liberty could be rendered meaningless if we were deprived of the material independence that property ensures. This is why for Locke an assault on one's property is an assault on the entire order of rights: An individual who would take one's possessions endangers the liberty and life that depend on them. Rights form a seamless garment whose integrity can be destroyed by a rip anywhere. Locke was prepared to follow the logic of this conviction even to the point of claiming a right to kill a thief: "I have no reason to suppose, that he, who would *take away my liberty,* would not when he had me in his power, take away everything else" (par. 17). To be consistent, he added that this provided no entitlement to the property of the malefactor beyond restoration of the property appropriated. The reason is that the **right to the property** of the thief belongs to his wife and children because on this their lives and liberty depend.

Property is therefore for Locke embedded in the very idea of the person. His most extended discussion of property occurs within the account of the prepolitical state of nature. Locke states: "Though the Earth, and all inferior Creatures be common to all Men, yet every Man has a *Property* in his own *Person.* This no Body has any Right to but himself. The Labor of his Body, and the *Work* of his Hands, we may say, are properly his. Whatsoever then he removes out of the State of Nature hath provided, and left it in, he hath mixed his *Labor* with, and joined to it something that is his own, and thereby makes it his Property" (par. 27). In the most elementary sense, he explains, we have a property in our persons. This does not mean we own ourselves; we have already seen that we are God's property but that we own our labor. Physical objects become our property through the application of our labor by which we attach them uniquely to ourselves. In the state of nature the world is given to human beings in common, but it can be enjoyed only by becoming the property of individual human beings. Locke's chapter on property is among the most carefully nuanced treatments in all his writing, and he was very much aware of treading a fine line between the modern and the traditional, between the unfettered rights of property and responsibility for the common good. The most vivid aspect of his discussion is that labor alone establishes the claim of ownership. It is not mere possession, however lengthy. In other words, Locke as far as possible links property with the integrity of the person. Initially, according to his sketch, this acquisition through labor promotes few conflicts. It may even alleviate them because the development of nature, by which a smaller area is utilized, leaves more of it available to others. No one can accumulate more property than they can use before it spoils. Conflict arises only when the possibility of storing up unlimited wealth is made possible by the introduction of money. What is notable about Locke's analysis here is not that he endorses a regime of unlimited acquisition, but that he depicts it with such unrelievedly negative overtones. There is even a veiled threat that government might later intervene to regulate such limitless accumulation. Property, it turns out, is not a private affair at all; it has its genesis in the prepolitical community that is Locke's state of nature. Indeed Locke treats the grounding of property within the mutual recognition of rights so lightly precisely because he takes it so much for granted.

TRANSITION TO CIVIL SOCIETY

The transition from the state of nature to the state of civil society, the creation of a **civil commonwealth,** is comparatively unproblematic for the same reason. Men in Locke's conception do not have to agree to form a community because they already find

PRIMARY SOURCE 8.2 | OF PROPERTY, FROM *SECOND TREATISE*, CHAPTER 5

Sect. 25. Whether we consider natural *reason*, which tells us, that men, being once born, have a right to their preservation, and consequently to meat and drink, and such other things as nature affords for their subsistence: or *revelation*, which gives us an account of those grants God made of the world to *Adam*, and to *Noah*, and his sons, it is very clear, that God, as King *David* says, *Psal.* cxv. 16. *has given the earth to the children of men*; given it to mankind in common. But this being supposed, it seems to some a very great difficulty, how any one should ever come to have a *property* in any thing: I will not content myself to answer, that if it be difficult to make out *property*, upon a supposition that God gave the world to *Adam*, and his posterity in common, it is impossible that any man, but one universal monarch, should have any property upon a supposition, that God gave the world to Adam, and his heirs in succession, exclusive of all the rest of his posterity. But I shall endeavor to show, how men might come to have a *property* in several parts of that which God gave to mankind in common, and that without any express compact of all the commoners.

Sect. 26. God, who hath given the world to men in common, hath also given them reason to make use of it to the best advantage of life, and convenience. The earth, and all that is therein, is given to men for the support and comfort of their being. And though all the fruits it naturally produces, and beasts it feeds, belong to mankind in common, as they are produced by the spontaneous hand of nature; and no body has originally a private dominion, exclusive of the rest of mankind, in any of them, as they are thus in their natural state: yet being given for the use of men, there must of necessity be *a means to appropriate* them some way or other, before they can be of any use, or at all beneficial to any particular man. The fruit, or venison, which nourishes the *wild Indian*, who knows no enclosure, and is still a tenant in common, must be his, and so his, i.e. a part of him, that another can no longer have any right to it, before it can do him any good for the support of his life.

Sect. 27. Though the earth, and all inferior creatures, be common to all men, yet every man has a *property* in his own *person*: this no body has any right to but himself. The *labor* of his body, and the *work* of his hands, we may say, are properly his. Whatsoever then he removes out of the state that nature hath provided, and left it in, he hath mixed his *labor* with, and joined to it something that is his own, and thereby makes it his *property*. It being by him removed from the common state nature hath placed it in, it hath by this *labor* something annexed to it, that excludes the common right of other men: for this *labor* being the unquestionable property of the laborer, no man but he can have a right to what that is once joined to, at least where there is enough, and as good, left in common for others.

Sect. 34. God gave the world to men in common; but since he gave it them for their benefit, and the greatest conveniences of life they were capable to draw from it, it cannot be supposed he meant it should always remain common and uncultivated. He gave it to the use of the industrious and rational (and *labor* was to be his *title* to it), not to the fancy or covetousness of the quarrelsome and contentious. He that had as good left for his improvement, as was already taken up, needed not complain, ought not to meddle with what was already improved by another's labor: if he did, it is plain he desired the benefit of another's pains, which he had no right to, and not the ground which God had given him in common with others to labor on, and whereof there was as good left, as that already possessed, and more than he knew what to do with, or his industry could reach to.

Sect. 35. It is true, in *land* that is common in *England*, or any other country, where there is plenty of people under government, who have money and commerce, no one can enclose or appropriate any part, without the consent of all his fellow-commoners; because this is left common by compact, i.e. by the law of the land, which is not to be violated. And though it be common, in respect of some men, it is not so to all mankind; but is the joint property of this country, or this

PRIMARY SOURCE 8.2 | OF PROPERTY, FROM *SECOND TREATISE*, CHAPTER 5 *continued*

parish. Besides, the remainder, after such enclosure, would not be as good to the rest of the commoners, as the whole was when they could all make use of the whole; whereas in the beginning and first peopling of the great common of the world, it was quite otherwise. The law man was under, was rather for appropriating. God commanded, and his wants forced him to *labor*. That was his *property* which could not be taken from him wherever he had fixed it. And hence subduing or cultivating the earth, and having dominion, we see are joined together. The one gave title to the other. So that God, by commanding to subdue, gave authority so far to *appropriate*: and the condition of human life, which requires labor and materials to work on, necessarily introduces private possessions.

Sect. 36. The *measure of property* nature has well set by the extent of men's *labor* and the *conveniences of life*: no man's labor could subdue, or appropriate all; nor could his enjoyment consume more than a small part; so that it was impossible for any man, this way, to entrench upon the right of another, or acquire to himself a property, to the prejudice of his neighbor, who would still have room for as good, and as large a possession (after the other had taken out his) as before it was appropriated. This *measure* did confine every man's *possession* to a very moderate proportion, and such as he might appropriate to himself, without injury to any body, in the first ages of the world, when men were more in danger to be lost, by wandering from their company, in the then vast wilderness of the earth, than to be straitened for want of room to plant in. And the same *measure* may be allowed still without prejudice to any body, as full as the world seems: for supposing a man, or family, in the state they were at first peopling of the world by the children of *Adam*, or *Noah;* let him plant in some inland, vacant places of *America,* we shall find that the *possessions* he could make himself, upon the *measures* we have given, would not be very large, nor, even to this day, prejudice the rest of mankind, or give them reason to complain, or think themselves injured by this man's encroachment, though the race of men have now spread themselves to all the corners of the world, and do infinitely exceed the small number was at the beginning. Nay, the extent of *ground* is of so little value, *without labor,* that I have heard it affirmed, that in *Spain* itself a man may be permitted to plough, sow, and reap, without being disturbed, upon land he has no other title to, but only his making use of it. But, on the contrary, the inhabitants think themselves beholden to him, who, by his industry on neglected, and consequently waste land, has increased the stock of corn, which they wanted. But be this as it will, which I lay no stress on; this I dare boldly affirm, that the same *rule of propriety, (viz.)* that every man should have as much as he could make use of, would hold still in the world, without straitening any body; since there is land enough in the world to suffice double the inhabitants, had not the invention of money, and the tacit agreement of men to put a value on it, introduced (by consent) larger possessions, and a right to them; which, how it has done, I shall by and by show more at large.

Sect. 37. This is certain, that in the beginning, before the desire of having more than man needed had altered the intrinsic value of things, which depends only on their usefulness to the life of man; or had *agreed, that a little piece of yellow metal,* which would keep without wasting or decay, should be worth a great piece of flesh, or a whole heap of corn; though men had a right to appropriate, by their labor, each one of himself, as much of the things of nature, as he could use: yet this could not be much, nor to the prejudice of others, where the same plenty was still left to those who would use the same industry. To which let me add, that he who appropriates land to himself by his labor, does not lessen, but increase the common stock of mankind: for the provisions serving to the support of human life, produced by one acre of enclosed and cultivated land, are

continued

PRIMARY SOURCE 8.2

OF PROPERTY, FROM *SECOND TREATISE*, CHAPTER 5 *continued*

(to speak much within compass) ten times more than those which are yielded by an acre of land of an equal richness lying waste in common. And therefore he that encloses land, and has a greater plenty of the conveniences of life from ten acres, than he could have from an hundred left to nature, may truly be said to give ninety acres to mankind: for his labor now supplies him with provisions out of ten acres, which were but the product of an hundred lying in common. I have here rated the improved land very low, in making its product but as ten to one, when it is much nearer an hundred to one: for I ask, whether in the wild woods and uncultivated waste of *America,* left to nature, without any improvement, tillage or husbandry, a thousand acres yield the needy and wretched inhabitants as many conveniences of life, as ten acres of equally fertile land do in *Devonshire,* where they are well cultivated?

—Before the appropriation of land, he who gathered as much of the wild fruit, killed, caught, or tamed, as many of the beasts, as he could; he that so employed his pains about any of the spontaneous products of nature, as any way to alter them from the state which nature put them in, *by* placing any of his *labor* on them, did thereby *acquire a propriety in them*: but if they perished, in his possession, without their due use; if the fruits rotted, or the venison putrefied, before he could spend it, he offended against the common law of nature, and was liable to be punished; he invaded his neighbor's share, for he had *no right, farther than his use* called for any of them, and they might serve to afford him conveniences of life.

themselves bound up with one another. They have only to form a government, to agree on the mode by which they are to govern themselves collectively. In the state of nature each was responsible for exercising the power of government in enforcing the law of nature. Now they must find a mechanism of transferring that authority to their representative. Throughout his account of the **genesis of civil society** Locke has the example of Hobbes in the background. Representation for Hobbes is effected through submission to a Leviathan, an absolute ruler who stands above the contracting parties as the only means of compelling their fidelity to the agreement. To Locke, submission to an absolute monarch defeats the purpose of quitting the state of nature. Among the inconveniences that induce us to construct civil society, none ranks higher than the burden of **men being judges in their own case.** Locke states: "*Want of a common Judge with Authority, puts all Men in a State of Nature: Force without Right, upon a Man's Person, makes a State of War,* both where there is, and is not, a common judge" (par. 19). An absolute ruler is precisely one who recognizes no common authority for resolving disputes affecting him. He is alone the one who judges what is lawful. To enter civil society on such a basis would negate the purpose of the undertaking because, as Locke so tellingly phrases it, an absolute ruler would still be in the state of nature with respect to the rest of the community (par. 90). The essence of civil society is that it constitutes a genuinely common measure by which differences are to be resolved. To the extent that any, especially its most powerful member, remains outside the law, it is to that extent not a genuine commonwealth. The arrangement has merely substituted the partiality of all in the state of nature for the partiality of the most powerful. In a move that underscores the constitutional thrust of his thought, Locke insists on the rule of law as the only guarantee of the liberty of all.

QUESTIONS FOR REFLECTION

How, according to Locke, does property become private when everything is given to human beings in common in the state of nature? Can you think of any other way of distributing property? Reflect on the inherently social character of any conception of property.

He recognizes that kingship played a historical role in the formation of commonwealths, as human societies had initially placed their trust in individuals acknowledged for the preeminence of their virtue. But that could not remain a permanent condition. Not only is the supply of virtuous monarchs notoriously short, but the paternalistic character of their rule implies the perpetual childhood of their subjects. And so it was, he explained, "the people finding their Properties not secure under the Government, as then it was, (whereas Government has no other end than the preservation of Property) could never be safe nor at rest, *nor think themselves to be in Civil Society,* till the Legislature was placed in collective Bodies of Men, call them Senate, Parliament, or what you please" (par. 94). He goes on to explain what this mutual constitution of a common authority must mean. It is nothing less than the **transfer of liberty** that each enjoyed in the state of nature to the state of civil society whereby the same legislative function that each performed individually is now enacted collectively. According to Locke, "The Natural Liberty of Man is to be free from any Superior Power on Earth, and not to be under the Will of Legislative Authority of Man, but to have only the Law of Nature for his Rule. The Liberty of Man, in Society, is to be under no other Legislative Power, but that established, by consent, in the Commonwealth, nor under the Dominion of any Will, or Restraint of any Law, but what the Legislative shall enact, according to the Trust put in it" (par. 22). Only when all are free equally are all equally free. "By which means every single person became subject, equally with other the meanest Men, to those laws, which he himself, as part of the Legislative had established: nor could any one, by his own Authority, avoid the force of the Law, when once made, nor by any pretense of Superiority, plead exemption, whereby to License his own, or the Miscarriages of any of his Dependants" (94). The analytic clarity Locke reaches in such formulations is directly related to the resistance mounting within him as he contemplated the superiority asserted by the Stuart monarchs. Encroachments on liberty were real and threatened its abolition entirely. The principal line of defense lay in insistence on the sovereignty of law and not of men. Civil society (or what is known today as liberal democracy) is the community of free people bound by their equal consent to law. "*No man in Civil Society,*" Locke proclaims in a culminating formulation, "*can be exempted from the Laws of it*" (94).

LIMITED GOVERNMENT

The absorption of consent into a legislative process that is the origin of civil society does not, of course, mean consent to all its decisions. Unanimity is hardly to be expected within collective bodies. Nor can a legislature remain paralyzed by the

PRIMARY SOURCE 8.3 | OF PATERNAL POWER, FROM *SECOND TREATISE*, CHAPTER 6

Sect. 87. Man being born, as has been proved, with a title to perfect freedom, and an uncontrolled enjoyment of all the rights and privileges of the law of nature, equally with any other man, or number of men in the world, hath by nature a power, not only to preserve his property, that is, his life, liberty, and estate, against the injuries and attempts of other men; but to judge of, and punish the breaches of that law in others, as he is persuaded the offense deserves, even with death itself, in crimes where the heinousness of the fact, in his opinion, requires it. But because no political society can be, nor subsist, without having in itself the power to preserve the property, and in order thereunto, punish the offenses of all those of that society; there, and there only is political society, where every one of the members hath quitted this natural power, resigned it up into the hands of the community in all cases that exclude him not from appealing for protection to the law established by it. And thus all private judgment of every particular member being excluded, the community comes to be umpire, by settled standing rules, indifferent, and the same to all parties; and by men having authority from the community, for the execution of those rules, decides all the differences that may happen between any members of that society concerning any matter of right; and punishes those offenses which any member hath committed against the society, with such penalties as the law has established: whereby it is easy to discern, who are, and who are not, in *political society* together. Those who are united into one body, and have a common established law and judicature to appeal to, with authority to decide controversies between them, and punish offenders, are in *civil society* one with another: but those who have no such common appeal, I mean on earth, are still in the state of nature, each being, where there is no other, judge for himself, and executioner; which is, as I have before showed it, the perfect *state of nature*.

Sect. 88. And thus the commonwealth comes by a power to set down what punishment shall belong to the several transgressions which they think worthy of it, committed amongst the members of that society (which is the *power of making laws*), as well as it has the power to punish any injury done unto any of its members, by any one that is not of it (which is the *power of war and peace*); and all this for the preservation of the property of all the members of that society, as far as is possible. But though every man who has entered into civil society, and is become a member of any commonwealth, has thereby quitted his power to punish offenses, against the law of nature, in prosecution of his own private judgment, yet with the judgment of offenses, which he has given up to the legislative in all cases, where he can appeal to the magistrate, he has given a right to the commonwealth to employ his force, for the execution of the judgments of the commonwealth, whenever he shall be called to it; which indeed are his own judgments, they being made by himself, or his representative. And herein we have the original of the *legislative* and *executive power* of civil society, which is to judge by standing laws, how far offenses are to be punished, when committed within the commonwealth; and also to determine, by occasional judgments founded on the present circumstances of the fact, how far injuries from without are to be vindicated; and in both these to employ all the force of all the members, when there shall be need.

Sect. 89. Wherever therefore any number of men are so united into one society, as to quit every one his executive power of the law of nature, and to resign it to the public, there and there only is a *political*, or *civil society*. And this is done, wherever any number of men, in the state of nature, enter into society to make one people, one body politic, under one supreme government; or else when any one joins himself to, and incorporates with any government already made: for hereby he authorizes the society, or which is all one, the legislative thereof, to make laws for him, as the public good of the society shall require; to the execution whereof, his own assistance (as to his own decrees) is due. And this *puts men* out of a state of nature

PRIMARY SOURCE 8.3 | OF PATERNAL POWER, FROM *SECOND TREATISE*, CHAPTER 6 *continued*

into that of a *commonwealth,* by setting up a judge on earth, with authority to determine all the controversies, and redress the injuries that may happen to any member of the commonwealth; which judge is the legislative, or magistrates appointed by it. And wherever there are any number of men, however associated, that have no such decisive power to appeal to, there they are still in *the state of nature.*

Sect. 90. Hence it is evident, that *absolute monarchy*, which by some men is counted the only government in the world, is indeed *inconsistent with civil society*, and so can be no form of civil government at all: for the *end of civil society*, being to avoid, and remedy those inconveniencies of the state of nature, which necessarily follow from every man's being judge in his own case, by setting up a known authority, to which every one of that society may appeal upon any injury received, or controversy that may arise, and which every one of the[1] society ought to obey; wherever any persons are, who have not such an authority to appeal to, for the decision of any difference between them, there those persons are still *in the state of nature*; and so is every *absolute prince*, in respect of those who are under his *dominion.*

Sect. 91. For he being supposed to have all, both legislative and executive power in himself alone, there is no judge to be found, no appeal lies open to any one, who may fairly, and indifferently, and with authority decide, and from whose decision relief and redress may be expected of any injury or inconvenience, that may be suffered from the prince, or by his order: so that such a man, however entitled, *Czar*, or *Grand Seignior*, or how you please, is as much in the state of nature, with all under his dominion, as he is with the rest of mankind: for wherever any two men are, who have no standing rule, and common judge to appeal to on earth, for the determination of controversies of right betwixt them, there they are still *in the state of nature,*[2] and under all the inconveniencies of it, with only this woeful difference to the subject, or rather slave of an absolute prince: that whereas, in the ordinary state of nature, he has a liberty to judge of his right, and according to the best of his power, to maintain it; now, whenever his property is invaded by the will and order of his monarch, he has not only no appeal, as those in society ought to have, but as if he were degraded from the common state of rational creatures, is denied a liberty to judge of, or to defend his right; and so is exposed to all the misery and inconveniencies, that a man can fear from one, who being in the unrestrained state of nature, is yet corrupted with flattery, and armed with power.

Sect. 92. For he that thinks *absolute power purifies men's blood*, and corrects the baseness of human nature, need read but the history of this, or any other age, to be convinced of the contrary. He that would have been insolent and injurious in the woods of *America,* would not probably be much better in a throne; where perhaps learning and religion shall be found out to justify all that he shall do to his subjects,

[1]The public power of all society is above every soul contained in the same society; and the principal use of that power is, to give laws unto all that are under it, which laws in such cases we must obey, unless there be reason showed which may necessarily enforce, that the law of reason, or of God, doth enjoin the contrary (*Hook. Eccl. Pol. l. i. sect. 16*)

[2]To take away all such mutual grievances, injuries and wrongs, i.e., such as attend men in the state of nature, there was no way but only by growing into composition and agreement amongst themselves, by ordaining some kind of government public, and by yielding themselves subject thereunto, that unto whom they granted authority to rule and govern, by them the peace, tranquility and happy estate of the rest might be procured. Men always knew that where force and injury was offered, they might be defenders of themselves; they knew that however men may seek their own commodity, yet if this were done with injury unto others, it was not to be suffered, but by all men, and all good means to be withstood. Finally, they knew that no man might in reason take upon him to determine his own right, and according to his own determination proceed in maintenance thereof, in as much as every man is toward himself, and them whom he greatly affects, partial; and therefore that strifes and troubles would be endless, except they gave their common consent, all to be ordered by some, whom they should agree upon, without which consent there would be no reason that one man should take upon him to be lord or judge over another (*Hooker's Eccl. Pol. l. i. sect. 10*)

continued

PRIMARY SOURCE 8.3 | OF PATERNAL POWER, FROM *SECOND TREATISE*, CHAPTER 6 *continued*

and the sword presently silence all those that dare question it: for what the *protection of absolute monarchy* is, what kind of fathers of their countries it makes princes to be and to what a degree of happiness and security it carries civil society, where this sort of government is grown to perfection, he that will look into the late relation of *Ceylon,* may easily see.

Sect. 93. In *absolute monarchies* indeed, as well as other governments of the world, the subjects have an appeal to the law, and judges to decide any controversies, and restrain any violence that may happen betwixt the subjects themselves, one amongst another. This every one thinks necessary, and believes he deserves to be thought a declared enemy to society and mankind, who should go about to take it away. But whether this be from a true love of mankind and society, and such a charity as we owe all one to another, there is reason to doubt: for this is no more than what every man, who loves his own power, profit, or greatness, may and naturally must do, keep those animals from hurting, or destroying one another, who labor and drudge only for his pleasure and advantage; and so are taken care of, not out of any love the master has for them, but love of himself, and the profit they bring him: for if it be asked, what security, *what fence* is there, in such a state, *against the violence and oppression of this absolute ruler?* the very question can scarce be borne. They are ready to tell you, that it deserves death only to ask after safety. Betwixt subject and subject, they will grant, there must be measures, laws and judges, for their mutual peace and security: but as for the *ruler,* he ought to be *absolute,* and is above all such circumstances; because he has power to do more hurt and wrong, it is right when he does it. To ask how you may be guarded from harm, or injury, on that side where the strongest hand is to do it, is presently the voice of faction and rebellion: as if when men quitting the state of nature entered into society, they agreed that all of them but one, should be under the restraint of laws, but that he should still retain all the liberty of the state of nature, increased with power, and made licentious by impunity. This is to think, that men are so foolish, that they take care to avoid what mischiefs may be done them by *pole-cats,* or *foxes;* but are content, nay, think it safety, to be devoured by *lions.*

Sect. 94. But whatever flatterers may talk to amuse people's understandings, it hinders not men from feeling; and when they perceive, that any man, in what station soever, is out of the bounds of the civil society which they are of, and that they have no appeal on earth against any harm, they may receive from him, they are apt to think themselves in the state of nature, in respect of him whom they find to be so; and to take care, as soon as they can, to have that *safety and security in civil society,* for which it was first instituted, and for which only they entered into it. And therefore, though perhaps at first (as shall be showed more at large hereafter in the following part of this discourse), some one good and excellent man having got a preeminency amongst the rest, had this deference paid to his goodness and virtue, as to a kind of natural authority, that the chief rule, with arbitration of their differences, by a tacit consent devolved into his hands, without any other caution, but the assurance they had of his uprightness and wisdom; yet when time, giving authority, and (as some men would persuade us) sacredness of customs, which the negligent, and unforeseeing innocence of the first ages began, had brought in successors of another stamp, the people finding their properties not secure under the government, as then it was (whereas government has no other end but the preservation of[3] property) could never be safe

[3] At the first, when some certain kind of regiment was once appointed, it may be that nothing was then farther thought upon for the manner of governing, but all permitted unto their wisdom and discretion, which were to rule, till by experience they found this for all parts very inconvenient, so as the thing which they had devised for a remedy, did indeed but increase the sore, which it should have cured. They saw, that *to live by one man's will, became the cause of all men's misery.* This constrained them to come unto laws, wherein all men might see their duty beforehand, and know the penalties of transgressing them. (*Hooker's Eccl. Pol. l. i. sect. 10*)

PRIMARY SOURCE 8.3

OF PATERNAL POWER, FROM *SECOND TREATISE*, CHAPTER 6 *continued*

nor at rest, *nor think themselves in civil society*, till the legislature was placed in collective bodies of men, call them senate, parliament, or what you please. By which means every single person became subject, equally with other the meanest men, to those laws, which he himself, as part of the legislative, had established; nor could any one, by his own authority; avoid the force of the law, when once made; nor by any pretense of superiority plead exemption, thereby to license his own, or the miscarriages of any of his dependents.[4] *No man in civil society can be exempted from the laws of it*: for if any man may do what he thinks fit, and there be no appeal on earth, for redress or security against any harm he shall do; I ask, whether he be not perfectly still in the state of nature, and so can be *no part or member of that civil society*; unless any one will say, the state of nature and civil society are one and the same thing, which I have never yet found any one so great a patron of anarchy as to affirm.

[4]Civil law being the act of the whole body politic, cloth therefore overrule each several part of the same body. (*Hooker, ibid.*)

failure to obtain the support of all. **Consent** is rather the assent to the *process* that includes the expectation that the minority will dissent from the majority. We have in that sense consented to laws from which we may dissent because we have participated in the process by which they were made. **Majority rule** is the only principle on which assemblies can effectively operate. "For when any number of Men have, by the consent of every individual, made a *Community*, they have thereby made that *Community* one Body, with a Power to Act as one Body, which is only the will and determination of the *majority*" (par. 95). That consideration determines the direction of the remainder of the *Second Treatise*, which, having established the principle of majority rule as the operative principle of civil society, then turns to the task of ensuring that it remains within the boundaries of the law of nature it was instituted to preserve. Chief among the means of restraining majority tyranny is continuous recollection of the "ends of political society and government." Locke seeks to make men responsible by calling them to their responsibilities. While not neglecting institutional devices designed to minimize the opportunities for overreaching, Locke places far greater reliance on the spirit that animates the legislative majority. This is largely in keeping with his conviction that the bond of trust makes the compact of civil society possible rather than the other way around. What his political reflections lack in precision, they make up for in rhetorical force. Locke's vision, rather than his details, has made the *Second Treatise* the most powerful evocation of liberal democracy.

Locke is thus at his evocative best when he reminds his readers that "the great and *chief end*" of men's formation of commonwealths "*is the Preservation of their Property*" (par. 124). He recognizes that the assault on property is the thin end of the wedge by which lawlessness seeps into civil society. The supreme legislative power exercised by the majority is corralled by principles that maintain it within the bounds for which it was instituted. First among its self-restraining principles is that it cannot be arbitrary because, even in the state of nature, none possess such power over themselves. It can legislate only within the bounds of the law of nature. Second, to avoid such arbitrariness, the legislative power is "*bound to dispense Justice,* and decide the Rights of the Subject *by promulgated standing Laws, and known Author-is'd Judges*" (par. 136). Third, it cannot " take from any Man any part of his *Property* without his consent" (par. 138). At this point Locke introduces the illustration of the absolute power over life and death that an official may exercise over an individual, as when a general orders a soldier to the mouth of a cannon, yet he "cannot dispose of one farthing of that Soldiers Estate" (139). Absolute power is not arbitrary power because it is fixed within the limits of law. Fourth, as the final bulwark against the rise of absolute rule, Locke insists that "*the Legislative cannot transfer the Power of Making Laws* to any other hands" (141). As if to underline the extent to which the legislative power constitutes a community under law, he insists on a separation of the executive and legislative powers. This idea is introduced in the form of an institutional check on the potential abuse of power because "it may be too great a temptation for humane frailty apt to grasp after Power, for the same Persons to have the Power of making Laws, to have also in their hands the power to execute them, whereby they may exempt themselves from Obedience to the Laws they make. . . ." But it is not simply the danger of abuse that is Locke's concern. It is the destruction of community by which the legislators might come to have an interest separate from the whole. Thus he insists that the legislative power be exercised by an assembly whose members "being separated again, they are subject to the Laws, they have made; which is a new and near tie upon them, to take care that they make them for the publick good" (par. 143).

RIGHT OF REVOLUTION

The executive power, in contrast, requires a more permanent existence and carries therefore the greatest potential of abuse. From this point on in the *Second Treatise,* Locke's reflections center on the restraint of executive power that cannot easily be limited in advance. By nature executive power is limited to the laws it is charged with enforcing and extends no further. But in reality, Locke recognizes, **executive power** is united with the **federative power** by which foreign policy is conducted. This latter power must remain open, flexible, and potentially unlimited because no one can determine in advance what may be required to ensure the survival of civil society in its relationships with other states. The challenge for Locke and for all constitutional government is to find a means of recapturing that unlimited power of war and peace within the boundaries of law that must occasionally be breached. Succeeding chapters are carefully structured to walk us through a series of steps that leads to the heart of the matter. Locke begins (Chapter 13) by reminding us that the community retains the supreme power of overruling its legislative or executive leaders when they step outside the law. The difficulty, however, is that the vital interests of the political community may from time to time require such illegality. **Prerogative** is the term by which this indeterminate power is known. While it may be indispensable to the viability of a constitutional order, it also opens an abyss of unlimited power. "This power to act according to discretion, for the publick good, without the prescription of the Law, and sometimes even against it, *is* that which is called *Prerogative*" (par. 160). Like Hobbes, Locke recognizes that no civil society can erect a power that can check the exercise of its sovereignty. Yet unlike Hobbes he insists that the community, even without a defender,

CASE STUDY 8.1 | LOCKE AND EXECUTIVE PREROGATIVE

Locke defines *prerogative* as the "power to act according to discretion, for the public good, without the prescription of the law, and sometimes even against it . . . for since in some governments the law-making power is not always in being, and is usually too numerous, and so too slow, for the dispatch requisite to execution; and because also it is impossible to foresee, and so by laws to provide for, all accidents and necessities that may concern the public, or to make such laws as will do not harm, if they are executed with an inflexible rigor, on all occasions, and upon all persons that may come in their way; therefore there is a latitude left to the executive power, to do many things of choice which the laws do not prescribe."

In sum, prerogative is the power of the executive to act in an extraconstitutional manner to preserve the nation in times of grave crisis, particularly when ordinary legal procedures are inadequate to the task. This may even involve breaking the constitution or the rule of law in the short-term in order to save it in the long-term. Locke's recognition of the power of prerogative reveals a tension in his thought between his defense of limited government and the need for executive energy in times of crisis. Can the precarious balance between liberty and security be maintained?

The Civil War placed enormous strains on the rule of law, testing whether the Constitution would become a casualty of the war. By the time of Abraham Lincoln's inauguration on March 4, 1861, seven states had seceded from the Union. On April 12, the Confederates opened fire on Fort Sumter in Charleston, South Carolina, thereby beginning the Civil War. Washington, D.C., was encircled by belligerents. The adjacent states of Maryland and Virginia were teetering on secession. Virginia would secede after Lincoln called up the militia. In Baltimore confederate sympathizers mobbed Union forces en route to Washington. Insurgents were burning bridges and sabotaging railways to prevent the capital's defense and reinforcement. With Congress out of session at the time, Lincoln undertook extraordinary measures to put down the rebellion and to protect the Union from a preemptive strike or invasion. He suspended the writ of habeas corpus, which guarantees the accused the right to have a judge review the grounds for their arrest; ordered a blockade of the South; called up state militias; and borrowed money from the treasury—all without congressional approval. When Congress was called into session on July 4, 1861, Lincoln justified his actions in the following manner:

> ". . . [A]re all the laws, *but one,* to go unexecuted, and the government itself go to pieces, lest that one be violated? Even in such a case, would not the official oath be broken, if the government should be overthrown, when it was believed that disregarding the single law, would tend to preserve it? But it was not believed that this question was presented. It was not believed that any law was violated. The provision of the Constitution that 'The privilege of the writ of habeas corpus, shall not be suspended unless when, in cases of rebellion or invasion, the public safety may require it,' is equivalent to a provision—is a provision—that such privilege may be suspended when, in cases of rebellion, or invasion, the public safety *does* require it. It was decided that we have a case of rebellion, and that the public safety does require the qualified suspension of the privilege of the writ which was authorized to be made. Now it is insisted that Congress, and not the Executive, is vested with this power. But the Constitution itself, is silent as to which, or who, is to exercise the power; and as the provision was plainly made for a dangerous emergency, it cannot be believed the framers of the instrument intended, that in every case, the danger should run its course, until Congress could be called together; the very assembling of which might be prevented, as was intended in this case, by the rebellion."

has not for that reason yielded its right of judging when its interests have been subverted (168). In the next chapter (15), Locke reminds us that such despotic power is not to be confused with paternal power that lasts only as long as childhood itself. Nor is tyranny to be confused with the rights of conquest, which extend no further than requiring satisfaction for injuries done. No government, Locke insists, "can have a right to

QUESTIONS FOR REFLECTION

Given Lincoln's extraordinary use of executive power during the Civil War, some scholars have claimed that he established a constitutional dictatorship. Are Lincoln's actions consistent with Locke's view of executive prerogative? Can the notion of a constitutional dictatorship be reconciled with limited and free government?

obedience from people who have not consented to it" (par. 192). This is such an immovable principle of the law of nature that princes can never dispense with it. Consent is the foundation of all moral relationships. To abrogate it would be to set aside all possibility of community—that is, of a relationship based on anything other than force. Even God himself is bound by consent. "*Grants, Promises* and *Oaths* are Bonds that *hold the Almighty:* Whatever some flatterers say to Princes of the World who all together, with all their People joined to them, are in comparison to the great God, but as a drop of the Bucket, or a Dust on the Balance, inconsiderable nothing" (195).

Consideration of **usurpation** (Chapter 17) and **tyranny** (Chapter 18) leads to the final phase of Locke's inquiry, which logically concerns the means by which the exercise of power without right might be resisted. In this discussion Locke goes through most of the standard arguments that had traditionally been adduced to resist a tyrant. Force may not be used against the legitimate exercise of power but only against "against unjust and unlawful Force" (204). There is no danger from such readiness to defend one's rights because it is in reality a defense of the boundaries of law itself. The logic of this position is fully unfolded in Chapter 19, "Of the Dissolution of Government." Here Locke makes clear that the unlawful use of force against members of the political community does not require or legitimate a revolt. Rather, rebellion becomes redundant when government has dissolved itself by setting the source of its own legal authority at naught. This is Locke's culminating affirmation of the bonds of community from which government is derived and which it is never entitled to abrogate. Rebellion does not so much remove a government that has become illegitimate as recognize a condition in which government has abolished itself by becoming illegitimate. What remains is for the community to institute a new government in recognition of its own desire to continue as a commonwealth under law. Everything that Locke says here follows from the crucial distinction he insists upon at the opening of the chapter between the community that endures and the government that may be dissolved. "He that will with any clearness speak of the *Dissolution of Government,* ought, in the first place to distinguish between the *Dissolution of the Society* and the *Dissolution of the Government*" (211). Because Locke places so much weight on this distinction, recognizing the permanence of civil society even in the impermanence of its governmental representative, he can accept the possibility of rebellion with equanimity. The specter of anarchy hardly seems to affect him because the bonds of community have not been broken. Even when government itself becomes a lawbreaker, a defense remains within the law-abiding community. In words that would later find their way into the *Declaration of Independence,* he can reassure us that such rejection of government will not happen "upon every little mismanagement of publick affairs." It is only when "a long train of Abuses, Prevarications, and Artifices, all tending the same way, make the design visible to the People" that they "then rouse themselves, and endeavor to put the rule into such hands, which may secure to them the ends for which Government was at first erected. . . ." (par. 225). The centrality of this idea of community recurs in the final paragraph of the *Treatise,* where Locke reiterates that the **dissolution of government** restores individuals not to the state of nature but rather to the prepolitical state of community that characterized it. The ambivalence of Locke's thought operating within the tension between the individual and the community remains to the very end. Hobbes is clear that there is no community without a government, without a representative through whom collective action is possible. Locke knows this too, but he cannot quite shake off the awareness that such sovereign authority has its source within self-governing individuals who must at some point come together to give effect to the common order they bear within them. The community can act only through a representative, but the representative cannot create himself. Government ultimately emerges in a mysterious process from individuals who are already inwardly united before they become visibly so. A large part of the secret of Locke's enormous influence is that the elusiveness of his thought respects the elusiveness of the situation in which human beings find themselves. We are individuals who determine our own existence and cannot be properly human if we are less than responsible for ourselves. Yet we cannot function alone. We find ourselves in a network of mutual obligations before we even become conscious of our self-determining prerogative. Politically this ambivalence is of great moment because it means that the breakdown or the failure of government is never ultimate. As individuals we carry the capacity for improvising government within ourselves.

It is because community is such an inner reality of human beings that Locke regards the breach of its bonds as such an outrage. The person who would break faith with his fellows has not merely failed morally or socially. He has set himself outside humanity itself. A particular invective is reserved for a prince who would turn rapaciously on his own people. He has become, in Locke's words, "a wolf or a lyon" who would stop at nothing short of the complete destruction of his victims. Like all criminals, "such men are not under the ties of the common law of reason, have no other rule, but that of force and violence, and so may be treated as beasts of prey" (par. 16). The blood-curdling quotation from Livy that Locke selects as the motto of the *Two Treatises* highlights the sentiment that animates the whole work. We must read the *Two Treatises,* therefore, primarily as a guide not to Locke's thoughts on politics but to the powerful conviction through which he thinks politics should be viewed. The work seeks to evoke a certain recognition in the reader and only subsequently to convince us of its political implications. That evocative vision at its core is the community of human beings. Harshness in the treatment of lawbreakers is one of the principal means by which Locke impresses the inviolability of the social and political bonds upon us. An assault on the rights of one becomes an assault on the rights of all. He who would set aside the rights of another has demonstrated a readiness to overturn the entire order of rights and can properly be treated as one who has turned his back on his own humanity. One reason why Locke was convinced that the mutual recognition and preservation of rights constituted a sufficient bond of political society was that he was intensely aware of the underlying sense of community on which it drew. The indivisibility of rights is not merely a slogan of later popularity, but is embedded in the very logic of the idea of rights. The genius of Locke and of the form of **liberal democracy** to which he gave rise is the realization of this unbreakable connection.

PRIMARY SOURCE 8.4

Of the Dissolution of Government, from *Second Treatise*, Chapter 19

Sect. 223. To this perhaps it will be said, that the people being ignorant, and always discontented, to lay the foundation of government in the unsteady opinion and uncertain humor of the people, is to expose it to certain ruin; and *no government will be able long to subsist,* if the people may set up a new legislative, whenever they take offense at the old one. To this I answer, Quite the contrary. People are not so easily got out of their old forms, as some are apt to suggest. They are hardly to be prevailed with to amend the acknowledged faults in the frame they have been accustomed to. And if there be any original defects, or adventitious ones introduced by time, or corruption; it is not an easy thing to get them changed, even when all the world sees there is an opportunity for it. This slowness and aversion in the people to quit their old constitutions, has, in the many revolutions which have been seen in this kingdom, in this and former ages, still kept us to, or, after some interval of fruitless attempts, still brought us back again to our old legislative of king, lords, and commons: and whatever provocations have made the crown be taken from some of our princes' heads, they never carried the people so far as to place it in another line.

Sect. 224. But it will be said, this *hypothesis* lays a *ferment for* frequent *rebellion.* To which I answer, *First,* No more than any other *hypothesis:* for when the people are made miserable, and find themselves *exposed to the ill usage of arbitrary power,* cry up their governors, as much as you will, for sons of *Jupiter*; let them be sacred and divine, descended, or authorized from heaven; give them out for whom or what you please, the same will happen. *The people generally ill treated,* and contrary to right, will be ready upon any occasion to ease themselves of a burden that sits heavy upon them. They will wish, and seek for the opportunity, which in the change, weakness, and accidents of human affairs, seldom delays long to offer itself. He must have lived but a little while in the world, who has not seen examples of this in his time; and he must have read very little, who cannot produce examples of it in all sorts of governments in the world.

Sec. 225. *Secondly,* I answer, such *revolutions* happen not upon every little mismanagement in public affairs. *Great mistakes* in the ruling part, many wrong and inconvenient laws, and all the *slips* of human frailty, will be *borne by the people* without mutiny or murmur. But if a long train of abuses, prevarications, and artifices, all tending the same way, make the design visible to the people, and they cannot but feel what they lie under, and see whither they are going; it is not to be wondered, that they should then rouse themselves, and endeavor to put the rule into such hands which may secure to them the ends for which government was at first erected; and without which, ancient names, and specious forms, are so far from being better, that they are much worse, than the state of nature, or pure anarchy; the inconveniencies being all as great and as near, but the remedy farther off and more difficult.

Sect. 226. *Thirdly,* I answer, that *this doctrine* of a power in the people of providing for their safety anew, by a new legislative, when their legislators have acted contrary to their trust, by invading their property, is *the best fence against rebellion,* and the probablest means to hinder it: for *rebellion* being an opposition, not to persons, but authority, which is founded only in the constitutions and laws of the government; those, whoever they be, who by force break through, and by force justify their violation of them, are truly and properly *rebels:* for when men, by entering into society and civil government, have excluded force, and introduced laws for the preservation of property, peace, and unity amongst themselves, those who set up force again in opposition to the laws, do *rebellare,* that is, bring back again the state of war, and are properly rebels: which they who are in power (by the pretense they have to authority, the temptation of force they have in their hands, and the flattery of those about them) being likeliest to do; the properest way to prevent the evil, is to show them the danger and injustice of it, who are under the greatest temptation to run into it.

Sect. 227. In both the fore-mentioned cases, when either the legislative is changed, or the legislators act contrary to the end for which they were constituted; those who are guilty are *guilty of rebellion:* for if any one by force takes away the established legislative of any society, and the laws by them made, pursuant to their trust, he thereby takes away the umpirage, which every one had consented to, for a peaceable decision of all their controversies, and a bar to the state of war

PRIMARY SOURCE 8.4 | OF THE DISSOLUTION OF GOVERNMENT, FROM *SECOND TREATISE*, CHAPTER 19 *continued*

amongst them. They, who remove, or change the legislative, take away this decisive power, which no body can have, but by the appointment and consent of the people; and so destroying the authority which the people did, and nobody else can set up, and introducing a power which the people hath not authorized, they actually *introduce a state of war,* which is that of force without authority: and thus, by removing the legislative established by the society, (in whose decisions the people acquiesced and united, as to that of their own will) they untie the knot, and *expose the people anew to the state of war.* And if those, who by force take away the legislative, are *rebels,* the *legislators* themselves, as has been shown, can be no less esteemed so; when they, who were set up for the protection, and preservation of the people, their liberties and properties, shall by force invade and endeavor to take them away; and so they putting themselves into a state of war with those who made them the protectors and guardians of their peace, are properly, and with the greatest aggravation, *rebellantes,* rebels.

Sec. 228. But if they, who say *it lays a foundation for rebellion,* mean that it may occasion civil wars, or intestine broils, to tell the people they are absolved from obedience when illegal attempts are made upon their liberties or properties, and may oppose the unlawful violence of those who were their magistrates, when they invade their properties contrary to the trust put in them; and that therefore this doctrine is not to be allowed, being so destructive to the peace of the world: they may as well say, upon the same ground, that honest men may not oppose robbers or pirates, because this may occasion disorder or bloodshed. If any *mischief* come in such cases, it is not to be charged upon him who defends his own right, but *on him that invades* his neighbors. If the innocent honest man must quietly quit all he has, for peace sake, to him who will lay violent hands upon it, I desire it may be considered, what a kind of peace there will be in the world, which consists only in violence and rapine; and which is to be maintained only for the benefit of robbers and oppressors. Who would not think it an admirable peace betwixt the mighty and the mean, when the lamb, without resistance, yielded his throat to be torn by the imperious wolf? *Polyphemus's* den gives us a perfect pattern of such a peace, and such a government, wherein *Ulysses* and his companions had nothing to do, but quietly to suffer themselves to be devoured. And no doubt *Ulysses,* who was a prudent man, preached up *passive obedience,* and exhorted them to a quiet submission, by representing to them of what concernment peace was to mankind; and by showing the inconveniences might happen, if they should offer to resist *Polyphemus,* who had now the power over them.

Sect. 229. The end of government is the good of mankind; and which is *best for mankind,* that the people should be always exposed to the boundless will of tyranny, or that the rulers should be sometimes liable to be opposed, when they grow exorbitant in the use of their power, and employ it for the destruction, and not the preservation of the properties of their people?

Sect. 230. Nor let any one say, that mischief can arise from hence, as often as it shall please a busy head, or turbulent spirit, to desire the alteration of the government. It is true, such men may stir, whenever they please; but it will be only to their own just ruin and perdition: for till the mischief be grown general, and the ill designs of the rulers become visible, or their attempts sensible to the greater part, the people, who are more disposed to suffer than right themselves by resistance, are not apt to stir. The examples of particular injustice, or oppression of here and there an unfortunate man, moves them not. But if they universally have a persuasion, grounded upon manifest evidence, that designs are carrying on against their liberties, and the general course and tendency of things cannot but give them strong suspicions of the evil intention of their governors, who is to be blamed for it? Who can help it, if they, who might avoid it, bring themselves into this suspicion? Are the people to be blamed, if they have the sense of rational creatures, and can think of things no otherwise than as they find and feel them? And is it not rather *their fault,* who put things into such a posture, that they would not have them thought to be as they are? I grant, that the pride, ambition, and turbulence of private men have sometimes caused great disorders in commonwealths, and factions have been fatal to states and kingdoms. But whether *the mischief* hath *oftener* begun *in the peoples wantonness,* and a desire to cast off the lawful authority of their rulers, or *in the rulers insolence,* and endeavors to get and exercise

continued

PRIMARY SOURCE 8.4

OF THE DISSOLUTION OF GOVERNMENT, FROM *SECOND TREATISE*, CHAPTER 19 *continued*

an arbitrary power over their people; whether oppression, or disobedience, gave the first rise to the disorder, I leave it to impartial history to determine. This I am sure, whoever, either ruler or subject, by force goes about to invade the rights of either prince or people, and lays the foundation for *overturning* the constitution and frame of *any just government,* is highly guilty of the greatest crime, I think, a man is capable of, being to answer for all those mischiefs of blood, rapine, and desolation, which the breaking to pieces of governments bring on a country. And he who does it, is justly to be esteemed the common enemy and pest of mankind, and is to be treated accordingly.

QUEST FOR RELIGIOUS CONSENSUS

Locke remained supremely confident that rights and community were inseparable. Unconcerned with the individualistic implications of his thought, he was free to explore how such fragmented perspectives lead again toward unity. Such was the task Locke set himself in his philosophical and religious writings, with results that are quite different. Whereas Locke's political reflections have constituted a permanent success in the advent of liberal democracy, his philosophical and religious analyses have generally receded in historical developments that have overtaken them. Impressive as the latter writings are, they no longer define the present state of the questions. The contrast with the continuing relevance of the *Two Treatises* could not be greater. Yet it would be a pity to neglect his philosophical and religious works as historically obsolete: They were celebrated in his own day, and they are classic statements of a particular phase of the questions in their own right. They also help us complete the picture of Locke's political theory in that they move in the same direction of evoking the community of human beings that is always inchoately present. Philosophically Locke sought the common ground of reason by which all intellectual, moral, and religious disagreements might be resolved. Theologically he sought to find a consensus understanding of Christianity that would stand on the common grounds of scripture. The fact that neither project succeeded does not demonstrate their futility; even in their failure they show the inspiration under which Locke labored to reconcile divergences.

Nowhere is this conception better captured than in the anecdote in which he explains, in an "Epistle to the Reader," the genesis of his philosophical masterpiece, *An Essay Concerning Human Understanding*. He recounts how a dinner conversation among friends, "meeting at my chamber and discoursing on a subject very remote from this, found themselves quickly at a stand, by the difficulties that arose on every side." One of the friends, James Tyrell, supplied the topic of their colloquium as "the principles of morality and revealed religion." In other words, Locke's focus, even in his philosophically most ambitious work, remains on the resolution of the differences that fracture the community in which human beings find themselves. He was willing to confront the plurality of perspectives that has come to characterize modern societies because he remained convinced of the single truth that lay behind them. *The Essay Concerning Human Understanding* has from its first appearance been recognized as just such a fearless undertaking. Locke was prepared to adopt a radical method of returning to the most elementary building blocks of thought in sensation and

QUESTIONS FOR REFLECTION

Consider the relationship between Locke and the American founders. The Declaration of Independence virtually quotes Locke in asserting a right of revolution, but the Constitution is completely silent about such a right. Is there such a thing as a right of revolution? If so, what kind of right is it—natural or legal?

reflection, our irreducible experience of the outer and inner reality in which we find ourselves. He well understood the risk of an approach that put traditional ideas of human nature, the world, and God to the test to probe their ultimate coherence. It was a project of similar ambition to that of Descartes, who had sought to rebuild philosophy anew from the ground up. There was no guarantee that it would find its way back to the traditional worldview. This intellectual daring has given Locke the reputation of an innovator, inclined to question conventional assumptions and even to expose the weaknesses of a tradition still regnant from the medieval Christian past. But keep in mind that Locke still subscribed to that essentially Christian vision of reality. He sought only to place it on a more impregnable basis.

The results may not always have been in line even with his own traditional inclinations. This is particularly the case if one traces the line of philosophical development from his *Essay* into the full-blown skepticism, and even atheism, of the 18th century. Some have concluded from this pattern that Locke's own avowed piety was not genuine, that he too was a skeptic and subverter at heart. The problem with this suggestion is that it contradicts the purpose that prompted his philosophical odyssey, which was to find a more secure basis for "the principles of morality and revealed religion." Locke was, in other words, a highly unusual thinker. He placed his philosophically radical reflection in the service of reinforcing the traditional order. We may still conclude that the assistance he rendered was more of a hindrance than a help, but we can hardly deny his intention. Perhaps of greater interest is to understand how he reconciled the apparently divergent tendencies of his thought. How was it possible for him to simultaneously undermine and defend traditional morality and religion? The answer is the faith that constituted the bedrock of his own worldview. Reason could be trusted as a guide to the truth of reality because ultimately God would not allow it to be deceived. Locke's faith in reason turns out therefore to be a faith in the God who created it. Even when he could not demonstrate the truth of the moral life, he nevertheless felt there was such a truth because God guaranteed it. "That God has given a rule whereby men should govern themselves, I think there is nobody so brutish as to deny. He has a right to do it; we are his creatures; he has goodness and wisdom to direct our actions to that which is best, and he has power to enforce it by rewards and punishments of infinite weight and duration in another life; for nobody can take us out of his hands. This is the only true touchstone of moral rectitude" (*Essay Concerning Human Understanding*, Book II, Chapter 28, par. 5).

Perhaps the inconclusiveness of his philosophical project led Locke to devote much of the remaining 15 years of his life more directly to the question of religion. In 1695 he published his most famous work in this area, *On the Reasonableness of Christianity*, in which he sketched what a plain reading of the scripture might yield. Once again his focus was on the common ground that Christians of all denominations might share once they confined themselves to the minimal consensus supportable by scripture alone. The result was a **Latitudinarian Christianity** in which the great theological dogmas of the divinity of Christ and his redemptive atonement for sin were muted to minimize the kind of religious conflict that had ravaged England during its civil war. Many accused Locke of being antitrinitarian, as well as of embracing a purely rational religion from which God's saving grace is absent. To all such critics his consistent reply was that he was neither for nor against the dogmas but simply could not find an incontrovertible basis for them in scripture. The discipline of his reading, on which alone a consensus form of Christianity might be articulated, was to add nothing more than a plain reading of the text would justify. He could moreover adduce a strong theological rationale for this strict construction. To the extent that Christians regard scripture as the inspired word of God, they owe it to God not to introduce their own private opinions into that authoritative communication. In insisting on this minimalist principle of interpretation, Locke had once again staked out an elusive middle ground that, while it did not satisfy the denominations, continued to play a role in the form of nondenominational Christianity that has often performed a unifying political role. Consider, for example, the kind of broadly Christian service that is employed at state funerals when the religious and the political are inevitably commingled.

The real contribution of Locke's *On the Reasonableness of Christianity* lies not in the ambiguous service it provides to Christianity, but in the clarification it renders toward the role of reason in grounding a political order. In the *Two Treatises* Locke pulls no punches concerning the theological source of the natural law; he had not yet confronted the possibility that natural law might be able to function without explicit reference to a divine lawgiver. Grotius had already suggested the possibility of such a purely rational basis for law, and this is of course a question of great significance within the contemporary understanding of the secular state. It is widely assumed that the form of liberal democracy evolves, whatever its historical roots may have been, in a fully secular direction. Much of the confidence that liberal democracy can be transmitted to regions of the world unconnected with Christianity relies on this conception. Islamic societies are today asked to embrace a secular form of government. But can liberal democracy be so neatly separated from its spiritual roots? Locke certainly tilts in this direction, although he concludes that the separation can never be complete. As we struggle today with the same question of Islamic societies and those of other faiths that are nevertheless liberal, it is instructive to return again to the nuanced position that Locke works out for this difficulty. In many ways it is reminiscent of the balance that the greatest medieval thinker, St. Thomas Aquinas, elaborates concerning the self-sufficiency of the law of nature. Both Aquinas and Locke recognize the natural law as a law of reason that is therefore in principle accessible to all men on that basis. Yet they also acknowledge that few are likely to reach its fullness without the aid of revelation. Locke goes even further, insisting that as a matter of fact none had done so. The evidence of history demonstrated that it was only through Christ that humanity had embraced the full implications of the law of nature. "It should seem," he concludes, "by the little that has hitherto been done in it, that 'tis too hard a task for unassisted reason, to establish morality, in all its parts, upon its true foundations, with a clear and convincing light" (*On the Reasonableness of Christianity,* par. 241). The moral law cannot ultimately dispense with its divine authorization. Like reason, morality is incapable of fully grounding itself.

TOLERANCE AS CORE SPIRITUAL TRUTH

The political implications of this admission are momentous because they seem to suggest what many have embraced: a theocratic state. If reason and morality are insufficient on their own, then only the rule of divine law can supply the authority needed. Locke and the liberal democracy he fostered of course resolutely reject that implication. The unraveling of this final tension in his thought brings us into the deepest level of its elusiveness. We now enter the innermost core that enabled Locke to hold together these two most divergent strands of the political reality in which he lived. On one hand, the moral and political law cannot do without its divine authorization; on the other, that divine authorization cannot displace the liberty that each person enjoys in self-government. How is it possible for authority and liberty to be reconciled? Locke's answer is that their coincidence is reached in the realization that liberty is divinely authorized. This insight is the central principle of his *Letter Concerning Toleration,* which forms an integral and culminating text within his political thought. Its influence has been perhaps even more far-reaching than that of the *Second Treatise:* Within the space of a 50-page letter Locke describes the self-evident formulation of the principle of religious liberty that had hitherto eluded statesmen and thinkers alike. His achievement in the *Letter* is nothing short of revolutionary. It consists in taking the term that had conventionally applied to "tolerating," or putting up with, religious differences one was powerless to change and transforming its largely negative meaning into an avowedly positive direction. From that point on **religious toleration** ceased to imply a concession of weakness and became the pivot for the affirmation of liberty that civil society had been instituted to preserve. Higher than the question of religious truth stood the human beings who must find their way toward it. The priority of liberty over truth now became the truth of liberal democracy.

There is every indication that Locke understood the significance of the path he was charting if we give full weight to the sentence with which he magisterially opens the letter. "Since you are pleased to inquire what are my thoughts about the mutual toleration of Christians in their different professions of religion, I must needs answer you freely, that I esteem that toleration to be the chief characteristical mark of the true Church." The argument on which he was about to embark drew on a theological justification. Rather than seeing toleration simply as an article of political peace, Locke sought to grasp it as a requirement of Christianity itself. He knew that only if toleration could be justified in principle could it be more than a compromise of temporary effect. Once again Locke had seized upon the essential point toward which his world had been inarticulately groping. No one wants religious liberty to hang on the shifting political fortunes or precarious goodwill of those in power. Somehow it must be established as a matter of principle—that is, as a right secured beyond political negotiation. But that would require finding a justification for toleration that is more than political. Liberty must be divinely authorized if it is to be regarded as ultimately impregnable. Locke understood the nature of the challenge this intuition presented: The impossibility of reaching a religious agreement had provoked the necessity of embracing toleration in the first place. Could there be a religious agreement that prescinded from religious differences? Would it be possible to reach a theological viewpoint above the confessional disputes? Locke was headed in the direction that is now familiar to us—toward the consensus that is already present between human beings even before they are aware of being in community with one another. His *Letter Concerning Toleration* is the great evocation of "religion without religion" that still represents the limit of the self-understanding of liberal democracy today.

When toleration has become the mark of the true church, then the true church seems to overlap with the true state. Locke seems less concerned with locating the distinction between church and state than with articulating it. The ambiguity of whether the distinction is theological or political is one with which he was prepared to live, for it served his fundamental goal of defining the meaning of what it is to be human. His *Letter* is carefully structured. It moves from an elementary consideration of the commonwealth as concerned with external matters (the protection of life, liberty, and property) into a deeper consideration of what the exercise of those rights must mean in the realm of religion. Civil society is instituted, we might say, to secure the conditions of freedom, not to determine the direction in which it is to be exercised. It is for this reason that "the care of souls is not committed to the civil magistrate, any more than to other men." Besides, the magistrate is in no better a position than other men to determine the truth and has at his disposal only external means of compulsion. A church, in contrast, is precisely the kind of institution equipped to lead people toward theological truth: It is led by people devoted to the task and committed only to spiritual means of persuasion. As a wholly voluntary society, a church is the appropriate community through which the exercise of individual liberty should be exercised. But this means that the church is also free to set its own rules, accepting or rejecting whom it pleases without attaching any civil penalties or consequences to its actions. Just as the church cannot call on the magistrate for special support in enforcing its discipline, so the magistrate cannot presume the wisdom of judging theological matters. Not only are they in different worlds but, Locke concludes, they are likely to struggle over issues that are remote from the most elemental truth that all denominations share. His reference here to "indifferent matters" has often been taken as suggesting Locke's indifference to religion. The contrary, as we have seen, is more likely to be the case. Locke takes religion so seriously that he is willing to surrender its details for the sake of preserving its core.

That is the position he stakes out at the very center of the *Letter*. Religion, if it is true to itself, must be a religion of liberty. Having extensively demarcated in the previous pages the roles of the magistrate and the church, he concedes that "after all, the principal consideration, and which absolutely determines this controversy, is this: although the magistrate's opinion in religion be sound, and the way that he appoints be truly evangelical, yet if I be not thoroughly persuaded thereof in my own mind, there will be no safety for me in following it." A faith that is coerced is not faith because its essence is that the response must be free. "Men cannot be forced to be saved" in the same way that they cannot be forced to be cured of various illnesses or compelled to receive external benefits against their will. The benefits of faith are inseparable from the freedom through which it is exercised. Over and above the content of all religion is the person whose assent cannot be coerced in the slightest, because that would rob religion of all value. The meaning of religion is, in other words, tied up with the inviolability of the person. Even God does not breach the boundary by which the freedom of the person is guarded. Respect for that innermost freedom is the core of all freedom because it is the core of what it means to be human. As possessors of a freedom impervious to foreclosures, we all possess a transcendent dignity. In evoking the very apex of his thought, Locke here finds the point at which the irremovable community of all human beings is recognized. Higher than all religions stands the truth of the person who is open to them. "In a word: whatsoever may be doubtful in religion, yet this at least is certain, that no religion which I believe not to be true, can be either true or profitable unto me."

Having established the indispensability of religious liberty, Locke still faced the question of its regulation. Religious liberty does not license an unfettered self-interpretation of its meaning. The magistrate remains responsible for the public good and therefore is charged with regulating the external conditions for the exercise of liberty. Concerning the rites and services of any church, his position is clear. Just as the magistrate cannot prohibit actions that are otherwise lawful within the commonwealth, neither can he excuse actions that are unlawful merely because they are performed in the name of religion. So human sacrifice as part of religious worship, for example, is not protected by the liberty presumption. "These things are not lawful in the ordinary course of life, nor in any private house; and therefore neither are they so in the worship of God, or in any religious meeting" (415). The matter is more complicated when it comes to the regulation of religious teaching. That seems to infringe on the very essence of liberty of conscience. Yet even here Locke is prepared to countenance significant limits. In the case of a clash between conscience and the law, the individual cannot presume the right to set aside his legal obligations; he may simple have to bear the consequences of punishment for his refusal to obey. More generally, Locke insists, certain categories of religious teaching are not to be tolerated. They included teachings contrary to the morality essential for human society, claims of special exemptions from the law, those who "deliver themselves up to the service and protection of another prince," and those that "deny the being of God." Looking back from our own broader conception of religious liberty, it is difficult to resist the conclusion that Locke has narrowed its application almost to the point of self-contradiction. We would be hard pressed to exclude Catholics and atheists, the targets of his last two categories. But fairness requires not only that we place Locke's restrictions within the historical context, especially the fear of Catholic absolutism in politics, but that we also acknowledge the wholly political justification for the limitations applied. The magistrate has no theological agenda at work. His only concern is with the political effect of their teaching. "Promises, covenants, and oaths, which are the bonds of human society, can have no hold on an atheist." They are proscribed, not because of what they believe, but because they are incapable of becoming citizens.

Locke's evocation of community, the bond of trust that makes political society possible, remains his principal concern. Like those who set aside the rights of others, be they princes or legislators, so also any who have placed themselves outside the common order that holds human beings together have already determined their own fate. Exclusion, like revolution, is redundant because they have already made the separation themselves. Even if we wanted to include those who claim that the rules no longer apply to them, we would not be able to do it. By the logic of their own actions they have made submission to a common law impossible. "That we may draw toward a conclusion," Locke declares, "the sum of all we drive at is that every man may enjoy the same rights that are granted to others." This is the bright center of Locke's political reflections. What those rights are may be insufficiently defined, and how we are to adjudicate conflicts between them may be left unaddressed; but we are in no doubt

PRIMARY SOURCE 8.5 | FROM A LETTER CONCERNING TOLERATION

Let us now consider what is the magistrate's duty in the business of toleration, which certainly is very considerable.

We have already proved that the care of souls does not belong to the magistrate. Not a magisterial care, I mean (if I may so call it), which consists in prescribing by laws and compelling by punishments. But a charitable care, which consists in teaching, admonishing, and persuading, cannot be denied unto any man. The care, therefore, of every man's soul belongs unto himself and is to be left unto himself. But what if he neglect the care of his soul? I answer: What if he neglect the care of his health or of his estate, which things are nearlier related to the government of the magistrate than the other? Will the magistrate provide by an express law that such a one shall not become poor or sick? Laws provide, as much as is possible, that the goods and health of subjects be not injured by the fraud and violence of others; they do not guard them from the negligence or ill husbandry of the possessors themselves. No man can be forced to be rich or healthful whether he will or no. Nay, God Himself will not save men against their wills. Let us suppose, however, that some prince were desirous to force his subjects to accumulate riches, or to preserve the health and strength of their bodies. Shall it be provided by law that they must consult none but Roman physicians, and shall everyone be bound to live according to their prescriptions? What, shall no potion, no broth, be taken, but what is prepared either in the Vatican, suppose, or in a Geneva shop? Or, to make these subjects rich, shall they all be obliged by law to become merchants or musicians? Or, shall everyone turn victualler, or smith, because there are some that maintain their families plentifully and grow rich in those professions? But, it may be said, there are a thousand ways to wealth, but one only way to heaven. It is well said, indeed, especially by those that plead for compelling men into this or the other way. For if there were several ways that led thither, there would not be so much as a pretense left for compulsion. But now, if I be marching on with my utmost vigor in that way which, according to the sacred geography, leads straight to Jerusalem, why am I beaten and ill-used by others because, perhaps, I wear not buskins; because my hair is not of the right cut; because, perhaps, I have not been dipped in the right fashion; because I eat flesh upon the road, or some other food which agrees with my stomach; because I avoid certain by-ways, which seem unto me to lead into briars or precipices; because, amongst the several paths that are in the same road, I choose that to walk in which seems to be the straightest and cleanest; because I avoid to keep company with some travelers that are less grave and others that are more sour than they ought to be; or, in fine, because I follow a guide that either is, or is not, clothed in white, or crowned with a miter? Certainly, if we consider right, we shall find that, for the most part, they are such frivolous things as these that (without any prejudice to religion or the salvation of souls, if not accompanied with superstition or hypocrisy) might either be observed or omitted. I say they are such-like things as these which breed implacable enmities amongst Christian brethren, who are all agreed in the substantial and truly fundamental part of religion.

But let us grant unto these zealots, who condemn all things that are not of their mode, that from these circumstances are different ends. What shall we conclude from thence? There is only one of these which is the true way to eternal happiness: but in this great variety of ways that men follow, it is still doubted which is the right one. Now, neither the care of the commonwealth, nor the right enacting of laws, does discover this way that leads to heaven more certainly to the magistrate than every private man's search and study discovers it unto himself. I have a weak body, sunk under a languishing disease, for which (I suppose) there is one only remedy, but that unknown. Does it therefore belong unto the magistrate to prescribe me a remedy, because there is but one, and because it is unknown? Because there is but one way for me

PRIMARY SOURCE 8.5 | FROM A LETTER CONCERNING TOLERATION *continued*

to escape death, will it therefore be safe for me to do whatsoever the magistrate ordains? Those things that every man ought sincerely to inquire into himself, and by meditation, study, search, and his own endeavors, attain the knowledge of, cannot be looked upon as the peculiar possession of any sort of men. Princes, indeed, are born superior unto other men in power, but in nature equal. Neither the right nor the art of ruling does necessarily carry along with it the certain knowledge of other things, and least of all of true religion. For if it were so, how could it come to pass that the lords of the earth should differ so vastly as they do in religious matters? But let us grant that it is probable the way to eternal life may be better known by a prince than by his subjects, or at least that in this incertitude of things the safest and most commodious way for private persons is to follow his dictates. You will say: "What then?" If he should bid you follow merchandise for your livelihood, would you decline that course for fear it should not succeed? I answer: I would turn merchant upon the prince's command, because, in case I should have ill-success in trade, he is abundantly able to make up my loss some other way. If it be true, as he pretends, that he desires I should thrive and grow rich, he can set me up again when unsuccessful voyages have broken me. But this is not the case in the things that regard the life to come; if there I take a wrong course, if in that respect I am once undone, it is not in the magistrate's power to repair my loss, to ease my suffering, nor to restore me in any measure, much less entirely, to a good estate. What security can be given for the Kingdom of Heaven?

Perhaps some will say that they do not suppose this infallible judgment, that all men are bound to follow in the affairs of religion, to be in the civil magistrate, but in the Church. What the Church has determined, that the civil magistrate orders to be observed; and he provides by his authority that nobody shall either act or believe in the business of religion otherwise than the Church teaches. So that the judgment of those things is in the Church; the magistrate himself yields obedience thereunto and requires the like obedience from others. I answer: Who sees not how frequently the name of the Church, which was venerable in time of the apostles, has been made use of to throw dust in the people's eyes in the following ages? But, however, in the present case it helps us not. The one only narrow way which leads to heaven is not better known to the magistrate than to private persons, and therefore I cannot safely take him for my guide, who may probably be as ignorant of the way as myself, and who certainly is less concerned for my salvation than I myself am. Amongst so many kings of the Jews, how many of them were there whom any Israelite, thus blindly following, had not fallen into idolatry and thereby into destruction? Yet, nevertheless, you bid me be of good courage and tell me that all is now safe and secure, because the magistrate does not now enjoin the observance of his own decrees in matters of religion, but only the decrees of the Church. Of what Church, I beseech you? of that, certainly, which likes him best. As if he that compels me by laws and penalties to enter into this or the other Church, did not interpose his own judgment in the matter. What difference is there whether he lead me himself, or deliver me over to be led by others? I depend both ways upon his will, and it is he that determines both ways of my eternal state. Would an Israelite that had worshipped Baal upon the command of his king have been in any better condition because somebody had told him that the king ordered nothing in religion upon his own head, nor commanded anything to be done by his subjects in divine worship but what was approved by the counsel of priests, and declared to be of divine right by the doctors of their Church? If the religion of any Church become, therefore, true and saving, because the head of that sect, the prelates and priests, and those of that tribe, do all of them, with all their might, extol and praise it, what religion can ever be accounted erroneous, false, and destructive? I am doubtful concerning the doctrine of the Socinians, I am suspicious of the way of worship practiced by the Papists, or Lutherans; will it be

continued

PRIMARY SOURCE 8.5 | From A Letter Concerning Toleration *continued*

ever a jot safer for me to join either unto the one or the other of those Churches, upon the magistrate's command, because he commands nothing in religion but by the authority and counsel of the doctors of that Church?

But, to speak the truth, we must acknowledge that the Church (if a convention of clergymen, making canons, must be called by that name) is for the most part more apt to be influenced by the Court than the Court by the Church. How the Church was under the vicissitude of orthodox and Arian emperors is very well known. Or if those things be too remote, our modern English history affords us fresh examples in the reigns of Henry VIII, Edward VI, Mary, and Elizabeth, how easily and smoothly the clergy changed their decrees, their articles of faith, their form of worship, everything according to the inclination of those kings and queens. Yet were those kings and queens of such different minds in point of religion, and enjoined thereupon such different things, that no man in his wits (I had almost said none but an atheist) will presume to say that any sincere and upright worshipper of God could, with a safe conscience, obey their several decrees. To conclude, it is the same thing whether a king that prescribes laws to another man's religion pretend to do it by his own judgment, or by the ecclesiastical authority and advice of others. The decisions of churchmen, whose differences and disputes are sufficiently known, cannot be any sounder or safer than his; nor can all their suffrages joined together add a new strength to the civil power. Though this also must be taken notice of—that princes seldom have any regard to the suffrages of ecclesiastics that are not favorers of their own faith and way of worship.

But, after all, the principal consideration, and which absolutely determines this controversy, is this: Although the magistrate's opinion in religion be sound, and the way that he appoints be truly Evangelical, yet, if I be not thoroughly persuaded thereof in my own mind, there will be no safety for me in following it. No way whatsoever that I shall walk in against the dictates of my conscience will ever bring me to the mansions of the blessed. I may grow rich by an art that I take not delight in; I may be cured of some disease by remedies that I have not faith in; but I cannot be saved by a religion that I distrust and by a worship that I abhor. It is in vain for an unbeliever to take up the outward show of another man's profession. Faith only and inward sincerity are the things that procure acceptance with God. The most likely and most approved remedy can have no effect upon the patient, if his stomach reject it as soon as taken; and you will in vain cram a medicine down a sick man's throat, which his particular constitution will be sure to turn into poison. In a word, whatsoever may be doubtful in religion, yet this at least is certain, that no religion which I believe not to be true can be either true or profitable unto me. In vain, therefore, do princes compel their subjects to come into their Church communion, under pretense of saving their souls. If they believe, they will come of their own accord, if they believe not, their coming will nothing avail them. How great soever, in fine, may be the pretense of goodwill and charity, and concern for the salvation of men's souls, men cannot be forced to be saved whether they will or no. And therefore, when all is done, they must be left to their own consciences.

Having thus at length freed men from all dominion over one another in matters of religion, let us now consider what they are to do. All men know and acknowledge that God ought to be publicly worshipped; why otherwise do they compel one another unto the public assemblies? Men, therefore, constituted in this liberty are to enter into some religious society, that they meet together, not only for mutual edification, but to own to the world that they worship God and offer unto His Divine Majesty such service as they themselves are not ashamed of and such as they think not unworthy of Him, nor unacceptable to Him; and, finally, that by the purity of doctrine, holiness of life, and decent form of worship, they may draw others unto the love of the true religion, and perform such other things in

PRIMARY SOURCE 8.5 | FROM A LETTER CONCERNING TOLERATION *continued*

religion as cannot be done by each private man apart.

These religious societies I call Churches; and these, I say, the magistrate ought to tolerate, for the business of these assemblies of the people is nothing but what is lawful for every man in particular to take care of—I mean the salvation of their souls; nor in this case is there any difference between the National Church and other separated congregations.

But as in every Church there are two things especially to be considered—the outward form and rites of worship, and the doctrines and articles of things must be handled each distinctly that so the whole matter of toleration may the more clearly be understood.

Concerning outward worship, I say, in the first place, that the magistrate has no power to enforce by law, either in his own Church, or much less in another, the use of any rites or ceremonies whatsoever in the worship of God. And this, not only because these Churches are free societies, but because whatsoever is practiced in the worship of God is only so far justifiable as it is believed by those that practice it to be acceptable unto Him. Whatsoever is not done with that assurance of faith is neither well in itself, nor can it be acceptable to God. To impose such things, therefore, upon any people, contrary to their own judgment, is in effect to command them to offend God, which, considering that the end of all religion is to please Him, and that liberty is essentially necessary to that end, appears to be absurd beyond expression.

But perhaps it may be concluded from hence that I deny unto the magistrate all manner of power about indifferent things, which, if it be not granted, the whole subject matter of law making is taken away. No, I readily grant that indifferent things, and perhaps none but such, are subjected to the legislative power. But it does not therefore follow that the magistrate may ordain whatsoever he pleases concerning anything that is indifferent. The public good is the rule and measure of all law making. If a thing be not useful to the commonwealth, though it be never so indifferent, it may not presently be established by law.

about their source. People have rights because they are all equally people. To overlook their common human nature is to enter an abyss without boundaries where disputes become irresolvable. The equal rule of law is more than a formal requirement of legality for Locke. It is the principle of the community that exists between human beings even before they have given it any legal expression. Just as in the state of nature rights and obligations bind human beings together within a form of community without government, so the advent of government merely solidifies an order that existed before it and can never be removed by it. Equal rights cannot be compromised without jeopardizing the entire purpose of political society itself. The genius of Locke that made him the father of liberal democracy, if there is any claimant to the role, is that he makes this intuition transparent. The rights of some cannot be sacrificed for the

QUESTIONS FOR REFLECTION

What is the basis for religious toleration? Does Locke propose it because it will lead to political peace or because it is inherent in the freedom of the person? Think about what your answer may suggest concerning the nature of human rights—the core of the Lockean political language that now dominates our world.

The Elusive Locke

Given Locke's enormous impact on modernity in general and on the American political tradition more specifically, it should be no surprise that his political teaching has been interpreted in significantly different ways. Included here are brief summaries of some differing interpretations of Locke's political thought:

The possessive individualist Locke: Most notably argued by Professor C.B. MacPherson, this interpretation tends to emphasize Locke's teachings on property rights, materialism, and the limited state as fostering capitalist development.

The Straussian Locke: Put forth by Professor Leo Strauss and his students, this interpretation considers Locke to be a Hobbes in "sheep's clothing." According to the Straussian reading, Locke conceals the Hobbesian aspects of his political thought by offering a milder view of the conflicts and inconveniences of the state of nature. Locke's liberalism justifies a strong capitalist state that protects the natural right of property.

The Christian Locke: This interpretation views Locke's egalitarianism in terms of Christian revelation. It takes seriously Locke's protestant spirituality as it influenced his political and economic liberalism. John Dunn is a representative of this school of thought.

The liberal–communitarian Locke: This is the interpretation of David Walsh, the author of this chapter. In contrast to those who stress the possessive individualist Locke, Walsh emphasizes a more communitarian Locke who seriously applies Christian teachings of individual dignity and free will as the basis of a shared, equal, and free civil society. Locke provides a coherent defense of liberal values anchored in the spiritual dignity of all human beings.

sake of the rights of others without toppling the whole structure of rights. Realizing that rights are indivisible, we also see the extent to which we are never simply defenders of our individual rights. In asserting the rights of one, we assert the rights of all. This idea of community Locke has incorporated into the political form that seems to have given priority to the individual. Within the elusiveness of that relationship stands the elusiveness of his political thought.

Key Terms

The Glorious Revolution of 1688
law of nature
natural rights
royal absolutism
priority of the moral community
civil society
divine right of kings
consent of the governed
tacit consent
state of nature
inconveniences
prepolitical community
compact
property
right to life
right to the property
civil commonwealth
genesis of civil society
men being judges in their own case
transfer of liberty
majority rule
consent
executive power
federative power
prerogative
usurpation
tyranny
dissolution of government
liberal democracy
Latitudinarian Christianity
religious toleration

Sources and Resources

Key Texts

First and Second Treatises on Government
Letter Concerning Toleration

Secondary Texts

Ashcraft, Richard. *Locke's Two Treatises on Government* (London: Allen & Ulwin, 1987).

Cranston, Maurice. *John Locke: A Biography* (London: Longmans Green, 1957).

Cox, Richard. *Locke on War and Peace* (Oxford: Clarendon Press, 1960).

Dunn, John. *The Political Thought of John Locke* (Cambridge: Cambridge University Press, 1969).

MacPherson, C.B. *Political Theory of Possessive Individualism: Hobbes to Locke* (Oxford: Clarendon Press, 1962).

Schochet, Gordon J. (ed.). *Life, Liberty, and Property: Essays on Locke's Political Ideas* (Belmont, CA: Wadsworth, 1971).

Strauss, Leo, *Natural Right and History* (Chicago: University of Chicago Press, 1953).

Web Sites

Stanford Encyclopedia of Philosophy entry online at http://plato.stanford.edu/entries/locke/

Free, full-text works by Locke online at http://onlinebooks.library.upenn.edu/webbin/book/search?amode=start&author=Locke,%20John

The Digital Locke Project online at www.digitallockeproject.nl/

ROUSSEAU

CHAPTER 9

By Joseph R. Fornieri *Rochester Institute of Technology*

LIFE

The French Poet Baudelaire claimed that reading Rousseau was like smoking hash—both experiences were euphoric. Certainly the main actors in the drama of the French Revolution were intoxicated by Rousseau's narcotic spell. They revered him as a secular political saint, parading his bust through the streets of Paris, placing an iconic figure of him in the assembly, and exhuming his body so it could be ceremoniously laid to rest in the Pantheon. Rousseau's influence on the French Revolution—one of the pivotal events in history—validates the oft-quoted expression in political philosophy that "ideas have consequences." For the intellectually adventurous, Rousseau's thought and style remain seductive. His provocative ideas are communicated not in bland treatises but through captivating narratives. These, in turn, often culminate in shocking epiphanies meant to awaken the reader from his or her complacent slumber: "Man was born free, but everywhere he is in chains." Ever since Socrates placed Athens on trial, the epic political philosophers have challenged the conventional wisdom of their time by measuring it against a normative vision of a better life. In an effort to rescue humanity from a downward spiral of debasement, Rousseau exploded the alienating patterns of modern life that he believed divided, corrupted, and enslaved the human spirit. To remedy this unfortunate condition, he prescribed an alternative vision of a free, cooperative, and virtuous society informed by man's original freedom in the state of nature. Indeed, his political project may be seen as an attempt to redeem fallen humanity, recapturing by means of human artifice and the grace of an enlightened lawgiver something of the unity, vigor, and freedom of its original condition in the state of nature. Before turning to that project, however, it is first worth examining the strange and tormented life that yielded such an extraordinary and controversial legacy.

Rousseau's personal odyssey began in the Swiss town of Geneva in 1712, where his mother died shortly after giving birth to him. The communal lifestyle and moral austerity of this republican city–state, which still bore the influence of the theologian John Calvin, left a lasting impression on his political thought. In his writing Rousseau would identify himself as a citizen of Geneva, consistently pointing to it, along with Sparta, as a model of republican virtue. After his volatile father was imprisoned for dueling, the 10-year-old Rousseau was sent to live with a country minister and then his uncle. Remarkably, the young Rousseau received little formal education. Yet he was a supreme autodidact who mastered a variety of subjects. In 1728, at 16, he ran away from home to sojourn through Europe. This was the beginning of a lifelong wanderlust. The rootless Rousseau would roam from job to job, from woman to woman, and from country to country—a vagabond philosopher. Later the same year, while in Italy, he converted to Roman Catholicism. He then took up residence with a fellow convert, the Swiss Baroness Madame de Warens, who was 12 years his senior. He would become her lover, living with her at her expense for some 14 years (1728–1742). Ripe with Freudian implications, Rousseau called his older lover "Mamam" (Mama); she affectionately referred to him as "Petit" (little one). Rousseau tried his hand at several jobs: tutor, musician, farmer, civil servant, and writer. As an aspiring musician, he even composed an opera, which would later be performed for King Louis XV. In 1742 he moved to Paris. Shortly thereafter he met Therese Levasseur, a maid and washwoman who would bear him five children. In his autobiography, *Confessions,* Rousseau explains that he abandoned all five of these children to a foundling hospital (an orphanage), claiming that the state would serve as a better parent than he would. While in Paris, Rousseau befriended the *philosophe* (French literary intellectual) and father of the encyclopedia, Denis Diderot. Like many of his relationships, Rousseau's friendship with Diderot followed a familiar pattern: An initial friend and supporter morphed into an enemy and a diabolical persecutor.

1750 marked a turning point in Rousseau's life and the beginning of his celebrity. This was the year he won the prize of the Dijon Academy for his essay in response to the question, "*Has the restoration of the sciences and arts tended to purify morals*?" Rousseau's ironic reply in his *First Discourse* established him as one of the foremost critics of the Enlightenment. Turning the Enlightenment dogma of progress upside down, Rousseau contended that the spread of the arts and sciences led not to the improvement but to the moral debasement of both man and society. The advance of science led not to progress but to moral regress. Rousseau's literary success made him the toast of the Paris Salon. In 1762 he published perhaps two of his greatest works, *The Social Contract* and *Emile*. Both were condemned for their religious and political heterodoxy. Though he had abandoned Roman Catholicism, Rousseau protested that he nonetheless still believed in God. In fact, he declared that he was the only man in France who still believed! Unlike many of the *philosophes,* he was not an atheist. Rather, he sought to remedy a corrupt version of religion, thereby providing a salutary alternative that would truly benefit man and society. As will be seen, Rousseau believed that civil religion plays an important role in the good society. After his works' condemnation, Rousseau became an international fugitive. He fled to England, where he was the guest of Scottish philosopher David Hume. Upon quarreling with Hume, he returned to the continent in 1767. For the rest of his life he lived a nomadic existence, turning to the solitary pleasure of botany for repose. Toward the end of his life, Rousseau's many physical ailments were compounded by mental anguish. He showed signs of paranoia, convinced of an international plot to destroy his reputation. To defend his name, he wrote the *Confessions,* regarded by many as the first autobiographical account of the modern self, a secular alternative to St. Augustine's *Confessions.* Rousseau died on July 2, 1778, leaving an intellectual and political legacy that was as complicated as his life.

ROUSSEAU'S GARDEN: WORLDVIEW AND HUMAN NATURE

Rousseau's political philosophy is informed by his understanding of human nature in the *Second Discourse on the Origins and Foundations of Inequality among Men.* This work provides the descriptive cornerstone on which he builds his prescriptive edifice in *The Social Contract.* Here Rousseau provides a narrative of how man's original freedom as a solitary, naturally good, happy being was lost. He tells how man was transformed through a gradual process of socialization into a rapacious, miserable, and divided soul trapped in a cycle of mutual exploitation, codependence, and domination.

Indeed, the *Second Discourse* provides a secular version of the Bible's account of man's fall from the Garden of Eden. Yet it modifies the biblical narrative in significant ways. The hand of God is noticeably absent in Rousseau's telling of the story. There are no miracles or divine intervention. Events in Rousseau's Garden occur randomly, without the guidance of divine grace. They are explained not in reference to some grand design or providence, but in terms of naturalistic processes that seem to occur by chance. In what may be considered an anticipation of Charles Darwin's theory of evolution, Rousseau argues that human nature evolves or changes over time. Random events like earthquakes and floods draw people out of their solitary condition, prompting them to adapt to their particular environmental circumstances. These social conditions, in turn, lead to the development of new faculties like speech and understanding. Rousseau's naturalistic account of the transformation of human nature reveals that man's humanity is not fixed but rather is acquired through the force of historical circumstances.

The complexity of Rousseau's political thought may be unpacked in terms of his own modified version of Christianity's Garden–Fall–Redemption narrative, which he creatively combines with a naturalistic, conjectural history of human origin and development. During the Enlightenment, Scottish and French thinkers speculated about the condition of the state of nature and the movement of humanity through various stages of development. Rousseau provides his own version of this conjectural history in his *Second Discourse.*

Rousseau's narrative of human history may be divided into three major stages, which borrow from, yet profoundly modify, the biblical narrative:

1. He begins his saga with a description of humanity's original innocence in the Garden (the original state of nature).
2. He then diagnoses the evil that entered through the fall (vanity—*amour propre;* dependence; private property; and inequality).
3. Finally he offers different paths of redemption or liberation—one public and one private—that lead out of this fallen condition.

In each case the particular historical, political, and economic conditions of each stage are crucial in shaping human nature.

A Preview of Rousseau's Three Major Stages of Historical Development

1. ***Original innocence and solitude in state of nature:*** Man's original condition was marked by natural goodness, self-sufficiency, radical freedom, and *amour de soi*—the sentiment of his own existence.
2. ***The fall—sociality and private property:*** The qualities of reason and *amour propre* (vanity or pride) emerge. All vice—greed, lust, jealousy, envy, wrath—stems from *amour propre*—the prideful comparison of oneself to others. Natural goodness and innocence are lost. Compassion and pity are weakened. The human condition is now marked by war, inequality, inner division between one's public duty and private inclination, and dependence on others. A bogus social contract provides legal sanction to inequality. These inequalities reach high levels of corruption in civilized bourgeois society, where money defines morality and where there is dependence on elites.
3. ***Redemption and liberation—the general will:*** Man's condition in the good society is marked by political equality, civic virtue, and the reconciliation of one's particular will with the general will. This prescription for the good society will break down the evils of mass dependence on organized economic, social, and political elites. A legitimate social contract will be based on the general will, in which it will be necessary to force individuals to be free.

Let us begin by exploring human nature in Rousseau's Garden. As noted, while Rousseau retains the powerful biblical symbolism of the Garden and Fall, he offers an alternative, naturalistic account of human origins based on a conjectural history informed by ethnographic studies of aboriginal peoples and primates. Indeed, Rousseau is among the first political philosophers to understand human nature in terms of the primitive. Though he retains the concept of nature as a standard to judge political things, Rousseau significantly modifies the meaning of this term. Whereas the ancients viewed nature in terms of a *telos* or end—a final fulfillment, a completion, a terminal excellence—Rousseau understands it in terms of primitive origins that are as yet undeveloped. *Nature* thus refers to the primeval beginnings of mankind in the state of nature, not to its end (*telos*) or moral perfection in civilization. It points to the untamed savage in the wilds, not to Aristotle's philosopher as the supreme manifestation of moral and intellectual virtue in society. Today we take for granted that the term *natural* applies to the instinctual, primitive, or wild. In so doing, we reveal our debt to Rousseau.

In seeking the original state of nature, Rousseau criticizes his predecessors, Hobbes and Locke, for not going far enough back to discover its true character. "The philosophers who have examined the foundations of society have all felt the necessity of going back to the state of nature, but none of them has reached it."[1] With this criticism, Rousseau begins a schism in modern political thought over the status and meaning of the state of nature. He accuses Hobbes and Locke of carrying over to the state of nature vicious qualities like jealousy, vanity, and greed that emerged later when human beings entered society. Hobbes and Locke spoke of savage man when, in fact, they were simply describing the debased men of their own time. Probing further than his predecessors, Rousseau seeks to peel off the many layers of social and intellectual tradition about civil man in order to glimpse the most basic, primordial inclinations that moved savage man while he was in the Garden.

Beginning with the modern assumption that understands human beings primarily as individuals living within a prepolitical state of nature, Rousseau draws the remarkable conclusion that within this original state we were radically asocial creatures who lived in utter solitude. Here it is important to mention that Rousseau's understanding of human nature relied on ethnographic studies of orangutans, the only solitary members of the great apes.

Rousseau denies man's sociopolitical nature altogether. If human beings were radically solitary creatures, it follows that they must have lacked both rational speech and understanding because these mutual qualities necessarily depend on social relations. Contrary to Aristotle, Rousseau denies that *logos* or rational speech is an intrinsic characteristic of human beings. Rather, he maintains that reason was an acquired quality that occurred at a much later stage of human development. Furthermore, according to Rousseau, human reasoning differs from that of an animal only by degree, not in kind. It is not the faculty of reason, he contends, that truly distinguishes man from the animals, but something else—namely freedom of the will or freedom of choice.

According to Rousseau, human beings are distinguished from animals in terms of two defining characteristics: **freedom of the will** and the **capacity of self-perfection.** He states, "it is not so much understanding which constitutes the distinction of man among

---

[1]Jean-Jacques Rousseau, *The First and Second Discourses,* (ed.) Robert D. Masters, trans. Roger D. and Judith R. Masters (New York: St. Martin's Press, 1964), p. 102.

QUESTIONS FOR REFLECTION

Rousseau's Savage Man as Neither Beast Nor God

Aristotle explains that human beings by nature are political animals, and that those who live apart from the city–state are either beasts or gods. How would Aristotle understand the solitary creatures in Rousseau's Garden—as men? As beasts? Or as something in between?

the animals as it is his being a free agent."[2] Rousseau thus emphasizes that freedom, rather than understanding, is the defining trait of human nature. Unlike an animal whose actions are governed entirely by instinct, human action is self-determining. "[N]ature alone does everything in the operations of a beast," Rousseau observes, "whereas man contributes to his operations by being a free agent. The former chooses or rejects by instinct and the latter by an act of freedom."[3] Unlike an animal, human beings possess a free will that can act in cooperation with or in opposition to their drive for self-preservation. Unfortunately, this freedom allows them to act in ways that are detrimental to their own well being and to the well being of others. Rousseau's prescription in *The Social Contract* may be seen as an attempt to restore through human artifice and convention the lost freedom of original inclination described in the *Second Discourse.*

Nature's solitaire—or savage man as he is called by Rousseau—was thus naturally free in the Garden to follow the inclinations of his self-preservation. His solitary condition made him radically independent. His freedom was utterly self-regarding. His actions were unbounded by an awareness of a moral obligation to himself or to others. As will be seen, however, once human beings entered civil society, this **natural freedom** was gradually lost and replaced by a more ambiguous **moral freedom,** which carried the potential for either the ennoblement or debasement of the species. Judith Best summarizes the crucial role that freedom plays in Rousseau's political thought when she explains that "man by nature is free, radically independent and undetermined. Natural freedom is the highest, the essential 'right' or characteristic of man as man. It is what distinguished men from beasts."[4]

The second distinctive faculty or characteristic of human nature is the capacity for **self-perfection.** By this Rousseau means the ability of human beings to acquire, adapt, and add other faculties or traits to themselves, which they then transmit to their offspring. Unlike an animal, whose nature is forever fixed, human nature is malleable—and transformable. This elastic quality is responsible for human beings acquiring the abilities to reason, to speak, and to use tools for self-preservation. Rousseau describes the faculty of self-perfection as "a faculty which, with the aid of circumstances, successively develops all the others, and resides among us as much in the species as in the individual."[5] This morally ambiguous faculty of self-perfection accounts for the transformation of savage man into civil man. And as will be seen, this faculty also gives rise to vanity or prideful self-love (*amour propre*)—a trait that accounts for much of man's misery in society. Foreshadowing the ironic role that the capacity of

[2] *Discourses,* p. 114.

[3] *Discourses,* p. 113.

[4] Judith Best, *The Mainstream of Western Political Thought* (New York: Human Sciences Press, 1980), p. 101.

[5] *Discourses,* p. 114.

self-perfection will play in the corruption of mankind, Rousseau explains that "this distinctive and almost unlimited faculty is the source of all of man's misfortunes; that it is this faculty which, by dint of time, draws him out of that original condition in which he would pass tranquil and innocent days; that it is this faculty which, bringing to flower over centuries his enlightenment and his errors, his vices and his virtues, in the long run makes him the tyrant of himself and of nature."[6]

Given Rousseau's understanding of the faculty of self-perfection, it follows that man's humanity was not fixed but was acquired through the force of historical circumstances, conditions, and environmental changes over time that shaped human nature. Rousseau relates how natural events such as catastrophes, earthquakes, scarcity, and animal migrations eventually led to the accidental commingling of our species and the emergence of human capacities like rational speech. Once human beings were drawn out of solitude, they were compelled by necessity to find novel and useful means to work together in satisfying their basic needs. The cliché that "necessity is the mother of invention" certainly applies to Rousseau's account of early humans in the state of nature. Signs and gestures led to the development of language. In turn, language led to the development of reason, which greatly assisted human beings in their self-preservation. As a result of greater cohabitation, humans increasingly became dependent on one another for their mutual survival and self-preservation. This transition from solitude to sociality actually changed human nature. Rousseau explains that those who study history carefully will

> sense that, the human race of one age not being the human race of another, the reason Diogenes did not find a man was that he sought among his contemporaries the man of a time that no longer existed. Cato, he will say, perished with Rome and freedom because he was out of place in his century; and the greatest of men only astonished the world, which he would have governed five hundred years earlier. In a word, he will explain how the soul and human passions, altering imperceptibly, change their nature so to speak; why our needs and our pleasures change their objects in the long run; why, original man vanishing by degrees, society no longer offers to the eyes of the wise man anything except an assemblage of artificial men and factitious passions which are the work of all these new relations and have no true foundation in nature.[7]

In addition to possessing the distinct characteristics of self-perfection and freedom of the will, savage man was animated by two sentiments in the Garden: self-love (*amour de soi*) and pity—(compassion). Rousseau is considered the father of Romanticism in view of his emphasis on the crucial role that sentiment plays in our humanity. He believed that the Enlightenment's celebration of reason overlooked those qualities that made human beings distinctively human—feeling and freedom. Furthermore, he believed that the Enlightenment's reduction of reason to rational self-interest failed to do justice to our loftier aspirations and achievements as human beings. Rational calculation alone cannot explain the heroic; narrow rational self-interest cannot induce someone to lay down his or her life for the homeland. By *sentiment* Rousseau means the distinctive human feelings, loves, passions, yearnings, longings, hopes, fears, aversions, and attachments. Sentiment may be contrasted to both intellect and instinct. It resides neither in the head nor in the belly, but in the heart.

---

[6]*Discourses,* p. 115.

[7]*Discourses,* p. 178.

QUESTIONS FOR REFLECTION

Rousseau's Historicism

By claiming that human nature changes as it passes through stages of historical development, does Rousseau's political thought contribute to the rise of historicism—the idea that human nature and consciousness are not fixed but are relative throughout time, place, and circumstance? If this is the case, it follows that the flux of history, rather than the qualities of an unchanging nature, becomes crucial to understanding the dynamics of man and society. In *Natural Right and History,* Leo Strauss argues that Rousseau's political thought represents an early version of historicism and moral relativism that culminates in the 19th-century political philosophies of Marx, Hegel, and Nietzsche. Is Strauss correct? What do you think?

Rousseau makes a crucial distinction between two types of sentiments of self-love: ***amour de soi*** and ***amour propre.*** *Amour de soi* is the original self love that existed in the state of nature as a benign egoism. In contrast, *amour propre*—that is, vanity or pride, developed subsequently along with reason and social relations. Whereas *amour de soi* is purely self-regarding, *amour propre* is based on comparisons and the judgments of others.

Rousseau describes the elusive concept of *amour de soi* as the sentiment of savoring one's own existence. The soul of savage man, he states, is "agitated by nothing, is given over to the sole sentiment of its present existence without any idea of the future, however near it may be, and his projects, as limited as his views, barely extend to the end of the day."[8] In *Reveries of a Solitary Walker* he describes how a residual experience of *amour de soi* can be retrieved through man's solitary communion with nature:

> Entirely taken up by the present, I could remember nothing; I had no distinct notion of myself as a person, nor had I the least idea of what had just happened to me. I did not know who I was, nor where I was; I felt neither pain, fear, nor anxiety. I watched my blood flowing as I might have watched a stream, without even thinking that the blood had anything to do with me. I felt throughout my whole being a wonderful calm, that whenever I recall this feeling I can find nothing to compare with it in all the pleasures that stir our lives.[9]

The other sentiment that animated in the state of nature was **pity,** defined by Rousseau as an innate repugnance to seeing one's fellow men suffer. While pity and *amour de soi* were both operative in the state of nature, the former trait is entirely self-regarding while the latter extends to others. Consequently, Rousseau describes pity or fellow feeling as the "sole natural virtue" in the state of nature. Unlike the conventional virtues born of society, the sentiment of pity does not depend on reflection or understanding. It is purely a matter of the heart—of feeling and passion. Indeed, according to Rousseau, both animals and humans are capable of pity; both have the ability to empathize with others of the same species. Pity tempers the chance conflicts that may occur between the solitaires in the state of nature, thereby helping to make the Garden a habitable state. According to Rousseau, pity, which "moderat[es] in each

[8] *Discourses,* p. 117.

[9] Jean-Jacques Rousseau, *Reveries of the Solitary Walker* (New York: Penguin Publishing, 1979), p. 39.

QUESTIONS FOR REFLECTION | **Rousseau and Animal Rights**

Should Rousseau be considered a forerunner of animal rights? He looks to orangutans as early humans in the state of nature, claiming that human intelligence differs from that of an animal only by degree and that animals, like humans, are capable of pity or commiseration.

individual the activity of love of oneself, contributes to the mutual preservation of the entire species."[10]

Pity continues to play an important role in society as the emotional glue that helps cement social bonds. Rousseau goes so far as to say that pity is the underlying source of the modern virtues of generosity, clemency, and humanity. Indeed, these modern traits are nothing other than pity applied to the weak, the guilty, and the human species respectively. Rousseau further emphasizes that pity—a sentiment and feeling—is a much more reliable guide in morals than calculation or reflection. The "human race," he argues, "would have perished long ago if its preservation had depended only on the reasonings of its members. . . ."[11] It is worth repeating that Rousseau casts freedom and feeling, rather than reason, as crucial to the success of his political project. As will be seen, religion and virtue play supporting roles in his account of the good society.

In sum, the unbounded freedom of savage man, his solitude, his benign self-love (*amour de soi*), and his natural pity made the Garden a habitable, idyllic place. Contrary to Hobbes and Locke who view the state of nature as a negative pole—a condition to be avoided—Rousseau envisions the original state of nature as a positive pole: a desirable and peaceful condition where humans were contented to live. "[T]hat state" he exclaims "was consequently the best suited to peace and the most appropriate for the human race."[12] According to Rousseau, the state of war described by Hobbes and Locke occurred at a much later stage in the history of man.

Rousseau attributes savage man's bliss in the original state of nature to both his solitude and self-sufficiency. In *Emile* he maintains that "a truly happy being is a solitary being." Savage man was happy because he depended on himself, not others, for contentment. Perhaps most importantly, his wants were proportioned to his basic needs. His "desires do not exceed his physical needs, the only goods he knows in the universe are nourishment, a female, and repose; the only evils he fears are pain and hunger. I say pain and not death because an animal will never know what it is to die; and knowledge of death and its terrors is one of the first acquisitions that man has made in moving away from the animal condition."[13] Remarkably, Rousseau goes so far as to claim that savage man had no awareness of death. Because he could not even project into the future, he was free from any anxiety over his self-preservation.

And unlike civil man, savage man did not yearn for those artificially induced wants or faux needs that society tells us will make us happy, such as superfluous consumer goods like expensive cars and designer clothes. These "faux or bogus needs

[10]*Discourses,* p. 133.

[11]*Discourses,* p. 133.

[12]*Discourses,* p. 129.

[13]*Discourses,* p. 116.

9

ERN POLITICAL THINKERS: HOBBES, LOCKE, AND ROUSSEAU

	Hobbes	Locke	Rousseau
Human Nature	• Egocentric, vicious. • "Man is a wolf to his fellow Man." • Reason is limited to calculation. The mind generates thoughts as "scouts" and "spies" to achieve one's desire. Reason is thus "the slave" of one's passions and desires.	• Rationally self-interested. • Incapable of being an objective judge in conflict with others.	• Naturally good. • Grounded in free will and pity. • In state of innocence, human nature is motivated by sentiments of *amour de soi* and pity. In society, human nature is motivated by the sentiment of *amour propre,* which may weaken natural pity.
State of Nature	• Negative pole where life is nasty, brutish, and short. • State of nature = state of war.	• "Inconveniences" in which there is no common judge who can resolve occasional conflicts between individuals.	• Positive pole, at first characterized by benign self-preservation, peaceful, habitable. • Later on, characterized by private property, inequality, and war.
Consent	• Everyone surrenders absolute freedom to common power, which takes on the character of an absolute sovereign.	• Surrender one's right to judge in own case, but retain inalienable right to life, liberty, and property.	• Particular will must conform to general will. • Obedience to a law one prescribes for oneself.
Rights	• Right to physical self-preservation in which the state can never require an individual to put his life in jeopardy involuntarily.	• Inalienable rights of life, liberty, and property, which cannot be surrendered or given up.	• Man born free and equal. • Free will to direct the course of one's own life. • No inalienable right to property. • Property may be regulated by general will.
Social Contract and Civil Society/ State	• Absolute sovereign created with above exception.	• Government establishes common judge whose rules are grounded in protection of inalienable rights of life, liberty, and property.	• Enlightened lawgiver shepherds the establishment of the institutions of popular government. • Government executes general will.
Revolution	• No right to resist. However, if the sovereign is incapable of regulating conflict and diminishing the fear of violent death, then the civil society will revert to the state of nature and a new social contract will be necessary.	• Right to revolution by majority judgment when inalienable rights are habitually abridged.	• Popular sovereignty guided by an enlightened lawgiver in the early stages of the formation of an effective popular government.

far exceed our true needs and our ability to satisfy them. Guided exclusively by his original inclinations and primeval urges, savage man sought pleasure and avoided pain. He was a benign hedonist. Rousseau contrasts the original freedom and happiness of savage man to the servitude, dependence, and misery of civilized man in these poignant terms:

> What reflection teaches us on this subject, observation confirms perfectly: savage man and civilized man differ so much in the bottom of their hearts and inclination that what constitutes the supreme happiness of one would reduce the other to despair. The former breathes only repose and freedom; he wants only to live and remain idle; and even the perfect quietude of the Stoic does not approach his profound indifference for all other objects. On the contrary, the citizen, always active, sweats, agitates himself, torments himself incessantly in order to seek still more laborious occupations; he works to death, he even rushes to it in order to get in condition to live, or renounces life in order to acquire immortality. He pays court to the great whom he hates, and to the rich whom he scorns. He spares nothing in order to obtain the honor of serving them; he proudly boasts of his baseness and their protection; and proud of his slavery, he speaks with disdain of those who do not have the honor of sharing it. What a sight the difficult envied labors of a European minister are for a Carib! How many cruel deaths would that indolent savage not prefer to the horror of such a life, which often is not even sweetened by the pleasure of doing good. But in order to see the goal of so many cares, the words *power* and *reputation* would have no meaning in his mind; he would have to learn that there is a kind of man who set some store by the consideration of the rest of the universe and who know how to be happy and content with themselves on the testimony of others rather than on their own. Such is, in fact, the true cause of all these differences: the savage man lives within himself; the sociable man, always outside of himself, knows how to live only in the opinion of others; and it is, so to speak, from their judgment alone that he draws the sentiment of his own existence.[14]

This idyllic description of human nature in the Garden reveals the natural goodness of savage man. In affirming **man's natural goodness,** Rousseau does not mean that human beings were virtuous in terms of possessing perfected moral habits and dispositions like prudence, justice, courage, and moderation. Such habits presume sociality and moral understanding, which savage man originally lacked. In speaking of man's natural goodness, therefore, it is much more accurate to say that the solitaires in Rousseau's Garden were amoral creatures, blissfully ignorant of good and evil, living in an idyllic state of innocence. Savage man was "naturally good" insofar as he lacked malice toward others of his own species. Whereas Nietzsche will speak of man at the end of history as being "beyond good and evil," Rousseau speaks of savage man at the beginning of history as living "before good and evil." He thus explains,

> Men are wicked; sad and continual experience spares the need for proof. However, man is naturally good; I believe I have demonstrated it. What then can have depraved him to this extent, if not the changes that have befallen his constitution, the progress he has made, and the knowledge he has acquired? Let human society be as highly admired as one wants; it is nonetheless true that it necessarily brings men to hate each other in proportion to the conflict of their interests, to render each other apparent services and in fact do every imaginable harm to one another.[15]

---

[14]*Discourses,* pp. 178–179.

[15]*Discourses,* p. 193.

QUESTIONS FOR REFLECTION

The Natural Goodness of Man and the Problem of Evil

If man is naturally good, in Rousseau's sense of the term, does it follow that he is corrupted or made bad by his environment? Does evil reside in the human heart or is it acquired through flawed social conditions—for example, vast inequalities and multigenerational dependence on welfare within inner-city neighborhoods? If evil is indeed the result of society, can it be remedied through proper social engineering? How might Bill Cosby and Rousseau differ in their understanding of the poor attitude that many inner-city young people have toward their education?

Rousseau's conception of the natural goodness of man may be understood further in terms of one who is good both for himself and for others. Savage man was good for himself because he was free, happy, and self-sufficient. He blithely enjoyed the sentiment of his existence—*amour de soi.* He satisfied his most basic needs of self-preservation without inner division. As yet, he was not addicted to the many faux needs marketed by society as good though they are actually harmful. Neither was he dependent on on socioeconomic elites for his well-being. On the contrary, "first sentiment was that of his existence, his first care that of his preservation."[16] Savage man was also good for others because his egoism was benign, and his solitary condition minimized conflict in the state of nature. If conflict did occur by chance, it was moderated by the sentiment of pity.

As stated earlier, to say that savage man's "first care was that of his self-preservation" does not imply, as Hobbes believed, that man was "a wolf to his fellow man," an aggressive predator, agitated by an insecure frenzy to escape violent death. By contrast, savage man's self-preservation was satisfied in a manner that was the least prejudicial to others. To convey the benign self-preservation of savage man, Rousseau reformulates the Golden Rule as it must have applied to solitaires in the state of nature: "Do what is good for you with the least possible harm to others."[17] In Rousseau's Garden, there is no Hobbesian fear of violent death (*summum malum*) that would motivate humans to act in hostile ways toward their fellow creatures. Furthermore, savage man's solitude made contacts with members of the same species rare, thereby minimizing opportunities for conflict. Thus taken altogether, savage man's pity, his benign self-preservation, and his solitude made the state of nature a peaceful place—a peaceful, contented, and desirable condition or "a positive pole".

If by chance solitaires encountered one another in the state of nature, their conflict over self-interest would be resolved with little incident. Consider, for example, the case of two savages racing for a coconut that dropped from a tree. According to Rousseau, the matter would be resolved with little controversy and without malice. Once the stronger secured the coconut by physically overpowering the weaker, the two would simply part ways without harboring any feelings of wounded pride, revenge, or jealousy. Notably, human nature had not yet acquired pride or vanity. Neither would savage man attribute the complex ideas of justice and injustice to this struggle over the coconut To be sure, the episode would be forgotten

[16]*Discourses,* p. 142.

[17]*Discourses,* p. 133.

within moments because savage man had no sense of time beyond the immediate present.

Significantly, Rousseau's conception of the natural goodness of man advances a radically new understanding of human nature that rejects the Christian view of original sin—the belief that pride and sin are intrinsic parts of the fallen human condition. Rousseau's teaching on natural goodness also rejects the biblical command that we are to be "our brother's keeper." Though capable of pity, savage man was completely unaware of any binding moral duty owed to others. As an asocial, amoral, and solitary being, he was incapable of discerning the rational dictates of conscience or the commands of a preexisting natural law that imposed moral and religious obligations upon him.

Finally, while Rousseau's conception of natural goodness rejects the Christian teaching of original sin, it also challenges the Enlightenment notion of progress. According to Rousseau, the march of history leads to the regression, not the progression, of human beings and society. If these earlier, more primitive times were happier, what happened? How did savage man fall from the state of natural innocence? How and why did he leave the Garden?

THE FALL: ROUSSEAU'S DIAGNOSIS

Man's fall proceeded step by step with his social relations and his dependence on others. In exchanging solitude for sociality, human beings lost their freedom, self-sufficiency, and natural goodness.

But how did human beings acquire sociality? There must have been some interaction between the sexes to propagate the human race. Rousseau argues that in the early state of nature sexual encounters were random and purely physical. They were done merely to satisfy what he refers to as the "simple impulsion of nature" without attachment to a particular mate or awareness of potential offspring from this union. After the urge was satisfied, the two sexes went their separate ways. No lasting psychological, physical, and emotional attachments or dependencies were formed. Notably, in the state of nature, men had a distinct advantage over women because they are physically stronger and did not have to bear the burden of pregnancy and childbirth.

However, man's radical independence changed with the advent of sociality and conjugal love. In addition to the chances of natural disaster, the discovery of agriculture and metallurgy hastened the permanent commingling of the species and the establishment of society. The sexes began to cohabitate in huts where they started families. Rousseau maintains that this "hut stage" was the most pleasant and happiest in the Garden because human beings enjoyed some of the benefits of society while retaining much of their original freedom and feeling. They were domesticated just enough to enjoy the feeling or sentiment of conjugal love and the domestic bliss that accompanies it, while still retaining much of their natural vigor and self-sufficiency. Each family hut was more or less self-sufficient in providing for its basic, true needs. To the extent that families had to rely on each other, there was cooperation and peace. Most importantly, vast inequities in private property had not yet been introduced. For a time, human beings were content to live alongside one another in the domestic bliss of their huts with their mates and children. But after a while, something went terribly wrong, leading to misery, mutual exploitation, and degradation.

A defining moment in history occurred when someone began to notice that the person in the neighboring hut sang louder and danced better than he did. Rousseau artistically narrates this conjectural event to illustrate the first stirrings of human pride or vanity (*amour propre*)—the source of untold and future misery for humankind. While the singer was filled with pride over his superior abilities, the musically challenged seethed with envy toward the more talented singer and dancer. Thus the first prima donna and the first music critic were born at the same time! Since Rousseau was a musician himself, perhaps it is no surprise that music plays a crucial role in his account of the origins of pride or *amour propre.*

In Rousseau's conjectural state of nature, pride (*amour propre*), and dependence are the twin evils that replace original sin in the Garden of Eden. He explains, "The bonds of servitude are formed only from the mutual dependence of men and the reciprocal needs that unite them; it is impossible to enslave a man without first putting him in the position of being unable to do without another; a situation which, as it did not exist in the state of nature, leaves each man there free of the yoke, and renders vain the law of the stronger."[18] *Amour propre* or pride, which involves pernicious and invidious comparisons, leads to a psychological dependence on others insofar as each measures himself or herself in terms of what the other has or does not have. Today we might say that it involves a codependence. Whereas the original self-love, *amour de soi,* of savage man was completely inner-regarding, the subsequent type of self-love, the *amour propre* or pride of civil man, is outer-regarding. Indeed, it is this pride which inspires some to revel in the domination of others.

In the early state of nature, reason and pride were dormant. Wants were proportioned to basic, true needs. These needs, in turn, were satisfied easily, without depending on others. However, with the development of *amour propre,* wants began to swell beyond our ability to satisfy them. The ambiguity of freedom allowed human beings to pursue illusory wants to their own detriment. Whereas savage man's natural goodness made him good for himself and for others, civil man's wickedness makes him bad for himself and for others. No longer satisfied with basic needs, he seeks to outdo his neighbor—"keeping up with the Jones'." In *Emile,* Rousseau clearly explains that "what makes a man essentially good is to have few needs and to compare himself little to others; what makes him essentially wicked is to have many needs and to depend very much on opinions." Civil man is thus at constant war with himself and others in a ceaseless competition for power, prestige, and possessions. And there is no going back! The solitaire's original innocence is irrevocably replaced by civil man's acquired propensity for evil. So acquired, human beings cannot divest themselves of vanity or pride. While born naturally good and free, human beings have become corrupt and enslaved. To regain intimations of their original felicity and freedom, their vicious qualities must be managed, contained, and redirected through the proper social conditions and political institutions. This is the concern addressed by Rousseau's social contract.

---

[18]*Discourses,* p. 140.

PRIMARY SOURCE 9.1 | THE CIVIL STATE, FROM *THE SOCIAL CONTRACT*, BOOK I, CHAPTER 8

THE passage from the state of nature to the civil state produces a very remarkable change in man, by substituting justice for instinct in his conduct, and giving his actions the morality they had formerly lacked. Then only, when the voice of duty takes the place of physical impulses and right of appetite, does man, who so far had considered only himself, find that he is forced to act on different principles, and to consult his reason before listening to his inclinations. Although, in this state, he deprives himself of some advantages which he got from nature, he gains in return others so great, his faculties are so stimulated and developed, his ideas so extended, his feelings so ennobled, and his whole soul so uplifted, that, did not the abuses of this new condition often degrade him below that which he left, he would be bound to bless continually the happy moment which took him from it for ever, and, instead of a stupid and unimaginative animal, made him an intelligent being and a man.

Let us draw up the whole account in terms easily commensurable. What man loses by the social contract is his natural liberty and an unlimited right to everything he tries to get and succeeds in getting; what he gains is civil liberty and the proprietorship of all he possesses. If we are to avoid mistake in weighing one against the other, we must clearly distinguish natural liberty, which is bounded only by the strength of the individual, from civil liberty, which is limited by the general will; and possession, which is merely the effect of force or the right of the first occupier, from property, which can be founded only on a positive title.

We might, over and above all this, add, to what man acquires in the civil state, moral liberty, which alone makes him truly master of himself; for the mere impulse of appetite is slavery, while obedience to a law which we prescribe to ourselves is liberty. But I have already said too much on this head, and the philosophical meaning of the word liberty does not now concern us.

THE BIRTH OF CONVENTIONAL INEQUALITY AND THE SWINDLE

The tendency to make comparisons led to the first awareness of inequality. Though differences in ability, strength, and appearance existed in the early state of nature, they were dormant. That is to say, they were not yet manifest or recognizable given savage man's solitary existence. However, once humans entered society and developed reason, their differences became apparent to one another, as in the case of the vain singer. Inequality blossomed. Some became conscious that they were more musical, more intelligent, and better-looking than others. To make matters worse, society began to sanction this inequality by rewarding those individuals who possessed a greater share of these qualities.

Rousseau thus distinguishes between natural and conventional inequality. **Natural inequality** refers to the innate differences between human beings in the early state of nature that were not yet apparent due to man's solitary condition. **Conventional inequality** represents the many customs, laws, and practices of society that sanction these differences. While Rousseau acknowledges natural differences in ability, strength, and intellect among human beings, he denies that such differences or inequalities provide a natural title for some to rule over others. The conventional inequality established by society robs human beings of the original freedom they once enjoyed in the state of nature. Most perniciously, it seeks to justify the plundering of the many by the few.

The development of *amour propre* (the wellspring of all vice) eventually led to malicious and vindictive struggles over land, possessions, love, and status. It was at this much later point in history that the state of nature devolved into the state of war famously described by Hobbes. Seeing how insecure their possessions were in this vulnerable state, the few rich schemed to protect their own self-interest at the expense of the many poor. They devised the ultimate swindle to protect their interests: the **bogus social contract.** The wealthy persuaded the poor that it was in their best interest to "gather... into one supreme power which governs us according to wise laws, protects and defends all the members of the association, repulses common enemies, and maintains us in an eternal concord."[19] They promised that the contract would secure each in the enjoyment of his life, freedom, and possessions. In fact, however, this contract was nothing more than a sham, a ploy, a ruse designed to perpetuate the inequality of the rich. It merely confirmed the power and supremacy of the few rich by convincing the many poor that of the bogus claim that some people by nature were entitled to a much greater share of land, resources, and wealth than their fellows.

We have now arrived at the origins of human inequality: the institution of **private property.** For Rousseau property generates both inequality and dependence. Indeed, Rousseau makes the radical claim that the foundations of almost all civil societies are illegitimate in sanctioning the unequal distribution of property. Poignantly describing the role that private property played in robbing man of his natural equality and original innocence, he states,

> The first person who, having fenced off a plot of ground, took it into his head to say *this is mine* and found people simple enough to believe him, was the true founder of civil society. What crimes, wars, murders, what miseries and horrors would the human race have been spared by someone who, uprooting the stakes or filling in the ditch, had shouted to his fellow-men: Beware of listening to this impostor; you are lost if you forget that the fruits belong to all and the earth to no one![20]

Thinking that the contract would secure them in their meager possessions, the poor all "ran to meet their chains." The simplemindedness of the people in accepting this "theft" was further compounded by their stupidity in comparing themselves to others in regard to their possessions. Private property inflames *amour propre* insofar as it arouses greed, spurs competition, intensifies rivalry, exacerbates jealousies, and promotes the worst kind of dependence in which the very life, freedom, and happiness of some are completely subject to the will of another. Once the more resourceful and industrious begin to secure a greater share of property, they also begin to think that they may accumulate as much as they can at the expense of others—and that they may even do so as a matter or "right" and "justice." The rich become arrogant and the poor become envious. The bonds of pity are weakened, if not broken entirely. The two become locked in a cycle of mutual dependence and exploitation. The master becomes enslaved to his unbridled appetite for more power, possessions, and prestige, while the poor are enslaved to the will of the master.

Contrary to Locke, Rousseau denies that there is an inalienable right to property in the state of nature. Nature simply does not sanction the unbounded accumulation of

[19]*Discourses,* p. 159.

[20]*Discourses,* pp. 141–142.

wealth and property for some and the abject penury of others. For Rousseau, the right to private property is conventional or customary. In most cases, it is a notorious example of the arbitrary inequality sanctioned by society to protect the "haves" from the "have nots." Moreover, it leads to conflicts that further disfigure the natural goodness of man, pitting human beings against each other in a ceaseless conflict that exacerbates pride and vanity. Prefiguring Karl Marx, Rousseau sees property as a source of division between members of society. Tracing the downward spiral that begins with the inequality of property and culminates with despotism of the rich over the poor, Rousseau explains, "If we follow the progress of inequality in these different revolutions, we shall find that the establishment of the law and the right of property was the first stage, the institution of the magistracy the second, and the third and last was the changing of legitimate power into arbitrary power."[21]

THE BOURGEOIS AND THE CORRUPT SOCIETY

Rousseau's narrative of the Garden, the Fall, and the origins of inequality bring us full circle to the plight of modern man, who is good for neither himself nor others. Rousseau's critique of civilization shatters the Enlightenment's faith in progress—the belief that the general diffusion of knowledge, science, and the arts would bring forth a new dawn of light for humanity, thereby improving the human condition both morally and materially. The diffusion of the arts and sciences only spread garlands over the chains of despotism and dependence, addicting people to superfluous luxuries, and rendering them decadent, soft, and effeminate. Given his debased condition, modern man is unable to make the necessary sacrifices in defense of liberty: "the people, already accustomed to dependence, repose, and the conveniences of life, and already incapable of breaking their chains, consented to let their servitude increase in order to assure their tranquility."[22]

The decadence of modern society culminates with the appearance of the **bourgeois**: the sophisticated urbanite, the modern professional—the banker, lawyer, and CEO. The bourgeois is the soulless product of a commercial society that measures happiness and success in terms of the market. He is a poser, pretending to be concerned with the public good, but in fact caring for nothing more than his own private, selfish interests. Rousseau notes that the bourgeois obsessions with commerce and luxury are particularly inimical to civic life since they intensify greed, selfishness, and inequality. Money corrupts the political process by allowing the wealthy to buy influence and access to politicians. Business occupies a privileged position in bourgeois societies. The principle of the market and supply and demands governs almost all human relations. The common good is perversely defined in terms of the selfish interests of the corporation. After all, "what is good for General Motors is good for the nation."

The bourgeois gluts his life with petty pleasures in an effort to prolong a comfortable existence, allowing others to do the fighting for him. For example, in times of war, the poor are either drafted or compelled by economic hardship to enlist while the rich are exempted and even profit off the war. With nothing to die for, the bourgeois really has nothing to live for. He or she ends the frantic race of life without ever truly having lived it.

---

[21]*Discourses,* p. 172.

[22]*Discourses,* p. 172.

Rousseau versus Mary Wollstonecraft on Sex and Politics

According to Rousseau, bourgeois society is further corrupted by the confusion of gender roles. He maintains that the vigor and health of the family and society depend on an education that properly divides the sexes into public and private spheres. These divided roles are interdependent and mutually beneficial. Rousseau argues that by nature men are intended for public life and women are intended for private domestic life. Women nonetheless play an important supporting role in the public sphere by raising virtuous children and by inspiring their husbands to sacrifice for country. According to Rousseau, the model of female republican virtue is the Spartan mother who rejoiced after hearing that her three sons died bravely in a battle that brought glory and victory to the city–state. Indeed, Rousseau believed that women had a civilizing and domesticating effect on men. A man's love and defense of his country are an extension of his love of home and hearth. In *Emile* and his novel, *Julie or the Nouvelle Heloise*, Rousseau prescribes a different course of education for men and women that will respect their sexual differences and interdependence. Unlike men, women should not be taught the abstract subjects of math, science, and philosophy. Instead they should practice the art of coquetry (flirtation); follow etiquette, protocol, and convention much more

Rousseau versus Mary Wollstonecraft on Sex and Politics *continued*

closely than men; and learn through concrete examples in literature.

Mary Wollstonecraft, considered by many to be the first feminist political thinker, provides a stinging rebuttal to Rousseau in *A Vindication of the Rights of Woman.* Wollstonecraft maintains that Rousseau's division of sex roles into the public and private spheres harms both sexes and society by impoverishing women's minds and by depriving men of true friendship and felicity. The following is an excerpt from her reply to Rousseau:

> I now appeal from the reveries of fancy and refined licentiousness to the good sense of mankind, whether, if the object of education be to prepare women to become chaste wives and sensible mothers, the method so plausibly recommended [by Rousseau] . . . be the one calculated to produce those ends? Will it be allowed that the surest way to make a wife chaste, is to teach her to practice the wanton arts of a mistress, termed virtuous coquetry, by the sensualist who can no longer relish the artless charms of sincerity, or taste the pleasure arising from a tender intimacy, when confidence is unchecked by suspicion, and rendered interesting by sense?
>
> The man who can be contented to live with a pretty, useful companion, without a mind, has lost in voluptuous gratifications a taste for more refined enjoyments; he has never felt the calm satisfaction, that refreshes the parched heart, like the silent dew of heaven, of being beloved by one who could understand him. . . .
>
> Why was Rousseau's life divided between ecstasy and misery? Can any other answer be given than this, that the effervescence of his imagination produced both. . . .[23]

Is Mary Wollstonecraft correct in her critique of Rousseau's sexual politics? What do you think might be Rousseau's rejoinder?

[23]Mary Wollstonecraft, *A Vindication of the Rights of Women* (New York: Norton Critical Edition, 1994), pp. 90–91.

Rousseau laments the fact that the grand, noble soul of the ancients has been reduced to the petty, selfish soul of the bourgeois. Whereas ancient man was elevated by civic virtue and love of country, modern soulless man believes in nothing other than his own narrow self-interest and the love of profit. "Ancient politicians incessantly talked about morals and virtue," exclaims Rousseau; "those of our time talk only of business and money."[24] Tragically, the narrow self-interest of the bourgeois diminishes the natural sentiment of pity, thereby weakening the emotional ties that bind citizens together. According to Rousseau, the public-spiritedness and proper sexual politics of the ancient city is epitomized by the aforementioned Spartan mother. Rousseau's prescription in *The Social Contract* emerges as an effort to save modern man from his tragic degradation and to restore the lost greatness of soul represented by the ancient republics of Rome and Sparta.

Though the original freedom, innocence, and felicity of the state of nature were irrevocably lost in society, the debasement of bourgeois society was neither inevitable nor necessary. Rousseau's paradox, "Man was born free and yet everywhere he is in chains," observes both the reality of human domination and the possibility of human liberation. Despite the tragedy of man's fall from the Garden, it must be emphasized that Rousseau does not call for a return to the condition of savage man. In fact, he

[24]*Discourses,* p. 51.

CASE STUDY 9.1 | THE ENRON SCANDAL

Enron was a Houston-based energy corporation that began as a gas pipeline manufacturer. It was transformed by its CEO Ken Lay into a "virtual corporation" that bought and sold energy stock on the world market. From October 1998 to November 2001 the top 30 executives at Enron sold over 20 million shares of their company's stock with gross proceeds of over a billion dollars. Chairman Ken Lay sold over 4 million shares with gross proceeds of over 184 million dollars.[25] While top executives were furiously selling shares of their own stock for outlandish personal profits, they reassured investors that the company was doing well, citing bogus earnings that had been fabricated by their bribed accounting firm, Arthur Andersen. In a word, they created imaginary earnings by "cooking the books." Incriminating documents were later shredded. When stock prices began to decline, the company's top executives, who had sold their own stock by the millions before the decline, prohibited their employees from doing the same. The house of cards tumbled in 2001 when Enron filed for Chapter 11 bankruptcy. Twenty thousand employees were fired, many losing their life savings and retirement, which were invested in the company's stocks. In some cases, employees were given half an hour to clear their offices out.

Enron's wealth was also used to buy influence and access to government. On January 28, 2002, *BusinessWeek* reported, "The corporation and its executives contributed almost $5.8 million to political war chests since 1989, including $1.9 million in soft money to both parties. While 73% went to Republicans including President Bush—whose campaign inauguration received $424,000—Enron also donated to prominent Democrats, such as . . . Senator Chuck Schumer (N.Y.). . . . In 1996, Enron donated $100,000 in soft money to the Democratic Party after the Clinton White House helped with troubled negotiations over a power plant in India."

Is Enron a modern example of Rousseau's teaching on bourgeois selfishness and the corrupt society where money buys power, access, and influence, and where unequal extremes of wealth lead to the vanity of conspicuous consumption, as well as the dependence of citizens on the will of economic elites?

[25]"Pipe Dreams, Greed, Ego, and the Death of Enron." Sources from *Mark Newby, et al. vs. Enron Corp., et al.* Securities and Exchange Commission filings, Congressional testimony, Enron Corp. Press release.

argues that a return to the primeval condition of savage man is not even desirable! Once human nature made the transition from the state of nature to society, this is impossible. Rousseau notes that "it is slavery to be ruled by appetite alone." Notwithstanding their fall, human beings actually benefited from the development of sociality. The acquisition of morality provided opportunities to exercise their freedom in a noble fashion. These opportunities for virtue were best realized in the ancient republics. In an important passage from *The Social Contract,* Rousseau explains:

> Although in civil society man surrenders some of the advantages that belong to the state of nature, he gains in return far greater; his faculties are so exercised and developed, his mind is so enlarged, his sentiments so ennobled, and his whole spirit so elevated that, if the abuse of his new condition did not in many cases lower him to something worse than what he had left, he should constantly bless the happy hour that lifted him forever from the state of nature and from a narrow, stupid animal made a creature of intelligence and a man.[26]

[26]Jean-Jacques Rousseau, *On Social Contract or Principles of Political Right,* in *Rousseau's Political Writings,* (eds.) Alan Ritter and Julia Conaway Bondella, trans. Julia Conaway Bondella (New York: Norton & Company, 1988), p. 95.

Rousseau fully recognizes that human freedom can lead to either high or low pursuits. The ancient examples of Rome and Sparta—not to mention the modern example of Geneva—demonstrate the possibility of human nobility and grandeur. In each case, these good societies are defined by a strong communal emphasis in which the individual self-interest and private life are subsumed by common good and public life.

Before considering more specifically Rousseau's prescription in the social contract, let us consider the relevance of his description of human nature thus far. How is this description still relevant if human nature has changed over time, and if human beings can no longer return to their original solitary condition in the Garden? First, Rousseau's description reveals the conventional nature of all societies—morality, customs, laws, and governments are all artificial human constructs. Second, it provides a telling critique of the foundations of most societies as illegitimate. Most societies merely sanction a conventional and arbitrary inequality that robs people of the freedom they were born to enjoy. Third, it posits freedom and feeling as distinctive qualities of human nature, and *amour propre* as an ineradicable, acquired trait of human nature. Rousseau teaches that the proper end of government is to guarantee each an equal freedom from dependence on another's particular will: "If we enquire wherein lies precisely the greatest good of all, which ought to be the goal of every system of law, we shall find that it comes down to two main objects, freedom and equality. . . ." It is worth repeating that because all human beings are born free, it follows that there is no natural title to authority: "Since no man has any natural authority over his fellows, and since force alone bestows no right, all legitimate authority among men must be based on covenants." Fourth, Rousseau's conception of human nature emphasizes the role of sentiment rather than rational understanding as the key to freedom and happiness: "I shall reply that the estimation of happiness is less a concern of reason than of sentiment." Finally, Rousseau's diagnosis of man's fallen condition points to his role as a philanthropist, a rare genius who can benefit mankind through an enlightened understanding of human nature and society.

ROUSSEAU'S PRESCRIPTION: THE GENERAL WILL

Rousseau's prescription in *The Social Contract* offers a public path of redemption that will restore something of the lost freedom and happiness of man's original condition by means of the general will. The political edifice in *The Social Contract* is informed by Rousseau's understanding of the core inclinations of human nature in the Garden—freedom and pity. These qualities are buried but still alive. They must be reawakened and redirected. Rousseau's prescription seeks to manage the acquired twin evils of *amour propre* and dependence through the proper social structures and conditions. If equal freedom is lost through bad customs, it may be recovered through good ones. If *amour propre* is an acquired source of misery, it must be managed accordingly.

Through human artifice or construct, Rousseau's prescription in *The Social Contract* attempts to replace the natural freedom and equality lost by man in the state of nature with civil freedom: "instead of destroying natural equality, the fundamental pact, on the contrary, substitutes a moral and legitimate equality for whatever physical equality nature had been able to impose among men, and, although they may be unequal in strength or in genius, they all become equal through agreements and law."[27] For most men, this civil freedom is the closest approximation to the lost natural freedom. Unlike prior covenants (the bogus social contract of the rich that sanctioned vast inequality of property), Rousseau's **social contract** seeks to provide a legitimate foundation for government.

In bourgeois societies, human beings are divided between their own private, selfish interests and the shared responsibilities of the public good. Rousseau attempts to find a way whereby individuals remain as free as they were in the state of nature (**freedom from** dependence on the particular will of another) while still performing their duties to society (**freedom to** fulfill their duties in society). In sum, through the social contract, Rousseau seeks to **reconcile freedom and duty.** "[W]hat makes us miserable as human beings," he explains, "is the contradiction between our situation and our desires, our duties and our inclinations, our nature and social institutions between man and the citizen; make man one, and you will render him as happy as he can be. Give him entirely to the state or leave him entirely to himself; but if you divide his heart, you tear him to pieces."[28]

The social contract transforms private individuals into public citizens who are capable of recognizing that their individual good and the public good now coincide. In one of his most famous quotations, Rousseau describes the purpose of the social contract: ". . . to find a form of association which will defend the person and goods of each member with the collective force of all, and under which each individual, while uniting himself with others, obeys no one but himself and remains as free as before."[29] The voice of the private individual answers every question about the good of society in reference to "me," whereas the voice of the public citizen transformed by the social contract answers it in terms of "we."

According to Rousseau, once human beings left the state of nature and entered into civil society, they tacitly agreed to exchange natural liberty (freedom from) for civil or public liberty (freedom to)—that is, they tacitly agreed to the self-imposed rule of law and to the obligation of social duties. The general will thus substitutes public or civil liberty for private liberty. Whereas civil or public liberty is the power of free, self-determining citizens to decide their collective destiny as a society, private liberty refers to the freedom of selfish individuals, elites, or corporations who pursue false wants at the public expense. Perhaps a current example of this civic or public liberty associated with the general will is found in the public-spiritedness of citizens who unite against Wal-Mart in a common effort to retain the autonomy and character of their local communities.

Can individuals fulfill their civic obligations on terms of equality, without mutual exploitation or domination? Unfortunately, as we have seen, the terms of the original social contract were unfair and bogus, merely sanctioning the artificial inequality that existed at the time. However, the legitimate social contract proposed by Rousseau

---

[27] *On Social Contract,* p. 98.

[28] Jean-Jacques Rousseau, *Fragments Politiques* (Paris: Gallimard, 1964), vol. 2, p. 510; quoted from Benjamin R. Barber, *Consumed: How Markets Corrupt Children, Infantilize Adults, and Swallow Citizens Whole* (New York: Norton & Company, 2007), p. 331.

[29] *On Social Contract,* p. 92.

remedies this problem by generating duties to others without making some dependent on the will of others.

Rousseau's definition of **civil freedom** as "obedience to a law one prescribes to oneself" is fundamental to his prescription in *The Social Contract* and his attempt to reconcile freedom and duty. If freedom consists in obeying a law one makes for oneself, then it follows that one's obedience to such a law is legitimate only when each individual freely gives laws to himself and is therefore no longer dependent on another's will. Furthermore, if obedience to a law one prescribes to oneself is the essence of civil freedom, then submission to a law prescribed by another without one's consent is the essence of despotism. Given that man was born free, consent among those equally free is the only legitimate principle of governance. "Since every man is born free and master of himself, no one can, under any pretext whatsoever, subjugate him without his consent."[30] In the following passage, Rousseau explains how the social contract emerges through the alienation—surrendering and uniting of the particular will of each to all—on terms of equality:

> . . . the social pact establishes such an equality among citizens that they all commit themselves under the same conditions and should all enjoy the same rights. Thus, by the very nature of the pact, every act of sovereignty, that is to say, every authentic act of the general will, obligates or favors all citizens equally, so that the sovereign knows only the body of the nation and makes no distinctions between any of those who compose it. What in fact is an act of sovereignty? It is not an agreement between a superior and an inferior, but an agreement between the body and each of its members, a legitimate agreement, because it is based upon the social contract; equitable because it is common to all; useful, because it can have no other purpose than the general good; and reliable, because it is guaranteed by public force and supreme power. As long as the subjects are only bound by agreements of this sort, they obey no one but their own will . . .[31]

Most importantly, the legitimacy of the social contract is grounded in the **general will,** which is an expression of the collective or common good among free and equal people.

Significantly, for Rousseau, the general will necessarily reflects the particular history, customs, habits, and manners of a people. On one hand, the general will is present as the guiding principle that animates virtuous citizens to unite for the common good. On the other, it is reflected in the outcome of public policies that have followed the proper democratic procedures. Some have interpreted the general will as a purely formal concept, claiming that it involves nothing more than following formal, fair democratic procedures. Others take the view that the general will has an objective moral status similar to Aristotle's and Aquinas' understanding of the common good, as a principle of justice that exists prior to any formal process. Rousseau invites this debate when he states, "the most general will is also the most just, and that the voice of the people is indeed the voice of God."[32]

---

[30] *On Social Contract,* p. 151.

[31] *On Social Contract,* p. 103.

[32] *On Social Contract,* p. 62.

QUESTIONS FOR REFLECTION

The General Will—Created or Discovered?

Is the general will discovered as something that is preexisting, or is it created by formal political processes through an agreement between the people? In either case, is the general will morally relative to the particular character of each people, or does it enjoin just moral principles that are universal to all?

Significantly, Rousseau distinguishes the **will of all** from the general will. The will of all is the summation of selfish, private interests or wills without regard for the common good. According to Rousseau, it is an illegitimate principle of governance. Rousseau's political philosophy thus appreciates the problem of the tyranny of the majority. The general will may be understood further in contrast to the particular will of each individual. The particular will of each may potentially reflect either one's selfish interest or the common good of all—that is, the general will. When legitimate, the social contract transforms each particular will into a public will through its participation in the general will: "Since each man gives himself to all, he gives himself to no one. . . . Each one puts into the community his person and all his powers under the supreme direction for the general will; and as a body incorporates every member as an individual part of the whole." The tension between the interests of a private or selfish will and the general or public will is raised when considering the actions of an unregulated free market that pollutes the environment, markets harmful and addictive products to children, and infiltrates every area of civic life with advertising and shopping. Rousseau clearly disagrees with the idea that what is good for big businessis necessarily good for the nation.

Yet it would be wrong to assume that the social contract seeks to abolish property. Rather it seeks to ensure a more equitable, fair, and secure protection of citizens' lives and property. The social pact requires the alienation or transfer of private property to the sovereign to ensure a just and equitable distribution of possessions: "What is remarkable about this alienation, far from robbing private individuals by accepting their property, the community only assures them of legitimate possession, and changes usurpation into a genuine right and possession into ownership."[33] Although Rousseau denies an inalienable right to property, the social contract nonetheless confers a **conventional right to property** upon first occupants, thereby making property more secure through the collective, public force of the general will. The sovereign seeks to prevent vast inequality of property from occurring in order to minimize dependence and to protect the freedom and lives of each. In the good society, private property is not to be treated as a limitless good that some can accumulate at the expense of others; rather, it is to be placed in service of the common good and general will: "The right of each individual to his own piece of land is always subordinate to the community's right to everything, without which there would be neither solidity in the social bond nor real power in the exercise of sovereignty."[34]

---

[33] *On Social Contract,* p. 97.

[34] *On Social Contract,* p. 98.

QUESTIONS FOR REFLECTION

How far is Rousseau willing to permit popular government to apply the political principle of forcing people to be free? To seat belts? Mandatory inoculations? Limitations on CEO salaries? Environmental regulations?

Because each individual has consented to the general will and has participated in it directly, no one has a right to oppose its outcome. If one persists, Rousseau states that he must be **forced to be free.** Though this may sound shocking, it is important to note that almost every society forces citizens to be free. When a citizen agrees to the terms of the social contract on an equal basis, he tacitly agrees to obey the rule of law. It is only through participation in the social contract, whereby each gives himself to others on terms of equality, that one is truly freed from the potential dependence on a particular will of another. One cannot renege on the contract if the determination of the general will varies from one's selfish, particular will, civic virtue, and freedom dictate that one must follow what is truly good for oneself and the community as a whole. For example, through the enforcement of traffic regulations a society forces individuals to do what is likely to secure their lives and establish the effective transportation of goods and services to benefit the common good. Unlike Hobbes' sovereign, Rousseau's sovereign may even demand that the citizen make the supreme sacrifice of his life.

ROUSSEAU'S GOOD SOCIETY

Rousseau makes clear that the general will is possible only under rare and special circumstances. In *The Social Contract,* he specifies those enabling conditions necessary for its emergence. First, the general will can be operative only in a small territory. Rousseau rejects the American founders' teaching that liberty is best secured in an extensive republic. On the contrary, he maintains that freedom is best secured in a small republic where social bonds are stronger.

Moreover, Rousseau argues that participatory democracy is the only legitimate form of association. This follows from his definition of freedom as obedience to a law one prescribes to oneself. For the general will to be operative, citizens must be self-determining in voting directly on laws themselves. Every citizen is, in effect, a lawmaker. The same person is both an author of and subject to the same law. All good governments are participatory and republican. In general, representative forms of government are illegitimate because citizens do not participate directly in lawmaking.

According to Rousseau, government serves a purely ministerial function in carrying out and executing the laws, whether it is administered by one, a few, or many. Moreover, he maintains that sovereignty is indivisible and therefore cannot be shared or divided between a state and a national authority.

Finally, Rousseau discourages the formation of interest groups or factions. Any groups that mediate between the state and citizens are dangerous because they inevitably become a power in and of themselves, privileging their particular group interest to the common good of all. Rousseau notes that "anything that destroys social unity is worthless." He would be appalled at the role that special interest groups today

PRIMARY SOURCE 9.2

On the Social Contract and the General Will, from *The Social Contract*, Book I, Chapter 6

6. The Social Compact

I SUPPOSE men to have reached the point at which the obstacles in the way of their preservation in the state of nature show their power of resistance to be greater than the resources at the disposal of each individual for his maintenance in that state. That primitive condition can then subsist no longer; and the human race would perish unless it changed its manner of existence.

But, as men cannot engender new forces, but only unite and direct existing ones, they have no other means of preserving themselves than the formation, by aggregation, of a sum of forces great enough to overcome the resistance. These they have to bring into play by means of a single motive power, and cause to act in concert.

This sum of forces can arise only where several persons come together: but, as the force and liberty of each man are the chief instruments of his self-preservation, how can he pledge them without harming his own interests, and neglecting the care he owes to himself? This difficulty, in its bearing on my present subject, may be stated in the following terms:

"The problem is to find a form of association which will defend and protect with the whole common force the person and goods of each associate, and in which each, while uniting himself with all, may still obey himself alone, and remain as free as before." This is the fundamental problem of which the Social Contract provides the solution.

The clauses of this contract are so determined by the nature of the act that the slightest modification would make them vain and ineffective; so that, although they have perhaps never been formally set forth, they are everywhere the same and everywhere tacitly admitted and recognized, until, on the violation of the social compact, each regains his original rights and resumes his natural liberty, while losing the conventional liberty in favor of which he renounced it.

These clauses, properly understood, may be reduced to one—the total alienation of each associate, together with all his rights, to the whole community; for, in the first place, as each gives himself absolutely, the conditions are the same for all; and, this being so, no one has any interest in making them burdensome to others.

Moreover, the alienation being without reserve, the union is as perfect as it can be, and no associate has anything more to demand: for, if the individuals retained certain rights, as there would be no common superior to decide between them and the public, each, being on one point his own judge, would ask to be so on all; the state of nature would thus continue, and the association would necessarily become inoperative or tyrannical.

Finally, each man, in giving himself to all, gives himself to nobody; and as there is no associate over whom he does not acquire the same right as he yields others over himself, he gains an equivalent for everything he loses, and an increase of force for the preservation of what he has.

If then we discard from the social compact what is not of its essence, we shall find that it reduces itself to the following terms:

"Each of us puts his person and all his power in common under the supreme direction of the general will, and, in our corporate capacity, we receive each member as an indivisible part of the whole."

At once, in place of the individual personality of each contracting party, this act of association creates a moral and collective body, composed of as many members as the assembly contains votes, and receiving from this act its unity, its common identity, its life, and its will. This public person, so formed by the union of all other persons formerly took the name of city, and now takes that of Republic or body politic; it is called by its members State when passive, Sovereign when active, and Power when compared with others like itself. Those who are associated in it take collectively the name of people, and severally are called citizens, as sharing in the sovereign power, and

PRIMARY SOURCE 9.2

On the Social Contract and the General Will, from *The Social Contract*, Book I, Chapter 6 *continued*

subjects, as being under the laws of the State. But these terms are often confused and taken one for another: it is enough to know how to distinguish them when they are being used with precision.

7. The Sovereign

THIS formula shows us that the act of association comprises a mutual undertaking between the public and the individuals, and that each individual, in making a contract, as we may say, with himself, is bound in a double capacity; as a member of the Sovereign he is bound to the individuals, and as a member of the State to the Sovereign. But the maxim of civil right, that no one is bound by undertakings made to himself, does not apply in this case; for there is a great difference between incurring an obligation to yourself and incurring one to a whole of which you form a part.

Attention must further be called to the fact that public deliberation, while competent to bind all the subjects to the Sovereign, because of the two different capacities in which each of them may be regarded, cannot, for the opposite reason, bind the Sovereign to itself; and that it is consequently against the nature of the body politic for the Sovereign to impose on itself a law which it cannot infringe. Being able to regard itself in only one capacity, it is in the position of an individual who makes a contract with himself; and this makes it clear that there neither is nor can be any kind of fundamental law binding on the body of the people—not even the social contract itself. This does not mean that the body politic cannot enter into undertakings with others, provided the contract is not infringed by them; for in relation to what is external to it, it becomes a simple being, an individual.

But the body politic or the Sovereign, drawing its being wholly from the sanctity of the contract, can never bind itself, even to an outsider, to do anything derogatory to the original act, for instance, to alienate any part of itself, or to submit to another Sovereign. Violation of the act by which it exists would be self-annihilation; and that which is itself nothing can create nothing...

In fact, each individual, as a man, may have a particular will contrary or dissimilar to the general will which he has as a citizen. His particular interest may speak to him quite differently from the common interest: his absolute and naturally independent existence may make him look upon what he owes to the common cause as a gratuitous contribution, the loss of which will do less harm to others than the payment of it is burdensome to himself; and, regarding the moral person which constitutes the State as a persona ficta, because not a man, he may wish to enjoy the rights of citizenship without being ready to fulfill the duties of a subject. The continuance of such an injustice could not but prove the undoing of the body politic.

In order then that the social compact may not be an empty formula, it tacitly includes the undertaking, which alone can give force to the rest, that whoever refuses to obey the general will shall be compelled to do so by the whole body. This means nothing less than that he will be forced to be free; for this is the condition which, by giving each citizen to his country, secures him against all personal dependence. In this lies the key to the working of the political machine; this alone legitimizes civil undertakings, which, without it, would be absurd, tyrannical, and liable to the most frightful abuses.

* * * *

9. Real Property

EACH member of the community gives himself to it, at the moment of its foundation, just as he is, with all the resources at his command, including the goods he possesses. This act does not make possession, in changing hands, change its nature, and become property in the hands of the Sovereign; but, as the forces of the city are incomparably greater than those of an individual, public possession is also, in fact, stronger and more irrevocable, without being

continued

PRIMARY SOURCE 9.2

On the Social Contract and the General Will, from *The Social Contract*, Book I, Chapter 6 *continued*

any more legitimate, at any rate from the point of view of foreigners. For the State, in relation to its members, is master of all their goods by the social contract, which, within the State, is the basis of all rights; but, in relation to other powers, it is so only by the right of the first occupier, which it holds from its members.

The right of the first occupier, though more real than the right of the strongest, becomes a real right only when the right of property has already been established. Every man has naturally a right to everything he needs; but the positive act which makes him proprietor of one thing excludes him from everything else. Having his share, he ought to keep to it, and can have no further right against the community. This is why the right of the first occupier, which in the state of nature is so weak, claims the respect of every man in civil society. In this right we are respecting not so much what belongs to another as what does not belong to ourselves.

In general, to establish the right of the first occupier over a plot of ground, the following conditions are necessary: first, the land must not yet be inhabited; secondly, a man must occupy only the amount he needs for his subsistence; and, in the third place, possession must be taken, not by an empty ceremony, but by labor and cultivation, the only sign of proprietorship that should be respected by others, in default of a legal title.

play in the financing of campaigns and elections. For him, the pluralism of special interest groups would be a clear indication that what prevails in society is not the general will, but either the will of all—the aggregate of private interests—or a particular elite's selfish will.

Although the general will always wills the common good and is always valid, it is not always enlightened; that is, it is not always discerned and applied properly. Rousseau states that "by themselves the people always will what is good, but by themselves they do not always discern it. The general will is always rightful, but it is not always enlightened." It thus falls upon the lawgiver or enlightened statesman to illuminate the general will.

But how can Rousseau call for a philanthropic genius and an enlightened lawgiver given his critique of the Enlightenment in the *First Discourse*? This paradox or seeming contradiction is resolved through a careful reading of Rousseau's teaching in the *First Discourse*. In fact, Rousseau's critique of the Enlightenment is qualified to the *general* diffusion or vulgar *popularization* of the arts and sciences to the mass of people. It does not extend to the rare individual genius, like Rousseau himself. Indeed, though he critiques the Enlightenment notion of progress in the *First Discourse*, in the same essay, Rousseau nonetheless praises Newton, Descartes, and Galileo as benefactors of mankind. He thus points to himself as a philanthropic genius who can benefit mankind in the realm of morals and politics. Kant's description of Rousseau as the Newton of the moral world is therefore apt in describing the latter's role as a genius whose philanthropy in the realm of politics and morals would likewise benefit mankind, if only we were to listen.

The enlightened lawgiver's task is analogous to that of a sculptor who molds a malleable slab of marble. To procure freedom for the community, the lawgiver must repress the human inclination to act selfishly: "The nearer men's natural powers are to

PRIMARY SOURCE 9.3 | ON THE SOCIAL CONTRACT AND THE GENERAL WILL, FROM *THE SOCIAL CONTRACT*, BOOK II

1. That Sovereignty Is Inalienable

THE first and most important deduction from the principles we have so far laid down is that the general will alone can direct the State according to the object for which it was instituted, i.e., the common good: for if the clashing of particular interests made the establishment of societies necessary, the agreement of these very interests made it possible. The common element in these different interests is what forms the social tie; and, were there no point of agreement between them all, no society could exist. It is solely on the basis of this common interest that every society should be governed.

I hold then that Sovereignty, being nothing less than the exercise of the general will, can never be alienated, and that the Sovereign, who is no less than a collective being, cannot be represented except by himself: the power indeed may be transmitted, but not the will.

In reality, if it is not impossible for a particular will to agree on some point with the general will, it is at least impossible for the agreement to be lasting and constant; for the particular will tends, by its very nature, to partiality, while the general will tends to equality. It is even more impossible to have any guarantee of this agreement; for even if it should always exist, it would be the effect not of art, but of chance. The Sovereign may indeed say, "I now will actually what this man wills, or at least what he says he wills"; but it cannot say, "What he wills tomorrow, I too shall will" because it is absurd for the will to bind itself for the future, nor is it incumbent on any will to consent to anything that is not for the good of the being who wills. If then the people promises simply to obey, by that very act it dissolves itself and loses what makes it a people; the moment a master exists, there is no longer a Sovereign, and from that moment the body politic has ceased to exist.

This does not mean that the commands of the rulers cannot pass for general wills, so long as the Sovereign, being free to oppose them, offers no opposition. In such a case, universal silence is taken to imply the consent of the people. This will be explained later on.

* * * *

3. Whether the General Will Is Fallible

IT follows from what has gone before that the general will is always right and tends to the public advantage; but it does not follow that the deliberations of the people are always equally correct. Our will is always for our own good, but we do not always see what that is; the people is never corrupted, but it is often deceived, and on such occasions only does it seem to will what is bad.

There is often a great deal of difference between the will of all and the general will; the latter considers only the common interest, while the former takes private interest into account, and is no more than a sum of particular wills: but take away from these same wills the pluses and minuses that cancel one another, and the general will remains as the sum of the differences.

extinction or annihilation, and the stronger and more lasting their acquired powers, the stronger and more perfect is the social institution." Through political artifice, the enlightened statesman must establish the basic political procedures that will enable human beings to reconcile freedom and duty within a moral and communal existence. In transforming private will into a collective, public will, the lawgiver must "change human nature, to transform each individual, who by himself is entirely complete and solitary, into a party of a greater whole. . . . to replace the physical and independent existence we have received from nature with a moral and communal existence." The enlightened lawgiver is comparable to Moses who led the Jews, or to Lycurgus who

Rousseau's Major Stages of Historical Development and the Sociopolitical Conditions Produced by Each

Stage	Condition
Original solitude in state of nature	Man's condition is marked by natural goodness, self-sufficiency, radical freedom, and *amour de soi*—the sentiment of his own existence.
Sociality	Man's condition is marked by the development of reason and *amour propre*—vanity. All vices—greed, lust, jealousy, envy, wrath—proceed from *amour propre.* Loss of innocence and natural goodness.
Private property	Man's condition is marked by war, inequality, inner division between duty and inclination, and dependence on others. A bogus social contract provides legal sanction to inequality. The height of this corruption is reached with bourgeois society.
The General Will as remedy	Man's condition in the good society is marked by equality, virtue, and the reconciliation of duty and inclination. This good society presumes a legitimate social contract based upon the General Will.

led the Spartans. In each case, these semidivine leaders bound a people together into a collective union based on shared customs, traditions, and cultures. Rousseau applauds Moses for incorporating into Jewish law specific rituals, practices, and customs (circumcision for example) that would constantly remind the Jewish people of their unique ethnic and political identity.

Most importantly, Rousseau demands that citizens in the good society be virtuous. He defines **virtue** or moral excellence as the disposition to act in conformity with the general will. In particular, Rousseau closely identifies civic virtue with the sentiment of patriotism. He understands such virtue not so much as an end in itself, but more as a means to an end: Virtue or patriotism is indispensable to the end of maintaining civil freedom and the civil autonomy of the individual who is freed from dependence upon the particular will of another. In his *Discourse on Political Economy,* Rousseau explains that the natural sentiment of pity is weakened and dissipated in a larger society. In a small republic, the sentimental bonds of patriotism are cemented through both pity and pride (*amour propre*). The love of oneself must be transformed into the love of one's country as a projection of oneself. Rousseau states,

> Interest and commiseration must be limited and compressed in some way to make them active. Now, since this inclination in us can be useful only to those with whom we have to live, it is good that the humanity concentrated among fellow citizens acquires new force within them through the habit of seeing each other and through the common interest that unites them. It is certain that the greatest marvels of virtue have been produced by love for the homeland. Its combination of self-love with all the beauty of virtue gives this sweet and lively sentiment an energy that, without disfiguring it, makes it the most heroic of all the passions.... the love for one's homeland [is] a hundred times more lively and delightful than the love for a mistress.[37]

CASE STUDY 9.2 — Participatory Democracy and the SDS's Port Huron Statement

The Port Huron Statement of 1962 was the manifesto of the Students for a Democratic Society (SDS), "the leading voice of the student movement in the early 1960s."[35] Over 100,000 copies of the Port Huron Statement were distributed throughout campuses across the nation. The SDS condemned the materialism, consumerism, greed, alienation, and racism of American society. They described America's political system as "corporate liberalism," referring to the corrupt influence of wealthy elites and special interests in running the government. The following excerpt from the Port Huron Statement conveys the students' diagnosis of the ills of "corporate liberalism" and their remedy of "participatory democracy":

Loneliness, estrangement, isolation describe the vast distance between man and man today. These dominant tendencies cannot be overcome by better personal management, nor by improved gadgets, but only when a love of man overcomes the idolatrous worship of things by man. As the individualism we affirm is not egoism, the selflessness we affirm is not self-elimination. On the contrary, we believe in generosity of a kind that imprints one's unique individual qualities in the relation to all human activity....

We would replace power rooted in possession, privilege, or circumstance by power and uniqueness rooted in love, reflectiveness, reason, and creativity. As a social system we seek the establishment of a democracy of individual participation, governed by two central aims: that the individual share in those social decisions determining the quality and direction of his life; that society be organized to encourage independence in men and provide the media for their common participation.

In a participatory democracy, the political life would be based in several root principles:

- That decision making of basic social consequence be carried out by public groupings.
- That politics be seen positively, as the art of collectively creating an acceptable pattern of social relations.
- That politics has the function of bringing people out of isolation and into community, thus being a necessary, though not sufficient, means of finding meaning in personal life.
- That the political order should serve to clarify problems in a way instrumental to their solution; it should provide outlets for the expression of personal grievance and aspiration; opposing views should be organized so as to illuminate choices and facilitate the attainment of goals; channels should be commonly available to relate men to knowledge and to power so that private problems—from bad recreation facilities to personal alienation—are formulated as general issues.

The economic sphere would have as its basis the principles:

- That work should involve incentives worthier than money or survival. It should be educative, not stultifying; creative, not mechanical; self-directed, not manipulated, encouraging independence, a respect for others, a sense of dignity and a willingness to accept personal responsibility, since it is this experience that has crucial influence on habits, perceptions, and individual ethics.
- That the economic experience is so personally decisive that the individual must share in the full determination.
- That the economy itself is of such social importance that its major resources and means of production should be open to democratic participation and subject to democratic social regulation.

Like the political and economic ones, major social institutions—cultural, educational, rehabilitative, and others—should be generally organized with the well-being and dignity of man as the essential measure of success."[36]

To what extent does the Port Huron Statement reflect Rousseau's vision of a Romantic democracy informed by the general will? To what extent does it accord with his critique of bourgeois society?

---

[35]Leonard Levy, *American Political Thought,* p. 459.

[36]Levy, p. 463.

PRIMARY SOURCE 9.4 | "ROUSSEAU'S LAWGIVER," FROM *THE SOCIAL CONTRACT*, BOOK II, CHAPTER 7

7. The Lawgiver

IN order to discover the rules of society best suited to nations, a superior intelligence beholding all the passions of men without experiencing any of them would be needed. This intelligence would have to be wholly unrelated to our nature, while knowing it through and through; its happiness would have to be independent of us, and yet ready to occupy itself with ours; and lastly, it would have, in the march of time, to look forward to a distant glory, and, working in one century, to be able to enjoy in the next. It would take gods to give men laws.

* * * *

He who dares to undertake the making of a people's institutions ought to feel himself capable, so to speak, of changing human nature, of transforming each individual, who is by himself a complete and solitary whole, into part of a greater whole from which he in a manner receives his life and being; of altering man's constitution for the purpose of strengthening it; and of substituting a partial and moral existence for the physical and independent existence nature has conferred on us all. He must, in a word, take away from man his own resources and give him instead new ones alien to him, and incapable of being made use of without the help of other men. The more completely these natural resources are annihilated, the greater and the more lasting are those which he acquires, and the more stable and perfect the new institutions; so that if each citizen is nothing and can do nothing without the rest, and the resources acquired by the whole are equal or superior to the aggregate of the resources of all the individuals, it may be said that legislation is at the highest possible point of perfection.

The legislator occupies in every respect an extraordinary position in the State. If he should do so by reason of his genius, he does so no less by reason of his office, which is neither magistracy, nor Sovereignty. This office, which sets up the Republic, nowhere enters into its constitution; it is an individual and superior function, which has nothing in common with human empire; for if he who holds command over men ought not to have command over the laws, he who has command over the laws ought not any more to have it over men; or else his laws would be the ministers of his passions and would often merely serve to perpetuate his injustices: his private aims would inevitably mar the sanctity of his work...

He, therefore, who draws up the laws has, or should have, no right of legislation, and the people cannot, even if it wishes, deprive itself of this incommunicable right, because, according to the fundamental compact, only the general will can bind the individuals, and there can be no assurance that a particular will is in conformity with the general will, until it has been put to the free vote of the people. This I have said already; but it is worth while to repeat it.

Thus in the task of legislation we find together two things which appear to be incompatible: an enterprise too difficult for human powers, and, for its execution, an authority that is no authority.

There is a further difficulty that deserves attention. Wise men, if they try to speak their language to the common herd instead of its own, cannot possibly make themselves understood. There are a thousand kinds of ideas which it is impossible to translate into popular language. Conceptions that are too general and objects that are too remote are equally out of its range: each individual, having no taste for any other plan of government than that which suits his particular interest, finds it difficult to realize the advantages he might hope to draw from the continual privations good laws impose. For a young people to be able to relish sound principles of political theory and follow the fundamental rules of statecraft, the effect would have to become the cause; the social spirit, which should be created by these institutions, would have to preside over their very foundation; and men would have to be before law what they should become by means of law. The legislator therefore, being unable to appeal to either force or reason, must have recourse to

PRIMARY SOURCE 9.4

"Rousseau's Lawgiver," from *The Social Contract*, Book II, Chapter 7 *continued*

an authority of a different order, capable of constraining without violence and persuading without convincing.

This is what has, in all ages, compelled the fathers of nations to have recourse to divine intervention and credit the gods with their own wisdom, in order that the peoples, submitting to the laws of the State as to those of nature, and recognizing the same power in the formation of the city as in that of man, might obey freely, and bear with docility the yoke of the public happiness.

This sublime reason, far above the range of the common herd, is that whose decisions the legislator puts into the mouth of the immortals, in order to constrain by divine authority those whom human prudence could not move. But it is not anybody who can make the gods speak, or get himself believed when he proclaims himself their interpreter. The great soul of the legislator is the only miracle that can prove his mission. Any man may grave tablets of stone, or buy an oracle, or feign secret intercourse with some divinity, or train a bird to whisper in his ear, or find other vulgar ways of imposing on the people. He whose knowledge goes no further may perhaps gather round him a band of fools; but he will never found an empire, and his extravagances will quickly perish with him. Idle tricks form a passing tie; only wisdom can make it lasting. The Judaic law, which still subsists, and that of the child of Ishmael, which, for ten centuries, has ruled half the world, still proclaim the great men who laid them down; and, while the pride of philosophy or the blind spirit of faction sees in them no more than lucky impostures, the true political theorist admires, in the institutions they set up, the great and powerful genius which presides over things made to endure.

We should not, with Warburton, conclude from this that politics and religion have among us a common object, but that, in the first periods of nations, the one is used as an instrument for the other.

In loving his country, each citizen sees a reflection of something of himself. Each citizen takes pride in the contribution and achievement of the collective to which he or she participates. Each citizen regards his or her fellow citizen as an equal who is involved in a common enterprise to further the public good. Insofar as each individual places the common good before his or her selfish interests, he or she is acting virtuously and in accordance with the general will. The citizen's private life and interests are thus subsumed by dedication to the public good.

In the good society, proper laws and moral habituation redirect vanity (*amour propre*) from a narrow love of self to the broader and more elevated sentiment of the love of one's own country. Allan Bloom thus describes patriotism or the love of country as the sublimated love of self (*amour propre*). Through the proper conditions that enable the general will, the negative love of *amour propre* can be transformed into a positive, self-sacrificing love of one's country and community. One's private interest and the public good thus merge into one. Freedom and duty are reconciled. Furthermore, the solidarity of the tightly knit community formed through the social contract strengthens the natural sentiment of pity, thereby cementing social bonds amongst citizens. Once pitted against each other by narrow self-interest, citizens are

[37] *Political Economy*, p. 69.

now united through pity and the very pride (*amour propre)* that formerly divided them.

Civic virtue, however, depends on strenuous moral habituation that disposes citizens to sacrifice for the common good. Rousseau thus emphasizes the need for a civic education that cultivates public-spiritedness and devotion to the republic. For Rousseau "statecraft is soulcraft": Laws shape the moral character. He argues that public education should be funded by the state and that citizens should be rewarded on the basis of their contribution to the common good. All practices and activities in the republic should seek to inspire public spiritedness. Festivities and games should build solidarity and physical vigor and honor national heroes. All forms of entertainment that corrupt morals by arousing selfish interests should be banned and censored. Rousseau is particularly concerned about the moral effects that theater or any private activities have on the character of citizens. Private life must serve public virtue. In his most recent book, *Consumed: How Markets Corrupt Children, Infantilize Adults, and Swallow Citizens Whole,* Benjamin R. Barber calls for a return to Rousseau's understanding of civic virtue and education:

> We need to understand that there can be no viable idea of public liberty outside of the quest for a moral and a common life defined by purposes that are some degree public in character. There can be no securing of liberty that is not also grounded in moral limits and hence in education and civic participation. . . . To be politically relevant, liberty in our era must be experienced as positive rather than negative, must be public rather than private. This means education for liberty must also be public rather than private. Citizens cannot be understood as mere consumers because individual desire is not the same thing as common ground and public goods are always something more than an aggregation of private wants. . . . The consumers' republic is quite simply a oxymoron. Consumers cannot be sovereign, only citizens can. Public liberty demands public institutions that permit citizens to address the public consequences of private market choices. . . . When the market is encouraged to do the work of democracy our culture is perverted and the character of our commonwealth undermined. Moreover, my sense of self—me as a moral being embedded in a free community—is lost. Liberty understood is the capacity to make public choices (in Rousseau's terms to engage in "general willing") is a potential faculty that must be learned rather than a natural one that is exercised from birth.[38]

Furthermore, in Rousseau's good society, inequalities of wealth and poverty must be minimized. Such inequalities weaken social bonds and undermine equality, pitting different classes against one another, thereby inflaming *amour propre* of the rich against the poor. The rich become filled with arrogance while the poor become filled with envy. Such malicious sentiments undermine a common, public life. Rousseau envisions a simple, tightly knit, agrarian society with little luxury to soften the morals of the citizens. Perhaps the Amish serve as the nearest contemporary example of the close communal binds that he envisions.

Finally, Rousseau's good society depends on a **civil religion** as a means to promote virtue. In *The Social Contract* he distinguishes between three types of religion: the religion of man, the religion of the citizen, and the religion of the priests. The religion

---

[38]Benjamin R. Barber, *Consumed: How Markets Corrupt Children, Infantilize Adults, and Swallow Citizens Whole* (New York: Norton & Company, 2007), pp. 125–126.

of man is an otherworldly, ascetic Christianity that practices benevolence toward all. It involves a purely internal worship without temples, rituals, or rites. It follows the simple teaching of the gospel. While the religion of man is benign, its otherworldly focus divides human beings between this life and the next life. It is not politically useful in training good citizens. The Christian's homeland is not of this world. Rousseau explains, "But I am mistaken in speaking of a Christian republic, these two words are mutually exclusive. Christianity preaches nothing but servitude and dependence. Its spirit is too favorable to tyranny for tyranny not always to take advantage of it. True Christians are made to be slaves; they know it and are scarcely moved by it; this short life has too little worth in their eyes."[39]

The second kind of religion, the religion of the citizen, was practiced in pagan times where every city has its own patron god. In antiquity, every war thus became a religious war to defend one's gods. However, the religion of the citizen is chauvinistic and intolerant. It is prone to fanaticism. Furthermore, the victory of Christianity over paganism makes a return to this religion almost impossible.

The third kind of religion, the religion of the priests—a thinly veiled reference to Roman Catholicism—is strongly condemned by Rousseau as superstitious, authoritarian, intolerant, and divisive. The religion of the priests is nothing more than a perversion of the religion of man. It has created a priestly hierarchy that perpetuates the worst kind of dependence. And it doubly divides citizens—not only between this life and the next life, but also within this life, between their secular loyalties to a particular state and their religious allegiance to the Catholic Church. "Everything that breaks down social unity is worthless: all institutions that place man in contradiction with himself are worthless." With this principle in mind, Rousseau praises Mohammed for having the foresight to keep church and state within Islam unified.

Rousseau offers civil religion as an alternative to aforementioned religions. The civil religion pertains to those opinions and actions that are relevant to the community. It is concerned not with the eternal life but with one's life on earth as a good citizen. The civil religion encourages and supports morality and duties that are necessary to a virtuous republic. Rousseau outlines the simple dogmas of this civil religion:

> The existence of a powerful, intelligent, beneficent, prescient, and provident divinity, the life to come, the happiness of the just, the punishment of the wicked, the sanctity of the social contract and the laws: these are the positive dogmas. As for the negative dogmas, I limit them to one alone: this is intolerance; it is part of the cults we have excluded.[40]

Those who cannot assent to this simple creed should be banished from the republic. Rousseau's civil religion seems to be an accommodation to a Christian civilization in which paganism is no longer desirable or possible, and in which the tendencies of asceticism and fanaticism must be avoided. It makes use of the political benefits of Christian teaching while sifting out fanatical tendencies that are adverse to good political order. God is useful, from a social and political standpoint, in sanctioning the laws and as a guarantor of justice who assures citizens that their virtue in this world will be rewarded in the next. According to Rousseau, the enlightened lawgiver must claim divine sanction for laws if he is to persuade the public to accept them.

---

[39] *On Social Contract*, p. 171.

[40] *On Social Contract*, p. 172.

PRIMARY SOURCE 9.5 — CIVIL RELIGION, FROM *THE SOCIAL CONTRACT*, BOOK IV, CHAPTER 8

But, setting aside political considerations, let us come back to what is right, and settle our principles on this important point. The right which the social compact gives the Sovereign over the subjects does not, we have seen, exceed the limits of public expediency. The subjects then owe the Sovereign an account of their opinions only to such an extent as they matter to the community. Now, it matters very much to the community that each citizen should have a religion. That will make him love his duty; but the dogmas of that religion concern the State and its members only so far as they have reference to morality and to the duties which he who professes them is bound to do to others. Each man may have, over and above, what opinions he pleases, without it being the Sovereign's business to take cognizance of them; for, as the Sovereign has no authority in the other world, whatever the lot of its subjects may be in the life to come, that is not its business, provided they are good citizens in this life.

There is therefore a purely civil profession of faith of which the Sovereign should fix the articles, not exactly as religious dogmas, but as social sentiments without which a man cannot be a good citizen or a faithful subject. While it can compel no one to believe them, it can banish from the State whoever does not believe them—it can banish him, not for impiety, but as an antisocial being, incapable of truly loving the laws and justice, and of sacrificing, at need, his life to his duty. If any one, after publicly recognizing these dogmas, behaves as if he does not believe them, let him be punished by death: he has committed the worst of all crimes, that of lying before the law.

The dogmas of civil religion ought to be few, simple, and exactly worded, without explanation or commentary. The existence of a mighty, intelligent, and beneficent Divinity, possessed of foresight and providence, the life to come, the happiness of the just, the punishment of the wicked, the sanctity of the social contract and the laws: these are its positive dogmas. Its negative dogmas I confine to one, intolerance, which is a part of the cults we have rejected.

Those who distinguish civil from theological intolerance are, to my mind, mistaken. The two forms are inseparable. It is impossible to live at peace with those we regard as damned; to love them would be to hate God who punishes them: we positively must either reclaim or torment them. Wherever theological intolerance is admitted, it must inevitably have some civil effect; and as soon as it has such an effect, the Sovereign is no longer Sovereign even in the temporal sphere: thenceforce priests are the real masters, and kings only their ministers.

Now that there is and can be no longer an exclusive national religion, tolerance should be given to all religions that tolerate others, so long as their dogmas contain nothing contrary to the duties of citizenship. But whoever dares to say: *Outside the Church is no salvation*, ought to be driven from the State, unless the State is the Church, and the prince the pontiff. Such a dogma is good only in a theocratic government; in any other, it is fatal. The reason for which Henry IV is said to have embraced the Roman religion ought to make every honest man leave it, and still more any prince who knows how to reason.

THE INDIVIDUAL PATH

Rousseau's prescription in *The Social Contract* offers a public path of redemption with strong communal elements. Yet this is not the only route he offers. In his *Confessions* and *Reveries of a Solitary Walker*, Rousseau points to an alternative, private path of redemption and liberation from the corruption of society. Here the price of freedom is high: a withdrawal from society and its corrupting effects into solitary existence.

CASE STUDY 9.3 Civil Religion in America

Benjamin Franklin spoke of a "public religion" that would provide moral support to the republic while safeguarding religious liberty. He stated, "History will also afford frequent opportunities of showing the necessity of a public religion, from its usefulness to the public; the advantages of a religious character among private persons; the mischiefs of superstition, and the excellency of the Christian religion above all others ancient or modern." In 1790, in a letter to Yale President Erza Stiles, Franklin revealed the articles of his personal faith, which happened to coincide with the dogmas of his public religion as well:

> I believe in one God, creator of the universe. That he governs it by his Providence. That he ought to be worshiped. That the most acceptable service we can render to him is doing good to his other children. That the soul of man is immortal, and will be treated with justice in another life respecting its conduct in this. These I take to be the fundamental principles of all sound religion, and I regard them as you do, in whatever sect I meet them.

To what extent does Franklin's discussion of a public religion and the articles of his personal creed accord with Rousseau's teaching on civil religion? Given the importance of religion to American public life, what might Franklin, or Rousseau for that matter, think of recent Supreme Court cases involving prayer in public schools, "intelligent design," "under God" in the pledge, and the public display of the Ten Commandments?

Because most societies are corrupt, and because the circumstances leading to the emergence of the general will are rare, the solitary path remains open to only a few people of considerable genius, idiosyncrasy, and individuality—like Rousseau himself. It is closed to the mass of human beings who are unable to "transcend" society and who could not bear to live a life of solitude.

The originality and impact of the *Confessions* are worth mentioning further in the context of Rousseau's life and legacy. In this work, Rousseau bares the most intimate details of his private life, recounting in gory detail his erotic pleasure in being spanked, his penchant for masturbation, his affair with "Mamam," his attempted seduction by a homosexual, his repulsion by a woman who lacked a nipple, his *ménage à trois* with a young prostitute, and his delight in exhibitionism. The *Confessions* originates the modern cult of sincerity, which redefines virtue as the quality of simply being in touch with one's feelings rather than acting in conformity with a preexisting moral standard. Unlike St. Augustine's *Confessions,* Rousseau's *Confessions* is not a story of conversion and salvation by God's grace; it is not a personal quest to know and love God. Instead it is a celebration of **authenticity** and **sincerity,** as when Rousseau forthrightly proclaims, "But I am made unlike any one I have ever met; I will even venture to say that I am like no one in the whole world. I may be no better, but at least I am different."[41] The sincere person is authentic—true to himself or herself as a unique individual in following his or her own spontaneously self-defined values that emanate from the heart. In any event, the continuing appeal of Frank Sinatra's personal anthem, "I Did It My Way" (remade by Sid Vicious of the Sex Pistols for a new generation of punk rockers), surely testifies to the vitality of the

[41]Jean-Jacques Rousseau, *Confessions* (New York: Penguin, 1953).

QUESTIONS FOR REFLECTION

What accounts for the differing paths to liberation in Rousseau's thought? Are these paths compatible with one another?

cult of sincerity in our own time. To be sure, these lyrics equally apply to Jean-Jacques Rousseau.

In *Emile,* Rousseau provides yet another path of redemption, one that stands between the fully communal life of *The Social Contract* and the fully private life of the *Reveries of a Solitary Walker*. *Emile's* path may be seen as one that is partly private and partly public. The educational program of *Emile* is intended for the average person living in the midst of a corrupt society who may still enjoy a domestic life while fulfilling his civic duties. Rousseau's solution in *Emile* seeks to shelter the natural goodness of the individual through a rigorous education that secludes him from corrupt influences of society until he is prepared to enter into it. However, Rousseau seems pessimistic about the prospects of this path as well: In the sequel to *Emile* the main character is corrupted, and his idyllic life ruined when he enters Paris.

CONCLUSION: AN EXTRAORDINARY LEGACY—WHO IS THE "REAL" ROUSSEAU?

Rousseau's intellectual legacy matches the twists and turns of his volatile life. His inspiration to the French revolutionaries has already been mentioned. Immanuel Kant regarded him as the Isaac Newton of the moral world. His critique of the Enlightenment's overweening faith in rationality and his counteremphasis on the role of sentiment in human flourishing make him the father of the Romantic movement. His celebration of a people's particular cultural heritage and history prefigured the nationalist movements of the 19th century. His effort to understand modern man by returning to primitive origins presaged the field of anthropology. His critique of economic inequality as the foundation of civil society, his view of the role that historical circumstances play in transforming human nature, and his diagnosis of the alienation of modern man anticipated Karl Marx. His iconoclastic behavior and critique of pseudo-bourgeois sophistication introduced us to the bohemian personality type. His view of love as the sublimation of sexual instinct was a precursor to Freud. And his educational teaching in *Emile* inaugurated an entirely new method of rearing children based on the novel insight that child growth and development pass through discrete stages that must be respected on their own terms. This pedagogical approach was in stark contrast to the traditional view that children should be treated like miniature, imperfect adults.

The complexity of Rousseau's political thought has led to widely divergent interpretations of him as a liberal, a totalitarian, and a republican. Those who support the liberal Rousseau point to his teaching on the natural goodness of man, his devotion to freedom, his critique of inequality at the root of society, and his reliance on institutions to mold human nature. Advocates of the totalitarian

Rousseau repudiate the collectivism of *The Social Contract,* citing his controversial statement in that work that citizens who oppose the general will are "forced to be free." Proponents of the republican Rousseau note his praise of ancient city–states of Rome and Sparta, his defense of civic virtue, and his call for a civil religion. Traditionally, Rousseau has been viewed as the nemesis of conservatives, who maintain that his teaching of man's natural goodness is dangerously utopian. Indeed, the father of modern conservatism, Edmund Burke, labeled Rousseau "the insane Socrates of the French Assembly." As we will see in our next chapter on Burke, in his *Reflections on the Revolution in France,* he blamed Rousseau for inspiring the revolutionaries to wipe away completely the *ancien regime* with the utopian expectation of creating a perfect society. This blindness to the limits of human nature and politics resulted in the unintended consequence of plunging society headlong into the extremes of demagoguery, anarchy, and tyranny of the majority. Yet, even this traditional interpretation has been questioned by scholors like Bertrand de Jouvenal who see Rousseau's teaching as genuinely conservative.[42] Students of political thought will never stop asking which is the "real" Rousseau. In seeking to answer this question, we should perhaps heed Rousseau's own advice of resisting the temptation of confining him to an ideological straitjacket. Like his personality, his thought defies simple classification.

Key Terms

freedom of the will
capacity of self-perfection
natural freedom
moral freedom
self-perfection
amour de soi
amour propre
pity
man's natural goodness
natural inequality
conventional inequality
bogus social contract
private property
bourgeois
social contract
freedom from
freedom to
reconcile freedom and duty
civil freedom
general will
will of all
conventional right to property
forced to be free
virtue
civil religion
authenticity
sincerity

Sources and Resources

Key Texts

The Social Contract
First Discourse
Second Discourse
Confessions
Reveries of a Solitary Walker
Government of Poland
Emile

[42]Bertrand de Jouvenal, "An Essay on Rousseau's Politics" in *Jean-Jacques Rousseau: Critical Assessments of Leading Political Philosophers,* Volume 1, Paradoxes and Interpretations, (ed.) John T. Scott (New York: Routledge, 2006), pp. 79–140.

Secondary Texts

Bloom, Allan. *Introduction to Emile or On Education* (New York: Basic Books, 1979).

Cladis, Mark S. *Public Vision, Private Lives: Rousseau, Religion, and 21st-Century Democracy* (Oxford: Oxford University Press, 2003).

Cranston M., and R. S. Peters, eds. *Hobbes and Rousseau: A Collection of Critical Essays* (Garden City, NY: Doubleday Anchor, 1972).

Masters, R. D. *The Political Philosophy of Rousseau* (Princeton, NJ: Princeton University Press, 1968).

Melzer, Arthur M. *The Natural Goodness of Man: On the System of Rousseau's Thought* (Chicago: University of Chicago Press, 1990).

Scott, John T. (ed.), *Jean-Jacques Rousseau: Critical Assessments of Leading Political Philosophers,* Volume 1, Paradoxes and Interpretations (New York: Routl edge, 2006).

Viroli, Maurizio. *Jean-Jacques Rousseau and the "Well-Ordered" Society* (Cambridge: Cambridge University Press, 1988).

Web Sites

Internet Encyclopedia of Philosophy entry online at www.iep.utm.edu/r/rousseau.htm

Free, full-text works by Rousseau online at www.gutenberg.org/browse/authors/r#a1286

Association dedicated to the study of Rousseau online at www.rousseauassociation.org/

BURKE

By Gary D. Glenn *Northern Illinois University*

LIFE AND TIMES

Edmund Burke (1729–1797) was a British man of letters, statesman, and orator, born and educated in Ireland, who served in Parliament from 1765 to 1794 during both the American and French Revolutions. Although he wrote an early philosophic treatise on aesthetics, his enduring reputation rests on his political speeches, letters, and pamphlets. Other than the treatise on aesthetics, he did not write a book. However, some of his letters, notably his most famous work *Reflections on the Revolution in France* (1790), and pamphlets, such as *Thoughts on the Causes of the Present Discontents* (1770), are "book-like" and serve the purpose of books. *Reflections,* at least, would be included in anyone's list of great books produced by the Western world.

In Parliament, he unsuccessfully defended the Americans between 1768 and 1776 in their constitutional objections to being taxed for revenue by the British government. Burke attempted to persuade Parliament of the impracticality as well as the injustice of such taxation.[1]

Although Burke adhered to the Church of England, he was a leader in largely unsuccessful Parliamentary attempts to mitigate the harsh anti-Catholic Irish penal laws and similarly oppressive laws against English Protestant dissenters.

Slavery was illegal in England during Burke's time but was legal in the American and West Indian colonies. Hence British companies and ships conducted a flourishing African slave trade. While there was no practical possibility of abolishing either this trade or slavery in the British colonies, Burke attempted and failed to persuade his party to adopt a Negro Code he had drafted (1780) that aimed to mitigate some of the worst slave trade abuses.

In the last years of his life, Burke said that he thought his greatest contribution was his failed but utterly just and selfless attempt to protect the people of India against the depredations of the British East India Company. He spent eight years (1786–1794) attempting to impeach the company's Governor General Warren Hastings. A third of his collected speeches and writings (4 of the 12 volumes) are devoted to this effort.

His attack on **the French Revolution** in 1790 resulted in the public rupture of his lifelong friendship with Charles James Fox, the leader of the party to which Burke belonged for his entire Parliamentary career. His party then threw him out of Parliament and denied him the customary retirement pension given to nonwealthy representatives. Later, when the revolution turned out to be as bloody and tyrannical as Burke had foreseen, this injustice was remedied by the king. But there was never a healing of the rupture with his party or with Fox.

In summary, Burke was frequently on the losing side of the politics of his time. The wisdom of his defense of the Americans was ultimately vindicated by the loss of the colonies; his failed defense of the East Indians was vindicated long after Burke's death by a more lenient and just British imperial rule; his failed defense of Irish Catholics and British Protestant defenders was ultimately vindicated, again after his death, by laws granting them tolerating and religious liberty; his personally costly opposition to the French Revolution (which he saw as tyrannical rather than liberating) became widely seen, in his own lifetime, as correct. Yet throughout his political life, he suffered

---

[1]The American speeches and the other speeches are writings alluded to in this biographical sketch are identified at the end of this chapter.

mistreatment and rejection for standing almost alone against his Whig friends, who thought Burke had abandoned his lifelong defense of liberty in order to defend absolute monarchy.

This willingness to stand alone is worth our trying to understand. Few politicians, then or now, will do this; but Burke, despite serving in Parliament, was no ordinary politician. Another indication of his extraordinary qualities is that he has left elaborate expositions of his thought on each of these issues. These are the primary means for us to learn what accounts for his persistent willingness to stand against the wind. We will see that his thought is grounded in an understanding of politics and statesmanship that transcends his time—in permanent things that persist while temporary circumstances, interests, and party configurations come along and pass. This is what it means to say that his thought is philosophically informed.

Despite his custom of defending just but losing causes, Burke's *Speech on American Taxation* (April 19, 1774), *Speech on Conciliation with the Colonies* (March 22, 1775), and *Letter to the Sheriffs of Bristol* (April 3, 1777) were still remembered a century after his death as "the most perfect manual in our literature, or in any literature, for one who approaches the study of public affairs, whether for knowledge or for practice."[2] And his *Reflections on the Revolution in France* (1790) remains today the standard critique of the French Revolution's natural rights theory, its ruthless and tyrannical political practice, and its proto-totalitarian claims, ambitions, and tendency. When puzzled and thoughtful people in the middle 20th century looked to the history of political philosophy for help in understanding the apparently unprecedented political form that had arisen in Lenin and Stalin's Soviet Union, in Hitler's Germany, and in Mussolini's Italy (to which they gave the name *totalitarianism*), some of them found Burke's *Reflections* helpful both for understanding and resistance.[3]

WORLDVIEW AND METHOD

It is disputed by informed and thoughtful people whether Burke should be regarded as a political philosopher at all. Burke fosters this impression by his characteristically negative and deprecatory use of terms like *theory, metaphysics, speculation,* and *abstract principles*—and by rarely speaking positively of philosophy or philosophers.

The clearest scholarly denial that Burke is a political philosopher comes from Leo Strauss. Strauss says that no one can be a political philosopher who does not regard the theoretical life, a life devoted to contemplation of eternal and unchanging things, as above the practical life. But Burke mostly lived a life devoted to practice, largely dealing with the British constitution—that is, a particular political arrangement of a particular people in a particular historical epoch. To prefer the particular over the permanent is not philosophic, as Strauss (following Plato) understands it.

More important for Strauss, Burke's understanding of political practice seems to rest on the historical development of the British constitution and thus takes its bearings

---

[2]John Morley, *Studies in Literature,* (London: Macmillan and Co. Limited, 1907).

[3]Notably Hannah Arendt, *The Origins of Totalitarianism* (Harvest Books, 1973; 1st ed., 1951). See especially Part III, "Totalitarianism." For Burke, see esp. pp. 283–284, 299ff, 474.

from history (the changeable) rather than from human nature (the permanent). Strauss regards Burke as a philosophically informed statesman. As a statesman, Burke's fundamental commitment is to the British political order, which he spent his life attempting to defend, preserve, and improve. He did so in light of what he understood to be sound or true everywhere, always focusing on such matters as human nature, justice, liberty, law, the relation of change and preservation, and the nature of the social contract. Still, his commitment is more to preserving and improving the British constitution than to attempting to understand and defend the regime that is best always and everywhere. Finally, Strauss goes so far as to accuse Burke of "misology" (distrust of reason) and of opening the door to historicism (the replacement of human nature with history as the basis of reasoning about political and human things).

Nevertheless, Strauss includes a chapter on Burke in *Natural Right and History,* his central book attempting to restore the possibility of political philosophy and especially classical political philosophy; he also discusses Burke in his co-edited *History of Political Philosophy.* So even though Strauss clearly denied Burke was a political philosopher, he nonetheless thought him relevant to political philosophy. Perhaps, for Strauss, Burke the statesman stands in company with Thucydides the philosophic historian, as well as the political theologian–philosophers Farabi, Maimonides, Suarez, and Aquinas, as important to the tradition of political philosophy. These examples seemingly indicate that unaided rational knowledge of the "everywhere and always," which is how Strauss understands political philosophy, cannot dogmatically reject how "the mysterious unity of oneness and variety in human things"[4] can be learned through both history and revelation-based theology.

Burke's political thought is directly concerned with the 18th-century British constitution but in such a way that it is still relevant for us, though we have no stake in that constitution. For example, in his *Speech on Conciliation with the Colonies* (1775) he said the Americans are "devoted to Liberty . . . according to English ideas and on English principles. Abstract Liberty, like other mere abstractions, is not to be found."[5] This formulation captures nicely both his philosophical method and a characteristic theme. Burke's method is always to think of, and try to understand, political ideas as embodied in a particular regime, history, and tradition. He is distrustful of arguments that base practical policies on abstract political ideas—that is, ideas formulated outside the political practice and tradition in which they are embodied. In particular, he distrusts and rejects the way of thinking characteristic of Hobbes, Locke, and Rousseau. These writers consider human nature, human life, and politics in abstract contexts like the prepolitical state of nature. Hence they think of the meaning of natural rights apart from any particular concrete embodiment. Burke does not deny the existence of natural rights in a prepolitical state; indeed he affirms them. But rhetorically he downplays their relevance; and as precise thought he absolutely rejects their direct relevance, unmediated by existing tradition, to any specific political order or policy.

---

[4]Strauss speaking of Herodotus in "Liberal Education and Mass Democracy" published in *Higher Education and Modern Democracy: The Crisis of the Few and Many,* (ed.) Robert A. Goldwin (Chicago: Rand McNally & Co., 1967), pp. 73–96, near the end.

[5]www.gutenberg.org/files/15198/15198-h/15198-h.htm#CONCILIATION_WITH_THE_COLONIES.

The safest way to approach Burke's thought is to assume that he is a philosophic statesman. If he is not a political philosopher, he makes those who study him political philosophers.

THE NATURE OF THE POLITICAL COMMUNITY: THE NATURAL RIGHT TO EQUAL POLITICAL POWER, THE "SOVEREIGNTY OF THE PRESENT GENERATION," AND THE MODERN SOCIAL CONTRACT

A relevant and enduring aspect of Burke's thought is his understanding of the nature of the political community. That understanding emerges in all the important events to which he devoted himself. But the French Revolution summoned forth his most complete and deepest reflection.

Burke early understood that this revolution was led by avowed followers of Rousseau, whom he called "the insane Socrates of the National Assembly":[6]

> The [National] Assembly recommends to its youth a study of the bold experimenters in morality. Every body knows that there is a great dispute amongst their leaders, which of them is the best resemblance to Rousseau. In truth, they all resemble him. His blood they transfuse into their minds and into their manners. Him they study; him they meditate; him they turn over in all the time they can spare from the laborious mischief of the day, or the debauches of the night. Rousseau is their canon of holy writ; in his life he is their canon of Polycletus; he is their standard figure of perfection.[7]

Burke also was one of the first to grasp both how unprecedented and decisively important it was for a political revolution to be inspired by the thought of a philosopher.[8] For this was a revolution of ideas rather than merely another overthrow of an oppressive or tyrannical ruler. One of those ideas, **tyrannicide,** had been justified by political thinkers throughout the Middle Ages. But the French Revolution did not merely assert that this particular king was a tyrant and hence an illegitimate ruler who should be overthrown. It asserted, on the basis of Rousseau's political theory, that hereditary monarchy as such is an illegitimate form of government; that an aristocratic social order as such violates the natural equality of all men; that inheritance as a title to rule, to property, and to ideas of justice violates the right of each generation to order and reorder society and government according to its will.

The philosophic basis of these claims is an abstract idea of the natural right of all human beings—that is, all living human beings—to equal power in deciding how society and government are governed and ordered. The great practical consequence is the right of the majority (of those now living) to define and do with the life, liberty, and property of others as they see fit, without regard to inherited ideas of justice concerning

---

[6] *Letter to a Member of the National Assembly,* 1791.

[7] *Letter to a Member of the National Assembly in Answer to Some Objections to his Book on French Affairs* (January 1791).

[8] "The present Revolution in France seems to me . . . to bear little resemblance or analogy to any of those which have been brought about in Europe, upon principles merely political. It is a Revolution of doctrine and theoretic dogma." *Thoughts on French Affairs,* 1791.

these matters. This justifies the destruction of the current rich, the nobles, the church, and all hierarchy except that consented to by each current generation. It implies, as Burke saw, the right of "the people" to make continuous and permanent revolution in the laws and order of society.

The foremost advocate of the French Revolution in English, Thomas Paine's *Rights of Man* (1791–1792), defends this idea that what makes both a political community, and legitimate government of that community, is consent of the people understood in a **radical** way—radical in the sense that it goes all the way to the roots. This **modern consent theory** came to be known as the **sovereignty of the present generation** and was made influential in the American founding thought by Paine's ally Jefferson.[9] Jefferson argued that the bindingness of every law and every constitution expires with the expiration of a majority of the generation that had consented to it (about every 20 years according to Jefferson's mortality tables). James Madison argued against this on the practical (and recognizably Burkean) ground that constitutions and laws gain greater authority as people become used to obeying them and look to them as legitimizing government's actions and authority. Thus willing obedience derives from such **habituation,** which in turn derives from longevity.

In the middle 20th century, under the impact of the constitutional crisis occasioned by the New Deal, American **progressive thinkers** and the courts found a way to combine these two views., They called it "the living constitution." This means the Constitution's words remain unchanged, but the courts give them new meaning to keep the Constitution in touch with the needs of the times. Thus each generation benefits from the willingness of the people to credit the old Constitution's customary authority, while simultaneously those who control constitutional interpretation in the present generation are sovereign. The original meaning of the Constitution as amended is dismissed as "the dead hand of the past." One important implication is that each generation is radically free of any Burkean obligation of gratitude to the benefits received from past generations.

Against this modern consent theory of the French Revolution, Paine, and Jefferson, Burke argues that we "claim and assert our liberties, as an entailed inheritance derived to us from our forefathers, and to be transmitted to our posterity as an estate specially belonging to the people of this kingdom without any reference whatever to any other more general or prior right." Burke argues that we inherit our political rights as we inherit our names and our blood, and that this is a better, more certain method of conserving them. Burke was among the first to see that the radical theory of consent, upon which the French Revolution justified itself, undermined the claims of natural families, of nations based on kinship, and of political systems and constitutions to continue themselves from one generation to the next. The reason is that any generation is free to abandon or discontinue such an inheritance and is justified in doing so.

In contrast, the French Revolutionaries despise their political and societal inheritance. Seeing nothing good in it, therefore they see nothing worth preserving. They despise even the examples of how other countries have founded or refounded their regimes. Their implicit claim is that no founders or refounders before them understood

---

[9]See especially Thomas Jefferson to James Madison., September 6, 1789, The Founder's Constitution, http://press-pubs.uchicago.edu/founders/documents/v1ch2s23.html, accessed August 12, 2007.

PRIMARY SOURCE 10.1 | *REFLECTIONS ON THE REVOLUTION IN FRANCE*

You will observe, that from Magna Charta to the Declaration of Right, it has been the uniform policy of our constitution to claim and assert our liberties, as an entailed inheritance derived to us from our forefathers, and to be transmitted to our posterity; as an estate specially belonging to the people of this kingdom without any reference whatever to any other more general or prior right. By this means our constitution preserves a unity in so great a diversity of its parts. We have an inheritable crown; an inheritable peerage; and a house of commons and a people inheriting privileges, franchises, and liberties, from a long line of ancestors.

This policy appears to me to be the result of profound reflection; or rather the happy effect of following nature, which is wisdom without reflection, and above it. A spirit of innovation is generally the result of a selfish temper and confined views. People will not look forward to posterity, who never look backward to their ancestors. Besides, the people of England well know, that the idea of inheritance furnishes a sure principle of conservation, and a sure principle of transmission; without at all excluding a principle of improvement. It leaves acquisition free; but it secures what it acquires. Whatever advantages are obtained by a state proceeding on these maxims, are locked fast as in a sort of family settlement; grasped as in a kind of mortmain for ever. By a constitutional policy, working after the pattern of nature, we receive, we hold, we transmit our government and our privileges, in the same manner in which we enjoy and transmit our property and our lives. The institutions of policy, the goods of fortune, the gifts of Providence, are handed down, to us and from us, in the same course and order. Our political system is placed in a just correspondence and symmetry with the order of the world, and with the mode of existence decreed to a permanent body composed of transitory parts; wherein, by the disposition of a stupendous wisdom, molding together the great mysterious incorporation of the human race, the whole, at one time, is never old, or middle-aged, or young, but in a condition of unchangeable constancy, moves on through the varied tenor of perpetual decay, fall, renovation, and progression. Thus, by preserving the method of nature in the conduct of the state, in what we improve, we are never wholly new; in what we retain we are never wholly obsolete. By adhering in this manner and on those principles to our forefathers, we are guided not by the superstition of antiquarians, but by the spirit of philosophic analogy. In this choice of inheritance we have given to our frame of polity the image of a relation in blood; binding up the constitution of our country with our dearest domestic ties; adopting our fundamental laws into the bosom of our family affections; keeping inseparable, and cherishing with the warmth of all their combined and mutually reflected charities, our state, our hearths, our sepulchers, and our altars.

Through the same plan of a conformity to nature in our artificial institutions, and by calling in the aid of her unerring and powerful instincts, to fortify the fallible and feeble contrivances of our reason, we have derived several other, and those no small benefits, from considering our liberties in the light of an inheritance. Always acting as if in the presence of canonized forefathers, the spirit of freedom, leading in itself to misrule and excess, is tempered with an awful gravity. This idea of a liberal descent inspires us with a sense of habitual native dignity, which prevents that upstart insolence almost inevitably adhering to and disgracing those who are the first acquirers of any distinction. By this means our liberty becomes a noble freedom. It carries an imposing and majestic aspect. It has a pedigree and illustrating ancestors. It has its bearings and its ensigns armorial. It has its gallery of portraits; its monumental inscriptions; its records, evidences, and titles. We procure reverence to our civil institutions on the principle upon which nature teaches us to their age; and on account of those from whom they are descended. All your sophisters cannot produce any thing better adapted to preserve a rational and manly freedom than the course that we have pursued, who have chosen our nature rather than our speculations, our breasts rather than our inventions, for the great conservatories and magazines of our rights and privileges.

QUESTIONS FOR REFLECTION

If Burke is correct that the revolutionary theory of natural rights denies that our rights and liberties are best preserved when inherited like our names and blood, is he also right that this theory would tend to undermine the existence of families by emphasizing that they are merely based on consent? Are they therefore disposable when any of the parties withdraw their consent? Could the contemporary decline of family formation and maintenance be a consequence of modern ideas of rights?

the correct way to found a new regime or refound an existing one. The hitherto untested theory is superior to those experiences. These convictions will, Burke thinks, cause them great misery. Burke thinks there is an accumulated wisdom in the customs of every nation and in the history of how other nations have reformed themselves.

CONSENT OF THE GOVERNED AND BURKE'S ALTERNATIVE TO THE MODERN SOCIAL CONTRACT

Burke sometimes engages his adversaries through their theoretical language. An important example is that he presents his teaching as a correction to the revolutionaries' understanding of *consent* and of *social contract.* "Society is indeed a contract" but not in the way the revolutionaries, following Rousseau, think. Rather, it is an intergenerational contract about more than matters of a "temporary and perishable nature." It "is a partnership in all science; a partnership in all art; a partnership in every virtue, and in all perfection." The contract is about virtue, not will. The implication for consent is that "As the ends of such a partnership cannot be obtained in many generations, it becomes a partnership not only between those who are living, but between those who are living, those who are dead, and those who are to be born." *Consent* does not mean the consent only of the present generation.

Because it is intergenerational and aimed at moral perfection, rather than one-generational and aimed merely at self-government, no single generation has a right to abrogate the contract. The generations are bound together by moral obligations necessary to the moral ends of society. These duties, not will, define the contract.

Thus for Burke, in contrast to the revolutionary theory, society is not only the present generation but is extended in time (**tradition**). He argues that this is truly "following nature, which is wisdom without reflection, and above it." Notice, however, that Burke's defense of it is the result of reflection and so is not mere unphilosophic and uncritical following of tradition. In contrast, the philosophic revolutionaries' "natural rights" follow and encourage a "spirit of innovation" that, he claims, is "the result of a selfish temper and confined views. People will not look forward to posterity, who never look backward to their ancestors."[10]

Burke is attempting to restore a premodern meaning to the term *social contract.* The modern philosophers (Hobbes, Locke, Rousseau) had used "the phrase borrowed from the [16th-century] theologians and made it cover a political doctrine which they would have been the last to accept" by teaching that human nature is not

[10]*Reflections on the Revolution in France* (1790); www.gutenberg.org/files/15679/15679-h/15679-h.htm.

QUESTIONS FOR REFLECTION

What do you think Burke means by "the fallible and feeble contrivances of our reason?" Does he mean that we should follow our "instincts" rather than our reason? Or does he mean only that our reason by itself (abstract reason) is an insufficient basis for our liberties? Does Burke strike you as someone who thinks his reason is "feeble?" If reason is so feeble, why does Burke regard the theory and ideas of the French Revolution as so dangerous?

designed for people to live together.[11] According to the moderns, society is not natural. Instead it is brought into being and continues only by agreement or consent. This is **modern social contract.** In the same way, rule and government are not natural and are created as well as authorized by contract. No man by nature has a right to rule another. By nature all men are free from rule, so the only basis for legitimate rule is consent of the governed. In the Rousseau version, because society is not natural, it is not governed morally by natural law. It is governed by the abstract and purely formal general will, which requires that any inequalities be consented to in order to be legitimate. If the present generation does not consent to hereditary rule and hereditary inequalities, they are illegitimate and may be abolished at the will of that generation.

Burke seeks to inject into this modern social contract a Christian or Aristotelian idea of contract developed in the late Middle Ages and articulated particularly in the thought of **Robert Bellarmine S.J.**, a 16th-century political theologian and philosopher.[12] The older view followed Aristotle and Cicero in holding that society was natural in the sense that human nature is designed for human beings to live together. In particular, the family is natural in this sense and includes forms of natural rule—notably husband over wife and parents over children. Such rule is naturally just if it is for the benefit of both ruler and ruled—that is, for the **common good.** Similarly, political rule is required by human nature (Aristotle) and also sanctioned by divine providence (St. Paul/Augustine). However, *who* should exercise such political authority is not settled by either natural or divine law. Both laws leave this determination to the consent of the governed. But consent does not create government, legitimate its power, or create the right to rule. It only makes these possible and specifies who should exercise the right to rule.

In particular, **premodern social contract** denies what modern social contract affirms—namely, that the people are the *source* of government's lawful power and therefore are not limited by right or law that are not manmade. In the premodern view, the source of government's power is moral law—natural or divine or both. These authorize as well as limit the lawful power of any government. There are some things that government may not rightly do even if the people consent to it.

---

[11]Orestes A. Brownson, *The American Republic* (Wilmington, DE: ISI Press, 2002), p.45. Reprint of the edition published by P. O'Shea, New York, 1865.

[12]Kathleen E. Murphy, Ph.D., trans. Robert Bellarmine, *De Laicis or The Treatise on Civil Government* (New York: Fordham University Press, 1928). Introduction by M. F. X. Millar, S. J. Ch. V, pp. 20–23. Available online at www.catholicism.org/pages/Laity.htm.

Bellarmine acknowledges that while society is a human construct, it is still natural because it is according to nature's purposes. It is constructed in accordance with nature rather than opposed to it as Rousseau (following Hobbes and Locke) says. For Bellarmine, society is natural in the way the glasses that facilitate my reading of this chapter are natural. Both help fulfill natural human needs.

The main idea Burke takes from premodern contract thought is an understanding of society in terms of **intergenerational duties.** Bellarmine argues that important things people need to live well take longer to develop than one human lifetime. Human beings are born into a particular society and thereby receive the benefits of what that society has previously learned and developed. These advantages inherited from society include language, a way of life, and development of the arts and sciences.

Burke adds and emphasizes a society's political institutions and ideas of justice. The generation coming into being benefits from these gifts and from being taught, by the present generation, how to both learn and improve them. Thus the young generation incurs a natural (not consensual) obligation or debt of gratitude both to the generation that handed on these gifts and to preceding generations. This obligation can be repaid only by preserving these benefits, cultivating and perhaps improving them, and passing them on as gifts to the next generation. Thus arises both the obligation of the present generation to past generations of their society and their solicitude for future generations.

It is difficult to see how any society, but especially modern society, can do without acknowledging and acting on intergenerational moral duties. For example, the present generation of modern society incurs the national debt, which is to be repaid by future generations; but the latter cannot consent to this obligation. Social Security obligates the present generation to pay debts pledged by past generations to which the present generation did not consent; and similarly for future generations. Another example: Does not the present generation have a moral duty to leave future generations air fit to breathe, water fit to drink, unpolluted land, and so on? Yet these obligations cannot be consented to by those parties to the contract who are not yet in being. So the basis of these obligations must be understood to be natural and moral rather than consensual and legal. In that way, Burke's social contract differs from a Hobbes, Locke, or Rousseau social contract to which all parties have consented. To the extent that society cannot do without an idea of intergenerational duties, it seems Burke's social contract makes more sense than the Paine/Jefferson "sovereignty of the present generation."

Perhaps a further consequence of the Paine/Jefferson social contract has become visible in the late 20th and early 21st centuries. Every industrialized country, to which modernity has come by transforming ways of life into industrialization, urbanization, and secularization, appears to be breeding itself out of existence. The mechanisms appear to be widespread individual decisions not to marry and not to have enough children to maintain a stable population. The outcome is fertility rates below replacement levels. Policy makers already see this "birth dearth" leading to a crisis in the welfare state systems as the number of workers who are paying into them declines relative to the number drawing from them. Massive immigration, legal and illegal, seems required simply to keep these societies functioning.

QUESTIONS FOR REFLECTION

Who would be more likely to view the decline in birthrates just discussed as a problem—those who believe in the sovereignty of the present generation or those who believe that society is an intergenerational contract?

However, a less noticed but more fundamental problem has appeared on the horizon. Cumulative individual decisions not to hand down genetic and cultural inheritances to the next generation have, for some time now, been pointing modern industrialized nations toward self-extinction in a quite literal way.[13] The theory of the sovereignty of the present generation now seems to have seeped into the individual consciousness of modern human beings, giving the present generation the right to deny existence to future generations. The present generation's individual choices now appear to be producing cultural suicide in these countries; a "culture of death" in a literal, social way.

THE RELATION OF MORAL DUTIES TO RIGHTS (AND WILL) IN CIVIL SOCIETY

The modern sovereignty of the present generation view of the social contract takes its bearings from the idea that the **rights** of each present generation are of greatest importance; in contrast, Burke's intergenerational view of the social contract takes its bearings from the idea that the **moral duties** of each generations are of greatest importance. This difference reflects their opposing views of the source of moral duties and of the relation of those duties to consent or voluntary will.

FAMILY

The foregoing passage shows that Burke understood the revolutionary theory to involve a rejection of the naturalness of familial ties, affections, and moral obligations and that this has politically important consequences. One consequence concerns the love of country and of mankind. Here is Burke's conception of the relation between love of family and love of country:

> To be attached to the subdivision, to love the little platoon we belong to in society, is the first principle (the germ as it were) of public affections. It is the first link in the series by which we proceed towards a love to our country and to mankind. The interests of that portion of social arrangement is a trust in the hands of all those who compose it; and as none but bad men would justify it in abuse, none but traitors would barter it away for their own personal advantage.[14]

[13]For a recent thoughtful journalistic analysis along these lines by an unrepentant but sober "poster child for the anti-mom," see Lionel Shriver, "No Kids Please, We're Selfish," *The Guardian* (of London), September 17, 2005.

[14]*Reflections,* Payne (ed.), p. 136.

PRIMARY SOURCE 10.2 | *REFLECTIONS ON THE REVOLUTION IN FRANCE*

Society is indeed a contract. Subordinate contracts, for objects of mere occasional interest, may be dissolved at pleasure; but the state ought not to be considered as nothing better than a partnership agreement in a trade of pepper and coffee, calico or tobacco, or some other such low concern, to be taken up for a little temporary interest, and to be dissolved by the fancy of the parties. It is to be looked on with other reverence; because it is not a partnership in things subservient only to the gross animal existence of a temporary and perishable nature. It is a partnership in all science; a partnership in all art; a partnership in every virtue, and in all perfection. As the ends of such a partnership cannot be obtained in many generations, it becomes a partnership not only between those who are living, but between those who are living, those who are dead, and those who are to be born.

Each contract of each particular state is but a clause in the great primeval contract of eternal society, linking the lower with the higher natures, connecting the visible and invisible world, according to a fixed compact sanctioned by the inviolable oath which holds all physical and all moral natures, each in their appointed place. This law is not subject to the will of those, who by an obligation above them, and infinitely superior, are bound to submit their will to that law. The municipal corporations of that universal kingdom are not morally at liberty at their pleasure, and on their speculations of a contingent improvement, wholly to separate and tear asunder the bands of their subordinate community, and to dissolve it into an unsocial, uncivil, unconnected chaos of elementary principles.

In contrast, the French Revolutionaries, instructed by Rousseau's "ethic of vanity," reject natural familial obligations. This ethic led Rousseau to turn his illegitimate children over to be raised by "the hospital of foundlings" and then to write books trumpeting from the rooftop both his shameful behavior and his compassion for all of mankind. Burke takes this to show that Rousseau is "a lover of his kind but a hater of his kindred." He goes so far as to say that this combined "benevolence to the whole species" and lack of "one spark of common parental affection" "form the character of the new philosophy." Rousseau's private defects are reflected in his political philosophy. One effect is that he goes straight from ideas of political philosophy to the love of all mankind, thus denying, bypassing, and undermining the intermediate institutions (family, neighborhood, local community, even country) that provide the natural bridge between the love of one's own and the love of all. Burke doubts the wisdom of this radical disconnection between the closest ties of natural affection and an affection for all. He thinks it likely to produce tyranny and oppression rather than liberty and justice for all.

ARE THERE PREPOLITICAL NATURAL RIGHTS?

At first glance, Burke seems to deny the existence of such rights that belong to all human beings as such. After all, we "claim and assert our liberties, as an **entailed inheritance** derived to us from our forefathers, and to be transmitted to our posterity; as an estate specially belonging to the people of this kingdom without any reference whatever to any other more general or prior right." However, this need not be understood in the way it seems at first glance. Notice that he carefully says only that

PRIMARY SOURCE 10.3 | An Appeal from the New to the Old Whigs, from *Further Reflections on the Revolution in France*

I cannot too often recommend it to the serious consideration of all men, who think civil society to be within the province of moral jurisdiction, that if we owe to it any duty, it is not subject to our will. Duties are not voluntary. Duty and will are even contradictory terms. Now though civil society might be at first a voluntary act (which in many cases it undoubtedly was) its continuance is under a permanent standing covenant, coexisting with the society; and it attaches upon every individual of that society, without any formal act of his own. This is warranted by the general practice, arising out of the general sense of mankind. Men without their choice derive benefits from that association; without their choice they are subjected to duties in consequence of these benefits; and without their choice they enter into a virtual obligation as binding as any that is actual. Look through the whole of life and the whole system of duties. Much the strongest moral obligations are such as were never the results of our option. I allow, that if no supreme ruler exists, wise to form, and potent to enforce, the moral law, there is no sanction to any contract, virtual or even actual, against the will of prevalent power. On that hypothesis, let any set of men be strong enough to set their duties at defiance, and they cease to be duties any longer...

We have obligations to mankind at large, which are not in consequence of any special voluntary pact. They arise from the relation of man to man, and the relation of man to God, which relations are not matters of choice. On the contrary, the force of *all the pacts which* we enter into with any particular person or number of persons amongst mankind, depends upon those prior obligations. In some cases the subordinate relations are voluntary, in others they are necessary—but the duties are all compulsive. When we marry, the choice is voluntary, but the duties are not a matter of choice. They are dictated by the nature of the situation.... Our country is not a thing of mere physical locality. It consists, in a great measure, in the ancient order into which we are born. We may have the same geographical situation, but another country; as we may have the same country in another soil. The place that determines our duty to our country is a social, civil relation.

we "claim and assert our rights." But the grounds on which we *claim* our rights need not be the *ultimate basis* of those rights.

Burke explicitly affirms the existence of prepolitical natural rights but contrasts them with the Rousseau-derived, abstract, prepolitical natural rights of the French Revolutionaries. The following passage casts doubt on the common understanding of Burke as a merely traditionalist conservative who affirms that there are only "the rights of Englishmen" but no "rights of man." Some conservatives of this kind regard the admission of natural rights to be dangerous to the established order because such rights would be a standard for judging the justice of tradition and convention. It is not difficult to see how that could be disturbing to, and even subversive of, the established order. However, Burke's thought is not conservative in that way.

The question for Burke is not whether natural rights exist. They do. The question is how such rights are to be understood and in what manner they are related to rights in civil society. For instance, not everything in civil society is to be decided in light of natural rights. In particular, the question of who should rule is not decided by natural rights: There is no prepolitical natural right to rule. That question is to be answered entirely by convention—that is, by consent, which does not mean it is a mere matter of

PRIMARY SOURCE 10.4

A Letter to a Member of the National Assembly

It is that new-invented virtue which your masters [the National Assembly] canonize, that led their moral hero [Rousseau] constantly to exhaust the stores of his powerful rhetoric in the expression of universal benevolence; whilst his heart was incapable of harboring one spark of common parental affection. Benevolence to the whole species, and want of feeling for every individual with whom the professors come in contact, form the character of the new philosophy. Setting up for an unsocial independence, this their hero of vanity refuses the just price of common labor, as well as the tribute which opulence owes to genius, and which, when paid, honors the giver and the receiver; and then he pleads his beggary as an excuse for his crimes. He melts with tenderness for those only who touch him by the remotest relation, and then, without one natural pang, casts away, as a sort of offal and excrement, the spawn of his disgustful amours, and sends his children to the hospital of foundlings. The bear loves, licks, and forms her young; but bears are not philosophers. Vanity, however, finds its account in reversing the train of our natural feelings. Thousands admire the sentimental writer; the affectionate father is hardly known in his parish.

Under this philosophic instructor in the ethics of vanity, they have attempted in France a regeneration of the moral constitution of man. Statesmen, like your present rulers, exist by everything which is spurious, fictitious, and false; by every thing which takes the man from his house, and sets him on a stage, which makes him up an artificial creature, with painted theatric sentiments, fit to be seen by the glare of candlelight, and formed to be contemplated at a due distance. Vanity is too apt to prevail in all of us, and in all countries. To the improvement of Frenchmen it seems not absolutely necessary that it should be taught upon system. But it is plain that the present rebellion was its legitimate offspring, and it is piously fed by that rebellion, with a daily dole.

If the system of institution, recommended by the Assembly, is false and theatric, it is because their system of government is of the same character. To that, and to that alone, it is strictly conformable. To understand either, we must connect the morals with the politics of the legislators. Your practical philosophers, systematic in every thing, have wisely began at the source. As the relation between parents and children is the first among the elements of vulgar, natural morality, they erect statues to a wild, ferocious, low-minded, hard-hearted father, of fine general feelings; a lover of his kind, but a hater of his kindred. Your masters reject the duties of this vulgar relation, as contrary to liberty; as not founded in the social compact; and not binding according to the rights of men; because the relation is not, of course, the result of free election; never so on the side of the children, not always on the part of the parents.

will. There is a principle of natural justice that is relevant:, that unequal contributions to society justify inequality in political power.

THE RELATION OF PREPOLITICAL NATURAL RIGHTS TO "RIGHTS OF MAN IN CIVIL SOCIETY"

The consent involved in forming and reforming civil society drastically modifies prepolitical natural rights. Indeed, following the mode of reasoning in Hobbes' and Locke's discussion of why men decide to leave the prepolitical condition and enter civil society, Burke argues that civil society is formed precisely because the "abstract perfection" of rights prior to civil society is incompatible with securing them. Given human beings as they are, these abstractly perfect rights have to be given up to some

QUESTIONS FOR REFLECTION

Should we "connect the morals with the politics of the legislators?" Or do they have nothing to do with each other? What should we make of politicians who profess concern for the poor but fail to fulfill their moral responsibilities to their spouses and children? Are such politicians seeking to symbolically expiate their private failures toward those for whom they are directly and immediately responsible, by professing to care about those whose suffering they are powerless to address? Or is there some more charitable interpretation? Finally, does this matter?

extent in order to secure the rights that remain. Mere theory provides little guidance about the extent to which these rights must be given up. It is largely a matter of **convention**—that is, consent or agreement among citizens through laws and customs. This must be renegotiated from time to time as circumstances and opinions change.

Notice the potential difficulty this passage poses for our understanding of Burke's thought. On one hand, he appeals to the premodern view that society is natural. On the other hand, he appeals to the existence of primitive rights that exist outside of "common life." Now in Rousseau's thought (and modern social contract generally), the existence of such rights implies that "common life" is not natural. So it would be easy for us to think that Burke, in this passage, is adopting that assumption, which would be self-contradictory. However, if you reread the passage, notice that his disjunction is "primitive" rights and "common life"—not the modern disjunction between "the state of nature" and "civil society." And recall that the premodern contract granted that society is constructed but that it is nevertheless natural. Prepolitical is not presocial as shown by the natural necessity of families. So for Burke, the existence of **prepolitical rights** is consistent with the naturalness of civil society and does not imply a modern "state of nature."

The conclusion seems to be that Burke acknowledges the existence of natural rights that belong to all human beings. However, these are too complete or abstractly perfect to be the basis for the **real rights of man** in civil society. Every society has to truck and barter, to give up to some extent the theoretically unqualified rights they would have in the abstract, in order to secure some of them, to some extent, in practice. The result of this *giving up* in order to *secure* what remains constitutes the moral, political, and social inheritance or tradition of each society. And to that tradition each society should recur when it needs to reform itself.

PRESCRIPTION

Each generation of every society has to learn from its experience to what extent and in what respects it has to give up some natural rights and liberty in order to secure what can be kept, under ever-changing circumstances; and each generation hands down that learning to later generations. What those modifications and restrictions must be can be taught by no "abstract rule" but only by "long experience." In particular, "the science of government . . . requires . . . more experience than any person can gain in his whole life."[15]

---

[15]Short quotes from Burke in this and the next paragraph are from *Reflections on the Revolution in France.*

PRIMARY SOURCE 10.5 | *REFLECTIONS ON THE REVOLUTION IN FRANCE*

Far am I from denying in theory; full as far is my heart from withholding in practice (if I were of power to give or to withhold), the real rights of men. In denying their false claims of right, I do not mean to injure those which are real, and are such as their pretended rights would totally destroy. If civil society be made for the advantage of man, all the advantages for which it is made become his right. It is an institution of beneficence; and law itself is only beneficence acting by a rule. Men have a right to live by that rule; they have a right to justice; as between their fellows, whether their fellows are in politic function or in ordinary occupation. They have a right to the fruits of their industry; and to the means of making their industry fruitful. They have a right to the acquisitions of their parents; to the nourishment and improvement of their offspring; to instruction in life; and to consolation in death. Whatever each man can separately do, without trespassing upon others, he has a right to do for himself; and he has a right to a fair portion of all which society, with all its combinations of skill and force, can do in his favor. In this partnership all men have equal rights; but not to equal things. He that has but five shillings in the partnership, has as good a right to it, as he that has five hundred pound has to his larger proportion. But he has not a right to an equal dividend in the product of the joint stock; and as to the share of power, authority, and direction which each individual ought to have in the management of the state, that I must deny to be amongst the direct original rights of man in civil society; for I have in my contemplation the civil social man, and no other. It is a thing to be settled by convention.

This way of society discovering from experience what a practical civil liberty can be, and handing down that experience from generation to generation, results in what Burke calls **prescription.** Prescription is a claim to what one has based on long possession, but it is not merely tradition. It is "a part of the law of nature." Indeed, it is "a great fundamental part" of it. This claim, if taken seriously, would save Burke's thought from the historical or cultural relativism to which it might otherwise be prone owing to his sharp contrast of the "rights of men" with "the rights of Englishmen" and his assertion that Englishmen claim and assert liberties "without any reference whatever to any more general or prior right." It would be relativism either to deny that some universal standard like "rights of men" exists at all or that such rights exist but have no relation to the "rights of Englishmen." To save his thought from relativism, he distinguishes the *basis* for *claiming* liberty in civil society from its ultimate and transcendent, but remote and "primitive"[16] *source.*

This distinction also squares his claim that prescription is part of natural law with the seeming denial of "any more general or prior right." Although abstract natural rights are too dangerous to appeal to directly in civil society, what can be safely appealed to is this prescription. The intergenerational contract is preserved by the present generation learning their prescriptive rights and appealing to them as prescription.

However, prescription is a losing political argument against the influence of the "rights of man," and Burke knows it.

---

[16]*Thoughts on French Affairs* (December 1791); www.gutenberg.org/files/15700/15700-h/15700-h.htm#THOUGHTS.

PRIMARY SOURCE 10.6 | *REFLECTIONS ON THE REVOLUTION IN FRANCE*

If civil society be the offspring of convention, that convention must be its law. That convention must limit and modify all the descriptions of constitution which are formed under it. Every sort of legislative, judicial, or executory power are its creatures. They can have no being in any other state of things; and how can any man claim, under the conventions of civil society, rights which do not so much as suppose its existence? Rights which are absolutely repugnant to it? One of the first motives to civil society, and which becomes one of its fundamental rules, is, that no man should be judge in his own cause. By this each person has at once divested himself of the first fundamental right of uncovenanted man, that is, to judge for himself, and to assert his own cause. He abdicates all right to be his own governor. He inclusively, in a great measure, abandons the right of self-defense, the first law of nature. Men cannot enjoy the rights of an uncivil and of a civil state together. That he may obtain justice he gives up his right of determining what it is in points the most essential to him. That he may secure some liberty, he makes a surrender in trust of the whole of it.

Government is not made in virtue of natural rights, which may and do exist in total independence of it; and exist in much greater clearness, and in a much greater degree of abstract perfection: but their abstract perfection is their practical defect. By having a right to every thing they want every thing. Government is a contrivance of human wisdom to provide for human wants. Men have a right that these wants should be provided for by this wisdom. Among these wants is to be reckoned is the want, out of civil society, of a sufficient restraint upon their passions. Society requires not only that the passions of individuals should be subjected, but that even in the mass and body as well as in the individuals, the inclinations of men should frequently be thwarted, their will controlled, and their passions brought into subjection. This can only be done by a power out of themselves; and not, in the exercise of its function, subject to that will and to those passions which it is its office to bridle and subdue. In this sense the restraints on men, as well as their liberties, are to be reckoned among their rights. But as the liberties and the restrictions vary with times and circumstances, and admit of infinite modifications, they cannot be settled upon any abstract rule; and nothing is so foolish as to discuss them upon that principle.

The moment you abate any thing from the full rights of men, each to govern himself, and suffer any artificial positive limitation upon those rights, from that moment the whole organization of government becomes a consideration of convenience. This it is which makes the constitution of a state, and the due distribution of its powers, a matter of the most delicate and complicated skill. It requires a deep knowledge of human nature and human necessities, and of the things which facilitate or obstruct the various ends which are to be pursued by the mechanism of civil institutions. The state is to have recruits to its strength, and remedies to its distempers. What is the use of discussing a man's abstract right to food or to medicine? The question is upon the method of procuring and administering them. In that deliberation I shall always advise to call in the aid of the farmer and the physician, rather than the professor of metaphysics.

The science of constructing a commonwealth, or renovating it, or reforming it, is, like every other experimental science, not to be taught a priori. Nor is it a short experience that can instruct us in that practical science; because the real effects of moral causes are not always immediate; but that which in the first instance is prejudicial may be excellent in its remoter operation; and its excellence may arise even from the ill effects it produces in the beginning. The reverse also happens; and very plausible schemes, with very pleasing commencements, have often shameful and lamentable conclusions. In states there are often some obscure and almost latent causes, things which appear at first view of little moment, on which a very great part of its prosperity or adversity may most essentially depend. The science of government being therefore so practical in itself, and intended for such practical

continued

PRIMARY SOURCE 10.6 | *REFLECTIONS ON THE REVOLUTION IN FRANCE continued*

purposes, a matter which requires experience, and even more experience than any person can gain in his whole life, however sagacious and observing he may be, it is with infinite caution that any man ought to venture upon pulling down an edifice which has answered in any tolerable degree for ages the common purposes of society, or on building it up again, without having models and patterns of approved utility before his eyes.

These metaphysic rights entering into common life, like rays of light which pierce into a dense medium, are, by the laws of nature, refracted from their straight line. Indeed in the gross and complicated mass of human passions and concerns, the primitive rights of men undergo such a variety of refractions and reflections, that it becomes absurd to talk of them as if they continued in the simplicity of their original direction. The nature of man is intricate; the objects of society are of the greatest possible complexity; and therefore no simple disposition or direction of power can be suitable either to man's nature, or to the quality of his affairs. When I hear the simplicity of contrivance aimed at and boasted of in any new political constitutions, I am at no loss to decide that the artificers are grossly ignorant of their trade, or totally negligent of their duty. The simple governments are fundamentally defective, to say no worse of them. If you were to contemplate society in but one point of view, all these simple modes of polity are infinitely captivating. In effect each would answer its single end much more perfectly than the more complex is able to attain all its complex purposes. But it is better that the whole should be imperfectly and anomalously answered, than that, while some parts are provided for with great exactness, others might be totally neglected, or perhaps materially injured, by the overcare of a favorite member.

The pretended rights of these theorists are all extremes; and in proportion as they are metaphysically true, they are morally and politically false. The rights of men are in a sort of middle, incapable of definition, but not impossible to be discerned. The rights of men in governments are their advantages; and these are often in balances between differences of good; in compromises sometimes between good and evil, and sometimes, between evil and evil. Political reason is a computing principle; adding, subtracting, multiplying, and dividing, morally and not metaphysically or mathematically, true moral denominations.

What accounts for the greater power of the revolutionary appeal to nature as against prescription? Burke gives the following answer in speaking about the prospective influence of the "rights of men" theory on the Russians: "The Muscovites are no great speculators; but I should not much rely on their uninquisitive disposition, if any of their ordinary motives to sedition should arise. The little catechism of the Rights of Men is soon learned; and the inferences are in the passions."[17] A catechism has the great advantage of being easy, simple, uncomplicated, and short—and hence within the understanding of many. In contrast, prescription requires wisdom, subtlety, study, and prudence in understanding the value of long-standing, institutionalized embodiments of liberty and justice; hence this is within the understanding of only a few. But the "rights of men" goes right to the passions of ordinary, uneducated people and bypasses wisdom. Against these rights "no argument [that is, no reasoning] is binding." That is why it is so influential.

---

[17]*Thoughts on French Affairs* (December 1791); www.gutenberg.org/files/15700/15700-h/15700-h.htm#THOUGHTS.

QUESTIONS FOR REFLECTION

"Rays of light," from a source prior to and outside of this world, can both be an indispensable means to human life, if the source is kept far enough away, and also destroy it if the rays are not interfered with and moderated by "a dense medium." What is the source of these rays in the metaphor? What is the medium? How does the metaphor help show why "the primitive rights of men" cannot safely be brought too close to human life and also why they cannot be applied to it without modification?

All the philosophic founders of modern natural rights base their teachings on appeals to common passions of man—or to passions of common men. Partly the purpose in doing so is to provide a *realistic* teaching that would *work,* in contrast to the classical and Christian philosophers who aimed at high virtue and perfection. The rationale for this modern strategy is stated by Hobbes in *Elements of Law* (1640): "to put such principles down for a foundation, as passion not mistrusting may not seek to displace." Such a strategy reduces the need for, and hence the authority of, priests and the learned. Hobbes' teaching appeals to the passion of fear of violent death and the subsequent desire for self-preservation; Locke's appeals to the desire for property and comfortable self-preservation; and Rousseau's appeals to the resentment and envy of those who are "higher" or better off and the subsequent passion for equality.

And if prescription is weaker politically, why does Burke make such a determined defense of it? I do not claim to know; but notice that it is part of a pattern. Burke spent his life defending the politically weak (the Americans, Irish Catholics, Negro slaves, English dissenters, the East Indians) against the politically strong. There was little hope of prevailing. So why?

Burke was asked this question directly regarding his defense of the East Indians. Recall that he spent many years in a manifestly hopeless effort that filled 4 of the 12 volumes of his collected works, attempting to help them. In the midst of this, an acquaintance, Mary Palmer, wrote to him from India expressing the bewilderment of herself and her acquaintances. They could not see what Burke hoped to gain. They saw no personal advantage to him, and his party was divided; therefore there was no political advantage. So why?

Burke replied, "I have no party in this business, my dear Miss Palmer, but among a set of people, who have none of your Lilies and Roses in their face; but who are the images of the Great Pattern as well as you and I. I know what I am doing; whether the white people like it or not."[18]

Probably in any time, but surely in our relativist, cynical, and disbelieving age, it would not be believed that he defended the politically weak simply because he would rather be on the side of truth and justice, even if it was the politically losing side; perhaps out of conscience; or the love or fear of his God; or the love of his country which he wished to be lovable; or simply to love and vindicate the good against wickedness. But if any of that happened to be the explanation, it would suggest that Burke was more a defender of justice than a politician; more a lover of the truth than of power; and hence more a philosopher than a political man.

[18]Edmund Burke to Mary Palmer, January 19, 1786.

PRIMARY SOURCE 10.7 | *REFLECTIONS ON THE REVOLUTION IN FRANCE*

With the National Assembly of France possession is nothing, law and usage are nothing. I see the National Assembly openly reprobate the doctrine of prescription, which one of the greatest of their own lawyers tells us, with great truth, is a part of the law of Nature. He tells us that the positive ascertainment of its limits, and its security from invasion, were among the causes for which civil society itself has been instituted. If prescription be once shaken, no species of property is secure, when it once becomes an object large enough to tempt the cupidity of indigent power. I see a practice perfectly correspondent to their contempt of this great fundamental part of natural law.

PRESERVATION AND CHANGE

Nineteenth-century interpreters understood Burke as a "liberal" because he defended freedom for the oppressed (the Americans, Negro slaves, people of India, Irish Catholics, and English Protestant dissenters). Twentieth-century interpreters understood him as "conservative" because he defended the established social and political order against total revolution; and inequalities of rank and power; and individual freedom from indefinitely expanding government. Conservatives of the mid-twentieth century looked to Burke to defend existing democracies against Soviet totalitarianism. This use of Burke by recent "conservatives" has conveyed the sense that he opposed change. However, this is too simple.

First, Burke regards **change** as necessary and unavoidable:

> We must all obey the great law of change, it is the most powerful law of nature, and the means perhaps of its conservation. All we can do, and that human wisdom can do, is to provide that the change shall proceed by insensible degrees. This has all the benefits which may be in change, without any of the inconveniences of mutation. Every thing is provided for as it arrives. This mode will, on the one hand, prevent the unfixing old interests at once; a thing which is apt to breed a black and sullen discontent, in those who are at once dispossessed of all their influence and consideration. This gradual course, on the other side, will prevent men, long under depression, from being intoxicated with a large draft of new power, which they always abuse with a licentious insolence. But, wishing, as I do, the change to be gradual and cautious, I would, in my first steps, lean rather to the side of enlargement than restriction.[19]

Although change is inevitable, it may be either good or bad, and it is the duty of all those who love their country to strive to distinguish these. The good kind of change, which is a means to the **conservation** of a just, free, and reasonably decent state, Burke calls **reform.** It is exemplified by his understanding of what was done by the Whigs in the Glorious Revolution of 1688.

---

[19]A Letter from the Right Hon. Edmund Burke, M.P. in the Kingdom of Great Britain, to Sir Hercules Langrishe, Bart. M.P. [On the Subject of Roman Catholics of Ireland, and the Propriety of Admitting Them to the Elective Franchise, Consistently with the Principles of the Constitution as Established at the Revolution]. January 3, 1792; www.gutenberg.org/files/15700/15700-h/15700-h.htm#SIR_HERCULES_LANGRISHE.

PRIMARY SOURCE 10.8 | ***REFLECTIONS ON THE REVOLUTION IN FRANCE***

[I]t is vain to talk to them of the practice of their ancestors, the fundamental laws of their country, the fixed form of a Constitution whose merits are confirmed by the solid test of long experience and an increasing public strength and national prosperity. They despise experience as the wisdom of unlettered men; and as for the rest, they have wrought under ground a mine that will blow up, at one grand explosion, all examples of antiquity, all precedents, charters, and acts of Parliament. They have "the rights of men." Against these there can be no prescription; against these no argument is binding: these admit no temperament and no compromise: anything withheld from their full demand is so much of fraud and injustice.

There is also a bad kind of change, which Burke calls **innovation.** This is change that is too open to overturning the established moral and political traditions of a people. It underestimates the value of these established traditions and hence the costs of changing them. It is heedless of the difficulty of getting both rulers and rulers to obey the restraints of law on their passions. By its willingness to accept or encourage change that is not necessary or that goes farther than necessary, it undermines law-abidingness. It thereby tends to destroy all established order and is hence incompatible with any just or decent politics:

> Thanks to our sullen resistance to innovation, thanks to the cold sluggishness of our national character, we still bear the stamp of our forefathers. We have not, as I conceive, lost the generosity and dignity of thinking of the fourteenth century; nor as yet have we subtilized ourselves into savages. We are not the converts of Rousseau; we are not the disciples of Voltaire; Helvetius has made no progress amongst us. Atheists are not our preachers; madmen are not our lawgivers. We know that we have made no discoveries, and we think that no discoveries are to be made, in morality; nor many in the great principles of government, nor in the ideas of liberty, which were understood long before we were born, altogether as well as they will be after the grave has heaped its mold upon our presumption, and the silent tomb shall have imposed its law on our pert loquacity.

Innovation is a mode of change, or an attitude toward change, that is especially favored by certain interests that were influential in the French Revolution: financiers and bankers on the one hand, and philosophers and intellectuals on the other:

> Along with the monied interest, a new description of men had grown up, with whom that interest soon formed a close and marked union; I mean the political Men of Letters. Men of Letters, fond of distinguishing themselves, are rarely averse to innovation.

Of course every theory of change, and how to distinguish good change from bad, including Burke's, is more compatible with the private interest of some group or other. But that is not decisive for whether that theory is sound or unsound. What is decisive for Burke is whether a theory of change is compatible with preserving the good that a society embodies in its inherited institutions, customs, and morality. Burke insists that innovation is not reform and is in fact antithetical to it:

> So far from refusing itself to reformation, that [prerevolutionary French] government was open, with a censurable degree of facility, to all sorts of projects and projectors on the subject. Rather too much countenance was given to the spirit of innovation, which soon was turned against those who fostered it, and ended in their ruin.

QUESTIONS FOR REFLECTION

What if the kind of high-minded, philosophic conservatism Burke represents is generally a losing political position in the modern world as it was in Burke's time? Is the power or appeal to the common passions, especially the passion for equality, any less effective now? Is rational argument any more effective against it now than it was in Burke's lifetime? What lessons might people drawn to Burke learn from such questions as these?

As little genius and talent am I able to perceive in the plan of judicature formed by the national assembly. According to their invariable course, the framers of your constitution have begun with the utter abolition of the parliaments. These venerable bodies, like the rest of the old government, stood in need of reform, even though there should be no change made in the monarchy. They required several more alterations to adapt them to the system of a free constitution. But they had particulars in their constitution, and those not a few, which deserved approbation from the wise. They possessed one fundamental excellence; they were independent. The most doubtful circumstance attendant on their office, that of its being vendible, contributed however to this independency of character. They held for life. Indeed they may be said to have held by inheritance. Appointed by the monarch, they were considered as nearly out his power. The most determined exertions of that authority against them only showed their radical independence. They composed permanent bodies politic, constituted to resist arbitrary innovation; and from that corporate constitution, and from most of their forms, they were well calculated to afford both certainty and stability to the laws. They had been a safe asylum to secure these laws in all the revolutions of humor and opinion. They had saved that sacred deposit of the country during the reigns of arbitrary princes, and the struggles of arbitrary factions. They kept alive the memory and record of the constitution. They were the great security to private property; which might be said (when personal liberty had no existence) to be, in fact, as well guarded in France as in any other country. Whatever is supreme in a state, ought to have, as much as possible, its judicial authority so constituted as not only to depend upon it, but in some sort to balance it. It ought to give a security to its justice against its power. It ought to make its judicature, as it were, something exterior to the state.[20]

"It cannot, at this time, be too often repeated—line upon line; precept upon precept; until it comes into the currency of a proverb—to innovate is not to reform. The French revolutionists complained of every thing; they refused to reform any thing; and they left nothing, no, nothing at all unchanged."[21]

REVOLUTION

Revolution has been a theme of political science since Aristotle. It means regime change—from one form of rule (regime or *politeia*) to another, such as from kingship to tyranny, from aristocracy to oligarchy, from mixed regime to democracy, or some

[20]This and the three previous passages are from *Reflections on the Revolution in France* (1790); www.gutenberg.org/files/15679/15679-h/15679-h.htm.

[21]*Letter to a Noble Lord,* 1796; www.gutenberg.org/files/15701/15701-h/15701-h-htm.

PRIMARY SOURCE 10.9

Reflections on the Revolution in France

A state without the means of some change is without the means of its conservation. Without such means it might even risk the loss of that part of the constitution which it wished the most religiously to preserve. The two principles of conservation and correction operated strongly at the two critical periods of the Restoration and Revolution, when England found itself without a king. At both those periods the nation had lost the bond of union in their ancient edifice; they did not, however, dissolve the whole fabric. On the contrary, in both cases they regenerated the deficient part of the old constitution through the parts which were not impaired. They kept these old parts exactly as they were, that the part recovered might be suited to them. They acted by the ancient organized states in the shape of their old organization, and not by the organic molecule of a disbanded people. At no time, perhaps, did the sovereign legislature manifest a more tender regard to their fundamental principle of British constitutional policy, than at the time of the Revolution, when it deviated from the direct line of hereditary succession. The crown was carried somewhat out of the line in which it had before moved; but the new line was derived from the same stock. It was still a line of hereditary descent; still a hereditary descent in the same blood, though a hereditary descent qualified with Protestantism. When the legislature altered the direction, but kept the principle, they showed that they held it inviolable.

similar transformation. It means that the class of citizens who ruled (one, few, or many) and the kind of political good sought by the regime (honor, wealth, virtue, or freedom somehow understood) changes. The American Revolution was a revolution in this old sense. The ruling group changed from heredity aristocracy and monarchy to government by the many. But the purpose of rule, "liberty . . . according to English ideas and on English principles," as Burke said, was not changed. All the old common laws, contracts, and property remained intact and in force. The social order, in both America and England, remained intact. What changed was the rulers of America and how they were chosen. The American people declared themselves to be a separate people and separated themselves politically from England.

However, the French Revolution, though it called itself by the same name, was an entirely new thing; and Burke understood that both first and most profoundly. It did not merely overthrow a monarch; it overthrew the monarchy as a form of rule. It did not merely overthrow a hereditary ruler; it overthrew heredity as a legitimate claim to rule. It did not merely overthrow rule by a hereditary aristocracy; it slaughtered every aristocrat it could get its hands on, together with their families and even loyal servants. It overthrew not only the political order but also the social order. Before the Revolution there were various distinctions among the citizens: kings, nobles, priests, monks, nuns, and so on. Afterward there were only citizens—a radical leveling of all distinction and hierarchy and the denial of the legitimacy of anything else. It also threw out all the old laws and the notions of justice contained in them because they had not been established by the consent of the people understood after the manner of Rousseau and Locke. Henceforth, justice was what the people (or those who ruled in the name of the people) said it was. All property that had been held under the old regime was declared stolen and confiscated by the revolutionary regime or by mobs operating in its name. In totally overthrowing the

QUESTIONS FOR REFLECTION

Today innovation is commonly regarded as both a good thing and a good word. The new and modern are presumed to be better than the old; and innovative is thought to be a term of praise. Certainly this is true in the language of science, business, technology, medicine, clothing styles, and so forth. Can you think of any area of contemporary life in which tradition or old is commonly presumed to be better than innovation? What does the prevailing approval of innovation suggest about whether Burke's view or the French Revolutionary view toward change prevails in our time?

old social and political order, the French Revolution anticipated the totalitarian revolutions of the 20th century.

Burke thought hard about what made this new, unique kind of revolution what it was. One decisive element was that it was a revolution not merely of political forms but also of philosophic ideas. But these new ideas resemble religion in that they are **proselytizing.** They aimed to remake not merely the government but also the society of France—and not just France but all of Europe. The only historical comparison that Burke knew for this proselytizing revolution was the Reformation.

LIBERTY

Burke believed that liberty, rightly understood, is a good thing. In accordance with that belief, he defended the Americans in their dispute with the British government over taxation because he thought they were struggling for what every Englishman should recognize as the liberty "for which our ancestors have shed their blood." The French Revolutionaries also claimed to be struggling for liberty, and their English sympathizers agreed with them. Burke replied that whether liberty is a good or a bad thing depends on what is done with it. Liberty is a good not in the abstract but only in light of its consequences. In particular, good liberty protects and does not destroy other important political goods:

> I flatter myself that I love a manly, moral, regulated liberty as well as any gentleman of that society, be he who he will; and perhaps I have given as good proofs of my attachment to that cause, in the whole course of my public conduct. I think I envy liberty as little as they do to any other nation. But I cannot stand forward, and give praise or blame to anything which relates to human actions and human concerns on a simple view of the object, as it stands stripped of every relation, in all the nakedness and solitude of metaphysical abstraction. Circumstances (which with some gentlemen pass for nothing) give in reality to every political principle its distinguishing color and discriminating effect. The circumstances are what render every civil and political scheme beneficial or noxious to mankind. Abstractedly speaking, government, as well as liberty, is good; yet could I, in common sense, ten years ago, have felicitated France on her enjoyment of a government (for she then had a government) without inquiry what the nature of that government was, or how it was administered? Can I now congratulate the same nation upon its freedom? Is it because liberty in the abstract may be classed amongst the blessings of mankind, that I am seriously to felicitate a madman who has escaped from the protecting restraint and wholesome darkness of his cell on his restoration to the enjoyment of light and

PRIMARY SOURCE 10.10 *Thoughts on French Affairs*

There have been many internal revolutions in the Government of countries, both as to persons and forms, in which the neighboring States have had little or no concern. Whatever the Government might be with respect to those persons and those forms, the stationary interests of the nation concerned, have most commonly influenced the new Governments in the same manner in which they influenced the old; and the Revolution, turning on matter of local grievance or of local accommodation, did not extend beyond its territory.

The present Revolution in France seems to me to be quite of another character and description; and to bear little resemblance or analogy to any of those which have been brought about in Europe, upon principles merely political. It is a Revolution of doctrine and theoretic dogma. It has a much greater resemblance to those changes which have been made upon religious grounds, in which a spirit of proselytism makes an essential part.

The last Revolution of doctrine and theory which has happened in Europe, is the Reformation. It is not for my purpose to take any notice here of the merits of that Revolution, but to state one only of its effects.

That effect was to introduce other interests into all countries, than those which arose from their locality and natural circumstances. The principle of the Reformation was such, as by its essence, could not be local or confined to the country in which it had its origin. For instance, the doctrine of "Justification by Faith or by Works," which was the original basis of the Reformation, could not have one of its alternatives true as to Germany, and false as to every other country. Neither are questions of theoretic truth and falsehood governed by circumstances any more than by places. On that occasion, therefore, the spirit of proselytism expanded itself with great elasticity upon all sides; and great divisions were every where the result.

These divisions however, in appearance merely dogmatic, soon became mixed with the political; and their effects were rendered much more intense from this combination. Europe was for a long time divided into two great factions, under the name of Catholic and Protestant, which not only often alienated State from State, but also divided almost every State within itself. The warm parties in each State were more affectionately attached to those of their own doctrinal interest in some other country than to their fellow citizens, or to their natural Government, when they or either of them happened to be of a different persuasion. These factions, wherever they prevailed, if they did not absolutely destroy, at least weakened and distracted the locality of patriotism. The public affections came to have other motives and other ties. It would be to repeat the history of the two last centuries to exemplify the effects of this Revolution.

---

liberty? Am I to congratulate a highwayman and murderer who has broke prison upon the recovery of his natural rights?

When I see the spirit of liberty in action, I see a strong principle at work; and this, for a while, is all I can possibly know of it. The wild gas, the fixed air is plainly broke loose: but we ought to suspend our judgment until the first effervescence is a little subsided, till the liquor is cleared, and until we see something deeper than the agitation of a troubled and frothy surface. I must be tolerably sure, before I venture publicly to congratulate men upon a blessing, that they have really received one. Flattery corrupts both the receiver and the giver; and adulation is not of more service to the people than to kings. I should therefore suspend my congratulations on the new liberty of France, until I was informed how it had been combined with government; with public force; with the discipline and obedience of armies; with the collection of an effective and well-distributed revenue; with morality and religion; with the solidity of property; with peace and order; with civil and social manners. All these (in their way) are good

QUESTIONS FOR REFLECTION

Do you think an orderly and decent society can reject all inherited ideas of justice and right? Would you want to live in such a society, which could at any time completely reject the received idea of who owns property or what constitutes liberty and justice? Should your thinking presume that the established order is just? Or that proposals for fundamental change in institutions and public morality should be presumed to be equally worthy as, or even better than, inherited or traditional ideas? For example, are those who think like the French Revolutionaries or those who think like Burke more likely to support current proposals to allow same-sex marriages?

> things too; and, without them, liberty is not a benefit whilst it lasts, and is not likely to continue long. The effect of liberty to individuals is, that they may do what they please: We ought to see what it will please them to do, before we risk congratulations, which may be soon turned into complaints. Prudence would dictate this in the case of separate insulated private men; but liberty, when men act in bodies, is power. Considerate people, before they declare themselves, will observe the use which is made of power; and particularly of so trying a thing as new power in new persons, of whose principles, tempers, and dispositions, they have little or no experience, and in situations where those who appear the most stirring in the scene may possibly not be the real movers.[22]

The French revolutionary theory justified doing things in the name of liberty that Burke thought showed that the idea of liberty driving the Revolution was bad liberty.

THE BRITISH CONSTITUTION

Burke's thought moved within the framework of the British constitution, as far as possible. Yet it is a common opinion that there is no such thing as a British constitution. Those who say this mean that there is no written document called a constitution such as that which the United States and many other countries have. This view fails to understand or acknowledge that there is another understanding of *constitution* besides the American idea of a written document.

Burke's understanding of the constitution is identical to his idea that "society is indeed a contract" as discussed earlier in this chapter. Society so understood is held together (constituted) by a commonly shared faith that each institution of the state will fulfill its moral obligations to do its prescribed job, to serve those goods for which each is responsible, and to stay out of the prescribed rights, prerogatives, and responsibilities of other institutions:

> The engagement and pact of society, which generally goes by the name of the constitution, forbids such invasion and such surrender. The constituent parts of a state are obliged to hold their public faith with each other, and with all those who derive any serious interest under their engagements, as much as the whole state is bound to keep its faith with separate communities.

[22]*Reflections on the Revolution in France* (1790); www.gutenberg.org/files/15679/15679-h/15679-h.htm.

QUESTIONS FOR REFLECTION

Why was the French Revolution an innovation rather than a reform? What did philosophic ideas have to do with the revolution's innovative character?

Nor is Burke's British constitution founded on any preexisting theory, such as a Lockean contract that takes men out of their natural prepolitical condition, or on the prepolitical natural rights of the people. It nevertheless secures the "real rights of man in civil society" as described earlier. Strictly speaking, it is not a founded constitution at all. It is a grown constitution; but it is not authoritative merely because it is grown. It exists, continues in existence, and has authority only by each generation's acceptance of received intergenerational moral obligations, intergenerational choices, and intergenerational consent, all produced by intergenerational cumulative wisdom:

> Our Constitution is a prescriptive constitution; it is a constitution whose sole authority is, that it has existed time out of mind? It is settled in these *two* portions against one, legislatively—and in the whole of the judicature, the whole of the federal capacity, of the executive, the prudential, and the financial administration, in one alone. Nor was your House of Lords and the prerogatives of the crown settled on any adjudication in favor of natural rights: for they could never be so partitioned. Your king, your lords, your judges, your juries, grand and little, all are prescriptive; and what proves it is the disputes, not yet concluded, and never near becoming so, when any of them first originated. Prescription is the most solid of all titles, not only to property, but, which is to secure that property, to government. They harmonize with each other, and give mutual aid to one another. It is accompanied with another ground of authority in the constitution of the human mind, presumption. It is a presumption in favor of any settled scheme of government against any untried project, that a nation has long existed and flourished under it. It is a better presumption even of the *choice* of a nation—far better than any sudden and temporary arrangement by actual election. Because a nation is not an idea only of local extent and individual momentary aggregation, but it is an idea of continuity which extends in time as well as in numbers and in space. And this is a choice not of one day or one set of people, not a tumultuous and giddy choice; it is a deliberate election of ages and of generations; it is a constitution, made by what is ten thousand times better than choice; it is made by the peculiar circumstances, occasions, tempers, dispositions, and moral, civil, and social habitudes of the people, which, disclose themselves only in a long space of time. It is a vestment which accommodates itself to the body. Nor is prescription of government formed upon blind, unmeaning prejudices. For man is a most unwise and a most wise being. The individual is foolish; the multitude, for the moment, is foolish, when they act without deliberation; but the species is wise, and, when time is given to it, as a species, it almost always acts right.[23]

The constitution so understood is not a law, much less a fundamental law, as is the written American Constitution. It is not a document. It does not exist on parchment. "The body of the people is yet sound, the Constitution is in their hearts, while wicked

---

[23] *Speech on a Motion on the Representation of the Commons in Parliament* (May 7, 1782); www.gutenberg.org/files/16292/16292-h/16292-h.htm#STATE_OF_THE_REPRESENTATION_OF_THE_COMMONS.

QUESTIONS FOR REFLECTION

Compare the American Constitution to this understanding. What holds our Constitution together? Is it commonly accepted moral obligations? Or is it judicial review—the Supreme Court enforcing the Constitution as law for other institutions and the people? Do we Americans have any need for prescription in our constitutional understanding, or is judicial review sufficient?

men are endeavoring to put another into their heads."[24] And if those wicked men succeed, the constitution is corrupted. The greatest and most important attempt to corrupt the people's minds with wicked ideas, contrary to the constitution in their hearts, is the speech by Dr. Richard Price praising the French Revolution as based on the same theory of consent of the governed as is the British constitution—and saying that the revolution is identical in spirit and meaning to the Glorious Revolution of 1688. It is that speech to which Burke's *Reflections on the Revolution in France* is specifically addressed:

> His doctrines affect our Constitution in its vital parts. He tells the Revolution Society, in this political sermon, that his Majesty "is almost the only lawful king in the world, because the only one who owes his crown to the choice of his people." . . . .
>
> This doctrine, as applied to the prince now on the British throne, either is nonsense, and therefore neither true nor false, or it affirms a most unfounded, dangerous, illegal, and unconstitutional position. According to this spiritual doctor of politics, if his Majesty does not owe his crown to the choice of his people, he is no lawful king. Now nothing can be more untrue than that the crown of this kingdom is so held by his Majesty. Therefore, if you follow their rule, the king of Great Britain, who most certainly does not owe his high office to any form of popular election, is in no respect better than the rest of the gang of usurpers, who reign, or rather rob, all over the face of this our miserable world, without any sort of right or title to the allegiance of their people.[25]

This summary ends by returning to the observation with which this discussion of the constitution began. Burke's thought moves within the British constitution as far as possible. But what does it mean that the constitution is identical to the social contract, rightly understood? Why call one thing by two names? This seems to be a rhetorical strategy.

On the one hand, Burke wants to explicitly denigrate theory and metaphysics because explicit theorizing is the mode of thought of the enemies of the constitution he wishes to defend. The modern philosophers love innovation more than the British constitution; and their popularizers, such as Richard Price, seek to reinterpret the latter so as to foster the former. So Burke can neither look nor sound too theoretical or philosophic.

On the other hand, he needs to philosophize in order to both reveal and defend the latent wisdom in the constitutional tradition. He obscures the considerable extent to which he addresses his adversaries at the level of political philosophy by presenting his theoretical teaching behind the cover of the constitution. And he needs to do that in order not to publicly legitimize theorizing about the constitution.

---

[24]Ibid.

[25]*Reflections on the Revolution in France* (1790); www.gutenberg.org/files/15679/15679-h/15679-h.htm.

QUESTIONS FOR REFLECTION

Would you say Burke's manner of political philosophizing is a reform or an innovation, in Burke's meaning of those terms, from the perspective of both classical and modern political philosophers?

CONCLUSION: RHETORIC, PHILOSOPHY, AND POLITICS

This chapter has emphasized Burke's thought as being more explicitly philosophic than Burke himself claimed. The purpose in doing so is to make accessible his thought in the deepest possible context. The statesman turns out to be considerably more than a statesman. The disadvantage is that it reveals Burke's rhetorical caution in downplaying his philosophizing. In that way, it undermines the rhetorical form of his teaching in order to get at the most revealing substance.

Yet this undermining follows the spirit, if not the literal example, of that rhetoric. Burke thought that the modern political philosophers, in contrast to "the authors of sound antiquity,"[26] had made philosophy a means to political power instead of an umpire between rival regimes. The French Revolution showed that this would greatly intensify modern political conflict, dividing every country in a way that reminded Burke of the conflict introduced by the Reformation. And the politicization of philosophy also redirected philosophy away from the quest for wisdom toward the acquiring of power. This made it necessary for the philosopher more imbued with the spirit of sound antiquity, but contrary to the classical conception of philosophy's relation to political conflict, to battle against the modern development. But the danger to philosophy, as well as to the constitution, required obscuring what he was attempting as far as possible.

Consider this example, in which Burke describes the development of his thinking about the American problem:

> I set out with a perfect distrust of my own abilities, a total renunciation of every speculation of my own, and with a profound reverence for the wisdom of our ancestors, who have left us the inheritance of so happy a Constitution and so flourishing an empire, and, what is a thousand times more valuable, the treasury of the maxims and principles which formed the one and obtained the other.[27]

On the surface, everything necessary can be found in "the wisdom of our ancestors" contained in the inherited constitution. We need only remember it and have no need for philosophizing. However, Burke's speeches and writing leave a legacy of how to do political philosophy without obviously appearing to and even while denying doing so—and also how to turn philosophy to defending rather than undermining a reasonably decent existing regime. By so doing Burke makes a great reform—or an innovation—in the long and contested relation between philosophy and politics.

---

[26]*Letter to a Member of the National Assembly* (1791); www.gutenberg.org/files/15700/15700-h/15700-h.htm#MEMBER_OF_THE_NATIONAL_ASSEMBLY.

[27]*Speech on Conciliation with the Colonies* (1775); www.gutenberg.org/files/15198/15198-h/15198-h.htm#CONCILIATION_WITH_THE_COLONIES.

Key Terms

French Revolution
tyrannicide
radical
modern consent theory
sovereignty of the present generation
habituation
progressive thinkers
tradition
modern social contract
Robert Bellarmine S.J.
common good
premodern social contract
intergenerational duties
rights in contrast to moral duties
entailed inheritance
convention
prepolitical rights
real rights of man
prescription
change
conservation\reform
innovation
proselytizing

Sources and Resources

Key Texts

A Letter to Sir Hercules Langrishe on the Subject of the Roman Catholics of Ireland
An Appeal from the New to the Old Whigs
Letters on a Regicide Peace
Letter to the Sheriffs of Bristol on the Affairs of America
Reflections on the Revolution in France
Speech in Opening the Impeachment of Warren Hastings, Esquire, Late Governor-General of Bengal
Speech on American Taxation
Speech on Conciliation with the Colonies
Thoughts on French Affairs
Thoughts on the Causes of the Present Discontents

Secondary Texts

Canavan, Francis. *The Political Reason of Edmund Burke* (Durham, NC: Duke University Press, 1960).
Kirk, Russell. *The Conservative Mind from Burke to Santayana* (Washington, D.C.: Regnery Gateway, 1986).
Mansfield, Harvey. *Statesmanship and Party Government: A Study of Burke and Bolingbroke* (Chicago: University of Chicago Press, 1965).
Morley, John. *Edmund Burke: A Historical Study* (University Press of the Pacific, 2003).
Stanlis, Peter. *Edmund Burke and the Natural Law* (Shreveport, LA: Huntington House, 1986).
Strauss, Leo. *Natural Right and History* (Chicago: University of Chicago Press, 1953).

Web Sites

Stanford Encyclopedia of Philosophy entry online at http://plato.stanford.edu/entries/burke/

Free, full-text works by Burke at www.gutenberg.org/browse/authors/b#a842

Tocqueville

By Peter Augustine Lawler *Berry College*

LIFE AND LEGACY

Alexis de Tocqueville (1805–1859) was born and lived as an aristocrat in the village of Tocqueville in France.[1] But he rejected the old or prerevolutionary French regime in which aristocrats ruled, and he was a doubtful and very qualified supporter of the democratic revolution of 1789 in his country and the revolution of 1776 in America. He was a strange and moderate liberal who sought to employ political liberty to balance the democratic concern with egalitarian justice with the aristocratic concern for the greatness of a few remarkable individuals. Tocqueville wrote that he personally preferred greatness over justice, and it was only by abandoning his own point of view for God's more comprehensive one that he could take the side of democracy. What seemed from his personal view to be decadence is in the Creator's eyes progress.[2] He could not deny that aristocracy—the rule of the few over the many by hereditary right—depended on unjust illusions, and he had no desire to perpetuate most of those illusions. He wrote movingly about the sense of family extending long into the past and future that animated aristocrats, but he had no children and apparently no desire to extend his own family. He stood in a privileged place between aristocracy and democracy, where he could readily criticize democracy—or popular sovereignty (rule by the people's will)—from an aristocratic view and aristocracy from a democratic view.

Tocqueville's love of greatness was of **political liberty:** the proud sense of responsibility and achievement that comes through ruling oneself and others. Whenever he could, he entered France's political life, although he always failed to become a first-rate political actor. He wrote his three great books—*Democracy in America,* his *Souvenirs* (or recollections of his political engagement during the French Revolution of 1848), and *The Old Regime and the Revolution* (1856)—when he was denied a place on his country's political stage. He always wrote primarily to defend political liberty, not merely to satisfy his curiosity or present dispassionate insights. He did not write as a philosopher or even as a political philosopher. He did not share the love of metaphysical speculation characteristic of the classical political philosophers such as Plato; but neither did he join in the futile (allegedly liberal) efforts of modern philosophers such as Hobbes, Locke, and Descartes to purge the human soul of the depth that made both such speculation and outstanding statesmanship possible.

Following the Christian thinker **Blaise Pascal,** Tocqueville understood his political involvement as, in part, a diversion from the miserable, restless uncertainty that he felt when alone and in thought. But he was certain that the distinctions that constitute political life are real and worthy of our admiration and spirited defense. He thought of himself as much more of a genuinely political thinker than the Platonists immersed in proud, aristocratic illusions, the Christian extremist Pascal wallowing in his apolitical misery without God, or the moderns aiming to substitute decent materialism for the risky and noble pursuits of political life.

---

[1]For the details of Tocqueville's life, including his life's work, see Peter Augustine Lawler, *The Restless Mind: Alexis de Tocqueville on the Origin and Perpetuation of Human Liberty* (Lanham, MD: Rowman and Littlefield, 1993); Harvey C. Mansfield and Delba Winthrop, "Editor's Introduction" to their translation of Alexis de Tocqueville, *Democracy in America* (Chicago: University of Chicago Press, 2000); and Andre Jardin, *Tocqueville: A Biography,* trans. L. Davis (Baltimore, Maryland: Farrar, Strauss, Giroux, 1988).

[2]Tocqueville, *Democracy in America,* Volume 2, Part 4, Chapter 8.

Tocqueville's devotion to political life was partly based in his extraordinary insensitivity to the charms of ordinary life. He criticized severely and even chauvinistically those—such as devoted wives and pious priests—who were satisfied with their private lives. He experienced both writing about politics and political involvement in revolutionary times as freeing him from the anxious and doubtful misery that filled him in ordinary circumstances. He knew that his preference for greatness might be at the expense of a decent, ordinary life that would make most people happy enough. Love of political liberty, he said, animates the hearts of only a few. Because his political passion was so intense and his doubtful misery without it was so strong, Tocqueville knew that it was both dangerous and unjust that the lives of most people be held to his standard. He was sure that lives that bored him were still in many ways equal to his. He thought that the aristocrats were wrong not to believe that all human beings were equal under the personal God or Creator. And—with Pascal's Christian help—he was able to find some greatness in the seemingly ordinary lives of middle-class Americans.

Tocqueville saw that the middle-class view of the human being, properly understood, is true. That being he defined as the brute with the angel in him.[3] Democratic theorists characteristically err by seeing the human being as basically no different from the other brutes—as just another being governed by the materialistic laws of nature with no extraordinary or great qualities. Aristocratic theorists err by proudly understanding themselves as "angels," as wholly transcending their bodily limitations through their extraordinary virtue. But the aristocrat's proud passion for greatness and the ordinary person's desire for peace and prosperity both reveal part of the complicated, mixed truth of the elusive mystery of being human.

In Tocqueville's mind, the best or most truthful political order would serve both prosperity and greatness—roughly both the needs of our body and the needs of soul. Such a political achievement would require the statesmanship of those who could see further than both aristocratic and democratic partisans, those who could prudently balance the incoherent aspirations of the wonderful being who is part beast and part angel. It would require the transcendence of merely human partisanship in the direction of the genuinely comprehensive view of the Creator Himself. What Tocqueville called his new political science that would guide statesmanship in the modern, democratic world is inseparable from his theology.

DEMOCRACY IN AMERICA

Tocqueville's singular effort to see and perpetuate greatness in democracy was his two-volume *Democracy in America.* The first volume was published in 1835, the second in 1840. Harvey C. Mansfield and Delba Winthrop have rightly noticed that *Democracy* is "at once the best book ever written on democracy and the best book ever written on America."[4] It was based on Tocqueville's journey with his friend Gustave de Beaumont to America in 1831, when they spent over nine months traveling throughout the country. The pretext for their voyage was the study of American

---

[3] *Democracy in America,* 2, 2, 16.

[4] Mansfield and Winthrop, "Editor's Introduction," xvii.

penal reform, and they did quickly produce a book on that subject when they returned home. But their true purpose was to see the extent to which Americans had reconciled democracy and liberty. Because Tocqueville believed that the whole world was and would continue to become progressively more egalitarian, he journeyed to the world's most democratic country so far to see if there was any future for human liberty. He saw a nation in which democracy was not just a form of government but a way of life. The democratic ways of thinking, feeling, and acting seemed in the process of infusing themselves into every aspect of the Americans' minds and hearts.

Ancient democracy, whatever its injustices, did not, in Tocqueville's view, pose a threat to political life itself. The ancient democracies were composed of a fairly small number of citizens and many slaves and others excluded from political participation. So the ancient democracies of the Greeks and Romans, Tocqueville claimed, were really aristocracies.[5] They shared the proud idealism of aristocracies, and their citizens were largely free of the anxious restlessness that characterizes modern, relatively apolitical life.

Much of Tocqueville's project for **modern democracy** was the cultivation of the political activity characteristic of ancient democracy. His multifaceted participatory teaching—centered on his praise of America's free, local political life and Americans' facility in forming associations for political purposes—aimed to bring forth aristocratic or proudly political qualities in democratic characters. He even said that his chief aim in writing *Democracy* was to combat the democrat's tendency to have neither the time nor the taste for political life, and he aimed to show him that it was in his interest and his natural inclination to have the leisure and energy for that life, as the ancient democrats did.

Tocqueville's political science in *Democracy in America* is *both* more democratic *and* more aristocratic than the classic text of the American founding. *The Federalist* explains why the American Constitution aims to curb the irresponsible and bellicose assertiveness or unfettered liberty characteristic of ancient democracy on behalf of the more tranquil and private understanding of liberty of the modern large and diverse republic. America's political life, according to *The Federalist*, would be centered not in a popular assembly or a local community but, instead, in a representative Congress distant from and relatively unaffected by popular passions. There representatives of enlarged and refined or aristocratic views would engage in political deliberation for the nation, and the people would be limited to periodically passing judgment on their work through elections. The goal of the Constitution is to at least damp down the love of political liberty or greatness in most citizens, leaving them alone to pursue private pursuits as they please.

Tocqueville rejected what he saw as *The Federalist's* aristocratic tendency to exclude ordinary citizens from regular participation in political life, and its democratic or vulgar tendency to regard that participation as a threat to social stability and material pursuits. The liberty defended by *The Federalist* and the modern philosophers to which it is indebted, such as John Locke and Montesquieu, is the liberty of the solitary individual. Tocqueville thought these modern liberals were remarkably insensitive to the degradation such an apolitical or "state-of-nature" view of liberty

---

[5] *Democracy in America,* 2, 1, 15.

could do to the individual over the long-term. He, in effect, is freed for the disorienting and paralyzing experience of doubt and isolation that Tocqueville himself experienced when uninvolved in political life. Ordinary Americans living private lives in a large and diverse republic would eventually become lonely, alienated, and insignificant to the point of being anonymous. Individuals would disappear from view.

VOLUME I: THE MIDDLE CLASS AND THE TYRANNY OF THE MAJORITY

The two threats to the perpetuation of human liberty in a middle-class democracy on which Tocqueville focuses in Volume I are the absence of a cultivated leisure class and the **tyranny of the majority.** American law completely abolished **primogeniture**—the inheritance of the firstborn son of all the family's property. Primogeniture was the legal foundation of aristocratic stability. By keeping a few families' fortunes relatively intact, it fostered long-term attachment to one's family and class. The American, democratic law of equal division breaks fortunes up every generation by dividing property among all the family's children, causing property to change hands rapidly and making each individual somewhat responsible for securing his own fortune.

The result is that almost all Americans are members of the **middle class**—the class of free beings who work. Aristocrats are free and do not have to work. Members of the lower class (servants, serfs, slaves, or whatever) are not free and have to work. For the middle class, the good news is that we are free; the bad news is that we must work for ourselves and our own to live well or even live at all. So one key difference between ancient and modern democrats is that the latter are not dependent on the work of slaves. The major exceptions to the middle-class way of life Tocqueville discovered in America were the aristocratic masters and African-American slaves in the South, and he correctly thought that the Southern aristocracy was doomed. He also thought, correctly, that racially based slavery was a monstrously unjust if ultimately a futile attempt to extinguish the very souls of the African slaves. Few human institutions have more deserved to die.[6]

Middle-class democracy is more just than aristocracy; there's a much closer connection between what one has and one's talents and efforts. Opportunity is much more equal. The middle-class view of justice *is* equality of opportunity, and not the government's imposition of some egalitarian result. Middle-class Americans think those who work—themselves—deserve more than those who do not. And most of them are confident that they will succeed in gaining more for themselves than could ever be given to them.

The middle-class way of life is also the basis for unprecedented prosperity. In America, everyone works. In an aristocracy, in a sense nobody does. The aristocrats can get away with proudly thinking that work is not for them, and the lower class has no incentive to work hard because its members are not working for themselves. The love of money is universal in America, says Tocqueville. Nobody is above or below it, and that love in some measure influences every human endeavor. Americans are, Tocqueville says, almost all, in this crucial respect, equally middle-class. They are all equally mediocre, and the result is that they are the wealthiest, most powerful, and most free people ever.

---

[6]*Democracy in America,* 1, 2, 10.

But for the highest forms of human excellence, Tocqueville adds, that universal love of money can be devastating. No class in America thinks of itself as free from material influences for more noble, leisurely, and spiritual pursuits. Education becomes merely middle-class or practical or merely technical, and there is no audience for what the best human beings can accomplish in art, music, philosophy, theology, and so forth. In that sense, Tocqueville says that there is almost no genuinely higher education in America. Even literature becomes an industry.[7] What disappears in middle-class democracy is everything that flows from the proud opinion that human beings are made for purposes higher than mere work, and prosperity or material success is no longer understood as a means for the good life but as the end of life itself. Prosperity and justice can coexist with a boring sort of workaholic decency that may push every manifestation of great human individuality from the stage. Tocqueville's main worry is not that equal freedom of middle-class Americans may lead them to pursue forbidden pleasures and dangerous liaisons. Instead he worries that their materialism will be altogether too decent, or purged of the great longings that animate the most remarkable human minds and imaginations.[8]

Middle-class democrats do not share the opinion of ancient democrats and classical philosophers that leisure is the basis of culture, a vigorous and principled political life, and individual and civic greatness. The middle-class view is that politics is just an extension of economics—a clash of interests that might be reconciled or compromised without noble exertions, deep thought, or any concern for moral goods human beings share in common. Tocqueville, finally, is less concerned with the absence of the leisure class in America than with the people who thought so little of themselves that they did not believe that they were made, in part, to devote themselves to the pursuit of the truth about God and the good.

The omnipresence of this middle-class moral and intellectual opinion is part of the tyranny the majority exercises in America over thought. Tocqueville goes as far as to explain that the reason America has no great writers is that literary excellence depends on freedom of the mind, and there is no such freedom in America. The American method of imposing this tyranny is simply to isolate or ostracize anyone who would really exercise intellectual freedom. That method is effective; it is almost impossible to have the courage to speak the truth all by oneself. Not so long ago, American writer Walker Percy confessed to having Solzhenitsyn envy.[9] The Russian dissident, anticommunist writer was taken seriously enough by his country to be branded a criminal and thrown in prison. America's genuinely radical literary critics live freely but are ignored and marginalized. Socrates in America would not have been condemned to death; his life might well have passed by completely unnoticed. The gadfly would not have effectively irritated anyone of any importance. The majority loves those who flatter the people by saying that the cure for what ails democracy is just more democracy. But it tends to quickly dismiss as useless and authoritarian even friendly antidemocratic criticisms like those given by Solzhenitsyn, Socrates, and Percy.

---

[7] *Democracy in America,* 2, 1, 14.

[8] *Democracy in America,* 2, 2, 11.

[9] Walker Percy, *Lost in the Cosmos* (Baltimore, Maryland: Farrar, Strauss, Giroux, 1983).

PRIMARY SOURCE 11.1

Social Condition of the Anglo-Americans, from *Democracy in America*, Volume I, Part I, Chapter 3

Social condition is commonly the result of circumstances, sometimes of laws, oftener still of these two causes united; but when once established, it may justly be considered as itself the source of almost all the laws, the usages, and the ideas which regulate the conduct of nations: whatever it does not produce, it modifies. If we would become acquainted with the legislation and the manners of a nation, therefore, we must begin by the study of its social condition.

The Striking Characteristic of the Social Condition of the Anglo-Americans Is Its Essential Democracy

MANY important observations suggest themselves upon the social condition of the Anglo-Americans; but there is one that takes precedence of all the rest. The social condition of the Americans is eminently democratic; this was its character at the foundation of the colonies, and it is still more strongly marked at the present day. . . .

But the law of inheritance was the last step to equality. I am surprised that ancient and modern jurists have not attributed to this law a greater influence on human affairs. It is true that these laws belong to civil affairs; but they ought, nevertheless, to be placed at the head of all political institutions; for they exercise an incredible influence upon the social state of a people, while political laws show only what this state already is. They have, moreover, a sure and uniform manner of operating upon society, affecting, as it were, generations yet unborn. Through their means man acquires a kind of preternatural power over the future lot of his fellow creatures. When the legislator has once regulated the law of inheritance, he may rest from his labor. The machine once put in motion will go on for ages, and advance, as if self-guided, toward a point indicated beforehand. When framed in a particular manner, this law unites, draws together, and vests property and power in a few hands; it causes an aristocracy, so to speak, to spring out of the ground. If formed on opposite principles, its action is still more rapid; it divides, distributes, and disperses both property and power. Alarmed by the rapidity of its progress, those who despair of arresting its motion endeavor at least to obstruct it by difficulties and impediments. They vainly seek to counteract its effect by contrary efforts; but it shatters and reduces to powder every obstacle, until we can no longer see anything but a moving and impalpable cloud of dust, which signals the coming of the Democracy. When the law of inheritance permits, still more when it decrees, the equal division of a father's property among all his children, its effects are of two kinds: it is important to distinguish them from each other, although they tend to the same end.

As a result of the law of inheritance, the death of each owner brings about a revolution in property; not only do his possessions change hands, but their very nature is altered, since they are parceled into shares, which become smaller and smaller at each division. This is the direct and as it were the physical effect of the law. In the countries where legislation establishes the equality of division, property, and particularly landed fortunes, have a permanent tendency to diminish. The effects of such legislation, however, would be perceptible only after a lapse of time if the law were abandoned to its own working; for, supposing the family to consist of only two children (and in a country peopled as France is, the average number is not above three), these children, sharing between them the fortune of both parents, would not be poorer than their father or mother.

But the law of equal division exercises its influence not merely upon the property itself, but it affects the minds of the heirs and brings their passions into play. These indirect consequences tend powerfully to the destruction of large fortunes, and especially of large domains.

Among nations whose law of descent is founded upon the right of primogeniture, landed estates often pass from generation to

continued

PRIMARY SOURCE 11.1 | Social Condition of the Anglo-Americans, from *Democracy in America*, Volume I, Part I, Chapter 3 *continued*

generation without undergoing division; the consequence of this is that family feeling is to a certain degree incorporated with the estate. The family represents the estate, the estate the family, whose name, together with its origin, its glory, its power, and its virtues, is thus perpetuated in an imperishable memorial of the past and as a sure pledge of the future.

When the equal partition of property is established by law, the intimate connection is destroyed between family feeling and the preservation of the paternal estate; the property ceases to represent the family; for, as it must inevitably be divided after one or two generations, it has evidently a constant tendency to diminish and must in the end be completely dispersed. The sons of the great landed proprietor, if they are few in number, or if fortune befriends them, may indeed entertain the hope of being as wealthy as their father, but not of possessing the same property that he did; their riches must be composed of other elements than his. Now, as soon as you divest the landowner of that interest in the preservation of his estate which he derives from association, from tradition, and from family pride, you may be certain that, sooner or later, he will dispose of it; for there is a strong pecuniary interest in favor of selling, as floating capital produces higher interest than real property and is more readily available to gratify the passions of the moment.

Great landed estates which have once been divided never come together again; for the small proprietor draws from his land a better revenue, in proportion, than the large owner does from his; and of course he sells it at a higher rate. The reasons of economy, therefore, which have led the rich man to sell vast estates will prevent him all the more from buying little ones in order to form a large one.

What is called family pride is often founded upon an illusion of self-love. A man wishes to perpetuate and immortalize himself, as it were, in his great-grandchildren. Where family pride ceases to act, individual selfishness comes into play. When the idea of family becomes vague, indeterminate, and uncertain, a man thinks of his present convenience; he provides for the establishment of his next succeeding generation and no more. Either a man gives up the idea of perpetuating his family, or at any rate he seeks to accomplish it by other means than by a landed estate.

Thus, not only does the law of partible inheritance render it difficult for families to preserve their ancestral domains entire, but it deprives them of the inclination to attempt it and compels them in some measure to cooperate with the law in their own extinction. The law of equal distribution proceeds by two methods: by acting upon things, it acts upon persons; by influencing persons, it affects things. By both these means the law succeeds in striking at the root of landed property, and dispersing rapidly both families and fortunes...

I do not mean that there is any lack of wealthy individuals in the United States; I know of no country, indeed, where the love of money has taken stronger hold on the affections of men and where a profounder contempt is expressed for the theory of the permanent equality of property. But wealth circulates with inconceivable rapidity, and experience shows that it is rare to find two succeeding generations in the full enjoyment of it.

This picture, which may, perhaps, be thought to be overcharged, still gives a very imperfect idea of what is taking place in the new states of the West and Southwest. At the end of the last century a few bold adventurers began to penetrate into the valley of the Mississippi, and the mass of the population very soon began to move in that direction: communities unheard of till then suddenly appeared in the desert. States whose names were not in existence a few years before claimed their place in the American Union; and in the Western

PRIMARY SOURCE 11.1

SOCIAL CONDITION OF THE ANGLO-AMERICANS, FROM *DEMOCRACY IN AMERICA*, VOLUME I, PART I, CHAPTER 3 *continued*

settlements we may behold democracy arrived at its utmost limits. In these states, founded offhand and as it were by chance, the inhabitants are but of yesterday. Scarcely known to one another, the nearest neighbors are ignorant of each other's history. In this part of the American continent, therefore, the population has escaped the influence not only of great names and great wealth, but even of the natural aristocracy of knowledge and virtue. None is there able to wield that respectable power which men willingly grant to the remembrance of a life spent in doing good before their eyes. The new states of the West are already inhabited, but society has no existence among them.

It is not only the fortunes of men that are equal in America; even their acquirements partake in some degree of the same uniformity. I do not believe that there is a country in the world where, in proportion to the population, there are so few ignorant and at the same time so few learned individuals. Primary instruction is within the reach of everybody; superior instruction is scarcely to be obtained by any. This is not surprising; it is, in fact, the necessary consequence of what I have advanced above. Almost all the Americans are in easy circumstances and can therefore obtain the first elements of human knowledge.

In America there are but few wealthy persons; nearly all Americans have to take a profession. Now, every profession requires an apprenticeship. The Americans can devote to general education only the early years of life. At fifteen they enter upon their calling, and thus their education generally ends at the age when ours begins. If it is continued beyond that point, it aims only toward a particular specialized and profitable purpose; one studies science as one takes up a business; and one takes up only those applications whose immediate practicality is recognized.

In America most of the rich men were formerly poor; most of those who now enjoy leisure were absorbed in business during their youth; the consequence of this is that when they might have had a taste for study, they had no time for it, and when the time is at their disposal, they have no longer the inclination. There is no class, then, in America, in which the taste for intellectual pleasures is transmitted with hereditary fortune and leisure and by which the labors of the intellect are held in honor. Accordingly, there is an equal want of the desire and the power of application to these objects.

A middling standard is fixed in America for human knowledge. All approach as near to it as they can; some as they rise, others as they descend. Of course, a multitude of persons are to be found who entertain the same number of ideas on religion, history, science, political economy, legislation, and government. The gifts of intellect proceed directly from God, and man cannot prevent their unequal distribution. But it is at least a consequence of what I have just said that although the capacities of men are different, as the Creator intended they should be, the means that Americans find for putting them to use are equal.

In America the aristocratic element has always been feeble from its birth; and if at the present day it is not actually destroyed, it is at any rate so completely disabled that we can scarcely assign to it any degree of influence on the course of affairs.

The democratic principle, on the contrary, has gained so much strength by time, by events, and by legislation, as to have become not only predominant, but all-powerful. No family or corporate authority can be perceived; very often one cannot even discover in it any very lasting individual influence.

America, then, exhibits in her social state an extraordinary phenomenon. Men are there seen on a greater equality in point of fortune and intellect, or, in other words, more equal in their strength, than in any other country of the world, or in any age of which history has preserved the remembrance....

The majority, Tocqueville concludes, can pretty much do whatever it wants, and so assertive majority opinion clamps down hard in America on those who might be capable of singular greatness. Even the diversity *The Federalist* says is protected by our constitutional institutions is a diversity of *interests;* that limited diversity presupposes uniformity among a middle-class people who think primarily in terms of material interests. But majority tyranny is tempered in America, Tocqueville adds, by the absence of administrative centralization (which keeps the majority tyranny from being all that effective), the spirit of the legal profession (the closest thing in America to an aristocracy), and juries (which allow particularly talented lawyers and judges to instruct ordinary citizens to respect legal forms and limits).[10] The Americans are better than it first seems in moderating the form of tyranny specific to their way of life.

VOLUME II: THE DEMOCRATIC MIND AND HEART

While the concern of Volume I is the threat that an assertive majority poses to liberty, Volume II is far more concerned with the surrender of human assertiveness or free individuality. Tocqueville's fear is that democracy will culminate in the soft or seemingly **benign despotism** of meddlesome schoolmasters who will control every facet of lives so apathetic and passive that they will have fallen below the level of humanity. A prelude to that despotism is the deference of isolated and disoriented individuals to the rule of **public opinion**—or the rule of no one in particular. To be ruled by someone is an offense against democracy, a degrading submission to some form of personal, aristocratic authority. But being ruled by no one or by "forces"—such as public opinion, fashion, technology, "history," or scientific expertise—enslaves us all equally. No person with aristocratic pretensions tells any of us what to do.

People might become so passive, Tocqueville warns, that they will readily be seduced by deterministic theories that proclaim that human individuals—even or especially great human individuals—have no real effect at all on our personal or collective destiny. People will fatalistically believe that their futures are not in their hands. The democratic destruction of aristocratic respect for tradition caused people to lose concern for their past; the next step is the surrender of the future. Tocqueville imagines a people so isolated that each of them is more or less trapped alone in the present. Thinking of himself as liberated from every form of personal authority or dogma for self-determination as a free and equal individual, where will the democrat get the point of view to resist the various degrading forces that threaten to envelop him? Radical self-determination—making oneself by oneself out of nothing—is rather obviously impossible.

The topic of Part I of Volume II is the democratic mind. There Tocqueville says that **Americans are Cartesians** without ever having read a word of the philosopher Descartes.[11] As their way of deconstructing aristocratic privileging, they habitually apply the Cartesian or skeptical method to everything. Skeptical of the soul-based distinctions as aristocratic illusions, the Americans turn their minds exclusively to the body and its enjoyments. So they prize scientific knowledge far less for its own sake

---

[10] *Democracy in America,* 1, 2, 8.

[11] *Democracy in America,* 2, 1, 1.

PRIMARY SOURCE 11.2

The Tyranny of the Majority in America over Thought, from *Democracy in America*, Volume I, Part II, Chapter 7

It is in the examination of the exercise of thought in the United States that we clearly perceive how far the power of the majority surpasses all the powers with which we are acquainted in Europe. Thought is an invisible and subtle power that mocks all the efforts of tyranny. At the present time the most absolute monarchs in Europe cannot prevent certain opinions hostile to their authority from circulating in secret through their dominions and even in their courts. It is not so in America; as long as the majority is still undecided, discussion is carried on; but as soon as its decision is irrevocably pronounced, everyone is silent, and the friends as well as the opponents of the measure unite in assenting to its propriety. The reason for this is perfectly clear: no monarch is so absolute as to combine all the powers of society in his own hands and to conquer all opposition, as a majority is able to do, which has the right both of making and of executing the laws.

The authority of a king is physical and controls the actions of men without subduing their will. But the majority possesses a power that is physical and moral at the same time, which acts upon the will as much as upon the actions and represses not only all contest, but all controversy.

I know of no country in which there is so little independence of mind and real freedom of discussion as in America. In any constitutional state in Europe every sort of religious and political theory may be freely preached and disseminated; for there is no country in Europe so subdued by any single authority as not to protect the man who raises his voice in the cause of truth from the consequences of his hardihood. If he is unfortunate enough to live under an absolute government, the people are often on his side; if he inhabits a free country, he can, if necessary, find a shelter behind the throne. The aristocratic part of society supports him in some countries, and the democracy in others. But in a nation where democratic institutions exist, organized like those of the United States, there is but one authority, one element of strength and success, with nothing beyond it.

In America the majority raises formidable barriers around the liberty of opinion; within these barriers an author may write what he pleases, but woe to him if he goes beyond them. Not that he is in danger of an auto-da-fe' but he is exposed to continued obloquy and persecution. His political career is closed forever, since he has offended the only authority that is able to open it. Every sort of compensation, even that of celebrity, is refused to him. Before making public his opinions he thought he had sympathizers; now it seems to him that he has none any more since he has revealed himself to everyone; then those who blame him criticize loudly and those who think as he does keep quiet and move away without courage. He yields at length, overcome by the daily effort which he has to make, and subsides into silence, as if he felt remorse for having spoken the truth.

Fetters and headsmen were the coarse instruments that tyranny formerly employed; but the civilization of our age has perfected despotism itself, though it seemed to have nothing to learn. Monarchs had, so to speak, materialized oppression; the democratic republics of the present day have rendered it as entirely an affair of the mind as the will which it is intended to coerce. Under the absolute sway of one man the body was attacked in order to subdue the soul; but the soul escaped the blows which were directed against it and rose proudly superior. Such is not the course adopted by tyranny in democratic republics; there the body is left free, and the soul is enslaved. The master no longer says, "You shall think as I do or you shall die"; but he says, "You are free to think differently from me and to retain your life, your property, and all that you possess; but you are henceforth a stranger among your people. You may retain your civil rights, but they will be useless to you, for you will never be chosen by your fellow citizens if you solicit

continued

PRIMARY SOURCE 11.2

The Tyranny of the Majority in America over Thought, from *Democracy in America*, Volume I, Part II, Chapter 7 *continued*

their votes; and they will affect to scorn you if you ask for their esteem. You will remain among men, but you will be deprived of the rights of mankind. Your fellow creatures will shun you like an impure being; and even those who believe in your innocence will abandon you, lest they should be shunned in their turn. Go in peace! I have given you your life, but it is an existence worse than death."

Absolute monarchies had dishonored despotism; let us beware lest democratic republics should reinstate it and render it less odious and degrading in the eyes of the many by making it still more onerous to the few....

If America has not as yet had any great writers, the reason is given in these facts; there can be no literary genius without freedom of opinion, and freedom of opinion does not exist in America. The Inquisition has never been able to prevent a vast number of antireligious books from circulating in Spain. The empire of the majority succeeds much better in the United States, since it actually removes any wish to publish them. Unbelievers are to be met with in America, but there is no public organ of infidelity. Attempts have been made by some governments to protect morality by prohibiting licentious books. In the United States no one is punished for this sort of books, but no one is induced to write them; not because all the citizens are immaculate in conduct, but because the majority of the community is decent and orderly.

In this case the use of the power is unquestionably good; and I am discussing the nature of the power itself. This irresistible authority is a constant fact, and its judicious exercise is only an accident.

than for its applications in making lives more comfortable and secure. They view the proud and allegedly pure desire to know—characteristic of aristocratic minds—as an excuse to get out of real work. The pleasures of the mind, in truth, exist to serve those of the body. For democrats, Tocqueville explains, the most magnificent products of human intelligence are methods that quickly produce wealth and machines that shorten the hours of labor and reduce the cost of production.

Tocqueville himself embraces neither the democratic nor the aristocratic view of science. He positions himself as a sort of umpire determining what is true and what is false in each extreme view. The pride associated with the aristocratic science is "sterile"; it causes an inconsiderate neglect of what scientific knowledge might do to improve ordinary human lives. But the aristocrats are right that all scientific advances—including technological ones—find their roots in fundamental, disinterested inquiry. Democrats are so selfishly enthralled with science's practical benefits that they forget that technological progress depends on pure theory. Those who direct democratic nations, Tocqueville contends, should use their power and influence to go against the grain by raising minds up on occasion to the contemplation of first cause and some appreciation of the magnificence of theoretical life. Otherwise the result might be the near disappearance of scientific genius and the gradual decline of scientific progress itself. American wealth and power depend on the perpetuation of a way of life that shares the aristocratic contempt for merely useful endeavors in favor of the leisurely pursuit of truth itself.

Tocqueville also criticizes the effects of applied science on ordinary language in democratic times. Language becomes progressively more vague and impersonal.

CASE STUDY 11.1 | POLITICAL CORRECTNESS: TYRANNY OF THE MAJORITY OVER THE AMERICAN MIND?

Tocqueville observes that America's passion for equality is often at the expense of freedom. More particularly, he argues that the majority exercises a tyranny over the American mind. Subtle and not-so-subtle pressures lead to a homogenization and conformity of thought that is reduced to the lowest common denominator. Ironically, though America takes pride in its freedom of thought, it has been argued that it actually lacks intellectual diversity of thought due to the leveling pressures of the majority. Is political correctness on campuses today an example of the tyranny of the mind feared by Tocqueville? Is it possible to have a serious university-wide debate that challenges prevailing views on feminism, multiculturalism, affirmative action, abortion, and differences in racial and gender performances?

Human actions are described using words more appropriate for describing mechanical motion. Instead of saying "opinion," we say "input." All personal distinctions and assertions become suspect. Instead of saying "I think," those who aim to influence democratic opinion say "studies show." And skepticism about all spiritual matters causes metaphysics and theology to slowly lose linguistic ground; those in the know put "the soul" in quotes in anticipation of the discredited idea disappearing altogether. The danger is that in a basically technical society, we will lose the words required to articulate the real distinctions that constitute the human soul. The reality of the soul—or the nonmaterial foundations of human motivation—will always be seen better by proud aristocrats than excessively skeptical democrats.

Tocqueville recommends that democratic language be protected from this indiscriminate linguistic leveling by having those with literary talents study the aristocratic Greek and Roman authors in their original languages. Having everyone engage in such study would produce a whole people dissatisfied with the mediocrity of middle-class life; it would make them unfit to earn money. But those who devote themselves primarily to writing can elevate our language through their access to words meticulously describing great, beautiful, and rare experiences available to human beings alone that are too easily forgotten in a largely practical or technical time; and they will preserve individual greatness as a theme—if not, of course, the only theme—in our history and poetry.

Part II of *Democracy's* Volume II is an account of the democratic heart. Not only do people in democratic times seek all their beliefs and opinions in themselves, their "sentiments" or hearts also turn inward. Tocqueville calls this emotional withdrawal **individualism.** He distinguishes individualism from selfishness, which is based on a natural human instinct and is always present in one form or another. We can also distinguish it from the rugged or assertive self-sufficiency of, say, the Marlboro Man or a John Wayne character. We can, finally, distinguish it from manliness, or the proud or social display of one's indispensable individual courage or greatness. Individualism is the democrat's mistaken judgment that the main effect of social passions of love and hatred is to produce the aristocratic vices of injustice and cruelty. Love mainly makes us miserable and is more trouble than it is worth.

Individualism is indifference to the fate of others, and it comes from the democratic destruction of the ties that connect citizens, family members, and members of a class. Examples of Americans with the "heart disease" of individualism are the rich

PRIMARY SOURCE 11.3

The Study of Greek and Latin Literature Is Peculiarly Useful in Democratic Communities, from *Democracy in America*, Volume II, Part I, Chapter 15

What was called the People in the most democratic republics of antiquity was very unlike what we designate by that term. In Athens all the citizens took part in public affairs; but there were only twenty thousand citizens to more than three hundred and fifty thousand inhabitants. All the rest were slaves, and discharged the greater part of those duties which belong at the present day to the lower or even to the middle classes. Athens, then, with her universal suffrage, was, after all, merely an aristocratic republic, in which all the nobles had an equal right to the government.

The struggle between the patricians and plebeians of Rome must be considered in the same light: it was simply an internal feud between the elder and younger branches of the same family. All belonged to the aristocracy and all had the aristocratic spirit...

No literature places those fine qualities in which the writers of democracies are naturally deficient in bolder relief than that of the ancients; no literature, therefore, ought to be more studied in democratic times. This study is better suited than any other to combat the literary defects inherent in those times; as for their natural literary qualities, these will spring up of their own accord without its being necessary to learn to acquire them.

It is important that this point should be clearly understood. A particular study may be useful to the literature of a people without being appropriate to its social and political wants. If men were to persist in teaching nothing but the literature of the dead languages in a community where everyone is habitually led to make vehement exertions to augment or to maintain his fortune, the result would be a very polished, but a very dangerous set of citizens. For as their social and political condition would give them every day a sense of wants, which their education would never teach them to supply, they would perturb the state, in the name of the Greeks and Romans, instead of enriching it by their productive industry.

It is evident that in democratic communities the interest of individuals as well as the security of the commonwealth demands that the education of the greater number should be scientific, commercial, and industrial rather than literary. Greek and Latin should not be taught in all the schools; but it is important that those who, by their natural disposition or their fortune, are destined to cultivate letters or prepared to relish them should find schools where a complete knowledge of ancient literature may be acquired and where the true scholar may be formed. A few excellent universities would do more toward the attainment of this object than a multitude of bad grammar schools, where superfluous matters, badly learned, stand in the way of sound instruction in necessary studies.

All who aspire to literary excellence in democratic nations ought frequently to refresh themselves at the springs of ancient literature; there is no more wholesome medicine for the mind. Not that I hold the literary productions of the ancients to be irreproachable, but I think that they have some special merits, admirably calculated to counterbalance our peculiar defects. They are a prop on the side on which we are in most danger of falling.

and sophisticated emotional cripples mocked on the television shows *Seinfeld* and *Curb Your Enthusiasm,* and in a different way on *Friends,* where insipid individuals remain locked in a narrow circle of friends in the midst of a crowded and passionate city. We can also see American individualism criticized in Allan Bloom's instant classic *The Closing of the American Mind.* Bloom describes the best educated and most fortunate young Americans as having flat souls, of being incapable of being moved by either youth or death, of being emotional solitaries who are nothing more than "nice" and are moved only by music that reduces human eros to the rhythm of the mechanical rutting of animals. The mistaken judgment of individualism, Tocqueville fears, may be the modern, democratic result Nietzsche called the "last man," the being who, as Pierre Manent writes, "no longer knows the meaning of the verbs to love, to create, and to long for, verbs that express the transcendence of the self."[12]

Aristocratic societies have the advantage over democracies as societies because people's hearts or social passions are invigorated and enlarged by being connected in many ways to members of their families and class. But Tocqueville also shows us the price in injustice that is paid on the heart's behalf. Aristocrats characteristically feel no love, compassion, or any human feeling at all for those not of their class. The aristocrat Madame de Sevigne, Tocqueville observes, who was far from "a selfish and barbaric creature," simply could "not clearly conceive what it was to suffer when one is not a gentleman."

As democracy emerges, love may retreat but compassion advances; people are increasingly sensitive to the suffering all human beings share in common.[13] That is partly because they really do become more alike. So they think more and more in terms of laws that benefit everyone, even if that compassion is too weak to rouse them often to personal sacrifice on behalf of others. The movement from the love of a particular few to generalized compassion for everyone serves democratic justice, and we can see the place of the growth of compassion in our country in the emergence of our egalitarian, redistributive, welfare state.

Compassion, the problem is, is weaker and more diffuse than love, and it fades too much as democracy progresses further. The failure of the democratic heart goes through stages—from intensely focused and activist love to vague and rather passively sensitive compassion to generalized or utterly apathetic indifference. The democratic movement from compassion to indifference may explain the erosion of the redistributive institutions of our welfare state and the emergence of a less compassionate and more individualistic understanding of virtue among sophisticated Americans today.

For Tocqueville's individualist, virtue does not require that you love or pity, but only that you not hate. It requires saying and believing "not that there's anything wrong with that" (the familiar *Seinfeld* phrase) in response to almost anything your friends, neighbors, family members, and fellow citizens do. And it means carefully avoiding the inegalitarian injustice that inevitably accompanies love. It goes without saying that I cannot love everyone, and my intense love is for only a privileged few. The only way to perfect equality is to progressively diminish the power of love, and so family ties, citizenship, friendship, and so forth. Individualism, by isolating citizens from one another, makes them all easy prey for despots of one kind or another. It is the characteristic of the despot, Tocqueville writes, to call those who keep to themselves good citizens.[14]

Individualism points in the direction, of course, not of the participatory democracy of the ancients, but of the equality of unassertive and insignificant dependents

[12]Pierre Manent, *A World beyond Politics,* trans. M. LePain (Princeton, NJ: Princeton University Press, 2006), p. 127.

[13]*Democracy in America,* 2, 3, 1.

[14]*Democracy in America,* 2, 2, 4.

incapable of ruling themselves or others. We cannot help but notice how far we have gone to redefine citizenship in terms of rights without any corresponding duties, and we seem to have done the same with indispensable social institutions such as marriage. Obviously the America we see is both considerably more democratic and considerably more individualistic than the one Tocqueville observed, and the democratic descriptions in *Democracy's* Volume II generally become truer over time, as Tocqueville predicted.

The movement from the assertive tyranny of the majority to apathetic individualism as the chief threat to human liberty from Volume I to Volume II in *Democracy* actually mirrors the direction of American history. The founding generation was primarily concerned with protecting minority rights from an aroused majority. And they regarded the strong institutions of government as the equivalent of political Prozac: Democracy will not be compatible with liberty unless we can calm people down and make them less moody. Today some Americans still believe that the chief threat to our liberty is an aroused majority. Some members of the American Civil Liberties Union and other liberals worry about the "theocratic" threat of the religious right, but those critics are generally thought to worry too much about an very unlikely democratic possibility.

The dominant concern today, which is expressed both from the left and the right, centers on citizens' political apathy and degrading dependence on forces they do not even try to control. The worry is about the inability to arouse most Americans morally or politically for any reason. Against the stupefying, individualistic influences of fashion, technology—particularly the preference for the virtual reality of the computer screen over real human contact—the increasingly vulgar and idiotic electronic media, globalization, the market and our application of market reasoning of contract and consent into every area of life, and multiple dimensions of peer pressure—we need to be fortified by some equivalent of political Viagra.

The left bemoans our selfish withdrawal from compassionate social concern, our creeping and sometimes creepy libertarianism. Citizens no longer care enough to take responsibility for one another. The right complains that people no longer take care of themselves. Conservatives say that we no longer honor those who provide for their own futures. Our conservative president may talk about an "ownership society," but he is actually provided unprecedented entitlements. Our "heart disease" has become so severe that we are creeping toward the birth dearth that already plagues Europe, and the radical individualism that fuels much of Europe's immersion in an ultimately self-destructive, postpolitical, postfamilial, and postreligious fantasy seems to be emerging here. The democratic Europeans, as Tocqueville feared, seem to have stopped thinking about the future.

AMERICAN COMBAT AGAINST INDIVIDUALISM

We have to add, of course, that the conclusions that Americans today no longer think of themselves as citizens and are no longer concerned with their individual or national futures are rather large exaggerations. Americans, in fact, might be distinguished in the world today by their concern both for their nation and their obsession with their personal futures. Tocqueville himself distinguishes between democratic tendencies and American reality. He presents Americans as having identified the problem of

PRIMARY SOURCE 11.4

ON INDIVIDUALISM IN DEMOCRATIC COUNTRIES, FROM *DEMOCRACY IN AMERICA*, VOLUME II, PART II, CHAPTER 2

I HAVE shown how it is that in ages of equality every man seeks for his opinions within himself; I am now to show how it is that in the same ages all his feelings are turned toward himself alone. Individualism is a novel expression, to which a novel idea has given birth. Our fathers were only acquainted with egoism (selfishness). Selfishness is a passionate and exaggerated love of self, which leads a man to connect everything with himself and to prefer himself to everything in the world. Individualism is a mature and calm feeling, which disposes each member of the community to sever himself from the mass of his fellows and to draw apart with his family and his friends, so that after he has thus formed a little circle of his own, he willingly leaves society at large to itself. Selfishness originates in blind instinct; individualism proceeds from erroneous judgment more than from depraved feelings; it originates as much in deficiencies of mind as in perversity of heart.

Selfishness blights the germ of all virtue; individualism, at first, only saps the virtues of public life; but in the long run it attacks and destroys all others and is at length absorbed in downright selfishness. Selfishness is a vice as old as the world, which does not belong to one form of society more than to another; individualism is of democratic origin, and it threatens to spread in the same ratio as the equality of condition.

Among aristocratic nations, as families remain for centuries in the same condition, often on the same spot, all generations become, as it were, contemporaneous. A man almost always knows his forefathers and respects them; he thinks he already sees his remote descendants and he loves them. He willingly imposes duties on himself toward the former and the latter, and he will frequently sacrifice his personal gratifications to those who went before and to those who will come after him. Aristocratic institutions, moreover, have the effect of closely binding every man to several of his fellow citizens. As the classes of an aristocratic people are strongly marked and permanent, each of them is regarded by its own members as a sort of lesser country, more tangible and more cherished than the country at large. As in aristocratic communities all the citizens occupy fixed positions, one above another, the result is that each of them always sees a man above himself whose patronage is necessary to him, and below himself another man whose cooperation he may claim. Men living in aristocratic ages are therefore almost always closely attached to something placed out of their own sphere, and they are often disposed to forget themselves. It is true that in these ages the notion of human fellowship is faint and that men seldom think of sacrificing themselves for mankind; but they often sacrifice themselves for other men. In democratic times, on the contrary, when the duties of each individual to the race are much more clear, devoted service to any one man becomes more rare; the bond of human affection is extended, but it is relaxed.

Among democratic nations new families are constantly springing up, others are constantly falling away, and all that remain change their condition; the woof of time is every instant broken and the track of generations effaced. Those who went before are soon forgotten; of those who will come after, no one has any idea: the interest of man is confined to those in close propinquity to himself. As each class gradually approaches others and mingles with them, its members become undifferentiated and lose their class identity for each other. Aristocracy had made a chain of all the members of the community, from the peasant to the king; democracy breaks that chain and severs every link of it.

As social conditions become more equal, the number of persons increases who, although they are neither rich nor powerful enough to exercise any great influence over their fellows, have nevertheless acquired or retained sufficient education and fortune to satisfy their own wants. They owe nothing to any man, they

continued

PRIMARY SOURCE 11.4

On Individualism in Democratic Countries, from *Democracy in America*, Volume II, Part II, Chapter 2 *continued*

expect nothing from any man; they acquire the habit of always considering themselves as standing alone, and they are apt to imagine that their whole destiny is in their own hands.

Thus not only does democracy make every man forget his ancestors, but it hides his descendants and separates his contemporaries from him; it throws him back forever upon himself alone and threatens in the end to confine him entirely within the solitude of his own heart.

individualism and fighting against it. The two weapons Americans use against the progress of individualism are **free institutions** (Chapter 4) and **interest rightly understood** (Chapter 8). Americans engage in that combat because they are not simply democrats; they love not only equality but also their own liberty, one another, and God. Free institutions—democratic, local decision making—are a form of practical combat. The doctrine of interest is a theory about morality that aids American political practice. The theoretical and practical forms of combat are, in fact, interdependent.

Citizens in America are charged with taking care of the ordinary functions of government democratically and locally, and the institutions of administration are decentralized. Free, local institutions compel otherwise self-obsessed and socially apathetic modern individuals to take part in public affairs just to pursue their private interests. What begins out of interest turns into instinct, and participation in local government stimulates other heart-enlarging political activity and associations. If I want a bridge built, there is no central authority in some distant capital that will get it done; the decision of whether to build is made locally. So I must get my fellow citizens interested in the project, saying something like "I feel your pain at not having a bridge." At first I associate with you only out of selfish calculation; your pain is not really mine. But after a while I actually begin to enjoy pursuing with you a political good we have in common.

Individuals compelled to act as if they were citizens actually become citizens; in a way I actually start to feel your pain, to affectionately identify my good with yours. So what free institutions do is artfully create ties that exist much more readily or seemingly naturally in aristocracies. People who have an exaggerated sense of their individual independence as individuals need to be reminded of the truth that they are, among other things, political animals. Such a reminder, to be effective, has to come mostly from hands-on experience. Tocqueville does not say that participation in political life transforms Americans into citizens and *nothing more*. It allows them to see *part* of the truth about their being that might otherwise elude them.

Tocqueville credits American legislators or lawgivers for this political victory over individualism. The most fundamental of these lawgivers were the English settlers, who carried their free institutions and manly mores with them to America.[15] Our free local institutions were, in fact, an American inheritance of the aristocratic tradition of political localism, one that fortunately was not leveled by the American

[15] *Democracy in America,* 2, 2, 4.

Revolution. Our revolution, unlike the French or Bolshevik or Chinese ones, did not try to reduce individuals and institutions to nothing in order to create them completely anew.[16] Tocqueville adds that it is also fortunate that Americans, in their national chauvinism, do not regard their inherited institutions as aristocratic. They have incorporated them into their liberal view of their democracy.

That means, Tocqueville suggests, that American political localism remains vulnerable to egalitarian criticism. Over time, American political power has centralized, largely in the name of justice. Largely—but not completely—gone are the particularistic and passionate local institutions Tocqueville describes. Local democracy is activist democracy because it readily arouses pride and love and inevitably some inegalitarian privileging. National democracy—because it is more consistently impersonal—tends in some ways to be more just but also ordinarily more apathetic. Local democracy depends more on personal responsibility, which is somewhat unpredictable. Centralized democracy depends more on the predictable uniformity of bureaucracy. In some ways, the price to be paid for egalitarian justice and efficiency is the inability of individuals to connect their interest to their own effective political action.

Tocqueville's praise of free institutions is in the more general context of his emphasis on the importance of the **art of association.** What we now call voluntary or intermediate associations, he says, are both indispensable for the exercise of liberty in democratic times and inconceivable unaccompanied by the institutions of self-government. Associations, especially those formed for moral and intellectual purposes, both enlarge the heart and develop the mind, countering both the emotional isolation and the intellectual paralysis characteristic of excessive individualism.[17] Tocqueville makes an amusing and instructive point of praising temperance associations, by uniting morally against the evil of intoxication, citizens rouse themselves up against the democratic temptation of moral and intellectual indifference. He adds that specifically political associations—such as parties and interest groups—are "great schools" where citizens learn what it takes to combine effectively for common purposes in all their lives.[18] In general, the art of association in a democracy must be a deliberate effort to infuse in citizens qualities they would have more readily or "naturally" in the more social environment of aristocracy.

THE AMERICAN MORAL DOCTRINE

Tocqueville's affirmation of the American moral doctrine of interest rightly understood seems largely to depend on the political context of free local institutions. That doctrine is presented as the way Americans explain to themselves why they do not really surrender their individual freedom when they perform the duties of citizens. The challenge democratic moralists face is that they can't appeal to self-sacrifice based on pride or love. Self-sacrifice, the democratic thought goes, is for suckers, and the moralist who praises it is actually imposing some aristocratic claim to rule. A free individual acts only according to sober calculation of his own interest. So the

---

[16]*Democracy in America,* 2, 2, 3.

[17]*Democracy in America,* 2, 2, 5.

[18]*Democracy in America,* 2, 2, 7.

PRIMARY SOURCE 11.5

How the Americans Combat the Effects of Individualism with Free Institutions, from *Democracy in America*, Volume II, Part II, Chapter 8

DESPOTISM, which by its nature is suspicious, sees in the separation among men the surest guarantee of its continuance, and it usually makes every effort to keep them separate. No vice of the human heart is so acceptable to it as selfishness: a despot easily forgives his subjects for not loving him, provided they do not love one another. He does not ask them to assist him in governing the state; it is enough that they do not aspire to govern it themselves. He stigmatizes as turbulent and unruly spirits those who would combine their exertions to promote the prosperity of the community; and, perverting the natural meaning of words, he applauds as good citizens those who have no sympathy for any but themselves.

Thus the vices which despotism produces are precisely those which equality fosters. These two things perniciously complete and assist each other. Equality places men side by side, unconnected by any common tie; despotism raises barriers to keep them asunder; the former predisposes them not to consider their fellow creatures, the latter makes general indifference a sort of public virtue.

Despotism, then, which is at all times dangerous, is more particularly to be feared in democratic ages. It is easy to see that in those same ages men stand most in need of freedom. When the members of a community are forced to attend to public affairs, they are necessarily drawn from the circle of their own interests and snatched at times from self-observation. As soon as a man begins to treat of public affairs in public, he begins to perceive that he is not so independent of his fellow men as he had at first imagined, and that in order to obtain their support he must often lend them his cooperation...

The Americans have combated by free institutions the tendency of equality to keep men asunder, and they have subdued it. The legislators of America did not suppose that a general representation of the whole nation would suffice to ward off a disorder at once so natural to the frame of democratic society and so fatal; they also thought that it would be well to infuse political life into each portion of the territory in order to multiply to an infinite extent opportunities of acting in concert for all the members of the community and to make them constantly feel their mutual dependence. The plan was a wise one. The general affairs of a country engage the attention only of leading politicians, who assemble from time to time in the same places; and as they often lose sight of each other afterward, no lasting ties are established between them. But if the object be to have the local affairs of a district conducted by the men who reside there, the same persons are always in contact, and they are, in a manner, forced to be acquainted and to adapt themselves to one another.

It is difficult to draw a man out of his own circle to interest him in the destiny of the state, because he does not clearly understand what influence the destiny of the state can have upon his own lot. But if it is proposed to make a road cross the end of his estate, he will see at a glance that there is a connection between this small public affair and his greatest private affairs; and he will discover, without its being shown to him, the close tie that unites private to general interest. Thus far more may be done by entrusting to the citizens the administration of minor affairs than by surrendering to them in the control of important ones, toward interesting them in the public welfare and convincing them that they constantly stand in need of one another in order to provide for it. A brilliant achievement may win for you the favor of a people at one stroke; but to earn the love and respect of the population that surrounds you, a long succession of little services rendered and of obscure good deeds, a constant habit of kindness, and an established reputation for disinterestedness will be required. Local freedom, then, which leads a great number of citizens to value the affection of their neighbors and of their kindred, perpetually brings men together and forces them to help one another in spite of the propensities that veer them....

democratic moralist can only preach to at least understanding one's own interest well, and that means cooperating intelligently with others as the only way to effectively achieve one's own goals.

All moral doctrines, Tocqueville shows, are a form of bragging about one's own freedom. Aristocrats are vain when it comes to their exaggerations concerning their selfless transcendence of the domain of interests; democrats boast that they never lose their heads or stupidly forget their interests. The aristocratic point of pride is to never be animated by interest, and the American's is to never not be. Aristocrats claim to be free from self-interest, as God is. Democratic Americans claim to be free from both brutish determination by natural impulse—unconscious or instinctive enjoyment—and from imaginary, aristocratic illusion through the rational and willful calculation about what's best for themselves. The doctrine of interest is basically middle-class—or the moral self-understanding of free beings that are constantly at work for themselves. And it serves justice: The truth is that one way in which we are all equal is that nobody is above and nobody is below having interests. Every self-conscious being with a body, in truth, has interests.

Tocqueville's praise of the moral doctrine of interest acknowledges its justice. But it is still a form of bragging, not an accurate description of how Americans really live. A life constantly in pursuit of but never actually enjoying happiness would be the definition of hell. Americans, Tocqueville shows, actually take a certain pride in their miserable restlessness, but that pride is not at all adequate compensation for the absence of love or enjoyment. If Americans got too close to living the way they say they do, they would surely surrender their freedom as unendurably miserable. Their excessive restlessness could easily become a cause of their surrender to the apathy of individualism.

Americans take pride in explaining, Tocqueville observes, how their enlightened self-interest leads them to give up some of their time and wealth to the service of each other and their political community. They enjoy claiming that their democratic citizenship has nothing to do with love or self-sacrifice. They believe that their "philosophy" has led them to resolve the age-old tension between civic duty and individual self-interest. But Tocqueville claims that what they *say* does not actually account for why they do what they *do*. They often do themselves less than justice by sometimes giving way to the natural impulse that all social beings have to love and serve others. The truth is that their actions are, like all people's, partly selfish and partly not. And Tocqueville, of course, has already explained how free local institutions transform calculated sacrifices into instinctive or intrinsically enjoyable ones.

So the big question turns out to be this: Why does Tocqueville encourage the Americans to embrace a moral doctrine that does not tell the whole truth—or anywhere near it—about their experiences? Their bragging is really a cover or disguise. The fact of their affection for or emotional dependence on their fellow citizens offends their democratic pride in their individual liberty. They are reluctant to acknowledge their dependence, which limits their liberty; so they need a doctrine that exaggerates how free they are. With that verbal disguise, it becomes easier for them politically to combat individualism by arousing the love and friendship citizens can have for one another. The paradox Tocqueville displays is that a heartless moral doctrine serves to protect what enlarges the heart.

PRIMARY SOURCE 11.6

How the Americans Combat Individualism with the Doctrine of Interest Rightly Understood, from *Democracy in America*, Volume II, Part II, Chapter 8

I doubt whether men were more virtuous in aristocratic ages than in others, but they were incessantly talking of the beauties of virtue, and its utility was only studied in secret. But since the imagination takes less lofty flights, and every man's thoughts are centered in himself, moralists are alarmed by this idea of self-sacrifice and they no longer venture to present it to the human mind.

They therefore content themselves with inquiring whether the personal advantage of each member of the community does not consist in working for the good of all; and when they have hit upon some point on which private interest and public interest meet and amalgamate, they are eager to bring it into notice. Observations of this kind are gradually multiplied; what was only a single remark becomes a general principle, and it is held as a truth that man serves himself in serving his fellow creatures and that his private interest is to do good.

I have already shown, in several parts of this work, by what means the inhabitants of the United States almost always manage to combine their own advantage with that of their fellow citizens; my present purpose is to point out the general rule that enables them to do so. In the United States hardly anybody talks of the beauty of virtue, but they maintain that virtue is useful and prove it every day. The American moralists do not profess that men ought to sacrifice themselves for their fellow creatures because it is noble to make such sacrifices, but they boldly aver that such sacrifices are as necessary to him who imposes them upon himself as to him for whose sake they are made.

They have found out that, in their country and their age, man is brought home to himself by an irresistible force; and, losing all hope of stopping that force, they turn all their thoughts to the direction of it. They therefore do not deny that every man may follow his own interest, but they endeavor to prove that it is the interest of every man to be virtuous. I shall not here enter into the reasons they allege, which would divert me from my subject; suffice it to say that they have convinced their fellow countrymen.

Montaigne said long ago, "Were I not to follow the straight road for its straightness, I should follow it for having found by experience that in the end it is commonly the happiest and most useful track." The doctrine of interest rightly understood is not then new, but among the Americans of our time it finds universal acceptance; it has become popular there; you may trace it at the bottom of all their actions, you will remark it in all they say. It is as often asserted by the poor man as by the rich. In Europe the principle of interest is much grosser than it is in America, but it is also less common and especially it is less avowed; among us, men still constantly feign great abnegation which they no longer feel.

The Americans, on the other hand, are fond of explaining almost all the actions of their lives by the doctrine of interest rightly understood; they show with complacency how an enlightened regard for themselves constantly prompts them to assist one another and inclines them willingly to sacrifice a portion of their time and property to the welfare of the state. In this respect I think they frequently fail to do themselves justice, for in the United States as well as elsewhere people are sometimes seen to give way to those disinterested and spontaneous impulses that are natural to man; but the Americans seldom admit that they yield to emotions of this kind; they are more anxious to do honor to their philosophy than to themselves.

I might here pause without attempting to pass a judgment on what I have described. The extreme difficulty of the subject would be my excuse, but I shall not avail myself of it; and I had rather that my readers, clearly perceiving my object, would refuse to follow me than that I should leave them in suspense.

The doctrine of interest rightly understood is not a lofty one, but it is clear and sure. It does not aim at mighty objects, but it attains

PRIMARY SOURCE 11.6

How the Americans Combat Individualism with the Doctrine of Interest Rightly Understood, from *Democracy in America*, Volume II, Part II, Chapter 8 *continued*

without excessive exertion all those at which it aims. As it lies within the reach of all capacities, everyone can without difficulty learn and retain it. By its admirable conformity to human weaknesses it easily obtains great dominion; nor is that dominion precarious, since the principle checks one personal interest by another, and uses, to direct the passions, the very same instrument that excites them.

The doctrine of interest rightly understood produces no great acts of self-sacrifice, but it suggests daily small acts of self-denial. By itself it cannot suffice to make a man virtuous; but it disciplines a number of persons in habits of regularity, temperance, moderation, foresight, and self-command; and if it does not lead men straight to virtue by the will, it gradually draws them in that direction by their habits. If the principle of interest rightly understood were to sway the whole moral world, extraordinary virtues would doubtless be more rare; but I think that gross depravity would then also be less common. The principle of interest rightly understood perhaps prevents men from rising far above the level of mankind, but a great number of other men, who were falling far below it, are caught and restrained by it. Observe some few individuals, they are lowered by it; survey mankind, they are raised.

I am not afraid to say that the doctrine of interest rightly understood appears to me the best suited of all philosophical theories to the wants of the men of our time, and that I regard it as their chief remaining security against themselves. Toward it, therefore, the minds of the moralists of our age should turn; even should they judge it to be incomplete, it must nevertheless be adopted as necessary.

I do not think, on the whole, that there is more selfishness among us than in America; the only difference is that there it is enlightened, here it is not. Each American knows when to sacrifice some of his private interests to save the rest; we want to save everything, and often we lose it all. Everybody I see about me seems bent on teaching his contemporaries, by precept and example, that what is useful is never wrong. Will nobody undertake to make them understand how what is right may be useful?

No power on earth can prevent the increasing equality of conditions from inclining the human mind to seek out what is useful or from leading every member of the community to be wrapped up in himself. It must therefore be expected that personal interest will become more than ever the principal if not the sole spring of men's actions; but it remains to be seen how each man will understand his personal interest. If the members of a community, as they become more equal, become more ignorant and coarse, it is difficult to foresee to what pitch of stupid excesses their selfishness may lead them; and no one can foretell into what disgrace and wretchedness they would plunge themselves lest they should have to sacrifice something of their own well-being to the prosperity of their fellow creatures.

THE DOCTRINE OF INTEREST APPLIED TO THE FAMILY

The doctrine of interest protects, in an increasingly democratic context, the heart-enlarging effects of America's lucky inheritance of free, local political institutions. A wider glance at *Democracy*'s Volume II shows that it performs the same for two other American aristocratic institutions that were left basically intact by our revolution: **the family and religion.** These institutions also enlarge the heart and make liberty lovable. They are also vulnerable to the self-centered, democratic criticism of all forms of inegalitarian dependence.

Tocqueville's presentation of even the American nuclear family as an aristocratic inheritance is quite indirect.[19] His initial emphasis is on how democracy has transformed relationships among family members. In the short-term, democratic progress actually intensifies familial love by liberating it from the proud reserve of democratic formalities. But eventually democracy, as we see today, threatens the family's very future. The family cannot be held together by love alone, and even the love of particular members of one's own family is undermined by love of equality. The family is necessarily exclusive, and its existence will always be a barrier to the achievement of perfect justice, which is why it is abolished, of course, in the greatest book ever on justice—Plato's *Republic.* Tocqueville also observes that the restless, calculating materialism and truncated or unleisurely imaginations of American men cause them not to be able to focus on "lovemaking."

The **superiority of American women,** Tocqueville concludes, explains why the American family endures. They submit freely to a transformed but genuine form of patriarchy, one justified by the doctrine of interest well understood. That doctrine causes American men to speak of marriage in a strangely unerotic tone. Their distrust and disparagement of romantic love is one of many examples of their constant sacrifice of passionate enjoyment for the sake of business. American men take pleasure in explaining that the pursuit of prosperity is most efficient when labor is divided between men and women. "They have applied," Tocqueville observes, "to the sexes the great principle of political economy which now dominates industry." Women's work is in the home, men's in business and politics. Marriage is a labor-saving device that maximizes a man's personal productivity; it is clearly in his self-interest rightly understood.

That means that the husband remains the ruler of the family under the law, and the wife is socially subordinated and almost literally locked in the home. American women are allowed the choice of whom to marry, or even whether or not to marry. Girls are told that they must use their freedom to choose well, and that marry they must if they are to secure the happiness and dignity possible for them in this world. One reason American women are superior to American men is that they freely acknowledge the limits to their independence. They see clearly what American men do not: In order to live well, their liberty must be compatible with love.

American women, Tocqueville shows, humor the pride of American men. They know that much male pride is really chauvinism, and they secretly view it with some irony and contempt. They also secretly rule to some extent: They are the source of the effective American defense of sexual morality and even religion. They shape the souls of their children and even their husbands. They accept the responsibility of habituating or humanizing men, making love and enduring commitment possible in a materialistic and vulgar time. By calculating how best to constrain liberty with love, American women make liberty lovable and so combat effectively, in American men, the mistaken judgment of individualism.

American men pay their women egalitarian lip service, but they still exaggerate their freedom from dependence on them. They certainly do not acknowledge how anxious and miserable they would be without the self-denying efforts of women.

---

[19]This discussion of women and the family in America is drawn from *Democracy in America,* 2, 3, 8–12.

The doctrine of interest well understood, with which they explain their family ties, is a boastful cover, allowing them not to have to acknowledge the extent to which conjugal and family love and duty limit their liberty.

Tocqueville hints that it is unreasonable to expect that American women would allow their concern for family and love to trump their just claims to equality and liberty forever. But despite the justice of their recent liberation, it would be an exaggeration to say that American women no longer humor the pride of men. They still are the special partisans of the family, more inclined to sacrifice for its flourishing. And studies show that men still need marriage and children to be happy and control the self-destructive impulses of their natures.[20] Women might have abandoned their concerned calculation about their genuine self-interest rightly understood in their surrender of their insistence on social support for the virtue of chastity and sexual morality as a whole—as well as their astute judgment, described by Tocqueville, that if a man says he loves a woman (to get sex) he is, in America, free to prove it by marrying her.

THE DOCTRINE OF INTEREST APPLIED TO RELIGION

Tocqueville observes, again with irony, that Americans take pride in extending the doctrine of interest to their religious duties, their relationship with God, and their achievement of eternal happiness.[21] He notices that their view of religious practice is "so quiet, so methodical, and so calculated that it would seem that the head rather than the heart leads them to the altar." They do not want to sacrifice unnecessarily any of their pursuit of happiness or enjoyment in this world, so they calculate how to give the minimum amount of attention to their duty to God and still gain eternal life. In effect, they bargain with God; they claim to treat Him like just another businessman. The Americans proudly refuse to feign indifference to their "future state" because their moral doctrine concerning their freedom leads them to conclude that it is possible to plan for *all* of one's future. Nothing need elude the domain of interest, and neither God nor death is a real limit on one's independence. The American modern scientific view is that *all* reality—past, present, and future—can be mastered through individual calculation. Why does Tocqueville do no more than hint at the pretentious nuttiness of such democratic exaggerations? Why doesn't he subject the unreserved application of the American moral doctrine to religion to the withering criticism it deserves?

The American revolution did not aim to destroy religious belief in America, and Tocqueville calls any religion in democratic times the most precious and an especially vulnerable inheritance from aristocratic ages. Cartesian skepticism—with its quest of egalitarian consistency—dissolves even trust in love of God; and from that skeptical, democratic view, trust in the word of God really means being suckered by another man's interpretation of that word. Tocqueville holds that the democratic imagination is too distrustful of spiritual distinctions to generate a new religion, and the best hope for the future of the love of God is to work to perpetuate whatever religion a democracy is fortunate enough to have inherited.

---

[20]See, for example, James Q.Wilson, *The Moral Sense* (New York: Free Press, 1994).

[21]*Democracy in America,* 2, 1, 9.

So Tocqueville affirms the American application of the doctrine of interest to religion because it is not a complete description of American religious longing and behavior. It is true enough that interest is what usually leads human beings to religion. But the Americans really do love God and are anxious about death, and they really do know that they trust in a loving Creator because love and death are beyond their comprehension and control. Not only that, the confidence they sometimes have that they are somehow immortal is a source of pride indispensable for seeing spiritual greatness in themselves and enduring significance in their accomplishments.[22] All in all, religion, in part, functions in America something like free, local political life; it arouses in Americans some of the love and pride of aristocrats, genuine concerns of beings with souls. The American boast that the reduction of God and eternity to control by their self-interested calculation perpetuates by protecting their genuinely spiritual experiences from skeptically democratic criticism.

Tocqueville's account of the American combat against individualism is of the complex interplay of the distinctively human qualities of interest, pride, and love. The just but excessively modest view of freedom of the middle-class being with interests is deployed to aid in the perpetuation and flourishing of the true greatness of the proud, loving social being—the being capable of experiencing himself as a parent, spouse, child, friend, citizen, and creature.

Tocqueville probably underestimated the extent to which the moral doctrine of interest rightly understood could corrupt Americans' experience of their social ties. Over time, what Americans *say* seems to have transformed what they *do,* and today sophisticated Americans, at least, are much more self-absorbed and relentlessly calculating than the ones Tocqueville described. Citizenship, families, and churches have suffered as a result. We, much more than the Americans Tocqueville describes, believe that all our social connections are voluntary, and that we have the right of secession from any or all of them. Tocqueville regarded the moral doctrine of interest rightly understood as basically salutary, but surely it has become more pernicious. That is why we have to attend more closely to Tocqueville's full account of American religion.

RELIGION, POLITICAL LIBERTY, AND GREATNESS

What may best distinguish Tocqueville from other modern thinkers is the significance he gives to religion. He thinks that it is not only politically useful—as did John Locke and the American founders—but an indispensable support for individual greatness and actually true. Tocqueville begins his American political analysis not with the relatively secular liberalism that emerged out of the revolution of 1776, but with the Puritans, from whom the Americans got their true opinion concerning the interdependence of the spirit of religion and the spirit of liberty.

Complete religious liberty—or a wholly open mind about the "primordial" questions—leads, Tocqueville presents the Americans as believing, to a surrender of political liberty. If people are surrounded on all sides with the misery of fundamental uncertainty (what Pascal described as the misery of man without God), they too readily surrender their thought and will to a provident political authority. Without some authority or point of view to limit their mental independence, they cannot resist

[22] *Democracy in America,* 2, 2, 15.

political dependence for long. They are paralyzed by the anxious uncertainty that Tocqueville himself experienced when alone and without belief. They have to believe, to some extent, that either God or the government provides, because they cannot live well if they believe they are completely on their own.

Unlike early liberal thinkers such as Hobbes and Locke, Tocqueville did not think the free modern achievement of peace and prosperity could make the need for belief much less intense. Nor did he agree with Marx that religion would wither away once injustice was eradicated through revolution. He thought that the restless misery Pascal described was a psychological fact that would always plague human beings when they were without faith; so he disagreed with Marx that religious longings were merely historical creations or popular opiates that could be dispensed with through the right kind of historical change. The truth is that human beings will always have a natural disgust for the limitations of their biological existence and thus will have a natural longing, as Pascal explained, for a greatness that transcends those limitations.

Americans, Tocqueville explains, exempt religious dogma rather self-consciously from their habitual skepticism. They accept its truth "without discussion." It is, in a way, part of the tyranny of the majority; no one who seeks political power dares dissent from that dogma. Americans impose a limit on their personal isolation through shared beliefs in order to be free and active citizens. Any religion, Tocqueville explains, moderates the materialistic self-obsession of middle-class individuals by imposing on them obligations to be performed in common. Those duties, in America, are the Christian morality held in common by all the various Christian denominations. That morality is part of the unity that makes America a political whole.[23]

By *political liberty* Tocqueville means not only the activity of citizens but properly limited government. Religious dogma is also required to make freedom from political domination *for* something or someone greater—the highest end of the human being is to know God and live according to His will. Tocqueville embraces the American doctrine of separation of church and state as a way of keeping religion or spiritual life from being absorbed by the one-dimensional materialism that tends to animate democratic political life. The spiritual imagination of religion places limits on the political imagination, keeping Americans from embracing the tyrannical thought (characteristic of the French Revolution and later totalitarian ideologies of the 20th century) that *anything* might be done to achieve political reform or the perfection of justice in the world. Americans do not look to political transformation or revolution to satisfy every human longing.

Religion, Tocqueville explains, help shapes American **mores.** In his view, mores include not only "habits of the heart" but "habits of the mind" or the formation of fundamental opinion; and such habituation is just as important as the law itself in maintaining a republic that is both free and democratic. Religion, Tocqueville adds, "reigns as a sovereign over the sovereign over the soul of [American] woman, and it is woman who makes mores."[24] He explains that religious mores are perpetuated in America by women, who see that it is in their self-interest to habituate their husbands and children to to think not only in terms of self-interest and material gratification.

---

[23]The account of Tocqueville's view of religion in America here is drawn from *Democracy in America,* 1, 2, 9 and 2, 1, 2–5.

[24]*Democracy in America,* 2, 2, 9.

Women's shaping of souls through religion is so fundamental for the effective exercise of political liberty that Tocqueville does not hesitate to call that effort, in its way, a political institution.

According to Tocqueville, religion, properly understood, indirectly but powerfully both encourages and limits the political imagination. It helps teach human beings to be citizens. And it shows them that they are more than free beings who work. By connecting individuals to one another through God, it opposes both the extreme assertiveness and the extreme passivity that come through the experience of moral isolation. *Democracy*'s final discussion of religion—in the section about the democratic heart—adds that religion allows Americans to sometimes experience the Creator's (and so their own) personal greatness and goodness. Through religion they experience themselves as created and their souls as immortal.

Six days of the week, Tocqueville observed, Americans work constantly or restlessly pursue prosperity. They feverishly avoid leisure. The opinion that fuels their constant effort is that each individual is on his own: God does not provide, and leisurely reflection would only make them miserably conscious of His absence. That excessive restlessness is too hard; that is why Americans stand in danger of surrendering their individual assertiveness to the apathetic judgment of individualism. But Americans are saved by Sunday. On the seventh day their restlessness is replaced by a deep repose, and that rest is something like the leisure praised by the aristocratic philosophers. The soul finally comes into its own and meditates upon itself, and it finds that experience pleasurable and good.

On the seventh day, Americans think and act as if the soul has needs that must be satisfied—as if the restless avoidance of leisure on the other days is an error. They believe that there could be true happiness in the practice of virtue for its own sake, so their moral doctrine of interest rightly understood is also an error. They believe that God has guaranteed that their desire for immortality is satisfied. Religion diverts the individual American from what he often believes he really knows; it is an indispensable momentary escape into an ideal world beyond his ordinarily earthbound and time-obsessed existence.

But American religion is not merely a diversion. It teaches a real and ennobling truth that aristocrats proudly knew and we unreasonably modest democrats so easily forget or disparage: We really are more than material beings, and the belief that our transcendent longing for immortality is satisfied in some way or another is what leads us to perform all sorts of great deeds that stand the test of time. Today our believers perform the truthful, aristocratic service of insisting that the Darwinian view of the individual as an insignificant accident in an indifferent cosmos is an unrealistic (or unreasonably skeptical or democratic) denial of what we can see with our own eyes about individual importance or greatness.[25]

For Tocqueville, the truth about the beast with the angel in him stands somewhere between the two rather incompatible images the American individual has of himself. One is excessively material, the other excessively spiritual. (Consider here the very philosophic *Little House on the Prairie* books: Pa spent the week in restless movement away from civilized limitations into the isolation of the wilderness, but on Sunday he sat still—except when he turned to his fiddle—and would not even let his little girls play.)

---

[25]This point is defended ably and at length, with extensive use of Tocqueville, by Carson Holloway in *The Right Darwin? Evolution, Religion, and the Future of Democracy* (Dallas, TX: Spence, 2006).

PRIMARY SOURCE 11.7

How Religious Beliefs Sometimes Turn the Thoughts of Americans to Immaterial Pleasures, from *Democracy in America,* Volume II, Part II, Chapter 15

In the United States on the seventh day of every week the trading and working life of the nation seems suspended; all noises cease; a deep tranquility, say rather the solemn calm of meditation, succeeds the turmoil of the week, and the soul resumes possession and contemplation of itself. On this day the marts of traffic are deserted; every member of the community, accompanied by his children, goes to church, where he listens to strange language which would seem unsuited to his ear. He is told of the countless evils caused by pride and covetousness; he is reminded of the necessity of checking his desires, of the finer pleasures that belong to virtue alone, and of the true happiness that attends it. On his return home he does not turn to the ledgers of his business, but he opens the book of Holy Scripture; there he meets with sublime and affecting descriptions of the greatness and goodness of the Creator, of the infinite magnificence of the handiwork of God, and of the lofty destinies of man, his duties, and his immortal privileges.

Thus it is that the American at times steals an hour from himself, and, laying aside for a while the petty passions which agitate his life, and the ephemeral interests which engross it, he strays at once into an ideal world, where all is great, eternal, and pure.

I have endeavored to point out, in another part of this work, the causes to which the maintenance of the political institutions of the Americans is attributable, and religion appeared to be one of the most prominent among them. I am now treating of the Americans in an individual capacity, and I again observe that religion is not less useful to each citizen than to the whole state. The Americans show by their practice that they feel the high necessity of imparting morality to democratic communities by means of religion. What they think of themselves in this respect is a truth of which every democratic nation ought to be thoroughly persuaded. I do not doubt that the social and political constitution of a people predisposes them to adopt certain doctrines and tastes, which afterward flourish without difficulty among them; while the same causes may divert them from certain other opinions and propensities without any voluntary effort and, as it were, without any distinct consciousness on their part. The whole art of the legislator is correctly to discern beforehand these natural inclinations of communities of men, in order to know whether they should be fostered or whether it may not be necessary to check them. For the duties incumbent on the legislator differ at different times, only the goal toward which the human race ought ever to be tending is stationary; the means of reaching it are perpetually varied. If I had been born in an aristocratic age, in the midst of a nation where the hereditary wealth of some and the irremediable penury of others equally diverted men from the idea of bettering their condition and held the soul, as it were, in a state of torpor, fixed on the contemplation of another world, I should then wish that it were possible for me to rouse that people to a sense of their wants; I should seek to discover more rapid and easy means for satisfying the fresh desires that I might have awakened; and, directing the most strenuous efforts of the citizens to physical pursuits, I should endeavor to stimulate them to promote their own well-being. If it happened that some men were thus immoderately incited to the pursuit of riches and caused to display an excessive liking for physical gratifications, I should not be alarmed; these peculiar cases would soon disappear in the general aspect of the whole community...

Materialism, among all nations, is a dangerous disease of the human mind; but it is more especially to be dreaded among a democratic people because it readily amalgamates with that vice which is most familiar to the heart under such circumstances. Democracy encourages a taste for physical gratification; this taste, if it become excessive, soon disposes men to believe that all is matter only; and materialism, in

continued

PRIMARY SOURCE 11.7

HOW RELIGIOUS BELIEFS SOMETIMES TURN THE THOUGHTS OF AMERICANS TO IMMATERIAL PLEASURES, FROM *DEMOCRACY IN AMERICA,* VOLUME II, PART II, CHAPTER 15 *continued*

its turn, hurries them on with mad impatience to these same delights; such is the fatal circle within which democratic nations are driven round. It were well that they should see the danger and hold back.

Most religions are only general, simple, and practical means of teaching men the doctrine of the immortality of the soul. That is the greatest benefit which a democratic people derives from its belief, and hence belief is more necessary to such a people than to all others. When, therefore, any religion has struck its roots deep into a democracy, beware that you do not disturb it; but rather watch it carefully, as the most precious bequest of aristocratic ages. Do not seek to supersede the old religious opinions of men by new ones, lest in the passage from one faith to another, the soul being left for a while stripped of all belief, the love of physical gratifications should grow upon it and fill it wholly.

The doctrine of metempsychosis is assuredly not more rational than that of materialism; nevertheless, if it were absolutely necessary that a democracy should choose one of the two, I should not hesitate to decide that the community would run less risk of being brutalized by believing that the soul of man will pass into the carcass of a hog than by believing that the soul of man is nothing at all. The belief in a supersensual and immortal principle, united for a time to matter is so indispensable to man's greatness that its effects are striking even when it is not united to the doctrine of future reward and punishment, or even when it teaches no more than that after death the divine principle contained in man is absorbed in the Deity or transferred to animate the frame of some other creature. Men holding so imperfect a belief will still consider the body as the secondary and inferior portion of their nature, and will despise it even while they yield to its influence; whereas they have a natural esteem and secret admiration for the immaterial part of man, even though they sometimes refuse to submit to its authority. That is enough to give a lofty cast to their opinions and their tastes, and to bid them tend, with no interested motive, and as it were by impulse, to pure feelings and elevated thoughts.

The American mixture, in its way, truthfully reflects the authentically middle-class instability of the human soul itself.

But Tocqueville, as usual, makes us wonder how much of a future such an obviously incoherent self-understanding could have. Reflecting on his experience at a revival or camp meeting—to which people traveled for hundreds of miles to give themselves wholly over to fierce spiritual fervor for a while—Tocqueville considers the propensity of Americans' unreasonably decent or soul-denying materialism to generate its opposite: religious madness.

A significant countercultural minority of Americans have become "whole life" Christians. They turn to the Bible for advice on every feature of human life, and their churches are the center of almost all their family's activities. They increasingly homeschool under religious guidance. In the name of their souls' integrity, they are abolishing the difference between Sunday and the other days. In some ways, every day is becoming the Sabbath for them.

Only fanatical secularists would call this trend the emergence of religious madness in America; evangelical and orthodox believers are characteristically restrained and thoughtful. Camp meetings and their equivalents aren't sweeping the land, though

QUESTIONS FOR REFLECTION

Over the last generation or two in America we have seen the distinctiveness of Sunday disappear. For most Americans, Sunday is now just about like any other day; all the stores are now open, and there is plenty to do. Even those Americans who pride themselves in being "seventh day recreationalists" are often busily engaged in complicated, high-tech hobbies. (Tocqueville noticed that there are few things less leisurely than an American vacation.)[26] Americans' "leisure industry" is characteristic of beings incapable of being soulful or just relaxing—an activity that Tocqueville also thought was evidence of the goodness of life. What would Tocqueville think about the disappearance of Sunday? Why might he be concerned?

[26]*Democracy in America,* 2, 2, 13.

they are still around. Nonetheless, there really is a secessionist impulse animating whole life Christians; they are withdrawing from what they regard as the antireligious and immoral lives of mainstream America. They are still nowhere near the Amish; American evangelicals are mostly high-tech and entrepreneurial. But there is a movement in that direction. We now have "Crunchy Cons" who combine religious orthodoxy—with its moral conservativism—with a 1960s emphasis on developing anticapitalist, pro-environmental, totally organic, communal alternatives.[27]

The common Christian morality that united Americans and from which no one who wanted to be influential dared dissent is gone today. Tocqueville himself thought that might happen: He presented American Protestantism as an unstable compromise between adherence to religious authority and religious individualism. And he predicted that increasingly Protestant Americans would move in two directions—toward both Catholicism and unbelief.[28] That has not happened exactly. But it is true that Americans are moving toward either more orthodox, countercultural beliefs or beliefs that comport better with our dominant individualism; all of our denominations have split into what the sociologists call "orthodox" and "progressive" factions.

Tocqueville also writes that the most seductive theology in democratic times will be **pantheism**—the doctrine that everything that exists is identical and divine, that all the distinctions we perceive are illusions.[29] Pantheism is surely the most egalitarian of doctrines; but it achieves its result by abolishing the distinctions between brute, human being, and God that make human individuality possible. It is a lullaby that makes our personal assertiveness seem not only insignificant but unnecessary. Why strive for greatness if I am already God?

Soothing me with thought about my passive divinity, the theology of pantheism is that I cannot and need not do anything to transcend myself. I am already no less than and no different from the gods and heroes that allegedly used to populate the world, and I can have the self-sufficient serenity of the Buddhist without all that spiritual discipline. Pantheism locks the individual up in the divinity allegedly inside oneself. The belief of a creature in a Creator—an image of personal perfection infinitely greater than himself—draws the human being outside his puny self in the direction of a personal greatness that is not merely the product of his solitary imagination. It is no

[27]Rod Dreher, *Crunchy Cons* (New York: Crown Forum, 2006).

[28]*Democracy in America,* 2, 1, 6.

[29]*Democracy in America,* 2, 1, 7.

wonder that Tocqueville urges all partisans of the true greatness of human individuality in our time to resist the seduction of pantheism on behalf of the Creator.

It does seem that American believers have split into those who believe in a personal Creator that loves and judges particular human creatures, and those who believe more vaguely or generally in a pantheistic or Gnostic or New Age form of divinity. In some rough fashion, Americans appear to be divided into those moved by the personal suffering portrayed in Mel Gibson's *The Passion* and those who are attracted to the antiorthodox conspiracy theory of the *Da Vinci Code*. For many believers, of course, both of those works of art are extreme; but it is hard not to be inclined in one direction or the other. Tocqueville says that while pantheism opposes the greatness of human individuality, it is not incompatible with individualism. That is because the tendency of individualism is to empty particular individuals of their distinctive moral content. Our emerging pantheism—at least among our sophisticates—is evidence of both the extremity of our individualism and our hostility to acknowledging any form of personal greatness—even that of the personal Creator.

CONCLUSION: TOCQUEVILLE, ROUSSEAU, AND PASCAL

The reason Tocqueville wrote books, particularly *Democracy in America,* was to reconcile the truth of aristocracy with the truth of democracy—the great achievements that flow from proud individuality with egalitarian justice. That always imperfect reconciliation of the parts of the beast with the angel in him is a task always given to statesmen, the proud few among whom Tocqueville counted himself. There are always a few human beings who love the true greatness of human liberty over tyrannical aristocratic illusions, decent materialism, and the love of equality for its own sake.

Because Tocqueville finally identified himself with a small group of natural aristocrats, he admitted that he would personally choose justice over greatness. But by subordinating his own will to that of our Creator, he came to see greatness in the pursuit of justice. And with the help of Pascal, he came to see greatness in the seemingly ordinary experiences of Americans. In the strangest chapter in *Democracy,* Tocqueville stands amazed at the fact that Americans are restless in the midst of prosperity.[30] Their material successes only produce more feverish pursuits, and they seem much less capable of human enjoyment than their less enlightened and less successful ancestors. They are futilely trying to satisfy their genuinely spiritually longings through material pursuits because their Cartesian skepticism often trumps their religious belief in their souls. They are haunted by the death that will come before they have acquired enough of the good things of this world to really be happy. If we look carefully at sophisticated "post-Christian" Americans today, the truth may be that they talk the therapeutic language of morally indifferent individualism, but they act with relentless self-obsession and the pressing scarcity of time in mind. The emotional withdrawal produced by popularized Cartesian skepticism creates a soul-based vacuum that has to be filled somehow.

According to Pascal, the greatness of man is in his misery, and the restless, workaholic Americans clearly are miserable in the absence of God. Miserable

---

[30]*Democracy in America,* 2, 2, 13.

restlessness, Tocqueville adds, is not new in the world. What is unprecedented is that America is a whole nation under its sway. America, from that view, is evidence that the Christians are right and the classical philosophers were wrong about the human soul: Most human beings do not live trapped in some political "cave" oblivious to the truth about their natural human situation; the Americans all display the spiritual restlessness that the aristocrats believed was possible for only a few.[31] From this view, most workaholic American lives display undeniable greatness.

The good news about Americans' misery, Tocqueville says, is that it shows that the human soul has needs that must be satisfied. Materialistic efforts to divert ourselves from them will not work over the long run. The pursuit of egalitarian justice, which obliterates, in theory, the very distinction between Creator and creature in the pantheistic imagination, will not really be able to destroy the human longing for a Creator. The bad news might be the inability of democratic people to understand that their true longings might be fierce rebellions against the constraints of decent, materialistic life. The original Christians, Tocqueville reminds us, were in rebellion against the refined Epicurean materialism of the imperial Romans. Although Tocqueville did not really think that theocracy was an American option, he clearly suggests that democratic America will remain fertile ground for religious revivals, and surely a good part of our country is in the midst of one now.

But Tocqueville, perhaps inconsistently, also fears the withering away of human passion through the mistaken judgment of individualism. He also fears the coming of soft despotism of equally will-less dependents who no long care about securing their own futures. Sometimes Tocqueville seems to agree with the Christian psychology of Pascal: Our restlessness—our longing for our true home somewhere else—cannot be extinguished through any form of social or political reform. Sometimes he seems to agree with the modern philosophers such as Rousseau, Hegel, and Marx: Our restlessness is not natural but historical, and so it will come to an end when history comes to end. Distinctively human existence—historical existence—will be brought to its culmination through democratic political reform that definitively satisfies or eradicates our human desires.

One part of Tocqueville's distinctive genius is his awareness that Pascal's psychology describes the same human restlessness as Rousseau's history, and he seems to have waffled a bit about whether Pascal or Rousseau was right about the human future. For Pascal, the good news is that we cannot help but remain human, and the bad news is that if we continue to deny our soul-based needs, we cannot help but make ourselves more miserable. For Rousseau, the bad news is that we accidentally made ourselves miserable through our historical efforts, but the good news is that we can, through our own efforts, undo what we have done. Maybe we can return ourselves to our natural or subhuman condition of unconscious enjoyment devoid of any impetus toward self-transcendence or historical transformation. Only on the basis of Rousseau can we speak of a posthuman or subhuman future or a biotechnological brave new world or an end of history. For Pascal, each of us cannot help but remain human in this world and soon enough in another. For Pascal, the main effect of

[31]Tocqueville writes "it was necessary that Jesus Christ come to earth to make it understood that all members of the human species are naturally alike and equal." And that's because "The most profound and vast geniuses of Rome and Greece were never able to arrive at [that] idea" (*Democracy in America*, 2, 1, 3).

PRIMARY SOURCE 11.8

Why Some Americans Manifest a Sort of Fanatical Spiritualism, from *Democracy in America*, Volume II, Part II, Chapter 12

Although the desire of acquiring the good things of this world is the prevailing passion of the American people, certain momentary outbreaks occur when their souls seem suddenly to burst the bonds of matter by which they are restrained and to soar impetuously toward heaven. In all the states of the Union, but especially in the half-peopled country of the Far West, itinerant preachers may be met with who hawk about the word of God from place to place. Whole families, old men, women, and children, cross rough passes and untrodden wilds, coming from a great distance, to join a camp meeting, where, in listening to these discourses, they totally forget for several days and nights the cares of business and even the most urgent wants of the body.

Here and there in the midst of American society you meet with men full of a fanatical and almost wild spiritualism, which hardly exists in Europe. From time to time strange sects arise which endeavor to strike out extraordinary paths to eternal happiness. Religious insanity is very common in the United States.

Nor ought these facts surprise us. It was not man who implanted in himself the taste for what is infinite and the love of what is immortal; these lofty instincts are not the offspring of his capricious will; their steadfast foundation is fixed in human nature, and they exist in spite of his efforts. He may cross and distort them; destroy them he cannot.

The soul has wants which must be satisfied; and whatever pains are taken to divert it from itself, it soon grows weary, restless, and disquieted amid the enjoyments of sense. If ever the faculties of the great majority of mankind were exclusively bent upon the pursuit of material objects, it might be anticipated that an amazing reaction would take place in the souls of some men. They would drift at large in the world of spirits, for fear of remaining shackled by the close bondage of the body.

our egalitarian political reform and technological transformations will be to make us more anxious and restless than ever.

Tocqueville seems closest to Rousseau and Marx when he muses that excessive restlessness—extreme manifestations of the experiences of being an isolated and disoriented individual—might be the cause of extreme passivity or our surrender of our human individuality. For Marx, the revolution that brings history to an end will be against the very idea of the individual. And that is because the pride and love that sustained individuality will be revealed by modern historical progress to be nothing but oppressive illusions.

But for Tocqueville, pride and love are not, in fact, anything near complete illusions, so it may be possible to sustain them artfully and against the grain in a largely democratic context. Tocqueville, finally, has the same aristocratic objection to both Pascal and Rousseau (and Marx): Being distinctively human is more than being distinctively miserable, and he thought the socialists and the Christians disparaged the human world we actually experience by not seeing and appreciating the distinctions that constitute vigorous political life. Created human nature, understood in its properly political context, is more good than not. The American combat against individualism is, most deeply, on behalf of the middle-class truth about the creature. To be middle-class, properly understood, is to be political; only the being who exists between the other animals and the angels or God is capable of the greatness that accompanies a genuinely political life.

PRIMARY SOURCE 11.9 | SORT OF DESPOTISM DEMOCRATIC NATIONS HAVE TO FEAR, FROM *DEMOCRACY IN AMERICA*, VOLUME II, PART IV, CHAPTER 6

A more accurate examination of the subject, and five years of further meditation, have not diminished my fears, but have changed their object...

It would seem that if despotism were to be established among the democratic nations of our days, it might assume a different character [than that of the ancient world under the Roman emperors]; it would be more extensive and more mild; it would degrade men without tormenting them. I do not question that, in an age of instruction and equality like our own, sovereigns might more easily succeed in collecting all political power into their own hands and might interfere more habitually and decidedly with the circle of private interests than any sovereign of antiquity could ever do. But this same principle of equality which facilitates despotism tempers its rigor. We have seen how the customs of society become more humane and gentle in proportion as men become more equal and alike. When no member of the community has much power or much wealth, tyranny is, as it were, without opportunities and a field of action. As all fortunes are scanty, the passions of men are naturally circumscribed, their imagination limited, their pleasures simple. This universal moderation moderates the sovereign himself and checks within certain limits the inordinate stretch of his desires.

Independently of these reasons, drawn from the nature of the state of society itself, I might add many others arising from causes beyond my subject; but I shall keep within the limits I have laid down.

Democratic governments may become violent and even cruel at certain periods of extreme effervescence or of great danger, but these crises will be rare and brief. When I consider the petty passions of our contemporaries, the mildness of their manners, the extent of their education, the purity of their religion, the gentleness of their morality, their regular and industrious habits, and the restraint which they almost all observe in their vices no less than in their virtues, I have no fear that they will meet with tyrants in their rulers, but rather with guardians.

I think, then, that the species of oppression by which democratic nations are menaced is unlike anything that ever before existed in the world; our contemporaries will find no prototype of it in their memories. I seek in vain for an expression that will accurately convey the whole of the idea I have formed of it; the old words despotism and tyranny are inappropriate: the thing itself is new, and since I cannot name, I must attempt to define it.

I seek to trace the novel features under which despotism may appear in the world. The first thing that strikes the observation is an innumerable multitude of men, all equal and alike, incessantly endeavoring to procure the petty and paltry pleasures with which they glut their lives. Each of them, living apart, is as a stranger to the fate of all the rest; his children and his private friends constitute to him the whole of mankind. As for the rest of his fellow citizens, he is close to them, but he does not see them; he touches them, but he does not feel them; he exists only in himself and for himself alone; and if his kindred still remain to him, he may be said at any rate to have lost his country.

Above this race of men stands an immense and tutelary power, which takes upon itself alone to secure their gratifications and to watch over their fate. That power is absolute, minute, regular, provident, and mild. It would be like the authority of a parent if, like that authority, its object was to prepare men for manhood; but it seeks, on the contrary, to keep them in perpetual childhood: it is well content that the people should rejoice, provided they think of nothing but rejoicing. For their happiness such a government willingly labors, but it chooses to be the sole agent and the only arbiter of that happiness; it provides for their security, foresees and supplies their necessities, facilitates their pleasures, manages their principal concerns, directs their industry,

continued

PRIMARY SOURCE 11.9

Sort of Despotism Democratic Nations Have to Fear, from *Democracy in America*, Volume II, Part IV, Chapter 6 *continued*

regulates the descent of property, and subdivides their inheritances: what remains, but to spare them all the care of thinking and all the trouble of living?

Thus it every day renders the exercise of the free agency of man less useful and less frequent; it circumscribes the will within a narrower range and gradually robs a man of all the uses of himself. The principle of equality has prepared men for these things; it has predisposed men to endure them and often to look on them as benefits. . . .

Key Terms

political liberty
Blaise Pascal
ancient democracy
modern democracy
tyranny of the majority
primogeniture
middle class
benign despotism
public opinion
Americans are Cartesians
individualism
compassion
free institutions
interest rightly understood
art of association
the family and religion
superiority of American women
mores
pantheism

Sources and Resources

Key Texts

Democracy in America
The Old Regime and the Revolution

Secondary Texts

Bellah, Robert N., Richard Madsen, William M. Sullivan, Ann Swidler, and Steven M. Tipton. *Habits of the Heart: Individualism and Commitment in American Life* (Berkeley: University of California Press, 1985).

Frohnen, Bruce. *Virtue and the Promise of Conservatism: The Legacy of Burke and Tocqueville* (Lawrence: University Press of Kansas, 1993).

Kessler, Sanford. *Tocqueville's Civil Religion* (Albany: State University of New York Press, 1994).

Lawler, Peter Augustine. *The Restless Mind* (Lanham, MD: Rowman and Littlefield, 1993).

Tocqueville, Alexis de. *Democracy in America*, trans. Harvey C. Mansfield and Delba Winthrop (Chicago: University of Chicago Press, 2000).

Web Sites

Notes on Tocqueville and *Democracy in America* online at www.gradesaver.com/classicnotes/authors/about_alexis_tocqueville.html

Free, full-text works by Tocqueville online at www.gutenberg.org/browse/authors/t#a424

In search of Tocqueville's *Democracy in America* online at www.tocqueville.org/

Karl Marx

CHAPTER 12

By Ethan Fishman *University of South Alabama*

LIFE

Rarely has a political philosopher had as much practical influence on world affairs as Karl Marx. It is no exaggeration to say that Marxism swept like a tsunami over 20th-century politics. During that time the domestic and foreign policies of virtually every government on earth were affected profoundly by Marxism—both in support of and in opposition to his ideas.

Marx was born on May 5, 1818, in Trier, a part of the German Rhineland ceded to Prussia by the Congress of Vienna in 1815. His parents, whose ancestors included numerous Jewish scholars and rabbis, were converts to the Lutheran faith. The conversion represented an attempt by the family to overcome the obstacles to its socioeconomic ambitions posed by German anti-Semitism. In 1835, Marx left Trier for the University of Bonn. A year later he transferred to the University of Berlin, where he became immersed in urban life and the philosophical system, Hegelianism, from which his own thought evolved.

According to **Georg Hegel** (1770–1831), the chronology of human events progresses dialectically through periods of stability and violent change motivated by the relationship of each epoch to a metaphysical force that he called the underlying idea or spirit of history. Hegel used the term *dialectic* to mean a conflict between opposites. In Berlin Marx was part of a group of theorists, known as the **Young Hegelians,** that antagonized powerful supporters of the status quo by claiming the time had come to challenge the Prussian absolutism of King Frederick William III.

At the University of Berlin, Marx first majored in law but soon changed to philosophy. After earning a doctorate in 1841 he became the editor of the *Rheinische Zeitung,* a journal dedicated to revealing how Prussian authorities systematically oppressed Rhineland peasants. Two years later the journal was shut down by the government it had been denouncing.

To escape Prussian repression, Marx next traveled to Paris, where he began work on a series of essays that became known as *The Economic and Philosophic Manuscripts of 1844.* Under the influence of the philosopher **Ludwig Feuerbach** (1804–1872), these early writings seem to reveal a deep humanistic concern about alienation, an appreciation of free will, and a belief in the potential for human divinity that, for the most part, tend to be absent in Marx's mature work. Many scholars have argued that Marx later seems to have adopted a more deterministic approach that treats human relationships as products of environmental forces over which people have little or no real control.

In 1843 Marx married Jenny von Westphalen, the daughter of a relatively prominent Prussian government official from his home town of Trier. The Westphalen family did not approve of the match. Soon thereafter he established a friendship with **Friedrich Engels** (1820–1895), the son of a wealthy textile manufacturer and a like-minded exponent of radical political causes. For the rest of his life Marx found in these two people the emotional, financial, and intellectual support he needed to pursue his scholarship.

While in Paris, Marx continued to work as a journalist and editor of the *Deutsch-Franzoesische Jahrbuecher.* The radical quality of his work got him into trouble with the authorities once again and eventually led to his expulsion from France. Settling next in Brussels, he joined a group of German émigrés, calling themselves the

Communist League (formerly the League of the Just), who were attempting to organize a clandestine working-class revolutionary movement. Marx wrote the *Communist Manifesto of 1848* to explain the differences between the league's brand of socialism and rival approaches espoused by such theorists as Henri Comte de Saint-Simon (1760–1825), Charles Fourier (1772–1837), Robert Owen (1771–1858), Michael Bakunin (1814–1876), and Pierre Joseph Proudhon (1809–1865).

Marx's *Manifesto* ends with these famous words: "Let the ruling classes tremble at a Communist revolution. The proletarians have nothing to lose but their chains. They have a world to win. Working men of all countries, unite!" (Tucker 1978, 500). For a while in 1848 it appeared that his words would prove instantly prophetic. From the revolt against the so-called July Monarchy of Louis Philippe, who had ruled France since 1830, to similar uprisings in Italy, Germany, and elsewhere, open class warfare gained momentum throughout Europe. Before long, however, opponents of radical reform returned to power, and the hopes of Marx and his fellow socialists were dashed.

As an explicit call for working-class revolution, the *Manifesto* also represents Marx's insistence on the unity of theory and what he calls ***praxis*** or practice. Traditional Western political philosophers celebrate the life of the mind. Thinkers such as Aristotle profess to love knowledge for the sake of knowledge, not for some utilitarian purpose. They also seek to communicate primarily to other theorists. In contrast, Marx's goal is to stimulate action by communicating his ideas to the widest audience possible of intellectuals and workers alike. As he wrote in his 1845 *Theses on Feuerbach,* "The philosophers have only *interpreted* the world, in various ways; the point, however, is to change it" (145; all italics in this essay are the author's own).

In 1849, again in flight from the forces of reaction on the continent, Marx moved with his family to London. There he initially lived in such abject poverty that three of his children died from lack of food and medical care. What little money he had came in the form of stipends from Engels and other friends and from his work as a foreign correspondent for the *New York Daily Tribune,* a newspaper founded by American socialists and edited by the noted journalist Horace Greeley (1811–1872).

Much of Marx's time in London was spent alone in the reading room of the British Museum studying the economic treatises and statistical data that served as background material for his most important work, *Capital.* He also concentrated on organizing the International Workingmen's Association, a group dedicated to overthrowing feudal and capitalist regimes around the globe. Members of the International played a role in the 1871 **Paris Commune,** a radical faction that controlled Paris for a brief period after the defeat of France in the Franco–Prussian War. Government persecution caused the demise of the International in 1876.

Another factor that splintered the organization was Marx's notoriously caustic and intolerant personality. He was willing to neither compromise nor suffer fools. Of course Marx felt that anyone who disagreed with him was a fool. Because he considered the truth of his arguments to be self-evident, he never bothered to master the powers of personal persuasion. According to one of his contemporaries, "Marx belonged to the type of men who are all energy, a force of will and unshakeable conviction. With a thick black mop of hair on his head, with hairy hands and a crookedly buttoned frock coat, he had the air of a man used to commanding the respect of others. His movements were clumsy but self-assured. His manners defied the

QUESTIONS FOR REFLECTION

What did Marx mean by *praxis?*

accepted conventions of social intercourse and were haughty and almost contemptuous. His voice was disagreeably harsh, and he spoke of men and things in the tone of one who would tolerate no contradiction, and which seemed to express his own firm conviction in his mission to sway men's minds and dictate the laws of their being" (Berlin 1963, 106–107).

By the time he died in London in 1883, Marx was reputed to be the world's preeminent spokesman for revolutionary socialism. Finally, through the power of his prose and originality of his theories, he gained the fame and financial independence that had long eluded him. At Marx's funeral Engels summed up his friend's life and work. His mission "was to contribute in one way or another to the overthrow of capitalist society," Engels said:

> Fighting was his element. And he fought with a passion, a tenacity and a success which few could rival....(H)e died, beloved, revered and mourned by millions of revolutionary fellow workers—from the mines of Siberia to the coasts of California, in all points of Europe and America....His name will endure through the ages, and so also will his work. (Tucker 1978, 682)

THOUGHT

HISTORICAL MATERIALISM

At the heart of Marx's political philosophy, which Engels eulogized and helped to develop, lies his theory of **historical materialism.** From Hegel, Marx learned that history follows a meaningful pattern of progress and is not simply a process of only tangentially related events. Whereas Hegel considers this pattern to be abstract and metaphysical, Marx searches for it in the most concrete material aspects of human existence: production of the basic means to support life itself. After all, Marx argues, before human beings can engage in imaginative thought, they must first discover ways to feed, clothe, and house themselves. According to Marx, therefore, the manner in which people work to secure the means for survival provides the underlying connecting thread of history.

Marx also borrowed from Hegel the mechanism by which history progresses. Marx thus teaches that history proceeds **dialectically**—that is, through successive changes marked by periods of stability (referred to by Hegel as the *thesis*), violent upheaval (the *antithesis*), and a return to stability defined by the changes recently generated by violence (the *synthesis*). This synthesis becomes a new thesis that generates a new antithesis, and so on. The point, for both Hegel and Marx, is that life will continue to get better for human beings as history progresses. For Hegel, history progresses dialectically as a conflict of ideas. For Marx, history progresses as a conflict between economic classes. Despite this difference, they both expected that people will conquer nature and master time—either through a clearer understanding

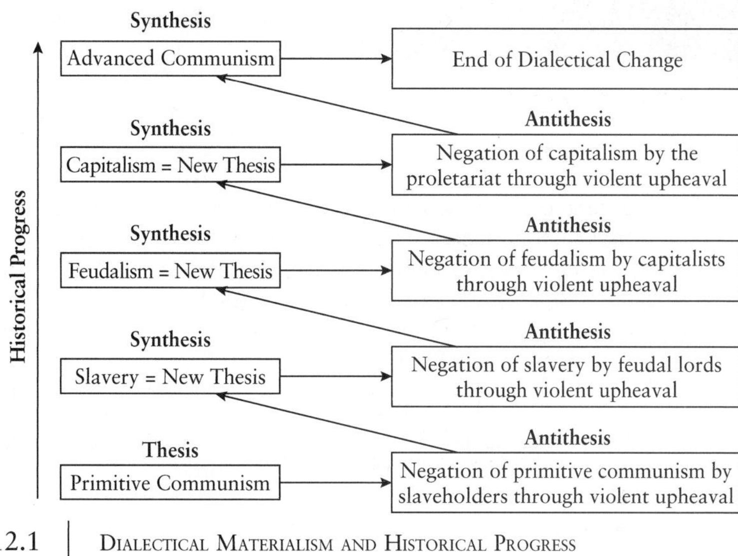

FIGURE 12.1 | DIALECTICAL MATERIALISM AND HISTORICAL PROGRESS

of the guiding idea or spirit of history, for Hegel, or through the invention of more economically effective and equitable ways to survive, for Marx (Figure 12.1).

For all his explicit reliance on Hegel's thought, Marx makes clear in his writings that he considers Hegel's references to immaterial ideals—such as justice, love, and honor—to be silly romantic notions upon which no sure knowledge ever can be based. Scholars disagree over how to interpret Marx's rejection of Hegelian metaphysics. Some count him among those social scientists who, in their dismissal of phenomena inaccessible to the senses, are led to conclude that material factors (such as socioeconomic status) are the sole determinants of human behavior. Others prefer to view Marx as a humanist who considers free will an essential part of human nature. From the humanist perspective, Marx's greatest achievement is his ability to reach up into the cosmos and bring Hegel's ideals down to earth for the sake of human autonomy and freedom.

In his *German Ideology,* written in 1845–1846, Marx tries to explain what he means by the **"materialist conception of history"** and how it differs from the theories of other Germans, including Hegel (See Primary Source 12.1).

In his *Socialism: Utopian and Scientific,* written in 1880, Engels, who contributed greatly to the development of Marxism, adds the following observations:

> The materialist conception of history starts from the proposition that the production of the means to support human life and, next to production, the exchange of things produced, is the basis of all social structure; that in every society that has appeared in history, the manner in which wealth is distributed and society divided into classes or orders is dependent upon what is produced, how it is produced, and how the products are exchanged. From this point of view the final causes of all social changes and political revolutions are to be sought, not in men's brains, not in men's better insight into eternal truth and justice, but in changes in the modes of production and exchange. They are to be sought not in *philosophy,* but in the *economics* of each particular epoch. (700–701)

PRIMARY SOURCE 12.1 | The Materialist Conception of History, from *German Ideology*

Since we are dealing with the Germans, who are devoid of premises, we must begin by stating the first premise of all existence and, therefore, of all history, the premise, namely, that men must be in a position to live in order to be able to make history. But life involves before everything else eating and drinking, a habitation, clothing and many other things. The first historical act is thus the production of the means to satisfy these needs, the production of material life itself. And indeed this is an historical act, a fundamental condition of all history, which, today, as thousands of years ago, must daily and hourly be fulfilled merely in order to sustain human life. Even when the sensuous world is reduced to a minimum, to a stick as with Saint Bruno, it presupposes the action of producing the stick. Therefore in any interpretation of history one has first of all to observe this fundamental fact in all its significance and all its implications and to accord it its due importance. It is well known that the Germans have never done this, and they have never, therefore, had an *earthly* basis for history and consequently never a historian. (155–156)

Marx offers historical materialism to explain not only the entire scope of human history but the qualities of particular epochs as well. He thus argues that legal, intellectual, political, social, religious, and cultural institutions—in other words, everything going on in a culture other than economics—are defined by the economic conditions that exist in that culture at any particular time. To Marx, economic conditions are composed of the forces and relations of production.

The term **forces of production** refers to the technology that people utilize to create the physical necessities of life. Some examples of technology are fire, wheels, fulcrums, assembly lines, computers, and robots. The term **relations of production** refers to the division of people into economic classes based on the function they perform in the production process. Slavery, feudalism, capitalism, and socialism constitute different relations of production. For Marx, the connection between economic classes is by definition manipulative. It always involves the subjugation of one class by another. As long as economic classes exist, he stipulates, the majority will always work and be exploited and the dominant class will always reap the profits.

During a specific period of history, Marx maintains, the forces and relations of production, which together make up what he calls the **substructure** of society, will complement each other and bring about a thesis. Ultimately, however, contradictions between the forces and relations of production will begin to surface, resulting in an antithesis that in turn will change existing political, social, and cultural institutions. Marx refers to these institutions as the **superstructure** of society, whose underlying purpose is to support the economic interests of the dominant class. He argues, moreover, that the changes moving society from its antithesis to synthesis stages necessarily involve violent forms of class conflict. To Marx, in summary, a society's superstructure at every point in its history is defined by its substructure (Figure 12.2).

Consider the following fictional scenario. A clan of prehistoric humans lives in a cave. During a terrible thunderstorm a huge boulder falls into the mouth of the cave, trapping the clan. Due to primitive forces of production or technology, in order to save themselves from certain doom, everyone must participate in moving the

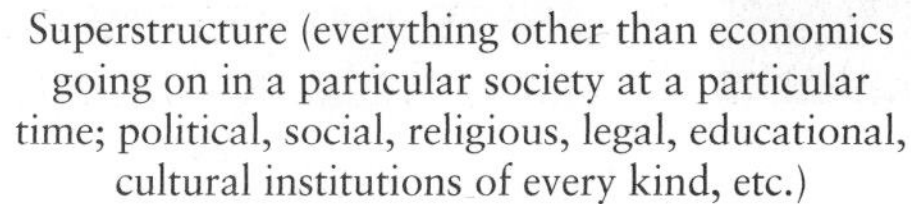

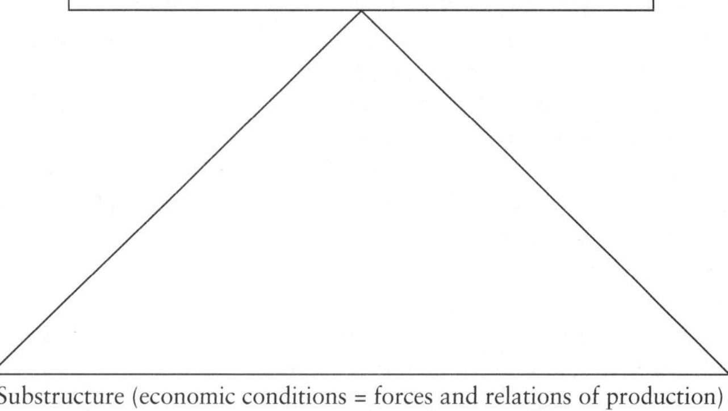

FIGURE 12.2

boulder. In other words, corresponding to the crude technological methods of the time are relations of production that require total cooperation within the clan community.

At a later date someone invents the fulcrum, claims its ownership, and seeks to withhold its use from fellow clan members unless they agree to work for him. A violent struggle between the owner and his fellows ensues. In the process a class structure, characterized by division of labor and private ownership, arises to both supplant the former cooperative relations of production and complement the new level of technology. This class structure will persist until technology advances again.

Marx's theory that economic conditions constitute the definitive feature of history is complicated by what he means by the word *define.* Those who prefer to view Marx as a humanist champion of free will read *define* to mean *influence,* as in economic conditions influence everything else that goes on in a particular society at a particular time. Economic conditions may be the primary cause of human behavior, the humanists maintain, but human beings also have some choice in how they live.

Those who interpret Marx as a social scientist read *define* to mean *determine,* as in economic conditions constitute the only true causal factors in history. This interpretation equates human beings with other living things that lack free will and are slaves to their environment. Just as environmental stimuli cause bears to hibernate during the winter, economic conditions determine human behavior. Among those who view Marx as a social scientist are totalitarian communist regimes and their apologists. Not surprisingly, these people would like the world to believe that totalitarian oppression—when practiced by communist dictators—represents the natural outcome of objective historical forces, not the invention of fallible human beings with their own agendas.

In a much-quoted passage from *A Contribution to the Critique of Political Economy,* written in 1859, Marx takes the deterministic route (See Primary Source 12.2).

PRIMARY SOURCE 12.2

MARX AND DETERMINISM, FROM *A CONTRIBUTION TO THE CRITIQUE OF POLITICAL ECONOMY*

The general result at which I arrived and which, once won, served as the guiding thread for my studies, can be briefly formulated as follows: In the social production of their life, men enter into definite relations that are indispensable and independent of their will, relations of production which correspond to a definite stage of development of their material productive forces. The sum total of these relations of production constitutes the economic structure of society, the real foundation, on which rises a legal and political superstructure and to which correspond definite forms of social consciousness. The mode of production of material life conditions the social, political and intellectual life process in general. It is not the consciousness of men that determines their being, but, on the contrary, their social being that determines their consciousness. At a certain stage of their development, the material productive forces of society come in conflict with the existing relations of production, or—what is but a legal expression for the same thing—with the property relations within which they have been at work hitherto. From forms of development of the productive forces these relations turn into their fetters. Then begins an epoch of social revolution. With the change of the economic foundation the entire immense superstructure is more or less rapidly transformed. In considering such transformations a distinction should always be made between the material transformation of the economic conditions of production, which can be determined with the precision of natural science, and the legal, political, religious, aesthetic or philosophic—in short, ideological forms in which men become conscious of this conflict and fight it out. Just as our opinion of an individual is not based on what he thinks of himself, so can we not judge such a period of transformation by its own consciousness; on the contrary, this consciousness must be explained rather from the contradictions of material life, from the existing conflict between the social productive forces and the relations of production. No social order ever perishes before all the productive forces for which there is room in it have developed; and new, higher relations of production never appear before the material conditions of their existence have matured in the womb of the old society itself. Therefore, mankind always sets itself only such tasks as it can solve; since, looking at the matter more closely, it will always be found that the task itself arises only when the material conditions for its solution already exist or are at least in the process of formation. In broad outlines Asiatic, ancient, feudal, and modern bourgeois modes of production can be designated as progressive epochs in the economic formation of society. The bourgeois relations of production are the last antagonistic form of the social process of production—antagonistic not in the sense of individual antagonism, but of one arising from the social conditions of life of the individuals; at the same time the productive forces developing in the womb of bourgeois society create the material conditions for the solution of that antagonism. This social formation brings, therefore, the prehistory of human society to a close. (4–5)

Yet some 30 years later, Engels contradicted his friend's definition in a letter he wrote to a Dr. Bloch:

> According to the materialist conception of history, the *ultimately* determining element in history is the production and reproduction of real life. More than this neither Marx nor I have ever asserted. Hence if somebody twists this into saying that the economic element is the *only* determining one, he transforms that proposition into a meaningless, abstract, senseless phrase. The economic situation is the basis, but the various elements of the superstructure: political forms of the class struggle and its results, to wit: constitutions established by the victorious class after a successful battle, etc., juridical forms, and then even the reflexes of all these actual struggles in the brains of the

QUESTIONS FOR REFLECTION

Would you describe Marx as a humanist or a determinist? Why?

participants, political, juristic, philosophical theories, religious views and their further development into systems of dogmas, also exercise their influence upon the course of the historical struggles and in many cases preponderate in determining their *form.* There is an interaction of all these elements in which, amid all the endless host of accidents (that is, of things and events, whose inner connection is so remote or so impossible of proof that we can regard it as nonexistent, as negligible) the economic movement finally asserts itself as necessary. (760–761)

Marxist Anthropology

In addition to borrowing from Hegel, Marxian scholarship also owes a debt to the research of **Lewis Morgan** (1818–1881), known as the father of American **anthropology.** In the 19th century, Morgan concluded that the first human beings lived in societies where there was no private property and everyone worked cooperatively on every task to meet the demands of the common good. To Marx, the societies Morgan identified are examples of **primitive communism.** The subsequent development of new tools, Marx maintains, made it possible for people to do their work more effectively to the point where not every person was required to complete every job. This division of labor, Marx argues, permitted a few to gain control over the means of production and left the vast majority to perform the manual labor. As a result a system of slavery arose to supplant primitive communism. When more complex technology was invented, he contends, slavery gave way to feudalism.

In Marx's own day capitalism had replaced feudalism and two new classes emerged: the **bourgeoisie,** who own the industries; and the **proletariat,** who work in them. Marx describes the relationship between the bourgeoisie and the proletariat as a form of wage slavery. He predicts that as the bourgeoisie continue to enrich themselves, the proletariat will continue to get poorer and poorer. Unemployment and economic crises will multiply. The proletariat will unite and become more militant. Eventually, a revolution will break out with the workers achieving total victory.

By Marx's estimation a period of **advanced communism** will then come into existence. A final equilibrium between the forces and relations of production will be achieved, resulting in the cessation of dialectical change. This period bears a marked resemblance to that of primitive communism. There will be no private property, no class structure, no division of labor, no exploitation, and neither rich people nor poor. The critical difference between the two periods has to do with levels of technology. Earlier, equality prevailed because everyone had to work cooperatively all the time. During advanced communism, according to Marx, equality will again prevail because machines will do all the work and everyone will own all the machines.

Marx argues that the period of advanced communism also will be characterized by the appearance of a "really human morality which stands above class antagonisms" (727). Marx denies the existence of universal moral truths such as "Thou shalt not steal." He considers ethical codes a relative part of a society's superstructure, invented by the powerful, who own considerable amounts of property, to subvert the weak,

PRIMARY SOURCE 12.3 | ENGELS, *ANTI-DUHRING*, 1878

From the moment when private ownership of movable property developed, all societies in which this private ownership existed had to have this moral injunction in common: Thou shalt not steal. Does this injunction thereby become an eternal moral injunction? By no means. In a society in which all motives for stealing have been done away with, in which therefore at the very most only lunatics would ever steal, how the preacher of morals would be laughed at who tried solemnly to proclaim the eternal truth: Thou shalt not steal!

We therefore reject every attempt to impose on us any moral dogma whatsoever as an eternal, ultimate and forever immutable ethical law on the pretext that the moral world, too, has its permanent principles which stand above history and the differences between nations. We maintain on the contrary that all moral theories have been hitherto the product, in the last analysis, of the economic conditions of society obtaining at the time. And as society has hitherto moved in class antagonisms, morality has always been class morality; it has either justified the domination and the interests of the ruling class, or, ever since the oppressed class became powerful enough, it has represented its indignation against this domination and the future interests of the oppressed. That in this process there has on the whole been progress in morality, as in all other branches of human knowledge, no one will doubt. A really human morality which stands above class antagonisms and above any recollection of them becomes possible only at a stage of society which has not only overcome class antagonisms but has even forgotten them in practical life. (726–727)

who might be tempted to steal it. Once a society's economic substructure is transformed into an authentically level playing field, he concludes, morality will become authentically respectful, tolerant, gentle, and kind in return. As Engels explains in his *Anti-Duhring,* written in 1878.

With this authentic equality, Marx argues, also will come the demise of government, religion, and the traditional family. Marx considers the belief in universal moral codes, government, religion, and the traditional family to be part of an ideological **"false consciousness,"** promulgated by the dominant class to justify the inferior status of the subordinate class in society. During the period of advanced communism when "there is no longer any social class to be held in subjection," Engels thus explains in his *Socialism: Utopian and Scientific,* "the government of persons is replaced by the administration of things" (713). Religion will no longer be necessary because, to Marx, its purpose is to drug or stupefy the subordinate class into passively accepting injustice on earth in favor of a perfect life after death in heaven. In his *Contribution to the Critique of Hegel's "Philosophy of Right,"* published in 1844, Marx thus referred to religion as "**the opium of the masses**" (54). And the traditional monogamous family will disappear because its hierarchical structure relegates children, and especially women, to an inferior status. According to Engels in *The Origin of the Family, Private Property, and the State,* written in 1884,

> We are now approaching a social evolution in which the hitherto existing economic foundations of monogamy will disappear just as certainly as will those of its supplement—prostitution. Monogamy arose out of the concentration of considerable wealth in the hands of one person—and that a man—and out of the desire to bequeath this wealth to this man's children and to no one else's. For this purpose monogamy was essential on the women's part....

QUESTIONS FOR REFLECTION

Was Marx mistaken in not calling for a strict political accountability of the political leadership to the rank-and-file proletariat?

> With the passage of the means of production into common property, the individual family ceases to be the economic unit of society. Private housekeeping is transformed into a social industry. The care and education of the children becomes a public matter. Society takes care of all children equally, irrespective of whether they are born in wedlock or not. (745–746)

During the period of advanced communism, in short, people will have all they could ever want. "In a higher phase of communist society," Marx writes in his *Critique of the Gotha Program,* published in 1891, "after the productive forces have also increased with the all-around development of the individual, and all the springs of cooperative wealth flow more abundantly—only then can the narrow horizon of bourgeois right be crossed in its entirety and society inscribe on its banner: From each according to his ability, to each according to his needs!" (531)

To facilitate the transition from the time of the workers' revolution to the period of advanced communism, Marx calls for an interim period of history known as the **dictatorship of the proletariat.** Although he leaves out the details of exactly how it would operate, Marx intends that this interim period will serve both to prepare workers emotionally for the radical new world of equality to come and to provide them with an enormously powerful political apparatus to physically force the bourgeoisie to surrender the last vestiges of their economic hegemony. Among the details that Marx disregards is when the violence and political repression associated with the dictatorship of the proletariat will run their course. As further analysis will reveal, these omissions were to have serious consequences for the development of Marxist thought after the death of Marx and Engels, as well as for the emergence of totalitarian communist regimes around the world in the 20th century.

Marx considered himself a socialist. While all socialists seek the same end of complete social, political, and economic equality, they disagree on the means to that end. For example, democratic socialists, such as the English Labor Party, believe they can achieve complete equality through the electoral process. What distinguishes Marxism from other types of socialism is the argument that significant change can come about only through violent revolution. Socialists who think that authentic equality can be achieved through peaceful, evolutionary means, Marx insists, are nothing less than delusional. To his mind, the bourgeoisie can never be persuaded to relinquish property and power voluntarily. For that reason he derides those he calls **utopian socialists** for what he considers their unmitigated naivete.

Theory of Alienation

Another aspect of Hegelianism that Marx adapts to suit his own materialistic orientation is Hegel's **theory of alienation.** According to Marx, when people are born the universe appears to them as a hostile and alien place. This insecurity derives

QUESTIONS FOR REFLECTION

What did Marx think of democratic socialists such as the Labor Party in England?

from the fear that what goes on in the cosmos may be beyond our control. To avoid feeling continually like strangers in a strange land, he observes, it becomes necessary to discover a way to appropriate the universe and become its master. Hegel maintains that the most effective method for appropriating the universe is to conquer it through mental concepts. By thinking about the universe, in other words, we can make it our mental property and achieve the peace of mind we so desperately desire.

For Marx, on the other hand, the correct means by which human beings can gain control of their lives and the universe is by working creatively to produce the necessary ingredients for survival. All living things act instinctively to survive. Marx recognizes that, for humans alone, imagination also is involved. Indeed, his fundamental criticism of class structure and division of labor is that they negate the opportunity for creativity and exacerbate human estrangement. He considers capitalism much worse than slavery and feudalism in that regard.

Marx's position is that capitalism combats creative labor in three significant ways. First, by separating the proletariat from their finished products, the capitalist assembly-line production technique robs them of a sense of pride in their work. "Owing to the extensive use of machinery and to division of labor, the proletarians have lost all individual character, and consequently, all charm for the workman. He becomes an appendage of the machine, and it is only the most simple, most monotonous, and most easily acquired knack, that is required of him," Marx writes in the *Communist Manifesto* (479). Second, the spirit of avaricious competition that capitalism engenders pits workers against each other and creates a work environment that stifles innovation and emphasizes quantity over quality, thereby reducing humans to the level of plants and animals. Third, capitalism degrades labor by encouraging the bourgeoisie to profit enormously from the work of the proletariat while permitting them only a subsistence wage. For Marx, indeed, the caliber of life for workers reaches its lowest level during the capitalist stage of history. At that point, the proletariat become estranged not only from themselves, but from their fellow workers and the productive process as well.

For all his criticism of capitalism, the irony is that Marx does not consider it an immoral system. This point of view is a function of his moral relativism: the belief that morality is defined by economic conditions and that, as these conditions change, ethical codes must change as well. Marx actually expresses gratitude toward capitalism for making advanced communism possible. By the terms of his theory of dialectical change, without slavery there could be no feudalism; without feudalism there could be no capitalism; and without capitalism there could be no advanced communism. Of course, for Marx, once the communist revolution occurs and the dictatorship of the proletariat ends, alienation will no longer be a problem for human beings. Machines will do all the boring work, and people will occupy their time in fully satisfying occupations. Perfection finally will be achieved on earth. Human beings finally will become "the real, conscious lord(s) of Nature."

PRIMARY SOURCE 12.4

THE ALIENATION OF LABOR, FROM *ECONOMIC AND PHILOSOPHIC MANUSCRIPTS*

What, then, constitutes the alienation of labor?

First, the fact that labor is *external* to the worker, i.e., it does not belong to his essential being; that in his work, therefore, he does not affirm himself but denies himself, does not feel content but unhappy, does not develop freely his physical and mental energy but mortifies his body and ruins his mind. The worker therefore only feels himself outside his work, and in his work feels outside himself. He is at home when he is not working, and when he is working he is not at home. His labor is therefore not voluntary, but coerced; it is *forced labor*. It is therefore not the satisfaction of a need; it is merely a *means* to satisfy needs external to it. Its alien character emerges clearly in the fact that as soon as no physical or other compulsion exists, labor is shunned like the plague. External labor, labor in which man alienates himself, is a labor of self-sacrifice, of mortification. Lastly, the external character of labor for the worker appears in the fact that it is not his own, but someone else's, that it does not belong to him, that in it he belongs, not to himself, but to another. . . .

As a result, therefore, man (the worker) no longer feels himself to be freely active in any but his animal functions—eating, drinking, procreating, or at most in his dwelling and in dressing-up, etc.; and in his human functions he no longer feels himself to be anything but an animal. What is animal becomes human and what is human becomes animal. (74)

PRIMARY SOURCE 12.5

ENGELS ON "THE KINGDOM OF FREEDOM," FROM *SOCIALISM: UTOPIAN AND SCIENTIFIC*

With the seizing of the means of production by society, production of commodities is done away with, and, simultaneously, the mastery of the product over the producer. Anarchy in social production is replaced by systematic, definite organization. The struggle for individual existence disappears. Then for the first time man, in a certain sense, is finally marked off from the rest of the animal kingdom, and emerges from mere animal conditions of existence into really human ones. The whole sphere of the conditions of life which environ man, and which have hitherto ruled man, now comes under the dominion and control of man, who for the first time becomes the real, conscious lord of Nature, because he has now become master of his own social organization. The laws of his own social action, hitherto standing face to face with man as laws of Nature foreign to, and dominating him, will then be used with full understanding, and so mastered by him. Man's own social organization, hitherto confronting him as a necessity imposed by Nature and history, now becomes the result of his own free action. The extraneous objective forces that have hitherto governed history pass under the control of man himself. Only from that time will man himself, more and more consciously, make his own history—only from that time will the social causes set in movement by him have, in the main and in a constantly growing measure, the results intended by him. It is the ascent of man from the kingdom of necessity to the kingdom of freedom. (715–716)

QUESTIONS FOR REFLECTION

Do you think that Marx has a realistic view of human nature?

CASE STUDY 12.1 | INDUSTRIAL REFORM

Through its use of the assembly-line technique that breaks the production process into hundreds of mindless tasks, Marx charges, capitalism negates craftsmanship and robs workers of any sense of professional fulfillment. The result is often a listless, apathetic, alienated labor force unconcerned about the quality of the product they are turning out. In the classic silent film *Modern Times,* Charlie Chaplin used his comedic genius to illustrate Marx's criticism of the capitalist work experience. In one unforgettable scene Chaplin plays a factory worker who becomes entangled in some gears and becomes literally a cog in the machine.

After World War II a number of industrial reforms were introduced to address the problem of worker apathy. One such reform sought to replace the assembly line with a team approach. By organizing workers into smaller groups sharing responsibility for the finished product as a whole, it was proposed, they would no longer see themselves as mere nut and bolt fasteners. They would begin to feel as if they had a stake in the company and regain at least some of their lost pride. In the 1950s several privately owned firms in Japan, Scandinavia, and the United States chose to adopt the reformers' proposals. Today they are regarded widely as standard industrial operating procedures.

What would have been Marx's reaction to these strategies? He would consider them superficial at best and deceitful at worst. He would see them as superficial because they are unable to solve the central problem of capitalist alienation: that, despite the stated objectives of the reformers, the commodity produced by the team of workers does not belong to them. He would call them deceitful because the real purpose of the strategies is not to help the proletariat but to multiply profits for the bourgeoisie by improving quality, discouraging absenteeism, and increasing productivity. In the final analysis, Marx would consider these post–World War II industrial reforms to be feeble attempts at delaying the inevitable. There is nothing capitalism can do to prevent the proletarian revolution, he would proclaim proudly. Only with the advent of advanced communism will workers' lives truly improve.

THEORY OF SURPLUS VALUE

Marx incorporates into his political philosophy the **labor theory of value** found in the work of John Locke (1632–1704) and others. The labor theory of value stipulates that a commodity's value or price depends on the number of human labor hours spent producing it. Marx observes that superior capitalist technology enables workers to produce enough value and make enough money in, say, four hours to feed, clothe, and house themselves for a day. Yet their bosses insist on, say, an eight-hour work day. What happens to the value created by the additional four hours of labor? Marx calls the hours exerted by workers, that produce value essential for their survival, **socially necessary labor.** He applies the term **surplus value** to the value produced by workers in excess of socially necessary labor. According to Marx, surplus value is the primary source of exploitation in capitalist societies. It represents, to him, value stolen from the proletariat by the bourgeoisie (Figure 12.3).

8-hour work day

−4 hours of socially necessary labor (wages paid to worker)

4 hours of surplus value or profit and overhead for the bourgeoisie

FIGURE 12.3

QUESTIONS FOR REFLECTION

Can reform of the industrial workplace forestall the proletarian revolution Marx predicts?

Marx's name for the power of human labor to create value is **variable capital.** His name for machinery, buildings, and raw materials is **constant capital.** According to Marx, cutthroat competition between the bourgeoisie will convince them that their businesses will prosper if they replace workers with labor-saving devices. What initially appears as good business sense will eventually backfire because, as he maintains, only human labor can produce value. In Marxian terms, any increase in the proportion of constant to variable capital will result in less profit, not more. He further predicts that as competition continues to grow, more firms will fail, more monopolies will arise, and more former owners will become part of the proletariat.

As the number of workers increases, but the number of jobs decreases (because they have been replaced by machines), Marx maintains, wages will follow the law of supply and demand and continue to fall until people no longer are making enough money even to subsist. Under these truly miserable conditions, the proletariat will have no choice but to organize and rebel. Victory will be ensured by the force of their numbers and the level of their desperation. And because capitalist monopolies previously had centralized ownership of the means of production, Marx argues, the proletariat will find it relatively easy to transfer economic ownership, and the political power that always accompanies it, from private to public hands.

MARXISM AFTER 1883

MARXISM–LENINISM

In the late 19th century Marxism spread to Russia, where bourgeois intellectuals used its theories to defend the peasants against their feudal overlords. Marx had argued that the dialectic proceeds according to a historically sequential pattern that requires capitalism to exist, a proletarian revolution to overthrow it, and a dictatorship of the proletariat to intervene before advanced communism could come into existence. Russian Marxists faced a problem: Their country had not yet progressed past feudalism to a full-blown capitalist economy. It remained for **V.I. Lenin** (1870–1924) to offer a solution to this apparent paradox—a solution that later would serve as the theoretical foundation for the successful Russian Revolution of 1917. Influenced by his comrade in arms **Leon Trotsky** (1877–1940), Lenin taught that it was possible for certain societies to skip the capitalist stage on their march toward advanced communism. These societies, he believed, could experience capitalism "vicariously." But what about the proletariat? Lenin maintained that the peasantry could substitute for the proletariat under certain circumstances. Their discontent, he claimed, also could be utilized to make advanced communism possible.

Another significant revision that Lenin contributed to orthodox Marxist doctrine was his theory of the Communist (formerly Bolshevik) Party as the **vanguard of the proletariat.** Marx had postulated that a transition period, known as the dictatorship of the proletariat, would be necessary between the fall of capitalism and the achievement

PRIMARY SOURCE 12.6 "THE KNELL OF CAPITALIST PRIVATE PROPERTY," FROM *CAPITAL*, 1867

As soon as this process of transformation has sufficiently decomposed the old society from top to bottom, as soon as the laborers are turned into proletarians, their means of labor into capital, as soon as the capitalist mode of production stands on its own feet, then the further socialization of labor and further transformation of the land and other means of production into socially exploited and, therefore, common means of production, as well as the further expropriation of private proprietors, takes a new form. That which is now to be expropriated is no longer the laborer working for himself, but the capitalist exploiting many laborers. This expropriation is accomplished by the action of the immanent laws of capitalistic production itself, by the centralization of capital. One capitalist always kills many. Hand in hand with this centralization, or this expropriation of many capitalists by a few, develop, on an ever-extending scale, the cooperative form of the labor process, the conscious technical application of science, the methodical cultivation of the soil, the transformation of the instruments of labor into instruments only usable in common, the economizing of all means of production by their use as the means of production of combined, socialized labor, the entanglement of all peoples in the net of the world market, and with this, the international character of the capitalistic regime. Along with the constantly diminishing number of the magnates of capital, who usurp and monopolize all advantages of this process of transformation, grows the mass of misery, oppression, slavery, degradation, exploitation; but with this too grows the revolt of the working class, a class always increasing in numbers, and disciplined, united, organized by the very mechanism of the process of capitalist production itself. The monopoly of capital becomes a fetter upon the mode of production, which has sprung up and flourished along with, and under it. Centralization of the means of production and socialization of labor at last reach a point where they become incompatible with their capitalist integument. This integument is burst asunder. The knell of capitalist private property sounds. The expropriators are expropriated. (437–438)

of advanced communism, during which power would be wrested violently from the hands of the bourgeoisie. On the specifics of just what this transition period would entail, however, Marx was vague. Lenin added the detail that it would involve a dictatorship of the Communist Party over the activities of the peasants and the proletariat in addition to the bourgeoisie. Without the stern intervention of the party's professional revolutionaries, he warned, the peasants and proletariat would impede dialectical progress by adopting a "trade union mentality"—that is, by accepting hastily only moderate reforms to their lifestyles instead of waiting patiently for the full equality that history had in store for them.

Lenin thus envisioned the Communist Party as having to forcefully impose a revolutionary consciousness on the Russian people. To execute this role, he argued, it would be necessary for the party to assume the form of a totalitarian government that would be intolerant of dissent and unafraid to utilize methods of terror and

QUESTIONS FOR REFLECTION

Do you agree with Marx that only human labor, and not machines, can produce economic value?

propaganda to enforce its decisions. "We are not Utopians, we do not indulge in 'dreams' of how best to do away *immediately* with all administration, with all subordination," Lenin wrote in his *State andRevolution,* published in 1917; "these Anarchist dreams, based upon a lack of understanding of the task of proletarian dictatorship, are basically foreign to Marxism, and, as a matter of fact, they serve to put off the Socialist revolution until human nature is different. No, we want the Socialist revolution with human nature as it is now, with human nature that cannot do without subordination, control, and 'managers'" (Lenin 1943, 42–43).

When did Lenin think totalitarian oppression would come to an end? Not until the Russian people could "grow accustomed to observing the *elementary conditions* of social existence *without force and without subjection,*" he responded (68). How long would it take the people to make such radical adjustments in their behavior? To that crucial question of dictatorship, Lenin, like Marx before him, had no ready answer. As it turned out, their mutual reluctance or inability to provide specific details about this period proved much more ominous in the case of Lenin. Immediately after taking control of the Soviet Union in 1917, he began initiating the kind of dictatorial control that Marx may have hinted at but that Lenin's thought explicitly endorsed. Among the first institutions he established, indeed, was a secret police force, the infamous Cheka, which brutalized any Russian who dared challenge him.

Under the leadership of **Joseph Stalin** (1879–1953), who came to power after Lenin's death in 1924, Soviet brutality increased exponentially. Untold millions of innocent Russian lives were lost to Stalin's farm collectivization plans, military and government purges, and forced labor camps, known as gulags. With Mao Zedong (1893–1976) in China, Kim Il Sung (1912–1994) in Korea, Ho Chi Minh (1890–1969) in Vietnam, Fidel Castro (1926–today) in Cuba, and Pol Pot (1925–1998) in Cambodia, the murder and oppression, if anything, got even worse.

With the realization of complete equality on earth at stake, these tyrants maintained, no price was too high for citizens to pay. No loss of careers, property, or lives was too great. Translating Marx's theoretical dictatorship of the proletariat into a practical mechanism for radical change, they claimed the right to bring about the transition from capitalism to advanced communism by any means at their disposal—no matter how cruel and inhumane.

Herbert Marcuse

One of Marx's most original late 20th-century interpreters was **Herbert Marcuse** (1898–1979), a German intellectual who immigrated to the United States to escape Nazi persecution. After working for the U.S. Office of Strategic Services (the forerunner of the CIA) during World War II, he taught political philosophy at a number of universities, including Columbia, Harvard, Brandeis, and the University of California–San Diego.

Marcuse tried to imagine what life would be like for human beings once they were liberated from the alienation that, according to Marx, keeps them from realizing their true potential. Among the benefits he envisions are that humans will participate in authentically creative labor, derive satisfaction from a dynamic culture prepared to defy convention, and enjoy sex without feeling guilty about it. The problem, from Marcuse's perspective, is that workers have become addicted to the material rewards conferred upon them by contemporary industrial society. They have been bought out by a one-dimensional consumer society, in other words. As a result, they lack the motivation to make the sacrifices Marx felt were necessary to challenge capitalism and move past the status quo to socialism and advanced communism.

Is the hope offered by Marx of a communist revolution that will end human exploitation a false hope, then? Not necessarily, Marcuse maintains. But if a revolution is to come, it will be initiated not by Marx's proletariat or Lenin's Communist Party, but by those strata of capitalist society that never were permitted to enjoy its affluence or somehow were able to resist being seduced by consumerism in the first place. (This description would seem to match the people abandoned in the New Orleans Superdome after Hurricane Katrina; see the final section of this chapter.)

"'The people,' previously the ferment of social change, have 'moved up' to become the fervent of social cohesion," Marcuse writes in his *One Dimensional Man*, published in 1964:

> However, underneath the conservative popular base is the substratum of the outcasts and outsiders, the exploited and persecuted of other races and colors, the unemployed and unemployable. They exist outside the democratic process; their life is the most immediate and the most real need for ending intolerable conditions and institutions. Thus their opposition is revolutionary even if their consciousness is not. Their opposition hits the system from without and is therefore not deflected by the system; it is an elementary force which violates the rules of the game and, in doing so, reveals it is a rigged game. (Marcuse 1964, 256–257)

Indeed, Marcuse's commitment to human liberation, antimaterialism, opposition to sexual repression, and willingness to stake humanity's future on capitalism's underclass led the hippie generation of the 1960s and 1970s to adopt him as one of their favorite academic speakers.

CONCLUSION

Any serious analysis of Marxism must begin with the controversy over whether he is a humanist champion of free will or a determinist. Because Marxian writings on the subject often are so contradictory, it is impossible to know for sure. If Marx teaches that history inevitably is marked by an enormous amount of tension and violence caused by economic conflicts and that this process unfairly targets the poor by taking away their power and freedom, his thought loses much of its originality because other humanists have said essentially the same thing: but at least the integrity of his thought remains intact. If, on the other hand, he teaches that economics alone determines what goes on in history, the reverse becomes true: Marx retains originality, but the integrity of his thought is compromised.

The point is that Marxism as determinism contains some notable inconsistencies. Marx the determinist argues that technology and economics constitute the sufficient cause of everything else going on in a specific society at a specific time—including the way people think. He also maintains that history reveals its inherent meaning gradually, so that people can comprehend only as much about it as the time in which they live will allow. At the end of history, when advanced communism has prevailed and the dialectic comes to a halt, he advises, it finally will be possible to grasp the knowledge that heretofore had been unavailable to human beings. Yet it is undeniable that Marx's thought, that the determinist considers to be merely an effect of economics, has had truly a profound influence on world history. It also is true that Marx claims to understand the entire course of historical development even though he did not live during the period he predicted would become advanced communism.

There are problems with the Marxian dialectic as well. Marx conceives of history as a dynamic, fluid process in which economic systems contain within themselves the seeds of their own destruction. At first the forces and relations of production exist in harmony. When contradictions inevitably occur, violent class conflict ensues. Primitive communism begets slavery, which begets feudalism, which begets capitalism. When advanced communism is achieved, however, the dialectic somehow comes to an abrupt halt. What remains unclear in Marxism is how a system that was once so vigorous can become so inert when class conflict alone has ended.

Marx's theory of alienation also generates controversy. Why would Marx claim that human beings consider the universe a hostile place in which to exist? Why did Engels predict that with the disappearance of alienation during the period of advanced communism, people will ascend "from the kingdom of necessity to the kingdom of freedom?" (Tucker 1978, 716). In his earlier writings especially Marx maintains that human beings have misconstrued their role in the universe. Once capitalism is overthrown, he proposes, people will gain a sense of empowerment from creative labor and conclude that God did not create them; they created God. Recognizing they possess the potential for perfection that in the past had been ascribed erroneously to divinity, Marx surmises, humans ultimately will realize that nothing is beyond their control.

This reversal of the traditional relationship between God and human beings leads to the impression that Marxism is a type of **secular religion.** It thus is possible to discover within Marxist doctrine the basic elements of Judaism in convoluted form. Marxism takes the place of Judaism. Jews as the chosen people now are replaced by the proletariat. Their Gentile oppressors are the bourgeoisie. Division of labor, which Marx claims was responsible for ending the period of primitive communism and undermining the potential for creative human work, supersedes original sin. The wandering of the Jews in the desert for 40 years, during which time Moses helped them lose the slave mentality they had acquired in Egypt and prepared them for freedom in Israel, is analogous to the dictatorship of the proletariat. Marx becomes the Messiah. The communist revolution represents the apocalypse, revealing true justice. The period of advanced communism becomes the kingdom of Heaven. Redemption is achieved through revolutionary activity, not through good works and faith in God. And God, once the motivating force of history, translates into history itself (Dawson 1935, 86–88).

Interpreting Marxism as a secular religion helps to explain why Marx felt the need to urge workers to engage in revolutionary activity against the bourgeoisie. Didn't he believe in historical inevitability? Wasn't the success of the proletarian revolution supposed to be a certainty? A similar apparent paradox exists in Judaism. Even though the apocalypse and the coming of the kingdom of Heaven are foretold in Judaic theology, Jews are taught that they must participate actively in their own redemption. The sooner they are able to achieve redemption, moreover, the sooner heaven and earth will become one. Jews are required to engage in redemptive *praxis,* in Marxian terms (Tucker 1961, 25). Of course the irony of the connection between Judaism and Marxism is that Marx supposedly relegated religion to society's peripheral superstructure, and the Marx family supposedly renounced all aspects of its Jewish ancestry.

QUESTIONS FOR REFLECTION

Why is Marxism sometimes described as a secular religion?

Moreover, questions need to be raised about the assumption of historical progress contained in Marxian political philosophy. Marx teaches that life is always getting technologically better for human beings. The hardships experienced during the periods of slavery, feudalism, and capitalism are temporary, he insists. They represent unfortunate but necessary stages in the ineluctable human march toward the dictatorship of the proletariat, advanced communism, and ultimately perfection on earth. A brief look at recent history might lead one to question Marx's faith. It is possible to argue that the two events most characteristic of the 20th century were the Holocaust and the development of nuclear weapons. Repression and murder of racial groups have been going on forever. But the Nazi attempt to completely eradicate Jews from the earth represented something new. The immense scope of their genocidal plan, which required the highest technology and most advanced bureaucratic methods then available, had no parallel in the past.

The development of the atomic bomb, and its subsequent use on the Japanese cities of Hiroshima and Nagasaki in 1945, also were events unique to the 20th century. Weapons of war have become deadlier with the passage of time. But nuclear bombs are not just powerful weapons. There is a eerie, doomsday quality to them. If World War III breaks out, the result will be a nuclear winter in which radioactivity and debris blocking sunlight from reaching the earth will combine to kill almost all living things.

Additional problems are posed by Marx's view of human nature. Marx suggests that once advanced communism is achieved and machines are performing all the grueling work, people will engage in fully satisfying occupations. What exactly is a fully satisfying occupation? Does he mean that people as a rule will refrain from watching television while lying on the couch with junk food and use their newfound free time to attend operas, visit museums, patronize libraries, and develop their latent literary and artistic talents? Is this a realistic expectation? Marx also implies that the vanguard of the proletariat will voluntarily relinquish its dictatorial power when bourgeois influences have been eradicated from society. Are dictators really that moral and rational? Did it ever occur to Lenin, Stalin, Mao, Kim, Ho, Castro, or Pol Pot to transfer power to the people?

In the *Communist Manifesto,* finally, Marx predicts the radical changes in society that will be brought about by the communist revolution. The implication is that the changes will rely on the revolution taking place and cannot take place without it. Among these changes are a graduated income tax, the establishment of a national bank to control a nation's credit rates, free public education for all children, and the

QUESTIONS FOR REFLECTION

To what extent have capitalist societies met the standards of political justice outlined by Marx in his *Communist Manifesto*?

CASE STUDY 12.2 | NEW ORLEANS

Marx speaks clearly and forcefully to the plight of the multitudes who have been dispossessed by capitalism through the ages. Especially when it is combined with a laissez-faire Social Darwinistic political philosophy, capitalism can be a heartless system in which intense competition sometimes leads to the law of the jungle. After Hurricane Katrina, tens of thousands of people were stranded without food, water, bathroom facilities, or police protection in the New Orleans Superdome and the New Orleans Convention Center. The local, state, and federal governments did not seem to care about these poor souls. This desperate situation in New Orleans is a testament to the fact that capitalism sometimes can combine with other cultural factors to create a society with a survival of the fittest mentality.

Because a majority of the people displaced by Katrina in New Orleans were African-Americans, the accusation has been made that racism was the primary cause of the fiasco there. Little was done to help those left behind in the Superdome and the Convention Center, it has been said, because the United States is a racist country. For authorities to issue a mandatory evacuation order without considering that poor African-Americans lacked access to transportation out of the city, this argument goes, demonstrates an utter lack of concern for their welfare.

Marx would disagree. The primary cause of the misfortune suffered by those abandoned in New Orleans by every level of American government, he would maintain, is the capitalist system itself. As he explains, the bourgeoisie actually encourage workers to play the race card. This strategy allows them to divide the proletariat from within on the basis of color. In this process the power of the workers as a group is diluted, their attention is diverted from their true problems, and the identity of their real enemies is concealed.

Exorbitant no-bid contracts have been awarded to giant multinational corporations to hire foreign laborers at minimum wages to clean up New Orleans. Marx would offer this information as additional proof that government in capitalist societies exists to make it possible for monied interests to profit from the misery of the poor. The hollow looks captured by the news media on the faces of those encamped in the Superdome and Convention Center were symptoms not only of physical distress, Marx would observe, but of an underlying feeling of powerlessness exacerbated by monotonous capitalist labor. And the poverty of the victims was a product of either the surplus value stolen from them by their employers or their jobs being taken by machines.

This is how Marx would explain what happened in New Orleans after Hurricane Katrina. While others blame the misery experienced in Louisiana, Mississippi, and Alabama on racism, Marx would focus on the injustices done to the proletariat by the bourgeoisie. What others may see as a race problem, Marx would see as a matter of class. It was not their skin color that caused government to ignore the plight of African-Americans, but their economic status. Impoverished African-American residents of New Orleans were exploited by the capitalist system after Katrina in the same way that workers of every color are exploited everyday. But not for long, Marx would argue. As soon as capitalism is overthrown by the proletarian revolution, all forms of exploitation and inequality will disappear.

---

abolition of child labor. In fact Marx is wrong. He clearly underestimates the ability of noncommunist societies to reform themselves. During the administration of Woodrow Wilson, for example, the United States provided for a graduated income tax with the passage of the Sixteenth Amendment to its Constitution in 1913. Under the leadership of Alexander Hamilton, this country chartered its first national bank in 1791 and set into motion what today is known as the Federal Reserve System. In 1827 Massachusetts, influenced by the reformer Horace Mann, passed a law requiring every town in the state with over 500 families to set up a public high school. Other states soon followed the Massachusetts example. And in 1941, during the administration of Franklin Roosevelt, Congress outlawed child labor.

QUESTIONS FOR REFLECTION

Did the Hurricane Katrina tragedy on the Gulf Coast illustrate the evils of capitalism about which Marx warns?

Key Terms

Georg Hegel
dialectically
Young Hegelians
Ludwig Feuerbach
Friedrich Engels
praxis
Paris Commune
historical materialism
materialist conception of history
forces of production
relations of production
substructure
superstructure
Lewis Morgan
anthropology
primitive communism
bourgeoisie
proletariat
advanced communism
false consciousness
the opium of the masses
dictatorship of the proletariat
utopian socialists
theory of alienation
labor theory of value
socially necessary labor
surplus value
variable capital
constant capital
V.I. Lenin
Leon Trotsky
vanguard of the proletariat
Joseph Stalin
Herbert Marcuse
secular religion

Sources and Resources

Key Texts

Economic and Philosophic Manuscripts of 1844
Contribution to the Critique of Hegel's "Philosophy of Right"
Theses on Feuerbach
The German Ideology
Communist Manifesto
The Eighteenth Brumaire of Louis Bonaparte
A Contribution to the Critique of Political Economy
Capital
Critique of the Gotha Program

Secondary Texts

Avineri, Shlomo. *The Social and Political Thought of Karl Marx* (New York: Cambridge University Press, 1968).

Berlin, Isaiah. *Karl Marx: His Life and Environment* (New York Oxford University Press, 1963).

Bober, M. M. *Karl Marx's Interpretation of History* (Cambridge: Harvard University Press, 1950).

Dawson, Christopher. *Religion and the Modern State* (London: Sheed and Ward, 1935).

Kolakowski, Leszek. *Main Currents of Marxism*, 3 vols. (New York: Oxford University Press, 1978).

Lenin, V. I. *State and Revolution* (New York: International Publishers, 1943).

Lichtheim, George. *Marxism: An Historical and Critical Study* (New York: Praeger, 1965).

Marcuse, Herbert. *One Dimensional Man* (Boston: Beacon Press, 1964).

McLellan, David. *Karl Marx: His Life and Thought* (New York Harper & Row, 1973).

Meyer, Alfred. *Marxism: The Unity of Theory and Practice* (Ann Arbor: The University of Michigan Press, 1963).

Tucker, Robert. *Philosophy and Myth in Karl Marx* (New York: Cambridge University Press, 1961).

Tucker, Robert. (ed.) *The Marx–Engels Reader* (New York: Norton, 1978).

Web Sites

Stanford Encyclopedia of Philosophy entry online at http://plato.stanford.edu/entries/marx/

Marxists Internet archive online at www.marxists.org/

The writings of Marx and Engels online at http://marx.eserver.org/

JOHN STUART MILL

CHAPTER 13

By Samuel Gregg *Acton Institute for the Study of Religion and Liberty*

LIFE

In the view of both his admirers and critics, the 19th-century English philosopher John Stuart Mill (1806–1873) has exerted one of the most powerful influences on contemporary understanding of subjects ranging from the nature and purposes of government, to the character of economic life, to the essential character and ends of human liberty. The eldest son of the utilitarian philosopher **James Mill**, author of among other texts *The History of British India*—(and himself a noted disciple of the founder of modern utilitarian thought, **Jeremy Bentham**), John Stuart Mill was educated largely by his father. Though, as we will see, Mill was to modify the **utilitarianism** of his father and Bentham considerably, the utilitarian approach exerted the greatest influence on Mill's thought for the rest of his life.

Mill's education was especially rigorous, even for the standards of highly educated people of his time. At the age of 3, for instance, he was introduced to Greek. He first encountered Latin at the age of 8. He read widely in the field of history, including texts by David Hume and Edmund Gibbon, as well as Greek and Roman works, such as Livy, Cicero, Ovid, Xenophon, Thucydides, and Aristotle's *Rhetoric*.

There was little to no formal religious influence on Mill during his upbringing. His father, a nominal Presbyterian, essentially opted for a type of agnosticism, believing the claims of atheism to be absurd while simultaneously believing that the conundrum of evil created significant obstacles to belief in a loving Creator. It is clear, nonetheless, that Mill absorbed a type of intellectual hostility toward the claims of Christianity from his father. Writing in his posthumously published *Autobiography* (1873), Mill refers to what he describes as Christianity's "slovenliness of thought" and its "subjection of the reason to fears, wishes, and affections." Only these, Mill believes, could enable Christians "to accept a theory involving a contradiction in terms." Mill also describes his father's "standard of morals" as "Epicurean, inasmuch as it was utilitarian, taking as the exclusive test of right and wrong, the tendency of actions to produce pleasure or pain."

This reference to utilitarianism is telling, especially because Mill's whole education was underpinned by a tacit commitment to utilitarian logic and philosophy. Looking back on his youth, Mill records that his "education had been, in a certain sense, already a course of Benthamism." Mill records in his *Autobiography* that when he first read Bentham, perhaps at the age of 15, he was engulfed by a sense that "that all previous moralists were superseded and that here indeed was the commencement of a new era in thought." Rejecting theories of natural law, human flourishing, and even natural rights, Bentham's principle of utility, Mill records, "gave unity to my conception of things. I now had opinions; a creed, a doctrine, a philosophy; in one among the best senses of the word, a religion; the inculcation and diffusion of which could be made the principal outward purpose of a life."

Upon turning 14, Mill was sent abroad to study for a year in the south of France in Montpellier, where he resided with Sir Samuel Bentham, the brother of Jeremy. Returning to England in 1821, Mill began to read the works of the French philosopher Etienne Bonnot, Abbé de Condillac, under the supervision of John Austin, the legal scholar now most commonly regarded as one of the founding fathers of legal positivism. The irony is that in doing so Mill chose to read the works of one of the few French thinkers whose ideas are remarkably similar to the British empiricist philosophical tradition of Locke, Berkeley, Hume, and, to an extent, Bentham. Exposure to Condillac was therefore likely only to confirm the type of intellectual outlook that Mill had absorbed from his father. It is also likely that Condillac's economic ideas, especially those concerning the utility-cum-scarcity theory of value, also reinforced in Mill's mind the economic implications of Benthamite thought.

While reading Condillac under Austin, Mill also had the opportunity to immerse himself in jurisprudence and legal theory. Austin's later works on this subject, especially *The Province of Jurisprudence Determined* (1832), focus on identifying law as a species of command and emphasize the need to draw distinctions between positive law and the demands of morality. Austin and his wife Sarah were also deeply committed utilitarians and close friends with both Mill Senior and Bentham. Austin was especially interested in law reform, serving on the Criminal Law Commission in 1833, from which he eventually resigned after being able to muster little support for his opinions. Perhaps the greatest impact of Austin's ideas was to be through the influence they exerted on Mill, especially when it came to Mill's thoughts about the nature and purpose of law and its relationship to questions of public morality.

Thus while Mill was certainly well educated, it seems clear that it was an education received almost entirely through the lens of utilitarian thinkers and utilitarian philosophy. Having been so thoroughly initiated into the English utilitarian circle, Mill spent the whole of 1825 editing Bentham's five volumes of *Rationale of Evidence.* The result, however, was not scholarly satisfaction, but rather prolonged overwork and the culmination of emotional and intellectual burdens. As a result, Mill experienced what would today be called a deep depression and an eventual nervous breakdown that same year.

In his *Autobiography,* Mill describes this event, which he experienced in the autumn of 1826, as the result of the mental and physical pressures he had experienced from the beginning of his life. No longer, Mill writes, could he take "any delight in virtue, or the general good, but also just as little in anything else." All that he had previously valued, Mill states, ceased to interest him. Dullness and lethargy dominated his senses, and Mill worried that his "constant habit of analysis had dried up the fountains of feeling within him." Mill's depression lasted for several months. Eventually, however, Mill sensed that "the cloud gradually drew off" when he found that he had not lost the ability to feel emotion. Describing this state of mind, Mill writes, "The oppression of the thought that all feeling was dead within me, was gone. I was no longer hopeless: I was not a stock or a stone. I had still, it seemed, some of the material out of which all worth of character, and all capacity for happiness, are made."

A lasting legacy of this experience was a gradual distancing of Mill's thought from the strict empiricist utilitarian tradition of Bentham and his father in which he has effectively been raised. He was now willing, Mill writes, "for the first time, [to give] proper place, among the prime necessities of human well-being, to the internal culture of the individual. I ceased to attach almost exclusive importance to the ordering of outward circumstances, and the training of the human being for speculation and for action." Though remaining a great admirer of Bentham, Mill now viewed Bentham as one who, while a rigorous thinker, had a distinctly limited vision of the world. Bentham's work, as Mill puts it, is "wholly empirical and the empiricism of one who has had little experience." Mill's intellectual interests and influences subsequently began to widen, as he read the work of Samuel Taylor Coleridge—not just his poetry but also his political and philosophical writings—and was taken with the idea that insight can provide people with knowledge that is just as valuable as the empirical method. Mill's romantic side was also awakened by reading the poetry of Alfred Tennyson and William Wordsworth. All of these developments would have concerned James Mill and Jeremy Bentham.

At the same time, the core of Mill's thinking remained firmly within the utilitarian orbit. The historian of philosophy Frederick Copleston correctly notes that "the effect of Mill's crisis should not be exaggerated. He remained a utilitarian, and, though modifying Benthanitism in important ways, he never went over to the opposite camp."[1] The primary reason that Mill continued to admire Bentham and his own father was for having brought what Mill regarded as clarity and order to fields of inquiry that seemed to Mill to have been marked by ambiguity and disordered thinking.

Not long after his mental breakdown Mill encountered the person who was to offer what he describes as "the friendship which has been the honor and chief blessing of my existence, as well as the source of a great part of all that I have attempted to do, or hope to effect hereafter, for human improvement." Mill records that he first met **Harriet Taylor** in 1830. A married woman whose husband shared the same liberal sentiments but had few intellectual interests, Mrs. Taylor suffered from what Mill described as all the social obstacles that hindered women's self-expression and intellectual development. Mill enjoyed a close personal and intellectual relationship with Taylor until her husband died, following which Mill married her in 1851.

Through his father, Mill had been able to secure a post in the Office of the Examiner of Correspondence at the East India Company in 1823. Mill's employment there for the next 35 years meant that he did not have to depend on writing to make his financial ends meet; his job also gave him sufficient time to pursue his intellectual interests. Apart from coauthoring articles with Mrs. Taylor, Mill published numerous articles in literary journals such as the *Westminster Review* and the *London Review* on subjects including economics, philosophy, religion, ethics, and politics. He also, however, found time to write much longer treatises. Mill's first major work is his *System of Logic* (1843). This was followed by texts that dealt with specific economic themes, including his *Essays on Some Unsettled Questions of Political Economy* (1844), and a more systematic work, his *Principles of Political Economy* (1848).

In terms of political thought, Mill's most important works are his relatively short book *On Liberty* (1859) and his famous *Utilitarianism* (1863), a text that originally appeared in journal form. Mill does not, however, confine his political thought to the theoretical. Entering politics, Mill sat in the Parliament of 1865–1868 as a radical MP for the seat of Westminster. In his short time as a parliamentarian, Mill displayed particular interest in establishing proportional representation for Parliament; alleviating the conditions of industrial workers, extending the electoral franchise in general and particularly to women; the interests of what Mill refers to as the laboring classes; and Irish issues, especially the question of home rule for Ireland. Some of the works he writes during this period, such as his 1868 pamphlet *England and Ireland* and his 1869 *The Subjection of Women,* outlines his thoughts about these specific

[1]Frederick Copleston, S.J., *A History of Philosophy,* Book Three, *Bentham to Russell,* Vol. VIII (New York: Image Books, 1985), p. 26.

PRIMARY SOURCE 13.1

Last Stage of Education, and First of Self-Education, from *Autobiography*, Chapter 3

My previous education had been, in a certain sense, already a course of Benthamism. The Benthamic standard of "the greatest happiness" was that which I had always been taught to apply; I was even familiar with an abstract discussion of it, forming an episode in an unpublished dialogue on Government, written by my father on the Platonic model. Yet in the first pages of Bentham it burst upon me with all the force of novelty. What thus impressed me was the chapter in which Bentham passed judgment on the common modes of reasoning in morals and legislation, deduced from phrases like "law of nature," "right reason," "the moral sense," "natural rectitude," and the like, and characterized them as dogmatism in disguise, imposing its sentiments upon others under cover of sounding expressions which convey no reason for the sentiment, but set up the sentiment as its own reason. It had not struck me before, that Bentham's principle put an end to all this. The feeling rushed upon me, that all previous moralists were superseded, and that here indeed was the commencement of a new era in thought. This impression was strengthened by the manner in which Bentham put into scientific form the application of the happiness principle to the morality of actions, by analysing the various classes and orders of their consequences. . . .

matters. At the same time, Mill spoke and wrote about less immediate matters, as indicated by his *Examination of Sir William Hamilton's Philosophy* (1865) and his 1867 inaugural address as rector of the University of St. Andrews in Scotland, which addressed the question of the value of culture. The last of Mill's intellectual achievements published in his lifetime was his 1869 edition of James Mill's *Analysis of the Phenomena of the Human Mind.*

John Stuart Mill died at Avignon on May 8, 1873. Several of his works, such as his *Autobiography* (1873) and his *Three Essays on Religion: Nature, the Utility of Religion, and Theism* (1874), were published posthumously. Many of his shorter writings were published between 1859 and 1875 under the title *Dissertations and Discussions* as a collected four-volume work.

UTILITARIANISM

Though Mill's name is perhaps most associated with his contributions to moral theory, his *Utilitarianism* is the only one of his texts that discusses this matter in any substantive detail. Mill may have decided that the essentials of his understanding of the science of morality had been firmly established by Jeremy Bentham and James Mill, so that John Stuart Mill's own work might be regarded as primarily introducing modifications and small corrections to Benthamite thinking about these matters. Of course Bentham's own version of utilitarianism was not something that he simply invented. In Bentham's *Fragment on Government,*[2] for example, we find Bentham's own acknowledgement that he found David Hume's claim in the *Treatise of Human Nature* that, in the final analysis, every virtue is derived from utility, to be especially enlightening. It was a theme found in Hume's other writings, such as his *Enquiry*

[2]Jeremy Bentham, *A Fragment on Government,* (ed.) Wilfred Harrison (Oxford: Basil Blackwell, 1948).

Concerning the Human Understanding and the Principles of Morals, which stressed that "public utility is the sole origin of justice."[3]

Central to his thought are Bentham's concern for **utility**—defined as the degree of conduciveness to the greater happiness of the greatest possible number of human beings in society—and his desire to apply this criterion to measure the efficacy of all social, economic, and political institutions and processes. His attention to utility is essentially grounded in a naturalist understanding of human beings: "Nature has placed mankind under the governance of two sovereign masters, pain and *pleasure.* It is for them alone to point out what we ought to do, as well as to determine what we shall do. On the one hand the standard of right and wrong, on the other the chain of causes and effects, are fastened to their throne. They govern us in all we do, in all we say, in all we think: every effort we can make to throw off our subjection, will serve but to demonstrate and confirm it. In words a man may pretend to abjure their empire: but in reality he will remain subject to it all the while."[4]

Bentham's statement about pain and pleasure is only a formal principle of morality—that is, a principle with no determinate content.[5] The word *good* is a synonym for that which gives someone **pleasure,** while the term *evil* refers to the experience of **pain.** As Bentham puts it, "On the one hand, the standard of right and wrong, on the other the chain of cause and effect, are fastened to their [pleasure and pain's] throne."[6] Given, then, that people are able to make a variety of choices concerning how they act, Bentham holds that it is reasonable to suggest that good actions tend to increase the total sum of happiness (that is, pleasure), and evil acts are those that reduce the sum of pleasure in society.

All of these claims are, of course, premised on Bentham's unspoken assumptions that we can know all the possible effects of our actions and then choose, having weighed all the possible pleasures and pains associated with several possible actions, the act likely to produce the most pleasure. The difficulty for Bentham—indeed the entire coherence of utilitarianism—is that such calculations appear to be impossible. Such assessment cannot be made without admitting that we must be ignorant of at least some possible effects that could follow from one choice. If so, the question becomes why we would even attempt to engage in such a calculation.

Bentham's effort to avoid this critique involves suggesting that we can restrict the range of necessary calculations by introducing quantitative distinctions. This insists that what brings people more pleasure should be given greater weight that whatever brings less pleasure or more pain. Unfortunately Benthamite utilitarianism now has a new problem: By what criteria do we determine that one pleasure or pain is greater than another? How do we assess, for instance, the pleasure involved in having a successful working career against the pleasure of a happy marriage? In other words,

---

[3]David Hume, *An Enquiry Concerning the Human Understanding and the Principles of Morals,* L.A. Selby-Brigge (Oxford: Clarendon Press, 1951), 3, I, p. 145.

[4]Jeremy Bentham, *An Introduction to the Principles of Morals and Legislation,* (ed.) L.K. Lafleur (Oxford: Basil Blackwell, 1948), Chapter 1, Sec. 1.

[5]See Johannes Messner, *Das Naturrecht: Handbuch der Gesellschaftsethik, Stattsethik und Wirstchaftsethik,* 3rd ed. (Innsbruck: Verlagsanstalt Tyrolia, 1958), p. 126.

[6]Bentham, *Introduction,* Chapter 1, Sec. 1.

BENTHAM'S HEDONISTIC CALCULUS

Very good act	High pleasure, high duration, high certainty of pleasure occurring
Moderately good act	High pleasure, low duration, high certainty of pleasure occurring
Less good act	High pleasure, low duration, low certainty of pleasure occurring
Bad act	Low pleasure, low duration, low certainty of pleasure occurring

Bentham's schema works only if benefits and harms in alternative actions are commensurable.

To address such criticisms, Bentham identifies a range of criteria—a type of hedonistic **calculus**[7]—by which people can assess the value of a pleasure or a pain, such as its intensity, its duration, its likelihood, and its degree of certainty or uncertainty. Bentham's hedonistic calculus looks something like the table at the top of the page.

Again, however, this calculus falters when confronted with commensurability questions. How do we assess the relative weights of these criteria against each other?

Much of John Stuart Mill's *Utilitarianism* is directed to addressing central objections to the theory proposed by Bentham. He does not, however, fundamentally disagree with Bentham's theory, and on other occasions he underlines his admiration for Bentham's essentially quantitative approach to moral theory.[8] According to Mill, there is only one phenomenon that we can assume all people experience: the sensations of pleasure or pain. From this, Mill claims, we can conclude that the yearning to experience pleasure and avoid pain is the only constant. It even, Mill argues, is the real motivation for people who say that they are pursuing virtue for its own sake. "There was," Mill writes, "no original desire of it, or motive to it, save its conduciveness to pleasure; and especially to protection from pain."[9]

Mill parts company, however, with Bentham when it comes to the definition of **happiness.** Unlike Bentham, Mill does not present happiness in essentially egotistical terms. "Actions are right," he states in Chapter 2 of *Utilitarianism,* "in proportion as they tend to promote happiness; wrong as they tend to produce the reverse of happiness." For Mill, however, happiness concerns "the greatest amount of happiness altogether"[10] rather than that of a particular individual. Mill also claims that true happiness requires a certain degree of competence in making such a judgment.

To address these and related concerns, Mill seeks to adjust Benthamite utilitarianism by altering the pain–pleasure calculus employed by Bentham. Mill claims that rather than judging the pleasure or pain produced by one person's action, we ought instead to focus on assessing the utility of rules that deal with all cases of a particular choice. Thus we might ask, for instance, about the likely effect on the net aggregate of pleasure and pain in society if we create and uphold a rule forbidding murder. Mill's calculus looks something like the following:

---

[7]See Bentham, *Introduction,* Chapter 1, Sec. 3.

[8]John Stuart Mill, *Dissertations and Discussions,* Vol. 1 (Boston: William V. Spencer 1867), pp. 339–340.

[9]Mill, *Utilitarianism,* pp. 56–57.

[10]Mill, *Utilitarianism,* p. 16.

Mill's Calculus

Good rule	High pleasure for most people
Bad rule	Low pleasure for most people

The difficulty with Mill's proposed alteration of shifting from Benthamite "act utilitarianism" to Mill's own "rule utilitarianism" is that the latter fails to diminish the number of requisite calculations. This becomes clear when we consider how to determine such rules on the basis proposed by Mill. If utilitarians are to be consistent with their underlying assumptions, it is only possible to know which rule is going to augment the cumulative sum of pleasure by considering every situation that might arise as a result of a particular choice and then determining the most pleasure-enhancing, pain-minimizing rule on the basis on that calculation. In other words, the process allowing the identification of such rules is compromised by its false assumption of commensurability and its reliance on an impossible calculation.

Mill, however, goes beyond Bentham in thinking about the process of weighing pleasure and pain. Perhaps reflecting his experience of life after his nervous breakdown, Mill suggests that we should examine the issue of the *quality* of a pleasure rather simply the question of quantity.[11] Some forms of pleasure are, in Mill's view, of a higher quality than others. Intellectual pleasures, he holds, ought to be given greater weight than merely sensual ones.

Some critics maintain that in advancing these ideas, Mill makes his version of utilitarianism inconsistent with its central principle of the explanatory power of utility. If the measure of utility remains pleasure and if people assign different qualitative weightings to different experiences of pleasure, then it appears that another reference point is necessary. Frederick Copleston points out that Mill essentially finds himself looking to other standards than pleasure itself.[12] The rationale Mill offers is that Bentham had an overly constricted vision of human nature that failed to reflect the fact that, as Mill writes in *On Liberty,* man is a "being capable of pursuing spiritual perfection as an end; of desiring for its own sake, the conformity of his own character to his standard of excellence, without hope of good or fear of evil from other source than his own inward consciousness."[13]

Another difficulty with Mill's utilitarianism is that Mill is remarkably slippery when it comes to defining what he means by *human nature.* When describing the features of human life upon which he wants to improve, Mill refers to "individuality,"[14] the "higher faculties,"[15] or "the permanent interests of man as a progressive being."[16] But Mill never defines what these "permanent interests" might be or what constitutes a "progressive being" or the content of "progressive."

[11]See Mill, *Utilitarianism,* pp. 11–12.

[12]Frederick Copleston, S.J., *A History of Philosophy,* Vol. VIII, Book 3 (New York: Image Books, 1985 [1966]), pp. 30–31.

[13]Mill, *On Liberty,* p. 9.

[14]Mill, *On Liberty,* p. 56.

[15]Mill, *Utilitarianism,* p. 16.

[16]Mill, *On Liberty,* p. 9.

Indeed Mill's utilitarianism can only work if one of two conditions prevails. One is a situation in which everyone has a single well-defined end (rather than something as broad and potentially ambiguous as pleasure) against which we can reasonably measure every act or every rule. Such an objective does not exist. Any single person can pursue many life plans, even in the most straitened circumstances. The second condition amounts to maintaining that all human desires must be considered equally valid. But this also is impossible. What reason, we might ask, can be found for considering one person's wish to stay ignorant as *validas* another person's desire to acquire knowledge?

THE QUESTION OF LIBERTY

Mill's *On Liberty* is a classic of modern political philosophy and is widely regarded as central to the various movements of liberalism that emerged in the 19th century. Mill himself tends to abstract himself from metaphysical and philosophical questions concerning the freedom of each person's will, a subject that has occupied the attention of philosophers and religious thinkers from the beginning of time. Instead he devotes his attention to questions of civil liberty. "The subject of this Essay," states the first chapter of *On Liberty,* "is not the so-called Liberty of the Will, so unfortunately opposed to the misnamed doctrine of Philosophical Necessity; but Civil, or Social Liberty: the nature and limits of the power which can be legitimately exercised by society over the individual."

The idea of the need of all human individuals to engage in self-development is central to Mill's justification for civil liberty. Like Bentham, Mill does not believe that humans enjoy a natural right to self-development. Rather, he grounds the idea of self-development in the principle of utility. Mill holds that the principle of utility provides the firmest foundation for a state of affairs in which people are allowed to shape themselves in accordance with the dictates of their own reason and will, provided that they do not do so in ways that unreasonably hinder the liberty of others to pursue the same end. "The free development of individuality," he writes, "is one of the principal ingredients of human happiness, and quite the chief ingredient of individual and social progress."[17] It is not, according to Mill, in the interests of the happiness of all that everyone follows the same path in life or shares the same views. Instead everyone's well-being is enhanced if everyone is allowed to develop freely, subject to the single restraint identified by Mill.

This being the case, much of Mill's thought about the nature of **liberty** is concerned with determining how far each individual's freedom to make choices can be reconciled with the need for a certain degree of social order. The essence of Mill's solution is to suggest that people's **freedom** should not be bounded, provided that the exercise of that liberty does not involve inciting others to criminal activity and that people do not interfere with the liberty of others. Hence Mill writes, "The only part of the conduct of anyone, for which he is amenable to society, is that which concerns others. In the part which merely concerns himself, his independence is, of right, absolute. Over himself, over his own body and mind, the individual is sovereign."[18]

---

[17]Mill, *On Liberty,* p. 9.

[18]John Stuart Mill, *On Liberty, Considerations on Representative Government,* (ed.) R.B. McCallum (Oxford: Oxford University Press, 1859/1946), p. 9.

PRIMARY SOURCE 13.2 | OF THE ULTIMATE SANCTION OF THE PRINCIPLE OF UTILITY, FROM *UTILITARIANISM*, CHAPTER 3

The question is often asked, and properly so, in regard to any supposed moral standard—What is its sanction? what are the motives to obey it? or more specifically, what is the source of its obligation? whence does it derive its binding force?. . . .

The principle of utility either has, or there is no reason why it might not have, all the sanctions which belong to any other system of morals. Those sanctions are either external or internal. Of the external sanctions it is not necessary to speak at any length. They are, the hope of favor and the fear of displeasure, from our fellow creatures or from the Ruler of the Universe, along with whatever we may have of sympathy or affection for them, or of love and awe of Him, inclining us to do his will independently of selfish consequences. There is evidently no reason why all these motives for observance should not attach themselves to the utilitarian morality, as completely and as powerfully as to any other. Indeed, those of them which refer to our fellow creatures are sure to do so, in proportion to the amount of general intelligence; for whether there be any other ground of moral obligation than the general happiness or not, men do desire happiness; and however imperfect may be their own practice, they desire and commend all conduct in others toward themselves, by which they think their happiness is promoted. With regard to the religious motive, if men believe, as most profess to do, in the goodness of God, those who think that conduciveness to the general happiness is the essence, or even only the criterion of good, must necessarily believe that it is also that which God approves. The whole force therefore of external reward and punishment, whether physical or moral, and whether proceeding from God or from our fellow men, together with all that the capacities of human nature admit of disinterested devotion to either, become available to enforce the utilitarian morality, in proportion as that morality is recognized; and the more powerfully, the more the appliances of education and general cultivation are bent to the purpose.

So far as to external sanctions. The internal sanction of duty, whatever our standard of duty may be, is one and the same—a feeling in our own mind; a pain, more or less intense, attendant on violation of duty, which in properly cultivated moral natures rises, in the more serious cases, into shrinking from it as an impossibility. This feeling, when disinterested, and connecting itself with the pure idea of duty, and not with some particular form of it, or with any of the merely accessory circumstances, is the essence of Conscience; though in that complex phenomenon as it actually exists, the simple fact is in general all encrusted over with collateral associations, derived from sympathy, from love, and still more from fear; from all the forms of religious feeling; from the recollections of childhood and of all our past life; from self-esteem, desire of the esteem of others, and occasionally even self-abasement. This extreme complication is, I apprehend, the origin of the sort of mystical character which, by a tendency of the human mind of which there are many other examples, is apt to be attributed to the idea of moral obligation, and which leads people to believe that the idea cannot possibly attach itself to any other objects than those which, by a supposed mysterious law, are found in our present experience to excite it. Its binding force, however, consists in the existence of a mass of feeling which must be broken through in order to do what violates our standard of right, and which, if we do nevertheless violate that standard, will probably have to be encountered afterward in the form of remorse. Whatever theory we have of the nature or origin of conscience, this is what essentially constitutes it.

The ultimate sanction, therefore, of all morality (external motives apart) being a subjective feeling in our own minds, I see nothing embarrassing to those whose standard is utility, in the question, what is the sanction of that particular standard? We may answer, the same as of all other moral standards—the conscientious feelings of mankind. Undoubtedly this sanction has no binding efficacy on those who do not possess the feelings it appeals to; but

PRIMARY SOURCE 13.2

OF THE ULTIMATE SANCTION OF THE PRINCIPLE OF UTILITY, FROM *UTILITARIANISM*, CHAPTER 3 *continued*

neither will these persons be more obedient to any other moral principle than to the utilitarian one. On them morality of any kind has no hold but through the external sanctions. Meanwhile the feelings exist, a fact in human nature, the reality of which, and the great power with which they are capable of acting on those in whom they have been duly cultivated, are proved by experience. No reason has ever been shown why they may not be cultivated to as great intensity in connection with the utilitarian, as with any other rule of morals...

It is not necessary, for the present purpose, to decide whether the feeling of duty is innate or implanted. Assuming it to be innate, it is an open question to what objects it naturally attaches itself; for the philosophic supporters of that theory are now agreed that the intuitive perception is of principles of morality and not of the details. If there be anything innate in the matter, I see no reason why the feeling which is innate should not be that of regard to the pleasures and pains of others. If there is any principle of morals which is intuitively obligatory, I should say it must be that. If so, the intuitive ethics would coincide with the utilitarian, and there would be no further quarrel between them. Even as it is, the intuitive moralists, though they believe that there are other intuitive moral obligations, do already believe this to one; for they unanimously hold that a large portion of morality turns upon the consideration due to the interests of our fellow creatures. Therefore, if the belief in the transcendental origin of moral obligation gives any additional efficacy to the internal sanction, it appears to me that the utilitarian principle has already the benefit of it.

On the other hand, if, as is my own belief, the moral feelings are not innate, but acquired, they are not for that reason the less natural. It is natural to man to speak, to reason, to build cities, to cultivate the ground, though these are acquired faculties. The moral feelings are not indeed a part of our nature, in the sense of being in any perceptible degree present in all of us; but this, unhappily, is a fact admitted by those who believe the most strenuously in their transcendental origin. Like the other acquired capacities above referred to, the moral faculty, if not a part of our nature, is a natural outgrowth from it; capable, like them, in a certain small degree, of springing up spontaneously; and susceptible of being brought by cultivation to a high degree of development. Unhappily it is also susceptible, by a sufficient use of the external sanctions and of the force of early impressions, of being cultivated in almost any direction: so that there is hardly anything so absurd or so mischievous that it may not, by means of these influences, be made to act on the human mind with all the authority of conscience. To doubt that the same potency might be given by the same means to the principle of utility, even if it had no foundation in human nature, would be flying in the face of all experience.

But moral associations which are wholly of artificial creation, when intellectual culture goes on, yield by degrees to the dissolving force of analysis: and if the feeling of duty, when associated with utility, would appear equally arbitrary; if there were no leading department of our nature, no powerful class of sentiments, with which that association would harmonize, which would make us feel it congenial, and incline us not only to foster it in others (for which we have abundant interested motives), but also to cherish it in ourselves; if there were not, in short, a natural basis of sentiment for utilitarian morality, it might well happen that this association also, even after it had been implanted by education, might be analyzed away. But there is this basis of powerful natural sentiment; and this it is which, when once the general happiness is recognized as the ethical standard, will constitute the strength of the utilitarian morality. This firm foundation is that of the social feelings of mankind; the desire to be in unity with our fellow creatures, which is already a powerful principle in human nature, and happily one of those which tend to become stronger, even without express inculcation, from the influences of advancing

continued

PRIMARY SOURCE 13.2 | OF THE ULTIMATE SANCTION OF THE PRINCIPLE OF UTILITY, FROM *UTILITARIANISM*, CHAPTER 3 *continued*

civilization. The social state is at once so natural, so necessary, and so habitual to man, that, except in some unusual circumstances or by an effort of voluntary abstraction, he never conceives himself otherwise than as a member of a body; and this association is riveted more and more, as mankind are further removed from the state of savage independence. Any condition, therefore, which is essential to a state of society, becomes more and more an inseparable part of every person's conception of the state of things which he is born into, and which is the destiny of a human being.

Now, society between human beings, except in the relation of master and slave, is manifestly impossible on any other footing than that the interests of all are to be consulted. Society between equals can only exist on the understanding that the interests of all are to be regarded equally. And since in all states of civilization, every person, except an absolute monarch, has equals, every one is obliged to live on these terms with somebody; and in every age some advance is made toward a state in which it will be impossible to live permanently on other terms with anybody. In this way people grow up unable to conceive as possible to them a state of total disregard of other people's interests. They are under a necessity of conceiving themselves as at least abstaining from all the grosser injuries, and (if only for their own protection) living in a state of constant protest against them. They are also familiar with the fact of cooperating with others and proposing to themselves a collective, not an individual interest as the aim (at least for the time being) of their actions. So long as they are cooperating, their ends are identified with those of others; there is at least a temporary feeling that the interests of others are their own interests. Not only does all strengthening of social ties, and all healthy growth of society, give to each individual a stronger personal interest in practically consulting the welfare of others; it also leads him to identify his feelings more and more with their good, or at least with an even greater degree of practical consideration for it. He comes, as though instinctively, to be conscious of himself as a being who of course pays regard to others. The good of others becomes to him a thing naturally and necessarily to be attended to, like any of the physical conditions of our existence. Now, whatever amount of this feeling a person has, he is urged by the strongest motives both of interest and of sympathy to demonstrate it, and to the utmost of his power encourage it in others; and even if he has none of it himself, he is as greatly interested as any one else that others should have it. Consequently the smallest germs of the feeling are laid hold of and nourished by the contagion of sympathy and the influences of education; and a complete web of corroborative association is woven round it, by the powerful agency of the external sanctions.

This mode of conceiving ourselves and human life, as civilization goes on, is felt to be more and more natural. Every step in political improvement renders it more so, by removing the sources of opposition of interest, and leveling those inequalities of legal privilege between individuals or classes, owing to which there are large portions of mankind whose happiness it is still practicable to disregard. In an improving state of the human mind, the influences are constantly on the increase, which tend to generate in each individual a feeling of unity with all the rest; which, if perfect, would make him never think of, or desire, any beneficial condition for himself, in the benefits of which they are not included. If we now suppose this feeling of unity to be taught as a religion, and the whole force of education, of institutions, and of opinion, directed, as it once was in the case of religion, to make every person grow up from infancy surrounded on all sides both by the profession and the practice of it, I think that no one, who can realize this conception, will feel any misgiving about the sufficiency of the ultimate sanction for the Happiness morality. To any ethical student who finds the realization difficult, I recommend, as a means of facilitating it, the second of M. Comte's two principle

PRIMARY SOURCE 13.2 | **OF THE ULTIMATE SANCTION OF THE PRINCIPLE OF UTILITY, FROM *UTILITARIANISM*, CHAPTER 3** *continued*

works, the *Traite de Politique Positive.* I entertain the strongest objections to the system of politics and morals set forth in that treatise; but I think it has superabundantly shown the possibility of giving to the service of humanity, even without the aid of belief in a Providence, both the psychological power and the social efficacy of a religion; making it take hold of human life, and color all thought, feeling, and action, in a manner of which the greatest ascendancy ever exercised by any religion may be but a type and foretaste; and of which the danger is, not that it should be insufficient but that it should be so excessive as to interfere unduly with human freedom and individuality.

Neither is it necessary to the feeling which constitutes the binding force of the utilitarian morality on those who recognize it, to wait for those social influences which would make its obligation felt by mankind at large. In the comparatively early state of human advancement in which we now live, a person cannot indeed feel that entireness of sympathy with all others, which would make any real discordance in the general direction of their conduct in life impossible; but already a person in whom the social feeling is at all developed, cannot bring himself to think of the rest of his fellow creatures as struggling rivals with him for the means of happiness, whom he must desire to see defeated in their object in order that he may succeed in his. The deeply rooted conception which every individual even now has of himself as a social being, tends to make him feel it one of his natural wants that there should be harmony between his feelings and aims and those of his fellow creatures. If differences of opinion and of mental culture make it impossible for him to share many of their actual feelings—perhaps make him denounce and defy those feelings—he still needs to be conscious that his real aim and theirs do not conflict; that he is not opposing himself to what they really wish for, namely their own good, but is, on the contrary, promoting it. This feeling in most individuals is much inferior in strength to their selfish feelings, and is often wanting altogether. But to those who have it, it possesses all the characters of a natural feeling. It does not present itself to their minds as a superstition of education, or a law despotically imposed by the power of society, but as an attribute which it would not be well for them to be without. This conviction is the ultimate sanction of the greatest happiness morality. This it is which makes any mind, of well-developed feelings, work with, and not against, the outward motives to care for others, afforded by what I have called the external sanctions; and when those sanctions are wanting, or act in an opposite direction, constitutes in itself a powerful internal binding force, in proportion to the sensitiveness and thoughtfulness of the character; since few but those whose mind is a moral blank, could bear to lay out their course of life on the plan of paying no regard to others except so far as their own private interest compels.

The heart of Mill's attempt to establish the limits for the exercise of civil liberty is what is commonly known as the **"harm principle." Coercion**, Mill holds, may be exercised on an individual only "to prevent harm to others. His own good, either physical or moral, is not a sufficient warrant."[19] There are some immediate and obvious objections to Mill's understanding of this principle. For one thing, where does one establish the line between activity that is "purely" self-regarding and that which involves, concerns, and affects others and their activities? Moreover, it could be

[19]Mill, *On Liberty,* p. 8.

QUESTIONS FOR REFLECTION

1. Describe how Mill's utilitarianism differs from that of Bentham. What is at the root of their differences?
2. Faced with the problem of the incommensurability of different desires, how might a utilitarian working in Mill's school resolve which is the right desire to fulfill? Are extra-utilitarian principles unavoidable as a reference point?

argued, from the standpoint of overall utility, that allowing an individual to engage in self-destructive actions lessens the sum of happiness in society.

When writing *On Liberty,* Mill is not blind to these objections. He believes that even some opinions lost their immunity from coercion when they lead to particular harms. He is also against the positive instigation of lawless acts. His suggested resolution is to maintain that society's well-being requires that individuals should enjoy as much liberty as possible consistent with the freedom of others. This involves defining harm to others in the most restrictive terms possible. Mill is deeply suspicious of any references to majority preference when it came to identifying what individuals ought and ought not to do. In Mill's view, the will of the state should prevail over that of individuals only when "there is a definite danger, or a definite risk of damage, either to the individual or to the public."[20] Of course one could argue that this still leaves much unresolved: What, for example, constitutes "definite danger" or a "definite risk of danger?"

In other works, however, Mill appears to have adapted aspects of his thought concerning the permissibility of coercing people for their own good. He agrees, for example, with proposals to legislate reductions in hours worked, and underlines the desirability of compulsory education. In both instances, Mill justifies his position by saying that such actions by government actually serve the best interests and real desires of individuals.

Government and its limits play a significant role in Mill's thoughts on liberty, especially representative government. While he believes in extending the electoral franchise, he is concerned about the volatility and limited experience of a large electorate. In is *Considerations on Representative Government,* Mill presents representative democracy as a political structure that engages the need for special skills and professionalism and expertise in administration, but also accommodates the need for public accountability. There is a "radical distinction," Mill writes, "between controlling the business of government and actually doing it." The size of contemporary states, Mill believes, make the notion of direct democracy (associated with the ancient Greeks) an impossibility. Though the people have the final say on who governs in a representative democracy, this need not imply that the people actually conduct the government's business. But Mill's desire to limit the people's voice in democracy is not limited to these distinctions. He also believes that more votes should be allocated to those wiser and more talented—people, presumably, such as himself. To this extent,

[20] Mill, *On Liberty,* p. 73.

CASE STUDY 13.1

James is studying political philosophy at an undergraduate level because he believes that it will help him get into law school. He needs, however, more than a passing grade—he requires the highest grade possible. His interest in going to law school is not primarily to work in the corporate world. He wants to provide legal counsel to nonprofit organizations working in the developing world. Everything hinges on his final exam.

Unfortunately James has managed only limited preparation for this exam. His aged mother suddenly became ill, and he had to spend several days assisting her. He knows that, given his state of preparedness, the only way he can achieve the highest grade is by cheating. While James is uneasy about cheating, he knows this may be the only way he can ensure his entry into law school, and then acquire the credentials to help others working with often starving, desperate people. Should James therefore cheat?

Questions

1. How might an act utilitarian and a rule utilitarian resolve this question?
2. How would a utilitarian deal with the wrongness of cheating in this instance?

Mill seems distrustful of the masses' judgment, which needs to be moderated by those with more wisdom and expertise.

MILL AS POLITICAL ECONOMIST

Like Bentham and James Mill, John Stuart Mill was always interested in the science of economics as well as the subject of political economy. His *Principles of Political Economy with Some of Their Applications to Social Philosophy* (1848) claims to be in the tradition of Adam Smith when it comes to such matters. It is also clear, however, that Mill believes that this tradition needs updating. "It appears to the present writer," Mill writes, "that a work similar in its object and general conception to that of Adam Smith, but adapted to the more extended knowledge and improved ideas of the present age, is the kind of contribution which Political Economy at present requires." The strength of Smith's *Wealth of Nations,* Mill contends, is that it insists on dealing with reality and disdains excessive abstraction. Because much of the world had changed since 1776, it was time, in Mill's view, for a fresh look at matters of political economy. It soon becomes apparent, however, that Mill's work in many respects goes beyond the insights of the Smith tradition and actually arrives at very different conclusions regarding the organization of the economy and the role played by governments in economic life.

Mill's political economy is not, as commonly supposed, a work of advocacy for laissez-faire economics. His ideas do not sit easily with strict libertarian approaches to political economy, but neither do they give enormous comfort to those of a socialist disposition. The key to understanding this is the manner in which Mill distinguishes between **state economic functions** that are **necessary** (such as protecting private property by criminalizing stealing) and those that Mill says are of "**the optional kind.**" The category of "optional" is further subdivided into functions that are "**nonauthoritative**" and those that are "**authoritative.**"

The functions of government in the economy that fall into the category of "necessary" are essentially identified by Mill by virtue not of a philosophical principle, but rather by the fact that few people object to them: "First, the means adopted by

PRIMARY SOURCE 13.3 | OF THE LIMITS TO THE AUTHORITY OF SOCIETY OVER THE INDIVIDUAL, FROM *ON LIBERTY*, CHAPTER 4

What, then, is the rightful limit to the sovereignty of the individual over himself? Where does the authority of society begin? How much of human life should be assigned to individuality, and how much to society?

Each will receive its proper share, if each has that which more particularly concerns it. To individuality should belong the part of life in which it is chiefly the individual that is interested; to society, the part which chiefly interests society.

Though society is not founded on a contract, and though no good purpose is answered by inventing a contract in order to deduce social obligations from it, every one who receives the protection of society owes a return for the benefit, and the fact of living in society renders it indispensable that each should be bound to observe a certain line of conduct toward the rest. This conduct consists, first, in not injuring the interests of one another; or rather certain interests, which, either by express legal provision or by tacit understanding, ought to be considered as rights; and secondly, in each person's bearing his share (to be fixed on some equitable principle) of the labors and sacrifices incurred for defending the society or its members from injury and molestation. These conditions society is justified in enforcing, at all costs to those who endeavor to withhold fulfilment. Nor is this all that society may do. The acts of an individual may be hurtful to others, or wanting in due consideration for their welfare, without going the length of violating any of their constituted rights. The offender may then be justly punished by opinion, though not by law. As soon as any part of a person's conduct affects prejudicially the interests of others, society has jurisdiction over it, and the question whether the general welfare will or will not be promoted by interfering with it, becomes open to discussion. But there is no room for entertaining any such question when a person's conduct affects the interests of no persons besides himself, or needs not affect them unless they like (all the persons concerned being of full age, and the ordinary amount of understanding). In all such cases there should be perfect freedom, legal and social, to do the action and stand the consequences...

What I contend for is, that the inconveniences which are strictly inseparable from the unfavorable judgment of others, are the only ones to which a person should ever be subjected for that portion of his conduct and character which concerns his own good, but which does not affect the interests of others in their relations with him. Acts injurious to others require a totally different treatment. Encroachment on their rights; infliction on them of any loss or damage not justified by his own rights; falsehood or duplicity in dealing with them; unfair or ungenerous use of advantages over them; even selfish abstinence from defending them against injury—these are fit objects of moral reprobation, and, in grave cases, of moral retribution and punishment. And not only these acts, but the dispositions which lead to them, are properly immoral, and fit subjects of disapprobation which may rise to abhorrence. Cruelty of disposition; malice and ill nature; that most antisocial and odious of all passions, envy; dissimulation and insincerity, irascibility on insufficient cause, and resentment disproportioned to the provocation; the love of domineering over others; the desire to engross more than one's share of advantages (the *pleonexia* of the Greeks); the pride which derives gratification from the abasement of others; the egotism which thinks self and its concerns more important than everything else, and decides all doubtful questions in his own favor—these are moral vices, and constitute a bad and odious moral character: unlike the self-regarding faults previously mentioned, which are not properly immoralities, and to whatever pitch they may be carried, do not constitute wickedness. They may be proofs of any amount of folly, or want of personal dignity and self-respect; but they are only a subject of moral reprobation when they involve a breach of duty to others, for whose sake the individual is bound to have care for himself. What are called duties to ourselves are not socially obligatory, unless

PRIMARY SOURCE 13.3

Of the Limits to the Authority of Society over the Individual, from *On Liberty,* Chapter 4 *continued*

circumstances render them at the same time duties to others. The term duty to oneself, when it means anything more than prudence, means self-respect or self-development; and for none of these is any one accountable to his fellow creatures, because for none of them is it for the good of mankind that he be held accountable to them.

The distinction between the loss of consideration which a person may rightly incur by defect of prudence or of personal dignity, and the reprobation which is due to him for an offense against the rights of others, is not a merely nominal distinction. It makes a vast difference both in our feelings and in our conduct toward him, whether he displeases us in things in which we think we have a right to control him, or in things in which we know that we have not. If he displeases us, we may express our distaste, and we may stand aloof from a person as well as from a thing that displeases us; but we shall not therefore feel called on to make his life uncomfortable. We shall reflect that he already bears, or will bear, the whole penalty of his error; if he spoils his life by mismanagement, we shall not, for that reason, desire to spoil it still further: instead of wishing to punish him, we shall rather endeavor to alleviate his punishment, by showing him how he may avoid or cure the evils his conduct tends to bring upon him. He may be to us an object of pity, perhaps of dislike, but not of anger or resentment; we shall not treat him like an enemy of society: the worst we shall think ourselves justified in doing is leaving him to himself, if we do not interfere benevolently by showing interest or concern for him. It is far otherwise if he has infringed the rules necessary for the protection of his fellow creatures, individually or collectively. The evil consequences of his acts do not then fall on himself, but on others; and society, as the protector of all its members, must retaliate on him; must inflict pain on him for the express purpose of punishment, and must take care that it be sufficiently severe. In the one case, he is an offender at our bar, and we are called on not only to sit in judgment of him, but, in one shape or another, to execute our own sentence: in the other case, it is not our part to inflict any suffering on him, except what may incidentally follow from our using the same liberty in the regulation of our own affairs, which we allow to him in his.

The distinction here pointed out between the part of a person's life which concerns only himself, and that which concerns others, many persons will refuse to admit. How (it may be asked) can any part of the conduct of a member of society be a matter of indifference to the other members? No person is an entirely isolated being; it is impossible for a person to do anything seriously or permanently hurtful to himself, without mischief reaching at least to his near connections, and often far beyond them. If he injures his property, he does harm to those who directly or indirectly derived support from it, and usually diminishes, by a greater or less amount, the general resources of the community. If he deteriorates his bodily or mental faculties, he not only brings evil upon all who depended on him for any portion of their happiness, but disqualifies himself for rendering the services which he owes to his fellow creatures generally; perhaps becomes a burden on their affection or benevolence; and if such conduct were very frequent, hardly any offense that is committed would detract more from the general sum of good. Finally, if by his vices or follies a person does no direct harm to others, he is nevertheless (it may be said) injurious by his example; and ought to be compelled to control himself, for the sake of those whom the sight or knowledge of his conduct might corrupt or mislead...

I fully admit that the mischief which a person does to himself, may seriously affect, both through their sympathies and their interests, those nearly connected with him, and in a minor degree, society at large. When, by conduct of this sort, a person is led to violate a distinct and assignable obligation to any other person or persons, the case is taken out of the self-regarding class, and becomes amenable to moral disapprobation in the proper sense of the term. If, for

continued

PRIMARY SOURCE 13.3

Of the Limits to the Authority of Society over the Individual, from *On Liberty*, Chapter 4 *continued*

example, a man, through intemperance or extravagance, becomes unable to pay his debts, or, having undertaken the moral responsibility of a family, becomes from the same cause incapable of supporting or educating them, he is deservedly reprobated, and might be justly punished; but it is for the breach of duty to his family or creditors, not for the extravagance. If the resources which ought to have been devoted to them, had been diverted from them for the most prudent investment, the moral culpability would have been the same. George Barnwell murdered his uncle to get money for his mistress, but if he had done it to set himself up in business, he would equally have been hanged. Again, in the frequent case of a man who causes grief to his family by addiction to bad habits, he deserves reproach for his unkindness or ingratitude; but so he may for cultivating habits not in themselves vicious, if they are painful to those with whom he passes his life, or who from personal ties are dependent on him for their comfort. Whoever fails in the consideration generally due to the interests and feelings of others, not being compelled by some more imperative duty, or justified by allowable self-preference, is a subject of moral disapprobation for that failure, but not for the cause of it, nor for the errors, merely personal to himself, which may have remotely led to it. In like manner, when a person disables himself, by conduct purely self-regarding, from the performance of some definite duty incumbent on him to the public, he is guilty of a social offense. No person ought to be punished simply for being drunk; but a soldier or a policeman should be punished for being drunk on duty. Whenever, in short, there is a definite damage, or a definite risk of damage, either to an individual or to the public, the case is taken out of the province of liberty, and placed in that of morality or law.

But with regard to the merely contingent or, as it may be called, constructive injury which a person causes to society, by conduct which neither violates any specific duty to the public, nor occasions perceptible hurt to any assignable individual except himself; the inconvenience is one which society can afford to bear, for the sake of the greater good of human freedom. If grown persons are to be punished for not taking proper care of themselves, I would rather it were for their own sake, than under pretense of preventing them from impairing their capacity of rendering to society benefits which society does not pretend it has a right to exact. But I cannot consent to argue the point as if society had no means of bringing its weaker members up to its ordinary standard of rational conduct, except waiting till they do something irrational, and then punishing them, legally or morally, for it. Society has had absolute power over them during all the early portion of their existence: it has had the whole period of childhood and nonage in which to try whether it could make them capable of rational conduct in life. The existing generation is master both of the training and the entire circumstances of the generation to come; it cannot indeed make them perfectly wise and good, because it is itself so lamentably deficient in goodness and wisdom; and its best efforts are not always, in individual cases, its most successful ones; but it is perfectly well able to make the rising generation, as a whole, as good as, and a little better than, itself. If society lets any considerable number of its members grow up mere children, incapable of being acted on by rational consideration of distant motives, society has itself to blame for the consequences. Armed not only with all the powers of education, but with the ascendency which the authority of a received opinion always exercises over the minds who are least fitted to judge for themselves; and aided by the natural penalties which cannot be prevented from falling on those who incur the distaste or the contempt of those who know them; let not society pretend that it needs, besides all this, the power to issue commands and enforce obedience in the personal concerns of individuals, in which, on all principles of justice and policy, the decision ought to rest with those who are to abide the consequences. Nor is there anything which tends more to discredit

PRIMARY SOURCE 13.3 | OF THE LIMITS TO THE AUTHORITY OF SOCIETY OVER THE INDIVIDUAL, FROM *ON LIBERTY*, CHAPTER 4 *continued*

and frustrate the better means of influencing conduct, than a resort to the worse. If there be among those whom it is attempted to coerce into prudence or temperance, any of the material of which vigorous and independent characters are made, they will infallibly rebel against the yoke. No such person will ever feel that others have a right to control him in his concerns, such as they have to prevent him from injuring them in theirs; and it easily comes to be considered a mark of spirit and courage to fly in the face of such usurped authority, and do with ostentation the exact opposite of what it enjoins; as in the fashion of grossness which succeeded, in the time of Charles II, to the fanatical moral intolerance of the Puritans. With respect to what is said of the necessity of protecting society from the bad example set to others by the vicious or the self-indulgent; it is true that bad example may have a pernicious effect, especially the example of doing wrong to others with impunity to the wrongdoer. But we are now speaking of conduct which, while it does no wrong to others, is supposed to do great harm to the agent himself: and I do not see how those who believe this, can think otherwise than that the example, on the whole, must be more salutary than hurtful, since, if it displays the misconduct, it displays also the painful or degrading consequences which, if the conduct is justly censured, must be supposed to be in all or most cases attendant on it.

But the strongest of all the arguments against the interference of the public with purely personal conduct, is that when it does interfere, the odds are that it interferes wrongly, and in the wrong place. On questions of social morality, of duty to others, the opinion of the public, that is, of an overruling majority, though often wrong, is likely to be still oftener right; because on such questions they are only required to judge of their own interests; of the manner in which some mode of conduct, if allowed to be practiced, would affect themselves. But the opinion of a similar majority, imposed as a law on the minority, on questions of self-regarding conduct, is quite as likely to be wrong as right; for in these cases public opinion means, at the best, some people's opinion of what is good or bad for other people; while very often it does not even mean that; the public, with the most perfect indifference, passing over the pleasure or convenience of those whose conduct they censure, and considering only their own preference. There are many who consider as an injury to themselves any conduct which they have a distaste for, and resent it as an outrage to their feelings; as a religious bigot, when charged with disregarding the religious feelings of others, has been known to retort that they disregard his feelings, by persisting in their abominable worship or creed. But there is no parity between the feeling of a person for his own opinion, and the feeling of another who is offended at his holding it; no more than between the desire of a thief to take a purse, and the desire of the right owner to keep it. And a person's taste is as much his own peculiar concern as his opinion or his purse. It is easy for any one to imagine an ideal public, which leaves the freedom and choice of individuals in all uncertain matters undisturbed, and only requires them to abstain from modes of conduct which universal experience has condemned. But where has there been seen a public which set any such limit to its censorship? or when does the public trouble itself about universal experience? In its interferences with personal conduct it is seldom thinking of anything but the enormity of acting or feeling differently from itself; and this standard of judgment, thinly disguised, is held up to mankind as the dictate of religion and philosophy, by nine tenths of all moralists and speculative writers. These teach that things are right because they are right; because we feel them to be so. They tell us to search in our own minds and hearts for laws of conduct binding on ourselves and on all others. What can the poor public do but apply these instructions, and make their own personal feelings of good and evil, if they are tolerably unanimous in them, obligatory on all the world?

continued

PRIMARY SOURCE 13.3

OF THE LIMITS TO THE AUTHORITY OF SOCIETY OVER THE INDIVIDUAL, FROM *ON LIBERTY,* CHAPTER 4 *continued*

The evil here pointed out is not one which exists only in theory; and it may perhaps be expected that I should specify the instances in which the public of this age and country improperly invests its own preferences with the character of moral laws. I am not writing an essay on the aberrations of existing moral feeling. That is too weighty a subject to be discussed parenthetically, and by way of illustration. Yet examples are necessary, to show that the principle I maintain is of serious and practical moment, and that I am not endeavoring to erect a barrier against imaginary evils. And it is not difficult to show, by abundant instances, that to extend the bounds of what may be called moral police, until it encroaches on the most unquestionably legitimate liberty of the individual, is one of the most universal of all human propensities.

As a first instance, consider the antipathies which men cherish on no better grounds than that persons whose religious opinions are different from theirs, do not practice their religious observances, especially their religious abstinences. To cite a rather trivial example, nothing in the creed or practice of Christians does more to envenom the hatred of Mahomedans against them, than the fact of their eating pork. There are few acts which Christians and Europeans regard with more unaffected disgust, than Mussulmans regard this particular mode of satisfying hunger. It is, in the first place, an offense against their religion; but this circumstance by no means explains either the degree or the kind of their repugnance; for wine also is forbidden by their religion, and to partake of it is by all Mussulmans accounted wrong, but not disgusting. Their aversion to the flesh of the "unclean beast" is, on the contrary, of that peculiar character, resembling an instinctive antipathy, which the idea of uncleanness, when once it thoroughly sinks into the feelings, seems always to excite even in those whose personal habits are anything but scrupulously cleanly and of which the sentiment of religious impurity, so intense in the Hindoos, is a remarkable example. Suppose now that in a people, of whom the majority were Mussulmans, that majority should insist upon not permitting pork to be eaten within the limits of the country. This would be nothing new in Mahomedan countries. Would it be a legitimate exercise of the moral authority of public opinion? and if not, why not? The practice is really revolting to such a public. They also sincerely think that it is forbidden and abhorred by the Deity. Neither could the prohibition be censured as religious persecution. It might be religious in its origin, but it would not be persecution for religion, since nobody's religion makes it a duty to eat pork. The only tenable ground of condemnation would be, that with the personal tastes and self-regarding concerns of individuals the public has no business to interfere.

governments to raise the revenue which is the condition of their existence. Secondly, the nature of the laws which they prescribe on the two great subjects of Property and Contracts. Thirdly, the excellence or defects of the system of means by which they enforce generally the execution of their laws, namely, their judicature and police."[21]

Looking at each of these functions in turn, Mill concludes that while each seems to restrict government intervention in the economy, the carrying out of these tasks necessitates many more functions on the part of the state than people usually realize. Thus as Mill notes, "The subject of protection to person and property, considered as afforded by government, ramifies widely, into a number of indirect channels.

[21]Mill, *Political Economy,* Book V, Chapter 1.

QUESTIONS FOR REFLECTION

1. Can you think of instances in which what Mill calls self-regarding behavior might be forbidden by law?
2. Are there any choices that may be legitimately described as purely self-regarding?
3. Is Mill's harm principle a genuine safeguard against excessive government coercion, or does it merely protect libertine attitudes?
4. What forms of private behavior constitute a risk of what Mill calls a "definite danger" to society?

It embraces, for example, the whole subject of the perfection or inefficiency of the means provided for the ascertainment of rights and the redress of injuries."[22] Then there is the constantly developing character of law—especially English common law—which is constantly altering the effect of government upon economic life. Conscious, however, of the effects of excessive government intervention upon economic prosperity, Mill tries to articulate a principle that will prevent government from growing. Unfortunately, he appears unable to find a philosophical maxim, and he opts to argue that government intervention ought to be permitted only in a powerful case of expediency. The problem with such a principle is its vagueness. What, for instance, constitutes expediency? And how might this differ from government officials seeking to promote their own interests over those of the wider society?

Ironically, Mill is able to give clearer definition to the types of "optional" government interference in the economy that he identifies. There ought, Mill argues, be a presumption against authoritative government interference in the economy. Such interference, understood as involving legal prohibitions and punishments, offends the principle of utility and individuality, and hence ought to be strongly presumed against. When it comes to "nonauthoritative" interference, Mill takes a different view. Provided that nonauthoritative government economic intervention in the economy serves as an adjunct to, rather than supplants, private economic activity, Mill holds that the same presumption does not apply.

In thinking about both the internal workings of an economy as well as the effects of growing wealth upon political society, Mill expresses ambiguous views, some of which have led scholars to characterize aspects of his thought as socialistic. Mill is concerned about the functional distinctions between owners and wage earners, and he worries that the conditions of industrial capitalism will damage the intellectual and cultural well-being of wage earners, especially in light of what he regards as their deprivation of being able to act in an entrepreneurial manner. As well as advocating proposals such as profit sharing, Mill's *Principles of Political Economy* also suggests that it would be best for society as a whole if economic life adopted what can be described as **"corporatist arrangements."** To cite Mill, "The form of association ... which if mankind continue to improve must be expected in the end to predominate is not that which can exist between a capitalist as Chief, and work people without a voice in the management, but the association of laborers themselves on forms of equality, collectively owning the capital with which they carry on their operations and working

[22]Mill, *Political Economy,* Book V, Chapter 8.

CASE STUDY 13.2

In the last decade of the 20th century, the pornography industry grew immensely in North America and Western Europe. What was once a relatively marginal (and in some jurisdictions criminal) activity is now a multibillion-dollar industry. This has been accompanied by the decriminalization of a variety of sexual acts since the 1960s, often by legislators and judges who have cited Mill's *On Liberty* as their intellectual inspiration for doing so.

At the same time, relatively few people—especially women—are willing to describe working in the pornography industry as an activity that enhances the dignity of the participants. Likewise, viewing pornography is regarded by many as itself being an immoral activity. There is also growing evidence that the increasingly widespread availability of pornography has changed how sex is understood by people, especially young men and women—not to mention how men and women regard each other. Pornography, it seems, is not a harmless activity, and yet many participating in the industry do so of their own free will.

Questions

1. Is Mill's harm principle a sufficient way to think through the problem of how we protect society from the cultural effects of pornography while simultaneously preserving civil liberty?
2. How might you draw the line between what society is and is not willing to tolerate concerning pornography? Explain your reasoning.

under managers elected and removable by themselves."[23] This, he believes, would do away with class antagonisms, as well as organizations that have emerged from such conflicts—including trade unions.

Mill's concerns about the cultural effects of capitalist economies are associated with what he saw as an increasingly consumerist social order and the apparent effects of capitalism upon the environment. Mill writes that there is little opportunity for contemplation of the natural world in economic conditions that emphasize growth, the unending acquisition of goods, and the increasingly important role played by technology and industrial production. To this extent, it seems that Mill parts company with the classical tradition of economics associated with figures such as Adam Smith. Indeed at various points in his *Principles,* Mill appears to advocate what might be called a **"stationary economy."** Like many people of his time, Mill was highly influenced by the thought of Thomas Malthus, who argued that the world possessed only finite resources—the limits of which, Malthus incorrectly believed, were being reached as a result of massive population growth as wealth-creating systems prolonged human life and enabled more people to have more children than would hitherto have been possible. Mill's "stationary state," as he calls it in the *Principles,* is underpinned by his lack of ease with "the ideal of life held out by those who think that the normal state of human beings is that of struggling to get on; that the trampling, crushing, elbowing and treading on each other's heels, which form the existing type of social life, are the most desirable lot of mankind, or anything but the disagreeable symptoms of one of the phases of industrial progress."[24] This argument for a "no-growth" economy presumes many things; but there seems little question that it takes Mill away from Smith's (and even, to an extent, Bentham's) economic ideas, bringing him closer to Marx's economic vision of a postcapitalist, postindustrial future.

[23]Mill, *Political Economy,* p. 133.

[24]Mill, *Political Economy,* p. 113.

PRIMARY SOURCE 13.4

Of the Functions of Government in General, from *Principles of Political Economy*, Book V, Chapter 1

1. One of the most disputed questions both in political science and in practical statesmanship at this particular period, relates to the proper limits of the functions and agency of governments. At other times it has been a subject of controversy how governments should be constituted, and according to what principles and rules they should exercise their authority; but it is now almost equally a question, to what departments of human affairs that authority should extend. And when the tide sets so strongly toward changes in government and legislation, as a means of improving the condition of mankind, this discussion is more likely to increase than to diminish in interest. On the one hand, impatient reformers, thinking it easier and shorter to get possession of the government than of the intellects and dispositions of the public, are under a constant temptation to stretch the province of government beyond due bounds: while, on the other, mankind have been so much accustomed by their rulers to interference for purposes other than the public good, or under an erroneous conception of what that good requires, and so many rash proposals are made by sincere lovers of improvement, for attempting, by compulsory regulation, the attainment of objects which can only be effectually or only usefully compassed by opinion and discussion, that there has grown up a spirit of resistance in limine [on the threshold] to the interference of government, merely as such, and a disposition to restrict its sphere of action within the narrowest bounds. From differences in the historical development of different nations, not necessary to be here dwelt upon, the former excess, that of exaggerating the province of government, prevails most, both in theory and in practice, among the Continental nations, while in England the contrary spirit has hitherto been predominant. The general principles of the question, in so far as it is a question of principle, I shall make an attempt to determine in a later chapter of this Book: after first considering the effects produced by the conduct of government in the exercise of the functions universally acknowledged to belong to it. For this purpose, there must be a specification of the functions which are either inseparable from the idea of a government, or are exercised habitually and without objection by all governments; as distinguished from those respecting which it has been considered questionable whether governments should exercise them or not. The former may be termed the necessary, the latter the optional, functions of government. By the term optional it is not meant to imply, that it can ever be a matter of indifference, or of arbitrary choice, whether the government should or should not take upon itself the functions in question; but only that the expediency of its exercising them does not amount to necessity, and is a subject on which diversity of opinion does or may exist.

2. In attempting to enumerate the necessary functions of government, we find them to be considerably more multifarious than most people are at first aware of, and not capable of being circumscribed by those very definite lines of demarcation, which, in the inconsiderateness of popular discussion, it is often attempted to draw round them. We sometimes, for example, hear it said that governments ought to confine themselves to affording protection against force and fraud: that, these two things apart, people should be free agents, able to take care of themselves, and that so long as a person practices no violence or deception, to the injury of others in person or property, legislatures and governments are in no way called on to concern themselves about him. But why should people be protected by their government, that is, by their own collective strength, against violence and fraud, and not against other evils, except that the expediency is more obvious? If nothing, but what people cannot possibly do for themselves, can be fit to be done for them by government, people might be required to protect themselves by their skill and courage even against force, or to beg or buy protection against it, as they actually do where the

continued

PRIMARY SOURCE 13.4

OF THE FUNCTIONS OF GOVERNMENT IN GENERAL, FROM *PRINCIPLES OF POLITICAL ECONOMY*, BOOK V, CHAPTER 1 *continued*

government is not capable of protecting them: and against fraud every one has the protection of his own wits. But without further anticipating the discussion of principles, it is sufficient on the present occasion to consider facts...

Nor is the function of the law in defining property itself, so simple a thing as may be supposed. It may be imagined, perhaps, that the law has only to declare and protect the right of every one to what he has himself produced, or acquired by the voluntary consent, fairly obtained, of those who produced it. But is there nothing recognized as property except what has been produced? Is there not the earth itself, its forests and waters, and all other natural riches, above and below the surface? These are the inheritance of the human race, and there must be regulations for the common enjoyment of it. What rights, and under what conditions, a person shall be allowed to exercise over any portion of this common inheritance, cannot be left undecided. No function of government is less optional than the regulation of these things, or more completely involved in the idea of civilized society.

The unresolved tension in Mill's thoughts on political economy in this area is how he proposes to reconcile his commitment to private property and free exchange, with the goal of a static economy, without reverting to something he clearly detests, which is a high degree of state coercive activity. Mill was aware of these tensions. He concedes that "a stationary condition of capital and population implies no stationary state of human improvement," something that appears difficult to reconcile with his often-mentioned commitment to progress as well as the natural disruption that occurs in the social order as a result of individuals making relatively uncoerced choices everyday.

CONCLUSION: MILL AS A CLASSICAL LIBERAL

Mill is a complex thinker, with thoughts on most subjects published in various forms. However, looking over the totality of his writings, it is difficult not to conclude that Mill and his ideas reflect a great deal of the confusion that riddles much contemporary

QUESTIONS FOR REFLECTION

1. Does Mill provide a way to preserve the institutions of modern capitalism such as private property and free exchange in his schema for a stationary economy? Is such a goal possible?
2. Identify different government economic activities that might fall into the categories of necessary, optional authoritative, and optional nonauthoritative. What other categories might be possible and yet consistent with Mill's schema?
3. To what extent does Mill remain within the tradition of political economy articulated by Adam Smith, and to what extent does he depart from it?
4. Is Mill's approach to political economy ultimately socialistic in its orientation?

CASE STUDY 13.3

Central banks have become an everyday feature of economic life in most countries since the Great Depression. Responsible for maintaining a stable money supply, central banks play a major role in preventing inflation and managing economies so that they avoid, as far as is possible, the boom–bust cycle that was so damaging in the 1930s.

Central banks, however, are an arm of the state. While they differ in their degree of closeness to the state, it is also true that capitalist economies were able to do without central banks for almost 250 years. They do not appear to be one of Mill's "necessary" functions of government. At the same time, they exercise a high degree of authority. In most countries, for example, they alone may issue legal tender.

Questions

1. How do central banks fit into Mill's tripartite distinction between necessary, optional authoritative, and optional nonauthoritative functions of government?
2. Is central banking something that Mill would justify primarily on grounds of utility, even though central banks exercise what might be called extragovernmental coercive authority?
3. How would Mill explain the growth of semiautonomous government institutions such as central banks?

thought claiming the title of *liberal.* Thus he favors universal suffrage and yet still wishes to maintain a privileged place for individuals like himself in his ideal political order. Likewise Mill advocates a high degree of economic liberty while simultaneously desiring the institutionalization of procedures and structures that undermine the workings of markets in the name of equality. He describes an idea of human dignity and yet remains essentially rooted in a utilitarian cast of mind that, by definition, disparages a notion like human dignity, grounded ultimately in metaphysical concepts that utilitarianism refuses to take seriously. Earnestly passionate about wanting to see a better world, Mill appears to have wrestled with some of the implications of his ideas that, while consistent with utilitarian thinking, were actually likely to make life less happy for many people—the same people he believed should be given fewer votes than more enlightened people such as himself. To this extent, exploring Mill's life and writings is an excellent way of studying the contradictions of classical and modern liberalism, as well as the apparent inability of liberal philosophers to escape the confines of their self-constructed cages.

Key Terms

James Mill
Jeremy Bentham
utilitarianism
Harriet Taylor
utility
pleasure
pain
calculus
happiness
liberty
freedom
harm principle
coercion
government
state economic functions
necessary
the optional kind
nonauthoritative
authoritative
corporatist arrangements
stationary economy

Sources and Resources

Key Texts

Autobiography
On Liberty
Principles of Political Economy
Utilitarianism
Discussions and Dissertations
Subjection of Women
System of Logic

Secondary Texts

Cowling, Maurice. Mill and Liberalism (New York: Cambridge University Press, 1990).

Gregg, Samuel. *On Ordered Liberty: A Treatise on the Free Society* (Lanham: Lexington, 2003).

Himmelfarb, Gertrude. *On Liberty and Liberalism: The Case of John Stuart Mill* (New York: Knopf, 1974).

Walsh, David. *The Growth of the Liberal Soul* (Columbia: University of Missouri Press, 1997).

Web Sites

Stanford Encyclopedia of Philosophy entry online at http://plato.stanford.edu/entries/mill/

Free, full-text works by Mill online at http://oll.libertyfund.org/Intros/MillJS.php

NIETZSCHE

CHAPTER 14

By David Walsh *The Catholic University of America*

LIFE AND LEGACY

Friedrich Nietzsche (1844–1900) is prominently featured in any discussion of contemporary political thought, yet he created no political writings. The passing references to politics within his philosophical reflections would not in themselves justify this attention. Rather, his philosophical works are themselves viewed in political terms. We discover with Nietzsche that political theory is broader than a consideration of the issues of governance. At stake in any political discussion is a deeper concern about what it means to be a human being. Who are we? Where are we going? Whence have we come? Such are the questions implicated in any approach to politics, which always takes a stand on the meaning and purpose of life. There cannot be a political order without a moral order, and there cannot be a moral order without some relationship to an order that transcends the human level. Politics cannot exist without reference to metaphysics. Normally such foundational questions of the dignity and worth of human life can be taken for granted; politics then becomes the means by which the rights of every individual are recognized and preserved. But what happens when a crisis of values overtakes a society? When doubt concerning the meaning and purpose of existence flickers across people's minds? A sense of the precariousness of civilization begins to take hold. Nietzsche was among the first to sound the alarm. As a consequence, he became the great diagnostician of the crisis that would become manifest in the global conflicts and totalitarian nightmare of the 20th century.

When politics collapses completely, the causes must lie in a failure deeper than the institutions involved. Nietzsche's relevance for political theory arises from the nonpolitical nature of the crisis that has engulfed it. Along with Dostoevsky, he sensed the explosions that would shatter the façade of progress in the 20th century. Dying at the very opening of the era of world wars, concentration camps, and weapons of mass destruction, he understood that the dangers had arisen not from external forces, but from the inner disintegration of humanity. Before any of these phenomena were visible, he intuited them as the darkness that had grown silently within modern civilization. This was because Nietzsche had an acute sensitivity to the nonpolitical factors of politics. He knew that what people believe makes all the difference. An orgy of destructiveness does not simply break out in human society. It is preceded by the disappearance of inner restraints. Politically, modern civilization was on the verge of a catastrophe because it had lost faith in the order that had sustained it for two millennia. Christianity and philosophy could no longer play their formative roles when people ceased to recognize their truth. The old order had collapsed, and nothing comparable had emerged to take its place. Many were of course likely to be misled by appearances, thinking that because nothing had visibly changed, the world was as it was. But Nietzsche understood that mere observance of the formalities was only a temporary phase before everyone realized that they now believed in nothing. The term he coined (although he did not invent it) to express the situation of modern humanity was **nihilism**. It appropriately indicates the "nihil" or nothing that now contaminates all meaning. When life has no higher meaning or purpose, everything in it becomes meaningless. The state of wandering aimlessly in a wasteland, the absurdity of existence that has become so familiar today, was first given a name by Nietzsche. It is because he seemed to understand this lost condition so well that he has remained one of the most widely read of all philosophers.

QUESTIONS FOR REFLECTION

Is modern existence experienced as absurd? You can verify the popularity of Nietzsche by checking the availability of his works in any bookstore. Has he tapped into a deep vein of absurdity in our modern experience? Is the mood of nihilism one that many people encounter in their lives today? What does this imply for the foundations of politics?

NIETZSCHE'S DIAGNOSIS OF THE MODERN CRISIS

To understand Nietzsche is of course a different matter. A reading of him is too frequently a reading into him of what we wish to find. This is because it is easier to locate a great thinker within our already settled understanding of reality, rather than confront the possibility that understanding him might entail a considerable enlargement of perspective on our part. Nietzsche is particularly prone to this misuse. His language is relatively nontechnical, giving the impression of accessibility. But superficial mastery masks our inability to go beneath the surface. His own advice about reading carefully was no doubt prompted by a premonition of distorted popularization. Nowhere is this more evident than in the familiarity with which his most famous remark, "God is dead," is bandied about. Easily repeated, the phrase seems to convey a recognizable meaning until we begin to realize that the whole of an era is contained in it. Then its multiple meanings proliferate. **"God is dead"** can be taken as a sociological observation that modern society no longer believes in God. Or it may be an autobiographical statement of Nietzsche's own inability to believe. Or it may indicate the inability of reason to philosophically reach the idea of God. Or it may represent a theological conception of the God who dies to redeem sinful humans from death. Perhaps the various meanings are interwoven. What is clear, however, is that the death of God constitutes a central preoccupation of Nietzsche. To the extent that God has become unbelievable in the modern world, that world had begun to lose the unifying principle by which it was sustained. Without religion politics would be utterly different. Concern about the presence or absence of religion in political life had its beginning in the Nietzschean realization that we live in a civilization without a space for the divine. Fundamentalists and secularists continue to do battle while seeking to hide the anxiety from which they operate. What does it mean to live without God? Nietzsche was really the first to courageously and honestly face this question.

As a result he has often been misunderstood as approving the condition in which he found himself. But that view overlooks his entire effort to overcome the theological vacuum. He foresaw what a civilization without its transcendent anchor would mean and struggled mightily to remedy it. This is why he claimed to be not only the first European nihilist, but the first to go beyond nihilism. His ambition was to find the way toward a spiritual renovation that would replace remaining tatters. What makes this project so remarkable, however, was that Nietzsche was also fully aware of the extent to which modern attempts to replace Greek philosophy and Christian revelation had failed. The crisis he addressed was dual. It was at once the exhaustion of ancient sources of meaning and the realization of the bankruptcy of modern alternatives. European Enlightenment had failed to deliver on the unlimited expectations it seemed to promise in the 18th century. All that was clear was that the ideological mass movements, the enthusiasms of nationalism, socialism, and liberalism—and the even more destructive successors of Nazism, fascism, and communism looming on the horizon—were hollow. To take the measure of Nietzsche, it is necessary to see the unrelieved bleakness of the moment in which he lived. The great spiritual heritage from the past was obsolete; the present held no prospect for the future. He was alone—the solitary individual called to respond to the crisis of a civilization. It is important to realize the weight he felt compelled to bear if we are to appreciate the faith that supported him in the struggle. Nietzsche may not have found the renovation he so desperately sought, but he was carried along by the confidence that it could be found.

This confidence sustained him on a philosophic odyssey that eventually took over his whole life. Gradually the realization dawned that he could not give himself only in part to the great questions of existence. But in the beginning he sought to follow a conventional path. Born in 1844, Nietzsche was the son of a Lutheran clergyman, benefiting from an excellent classical education and attendance at the universities of Bonn and Leipzig. He studied philology, the new science of textual interpretation in which the German universities excelled. Philology, with its rigorously impartial treatment of texts, locating everything within its historical setting, promised reliable access to the philosophical and religious scriptures so much in dispute. At last an objective path had opened up on what had long been the preserve of those who wielded authority, whether priests or princes. Scholars could now authenticate texts that had been declared off limits for the unconsecrated. With brilliant prospects ahead of him, Nietzsche was appointed to the chair of classical philology at Basel University at the age of 24. He discovered, however, that the academic world was not really interested in truth. It was instead devoted to the methods of scholarship as an end in itself. So it was not surprising that Nietzsche cast around for direction beyond the academic confines. The two mentors who captivated him both exemplified the independence of spirit he so ardently sought. **Arthur Schopenhauer** had shown how philosophy must turn its back on its pale academic imitation, while **Richard Wagner** was the creative genius whose musical dramas would remake the cultural soul of the nation. Both of these towering influences came together in the young scholar's first book, *The Birth of Tragedy from the Spirit of Music* (1872). While ostensibly a contribution to the discipline of classical philology, it was clear that Nietzsche's goal was far more than an investigation of Greek tragedy. He was searching for the inner life of tragedy that could once again give birth to cultural greatness within the modern world. Nietzsche's real interest was less in the birth of tragedy than in the possibility of its rebirth today. That notable difference did not escape his academic reviewers, who panned the book into which he had poured so much of himself. This began an inner break with a world from which he would soon break more visibly.

After several leaves occasioned by ill health, Nietzsche resigned his young professorship at the age of 35 to assume the very different life of a wandering seeker. Behind him was the early academic promise, his admiration for Schopenhauer and Wagner, and brief service as an ambulance orderly on the battlefield of the **Franco–Prussian war of 1870.** His service in the war included corpse collection, an experience that confronted him with the most gruesome atrocities human beings can inflict on one another. For the next two decades he would live without institutional structure or support, returning only for his last few years to a very different kind of institution, when the onset of mental illness caused by physiological disease made independent living impossible. He died just as the century he dreaded was about to begin. In the intervening period, without a publicly defined role, Nietzsche lived a wholly private life. Frequently suffering migraines and other health problems, he learned to triumph over adversities he could not eliminate. His modest pension from the university was sufficient to cover his material needs as he shuttled between various rented accommodations in Switzerland, France, and Italy. Nietzsche's proposal of marriage to Lou Salomé was rebuffed, and he did not seek any other female possibilities. His friendships with many individuals were particularly close at various stages in his life, although they often reached insuperable disagreements. This was particularly the case in his painful break with Richard Wagner and his wife. Two of his most faithful companions, who later oversaw the disposition of his literary effects, were his sister, Elizabeth Förster, and his friend, Peter Gast. One unfortunate effect of his sister's involvement with Nietzsche's work was that she enlisted it in support of her own anti-Semitic inclinations, thereby making it possible for the Nazis to eventually claim him, inaccurately, as one of their own. The suggestion that his mental collapse was brought on as a result of contracting syphilis remains a matter of speculation. All we know is that its onset occurred in 1889 when he embraced a horse to protect its head from the blows of a carriage driver. Later, his friend Overbeck found him huddled in a corner at home. Nietzsche was taken to a number of clinics for the insane, where he remained until his death in August 1900.

The details of his life remain a topic of fascination precisely because of their intimate relationship with his writings. He saw that philosophy could not be pursued as a wholly intellectual affair because it is taken seriously only if it is used as a guide to life. Philosophy has to be lived. This was the point of Nietzsche's determination to live outside any framework that could be mistaken for the truth of who he was. Intensely aware of the falsehood of masks, he sought to live without dissemblance, or even a social layer, of any kind. Honesty had become his vocation. This was a solitary but by no means lonely undertaking: He carried it out with intense awareness of its social significance. What he discovered in his own existence would henceforth become a path available to all human beings. By not being a part of modern civilization, he would serve it more deeply. The philosophy he sought would not be contained in books because it would be written first in his own life and, in that way, strike others with the same immediate truth. Without an institutional role to fall back on, he was compelled to address us out of the sheer force of his humanity. The difficulty we have in understanding him today is that we have not yet made the transition to this existential mode of philosophizing. We still expect to find Nietzsche's meaning in the books he left behind.

A more appropriate interpretation would be to take his writings as pointers toward the life that was lived outside them. At every step Nietzsche challenges both himself and us to go beyond what he has said. The literary form by which he seeks to suggest this dynamic quality is the **aphorism**, a polished nugget of reflection that seems to catch life on the run. It is a perfect means of suggesting a sideways glance at life that cannot be focused on directly without arresting its movement. Nietzsche's writing method was to take long walks with a notebook in which he could jot down his meditations as they occurred to him. Then from a wealth of penetrating observations he would organize selections of aphorisms around thematic unities. The first fruit of this distinctive approach to philosophizing is a volume titled *Human, All Too Human* (1878). It marked the beginning of his literary career after his break from the mentorship of Schopenhauer and Wagner. An earlier volume of essays, *Untimely Meditations,* had signaled that he found each of them wanting in the seriousness with which they took their own projects. Schopenhauer's philosophical inquiry had served only as a prelude to escape from all philosophizing into a kind of nirvana of unconsciousness; Wagner's dedication to a great cultural renewal had merely transformed tragedy into theater, not a way of life. For Nietzsche the imperative was to find an answer to the question of whether life is worth living, especially given the collapse of meaning that has become the modern experience. Anything that even suggested an escape was tantamount to a betrayal of the question. The affirmation he sought would have to lead toward an even fuller life and in this way establish its truth. Once he had begun, Nietzsche would have nothing to do with the sickly impulse that turns aside from the agony and the ecstasy of living. Instead of merely reflecting on life philosophy, he would now find its truth in the enhancement of life it made possible.

CAREER OF AN "IMMORALIST"

The first target of Nietzsche's critique is the morality that stood in the way of its own actual demands. He modeled *Human, All Too Human* on the French moralists who had honed the skill of exposing the hypocrisies of human society. But he was interested neither in entertaining nor in improving the subjects of his analysis. Nietzsche's ambition was to renovate the very conception of the moral life. He sought to respond to the long-noted tension between knowing what is right and doing it. Even Aristotle discusses the tendency for human beings to prefer to talk about virtue rather than practice it, thereby suggesting that the discussion of ethics can undermine its purpose. Now Nietzsche sought to eliminate the distance that intervenes between reflection and act—a distance for which he held "morality" responsible. This is the root of hypocrisy. Human beings are notoriously prone to act contrary to what they say, and Nietzsche could find an abundance of instances in an age of unrestrained "idealism." His aim was not, however, to eliminate hypocrisy. It was to remove its opportunity. Morality itself had become a great obstacle to the moral life because human beings had confused articulating the good with acting upon it. This was the most far-reaching revision of moral philosophy since its Greek discovery; Nietzsche was well aware of the difficulties entailed. He would not only have to go against the settled conventions of two millennia, but he would have to do so by challenging a language widely regarded as settled. That is why he found it necessary to shock his reader, declaring himself to be an **"immoralist"** who would lead them **beyond "good and evil."** His goal may have been to deepen the moral life, but his method had to assume the form of its radical rejection.

This is what makes Nietzsche a puzzling writer. Exposing the hollowness of conventional moralizing can hardly be reconciled with a root-and-branch rejection of the very idea of morality. It makes sense only if we keep in mind that his target is not hypocrisy as such, but the rationalizations that enable us to think well about ourselves while doing the opposite. "Morality" is the poison that fatally infects the moral life. At every turn it interposes a distance, a moment of self-congratulation that separates us from the good we might serve more fully. The delicious sense of superiority morality allows, robs the value of what is done. Self-reflection subtly but inexorably redirects the purpose of the action back upon the self. We fail to set aside the interest of the self, the selflessness we so loudly proclaim. The danger of doing "the right thing for the wrong reason" has always been recognized. Nowhere was it expressed more beautifully than by Christ in the Gospel when he counseled his followers in doing good "not to let your left hand know what the right hand is doing" (Mt 6:3). To really do good without any calculation of return to the self, it must be done unthinkingly. We cannot of course be unconscious in the process—actions performed while sleepwalking cannot be regarded as moral either. But as far as possible the self must be lost in the service that is performed with only the good itself in mind. How then is it possible to do good without thinking about it? This is the great question of moral philosophy to which Nietzsche was convinced he had found the answer. Only the beginnings of it are discernible in *Human, All Too Human;* it would take him another 10 years to find a satisfactory formulation of what he had in mind. Its essence, however, consists in recognizing that the moral life always exceeds the moral language that seeks to capture it. Morality is a boundary that the moral life constantly aims at surpassing. As a dynamic movement the moral life must never allow itself to be contained within any moral principles; otherwise it can never claim to be their source.

THE SELF-SUBLIMATION OF MORALITY

The conventional attribution of moral convictions to prior moral principles reverses the order between them. This was the big discovery Nietzsche makes in *Human, All Too Human.* The principles are not the source of our convictions; the convictions are the source of the principles. We can no more stand apart from our convictions than we can get outside our skins. Attributing our convictions to preexisting moral principles is merely a way of defining the movement in which we sense ourselves propelled. But definition carries with it an implication of stepping outside. It seems to let us view ourselves objectively, as if we have mastered the very conditions of our existence. Escaping once again into discourse about life rather than engaging in it, we reach only an illusory superiority. Morality escapes us as we turn it into its vain imitation. Wishing to seem moral, we lose the thread that would enable us to be moral. Nietzsche's exposure of the vanity of our moral posturing is in line with the withering dissection of respectability by the moralists, but now the critique is more conscious of its own source. Unlike his moralist predecessors, Nietzsche is intensely aware of the moral character of his analysis. The critique of morality is itself a moral critique. When we discover that our "good actions are sublimated evil ones,"[1] we have not really evacuated them of all moral worth. Rather, we have taken the first step toward the higher morality to which they point. The freedom of Nietzsche's analysis from this point on in his work arises from his discovery of the inner dynamic of all moral principles. They constantly aim beyond themselves, thereby demonstrating that the life within them is more than their expression.

---

[1]Nietzsche, *Human, All Too Human,* trans. R. J. Hollingdale (Cambridge: Cambridge University Press, 1986), Aphorism 107.

Once we recognize the radical novelty of this conception of philosophy, we begin to gain some appreciation of the struggle that unfolds in his writings. Nietzsche seeks to overcome the failure of all prior philosophy, which eventually imposes a conceptual straitjacket on the vitality from which it springs. But how was he to avoid turning his own formulations into just such an obstruction? Somehow he had to find the means of suggesting the provisional character of all linguistic expressions. It was always the movement by which the individual transcended himself and never the resting points along the way that counted. Whether in art or religion or politics, the products or the end results never mattered; it was the living dynamic that overflowed their boundaries and could never be contained within them. A painter, for example, is not a producer of works of art; she is herself the one on who is produced through a process to which she gives herself. What makes one mixture of colors on a canvas or one set of musical sounds superior to another is the greatness of soul discernible behind them. The external expressions are in themselves relatively slight; the art consists in the sublimity conveyed by the modesty of the means employed. Politics too operates in a similar way, according to Nietzsche. This is why he is skeptical of the democratic liberation of the private individual, which would no longer connect him up to a greatness beyond himself but rather spelled "the death of the state." Nietzsche's purpose, by contrast, is the celebration of the individual who could not be contained within any of the structures he had produced. "Dancing with chains" is one of the metaphors to which he returns over and over again. In this phrase Nietzsche finds the literary means of suggesting the vitality of the "free spirits" to whom the book is dedicated. For such individuals the chains remain an indispensable condition. Nietzsche does not seek to abolish them, to set humanity on an utterly uninhibited future. He foresaw the dismal vacuousness of such a prospect and maintained a wistful respect for the rule-bound traditions of the past. We cannot simply turn back the clock. But we can lay hold of the dynamic of life that has demonstrated the human capacity to rise above all circumstances. Living in a world without chains or limits, Nietzsche would still preserve the movement of ever going beyond. This is what accounts for the restlessness of his thought.

To do good unthinkingly is freedom in action. Even the vanity and egoism of our moral self-approval have their place within that endless movement by which human beings are ever thrust beyond themselves, realizing they are called to do more than they had ever counted on doing. "In us there is accomplished—supposing you want a formula," Nietzsche announces in his next book *Daybreak* (1881), "the **self-sublimation of morality**" (Aphorism 4). Nietzsche is struck by the enormous difference between the act of making a moral commitment and the paltry means of its expression. We are always in danger of confusing one with the other. Marriage, for example, can be seen as merely the contract by which it is expressed. Or we might think we have fulfilled the law merely by adhering to its letter. Even the spiritual language in which we clothe the moral life in terms of its eternal significance seems to substitute an ideal for the reality within which we actually exist. Unless the dynamic of the moral life continually aims at the overcoming of self, it is deflected toward the service of self. In this respect Christians are no different from anyone else; their Christianity is a consolation they seek rather than what they serve. "These serious, excellent, upright, deeply sensitive people who are still Christians from the very heart: they owe it to themselves to try for once the experiment of living for some length of time without

QUESTIONS FOR REFLECTION

Is the moral life larger than the principles in which it is expressed? Nietzsche is conscious of the originality of the question his writings pose. But are there other famous examples of it? Think about the Sermon on the Mount, in which Christ mounts a critique of the morality of the law. The static morality of the law seems to require an eye-for-an-eye strict justice; but the new morality of the gospel requires going beyond what the law requires to do good to those who injure you. Is this similar to Nietzsche's position that there is never a point where we can say we have done enough?

Christianity, they owe it to *their faith* in this way for once to sojourn 'in the wilderness'—if only to win for themselves the right to a voice on the question of whether Christianity is necessary" (Aphorism 61).[2] The "self-sublimation of morality" requires the elimination of any resting place that would impede the moral life. A true Christian, Nietzsche insists, should be willing to sacrifice his Christianity to remain faithful to its commandment. Aware of the self-delusion and vanity lodged even in his noblest moment, his love of the neighbor, he should seek to do away with everything that calls attention to the significance of his actions. Through the inexorable purifying of motives he will arrive at the reality of love itself. The transformation effected by divine grace will become a wholly internal reality as love eliminates any vestige of ego. "Well, if you are capable of this, go a step further: love yourselves as an act of clemency—then you will no longer have any need of your god, and the whole drama of Fall and Redemption will be played out to the end in yourselves" (Aphorism 79).[3]

THE DEATH OF GOD

At last Nietzsche has declared his most famous idea, the death of God, although it is not until his next book of aphorisms, *The Gay Science* (1882), that he makes it explicit. The dramatic nature of the announcement there and the notoriety attaching to it create, however, the impression of a rupture within his thought as a whole. This is the reason for the difficulty in pinning down the meaning of his most famous pronouncement. To avoid this difficulty we have tried to stress the continuity of the death of God with the fundamentally moral thrust of Nietzsche's reflections. His is not an atheism of rejection or revolt but an atheism of inevitability. Abandonment of belief in God is, he discovers, embedded in the logic of the moral life. It is a surrender of God in the name of God and therefore more profoundly theological in its own right. This ambivalent relationship to Christianity, by which Nietzsche internalizes the Christian message so completely that its doctrinal formulation is superceded, characterizes the mature phase of his thought inaugurated with *The Gay Science.* The term "anonymous Christian" might be applied to him, but it hardly covers the situation in which anonymity is deliberately sought. Yet the complexity of Nietzsche's theological relationships are only the beginning of the challenges confronting him. Now he must

---

[2]Nietzsche, *Daybreak: Thoughts on the Prejudices of Morality,* trans. R. J. Hollingdale (Cambridge: Cambridge University Press, 1982).

[3]Ibid.

elaborate a whole alternative language by which to convey the restless moral dynamic that eschews any conventional or static formulations. The distinctively Nietzschean terminology of the **will to power,** the **eternal return,** and the **self-overcoming** all make their first appearances in *The Gay Science.* Only the ***Übermensch,*** the "overman," remains to be announced in his succeeding work. For the rest of his literary career Nietzsche struggled with the danger that specifying terms would cause for the project of creating a living philosophy. Having named his thoughts, he risks the assumption that his readers may claim to know what they mean.

Even for Nietzsche himself self-knowledge could not necessarily be presumed. The prolific stream of writings that followed arose as much from the need to understand his own work as to make it intelligible to others. This is what accounts for the revelatory quality of his writings. We are on a journey of discovery that remains as much of a novelty for the author as it is for the reader. The writings are not simply the result of Nietzsche's life, they are his way of life. The **gay science** to which the title refers is the joyful life celebrated by the medieval troubadours that Nietzsche has learned to make his own. Through it he could affirm that he found life "truer, more desirable and mysterious every year—ever since the day the great liberator overcame me: the thought that life could be an experiment for the knowledge-seeker—not a duty, not a disaster, not a deception! . . . '*Life as a means to knowledge*'—with this principle in one's heart one can not only live bravely but also *live gaily and laugh gaily*" (Aphorism 324).[4] The reference to the "liberator" in this passage is to the advent of the figure with whom the first edition of *The Gay Science* culminates, Zarathustra. *Thus Spoke Zarathustra* (1883) is the title of the succeeding book that opens using the same paragraph with which *The Gay Science* concludes. It marks a literary shift by Nietzsche from aphorism to a more narrative style—but still with the same purpose of conveying the concreteness of existence. Where previously he sought to catch life on the run, now his imagination is seized by a figure whose own self-revelation performs the same task. **Zarathustra** is a type modeled on the Old Testament prophets; his name suggests an affinity with Zoroaster, founder of the ancient Persian religion that sought to hold together light and darkness, the principles of good and evil. He is one more embodiment of Nietzsche's insight that the source of morality lies beyond good and evil, as what makes the choice of such directions possible.

The limit of aphorism is reached in the vividness of character. Zarathustra connects too with Nietzsche's earlier interest in the rebirth of tragedy, which has now found its central character. As a result, *Thus Spoke Zarathustra* is both Nietzsche's most accessible and most inaccessible work. The literary inventiveness gives rise to a rich profusion of symbolism and character development readily apprehended by every reader, yet containing a depth of meaning that probably remains inexhaustible even for the author himself. Zarathustra is a discloser of mystery to Nietzsche. We must keep this in mind if we are to understand the content of his message, especially the key concepts of the will to power, the eternal return, and the overman, which have become virtually synonymous with Nietzsche's philosophy. It is important, therefore, to remind ourselves that they are not for Nietzsche such well-defined conceptions. Rather, they mark the boundaries toward which his thought

---

[4]Nietzsche, *The Gay Science,* (ed.) Bernard Williams (Cambridge: Cambridge University Press, 2001).

strained as he sought to acquire the knowledge that could be gained only by living it out. Zarathustra is a revelation of the path on which Nietzsche must embark. That of course means that Zarathustra too cannot reach his goal. He must remain a bridge or a signpost of the way on which he is proceeding—never a character whose fulfillment is reached. Yet that is enough; As the seeker he can be a great teacher. The book is structured around those twin dimensions as Zarathustra begins his odyssey in the world of human society, then withdraws to find what cannot be found there, returning again to the possibility of communicating with others. The high point is naturally in the third part, when Zarathustra reaches his own epiphany in the discovery of the eternal return that unites everything.

The way toward this epiphany begins with Zarathustra's departure from the world of men, the town of the Motley Cow from which he sets out. All he knows is that divinity is not to be found in any of the idols to which human beings have attached themselves. Gone are all external divinities as Zarathustra entrusts himself to the only divinity he knows: that which is within him. "*Dead are all gods: now we want the overman to live*—on that great noon, let this be our last will" (end of part one).[5] Zarathustra is a strange kind of prophet, one who speaks not with divine authority but with the confidence of finding his way toward it. That may account for some of the grandiose quality of his tone; he is never to be simply identified with Nietzsche. He is rather a character through whom Nietzsche can say certain things he cannot say directly himself. Among the most famous is the remark of Zarathustra as he proceeds along the journey of self-discovery: "Let me reveal my heart to you entirely, my friends: *if* there were gods, how could I endure not to be a god! Hence there are no gods."[6] The question is, however, what does it mean to be a god? The path toward divinity has already been disclosed in Zarathustra's intuition that "a gift-giving virtue is the highest virtue." Christian theology has failed to take this realization seriously enough because it has not seen that "if a little charity is not forgotten, it turns into a gnawing worm."[7] This extends even to the conception of God, who is pictured as an endlessly pitying man. Not only does this omnipresent compassion overshadow the independence of man; it eats away at the very essence of God, turning him into a voyeur who gains satisfaction from his superiority over the object of his contemplation. No one can any longer believe in such a God. "Thus spoke the devil to me once: 'God too has his hell; that is his love for man.' And most recently I heard him say this: 'God is dead; God died of his pity for man' " (90).[8] Divinity has drained away when the demand of love has outstripped such a static relationship to man. Love, if it is to be true to itself, cannot permit even the flash of self-awareness to remain within the movement by which it gives all for the other. That is the real divinity toward which Zarathustra strives: the love that sacrifices all, including itself, so that nothing remains but the purity of the movement itself. " 'Myself I sacrifice to my love, *and my neighbor as myself*—thus runs the speech of all creators. But all creators are hard" (92).[9]

---

[5]Nietzsche, *Thus Spoke Zarathustra,* in *The Portable Nietzsche,* trans. Walter Kaufmann (New York: Viking Press, 1968), p. 191.

[6]Ibid., p. 198.

[7]Ibid., p. 201.

[8]Ibid., p. 202.

[9]Ibid.

PRIMARY SOURCE 14.1

THE MADMAN, FROM *THE GAY SCIENCE*, BOOK III, SECTION 125

The madman.—Have you not heard of that madman who lit a lantern in the bright morning hours, ran to the market place and cried incessantly, "I seek God! I seek God!"—As many of those who did not believe in God were standing around just then, he provoked much laughter. Has he got lost? asked one. Did he lose his way like a child? asked another. Or is he hiding? Is he afraid of us? Has he gone on a voyage? emigrated?—Thus they yelled and laughed. The madman jumped into their midst and pierced them with his eyes. "Whither is God?" he cried. "I will tell you. *We have killed him*—you and I! All of us are his murderers! But how did we do this? How could we drink up the sea? Who gave us the sponge to wipe away the entire horizon? What were we doing when we unchained this earth from its sun? Whither is it moving now? Whither are we moving? Away from all suns? Are we not plunging continually? And backward, sideward, forward, in all directions? Is there still any up or down? Are we not straying as through an infinite nothing? Do we not feel the breath of empty space? Has it not become colder? Is not night continually closing in on us? Do we not need to light lanterns in the morning? Do we not hear nothing as yet of the noise of the gravediggers who are burying God? Do we smell nothing as yet of the divine decomposition?—Gods, too, decompose! God is dead! God remains dead! And we have killed him! How shall we comfort ourselves, the murderers of all murderers? What was holiest and mightiest of all that the world has yet owned has bled to death under our knives—who will wipe this blood off us? What water is there for us to clean ourselves? What festivals of atonement, what sacred games shall we have to invent? Is not the greatness of this deed too great for us? Must we ourselves not become gods simply to appear worthy of it? There has never been a greater deed—and whoever is born after us, for the sake of this deed he will belong to a higher history than all history hitherto!"—Here the madman fell silent and looked again at his listeners: they, too, were silent and stared at him in astonishment. At last he threw his lantern to the ground, and it broke into pieces and went out. "I have come too early," he said then; "my time is not yet. This tremendous event is still on its way, still wandering—it has not yet reached the ears of men. Lightning and thunder require time; the light of the stars requires time; deeds, though done, still require time to be seen and heard. This deed is still more distant from them than the most distant stars—*and yet they have done it themselves*!"—It has been related further that on the same day the madman forced his way into several churches and there struck up his *requiem aeternam deo*. Led out and called to account, he is said always to have replied nothing but "What after all are these churches now if they are not the tombs and sepulchers of God?"

ETERNAL RETURN

All the themes of Nietzsche's philosophy come together here in this conception of a love that creates, that brings forth rather than contemplating its own benevolence. This is what he means by the will to power, that which overcomes all, even itself. And it is what marks the man of the future, the overman, that great future toward which Zarathustra points. But we have not arrived at that goal; only the aspiration has become clear. There is still a Rubicon to be crossed, a test of the greatness of soul that alone constitutes the attainment of divinity that exists nowhere but within the inwardness of the overman. This is the **eternal return.** Without it not only is the will to power of the overman incomplete; he is hardly real at all. Everything is realized in the entry into the eternal return, which is the keystone of Nietzsche's entire philosophical project. It is the rock on which more than a few commentators have foundered. Many have settled for some approximation of the basic meaning of the term, such as that everything that has happened will recur. It is a cyclical view of reality that goes all the way back to the cosmological form of the most ancient civilizations. The cosmos periodically sets out on the cycle from which it begins again. Obviously this conflicts with the Christian understanding of history as linear progress through unrepeatable events. In particular, the eternal return challenges directly the notion of an end or a purpose that furnishes the meaning to reality as a whole. Some of Nietzsche's own remarks suggest that it converges with a scientific view of the world that in an infinite expanse of time all finite events are repeated. This meshes well with the overriding conception of nihilism as the defining feature of our existence, thereby making acceptance of the eternal return the last test of our capacity to live without meaning. The problem with such interpretations is that they contradict Nietzsche's own avowed purpose of reaching toward what is higher. We are on safer ground if we remain close to the question of living that was uppermost for him. As the least speculative thinker, his interest in metaphysics was confined to what it contributed to the way we should live. That is of course what makes him singularly important from the perspective of his contribution to metaphysics. The only caveat is that we must not tackle his metaphysical conceptions directly. They yield their meaning only through the indirect path of living them out.

As always, Nietzsche prioritizes "life as a means of knowledge." His most central conception of the eternal return arises, therefore, not from any theoretical breakthrough, but from the logic of life itself. In the overcoming of self that is the inexorable march of life there must be something inexhaustible; otherwise life would simply cease. This is particularly evident in the movement of the will through which life unfolds. If the will were to reach its goal, this movement would stop; so it is somehow implicit in the very notion of the will that its goal is unreachable. The pursuit of purpose may constitute the structure of the will, but its purpose cannot finally be reached without terminating the will itself. A movement can be sustained only by what is beyond movement. The whole vitality of the will is thus premised on the impossibility of consummating its purpose. We are familiar with this pattern in the ordinary course of life, whereby the goals we set for ourselves provide not a resting place but mere stepping-stones to the pursuit of further goals. Only by not paying attention to the futility of this pattern can we find the strength to carry on. But what about that moment when the realization of purposelessness dawns? This is the crisis in the life of an individual, and of a whole civilization, that Nietzsche addresses. His response is unique. It is not to find some higher purpose, theological or ideological, that can substitute for a false sense of ultimacy that previously characterized our goal-directedness. Instead he calls us to confront the **nihilism** embedded in all willing. Then we can recognize that our pursuit of purpose is utterly without purpose and accept it as the very condition of existence. Nothing is achieved because all that is gained is lost, and all that is lost is regained eternally. Willing is located within the eternal return. In order to will we must will the nonattainment of our purpose, even while we pursue specific purposes. All willing is therefore an eternal willing, a willing of the eternal return, because it "wants deep, wants deep eternity" (228).[10]

---

[10]Ibid., p. 340.

A will that seeks to remain in the moment, resting in its accomplishment, is a perversion of willing because it wills its own annihilation. That is the nihilism Nietzsche sees in the modern schemes of perfection and discerned in the otherworldliness of religion. Striving had become obsessed with putting an end to striving. Everywhere human beings seemed to be turning their backs on life. In response to this crisis Zarathustra rose in Nietzsche's imagination with the promise of redemption. Unlike the predecessors, however, Zarathustra's redemption was not to bring a release from existence. His was a redemption into existence, authenticated by the ever deeper life it made possible. As an unconditional affirmation that could not itself be comprehended, the eternal return was at once the confrontation with nihilism and its overcoming. "To redeem what is past in man," Zarathustra proclaims, "and to re-create all 'it was' until the will says, 'Thus I willed it!'—this I called redemption and this alone I taught them to call redemption" (198).[11] **Redemption** is not itself then a past event but the eternal affirmation that makes all affirmation possible. It is in that sense very close to the Christian idea of redemption, which, although it is dated by an event within time, is eternal in its encompassing of all times and places. Nietzsche is not so concerned with explaining the Christian derivation of his insight, but it helps to keep it in mind if we are to comprehend his intentions. He understands that redemption would simultaneously have to break into time without being tied to time. Eternal return performs just such a function of redeeming time because it is both within time and beyond it. The difficulty that Nietzsche has in explaining this notion is paralleled by the Christian difficulty of explaining redemption. Each attempts to lay hold of a mystery that, precisely because it encompasses the explainers themselves, cannot be adequately penetrated by them. All Nietzsche knows is that purpose cannot reach its conclusion without denying the movement that sustains it. There must therefore be, beyond purpose, a realm where its fulfillment and its frustration recur eternally. Affirmation of life cannot occur without the affirmation of its inexhaustibility.

The eternal return is not a thesis to be demonstrated. It is the condition of existence glimpsed as we rush headlong through life. The purposes we set for ourselves are not ultimately what defines us, for there is a yet further perspective beyond purpose from which we exist. We cannot reach our *telos* (or end) without literally bringing existence to a close. So it is a great liberation when Zarathusta declares that life is not governed by a teleological movement but rather by the chance that sustains the openness of freedom. " 'By Chance'—that is the most ancient nobility of the world, and this I restored to all things: I delivered them from their bondage under Purpose."[12] If we had such mastery over ourselves that the lines of development had all been laid down in advance, we would scarcely exist as human beings. The essence of human life is the power of living, of overcoming—the will to power that is epitomized in **the overman**. None of that is possible if there is a fixed human nature that all must follow. Nietzsche's rejection of the Greek conception of a universal human nature is based not on the proposal of an alternative anthropology, but on the imperative of human self-creation. In this sense it is a deepening of the account. The nature of human beings is that they have no nature in advance but engage in its self-creation. This is familiar in

---

[11]Ibid., p. 310.

[12]Ibid., p. 278.

the modern idea that every human being must determine himself or herself. Autonomy is the term on everyone's lips. What Nietzsche is doing, therefore, is supplying the metaphysical background to the ideas that dominate our social and political lives. To the extent that we really take seriously the conviction that every human being is responsible for himself, then we must also subscribe to the notion that the exercise of self-creation is never a completed process. Ultimately freedom is located within eternity. This is why the eternal return performs such a pivotal role in Nietzsche's thought. It perfectly captures the insight that we never get beyond the beginning; we are always recurring to it as the eternal moment we never leave behind. We live not in time—but within the eternal return that makes the unfolding of time possible.

Eternal return captures the idea that human existence is a participation in the divine. We live as creators outside of the time we create. Who we are to be is known only through the **process of self-creation** because good and evil cannot be known in advance. "I disturbed their sleepiness," Zarathustra observes, "when I taught: what is good and evil *no one knows yet,* unless it be he who creates."[13] The only imperative is the pouring forth of self by which creation happens. This extends to the sharing of the power of creation itself, the most divine gift of all. The "death of God" can be more properly understood as the death of a God of self-enclosing divinity. Zarathustra has come to announce the dispersion of the creative power as the most divine expression of all. There was no "twilight of the gods"; instead "they *laughed* themselves to death." The idea that God might seek to remain wrapped up in his divinity for himself had simply become incredible. The irruption occurs when one of the gods proclaimed himself the only God. "And then all the gods laughed and rocked on their chairs and cried, 'Is not just this godlike that there are gods but no God?' "[14] Conserving one's substance is the very opposite of what constitutes divinity. We might say that Nietzsche's theology is no longer centered on God because it is so heavily involved in the movement outward toward all others. The same pattern is generalized to all human relationships. To really relate to others, he recognizes, is to do everything to preserve their independence. Quite contrary to relationships of dependence, the whole point is to foster the maturity of their own self-creation, their own self-overcoming. This is what the politics of eternal return must entail. All human relationships, if they are to be genuinely free, must be relationships of indirection in which we give what cannot be given but only received if each finds it on his own. An unconditional love, whether of God or men, would scarcely even reveal itself. "If I love you, what does that concern you?" (*The Gay Science,* Aphorism 141).

THE PREJUDICE OF TRUTH

The challenge of communicating such unsurpassable maturity was to prove more daunting. No doubt this is in part what Nietzsche struggles with in the fourth part of *Zarathustra,* when the prophet returns to his uncomprehending disciples. The array of characters is a tour de force of Nietzsche's comic genius, culminating in the "festival of the ass" that parodies Zarathustra's high-flown expectations for humanity. It was a

---

[13]Ibid., p. 308.

[14]Ibid., p. 294.

QUESTIONS FOR REFLECTION

Is willing a dynamic or a static reality? The difficulty of unraveling Nietzsche's conception of the eternal return is that the term seems to be about the order of the universe, while its real source lies in his insight into the nature of will. Think about what it means to will to do something—for example, the decision to learn to swim or to help someone cross the street. Do we will anything else in the process? Is there a willing to go on willing? Not to rest on the achievements reached but to go beyond them? What would happen if we reached our goals in life? What happens to people who win the lottery? Is there something like winning the moral lottery?

fitting introduction to the final phase of Nietzsche's writings in which he struggles with the resistance he is likely to encounter in the world at large. Returning again to aphorisms, Nietzsche, in *Beyond Good and Evil* (1886), seeks to explain what Zarathustra was too busy living to explain. The philosophical questions could no longer be avoided. Even if Zarathustra's whole point was that life must be lived rather than discussed, that assertion itself needed some amplification. What happens, for example, to the notion of truth? Is it a matter of complete irrelevance that we seem to have left behind? Is the life of illusion the same as life in conformity with truth? These are difficult questions to resolve, and Nietzsche's struggle with them is by no means dispelled the confusion surrounding them. Many readers have concluded that in these works he embraces a version of relativism, the endless multiplicity of perspectives, as the truth about human existence. The difficulty with that interpretation is that it assumes Nietzsche was capable of patently contradicting himself. A serious thinker could hardly commit such an elementary error as to assert the nonexistence of truth as true. The explanation of the difficulty must be found elsewhere. It lies in the radical novelty of Nietzsche's project—which is to turn philosophy into the dynamic force everyone had always said it was before they mummified it in concepts. Zarathustra had shown him the defectiveness of all categories for capturing life: As soon as they are announced life had overleaped them. This is the whole point of the eternal return. Now Nietzsche tests the possibility of thinking beyond the limits of thought.

"I think therefore I am" was the famous formulation of Descartes that seemed to place the subject firmly in control of his thoughts and his existence. Scarcely anyone asked how this "I" could think before it exists because the Cartesian account conveyed a reassuring sense of our superiority over the objects of our thought. As everyone knows, however, we do not possess thoughts in the same way that we carry loose change in our pockets. Rather, "a thought comes when 'it' wishes," Nietzsche observes, "and not when 'I' wish, so that it is a falsification of the facts of the case to say that the subject 'I' is the condition of the predicate 'think'" (Aphorism 17).[15] We do not have thoughts; more accurately, thoughts have us. This is what Nietzsche aims at glimpsing when he talks about the limitations of "truth," all the while fully aware that his reflections are carried forward by their own underlying assumption of truth. He wants us to see that there are two fundamentally different conceptions of truth, one static and one dynamic. The dynamic is the one we can never discard because it is present even

[15]Nietzsche, *Beyond Good and Evil,* trans. Walter Kaufmann (New York: Vintage, 1966).

PRIMARY SOURCE 14.2

On the Vision and the Riddle, from *Thus Spake Zarathustra,* Part III, Chapter 46

Part 1

Part 2

"Halt, dwarf!" said I [Zarathustra]. "Either I—or you! I, however, am the stronger of the two: you knowest not my abysmal thought! It—could you not endure!"

Then happened that which made me lighter: for the dwarf sprang from my shoulder, the prying sprite! And it squatted on a stone in front of me. There was however a gateway just where we halted.

"Look at this gateway! Dwarf!" I continued, "it has two faces. Two roads come together here: these has no one yet gone to the end of.

This long lane backward: it continues for an eternity. And that long lane forward—that is another eternity.

They are antithetical to one another, these roads; they directly abut on one another: and it is here, at this gateway, that they come together. The name of the gateway is inscribed above: 'This Moment.'

But should one follow them further—and ever further and further on, think you, dwarf, that these roads would be eternally antithetical?"

"Everything straight lies," murmured the dwarf, contemptuously. "All truth is crooked; time itself is a circle."

"You spirit of gravity!" said I wrathfully, "do not take it too lightly! Or I shall let you squat where you squat, Haltfoot—and I carried you high!"

"Observe," continued I, "This Moment! From the gateway, This Moment, there runs a long eternal lane backward: behind us lies an eternity.

Must not whatever can run its course of all things, have already run along that lane? Must not whatever can happen of all things have already happened, resulted, and gone by?

And if everything has already existed, what think you, dwarf, of This Moment? Must not this gateway also—have already existed?

And are not all things closely bound together in such wise that This Moment draws all coming things after it? Consequently—itself also?

For whatever can run its course of all things, also in this long lane outward—must it once more run!

And this slow spider which creeps in the moonlight, and this moonlight itself, and you and I in this gateway whispering together, whispering of eternal things—must we not all have already existed?

And must we not return and run in that other lane out before us, that long weird lane—must we not eternally return?"

Thus did I speak, and always more softly: for I was afraid of my own thoughts, and arrear-thoughts. Then, suddenly did I hear a dog howl near me.

Had I ever heard a dog howl thus? My thoughts ran back. Yes! When I was a child, in my most distant childhood:

Then did I hear a dog howl thus. And saw it also, with hair bristling, its head upward, trembling in the still midnight, when even dogs believe in ghosts:

So that it excited my commiseration. For just then went the full moon, silent as death, over the house; just then did it stand still, a glowing globe—at rest on the flat roof, as if on some one's property:

Thereby had the dog been terrified: for dogs believe in thieves and ghosts. And when I again heard such howling, then did it excite my commiseration once more.

Where was now the dwarf? And the gateway? And the spider? And all the whispering? Had I dreamt? Had I awakened? 'Twixt rugged rocks did I suddenly stand alone, dreary in the dreariest moonlight.

But there lay a man! And there! The dog leaping, bristling, whining—now did it see me coming—then did it howl again, then did it cry: had I ever heard a dog cry so for help?

And verily, what I saw, the like had I never seen. A young shepherd did I see, writhing, choking, quivering, with distorted countenance, and with a heavy black serpent hanging out of his mouth.

continued

PRIMARY SOURCE 14.2 | ON THE VISION AND THE RIDDLE, FROM *THUS SPAKE ZARATHUSTRA,* PART III, CHAPTER 46 *continued*

Had I ever seen so much loathing and pale horror on one countenance? He had perhaps gone to sleep? Then had the serpent crawled into his throat—there had it bitten itself fast.

My hand pulled at the serpent, and pulled: in vain! I failed to pull the serpent out of his throat. Then there cried out of me: "Bite! Bite!

Its head off! Bite!"—so cried it out of me; my horror, my hatred, my loathing, my pity, all my good and my bad cried with one voice out of me.

You daring ones around me! You venturers and adventurers, and whoever of you have embarked with cunning sails on unexplored seas! You enigma-enjoyers!

Solve to me the enigma that I then beheld, interpret to me the vision of the most lonesome one!

For it was a vision and a foresight: what did I then behold in parable? And who is it that must come someday?

Who is the shepherd into whose throat the serpent thus crawled? Who is the man into whose throat all the heaviest and blackest will thus crawl?

The shepherd however bit as my cry had admonished him; he bit with a strong bite! Far away did he spit the head of the serpent—and sprang up.

No longer shepherd, no longer man—a transfigured being, a light-surrounded being, that laughed! Never on earth laughed a man as he laughed!

O my brothers, I heard a laughter which was no human laughter—and now gnaws a thirst at me, a longing that is never allayed.

My longing for that laughter gnaws at me: oh, how can I still endure to live! And how could I endure to die at present!

Thus spoke Zarathustra.

---

when we employ it to question the possibility of truth. "It is no more than a moral prejudice," he notes famously, "that truth is worth more than mere appearance; it is even the worst proved assumption there is in the world" (Aphorism 34). On its face this sentence illustrates the self-contradiction of which Nietzsche has often been accused, but that impression is removed when we recall that the sentence is uttered with full awareness of the self-contradiction. He is not about to talk about a "higher truth" or a "dynamic truth" because this would still suggest that there is another realm beyond appearance to which we can escape. Nietzsche's whole conviction is that truth is to be found only in the movement toward it, which is guaranteed only by the impossibility of reaching it.

The closest he comes to acknowledging his inescapable orientation toward truth, even in his denial of it, is when he reflects on the extent to which he still worships at the same altar as Plato. "We godless anti-metaphysicians," he admits, are compelled to recognize that "it is still a *metaphysical faith* upon which our faith in science rests" (*The Gay Science,* Aphorism 344). But this is more than a grudging realization of his inability to slough off the vestiges of Greek philosophy. It is also a deeper affirmation of the living source from which that philosophic beginning originated. Nietzsche's relationship to Greek philosophy is as ambivalent as that he has with Christianity. He is at once a devastating critic and, for that very reason, its most profound affirmer. The critique is powerful precisely because it comes from within, accusing both philosophy and Christianity of failing to be what they claim. He calls on them to be what they aspire to be and, in this way, affirms them more deeply than they have been affirmed since their beginning. Nietzsche may appear to be overturning the history of philosophy, but this is an

PRIMARY SOURCE 14.3

Before Sunrise, from *Thus Spake Zarathustra*, Part III, Chapter 48

For rather will I have noise and thunders and tempest blasts, than this discreet, doubting cat repose; and also amongst men do I hate most of all the soft treaders, and half-and-half ones, and the doubting, hesitating, passing clouds.

And "he who cannot bless shall LEARN to curse!"—this clear teaching dropt unto me from the clear heaven; this star standeth in my heaven even in dark nights.

I, however, am a blesser and a Yea-sayer, if thou be but around me, thou pure, thou luminous heaven! Thou abyss of light!—into all abysses do I then carry my beneficent Yea-saying.

A blesser have I become and a Yea-sayer: and therefore strove I long and was a striver, that I might one day get my hands free for blessing.

This, however, is my blessing: to stand above everything as its own heaven, its round roof, its azure bell and eternal security: and blessed is he who thus blesseth!

For all things are baptized at the font of eternity, and beyond good and evil; good and evil themselves, however, are but fugitive shadows and damp afflictions and passing clouds.

Verily, it is a blessing and not a blasphemy when I teach that "above all things there standeth the heaven of chance, the heaven of innocence, the heaven of hazard, the heaven of wantonness."

"Of Hazard"—that is the oldest nobility in the world; that gave I back to all things; I emancipated them from bondage under purpose.

This freedom and celestial serenity did I put like an azure bell above all things, when I taught that over them and through them, no "eternal Will"—willeth.

This wantonness and folly did I put in place of that Will, when I taught that "In everything there is one thing impossible—rationality!"

A LITTLE reason, to be sure, a germ of wisdom scattered from star to star—this leaven is mixed in all things: for the sake of folly, wisdom is mixed in all things!

A little wisdom is indeed possible; but this blessed security have I found in all things, that they prefer—to DANCE on the feet of chance.

O heaven above me! thou pure, thou lofty heaven! This is now thy purity unto me, that there is no eternal reason-spider and reason-cobweb:—

—That thou art to me a dancing-floor for divine chances, that thou art to me a table of the Gods, for divine dice and dice-players!—

But thou blushest? Have I spoken unspeakable things? Have I abused, when I meant to bless thee?

Or is it the shame of being two of us that maketh thee blush!—Dost thou bid me go and be silent, because now—DAY cometh?

The world is deep:—and deeper than e'er the day could read. Not everything may be uttered in presence of day. But day cometh: so let us part!

O heaven above me, thou modest one! thou glowing one! O thou, my happiness before sunrise! The day cometh: so let us part!—

Thus spake Zarathustra.

---

overturning that happens philosophically. He does philosophy in a new way when he insists that the movement toward truth takes precedence over any truth disclosed. That means we acknowledge that we do not know what truth is—that we cannot comprehend truth. All we can do is live within truth as the horizon that is larger than our existence. "We simply have no organ for *knowing*, for truth" (Aphorism 354). Admitting that the distinction between appearance and reality was based on the easy assumption that we stand outside them, that we had mastery over truth, we now can live within the openness that is made possible by the unattainability of truth. The key to all of these puzzling observations of Nietzsche is the priority he always assigns to life over its conceptualization. The life of truth exceeds the truth of life.

QUESTIONS FOR REFLECTION

Must truth be unattainable? Is the unattainability of truth one of the presuppositions of all thinking? What would happen to science if it answered all of its questions? Would there any longer be an investigation or search for the truth of things? What would life be like if we no longer searched but had all the answers?

MORALITY AS THE OVERFLOWING OF LIFE

Nietzsche repeats that it is not people's convictions that account for their lives but their lives that account for their convictions. This is the insight he seeks to elaborate in *On the Genealogy of Morals* (1887), the sequel to *Beyond Good and Evil* that targets the idea that there is a morality prior to the actions people take. "But there is no such substratum; there is no 'being' behind doing, effecting, becoming: 'the doer' is merely a fiction added to the deed—the deed is everything" (Section 13).[16] It is by throwing ourselves into existence that we discover who we are and the code by which we live, not by withdrawing from action behind abstract ideals. The **genealogy of morals**, the process by which morality came to dominate existence, is the story of the **resentment** of the weak against the strong. By means of an enormous deception the weak prevailed on the strong to turn their strength against themselves. This was the genesis of morality, the catastrophe that inverted the relationship of human nature to its expression. Now weakness would be valued more than strength and the withdrawal from existence over its resolute unfolding. Christianity both exacerbated this situation and sought to relieve it at the same time by introducing the idea that God himself dies on behalf of fallen mankind. But its inner contradiction cannot be sustained. Life itself requires what is owed to it. Even the spiritual refinement of its self-denial, what Nietzsche now sees as the genius of Christianity, cannot forever postpone the day of reckoning. Redemption cannot be permanently assigned to a beyond of existence but must somehow find its way into the affirmation of life lived in all its fullness. The turning point, he now realizes even more clearly, is the recognition that the source of the Christian idea of redemption is the intimation of its presence already within life. The drive toward life, the will to power that aims not just at life but at its fullness, is already the redemption that carries us forward. We do not await redemption but live within it. From this overflowing of existence our ideas follow—not from their elevation into a realm remote from all actual living.

Nietzsche now sees that his own question, whether life was worth living, is an "unapproachable problem" because it presupposes that we can take up a position outside life. "When we speak of values, we speak with the inspiration, with the way of looking at things, which is part of life: life itself forces us to posit values."[17] It is noteworthy that the book in which he announces this is titled *The Twilight of the Idols:* It is the idols who have fallen, not the gods. The way beyond nihilism is not the creation of new values that still bear the mark of their artificiality. It is to embrace more fully the life that all along has been the driving force behind the projection of values. Living renders all

[16]Nietzsche, *On the Genealogy of Morals,* trans. Walter Kaufmann (New York: Vintage, 1967).

[17]*The Twilight of the Idols* in *Portable Nietzsche,* trans. Walter Kaufmann (New York: Viking Press, 1963), p. 490.

talk of the value of living obsolete. "Here the most profound instinct toward the future of life, the eternity of life, is experienced religiously—and the way to life, procreation, as the *holy* way" (562).[18] Nietzsche can now affirm his faith as a faith in life that bears fruit in its bringing forth of life. The project he now set out for himself was to be called ***The Revaluation of All Values,*** a title that suggests the redirecting of all values to their source in life as the truth that has become obscured in their idealized separation from it. His health, however, did not permit the completion of this great summation of his work. Instead the final book was a far shorter piece that had been intended as the first essay within *The Revaluation.* It was called *Der Antichrist* (1895), which can be translated either as *The Antichrist* or *The Antichristian,* reflecting an ambivalence that pervades his entire relationship to the Christian and philosophic traditions. But this ambivalence is at the very core of Nietzsche's entire life. As the most harrowing critic of Christianity, he is also its most fervent disciple; these twin roles cannot be separated.

In *The Antichrist* we see the meaning of Nietzsche's earlier observation that "as soon as religion comes to dominate, it has as its opponents all those who would have been its first disciples" (*Human, All Too Human,* Aphorism 118). Nowhere is this more evident than in Nietzsche's admiration for the exemplary life and death of Christ and his execration of the misuse he has suffered at the hands of the Church. The distinction between Christ and Christianity is memorably underlined in Nietzsche's remark that "in truth, there was only *one* Christian, and he died on the cross" (612).[19] Christ's early band of followers utterly failed to grasp the central idea he tried to communicate in the only way possible—by living it. He showed them in his capacity to surmount the suffering of existence "the superiority over any feeling of *ressentiment*" [resentment],[20] which is the only real meaning of redemption. Instead they perverted his authentic witness into a dogma of redemption for all who care to believe. But what does such an empty formula signify if it has not become real in life? It is only "we spirits who have *become free*" who can understand what 19 centuries of Christianity have missed: that there is no immortality worthy of the name but the immortality exemplified by the way one lives. Nietzsche, we might say, prioritizes the Christian life over the Christian dogma. He is the latest in a long line of prophets and reformers who have continuously harangued the community of believers to make their actions speak for their faith. But he is also something more. Nietzsche seems to suggest that he may be the end of the line. When Christ has been completely internalized within a mode of life, the need for any historical or theological reference has been superseded. As the ultimate follower of Christ, Nietzsche is also the last. This is what accounts for his insistence on a thoroughgoing atheism to the very end. "That we find no God—either in history or in nature or behind nature—is not what differentiates *us,* but that we experience what has been revered as God, not as 'godlike' but as miserable, as absurd, as harmful, not merely as an error but as a *crime against life.* We deny God as God."[21]

The ambivalence persists, and the care of Nietzsche's formulation indicates his awareness of it. Ambivalence may even have been his principal discovery. One cannot

---

[18]Ibid., p. 562.

[19]*The Antichrist,* in *Portable Nietzsche,* p. 612.

[20]Ibid., p. 615.

[21]Ibid., p. 627.

be a critic of philosophy or Christianity without going more deeply into the life from which they arise. His new way of doing philosophy and of following Christ entail the refusal to allow any intermediary, least of all the categories of philosophy and Christianity themselves, to distance him from the life they require. Can philosophy and Christianity become entirely existential affairs? Is it possible to live the life without any reference to the intimations that might guide it? Those are certainly questions that might be posed to Nietzsche; they are just as valid as the scrutiny he brings to bear on the more conventional formulations. Can there be a life of faith that no longer believes in anything? Strange as it may sound, as indeed it has resounded in the whole strangeness of postmodern philosophy after Nietzsche, this is precisely where his trajectory points. The collapse of dogma defines the crisis of nihilism he sought to address. His response, after following many twists and turns, is to find a way of living without dogma. But the emphasis falls on living. Nietzsche's singular discovery is that life always and everywhere precedes its dogmatic formulation. The crisis can be surmounted, therefore, through a fullness of living that renders the need for reflection upon it utterly redundant. "By their fruits you shall know them" has long been a criterion of the moral truth of any spiritual movement. As with so much else in the tradition, Nietzsche's stance is radical only by virtue of his readiness to take it with the seriousness of his whole existence. By "upping the ante" he challenges believers of all types to the same commitment. In his account, morality and religion regain the shocking impact of the unconditional as they make demands upon us we are unsure we will be able to fulfill. That is the life beyond life from which Nietzsche writes.

The connection of this philosophic revolution with the world of politics is at once obvious and obscure. It is obvious in the sense that politics is already a mode of life and moves itself forward before anyone reflects on what it is. Political theory comes on the scene after a political reality, with its own working self-interpretation, is already in place. So politics exemplifies Nietzsche's insight that **life precedes its understandings.** Yet politics has also never quite shaken the conviction that it depends on some ideas about what it is. Constitutions, legal frameworks, and political rhetoric all seem to point to the centrality of argument about what shapes and sustains the common reality. Political theory reinforces the notion that politics originates in certain ideas about the nature of government. As a result, the emergence of political entities is often obscured as they acquire a self-understanding only after they have become stable realities. That frozen snapshot of a political community then becomes an obstacle to the unfolding of the more fluid reality that it really is. It is at this point that Nietzsche's philosophic breakthrough can be of great value. By calling attention to the fixities of all conventional accounts of human society, its morals and beliefs, he performs the inestimable service of pointing out that the community is always more than it thinks it is. The life of political society, like all human life, is more than what it is at any given stage. Life overflows all the boundaries that are set for it. That is what makes it life, capable of always going beyond what it is until its final demise. Short of that termination the crises that arise, especially crises in the principles by which human society seeks to guide itself, are never ultimate. This is because the principles are never themselves ultimate. They emerge from within the processes of life that precede them, and we can expect that the same dynamic will carry us forward with a momentum larger than any definitions assigned to it. Even when the loss of faith appears irreversible, the very meaning of an age of nihilism, there still remains faith in faith.

PRIMARY SOURCE 14.4 | *THE ANTICHRIST*, SECTIONS 39–41

39

I shall go back a bit, and tell you the *authentic* history of Christianity. The very word "Christianity" is a misunderstanding—at bottom there was only one Christian, and he died on the cross. The "Gospels" *died* on the cross. What, from that moment onward, was called the "Gospels" was the very reverse of what *he* had lived: "bad tidings," a *Dysangeliu.* It is an error amounting to nonsensicality to see in "faith," and particularly in faith in salvation through Christ, the distinguishing mark of the Christian: only the Christian *way of life,* the life *lived* by him who died on the cross, is Christian.... To this day *such* a life is still possible, and for *certain* men even necessary: genuine, primitive Christianity will remain possible in all ages.... *Not* faith, but acts; above all, an *avoidance* of acts, a different *state of being*.... States of consciousness, faith of a sort, the acceptance, for example, of anything as true—as every psychologist knows, the value of these things is perfectly indifferent and fifth-rate compared to that of the instincts: strictly speaking, the whole concept of intellectual causality is false. To reduce being a Christian, the state of Christianity, to an acceptance of truth, to a mere phenomenon of consciousness, is to formulate the negation of Christianity. *In fact, there are no Christians. The* "Christian"—he who for two thousand years has passed as a Christian—is simply a psychological self-delusion. Closely examined, it appears that, *despite* all his "faith," he has been ruled *only* by his instincts—and *what instincts!*—In all ages—for example, in the case of Luther—"faith" has been no more than a cloak, a pretense, a *curtain* behind which the instincts have played their game—a shrewd *blindness* to the domination of *certain* of the instincts....I have already called "faith" the specially Christian form of *shrewdness*—people always *talk* of their "faith" and *act* according to their instincts.... In the world of ideas of the Christian there is nothing that so much as touches reality: on the contrary, one recognizes an instinctive *hatred* of reality as the motive power, the only motive power at the bottom of Christianity. What follows therefrom? That even here, in *psychologicis,* there is a radical error, which is to say one conditioning fundamentals, which is to say, one in *substance.* Take away one idea and put a genuine reality in its place—and the whole of Christianity crumbles to nothingness!—Viewed calmly, this strangest of all phenomena, a religion not only depending on errors, but inventive and ingenious *only* in devising injurious errors, poisonous to life and to the heart—this remains a *spectacle for the gods*—for those gods who are also philosophers, and whom I have encountered, for example, in the celebrated dialogues at Naxos. At the moment when their *disgust* leaves them (—and us!) they will be thankful for the spectacle afforded by the Christians: perhaps because of *this* curious exhibition alone the wretched little planet called the earth deserves a glance from omnipotence, a show of divine interest.... Therefore, let us not underestimate the Christians: the Christian, false *to the point of innocence,* is far above the ape—in its application to the Christians a well-known theory of descent becomes a mere piece of politeness....

40

The fate of the Gospels was decided by death—it hung on the "cross."... It was only death, that unexpected and shameful death; it was only the cross, which was usually reserved for the canaille only—it was only this appalling paradox which brought the disciples face to face with the real riddle: "Who *was it? what was it?*"—The feeling of dismay, of profound affront and injury; the suspicion that such a death might involve a *refutation* of their cause; the terrible question, "Why just in this way?"—this state of mind is only too easy to understand. Here everything *must* be accounted for as necessary; everything must have a meaning, a reason, the highest sort of reason; the love of a disciple excludes all chance. Only then did the chasm of doubt yawn: "*Who* put him to death? who was his natural enemy?"—this question flashed like a lightning-stroke. Answer: dominant Judaism, its ruling class. From that moment, one found one's self in revolt *against* the established order, and began to understand Jesus as in *revolt against the established order.* Until then this militant, this

continued

PRIMARY SOURCE 14.4 | *THE ANTICHRIST*, SECTIONS 39–41 *continued*

nay-saying, nay-doing element in his character had been lacking; what is more, he had appeared to present its opposite. Obviously, the little community had not understood what was precisely the most important thing of all: the example offered by this way of dying, the freedom from and superiority to every feeling of *ressentiment*—a plain indication of how little he was understood at all! All that Jesus could hope to accomplish by his death, in itself, was to offer the strongest possible proof, or *example,* of his teachings in the most public manner. But his disciples were very far from *forgiving* his death—though to have done so would have accorded with the Gospels in the highest degree; and neither were they prepared to *offer* themselves, with gentle and serene calmness of heart, for a similar death.... On the contrary, it was precisely the most unevangelical of feelings, *revenge,* that now possessed them. It seemed impossible that the cause should perish with his death: "recompense" and "judgment" became necessary (—yet what could be less evangelical than "recompense," "punishment," and "sitting in judgment"!) —Once more the popular belief in the coming of a messiah appeared in the foreground; attention was riveted upon an historical moment: the "kingdom of God" is to come, with judgment upon his enemies.... But in all this there was a wholesale misunderstanding: imagine the "kingdom of God" as a last act, as a mere promise! The Gospels had been, in fact, the incarnation, the fulfillment, the *realization* of this "kingdom of God." It was only now that all the familiar contempt for and bitterness against Pharisees and theologians began to appear in the character of the Master was thereby *turned* into a Pharisee and theologian himself! On the other hand, the savage veneration of these completely unbalanced souls could no longer endure the Gospel doctrine, taught by Jesus, of the equal right of all men to be children of God: their revenge took the form of *elevating* Jesus in an extravagant fashion, and thus separating him from themselves: just as, in earlier times, the Jews, to revenge themselves upon their enemies, separated themselves from their God, and placed him on a great height. The One God and the Only Son of God: both were products of *resentment*....

41

And from that time onward an absurd problem offered itself: "how *could* God allow it!" To which the deranged reason of the little community formulated an answer that was terrifying in its absurdity: God gave his son as a *sacrifice* for the forgiveness of sins. At once there was an end of the gospels! Sacrifice for sin, and in its most obnoxious and barbarous form: sacrifice of the *innocent* for the sins of the guilty! What appalling paganism!—Jesus himself had done away with the very concept of "guilt," he denied that there was any gulf fixed between God and man; he *lived* this unity between God and man, and that was precisely *his* "glad tidings."... And *not* as a mere privilege!—From this time forward the type of the Savior was corrupted, bit by bit, by the doctrine of judgment and of the second coming, the doctrine of death as a sacrifice, the doctrine of the *resurrection,* by means of which the entire concept of "blessedness," the whole and only reality of the gospels, is juggled away—in favor of a state of existence *after* death!...
St. Paul, with that rabbinical impudence which shows itself in all his doings, gave a logical quality to that conception, that *indecent* conception, in this way: "*If* Christ did not rise from the dead, then all our faith is in vain!"—And at once there sprang from the Gospels the most contemptible of all unfulfillable promises, the *shameless* doctrine of personal immortality.... Paul even preached it as a *reward*....

Life is larger than its meaning. That is the great insight Nietzsche offers to a civilization that has lost its way, even as the tone of his last writings betrays his own descent into darkness. By ever inviting us to become better than we thought we were, he has made an enduring contribution to political theory.

QUESTIONS FOR REFLECTION

Is redemption in the present or in the future? Has Nietzsche succeeded in his project of superseding two millennia of philosophy and Christianity? Has he shown that a redemption in the future is meaningless? That the only meaningful understanding of redemption is in the way one lives now? Does this render the traditional understanding obsolete? Has he overcome the crisis of nihilism?

Key Terms

nihilism
God is dead
Arthur Schopenhauer
Richard Wagner
Franco–Prussian war of 1870
aphorism
immoralist
beyond good and evil
self-sublimation of morality
will to power
eternal return
self-overcoming
Übermensch
gay science
Zarathustra
eternal return
redemption
the overman
process of self-creation
genealogy of morals
resentment
The Revaluation of All Values
life precedes its understandings

Sources and Resources

Key Texts

Human, All Too Human
Daybreak
On the Genealogy of Morals
Beyond Good and Evil
The Gay Science
Twilight of the Idols
The Will to Power
Thus Spoke Zarathusa

Secondary Texts

Dannhauser, Werner. *Nietzsche's View of Socrates.* Ithaca: Cornell University Press, 1974.

Jaspers, Karl. *Nietzsche: An Introduction to the Undertanding of His Philosophical Activity.* Translated by Charles F. Wallraff and Frederck J. Schmitz. South Bend: Gateway, 1979.

Kaufmann, Walter. *Nietzsche: Philosopher, Psychologist, Antichrist.* 4th ed. Princeton: Princeton University Press, 1974.

Lampert, Laurence. *Nietzsche's Teaching: An Interpretation of "Thus Spoke Zarathustra."* New Haven: Yale University Press, 1986.

Lowith, Karl. *From Hegel to Nietzsche: The Revolution in Nineteenth Century Thought.* Translated by David E. Green. New York: Holt, Rinehart and Winston, 1964.

Web Sites

Stanford Encyclopedia of Philosophy entry online at http://plato.stanford.edu/entries/nietzsche/

The works of Nietzsche online at www.gutenberg.org/browse/authors/n#a779

The Nietzsche Circle online at www.nietzschecircle.com/